THE PENGUIN CLASSICS
FOUNDER EDITOR (1944–64): E. V. RIEU
PRESENT EDITORS:
BETTY RADICE AND ROBERT BALDICK
L 63

L · N · TOLSTOY

WAR AND PEACE

TRANSLATED AND
WITH AN INTRODUCTION
BY
ROSEMARY EDMONDS

VOLUME
2

PENGUIN BOOKS

Penguin Books Ltd, Harmondsworth, Middlesex, England
Penguin Books Inc., 3300 Clipper Mill Road, Baltimore 11, Md, U.S.A.
Penguin Books Pty Ltd, Ringwood, Victoria, Australia

—

First published 1869
This translation first published 1957
Reprinted 1961, 1964, 1965

—

Copyright © Rosemary Edmonds, 1957

—

Made and printed in Great Britain
by Hazell Watson & Viney Ltd
Aylesbury, Bucks
Set in Monotype Bembo

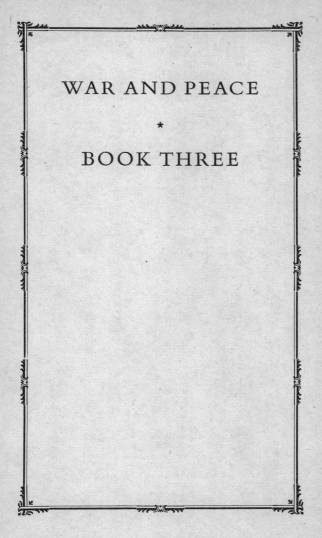

WAR AND PEACE

*

BOOK THREE

PART ONE

I

The last months of the year 1811 saw the sovereigns of Western Europe beginning to reinforce their armies and concentrate their strength, and in 1812 these forces – millions of men, reckoning in those concerned in the transport and victualling of the army – moved eastwards towards the Russian frontiers, where the Russians, too, had been massing since 1811. On the 12th of June 1812 the forces of Western Europe crossed the frontiers of Russia, and war began: in other words, an event took place counter to all the laws of human reason and human nature. Millions of men perpetrated against one another such innumerable crimes, deceptions, treacheries, robberies, forgeries, issues of false monies, depredations, incendiarisms and murders as the annals of all the courts of justice in the world could not muster in the course of whole centuries, but which those who committed them did not at the time regard as crimes.

What brought about this extraordinary occurrence? What were its causes? The historians, with naïve assurance, tell us that behind this event lay the wrongs inflicted on the Duke of Oldenburg, the non-observance of the Continental System forbidding trade with England, the ambition of Napoleon, the firmness of Alexander, the mistakes of the diplomats, and so on.

Of course, if that were so it would only have been necessary for Metternich, Rumyantsev or Talleyrand, in the interval between a levée and an evening party, to have taken a little trouble and penned a more judicious diplomatic note; or Napoleon to have written to Alexander: '*Monsieur mon frère*, I consent to restore the duchy to the Duke of Oldenburg' – and there would have been no war.

We can understand that this was not the view taken at the time. We can understand how it naturally seemed to Napoleon that the war was caused by England's intrigues (as in fact he said on the island of St Helena). We can understand how to the English Parliament

Napoleon's ambition seemed to be the cause of the war; to the Duke of Oldenburg it was the outrage done to him; to the merchants the cause of the war was the Continental System which was ruining Europe. Generals and veterans of the army traced the cause of the war to the necessity of providing them with employment, while to the legitimists of the day it was the vital need for re-establishing *les bons principes*; and the diplomats set it down to the alliance between Russia and Austria in 1809 not having been concealed tactfully enough from Napoleon, and to the awkward wording of Memorandum No. 178. We can understand how these and an incalculable and endless number of other reasons – the number corresponding to the infinite variety of points of view – presented themselves to men of that day; but for us of posterity, contemplating the accomplished fact in all its magnitude, and seeking to fathom its simple and terrible meaning, these explanations must appear insufficient. To us it is incomprehensible that millions of Christian men killed and tortured each other either because Napoleon was ambitious or Alexander firm, or because England's policy was astute or the Duke of Oldenburg wronged. We cannot grasp the connexion between these circumstances and the actual fact of slaughter and violence: why because the Duke was wronged thousands of men from the other end of Europe slaughtered and pillaged the inhabitants of Smolensk and Moscow, and were slaughtered by them.

For us their descendants, who are not historians and are not carried away by the process of research, and so can look at the facts with common sense unobscured, a countless number of causes offer themselves. The deeper we delve in search of these causes the more of them do we discover; and each separate cause or whole series of causes appears to us equally valid in itself and equally unsound by its insignificance in comparison with the size of the event, and by its impuissance (without the co-operation of all the other coincident causes) to occasion the event. To us the willingness or unwillingness of this or that French corporal to serve a second term has as much weight as Napoleon's refusal to withdraw his troops beyond the Vistula and to restore the duchy of Oldenburg; for had the corporal refused to serve, and a second and a third and a thousand corporals and soldiers with him, Napoleon's army would have been so greatly reduced that the war could not have occurred.

If Napoleon had not taken offence at the demand that he should retire beyond the Vistula, and had not ordered his troops to advance, there would have been no war. But if all his sergeants had objected to serving in a second campaign, then also there could have been no war. Nor could there have been a war had there been no English intrigues and no Duke of Oldenburg, and had Alexander not felt insulted, and had there not been an autocratic government in Russia, or a Revolution in France and consequent dictatorship and Empire, or all the things that produced the French Revolution, and so on. Had any one of these causes been absent, nothing could have happened. And so all these causes – these myriads of causes – coincided to bring about what happened. And so there was no exclusive reason for that occurrence: the war came about because it was bound to come about. Millions of men, renouncing their human feelings and their common sense, had to march from west to east to slay their fellows, just as some centuries previously hordes of men had moved from east to west, slaying their fellows.

The deeds of Napoleon and Alexander, on whose fiat the whole question of war or no war apparently depended, were as little spontaneous and free as the actions of every common soldier drawn into the campaign by lot or by conscription. This could not be otherwise, for in order that the will of Napoleon and Alexander (the people on whom the whole decision appeared to rest) should be effected a combination of innumerable circumstances was essential, without any one of which the event could not have taken place. It was necessary that millions of men in whose hands the real power lay – the soldiers who fired the guns or transported provisions and cannon – should consent to carry out the will of those weak individuals, and should have been induced to do so by an infinite number of diverse and complex causes.

We are forced to fall back on fatalism to explain the irrational events of history (that is to say, events the intelligence of which we do not see). The more we strive to account for such events in history rationally, the more irrational and incomprehensible do they become to us.

Every man lives for himself, using his freedom to attain his personal aims, and feels with his whole being that he can at any moment perform or not perform this or that action; but, so soon as he has done it, that action accomplished at a certain moment in time becomes irrevocable and belongs to history, in which it has not a free but a predestined significance.

There are two sides to the life of every man: there is his individual existence which is free in proportion as his interests are abstract; and his elemental life as a unit in the human swarm, in which he must inevitably obey the laws laid down for him.

Man lives consciously for himself but unconsciously he serves as an instrument for the accomplishment of historical and social ends. A deed done is irrevocable, and that action of his coinciding in time with the actions of millions of other men assumes an historical significance. The higher a man stands in the social scale, the more connexions he has with others and the more power he has over them, the more conspicuous is the predestination and inevitability of every act he commits.

'The hearts of kings are in the hand of God.'

A king is the slave of history.

History, that is, the unconscious, universal, swarm-life of mankind, uses every moment of the life of kings for its own purposes.

*

Though Napoleon at that time, in 1812, was more convinced than ever that to shed or not to shed the blood of his peoples – *verser ou ne pas verser le sang de ses peuples*, as Alexander expressed it in his last letter to him – depended entirely on his will, he had never been more in the grip of those inevitable laws which compelled him, while to himself he seemed to be acting on his own volition, to perform for the world in general – for history – what was destined to be accomplished.

The people of the west moved eastwards to slay their fellow-men. And, by the law of coincidence of causes, thousands of minute causes fitted together and co-ordinated to produce that movement and that war; resentment at the non-observance of the Continental System, the Duke of Oldenburg's wrongs, the advance of troops into Prussia – a measure undertaken (as Napoleon thought) solely for the purpose of securing armed peace – and the French Emperor's passion for war, and the habit of fighting which had grown upon him, coinciding with the inclinations of his people, who were carried away by the grandiose scale of the preparations, and the expenditure on those preparations, and the necessity of recouping that expenditure. Then there was the intoxicating effect of the honours paid to the French Emperor at Dresden, the diplomatic negotiations which in the opinion of contemporaries were conducted with a genuine desire to achieve a peace, though they only inflamed the *amour propre* of both sides, and millions upon millions of other coincident causes that adapted themselves to the fated event.

Why does an apple fall when it is ripe? Is it brought down by the force of gravity? Is it because its stalk withers? Because it is dried by the sun, because it grows too heavy, or the wind shakes it, or because the boy standing under the tree wants to eat it?

None of these is the cause. They only make up the combination of conditions under which every living process of organic nature fulfils itself. And the botanist who finds that the apple falls because the cellular tissue decays, and so forth, is just as right as the child who stands under the tree and says the apple fell because he wanted to eat it and prayed for it to fall. In the same way the historian who declares that Napoleon went to Moscow because he wanted to, and perished because Alexander desired his destruction, will be just as right and wrong as the man who says that a mass weighing thousands of tons, tottering and undermined, fell in consequence of the last blow of the pickaxe wielded by the last navvy. In historical events great men – so-called – are but labels serving to give a name to the event, and like labels they have the least possible connexion with the event itself.

Every action of theirs, that seems to them an act of their own free-will, is in the historical sense not free at all but is bound up with the whole course of history and preordained from all eternity.

2

ON the 29th of May Napoleon left Dresden, where he had spent three weeks surrounded by a Court that included princes, dukes, kings and even one emperor. Before his departure Napoleon lavished his favours on the princes, the kings and the emperor who had earned them, upbraided the kings and princes with whom he was displeased, presented his own diamonds and pearls – those, that is, which he had taken from other kings – to the Empress of Austria, and having, as his historian tells us, tenderly embraced the Empress Marie Louise (who regarded herself as his consort though he had left another consort in Paris), he proceeded on his way, leaving her deeply distressed by the parting, which she seemed scarcely able to bear. Although the diplomats still firmly believed in the possibility of peace, and were zealously working to that end; although the Emperor Napoleon penned a letter to Alexander calling him *Monsieur mon frère* and sincerely assuring him that he had no wish for war and would always hold him in affection and esteem – yet he set off to join his army, and at every station gave fresh orders to accelerate the progress of his troops from west to east. He travelled in a closed coach drawn by six horses, accompanied by pages, aides-de-camp and a bodyguard, along the road through Posen, Thorn, Dantzig and Königsberg. At each of these towns thousands of people rushed to greet him with enthusiasm and trepidation.

The army was moving from west to east, and relays of six horses bore him in the same direction. On the 10th of June, coming up with the army, he spent the night in quarters prepared for him on the estate of a Polish count in the Wilkowiski forest.

The following day Napoleon drove on ahead of the army, reached the Niemen and, changing into Polish uniform, went to the river bank in order to select a place for the crossing.

When he saw the Cossacks posted on the opposite bank and the expanse of the steppes, in the midst of which lay the holy city of Moscow – *Moscou, la ville sainte* – capital of an empire, like the Scythian empire into which Alexander the Great had marched, Napoleon unexpectedly, and contrary alike to strategic as well as diplomatic considerations, ordered an immediate advance, and the next day his army began to cross the Niemen.

Early on the morning of the 12th of June he came out of his tent, which was pitched that day on the steep left bank of the Niemen, and looked through a field-glass at his troops pouring out of the Wilkowiski forest and flowing over the three bridges thrown across the river. The troops, knowing of the Emperor's presence, were on the look-out for him, and when they caught sight of a figure in a greatcoat and cocked hat standing apart from his suite in front of his tent on the hill they threw up their caps and shouted '*Vive l'Empereur!*' And rank after rank, never ending, they streamed out of the vast forest that had concealed them, and splitting up crossed the three bridges to the other side.

'Now we shall get on! Things warm up when he himself takes a hand! ... By Jove! ... There he is! ... *Vive l'Empereur!* So those are the steppes of Asia! Nasty country, all the same. Good-bye, Beauché! I'll reserve the best palace in Moscow for you! Good-bye! Good luck! ... Did you see the Emperor? *Vive l'Empereur! ... pereur!* If they make me governor of the Indies, Gérard, I'll make you minister of Kashmir – that's a bargain. Hurrah for the Emperor! Hurrah! hurrah! hurrah! Those rascally Cossacks – see how they run! *Vive l'Empereur!* There he is! See him? I've seen him twice, plain as I'm seeing you now. *Le petit caporal.* ... I saw him present the Cross to one of our old 'uns. ... Hurrah for the Emperor!' came the voices of men, old and young, of the most diverse characters and stations in life. The faces of all alike wore one common expression of delight at the commencement of the long-expected campaign, and of enthusiasm and devotion for the man in the grey coat standing on the hill.

On the 13th of June a rather small, thoroughbred Arab horse was brought to Napoleon. He mounted and rode at a gallop to one of the bridges over the Niemen, deafened all the while by rapturous acclamations which he evidently endured only because it was impossible to forbid the men to express their love of him by such shouting; but this shouting, which accompanied him everywhere he went, fatigued him and distracted his attention from the military problems which beset him from the time he joined the army. He rode over one of the swaying pontoon bridges to the farther side, turned sharply to the left and galloped in the direction of Kovno, preceded by ecstatic horse guards who, wild with excitement, tore ahead to clear a passage for him through the troops. On reaching the broad river Viliya he pulled up beside a regiment of Polish Uhlans stationed on the bank.

'Long live the Emperor!' shouted the Poles no less enthusiastically, breaking their ranks and pushing against one another to get a sight of him. Napoleon looked up and down the river, got off his horse and sat down on a log that lay on the bank. At a mute sign from him he was handed a telescope which he rested on the back of a page, who ran up delighted. He gazed at the opposite bank and then, with absorbed attention, studied a map spread out between logs. Without lifting his head he said something, and two of his aides-de-camp galloped off to the Polish Uhlans.

'What? What did he say?' was heard in the ranks of the Polish Uhlans as one of the adjutants rode up to them.

The order was that they should look for a ford and cross the river. The colonel of the Polish Uhlans, a handsome old man, flushing and stammering in his excitement, asked the aide-de-camp whether he might be permitted to swim the river with his men instead of seeking a ford. In obvious dread of a refusal, like a boy asking permission to get on a horse, he begged to be allowed to swim across the river before the Emperor's eyes. The aide-de-camp replied that in all probability the Emperor would not be displeased at this excess of zeal.

No sooner had the aide-de-camp said this than the old whiskered officer, with beaming face and sparkling eyes, brandished his sabre in the air, shouted '*Vivat!*' and, calling on his men to follow him, spurred his horse and dashed down to the river. He gave a vicious thrust to his charger which had grown restive under him, and plunged into the water, heading for the deepest part where the current was swift. Hundreds of Uhlans galloped in after him. It was cold and forbidding in the middle in the rapid current. The Uhlans clung to one another as they fell from their horses. Some of the animals were drowned, some, too, of the men; the rest struggled to swim on and reach the opposite bank; and though there was a ford only about a quarter of a mile away they were proud to be swimming and drowning in the river under the eyes of the man who sat on the log and was not even looking at what they were doing. When the adjutant returned and, choosing an opportune moment, ventured to draw the Emperor's attention to the devotion of the Poles to his person, the little man in the grey overcoat got up and, having summoned Berthier, began pacing up and down the bank with him, giving him instructions and occasionally casting a glance of displeasure at the drowning Uhlans who distracted his thoughts.

It was nothing new in his experience and he did not need any convincing that his presence in any part of the world, from Africa to the steppes of Muscovy alike, was enough to turn men's heads and drive them to senseless acts of self-sacrifice. He ordered his horse and rode to his bivouac.

Some forty Uhlans were drowned in the river though boats were sent to their assistance. The majority scrambled back to the bank to which they had started. The colonel with several of his men got across and with difficulty clambered out on the other bank. But so soon as they were out of the water, their clothes soaked and streaming, they shouted '*Vivat!*' and looked ecstatically at the spot where Napoleon had stood, though he was there no longer, and at that moment considered themselves happy.

In the evening, between issuing two orders – one for hastening the arrival of the counterfeit paper money prepared for circulation in Russia, and the other that a Saxon who had been caught with a letter containing information concerning the dispositions of the French army should be shot – Napoleon also gave instructions for the Polish colonel who had quite unnecessarily flung himself into the river to be enrolled in the *Légion d'Honneur* of which Napoleon himself was the head.

Quos vult perdere – dementat.

3

THE Emperor of Russia had meanwhile been in Vilna for over a month, reviewing troops and holding manoeuvres. Nothing was ready for the war which everyone expected and to prepare for which the Emperor had come from Petersburg. There was no general plan of action. Hesitation between all the various schemes that were proposed was even more marked after the Tsar had been at Headquarters for a month. Each of the three armies had its own commander-in-chief, but there was no supreme commander of all the forces, and the Emperor did not see fit to assume that responsibility himself.

The longer the Emperor remained at Vilna the less did everybody – tired of waiting – do to prepare for the war. Every effort of the men who surrounded the Sovereign seemed directed solely to making his stay as pleasant as possible and enabling him to forget the impending clash of arms.

In June, after a series of balls and fêtes given by the Polish magnates, by members of the Court and by the Emperor himself, it occurred to one of the Polish aides-de-camp in attendance that all the generals on the staff should give a banquet and a ball for the Emperor. The idea was eagerly received. The Emperor expressed his consent. The imperial adjutants collected the necessary funds by subscription. The lady who was thought to be most pleasing to the Emperor was invited to act as hostess. Count Bennigsen, being a landowner in the Vilna province, offered his villa for the festivity, and the 13th of June was fixed for a ball, banquet, regatta and fireworks at Zakreto, Count Bennigsen's country seat.

The very day that Napoleon gave the order to cross the Niemen, and his vanguard, driving back the Cossacks, crossed the Russian frontier, Alexander was spending the evening at the entertainment given by his aides-de-camp at Bennigsen's country house.

It was a gay and brilliant fête. Connoisseurs of such matters declared that rarely had so many beautiful women been assembled in one place. Countess Bezuhov, who together with other Russian ladies had followed the Sovereign from Petersburg to Vilna, was at this ball, by her massive beauty – the Russian type, as it is called – eclipsing the dainty little Polish ladies. The Emperor noticed her and honoured her with a dance.

Boris Drubetskoy, having left his wife in Moscow and being for the present *en garçon*, as he said, was also there, and though not an aide-de-camp had subscribed a large sum towards the expenses. Boris was now a rich man who had risen to high honours and no longer sought patronage but stood on an equal footing with the most distinguished representatives of his own generation.

At midnight dancing was still going on. Hélène, finding no other partner to her taste, had herself offered to dance the mazurka with Boris. They were the third couple. Boris, glancing with cool indifference at Hélène's dazzling bare shoulders which emerged from a bodice of dark, gold-embroidered gauze, talked to her of old acquaintances, at the same time, though neither he himself nor anyone else was aware of it, never for an instant ceasing to observe the Emperor who was in the same room. The Emperor was not dancing: he stood in the doorway, stopping now one pair, now another with the gracious words that he alone knew how to utter.

As the mazurka began Boris saw that Adjutant-General Balashev, one of those in closest attendance on the Emperor, went up to him and, contrary to Court etiquette, stood near him while he conversed with a Polish lady. After a few remarks to her the Emperor looked inquiringly at Balashev and, evidently perceiving that only weighty considerations would have caused him to act thus, he gave the lady a slight bow and turned to the adjutant. Hardly had Balashev begun to speak before a look of amazement appeared on the Emperor's face. He took Balashev by the arm and crossed the room with him, unconsciously clearing a space three yards wide on each side of him as people hastily drew back. Boris noticed Arakcheyev's agitation when the Sovereign went out with Balashev. Arakcheyev looked at the Emperor from under his brows and, sniffing with his red nose, stepped forward from the crowd as though expecting the Emperor to turn to him. (It was clear to Boris that Arakcheyev was jealous of Balashev and annoyed that apparently important news had reached the Emperor otherwise than through himself.)

But the Tsar and Balashev walked on through the door into the illuminated garden, without noticing Arakcheyev. Arakcheyev, holding his sword and glancing wrathfully about him, followed some twenty paces behind them.

Boris continued to perform the figures of the mazurka but he was wondering all the time what the news could be that Balashev had brought, and how he could get hold of it before other people.

In the figure in which he had to choose two ladies, he whispered to Hélène that he meant to ask Countess Potocka who had, he thought, gone out on to the balcony, and gliding over the parquet floor he slipped through the door opening into the garden, where, seeing Balashev and the Emperor returning to the verandah, he stood still. They were moving towards the door. Boris, pretending he had not time to get out of the way, respectfully pressed back against the door-post and bowed his head.

The Emperor in the tone of a man resenting a personal insult was saying:

'To enter Russia with no declaration of war! I will not make peace so long as a single armed enemy soldier remains in my country!'

Boris fancied that the Tsar felt some satisfaction in saying these words: he was pleased with the form in which he had expressed his thought, but displeased that Boris had overheard it.

'Let no one know of this!' the Emperor added with a frown.

Boris understood that this was meant for him, and closing his eyes he inclined his head a little. The Emperor re-entered the ball-room and stayed another half an hour or so.

Boris was thus the first to learn that French troops had crossed the Niemen – which enabled him to give certain important personages to understand that much which was concealed from others was commonly known to him, and thereby he succeeded in rising still higher in their estimation.

*

The astounding information of the French having crossed the Niemen seemed particularly unexpected, coming after a month of unfulfilled expectancy, and at a ball! At the first instant of receiving the news, under the influence of indignation and resentment, the Emperor hit on the declaration which has since become famous – a declaration which pleased him and exactly expressed his feelings. On returning home from the ball at two o'clock in the morning, he sent for his secretary, Shishkov, and told him to write a general order to the troops, and a rescript to Field-Marshal Prince Saltykov, in which he insisted on the words being inserted that he would never make peace so long as a single armed Frenchman remained on Russian soil.

Next day the following letter was sent to Napoleon.

Monsieur mon frère,

Yesterday I learnt that, despite the fidelity with which I have adhered to my engagements with your Majesty, your troops have crossed the frontiers of Russia, and I have at this moment received a note from Petersburg in which Count Lauriston informs me, in explanation of this aggression, that your Majesty has considered yourself to be in a state of war with me from the time that Prince Kurakin requested his passports. The grounds on which the *duc de* Bassano based his refusal to deliver these passports would never have led me to suppose that that incident would serve as a pretext for aggression. In point of fact, my ambassador, as he himself has declared, was never authorized to make that request, and so soon as I was informed of it I manifested the extent of my disapproval by ordering him to remain at his post. If your Majesty is not bent upon shedding the blood of our peoples for such a *malentendu,* and consents to withdraw your troops from Russian territory, I will ignore what has happened, and a settlement between us will be possible. In the contrary case, your Majesty, I shall be forced to repel an invasion that nothing on my part has provoked. It is still in your Majesty's power to preserve humanity from the disasters of another war.

I am, etc.

(Signed) ALEXANDER

4

AT two in the morning of the 14th of June the Emperor, having sent for Balashev and read him his letter to Napoleon, ordered him to take and hand it personally to the French Emperor. As he dismissed Balashev the Sovereign once more repeated to him his declaration that he would never make peace so long as a single armed enemy soldier remained on Russian soil, and told him to be sure to quote those words to Napoleon. Alexander had not incorporated them in his letter to Napoleon because, with his characteristic tact, he felt that it would be injudicious to use them just when last attempts towards reconciliation were being made, but he expressly charged Balashev to give that message verbally to Napoleon.

Having set off in the small hours of the 14th, accompanied by a bugler and two Cossacks, Balashev reached the French outposts at the village of Rykonty on the Russian side of the Niemen, by dawn. There he was stopped by French cavalry sentinels.

A French subaltern officer of hussars, in a crimson uniform and a shaggy cap, shouted to the approaching envoy and ordered him to halt. Balashev did not obey at once but continued to advance along the road at walking pace.

The subaltern, with scowls and muttered abuse, blocked Balashev's way with his horse, put his hand to his sabre and shouted rudely at the Russian general, asking him whether he was deaf that he did not hear when he was spoken to. Balashev gave his name. The subaltern sent a soldier to his superior officer.

Paying no further attention to Balashev, the subaltern began talking with his comrades about regimental matters.

It was an exceedingly strange experience for Balashev, used to living close to the very fountain-head of power and might, having only three hours before been conversing with the Tsar, and in general being accustomed to the deference due to his rank in the Service, to be subjected in his own person and on his native soil to this hostile and, still more, this disrespectful display of brute force.

The sun was only just appearing from behind the clouds; the air was fresh and dewy. A herd of cattle was being driven along the road from the village. Over the fields, one after another, like bubbles floating to the surface of water, larks soared trilling into the sky.

Balashev looked about him as he awaited the arrival of an officer from the village. The Russian Cossacks and the bugler and the French hussars looked at one another from time to time but no one spoke.

A French colonel of hussars, evidently just out of bed, came riding up from the village on a handsome sleek grey horse, accompanied by two of his men. The officer, the soldiers and their horses all looked smart and content with life.

It was that first stage in a campaign when troops are still in full trim, almost like that of peace-time manoeuvres but enhanced by a touch of martial swagger in their apparel and the gay spirit of adventure which always accompany the beginning of an expedition.

The French colonel with difficulty repressed a yawn but was courteous and apparently appreciated Balashev's importance. He conducted him past his soldiers and behind the line of outposts, and informed him that his desire for an audience with the Emperor would in all probability be satisfied immediately, since the Imperial Headquarters, he believed, were not far distant.

They rode through the village of Rykonty, past French picket ropes, and sentinels and soldiers who saluted their colonel and stared with curiosity at a Russian uniform. They came out at the other end of the village, and the colonel told Balashev that they were only a mile and a quarter from the commander of the division, who would receive him and take him to his destination.

The sun had by now fully risen and was shining cheerfully on the vivid green of field and tree.

They had hardly ridden up a hill, past a tavern, before they saw a group of horsemen coming towards them, led by a tall figure in a scarlet cloak with plumes in his hat and black hair curling down to his shoulders. He was mounted on a raven-black horse whose trappings glittered in the sun, and his long legs were thrust forward in the fashion affected by French riders. This personage came towards Balashev at a gallop, plumes fluttering and gems and gold lace glittering in the bright June sunshine.

Balashev was already within ten yards of this rider with the bracelets, plumes, necklaces and gold lace, who was galloping towards him with a theatrically solemn countenance, when Julner, the French colonel, whispered with reverence: 'The King of Naples!' It was in fact Murat, now styled 'King of Naples'. Though it was wholly incomprehensible why he should be King of Naples, still he was called so, and was himself convinced that so it was, and therefore assumed an air of greater solemnity and dignity than before. So firmly did he believe that he really was the King of Naples that when on the eve of departure from that city, as he was strolling through the streets with his wife, some Italians acclaimed him with cries of *'Viva il re!'* he turned to her with a pensive smile and said: 'Poor souls, they little know that I am leaving them tomorrow!'

But, though he so implicitly believed himself to be King of Naples, and sympathized with his subjects' grief at losing him, after he had been ordered to return to military service, and especially after his last interview with Napoleon at Dantzig, when his august brother-in-law had told him, 'I made you king to rule in my way, not your own!' he had cheerfully resumed his familiar business; and, like a well-fed but not over-fat horse feeling himself in harness and prancing between the shafts, he decked himself out in the most gorgeous and costly array possible, and went gaily and contentedly galloping along the roads of Poland, with no notion where or why.

On seeing the Russian general he threw back his head, with its long hair curling to his shoulders, in royal majestic fashion and looked inquiringly at the French colonel. The colonel respectfully informed his Majesty of Balashev's mission, whose name he could not pronounce.

'De Bal-macheve!' said the King (overcoming by his assurance the difficulty that had presented itself to the colonel). 'Charmed to make your acquaintance, general!' he added with a gesture of regal condescension.

As soon as the King began to speak loudly and rapidly all his royal dignity instantly deserted him and, without himself being aware of it, he slipped into his natural tone of good-natured familiarity. He laid his hand on the withers of Balashev's horse.

'Well, general,' he said, 'everything looks like war,' as though he regretted a state of things on which he was unable to offer an opinion.

'Sire,' replied Balashev, 'the Emperor, my master, does not desire war, and as your Majesty sees ...' said Balashev, using the words *your Majesty* at every possible opportunity, with the affectation unavoidable when reiterating a title and addressing one to whom that title is still a novelty.

Murat's face beamed with foolish satisfaction as he listened to 'Monsieur de Balacheff'. But royalty has its obligations: he felt it incumbent on him, as a King and an ally, to confer on affairs of state with Alexander's envoy. He dismounted, took Balashev's arm and, moving a few steps away from his suite, who remained dutifully waiting, began walking up and down with him, trying to speak with grave significance. He referred to the fact that the Emperor Napoleon had resented the demand made upon him to withdraw his forces from Prussia, especially when that demand had been made public and the dignity of France was thereby offended.

Balashev replied that there was nothing offensive in the demand, seeing that ... but Murat interrupted him:

729

'Then you do not consider the Emperor Alexander the aggressor?' he asked suddenly, with a silly good-natured smile.

Balashev explained why he considered Napoleon to be the one responsible for the war.

'Ah, my dear general!' Murat interrupted him again, 'I hope with all my heart that the Emperors may settle the matter between themselves, and that the war begun by no desire of mine may finish as quickly as possible!' said he in the tone of a servant anxious to remain on friendly terms with another despite a quarrel between their masters. And he turned the conversation, inquiring after the health of the Grand Duke and recalling the agreeable and amusing time he had spent with him in Naples. Then suddenly, as if remembering his royal dignity, Murat solemnly drew himself up, struck the attitude in which he had stood at his coronation, and with a wave of his right arm, said:

'I will detain you no longer, general. I wish you success in your mission,' and with a flutter of his embroidered scarlet cloak and his plumes, and a flash of his jewels, he rejoined his suite who were respectfully awaiting him.

Balashev rode on, supposing from Murat's words that he would very shortly be brought before Napoleon himself. But, instead of any speedy meeting with Napoleon, at the next village he was stopped by the sentinels of Davoust's infantry corps, just as he had been at the outposts, and an adjutant of the corps commander was sent for to conduct him into the village to Marshal Davoust.

5

DAVOUST was to the Emperor Napoleon what Arakcheyev was to Alexander. Though not a coward like Arakcheyev he was as exacting and cruel, and as unable to express his devotion to his monarch otherwise than by cruelty.

In the mechanism of administration such men are as necessary as wolves are in the economy of nature, and they are always to be found, making their appearance and holding their own, however incongruous their presence and their proximity to the head of the administration may be. This indispensability alone can explain how a man so cruel as Arakcheyev, who tore out grenadiers' moustaches with his own hands yet whose weak nerves rendered him unable to face danger, who was ill-bred and boorish, could retain such influence with a sovereign of gentle chivalry and nobility of character like Alexander.

Balashev found Davoust seated on a barrel in the shed of a peasant's hut, writing – he was auditing accounts. An adjutant stood near him. Better quarters could have been found for him, but Marshal Davoust was one of those men who purposely make the conditions of life as uncomfortable for themselves as possible in order to have an excuse for being gloomy. For the same reason they are always hard at work and in a hurry. 'How can I think of the bright side of existence when, as you see, I sit perched on a barrel in a dirty shed, hard at work ?' the expression of his face seemed to say. The chief satisfaction and requirement of such people is to make a great parade of their own dreary, persistent activity, whenever they encounter anyone enjoying life. Davoust allowed himself that gratification when Balashev was brought in. He buried himself more deeply than ever in his work when the Russian general entered, and after a glance through his spectacles at Balashev's face, which was animated by the beauty of the morning and his talk with Murat, he did not rise, did not stir even, but scowled more blackly than before and smiled malignantly.

Perceiving the disagreeable impression produced on Balashev by this reception, Davoust raised his head and asked him frigidly what he wanted.

Thinking he could have been received in such a manner only because Davoust did not know that he was adjutant-general to the Emperor Alexander and, what was more, his envoy to Napoleon, Balashev hastened to inform him of his rank and mission. But, contrary to his expectations, Davoust, after listening to his communication, became still more surly and rude.

'Where is your despatch ?' he demanded. 'Give it to me. I will forward it to the Emperor.'

Balashev replied that he had been ordered to hand it personally to the Emperor.

'Your Emperor's orders are obeyed in your army, but here,' said Davoust, 'you must do as you're told.'

And, as though to make the Russian general still more sensible that he was at the mercy of brute force, the marshal sent an adjutant to call the officer on duty.

Balashev took out the packet containing the Tsar's letter and laid it on the table (which consisted of a door placed across two tubs with the hinges still hanging on it). Davoust picked up the packet and read the inscription.

'You are perfectly at liberty to show me respect or not, as you please,' protested Balashev, 'but permit me to observe that I have the honour to be adjutant-general to his Majesty. ...'

Davoust glanced at him in silence, plainly deriving satisfaction from the signs of disturbance and agitation on Balashev's face.

'You will be shown what is fitting,' said he and, putting the packet in his pocket, left the shed.

A minute later an adjutant of the marshal's, Monsieur de Castre, came in and conducted Balashev to the lodgings assigned him.

Balashev dined that day in the shed with the marshal, sitting down to the door laid across the tubs.

The following morning Davoust rode out early, but before starting he sent for Balashev and peremptorily requested him to remain where he was, to move on with the baggage-train should orders arrive for it to move, and to have no communication with anyone save Monsieur de Castre.

After four days of solitude, ennui and a continual sense of impotence and insignificance – all the more acutely felt by contrast with the atmosphere of power to which he had until so lately been accustomed – and after a number of marches with the marshal's baggage and the French troops, who occupied the whole district, Balashev was brought back to Vilna – now in possession of the French – re-entering the town through the very gate by which he had left it four days previously.

Next day the Emperor's gentleman-in-waiting, Comte de Turenne, came to Balashev to inform him of the Emperor Napoleon's wish to honour him with an audience.

Four days before, sentinels of the Preobrazhensky regiment had mounted guard in front of the very house to which Balashev was conducted, but now two French grenadiers stood there, wearing fur caps and blue uniforms open over the breast, while an escort of hussars and Uhlans and a brilliant suite of aides-de-camp, pages and generals were waiting for Napoleon to come out, forming a group round his saddle-horse and his Mameluke, Rustan. Napoleon received Balashev in the actual house in Vilna from which Alexander had despatched him on his mission.

6

Though Balashev was used to imperial pomp he was amazed at the luxury and magnificence of Napoleon's Court.

Comte de Turenne led him into the great reception-room, where a throng of generals, gentlemen-in-waiting and Polish magnates – several of whom Balashev had seen at the Court of the Emperor of Russia – were waiting. Duroc said that Napoleon would receive the Russian general before going for his ride.

After some minutes the gentleman-in-waiting who was on duty came into the great reception-room and, bowing politely, invited Balashev to follow him.

Balashev went into the small reception-room, one door of which led into a study, that same room from which the Russian Emperor had sent him forth. He stood for a couple of minutes waiting. Hasty steps were heard the other side of the door, both leaves of which were quickly thrown open, and in the ensuing silence came the sound of other steps, firm and resolute – those of Napoleon. He had just finished dressing for his ride, and wore a blue uniform opening in front over a white waistcoat, so long that it covered his round stomach, white doeskin breeches fitting tightly over the fat thighs of his stumpy legs, and Hessian boots. His short hair had evidently just been brushed, but one lock hung down in the middle of his broad forehead. His plump white neck stood out sharply above the black collar of his uniform, and he smelt of eau-de-Cologne. His youthful-looking, full face, with its prominent chin, wore an expression of benevolent welcome compatible with his imperial majesty.

He entered briskly, with a jerk at every step and his head slightly thrown back. The whole of his short corpulent figure with the broad thick shoulders and with the abdomen and chest unconsciously thrust forward had the imposing air of dignity common in men of forty who enjoy a life of ease. Moreover, it was evident that on this particular day he was in extremely good humour.

He nodded in response to Balashev's low and deferential bow, and, going up to him, at once began speaking like a man who values every moment of his time and does not condescend to prepare what he has to say but is sure of always saying the right thing and saying it well.

'Good day, general!' he began. 'I have received the letter you brought from the Emperor Alexander and am very glad to see you.' He scrutinized Balashev's face with his large eyes and then immediately looked past him.

It was plain that Balashev's personality did not interest him in the least. Nothing outside *his* own self held any significance for him, because everything in the world, it seemed to him, depended on his will alone.

'I do not, and did not, desire war,' he continued, 'but it has been forced on me. Even *now*' (he emphasized the word) 'I am ready to accept any explanations you can give me.'

And he proceeded clearly and concisely to state the grounds for his dissatisfaction with the Russian government.

Judging by the studiously composed and amicable tone of the French Emperor, Balashev was firmly persuaded that he was anxious for peace and intended to enter into negotiations.

'*Sire*, the Emperor, my master,' began Balashev when Napoleon had finished speaking and looked inquiringly at the Russian envoy. But the sight of the Emperor's eyes fastened upon him disconcerted him and drove from his mind the speech he had prepared long before. 'You are flurried – steady yourself!' Napoleon's gaze seemed to say, as with a scarcely perceptible smile he glanced at Balashev's uniform and sword.

Balashev recovered himself and began to speak. He said that the Emperor Alexander did not consider Kurakin's demand for his passports a sufficient ground for war; that Kurakin had acted on his own initiative and without his Sovereign's sanction; that the Emperor Alexander did not desire war and that he had no relations with England.

'Not *yet*!' interposed Napoleon and, as though fearing to give vent to his feelings, he frowned and nodded slightly as a sign that Balashev might continue.

Having said all he had been instructed to say, Balashev added that the Emperor Alexander wished for peace but that he would not enter into negotiations except on condition that ... Here Balashev stopped short: he remembered the words the Emperor Alexander had not written in his letter but had insisted on inserting in the rescript to Saltykov, and had commanded Balashev to repeat to Napoleon. Balashev remembered those words, 'so long as a single armed enemy soldier remains on Russian soil', but some complex feeling held him back. He could not utter those words, much as he had meant to do so. He hesitated, and said: 'On condition that the French army retires beyond the Niemen.'

Napoleon observed Balashev's embarrassment over this last sentence, and his face twitched and the calf of his left leg started to tremble rhythmically. Without moving from where he stood he began speaking in a louder and more hurried tone than before. During the speech that followed, Balashev, who more than once lowered his eyes, could not help watching the quivering of Napoleon's left calf, which increased as Napoleon raised his voice.

'I am no less desirous of peace than the Emperor Alexander,' he began. 'Have I not for the past eighteen months been doing everything to obtain peace? I have waited eighteen months for explanations. But in order to open negotiations what is it that is required of me?' he said, frowning and making a vigorous gesture of inquiry with his plump little white hand.

'The withdrawal of your forces beyond the Niemen, sire,' said Balashev.

'Beyond the Niemen?' echoed Napoleon. 'So now you want me to retire beyond the Niemen – only beyond the Niemen?' repeated Napoleon, looking straight at Balashev.

Balashev respectfully bowed his head.

Four months previously the demand had been for his withdrawal from Pomerania; now all that was required was a retirement beyond the Niemen. Napoleon swung round and began walking up and down the room.

'You say that I must retire across the Niemen before negotiations can be opened; but in exactly the same way two months ago the demand was that I should withdraw beyond the Oder and the Vistula, and yet you are willing to negotiate!'

He strode in silence from one corner of the room to the other and again stopped in front of Balashev. Balashev noticed that his left calf was twitching faster than ever and his face seemed petrified in its stern expression. This twitching of his left leg was something Napoleon was conscious of. 'The vibration of my left calf is a great sign with me,' he remarked at a later date.

'Such demands as to retreat beyond the Oder and the Vistula may be made to a prince of Baden, but not to me!' Napoleon almost screamed, quite to his own surprise. 'If you were to offer me Petersburg and Moscow, I would not accept such conditions. You say I began this war! But which of us was the first to join his army? The Emperor Alexander, not I! And you propose negotiations when I have expended millions, when you are in alliance with England, and when your position is weak – you propose negotiations with me! Yes, and what is the object of your alliance with England? What has she given you?' he continued hurriedly, obviously no longer thinking of enlarging on the benefits or possibility of peace but entirely bent on proving his own righteousness and his own power, and Alexander's improbity and blundering.

He had plainly entered on his speech with the intention of pointing out the advantages of his position and indicating that he was nevertheless willing to negotiate. But he had begun talking, and the more he talked the less able was he to control the tenor of his words.

The whole purport of his remarks now was clearly to exalt himself and insult Alexander – precisely what he had least intended to do at the outset of the interview.

'I hear you have concluded a peace with the Turks?'

Balashev bowed his head affirmatively.

'Yes, peace has been ...' he began.

But Napoleon did not let him speak. It was obvious that he wanted to do all the talking himself, and he went on with the vehemence and irritable impatience to which people spoilt by success are so prone.

'Yes, I know you have made peace with the Turks without obtaining Moldavia and Wallachia – while I would have given your Sovereign those, just as I presented him with Finland. Yes,' he went on, 'I promised Moldavia and Wallachia to the Emperor Alexander, and I would have given them to him, but now he will not get those fair provinces. Yet he might have united them to his Empire and in a single reign would have extended Russia from the Gulf of Bothnia to the mouth of the Danube. Catherine the Great could not have done more,' declared Napoleon, growing more and more excited as he paced up and down the room repeating to Balashev almost the very words he had used to Alexander himself at Tilsit. 'All that, he would have owed to my friendship. Ah, what a glorious reign, what a glorious reign ...!' he repeated several times, then paused, drew from his pocket a gold snuff-box, lifted it to his nose and greedily sniffed at it. 'What a glorious reign the Emperor Alexander's *might have been!*'

He turned a commiserating glance on Balashev, and as soon as the latter started to make some rejoinder hastily interrupted him again.

'What could he wish or look for that he would not have secured through my friendship? ...' demanded Napoleon, shrugging his shoulders with an air of perplexity. 'But no, he has preferred to surround himself with my enemies – and with whom? With the Steins, the Armfeldts, the Bennigsens, the Wintzingerodes! Stein, a traitor expelled from his own country; Armfeldt, a rake and an intriguer; Wintzingerode, a renegade French subject; Bennigsen, rather more of a soldier than the rest but all the same an incompetent, who was helpless in 1807 and who, I should have thought, must arouse horrible memories in the Emperor Alexander's mind. ... We will grant that were they efficient they might be made use of,' pursued Napoleon, hardly able to keep pace in speech with the rush of arguments proving to him his right or his might (which to his mind meant one and the same thing), 'but they are not even that! They are no good for war or peace! Barclay is said to be the most capable of the lot, but I shouldn't say so, judging by his first manoeuvres. And what are they doing, what are all these courtiers doing? Pfuhl formulates plans, Armfeldt argues, Bennigsen considers, while Barclay, called upon to act, does not know what to decide on, and time slips by. Bagration alone is a soldier. He's stupid but he has experience, a quick eye and determination. ... And what part does your young Emperor play in this unseemly crowd? They compromise him and throw upon him the responsibility for all that happens. A Sovereign should not be with the army unless he is a general!' said Napoleon, evidently intending these words as a direct challenge to the Russian Emperor. Napoleon knew Alexander's ambition to pass for a military commander.

'Why, the campaign opened a week ago, and you haven't even succeeded in defending Vilna. You are cut in two and have been driven out of the Polish provinces. Your army is discontented. ...'

'On the contrary, your Majesty,' began Balashev, hardly able to remember what had been said to him, and with difficulty following these verbal fireworks, 'the troops are wild with enthusiasm. ...'

'I know all that,' Napoleon interrupted him. 'I know all that, and I know the number of your battalions as well as I know that of my own. You have not two hundred thousand men, while I have three times as many. I give you my word of honour,' said Napoleon, forgetting that his word of honour could carry no weight – 'I give you my *parole d'honneur* that I have five hundred and thirty thousand men this side of the Vistula. The Turks will be no help to you. They are never any good, and have proved it by making peace with you. As for the Swedes, it's their destiny to be ruled by mad kings. Their king was insane. They changed him for another – Bernadotte, who promptly went mad, for no Swede would ally himself with Russia unless he were mad.'

Napoleon sneered maliciously and again lifted the snuff-box to his nose.

To each of Napoleon's remarks Balashev had a reply ready and would have come out with it: he kept making the gestures of a man who has something to say, but Napoleon always cut him short. The allegation that the Swedes were insane Balashev would have refuted with the argument that when Russia is on her side Sweden is practically an island; but Napoleon shouted an angry exclamation to drown his voice. Napoleon was in that state of irritation in which a man has to talk and talk and talk, simply to prove to himself that he is in the right. Balashev began to feel uncomfortable: as envoy he was anxious to keep up his dignity, and felt it incumbent upon himself to reply; but as a man he shrank before the assault of Napoleon's unreasonable fury. He was aware that nothing Napoleon might say now had any significance, and that Napoleon himself would be ashamed of his words when he came to his senses. Balashev stood with downcast eyes, watching Napoleon's fat legs as they moved to and fro, and trying to avoid his eyes.

'But what do I care about your allies?' said Napoleon. 'I have allies too – the Poles. There are eighty thousand of them and they fight like lions! And before long they will number two hundred thousand.'

And probably still further exasperated at having told this palpable falsehood, and at Balashev's continuing to stand mutely before him in that attitude of resignation to fate, Napoleon turned abruptly and going right up to Balashev and gesticulating rapidly and vigorously in his face with his white hands, he almost shouted:

'Let me tell you that if you stir up Prussia against me I'll wipe her off the map of Europe!' he declared, his face pale and distorted with anger, as he smote one little hand energetically against the other. 'And as for you, I'll throw you back beyond the Dvina, beyond the Dnieper, and I'll restore the frontier that Europe was criminal and blind to allow you to overrun. Yes, that's what is in store for you.

That is what you have gained by alienating me!' And he took several turns up and down the room in silence, his fat shoulders twitching.

He put his snuff-box into his waistcoat pocket, took it out again, held it several times to his nose, and halted in front of Balashev. He paused, looked sardonically straight into Balashev's eyes and said in a quiet voice:

'And yet what a glorious reign your master *might have had!*'

Balashev, feeling it imperative to make some rejoinder, declared that Russians did not take so gloomy a view of the position. Napoleon was silent, still looking derisively at him and evidently not listening. Balashev said that in Russia the best results were expected from the war. Napoleon nodded condescendingly, as much as to say: 'I know it is your duty to say so, but you don't believe it yourself. My arguments have convinced you.'

When Balashev was done, Napoleon again pulled out his snuff-box, took a pinch and stamped his foot twice on the floor as a signal. The door opened, a gentleman-in-waiting, bending respectfully, handed the Emperor his hat and gloves; another brought him a pocket-handkerchief. Napoleon, without bestowing a glance on them, turned to Balashev:

'Assure the Emperor Alexander from me,' said he, taking his hat, 'that I am devoted to him as before: I know him perfectly, and have the highest esteem for his lofty qualities. I will detain you no longer, general: you shall receive my letter to the Emperor.'

And Napoleon walked rapidly to the door. Everyone in the reception-room rushed forward and down the stairs.

7

AFTER all that Napoleon had said to him, after those outbursts of anger and the last dryly spoken words, 'I will detain you no longer, general: you shall receive my letter,' Balashev felt certain that Napoleon would not wish to see him again – indeed, that he would avoid another meeting with the envoy he had treated with contumely and, what was more, who had been the eye witness of his unbecoming vehemence. But to his astonishment Balashev received, through Duroc, an invitation to dine that day with the Emperor.

Bessières, Caulaincourt and Berthier were present at the dinner.

Napoleon met Balashev with a cheerful, affable air. There was not the slightest trace of constraint or self-reproach for his outburst of the morning: on the contrary, he did his best to put Balashev at his ease. It was plain that it had long been Napoleon's conviction that no possibility existed of his making a mistake, and that, according to his understanding of things, whatever he did was right, not because it harmonized with any preconceived notion of right or wrong but because it was *he* who did it.

The Emperor was in excellent spirits after his ride through Vilna, where he had been greeted and followed by the acclamations of crowds of the inhabitants. Every window in the streets through which he rode was hung with rugs, flags or draperies with his monogram, and the Polish ladies waved their handkerchiefs to him in welcome.

At dinner, having placed Balashev beside him, Napoleon not only addressed him amiably but behaved as though he regarded him as one of his own courtiers, one of those who sympathized with his plans and must surely rejoice at his successes. In the course of conversation he mentioned Moscow, and questioned Balashev about the Russian capital, not merely as an interested traveller asks about a new place which he has in mind to visit, but with the apparent conviction that Balashev, as a Russian, must be flattered by his curiosity.

'What is the population of Moscow? How many houses are there? Is it true that Moscow is called *Moscou la sainte*? How many churches are there in Moscow?' he asked.

And when he was told that Moscow had over two hundred churches, he said:

'What is the good of so many?'

'Russians are very devout,' replied Balashev.

'Incidentally, a large number of monasteries and churches is always a sign of the backwardness of a people,' remarked Napoleon, looking round to Caulaincourt for appreciation of this pronouncement.

Balashev ventured respectfully to disagree with the French Emperor.

'Every country has its own customs,' said he.

'But nowhere else in Europe is there anything like that,' declared Napoleon.

'I beg your Majesty's pardon,' returned Balashev, 'besides Russia there is Spain, which also has a vast number of churches and monasteries.'

This retort of Balashev's, which suggested a covert allusion to the recent discomfiture of the French in Spain, was highly appreciated when Balashev repeated it at Alexander's Court but was little esteemed at Napoleon's dinner and excited no attention.

From the indifferent and doubtful faces of the marshals it was obvious that they were puzzled as to what Balashev's tone suggested. 'If there is a point, we fail to see it', or 'It is not at all witty' their expressions seemed to say. So little was his rejoinder appreciated that Napoleon did not notice it at all, and naïvely asked Balashev through what towns the direct road from there (Vilna) to Moscow passed. Balashev, who was on his guard all through the dinner, replied that just as 'all roads lead to Rome' so all roads led to Moscow; that there were many roads and among them 'the road through *Poltava*, which Charles XII chose'. Balashev involuntarily flushed with pleasure at the aptness of this answer, but hardly had he uttered the word *Poltava* before Caulaincourt began talking of the badness of the road from Petersburg to Moscow and of his Petersburg reminiscences.

After dinner they adjourned to drink coffee in Napoleon's study, which four days previously had been the study of the Emperor Alexander. Napoleon sat down, toying with his Sèvres coffee-cup, and motioned Balashev to a chair beside him.

There is a well-known after-dinner mood which is more potent than any rational consideration in making a man contented with himself and disposed to regard everyone as his friend. Napoleon was in this comfortable humour, fancying himself surrounded by men who adored him, and persuaded that after his dinner Balashev, too, was his friend and worshipper. Napoleon turned to him with a pleasant though slightly ironic smile.

'They tell me this is the very room the Emperor Alexander occupied. Strange, isn't it, general?' he said, obviously without the least misgiving that this remark could be other than agreeable to the Russian since it went to show his, Napoleon's, superiority over Alexander.

Balashev could make no reply, and inclined his head in silence.

'Yes, in this room, four days ago, Wintzingerode and Stein were holding council,' pursued Napoleon with the same confident, satirical smile. 'What I cannot understand,' he went on, 'is that the Emperor Alexander has taken to himself all my personal enemies. That I do not ... understand. Has it never occurred to him that I might do the same?' and he turned inquiringly to Balashev, and obviously the question revived the hardly smothered furies of the morning.

'Aye, and I will, too: let him know that!' said Napoleon, rising and pushing his cup away with his arm. 'I'll drive all his kith and kin out of Germany – the Württembergs and Badens and Weimars. ... Yes, I'll drive them out. Let him prepare an asylum for them in Russia!'

Balashev bowed his head with an air indicating that he would be glad to take his leave and retire, and was simply listening because he had no alternative but to listen to what was said to him. Napoleon did not notice this expression; he was treating Balashev not as an envoy from his enemy but as a man now wholly devoted to him and certain therefore to rejoice at his former master's humiliation.

'And why has the Emperor Alexander assumed command of his armies? What is the good of that? War is my profession, but his business is to reign and not to command armies. Why has he taken such a responsibility on himself?'

Again Napoleon brought out his snuff-box, strode several times up and down the room in silence, and then suddenly and unexpectedly went up to Balashev, and with a slight smile, and as confidently, quickly and without ceremony as though he were doing something not merely important but even agreeable to Balashev, he raised his hand to the forty-year-old Russian general's face and taking him by the ear pulled it gently, smiling with his lips only.

To have one's ear pulled by the Emperor was considered the greatest honour and mark of favour at the French Court.

'Eh bien, adorer and courtier of the Emperor Alexander, why don't you say something?' he said, as though it were comic, in his presence, to be the adorer and courtier of anyone but himself, Napoleon. 'Are the horses ready for the general?' he added, with a slight nod in acknowledgement of Balashev's bow. 'Let him have mine. He has *a long way to go*. ...'

The letter carried back by Balashev was the last Napoleon sent to Alexander. Every detail of the interview was communicated to the Russian monarch, and the war began.

8

AFTER his meeting with Pierre in Moscow Prince Andrei went to Petersburg, on business as he told his family but in reality to seek out

Anatole Kuragin, whom he felt it necessary to see. Kuragin, for whom he inquired as soon as he reached Petersburg, was no longer there. Pierre had warned his brother-in-law that Prince Andrei was on his track. Anatole Kuragin had promptly obtained a commission from the minister of war, and gone to join the army in Moldavia. During this visit to Petersburg Prince Andrei met Kutuzov, his former commander, who was always well disposed towards him, and Kutuzov suggested that he should accompany him to the Moldavian army, of which the old general had been appointed commander-in-chief. So Prince Andrei, having received an appointment on the headquarters staff, left for Turkey.

Prince Andrei did not think it proper to write to Kuragin and challenge him. He considered that if he challenged him without some fresh cause it might compromise the young Countess Rostov, and so he was seeking to encounter Kuragin in person in order to pick a quarrel with him that would serve as a pretext for a duel. But in the Turkish army, too, Prince Andrei failed to come across Kuragin, who returned to Russia shortly after Prince Andrei's arrival. In a new country, amid new conditions, Prince Andrei found life easier to bear. After the faithlessness of his betrothed, which he felt the more acutely the more he endeavoured to conceal its effect on him, the surroundings in which he had been happy he now found painful, and the freedom and independence he had once prized so highly still more so. He not only no longer thought the thoughts which had first come to him as he lay gazing up at the heavens on the field of Austerlitz and which he had afterwards loved to enlarge upon with Pierre – the thoughts which had been the companions of his solitude at Bogucharovo, and later on in Switzerland and Rome: he even dreaded to recall them and the boundless vistas of light they had opened up to him. He now concerned himself solely with the practical interests lying closest to hand and in no way related to his old ideals. The more the latter were closed to him the more avidly he clutched at these new interests. It was as if that lofty infinite canopy of heaven that had once arched high above him had suddenly been transformed into a low solid vault that weighed him down, in which all was clear but nothing was eternal or mysterious.

Of the activities that presented themselves to his choice, army service was the simplest and most familiar. Accepting the duties of a general on the staff, he applied himself to his work so doggedly and perseveringly that Kutuzov was amazed at his zeal and conscientiousness. Having missed Kuragin in Turkey, Prince Andrei did not feel it necessary to gallop back to Russia after him, but all the same he knew that however long it might be before he met Kuragin, despite his contempt for him and despite all the arguments he used to convince himself that it was not worth stooping to a clash with him – he knew that when he did come across him he would not be able to resist calling him out, any more than a starving man can resist rushing at food. And the consciousness that the insult was not yet avenged, that his rancour had not been expended but was still stored up in his heart, poisoned the artificial tranquillity which he managed to obtain in Turkey in the form of strenuously preoccupied, and rather vainglorious and ambitious activity.

In the year 1812, when news of the war with Napoleon reached Bucharest (where Kutuzov had been living for two months, spending his days and nights with a Wallachian woman), Prince Andrei asked to be transferred to the western army. Kutuzov, who was already weary of Bolkonsky's energy, which he felt as a standing reproach to his own idleness, very readily let him go, and gave him a mission to Barclay de Tolly.

Before joining the army of the west, which was then, in May, encamped at Drissa, Prince Andrei visited Bald Hills, which was directly on his route, being only a couple of miles off the Smolensk high road. During the last three years there had been so many changes in his life, he had thought, felt and seen so much (having travelled both in the east and the west), that it surprised and struck him as strange when he reached Bald Hills to find life there continuing exactly as it always had, down to the smallest detail. He drove through the stone gateway into the avenue leading up to the house, feeling as though he were entering an enchanted castle where everything was fast asleep. The same sedate air, the same spotlessness, the same silence reigned in the house; there was the same furniture, the same walls, the same sounds and smells, and the same timid faces, only grown a little older. Princess Maria was still the same timid, plain girl, no longer in her first youth, wasting the best years of her life with her fears and eternal moral searchings, and getting no benefit or happiness out of her existence. Mademoiselle Bourienne was the same coquettish, self-satisfied young woman, enjoying every moment of the day and full of the blithest hopes for the future. Only she had become more sure of herself,

Prince Andrei thought. Dessalles, the tutor he had brought back from Switzerland, was wearing a coat of Russian cut and talking broken Russian to the servants, but he was still the same cultured, virtuous, pedantic preceptor of somewhat limited intelligence. The only physical change apparent in the old prince was the gap left at the side of his mouth caused by the loss of a tooth: in temper he was the same as ever, only even more irritable and sceptical concerning the good faith of what was happening in the world. Little Nikolai alone had grown and changed: his cheeks were rosier, his hair was dark and curly, and when he was laughing and happy he unconsciously lifted the lip of his pretty little mouth just as his dead mother had done. He alone did not obey the law of immutability in this spellbound sleeping castle. But though on the surface everything remained as of old, the relations to each other of all these people had altered since Prince Andrei had last seen them. The household was divided into two hostile camps, who came together now simply because he was there, on his account modifying their usual pattern of existence. To one camp belonged the old prince, Mademoiselle Bourienne and the architect; to the other – Princess Maria, Dessalles, little Nikolai and all the old nurses and maids.

During his stay at Bald Hills all the family dined together, but they were ill at ease and Prince Andrei felt that he was being treated as a guest for whose sake an exception was being made, and that his presence was a constraint upon them. On the first day at dinner, instinctively aware of this, he sat mute, and the old prince, remarking his unnatural quietness, relapsed into a moody silence, and immediately after dinner retired to his apartments. In the evening, when Prince Andrei joined him and began to tell him of young Count Kamensky's campaign, in the hope of rousing his interest, the old prince to his surprise began talking about Princess Maria, criticizing her for her religious superstitions and her dislike of Mademoiselle Bourienne, who was, he said, the only person really attached to him.

The old prince declared it was all Princess Maria's doing if he was not well: that she set out to plague and annoy him, and that she was spoiling little Nikolai with her coddling and silly talk. The old prince knew perfectly well that he tormented his daughter and that she had a very hard life; but he knew, too, that he could not help tormenting her and that she deserved it. 'Why does Prince Andrei, who sees this, say nothing about his sister?' wondered the old prince. 'Does he think me a scoundrel, or an old fool who for no reason has estranged himself from his daughter and taken the Frenchwoman in her place? He doesn't understand, so I must explain and he must hear me out,' thought the old prince. And he began expounding why it was he could not put up with his daughter's stupid character.

'If you ask me,' said Prince Andrei, not looking at the old man (it was the first time in his life that he was finding fault with his father), 'I had no wish to speak of it – but, if you ask me, I will give you my frank opinion. If there is misunderstanding and discord between you and Marie, I cannot lay the blame for it at her door. I know how she loves and reveres you. Since you ask me,' continued Prince Andrei, his temper rising, as of late it was apt to, 'I can only say that if there are misunderstandings the cause of them is that worthless woman, who is not fit to be my sister's companion.'

The old man at first stared at his son with fixed eyes, and a forced smile disclosed the fresh gap between his teeth to which Prince Andrei could not get accustomed.

'What companion, my dear boy? Eh? So you've already been talking it over, have you?'

'Father, I had no wish to pass judgement,' said Prince Andrei in a hard, bitter tone, 'but you insisted, and I have said, and always shall say, that Marie is not to blame. It is the fault of those – it is the fault of that Frenchwoman.'

'Ah, he has pronounced judgement ... pronounced judgement!' said the old prince in a low voice and, as it seemed to Prince Andrei, with some embarrassment. But the next moment he jumped to his feet and screamed: 'Get out of my sight, get out of my sight. Never let me lay eyes on you again.'

Prince Andrei would have left at once but Princess Maria persuaded him to stay another day, during which he did not see his father, who kept to his room and admitted no one save Mademoiselle Bourienne and Tikhon, and asked several times whether his son had gone. On the following day, just before setting out, Prince Andrei went to the part of the house where his son was to be found. The sturdy little boy, curly-headed like his mother, sat on his knee. Prince Andrei began telling him the story of Bluebeard but fell into a reverie before he got to the end. He was thinking not of the pretty child, his son whom he held on his knee, but of himself. He sought, and was horrified not to find in himself, either remorse for having angered his father or regret at leaving home for the first time in his life on bad terms with him. What disturbed him still more was that he could detect no trace in himself of the tenderness he had once felt for the boy and had hoped to revive in his heart when he petted the child and sat him on his knee.

'Well, go on!' said his son.

Prince Andrei, without replying, put him down from his knee and went out of the room.

As soon as Prince Andrei suspended his daily occupations, and especially the moment he returned to the old surroundings in which he had been happy, the anguish of life seized him with all its former strength, and he made haste to escape from these memories and to find some work to do without delay.

'Are you really leaving, André?' his sister asked him.

'Thank God that I can,' replied Prince Andrei. 'I am very sorry you can't.'

'Why do you say that?' exclaimed Princess Maria. 'How can you say that when you are going to this awful war, and he is so old? Mademoiselle Bourienne says he keeps asking about you. ...'

As soon as she began on that subject, her lips quivered while large tears rolled down her cheeks. Prince Andrei turned away and began walking up and down the room.

'Good God! And to think that such – such trash can bring misery on people!' he cried with a malignity that alarmed Princess Maria.

She realized that by the word 'trash' he was referring not only to Mademoiselle Bourienne, the cause of her misery, but also to the man who had destroyed his own happiness.

'André, one thing I beg, I entreat of you!' she said, touching his elbow and looking at him with eyes that shone through her tears. 'I understand you' (she looked down). 'Don't imagine that sorrow is the work of men. Men are His instruments.' She glanced upwards a little above Prince Andrei's head with the confident, accustomed look with which one glances towards the place where a familiar portrait hangs. 'Sorrow is sent by Him, not by men. Men are His instruments – they are not to blame. If it seems to you that someone has wronged you, forget it and forgive. We have no right to punish. And then you will know the happiness of forgiveness.'

'If I were a woman, I would, Marie. That is a woman's virtue. But a man should not and cannot forgive and forget,' he replied, and, though up to that minute he had not been thinking of Kuragin, all his unexpended anger suddenly surged up in his heart. 'If Marie is already hoping to persuade me to forgive, it is proof positive that I ought long ago to have punished him,' he thought. And making no further reply to her he began picturing to himself the glad vindictive moment when he would meet Kuragin, who he knew was now with the army.

Princess Maria besought her brother to stay one day more, telling him she knew how unhappy her father would be if Andrei left without being reconciled to him, but Prince Andrei answered that he would probably soon be back again from the army, and would write to his father, but that the longer he delayed now the more embittered would their difference become.

'Adieu, André! Remember that misfortunes come from God, and men are never to blame,' were the last words he heard from his sister as he said good-bye to her.

'Such is fate!' thought Prince Andrei as he drove out of the avenue of the Bald Hills mansion. 'She, poor innocent creature, is left to be victimized by an old man who has outlived his wits. The old man knows he is wrong but he can't help himself. My boy is growing up and smiling at life in which like everybody else he will deceive or be deceived. And I am off to the army – why? I have no idea. And I am anxious to meet with a man whom I despise, so as to give him a chance to kill me and sneer at me!'

Life had been made up of the same conditions before, but then these conditions had seemed to him all of a piece, whereas now they had all fallen apart. His mind flitted inconsequently from one thing to another, and there was no sense or meaning anywhere.

9

PRINCE ANDREI reached Army Headquarters at the end of June. The first army, with the Emperor, occupied a fortified camp at Drissa; the second army was retreating, in an effort to effect a junction with the first, from which it was said to be cut off by large French forces. Everyone was dissatisfied with the general course of military affairs in the Russian army, but no one even dreamed that the Russian provinces might be in danger of invasion or that the war would not be confined to the western, the Polish, provinces.

Prince Andrei found Barclay de Tolly, to whom he had been

assigned, on the bank of the Drissa. As there was not a single small town or sizeable village in the neighbourhood of the camp, the immense multitude of generals and court functionaries accompanying the army had taken possession of the best houses of the villages on both sides of the river, over a radius of about six miles. Barclay de Tolly was quartered nearly three miles from the Emperor. He received Bolkonsky stiffly, and frigidly informed him in his German accent that he would refer to the Emperor concerning his employment, and proposed that for the time being he should remain on his staff. Anatole Kuragin, whom Prince Andrei had hoped to find in the army, was not there: he was in Petersburg, and Bolkonsky was glad to hear it. He was absorbed by the interest of being at the heart of a mighty war that was just at its beginning, and was thankful for a short respite from the excitation of feeling which the thought of Kuragin provoked in him. Having no immediate duties, he spent the first four days in riding all round the camp's fortifications, endeavouring with the help of his own experience and talks with the well-informed to conceive a specific opinion about it. But the question whether the camp was an advantage or not remained an open one in his mind. He had already, from his own military experience, come to the conclusion that in war the most deeply deliberated plans mean nothing (he had seen that at Austerlitz), and that everything depends on the way unexpected movements on the part of the enemy – which cannot possibly be foreseen – are met with, and on how and by whom operations are directed. To get light on this last point Prince Andrei, availing himself of his position and acquaintances, took every opportunity of studying the character of the control of the army and of the persons and parties engaged in its organization, and deduced for himself the following idea of the position of affairs.

While the Emperor was at Vilna the forces had been divided into three armies. First, the army under Barclay de Tolly; secondly, the army under Bagration; and thirdly, the one commanded by Tormasov. The Emperor was with the first army but not in the capacity of commander-in-chief. In the order of the day it was announced, not that the Emperor would take command, but only that he would be with the army. Moreover, the Emperor had with him not a commander-in-chief's staff but the Imperial Headquarters staff. In attendance on him was the Chief of the Imperial Staff, Quartermaster-General Prince Volkonsky, as well as generals, Imperial aides-de-camp, diplomatic officials and a considerable number of foreigners, but it was not a military staff. Also accompanying the Emperor, in no definite capacity, were Arakcheyev, ex-minister of war; Count Bennigsen, the most senior in rank of the generals; the Tsarevich, the Grand Duke Constantine Pavlovich; Count Rumyantsev, the chancellor; Stein, a former Prussian minister; Armfeldt, the Swedish general; Pfuhl, the chief author of the plan of campaign; General-adjutant Paulucci, a Sardinian *émigré*; Wolzogen – and many others. Though these personages had no military appointment in the army their position gave them influence, and often a corps-commander or even one of the commanders-in-chief did not know in what capacity Bennigsen or the Tsarevich, Arakcheyev or Prince Volkonsky asked questions or proffered their counsel, and could not tell whether such and such an order, couched in the form of a piece of advice, emanated from the man who gave it or from the Emperor, and whether it had to be executed or not. But all this simply formed the external aspect of the situation: the inner import of the presence of the Emperor and all these other individuals was, from a courtier's point of view (and in an emperor's vicinity all men become courtiers), plain to everyone. All realized that, though the Emperor was not formally assuming the title of commander-in-chief, the control of all the armies was in his hands, and the persons about him were his assistants. Arakcheyev was the faithful custodian of law and order, and the Sovereign's bodyguard. Bennigsen was a landowner in the Vilna province who appeared to be doing the honours of the district but was in reality a good general, useful as an adviser and ready to hand to replace Barclay. The Tsarevich was there because it suited him. The former Prussian minister, Stein, was there because his advice was valuable and the Emperor Alexander had a high opinion of his personal qualities. Armfeldt had a violent hatred of Napoleon, and was a general possessed of great confidence in his own ability, a trait which never failed to have influence with Alexander. Paulucci was there because he was bold and decided in his utterances. The adjutants-general were there because they were always to be found where the Emperor was; and the last and principal figure, Pfuhl, was there because he had drawn up the plan of campaign against Napoleon, and, having induced Alexander to believe in the efficacy of this plan of his, was directing the entire action of the war. With Pfuhl was Wolzogen, who put Pfuhl's ideas in a more comprehensible form than Pfuhl himself – who was a rigid cabinet theorist, self-confident to the point of despising everyone else – was able to do.

In addition to the above-mentioned Russians and foreigners (with foreigners in the ascendancy and every day propounding new and startling suggestions with the audacity characteristic of people engaged in activities in spheres not their own) – there were many more persons of secondary importance who were with the army because their principals were there.

In this vast, restless, brilliant and haughty world, among all these conflicting opinions and voices, Prince Andrei distinguished the following sharply outlined sub-divisions of tendencies and parties.

The first party consisted of Pfuhl and his adherents: military theorists who believed in a science of war having its immutable laws – laws for oblique movements, outflankings and so forth. Pfuhl and his adherents demanded a retirement into the interior of the country in accordance with precise principles defined by a pseudo-theory of war, and in every deviation from this theory they saw only barbarism, ignorance or evil intention. To this party belonged the German princes, Wolzogen, Wintzingerode and others, but chiefly the Germans.

The second faction, diametrically opposed to the first, fell, as always happens, into the other extreme. The members of this party were those who had clamoured for an advance from Vilna into Poland, and freedom from all prearranged plans. Besides being advocates of bold action, this section also represented nationalism, which made them still more one-sided in the dispute. They were the Russians: Bagration, Yermolov (who was just beginning to make his mark) and others. It was at this time that Yermolov's famous joke was being circulated – that he had petitioned the Emperor to promote him to the rank of 'German'. The men of this party were never tired of quoting Suvorov and arguing that there was no need for cerebration and sticking pins into maps: the point was to fight, beat the enemy, keep him out of Russia, and not let the army lose heart.

To the third party – in which the Emperor had most confidence – belonged the courtiers, who tried to effect a compromise between the other two. The members of this group, chiefly civilians and including Arakcheyev among their number, thought and spoke in the way men who have no convictions but wish to pass for having some usually do speak. They said that war, especially against such a genius as Bonaparte (they called him Bonaparte again now) did undoubtedly call for the profoundest tactical considerations and scientific knowledge, and in that respect Pfuhl was a genius; but at the same time it had to be acknowledged that theorists were often one-sided, and so one should not place implicit faith in them but should also listen to what Pfuhl's opponents had to say, and to the views of practical men with experience in warfare, and then choose a middle course. They insisted that the camp at Drissa should be retained according to Pfuhl's plan, but advocated altering the disposition of the other two armies. Though by this course neither one aim nor the other could be attained, this seemed to the party of compromise the best line to adopt.

Of a fourth tendency of opinion the most conspicuous representative was the Grand Duke and heir-apparent, who could not get over his rude awakening at Austerlitz, where he had ridden out at the head of the Guards in casque and cuirass as to a review, expecting to rout the French with a flourish, but had suddenly found himself in the front line and had a narrow escape from the general *mêlée*. The men of this party had at once the merit and the defect of sincerity in their convictions. They feared Napoleon, recognized his strength and their own weakness, and had no hesitation in saying so. 'Nothing but misfortune, ignominy and defeat can come of all this,' they said. 'Here we have abandoned Vilna, abandoned Vitebsk, and we shall likewise abandon Drissa. The only rational thing left for us to do is to make peace, and as soon as possible, before we are driven out of Petersburg!'

This view was widely prevalent in the higher military circles, and found support in Petersburg too, and from the chancellor Rumyantsev, who for other reasons of state was in favour of peace.

Partisans of Barclay de Tolly, not so much as a man but as minister of war and commander-in-chief, formed the fifth faction. They said: 'Whatever else he is' (they always began like that), 'he is an honest, practical man, and we have nobody better. Give him real power, because war can never be prosecuted successfully under divided authority, and he will show what he can do, as he did in Finland. If our army is well-organized and strong, and has withdrawn to Drissa without suffering a single defeat, we owe it entirely to Barclay. If Barclay is now to be replaced by Bennigsen all will be lost, for Bennigsen proved his incapacity as far back as 1807.' Thus spoke the fifth party.

The sixth element – the Bennigsenites – argued, on the contrary, that after all there was no one more capable and experienced than Bennigsen, 'and however much you twist and turn you'll have to come to Bennigsen in the end'. Our whole retirement to Drissa, they maintained, was a shameful reverse and an uninterrupted series of blunders. 'The more mistakes that are made the better. At least it will teach them all the sooner that things cannot go on like this. And we want none of your Barclays, but a man like Bennigsen, who showed what he was made of in 1807, and to whom Napoleon himself had to do justice – a man whose authority would be willingly recognized. And the only man of that stamp is Bennigsen.'

The seventh party consisted of individuals such as are always to be found, especially in the entourage of young monarchs, and of whom there was a particularly plentiful supply around Alexander – generals and Imperial aides-de-camp passionately devoted to their Sovereign, not merely as a monarch but sincerely and whole-heartedly worshipping him as a man, just as Rostov had done in 1805, and who saw in him not only all the virtues but all the human talents as well. These men, though enchanted with the Sovereign for declining to assume command of the army, deplored such excess of modesty, and desired and urged one thing only – that their adored Tsar should overcome his diffidence and openly proclaim that he was placing himself at the head of the army, gather round him a staff appropriate to a commander-in-chief and, consulting experienced theoreticians and practical veterans where necessary, himself lead his forces, whose spirits would thereby be raised to the highest pitch of enthusiasm.

The eighth and largest group, numbering ninety-nine to every one of the others, consisted of men who were neither for peace nor for war, neither for offensive operations nor a defensive camp at Drissa or anywhere else; who did not take the side of Barclay or of the Emperor, of Pfuhl or of Bennigsen, but cared only for the one thing most essential – as much advantage and pleasure for themselves as they could lay hold of. In the troubled waters of those cross-currents of intrigue that eddied about the Emperor's headquarters it was possible to succeed in very many ways that would have been unthinkable at other times. One courtier simply interested in retaining his lucrative post would today agree with Pfuhl, tomorrow with Pfuhl's opponents, and the day after, merely to avoid responsibility or to please the Emperor, would declare that he had no opinion at all on the matter. Another, eager to curry favour, would attract the

Tsar's attention by loudly advocating something the Emperor had hinted at the day before, and would dispute and shout at the Council, beating his breast and challenging those who did not agree with him to a duel, thus displaying his readiness to sacrifice himself for the common weal. A third, while his enemies were out of the way, and in between two Councils, would simply solicit a special gratuity for his faithful services, well aware that it would be quicker at the moment to grant it than to refuse it. A fourth would contrive to be seen by the Tsar quite overwhelmed with work. A fifth, in order to achieve his long-cherished ambition to dine with the Emperor, would vehemently debate the rights or wrongs of some newly emerging opinion, producing more or less forcible and valid arguments in support of it.

All the members of this party were fishing after roubles, decorations and promotions, and in their chase simply kept their eye on the weathercock of Imperial favour: directly they noticed it shifting to one quarter the whole drone-population of the army began buzzing away in that direction, making it all the harder for the Emperor to change course elsewhere. Amid the uncertainties of the position, with the menace of serious danger which gave a peculiarly feverish intensity to everything, amid this vortex of intrigue, selfish ambition, conflicting views and feelings, and different nationalities, this eighth and largest party of men preoccupied with personal interests imparted great confusion and obscurity to the common task. Whatever question arose, a swarm of these drones, before they had done with their buzzing over the previous theme, would fly off to the new one, to smother and drown by their humming the voices of those who were prepared to examine it fully and honestly.

Out of all these groups, just at the time Prince Andrei reached the army, another and ninth party was coming into being and beginning to make its voice heard. This was the party of the elders, of sound men of experience in state affairs, sharing none of the conflicting opinions and able to take a detached view of what was going on at Staff Headquarters, and to consider means for escaping from the muddle, uncertainty, confusion and weakness.

The members of this party said and thought that the whole evil was primarily due to the Emperor's presence in the army with his military court, and the consequent introduction of that indefinite, conditional and fluctuating uncertainty of relations which may be convenient at Court but is mischievous in an army; that it was for a sovereign to reign but not command the army, and that the only solution of the difficulty would be for the Emperor and his Court to take their departure; that the mere presence of the Tsar paralysed fifty thousand troops required to secure his personal safety; and that the most incompetent commander-in-chief if he were independent would be better than the very best one hampered by the presence and authority of the Monarch.

Just at the time Prince Andrei was continuing at Drissa with nothing to do, Shishkov, secretary of state and one of the chief representatives of this last group, concocted a letter to the Emperor to which Balashev and Arakcheyev agreed to add their signatures. In this letter, availing himself of the Emperor's permission to discuss the general course of affairs, he respectfully suggested – on the plea of the vital necessity for the Sovereign to rouse the people of the capital to enthusiasm for the war – that the Emperor should leave the army.

The fanning of this flame by the Sovereign, and his appeal to them to rise in defence of their Fatherland – the very factors (in so far as they can be said to have resulted from the Tsar's personal presence in Moscow) which led to Russia's ultimate triumph – were suggested to the Emperor, and accepted by him, as a pretext for quitting the army.

10

THIS letter had not yet been presented to the Emperor when Barclay, at dinner one day, informed Bolkonsky that his Majesty wished to see him personally, to question him about Turkey, and that Prince Andrei was to appear at Bennigsen's quarters at six o'clock that evening.

That very day news had reached the Emperor's staff of a fresh movement on the part of Napoleon which might prove dangerous for the army – a report which subsequently turned out to be false. And that morning Colonel Michaud had accompanied the Tsar on a tour of inspection of the Drissa fortifications, and had pointed out to him that this fortified camp, constructed under Pfuhl's direction and hitherto regarded as a *chef d'œuvre* of tactical science which would ensure Napoleon's destruction, was a piece of folly and the ruin of the Russian army.

Prince Andrei proceeded to Bennigsen's quarters, a small manor-house on the very bank of the river. Neither Bennigsen nor the

Emperor was there but Tchernyshev, the Emperor's aide-de-camp, received Bolkonsky and informed him that the Tsar, with General Bennigsen and the Marchese Paulucci had set off for the second time that day to inspect the fortifications of the Drissa camp, of the utility of which they were beginning to entertain grave doubts.

Tchernyshev was sitting at a window of the outer room with a French novel in his hand. This room had at one time probably been a music-room: there was still an organ in it on which some rugs were piled, and in one corner stood the folding bedstead of Bennigsen's adjutant. This adjutant was also there, and sat dozing on the rolled-up bedding, apparently exhausted by work or festivities. Two doors led from the room, one straight into what had been the drawing-room, and another, on the right, opening into the study. Through the first came the sound of voices conversing in German and occasionally in French. In the former drawing-room were gathered, by the Emperor's request, not a Council of War (the Emperor preferred to have things vague) but certain persons whose opinions he wished to know, in view of the impending difficulties. It was not a Council of War but a sort of council to elucidate various questions for the benefit of the Tsar personally. To this semi-council had been invited the Swedish general, Armfeldt, Adjutant-General Wolzogen, Wintzingerode (whom Napoleon had referred to as a renegade French subject), Michaud, Toll, Count Stein – by no means a military man – and finally Pfuhl, who was, so Prince Andrei had heard, the mainspring of the whole affair. Prince Andrei had an opportunity of getting a good look at him, as Pfuhl arrived shortly after himself, and stopped for a minute to say a few words to Tchernyshev before passing on into the drawing-room.

At first glance Pfuhl, in his badly-cut uniform of a Russian general, which sat on him awkwardly like some fancy dress costume, seemed a familiar figure to Prince Andrei though he had never seen him before. He was of the same order as Weierother, Mack and Schmidt, and many other German theorist-generals whom Prince Andrei had come across in 1805, but he was more typical than any of them. Never in his life had Prince Andrei beheld a German theorist who so completely combined in himself all the characteristics of those other Germans.

Pfuhl was short and very thin but big-boned, of coarse, robust build, broad in the hips and with prominent shoulder-blades. His face was much wrinkled, and his eyes deep-set. His hair had obviously been hastily brushed smooth in front by the temples but it stuck up behind in odd little tufts. He walked in looking nervously and irritably about him, as if afraid of everything in that great room to which he was bound. Awkwardly holding up his sword, he addressed Tchernyshev, asking him in German where the Emperor was. It was evident that he was anxious to get across the room as speedily as possible, have done with the bows and greetings, and sit down to business in front of a map, where he would feel at home. He nodded abruptly in response to Tchernyshev, and smiled ironically on hearing that the Sovereign was inspecting the fortifications that he, Pfuhl, had planned in accord with his theory. He growled to himself in his bass voice, muttering something that might have been 'Stupid blockhead!' or '... Damn the whole business!' or 'A pretty state of affairs that will lead to!', after the manner of all conceited Germans. Prince Andrei did not catch his remarks, and would have passed on, but Tchernyshev introduced him to Pfuhl, observing that Prince Andrei had just come from Turkey, where the war had terminated so fortunately. Pfuhl gave a fleeting glance not so much at Prince Andrei as through him, and commented with a laugh: 'That war must have been a model of tactics!' And, laughing scornfully, he went on into the room from which the sound of voices came.

It was plain that Pfuhl, always inclined to be irritable and sarcastic, was particularly provoked that day by the fact of their having dared to inspect and criticize his camp in his absence. From this brief interview with Pfuhl, Prince Andrei, thanks to his Austerlitz experiences, was able to form a clear conception of the man's character. Pfuhl was one of those hopelessly, immutably conceited men, obstinately sure of themselves as only Germans are, because only Germans could base their self-confidence on an abstract idea – on science, that is, the supposed possession of absolute truth. A Frenchman's conceit springs from his belief that mentally and physically he is irresistibly fascinating both to men and women. The Englishman's self-assurance comes from being a citizen of the best-organized kingdom in the world, and because as an Englishman he always knows what is the correct thing to do, and that everything he does as an Englishman is undoubtedly right. An Italian is conceited because he is excitable and easily forgets himself and other people. A Russian is conceited because he knows nothing and does not want to know anything, since he does not believe that it is possible to know anything completely. A conceited German is the worst of them all, the most stubborn and unattractive, because he imagines that he possesses the truth in science – a thing of his own invention but which for him is absolute truth. Pfuhl was evidently of this breed. He had his science – the theory of oblique movements deduced by him from the history of Frederick the Great's wars, and everything he came across in more recent military history seemed to him preposterous and barbarous – crude struggles in which so many blunders were committed on both sides that such wars could not be called wars: they did not fit in with the theory, and therefore could not serve as material for science.

In 1806 Pfuhl had been one of those responsible for the plan of campaign that culminated in Jena and Auerstadt; but in the outcome of that war he did not see the slightest evidence of the fallibility of his theory. On the contrary, to his mind the disaster was entirely due to the deviations that were made from his theory, and with characteristically gleeful sarcasm he would remark: 'Didn't I always say the whole affair would go to the devil!' Pfuhl was one of those theoreticians who are so fond of their theory that they lose sight of the object of that theory – its application in practice. His passion for theory made him hate all practical considerations, and he would not hear of them. He even rejoiced in failure, for failures resulting from departures in practice from abstract theory only proved to him the accuracy of his theory.

He said a few words to Prince Andrei and Tchernyshev about the present war, with the air of a man who knows beforehand that everything will go wrong, and indeed is not displeased that it should do so. The little tufts of uncombed hair sticking up behind and the hastily brushed locks on his temples expressed this most eloquently.

He crossed into the other room, from where the querulous notes of his bass voice were at once audible.

I I

PRINCE ANDREI was still following Pfuhl with his eyes when Count Bennigsen came hurrying into the room and, nodding to Bolkonsky but not stopping, passed into the study, giving instructions to his adjutant as he went. The Emperor was behind him, and Bennigsen had hastened on ahead to make some preparations and to be there to receive him. Tchernyshev and Prince Andrei went out into the porch, where the Emperor, who looked tired, was dismounting from his horse. The Marchese Paulucci was addressing him with particular warmth and the Emperor, with his head inclined to the left, was listening with a look of displeasure. The Emperor moved forward, evidently wishing to cut short the conversation, but the flushed and excited Italian, oblivious of etiquette, followed him, still talking.

'As for the man who advised this camp at Drissa —' Paulucci was saying as the Emperor mounted the steps and, noticing Prince Andrei, scanned his unfamiliar face, 'as to that person, sire ...' Paulucci persisted desperately, apparently unable to restrain himself, 'the man who advised the Drissa camp – I see no alternative but the madhouse or the gallows.'

Without waiting for the Italian to finish, and as though not hearing his remarks, the Emperor, recognizing Bolkonsky, turned to him graciously.

'I am very glad to see you. Go in to the others and wait for me.'

The Emperor went into the study. He was followed by Prince Piotr Mihalovich Volkonsky and Baron Stein, and the door closed behind them. Prince Andrei, taking advantage of the Tsar's permission, accompanied Paulucci, whom he had met in Turkey, into the drawing-room where the Council was assembled.

Prince Piotr Mihalovich Volkonsky occupied the position, as it were, of chief of the Emperor's staff. He came out of the study into the drawing-room, bringing with him some maps which he spread on a table, and announced the points on which he wished to hear the opinion of the gentlemen present. What had happened was that news (which afterwards proved to be false) had been received during the night of a movement by the French to outflank the Drissa camp.

The first to speak was General Armfeldt, who, to counter the difficulty that presented itself, unexpectedly proposed that they should choose an entirely new position away from the Petersburg and Moscow roads, and, united there, await the enemy. No one could see any reason for his advocating such a scheme, unless it was a desire to show that he, too, could have ideas of his own. It was obviously a plan that Armfeldt had thought out long ago, and put forward now not so much with the object of meeting the problem – to which it offered no solution – as to avail himself of the opportunity of airing it. It was one of a myriad propositions, each as good as the other, which might be made in ignorance of what character the war would take. Some of those present attacked his suggestion, others defended it. The young Colonel Toll criticized the Swedish general's views with more heat than anyone, and in the course of the argument drew from his side-pocket a well-filled manuscript-book which he asked permission to read to them. In a voluminous note Toll propounded still another plan of campaign, totally different from Armfeldt's or Pfuhl's. Paulucci, in raising objections to Toll's ideas, suggested an advance and attack, which, he urged, was the only way to extricate ourselves from the present uncertainty and from the trap (as he called the camp at Drissa) in which we were placed. During all these discussions Pfuhl and his interpreter Wolzogen (his mouthpiece in his dealings with the court) sat silent. Pfuhl merely snorted contemptuously and turned his back to indicate that he would never stoop to reply to the rubbish he was hearing. So when Prince Volkonsky, who was in the chair, appealed to him for his opinion he simply answered:

'Why ask me ? General Armfeldt has proposed a first-rate position with our rear exposed to the enemy. Or why not this Italian gentleman's attack – a capital idea ! Or a retreat ? Excellent, too. Why ask me ?' he repeated. 'You all know better than I do, it appears.'

But when Volkonsky frowned and said that he asked his opinion in the name of the Emperor, Pfuhl rose to his feet and, suddenly animated, began to speak:

'Everything has been spoilt and thrown into a muddle. Everybody thought they knew better than I, and now you come to me ! "What shall we do to put things right ?" you say. There is nothing to be put right. You have only to carry out to the letter the principles laid down by me,' said he, drumming on the table with his bony knuckles. 'What is the difficulty ? It's nonsense ! Child's play !'

He went up to the table and, speaking rapidly and thrusting with his wrinkled finger at the map, began demonstrating that no contingency could affect the advantages of the Drissa camp, that everything had been foreseen and that if the enemy were actually to outflank them, then the enemy would infallibly be wiped out.

Paulucci, who did not know German, began questioning him in French. Wolzogen came to the assistance of his chief, who spoke French badly, and began translating for him, hardly able to keep pace with Pfuhl, who was demonstrating at top speed that everything – not only all that had happened but all that could possibly happen –

had been provided for in his plan, and that if difficulties had arisen now the whole fault lay in the fact that his plan had not been carried out with exactitude. He kept laughing sarcastically as he argued, and at last, like a mathematician who will waste no more time verifying the various steps in the solution of a problem already proved, he contemptuously abandoned his demonstration. Wolzogen took his place, continuing to explain his views in French and every now and then turning to Pfuhl with a 'Is that not right, your Excellency?' But Pfuhl, as a man in the heat of the fray will belabour those of his own side, shouted angrily at his supporter:

'To be sure – it's as plain as daylight.'

Paulucci and Michaud fell simultaneously on Wolzogen in French. Armfeldt addressed Pfuhl in German. Toll explained to Prince Volkonsky in Russian. Prince Andrei listened and watched the proceedings in silence.

Of all these men the irate, peremptory and absurdly conceited Pfuhl was the one who most attracted Prince Andrei's sympathy. He alone of all those present was obviously not seeking anything for himself, harboured no personal grudge, and desired one thing only – the adoption of his plan based on a theory arrived at after years of toil. He was ridiculous, he was disagreeable with his sarcasm, yet he inspired an involuntary feeling of respect by his boundless devotion to an idea. Besides this, with the single exception of Pfuhl, the remarks of every person present possessed a common trait, of which there had been no symptom at the council of war in 1805. This was a panic fear of Napoleon's genius, a dread which, though cloaked, betrayed itself in every argument. They took it for granted that Napoleon could do anything, expected him to appear from every quarter at once, and invoked his terrible name to demolish each other's proposals. Pfuhl alone, it seemed, considered Napoleon as much a barbarian as everybody else who opposed his theory. But, as well as respect, Pfuhl evoked pity in Prince Andrei. From the tone in which the courtiers addressed him, and the way in which Paulucci had ventured to speak of him to the Emperor, but above all from a certain desperation in Pfuhl's own utterances, it was clear that the others knew, and Pfuhl himself was aware, that his fall was at hand. And for all his conceit and querulous German irony he was pathetic with his hair flattened on the temples and sticking up in tufts behind. Although he did his best to conceal the fact under a show of irritation and contempt, he was visibly in despair that his sole remaining chance of testing his theory on a tremendous scale and proving its soundness to the whole world was slipping from him.

The discussion continued a long while, and the longer it lasted the more heated grew the arguments, culminating in shouts and personalities, and the less possible it was to arrive at any general conclusions from all that had been said. Prince Andrei, listening to this polyglot talk, to the presuppositions, plans, cries and objections, could only wonder in amazement. A thought which had early and often occurred to him during the period of his military activities – that there was not, and could not be any such thing as a science of war, and consequently no such thing as military genius – now appeared to him a completely obvious truth. 'What theory and science is possible where the conditions and circumstances of a subject are unknown and cannot be defined – and especially when the strength of the active forces engaged cannot be ascertained ? No one could know – no one can know – the relative positions of our army and the enemy twenty-four hours from now, and no one can gauge the potential of this or that detachment. Sometimes, when there is no coward in front to cry, "We are cut off!" and start to run, but a brave, spirited lad who leads the way with shouts of "Hurrah", a division of five thousand is as good as thirty thousand, as was the case at Schön Graben, while at other times fifty thousand will fly from eight thousand, as happened at Austerlitz. What science can there be where everything is vague and depends on an endless variety of circumstances, the significance of which becomes manifest all in a moment, and no one can foretell when that moment is coming ? Armfeldt says that our army is cut off, while Paulucci maintains that we have caught the enemy between two fires. Michaud asserts that the weak point of the Drissa camp is having the river behind it, while Pfuhl declares that that is what constitutes its strength. Toll proposes one plan, Armfeldt another, and all are good and all are bad, and the advantages of each and every suggestion can only be seen at the moment of trial. And why do they all talk of "military genius" ? Is a man a genius because he knows when to order army biscuits to be sent up, and when to march his troops to the right and when to the left ? He is called a genius merely because of the glamour and power with which the military are invested, and the crowds of sycophants always ready to flatter power and to ascribe to it qualities of genius it does not possess. Indeed the best generals I have known were stupid or absent-minded men. The best was Bagration, Napoleon himself admitted that. And Bonaparte himself! I remember his self-satisfied, insular expression on the field of Austerlitz. A good general has no need of any special qualities: on the contrary, he is the better for the absence of the loftiest and finest human attributes – love, poetry, tenderness and philosophic and inquiring doubt. He should be limited, firmly convinced that what he is doing is of great importance (otherwise he will not have the patience to go through with it), and only then will he be a gallant general. God forbid that he should be humane, should feel love or compassion, should stop to think what is just and unjust. It is understandable that a theory of their "genius" was invented for them long ago because they are synonymous with power! The success of a military action depends not on them but on the man in the ranks who first shouts "We are lost!" or "Hurrah!" And only in the ranks can one serve with the assurance of being useful.'

Thus mused Prince Andrei as he listened to the arguments, and he only roused himself when Paulucci called him and the meeting was breaking up.

At the review next day the Emperor asked Prince Andrei where he desired to serve, and Prince Andrei lost his standing in court circles for ever by asking permission to serve with the army, instead of begging for a post in attendance on the Sovereign's person.

12

BEFORE the beginning of the campaign Rostov had received a letter from his parents in which they told him briefly of Natasha's illness and the breaking off of her engagement to Prince Andrei (which they explained as having come about simply because Natasha rejected him), and again begged him to retire from the army and return home. On receiving this letter Nikolai made no attempt to secure either leave of absence or permission to go upon the retired list, though he wrote to his parents that he was very sorry about Natasha's illness and the rupture with her betrothed, and that he would do all he could to fall in with their wishes. To Sonya he wrote separately.

Adored friend of my heart [he wrote]. Nothing save honour could keep me from returning to the country. But now, at the commencement of a campaign, I should count myself disgraced not only in my comrades' eyes but in my own were I to put my personal happiness before my duty and my love for the Fatherland. But this shall be our last separation. Be sure that directly the war is over, if I am still alive and you still love me, I shall throw up everything and fly to you, to clasp you for ever to my ardent breast.

It was, in point of fact, only the inauguration of the campaign that held Rostov back and prevented him from returning home, as he had promised, and marrying Sonya. The autumn at Otradnoe with the hunting, and the winter with the Christmas holidays and Sonya's love, had opened out to him a vista of quiet country delights and contentment such as he had never known before and which now beckoned to him invitingly. 'A nice wife, children, a good pack of hounds, a dozen leashes of spirited borzois, the estate to look after, neighbours to entertain, perhaps an active share in the functions of the nobility,' he mused. But now the campaign was on them and he must remain with his regiment. And since it had to be so, Nikolai Rostov was characteristically able to be content too with the life he led in the regiment, and to make that life a pleasant one.

He had been hailed with joy by his comrades on returning from his furlough, and then sent to obtain remounts for the regiments. From the Ukraine he brought back some excellent horses which gave him great satisfaction and earned him commendation from his superior officers. During his absence he had been promoted to the rank of captain, and when the regiment was put on war-footing with an increased complement he was again allotted his old squadron.

The campaign began, the regiment was moved into Poland on double pay, new officers arrived, new men and horses, and, above all, everybody was infected with the excitement and enthusiasm which always accompany the beginning of a war; and Rostov, fully appreciating the advantages of his position in the regiment, devoted himself heart and soul to the pleasures and interests of military service, though he knew that sooner or later he would have to relinquish them.

The troops retired from Vilna for various complex considerations of state, of policy and of tactics. Every yard of the retreat stimulated a complicated interplay of interests, arguments and passions at Headquarters. For the Pavlograd Hussars, however, the whole of the withdrawal during the finest period of the summer and with ample supplies was a very simple and agreeable business. At Headquarters men might lose heart, grow nervous and intrigue but in the body of the army no one even thought of wondering where and why they were going. If they regretted having to retreat, it was only because it meant leaving billets they had become used to, or some pretty little Polish lady. If the idea did occur to anyone that things looked bad, he tried, as a good soldier should, to put a cheerful face on it, concentrating his attention on the task nearest to hand and forgetting the general trend of events. At first they pitched camp gaily before Vilna, making acquaintance with the Polish landowners of the neighbourhood, preparing for reviews and being reviewed by the Emperor and other high-ranking officers. Then came an order to retreat to Swienciany and destroy any stores that could not be carried away. Swienciany stuck in the hussars' memory simply as the *drunken camp*, the name given to the encampment there by the whole army, and as the scene of many complaints against the troops, who had taken advantage of orders to collect provisions and under this heading had included and taken horses, carriages and rugs from the Polish gentry. Rostov remembered Swienciany because on the first day of their arrival in that small town he had dismissed his quartermaster and been unable to do anything with the men of his squadron, all of whom were tipsy, having, without his knowledge, appropriated five barrels of old beer. From Swienciany they had retired farther, and then farther still, until they reached Drissa, and from Drissa the retreat had continued, till they were nearing the frontiers of Russia proper.

On the 13th of July the Pavlograds took part for the first time in a serious action.

On the 12th of July, on the eve of that engagement, there had been a heavy storm of rain and hail. In general, the summer of 1812 was remarkable for its tempestuous weather.

The two Pavlograd squadrons were bivouacking in a field of rye which was already in ear but had been completely trodden down by cattle and horses. Rain was falling in torrents, and Rostov was sitting with a young officer named Ilyin, a *protégé* of his, in a shelter that had been hastily rigged up for them. An officer of their regiment, with long moustaches hanging down from his cheeks, riding back from Staff Headquarters and caught in the rain, joined Rostov.

'I'm on my way from Staff, count. Heard about Raevsky's exploit?'

And the officer proceeded to relate the details of the Saltanov battle which had been told him at Headquarters.

Rostov, hunching his shoulders as the water trickled down his neck, smoked his pipe and listened carelessly, with an occasional glance at young Ilyin who was squeezed in close to him. This officer, a lad of sixteen who had recently entered the regiment, looked up to Nikolai in the same way as Nikolai had looked up to Denisov seven years before. Ilyin tried to copy Rostov in everything, and adored him as a girl might have done.

The officer with the twin moustaches, Zdrzhinsky by name, grandiloquently described the dam at Saltanov as being a 'Russian Thermopylae', and declared the heroic deed of General Raevsky on that dam to be worthy of antiquity. He recounted how Raevsky had led his two sons forward on to the dam under terrific fire, and had charged with them beside him. Rostov heard the story and not only said nothing to encourage Zdrzhinsky's enthusiasm but, on the contrary, looked like a man ashamed of what was being told him, though he had no intention of gainsaying it. After Austerlitz and the campaigns of 1807 Rostov knew from his own experience that men always lie when reporting deeds of battle, as he himself had done. In the second place his experience had taught him that in war nothing really happens exactly as we imagine and describe it. And so he did not care for Zdrzhinsky's tale, nor did he like Zdrzhinsky himself, who had, besides his moustaches, a habit of bending right over into the face of the person he was speaking to; and he took up too much room in the cramped little shelter. Rostov looked at him without speaking. 'To begin with, there must have been such a crush and confusion on the dam they were attacking that if Raevsky had really rushed forward with his sons it could have had no effect except perhaps on the ten or twelve men nearest to him,' thought Rostov. 'The rest could not have seen how or with whom Raevsky advanced on to the dam. And then even those who did see could not have been particularly inspired, for what did Raevsky's tender paternal feelings matter to them when they had their own skins to think about? And, moreover, the fate of the Fatherland did not depend on whether the Saltanov dam was taken, as we are told was the case at Thermopylae. So what was the use of such a sacrifice? And why expose his own children in battle? I wouldn't have taken my brother Petya there, nor even Ilyin, who's not my own kith and kin but he's a nice lad: I would have tried to keep them out of danger,' Nikolai reflected as he listened to Zdrzhinsky. But he did not give voice to his thoughts: in that, too, experience had taught him wisdom. He knew that this tale redounded to the glory of our arms, and so one had to pretend to take it in. And he acted accordingly.

'I can't stand this any more,' exclaimed Ilyin, perceiving that Rostov did not care for Zdrzhinsky's chatter. 'Stockings and shirt and all – I'm soaked through. I'm off to look for another place. I fancy the rain's not so heavy.'

Ilyin went out and Zdrzhinsky rode away.

Five minutes later Ilyin came splashing back through the mud to the shanty.

'Hurrah, Rostov! Stir your stumps, I've found somewhere. There's a tavern a couple of hundred yards from here and a lot of our fellows are there already. We can at least get dry, and Maria Hendrihovna's there.'

Maria Hendrihovna was the wife of the regimental doctor, a pretty young German woman whom he had married in Poland. The doctor, either because he could not afford to set up house for her or because he did not want to be parted from his young wife in the early days of their marriage, took her with him wherever he went in his travels with the regiment, and his jealousy became a standing joke among the hussar officers.

Rostov flung his cloak over his shoulders, shouted to Lavrushka to follow with their things, and set off with Ilyin, now slipping in the mud, now splashing straight through it, in the lessening rain and the darkness which was rent at intervals by distant lightning.

'Rostov, where are you?'

'Here. What a flash!' they called to one another.

13

In the tavern, before which stood the doctor's covered cart, there were already some half-dozen officers. Maria Hendrihovna, a plump, flaxen-headed little German in a dressing-jacket and night-cap, was sitting on a broad bench in the front corner. Her husband, the doctor, lay asleep behind her. Rostov and Ilyin were greeted with merry shouts and laughter as they entered the room.

'I say, how jolly we are!' said Rostov, laughing.

'And what are you gaping over?'

'Fine specimens they are! Why, the water's streaming from them! Don't swamp our parlour floor.'

'Mind you don't drip on Maria Hendrihovna's dress!' cried different voices.

Rostov and Ilyin made haste to look for a corner where they could change their wet clothes without offending Maria Hendrihovna's modesty. They started for a tiny recess the other side of a partition, but found it completely filled by three officers sitting on an empty chest playing cards by the light of a solitary candle, and nothing would induce them to budge. Maria Hendrihovna obliged with the loan of her petticoat which they hung up by way of a curtain, and behind this Rostov and Ilyin, assisted by Lavrushka, who had brought their kits, got out of their wet things and into dry ones.

They lit a fire in the dilapidated brick stove, discovered a board and propped it across two saddles and covered it with a horse-cloth. A small samovar was produced, together with a luncheon-basket and half a bottle of rum; and having asked Maria Hendrihovna to preside they all crowded round her. One offered her a clean handkerchief to wipe her charming hands; another spread his tunic under her little feet to keep them from the damp floor; a third hung a cape over the window to screen her from the draught; while a fourth waved the flies away from her husband's face lest he should wake up.

'Let him be,' said Maria Hendrihovna with a shy, happy smile. 'He will sleep sound anyhow after being up all night.'

'Oh no, Maria Hendrihovna,' replied the officer, 'one must look after the doctor. Anything may happen, and I dare say he'll take pity on me one day, when he has to cut off my leg or my arm.'

There were only three glasses, the water was so muddy that there was no telling whether the tea was strong or weak, and the samovar would only hold water enough for six; but this made it all the more fun to take turns in order of seniority to receive a glass from Maria Hendrihovna's plump little hands with their short and not over-clean nails. All the officers seemed to be genuinely in love with her for that evening. Even those who had been playing cards behind the partition soon left their game and came over to the samovar, catching the general mood of courting Maria Hendrihovna. She, seeing herself surrounded by all these brilliant and devoted young men, beamed with satisfaction, which she sought in vain to conceal, unmistakably alarmed as she was every time her husband moved in his sleep behind her.

There was only one spoon, sugar there was in plenty, but it took so long to melt that it was decided that Maria Hendrihovna should stir the sugar for each in turn. Rostov took his glass of tea, and adding some rum to it, begged Maria Hendrihovna to stir it for him.

'But you take it without sugar, don't you ?' she said, smiling all the while as though everything she said and everything the others said was as amusing as could be and held a double meaning.

'It's not the sugar I care about – all I want is for your little hand to stir my tea.'

Nothing loath, Maria Hendrihovna began looking for the spoon, which someone had pounced upon.

'Use your pretty little finger, Maria Hendrihovna,' said Rostov. 'I shall like that still better.'

'Too hot!' said Maria Hendrihovna, colouring with pleasure.

Ilyin put a few drops of rum into a bucket of water and brought it to Maria Hendrihovna, begging her to stir it with her finger.

'This is my cup,' he said. 'Only dip your finger in and I'll drink every drop.'

When they had emptied the samovar Rostov took a pack of cards and proposed a game of 'Kings' with Maria Hendrihovna. They drew lots to settle who should make up her set. At Rostov's suggestion it was agreed that whoever was 'king' should have the privilege of kissing Maria Hendrihovna's little hand, while the 'knave' should have to put the samovar on again for the doctor's tea when he awoke.

'Well, but supposing Maria Hendrihovna is "king" ?' asked Ilyin.

'She is our queen already, and her word is law!'

The game had scarcely begun before the doctor's dishevelled head suddenly popped up behind Maria Hendrihovna. He had been awake for some time, listening to the conversation, and apparently found nothing entertaining or amusing in what was going on. His face was glum and forlorn. He did not greet the officers but, scratching himself, asked them to move to let him get by. As soon as he had left the room all the officers burst into loud peals of laughter, while Maria Hendrihovna blushed till the tears came, which made her still more bewitching in the eyes of the young men. Returning from the yard, the doctor told his wife (who had lost her happy smile and was looking at him in dismay, in expectation of the sentence in store for her) that the rain had stopped and they must go and spend the night in their covered cart, or everything in it would be stolen.

'But I'll send an orderly ... I'll send a couple!' said Rostov. 'What an idea, doctor!'

'I will mount guard myself!' cried Ilyin.

'No, gentlemen, you have slept your fill but I've been up these two nights,' replied the doctor, and he sat gloomily down beside his wife to wait for the end of the game.

Seeing his sombre face lowering at his wife, the officers grew still more hilarious and many of them could not suppress their laughter, for which they hurriedly sought to invent plausible pretexts. When the doctor had gone, taking his wife with him, and had settled himself with her in their covered cart, the officers lay down in the tavern, covering themselves with their damp cloaks, but it was a long time before sleep came. They stayed awake talking, recalling the doctor's misgivings and his wife's glee, or running out on to the porch and coming back to report what was happening in the covered trap. Several times Rostov muffled up his head and tried to go to sleep, but some remark would rouse him again and the conversation would be resumed and again they would break out into nonsensical merry laughter, as though they were children.

14

It was going on for three o'clock but no one was yet asleep when the quartermaster appeared with orders that they were to move on to the small town of Ostrovna.

Still laughing and talking, the officers began hurriedly getting ready; once more the samovar was filled with dirty water. But Rostov went off to his squadron without waiting for tea. It was already light, the rain had ceased and the clouds were dispersing. It felt damp and cold, especially in clothes that had not dried. As they came out of the tavern in the twilight of the dawn, Rostov and Ilyin both glanced under the wet and glistening leather hood of the doctor's cart; the doctor's feet were sticking out from under the apron, and in the interior they caught a glimpse of his wife's night-capped head resting on a pillow, and heard her sleepy breathing.

'She's a dear little creature, isn't she?' said Rostov to Ilyin, who was following him.

'Yes, what a charming woman!' responded Ilyin with all the gravity of a boy of sixteen.

Half an hour later the squadron was lined up on the road. The command was given 'Mount!', and crossing themselves the soldiers climbed into their saddles. Rostov, riding in front, gave the order 'Forward!' and the hussars, with clanking sabres and the subdued buzz of voices, their horses' hooves splashing in the mud, filed off four abreast and trotted along the broad road planted with birch-trees on either side, following the infantry and a battery which had gone on ahead.

Tattered violet-grey clouds, reddening in the sunrise, were scudding before the wind. It was getting lighter every moment. The feathery grass which always grows by the roadside in the country could be seen quite plainly, still glistening from the night's rain. The drooping branches of the birch-trees, wet too, swayed in the wind and tossed sparkling drops of water aslant across the highway. The soldiers' faces showed more distinctly with the passing of every minute. Rostov, with Ilyin who never left him, rode along the side of the road between two rows of birch-trees.

On active service Rostov allowed himself the indulgence of a Cossack horse instead of a regimental horse of the line. A connoisseur and lover of horses, he had lately acquired a fine spirited animal from the Don steppes, a chestnut with light mane and tail, on whom he could out-gallop anyone. To be on this mount was a pleasure to him, and so he rode on, thinking of his horse, of the morning, of the doctor's wife, and never once of the peril awaiting him.

Advancing into action in the early days, Rostov had felt afraid, but now there was not the slightest sensation of fear. He was fearless not because he had grown used to being under fire (one cannot grow used to danger), but because he had learned how to control his thoughts in face of danger. He had schooled himself when going into action to think about anything except what one would have supposed to be the most pressing interest of all – the hazards that lay before him. During the first period of his service, earnestly as he had tried and bitterly as he had reproached himself with cowardice, he had not been able to do this, but with time it had come of itself. So now he rode beside Ilyin under the birch-trees, occasionally plucking leaves from a branch that met his hand, sometimes touching his horse's flank with his foot, or without turning his head, handing the pipe he had finished to an hussar behind him, all with as calm and careless an air as though he were merely out for a ride. He felt a pang of pity when he looked at the excited face of Ilyin, who talked fast and nervously. He knew from experience the agonizing state of anticipation of terror and death in which the cornet was plunged, and knew that only time could help him.

As soon as the sun appeared in the clear strip of sky below the clouds the wind died down, as though it dared not mar the beauty of the summer morning after the storm; the trees still dripped but now the drops fell vertically, and all was hushed. The sun came up full and round, poised on the horizon and then disappeared behind a long, narrow cloud that hung above it. A few minutes later it burst forth brighter than ever on the upper rim of the cloud, cutting its edge. Everything shone and sparkled with light. And with that light, as though in response to it, the sound of guns was heard ahead of them.

Before Rostov had had time to collect his thoughts and determine how far distant the firing was, Count Ostermann-Tolstoy's adjutant came galloping from Vitebsk with orders to advance at a trot along the road.

The squadron overtook and passed the infantry and the battery – which had also quickened their pace – rode down a hill and through an empty, deserted village and started to climb again. The horses were beginning to lather and the men looked hot.

'Halt! Dress ranks!' the command of the divisional colonel rang out in front. 'Forward by the left. Walking pace – forward!'

And the hussars made their way along the line of troops to the left flank of our position, and halted behind our Uhlans, who formed the front line. To the right stood our infantry in a dense column: they were the reserves. Higher up the hill, on the very horizon, our cannons could be seen in the crystal-clear air, shining in the slanting rays of the morning sun. In front, beyond a hollow dale, the enemy's columns and guns were visible. Down below in the hollow our advanced line had already gone into action and was briskly exchanging shots with the enemy.

At these sounds, which he had not heard for many a day, Rostov's spirits rose, as though the firing was the liveliest of music. *Trap-ta-ta-tap!* cracked the shots, now together, now in rapid succession. Again all was silent, and then again it sounded as though someone were walking on squibs and exploding them.

The hussars waited for about an hour in the same place. A cannonade began. Count Ostermann with his suite rode up behind the squadron, stopped to say a word to the colonel of the regiment and continued up the hill to the guns.

After Ostermann had gone, a command rang out to the Uhlans. 'Fall in! Prepare to charge!'

The infantry in front parted into platoons to allow the cavalry to pass. The Uhlans started forward, the pennons on their lances fluttering, and trotted downhill towards the French cavalry, which had come into sight below to the left.

As soon as the Uhlans moved down the slope the hussars were ordered up the hill to support the battery. As they took the places vacated by the Uhlans bullets came flying from the outposts, hissing and whining but falling wide.

This sound, which he had not heard for so long, had an even more joyous and exhilarating effect on Rostov than the previous crack of musketry. Drawing himself up in the saddle, he surveyed the field of battle opening out before him from the hill, and with his whole soul followed the Uhlans into the charge. The Uhlans swooped down close upon the French dragoons, there was a scene of confusion in the smoke, and five minutes later the Uhlans were dashing back, not towards the spot where they had been posted but more to the left, and among the orange-coloured ranks of Uhlans on chestnut horses, and in a great mass behind them, could be seen blue French dragoons on grey horses.

15

ROSTOV, with the keen eye of the hunting man, was one of the first to descry these blue French dragoons pursuing our Uhlans. Nearer and nearer came the disordered throng of Uhlans with the French dragoons in pursuit. He could already see separate figures – who looked so small at the foot of the hill – jostling and overtaking one another, and waving their arms or their sabres in the air.

Rostov gazed at what was happening before him as he might have watched a hunt. His instinct told him that if he were to charge with his hussars on the French dragoons now, the latter could not stand their ground; but if they were to strike it must be done immediately, on the instant, or it would be too late. He looked round. A captain, standing beside him, also had his eyes fixed on the cavalry below.

'Andrei Sevastyanich,' said Rostov, 'you know, we could hack 'em to bits. ...'

'Yes, glorious,' said the captain, 'in fact we could. ...'

Without waiting for him to finish, Rostov touched his horse and galloped to the front of his men; and before he had time to give the word of command the whole squadron, sharing his impulse, dashed after him. Rostov himself could not have said how or why he acted. He did it all without reflecting or considering, as he would have done out hunting. He saw the dragoons near and galloping in disorder; he knew they could not withstand an attack – knew that there was only that one minute in which to take action and that it would not return if he let it slip. The bullets were whizzing and whistling around him so stimulatingly, and his mount was so eager to be off, that he could not resist it.

He spurred his horse, shouted the command and at the same instant rode at full trot downhill towards the dragoons, hearing the tramp of his deployed squadron behind him. No sooner had they reached the bottom of the slope than their gait involuntarily changed from trot to gallop, which grew swifter and swifter as they approached our Uhlans and the French dragoons who were pursuing them. The dragoons were close now. The foremost, seeing the hussars, began turning back, those behind paused. With the same feeling with which he would have dashed forward in the path of a wolf Rostov gave full rein to his Don horse and speeded to cut off the broken ranks of the French dragoons. One Uhlan stopped, another who was on foot flung himself to the ground to avoid being knocked over, a riderless horse fell in with the hussars. Nearly all the French dragoons were galloping back. Rostov, picking out one on a grey horse, flew after him. On the way he found himself bearing down on a bush, his gallant horse cleared it, and almost before he had righted himself in the saddle he saw that he was within a few seconds of overtaking his man. This Frenchman, an officer to judge by his uniform, was crouching over his grey horse and urging it on with his sabre. An instant later Rostov's charger dashed its shoulder against the hindquarters of the officer's horse, almost knocking it over, and at the same second Rostov, without knowing why, raised his sword and struck at the Frenchman.

The instant he had done this all Rostov's eagerness suddenly vanished. The officer fell, not so much from the blow – which had but slightly grazed his arm above the elbow – as from fright and the collision of the horses. Rostov reined in, and his eyes sought his foe to see what sort of man he had vanquished. The French officer was hopping with one foot on the ground and the other caught in the stirrup. With eyes screwed up with fear, as though expecting another blow at any moment, he glanced up at Rostov in shrinking terror. His pale mud-stained face – fair-haired, boyish, with a dimple in the chin and clear blue eyes – was not at all warlike or suited to the battlefield, but a most ordinary homely countenance. Before Rostov could decide what to do with him the officer cried, 'I surrender!' He made frantic unavailing efforts to get his foot out of the stirrup, and kept his frightened blue eyes fixed on Rostov. Some hussars who galloped up freed his foot and helped him into the saddle. On all sides Rostov's men were busily engaged with the French dragoons: one dragoon was wounded but though his face was streaming with blood he would not give up his horse; another sat perched up behind an hussar with his arms round him; a third was being assisted on to his horse by an hussar. In front the French infantry were firing as they ran. The hussars galloped back in haste with their prisoners. Rostov spurred back with the rest, conscious of a sort of ache in his heart. With the capture of that French officer and the blow he had dealt him he had been overcome by a vague, confused feeling, which he could not at all account for.

Count Ostermann-Tolstoy met the returning hussars, sent for Rostov, thanked him and said he would report his gallant action to the Emperor and would recommend him for the St George Cross. When he was summoned to Count Ostermann, Rostov, remembering that he had charged without orders, had no doubt that his commanding-officer was sending for him to reprimand him for breach of discipline. Ostermann's flattering words and promise of a reward should, therefore, have been all the more pleasant a surprise, but he was still oppressed by that obscure, disagreeable feeling of moral nausea. 'What on earth is it that's worrying me so?' he asked himself as he rode back from the general. 'Is it Ilyin? No, he's safe and sound. Have I disgraced myself in any way? No, that's not it either.' Something else was fretting him, like remorse. 'Yes, yes, that French officer with the dimple. And I remember how my arm hesitated when I raised it.'

Rostov caught sight of the prisoners being led away, and galloped after them to have a look at his Frenchman with the dimple in his chin. He was sitting in his strange foreign uniform on an hussar pack-horse, glancing uneasily about him. The sword-cut on his arm could scarcely be called a wound. He simulated a smile for Rostov and waved his hand in greeting. Rostov still felt uncomfortable, as if something were weighing on his conscience.

All that day and the next his friends and comrades noticed that Rostov, without being exactly depressed or irritable, was silent, thoughtful and preoccupied. He drank under protest as it were, tried to be alone and obviously had something on his mind.

He was going over that brilliant exploit of his, which to his amazement had gained him the St George Cross and even given him a reputation for bravery, and there was something he could not make out at all. 'So they are even more afraid than we are!' he thought. 'Is this, then, all that is meant by what is called heroism? And did I do it for my country's sake? And where was he to blame, with his dimple and his blue eyes? And how frightened he was! He thought I was going to kill him. Why should I kill him? My hand trembled. But they have given me the St George Cross. I can't make it out, I can't make it out at all!'

But while Nikolai brooded over these questions in his mind, and still failed to arrive at any clear solutions to what puzzled him so, the wheel of fortune, where the Service was concerned, as often happens, turned in his favour. After the affair at Ostrovna he received recognition and was given the command of a battalion of hussars, and whenever an intrepid officer was needed it was he who was picked for the job.

16

As soon as she received news of Natasha's illness the countess, though still ailing and far from strong, set out for Moscow with Petya and the rest of the household, and the whole family moved from Maria Dmitrievna's house to their own, and settled down in town.

Natasha's illness was so serious that, fortunately for her and for her parents, all thought of what had caused it, of her conduct and the breaking off of the engagement, receded into the background. She was so ill that they could not stop to consider how far she was to blame for all that had happened, while she could not eat or sleep, was growing visibly thinner, coughed and, as the doctors gave them to understand, was in danger. There was only one thing to be thought of now, and that was how to get her well again. Doctors came to see her, both singly and in consultation, talked endlessly in French, German and

Latin, criticized one another and prescribed every sort of remedy to cure every complaint they had ever heard of. But it never occurred to one of them to make the simple reflection that the disease Natasha was suffering from could not be known to them, just as no complaint afflicting a living being can ever be entirely familiar, for each living being has his own individual peculiarities and whatever his disease it must necessarily be peculiar to himself, a new and complex malady unknown to medicine – not a disease of the lungs, liver, skin, heart, nerves, and so on, as described in medical books, but a disease consisting of one out of the innumerable combinations of the ailments of those organs. This simple reflection could not occur to the doctors (any more than it could ever occur to a sorcerer that he is unable to produce magic) because medicine was their life-work, because it was for that that they were paid and on that that they had expended the best years of their lives. But the chief reason why this reflection could never enter their heads was because they saw that they unquestionably were useful; and they certainly were of use to the whole Rostov family. Their help did not depend on making the patient swallow substances, for the most part harmful (the harm was scarcely appreciable because they were administered in such small doses), but they were useful, necessary and indispensable because they satisfied a moral need of the sick girl and those who loved her – and that is why there are and always will be pseudo-healers, wise women and homoeopathists. They satisfied the eternal human need for hope of relief, for sympathetic action, which is felt in the presence of suffering, the need that is seen in its most elementary form in the child which must have the bruised place rubbed to make it better. A child hurts itself and at once runs to the arms of mother or nurse to have the bad place kissed and rubbed, and feels better as soon as this is done. The child cannot believe that these people who are so much stronger and cleverer have no remedy for its pain. And the hope of relief and the expression of its mother's sympathy while she rubs the bump comforts it. The doctors in Natasha's case were of service because they kissed and rubbed the bad place, assuring her that the trouble would soon be over if the coachman drove down to the chemist's in Arbatsky square and got a powder and some pills in a pretty box for a rouble and seventy kopeks, and if she took those powders in boiled water at intervals of precisely two hours, neither more nor less.

What would have become of Sonya and the count and countess if they had had nothing to do but look on – if there had not been those pills to give by the clock, the warm drinks to prepare, the chicken cutlets, and all the other details ordered by the doctors, which supplied occupation and consolation to all of them? How could the count have borne his beloved daughter's illness had he not known that it was costing him a thousand roubles, and that he would not grudge thousands more, if that would do her any good; or had he not known that if her illness continued he would find still further thousands to take her abroad for consultations, and had he not been able to tell people how Métivier and Feller had not understood the symptoms, but Friez had diagnosed them, and Mudrov had succeeded even better? What would the countess have done had she not been able every now and then to scold the invalid for not obeying the doctor's instructions to the letter?

'You'll never get well like that,' she would say, vexation making her forget her distress, 'if you won't listen to the doctor and take your medicine properly! We can't play about, you know, or it may turn to *pneumonia*,' she would go on, finding great comfort in repeating this mysterious word, incomprehensible to others as well as to herself.

What would Sonya have done without the glad consciousness that at first she had not had her clothes off for three nights running, so as to be in readiness to carry out the doctor's injunctions promptly, and that she still kept awake at night so as not to miss the right time for giving Natasha the not very harmful pills from the little gilt box? Even Natasha herself, though she declared that no medicines could do her any good and that it was all nonsense, found it pleasant to see so many sacrifices being made for her, and to know that she had to take medicine at certain hours. And it was even pleasant to be able to show, by disregarding the doctor's prescriptions, that she did not believe in medical treatment and did not value her life.

The doctor came every day, felt her pulse, looked at her tongue and laughed and joked with her, paying no attention to her dejected face. But afterwards, when he had gone into the next room, where the countess hurriedly followed him, he would put on a grave expression and, thoughtfully shaking his head, say that, though the patient was in a critical state, still he placed high hopes on the efficacy of this last medicine, and that they must wait and see; that the illness was more psychological than...

And the countess, trying to conceal the action from herself and from him, would slip a gold piece into his hand, and always returned to the sick-room with a lighter heart.

The symptoms of Natasha's illness were loss of appetite, sleeplessness, a cough and continual depression. The doctors declared that she could not dispense with medical treatment, so they kept her in the stifling atmosphere of the city, and the Rostovs did not visit the country all that summer of 1812.

In spite of the vast number of little pills Natasha swallowed, and all the drops and powders out of the little bottles and boxes, of which Madame Schoss, who had a passion for such things, made a large collection, and in spite of being deprived of the country life to which she was accustomed, youth prevailed: Natasha's grief began to be overlaid by the impressions and incidents of everyday life, and ceased to press so painfully on her heart. The ache gradually faded into the past, and little by little her physical health improved.

17

NATASHA was calmer but she did not recover her spirits. She not merely avoided everything that might have amused and cheered her, such as balls, drives, concerts and theatres, but she never laughed without a note of tears in her laughter. She could not sing. As soon as she began to laugh or attempted to sing when she was by herself tears choked her: tears of remorse, tears of regret for that time of pure happiness which could never return, tears of vexation that she should so wantonly have ruined her young life which might have been so happy. Laughter and singing in particular seemed to her like a blasphemy in face of her sorrow. As to flirtation, there was no need for restraint – the idea never entered her head to desire admiration. She declared and felt at that time that all men were no more to her than Nastasya Ivanovna, the buffoon. Something stood sentinel within her and forbade her every joy. And indeed she seemed to have lost all the old interests of her girlish, carefree life that had been so full of hope. Those autumn months, the hunting, 'Uncle', and the Christmas holidays spent with Nikolai at Otradnoe were the memories over which she brooded most of all and with the sharpest pangs. What would she not have given to bring back even one single day of that time! But now it was gone for ever. Her presentiment at the time had not deceived her – the feeling that that state of freedom and readiness for every enjoyment would never come again. Yet she had to live on.

It comforted her to reflect that she was not better, as she had once fancied, but worse, far worse than anybody else in the world. But this was not enough. She knew that, and asked herself, 'What next?' But there was nothing to come. There was no gladness in life, yet life was passing. Natasha's sole idea was evidently not to be a burden or a hindrance to anyone, but for herself she wanted nothing at all. She held aloof from all the household, and only with her brother Petya did she feel at ease. She liked to be with him better than with the others, and when they were alone together she sometimes laughed. She rarely went out, and of those who came to call she was only glad to see one person – Pierre. No one could have been more tender, circumspect and at the same time serious than Count Bezuhov in his manner to her. Natasha unconsciously fell under the spell of this affectionate tenderness, and so took great solace in his society. But she was not even grateful to him for it – it seemed to her that Pierre did not have to make an effort to be good: it appeared to come so naturally to him that there was no merit in his kindness. Sometimes Natasha noticed embarrassment and awkwardness on his part in her presence, especially when he was apprehensive lest something in the conversation should revive memories painful to her. She observed this and put it down to his general kindliness and shyness, which she supposed would be the same with everyone else. After those involuntary words – that if he were free he would have asked on his knees for her hand and her love – uttered in a moment of violent stress for her, Pierre never mentioned his feelings to Natasha; and it seemed to her plain that those words, which had so comforted her at the time, held no more meaning than any thoughtless, unconsidered absurdities spoken to console a weeping child. It was not because Pierre was a married man but because Natasha was conscious that between him and her the moral barrier – which she had felt to be absent with Kuragin – stood firm and rigid that it never entered her head that her relations with Pierre might develop into love on her side, and still less on his, or even into that tender, self-conscious, romantic friendship between a man and a woman of which she had known several instances.

Towards the end of the fast of St Peter, Agrafena Ivanovna Byelov, a country neighbour of the Rostovs, came to Moscow to pay her devotions at the shrines of the saints there. She suggested that Natasha should prepare for the Sacrament with her, and Natasha gladly welcomed the idea. Although the doctors forbade her going out early in the morning Natasha insisted on fasting and preparing for the Sacrament, not as was generally done in the Rostov family, by taking part in three services in their own house, but in the way Agrafena Ivanovna was doing, and going to church every day for a whole week and not missing a single vespers, matins or Liturgy.

The countess was pleased with Natasha's zeal. After the poor results of medical treatment, at the bottom of her heart she hoped that prayer might do more for her daughter than medicines, and, though she concealed it from the doctor and had some inward misgivings, she fell in with Natasha's wishes and entrusted her to Mademoiselle Byelov.

Mademoiselle Byelov would go in at three o'clock in the morning to call Natasha but generally found her already awake. Natasha was afraid of oversleeping and being late for matins. Making hasty ablutions and humbly dressing in her shabbiest gown and an old mantle, Natasha, shivering in the chill air, went out into the deserted streets lit by the pale light of early dawn. On Mademoiselle Byelov's advice Natasha prepared herself not in her own parish but at a church where, according to the devout Mademoiselle Byelov, the priest was a man who led an austere and lofty life. There were never many people in the church. Natasha always stood beside Mademoiselle Byelov in the same place, before the icon of the Mother of God let into the screen by the choir on the left, and a new feeling of humility before something sublime and incomprehensible came over Natasha when at that unprecedented early hour she gazed at the dark face of Our Lady, lit up by the candles burning before it and the morning light falling from the window, and listened to the words of the service which she tried to follow with understanding. When she understood them, all the shades of her personal feeling became interwoven with her prayer. When she did not understand, it was sweeter still to think that the desire to understand all was pride, that it was impossible to comprehend everything, that all she had to do was to have faith and commit herself to God, Who was, she felt, at those moments guiding her soul. She crossed herself, bowed to the ground, and when she did not follow, in horror at her own vileness simply asked God to forgive her everything, everything, and have mercy on her soul. The prayers to which she surrendered herself most of all were the prayers of repentance. On the way home in the early morning when the only people about were bricklayers going to work or men sweeping the street, and everybody indoors was still asleep, Natasha experienced a new sense of the possibility of correcting her wickedness, and leading a fresh life of purity and happiness.

During all that week which she spent in this way the feeling grew with every day. And the happiness of communicating, or 'communing' as Mademoiselle Byelov liked to call taking Communion, seemed to Natasha so great that she thought she would never live till that blessed Sunday.

But the happy day did come, and on that memorable Sunday when Natasha, wearing a white muslin dress, returned from the Sacrament, for the first time for many months she felt at peace and not oppressed by the thought of the life that lay before her.

The doctor, who came to see her that day, ordered the powders to be continued, that he had begun prescribing a fortnight previously.

'She must certainly go on taking them morning and evening,' said he, with visible and simple-hearted satisfaction at the success of his treatment. 'Now please be careful and don't forget them. You may set your mind at rest, countess,' he continued playfully, as he deftly received the gold piece in the palm of his hand. 'She will soon be singing and frolicking about. The last medicine has done wonders. She is very much better.'

The countess looked at her finger-nails and spat a little for luck as she returned to the drawing-room with a cheerful face.

18

AT the beginning of July more and more disquieting reports about the war began to spread in Moscow: there was talk of an appeal by the Emperor to the people, and of his coming himself from the army to Moscow. And as up to the 11th of July no manifesto or appeal had been received the most exaggerated rumours became current about them and concerning the position of Russia. It was said that the Emperor was leaving because the army was in danger; it was said that Smolensk had surrendered; that Napoleon had a million men and that nothing short of a miracle could save the Fatherland.

On the 11th of July, a Saturday, the manifesto was received but was not yet in print, and Pierre, who happened to be at the Rostovs', promised to come next day, Sunday, to dinner, and bring a copy of the manifesto and appeal, which he would obtain from Count Rostopchin.

That Sunday the Rostovs attended divine service as usual in the private chapel of the Razumovskys. It was a hot July day. Even by ten o'clock, when the Rostovs got out of their carriage at the chapel, the sultry air, the shouts of the street-hawkers, the bright, gay clothes of the crowd, the dusty leaves of the trees along the boulevard, the martial music and white trousers of a battalion marching by to parade, the rattling of wheels on the cobble-stones, and the blazing sunshine were all full of that summer languor, that content and discontent with the present, which is felt with particular poignancy on a brilliant scorching day in town. All the rank and fashion of Moscow, all the Rostovs' acquaintances were in the Razumovskys' chapel. (This year, as if anticipating serious events, a great many of the wealthy families who usually spent the summer on their estates in the country were staying in the city.) As Natasha walked beside her mother, preceded by a footman in livery who cleared the way for them through the throng, she heard a young man make a remark about her in too loud a whisper.

'That's the young Countess Rostov, the one who ...'

'How thin she's got! But she's still pretty!'

She heard, or fancied she heard, the names of Kuragin and Bolkonsky. But that was always happening. She was always fancying that anyone who looked at her could only be thinking of what she had done. With a sinking heart, wretched as she always was now when she found herself in a crowd, Natasha, in her lilac silk dress trimmed with black lace, walked on, presenting an appearance – as women can – of ease and dignity all the greater for the pain and shame in her heart. She knew for a fact that she was pretty but the knowledge no longer gave her the pleasure it used to afford. On the contrary, it had been a source of more misery than anything of late, and especially so on this bright, hot summer day in town. 'Sunday again, and another week,' she said to herself, recalling how she had been here the previous Sunday, 'and for ever the same life which is no life; and the same circumstances in which it had been so easy to live before. I'm pretty, I'm young and I know that now I am good. Before I was wicked, but now I am good, I know,' she thought, 'but yet my best years, my very best years are slipping by and all for nothing.' She stood by her mother's side and exchanged nods with acquaintances who were standing near. From force of habit she scrutinized the dresses of the ladies, and criticized the *tenue* of a lady close to them, and the awkward cramped way in which she crossed herself; and then she thought again with vexation that she herself was being found fault with and was judging others, and suddenly, at the first sounds of the service, she was horrified at her sinfulness, horrified that her purity of heart should be lost to her again.

A venerable, neat-looking old man was conducting the service with that gentle solemnity which has so elevating and soothing an effect on the souls of the worshippers. The sanctuary doors were closed, the curtain was slowly drawn, and from behind it a soft mysterious voice pronounced some words. Tears that she could not have explained made Natasha's breast heave, and a feeling of joyful agitation came upon her.

'Teach me what to do, show me how to live my life and do right for ever and ever! ...' she prayed.

The deacon came out on to the raised space before the altar-screen and, holding his thumb extended, drew his long hair from under his dalmatic, and making the sign of the cross on his breast began in a loud and solemn voice to recite the words of the litany:

'In peace let us pray unto the Lord.'

'As one community, without distinction of class, without enmity, united in brotherly love – let us pray!' thought Natasha.

'For the peace which is from above, and for the salvation of our souls.'

'For the world of angels and the souls of all spiritual beings who dwell above us,' prayed Natasha.

When they prayed for the armed forces she thought of her brother and Denisov. When they prayed for all who travel on sea and land she thought of Prince Andrei and prayed for him, and asked God to forgive her the wrong she had done him. When they prayed for all who love us she prayed for the members of her own family, her father, her mother, Sonya, realizing now for the first time how wrongly she had acted towards them and how strong and deep was her love for them. When they prayed for those who hate us she tried to conjure up enemies and people who hated her, in order to pray for them. Among her enemies she reckoned her father's creditors and all those who had business dealings with him, and always at the thought of enemies and people who hated her she remembered Anatole, who had done her so much harm, and though he had not hated her she prayed gladly for him as for an enemy. Only at prayer was she able to think clearly and calmly of Prince Andrei and Anatole, with a sense that her feelings for them were as nothing compared with her awe and devotion to God. When they prayed for the Imperial family and the Synod she bowed and crossed herself more devoutly than ever, telling herself that even if she did not understand, still she could not doubt and, anyway, loved the ruling Synod and prayed for it.

When the litany was over, the deacon crossed the stole over his breast and said:

'Let us commit ourselves and our whole lives to Christ the Lord!'

'Commit ourselves to God,' Natasha repeated in her heart. 'O God, I submit myself to Thy will!' she thought. 'I ask for nothing, desire nothing: teach me how to act, what to do with my will! Take me, take me to Thee!' prayed Natasha, her heart filled with yearning impatience. She did not cross herself but stood with her thin arms hanging down as if expecting some invisible power at any moment to take her and deliver her from herself, from her regrets and desires, her remorse, her hopes and her sins.

Several times during the service the countess looked round at her daughter's rapt face and shining eyes, and prayed God to help her.

To the general surprise, in the middle of the service and contrary to the usual order of the Liturgy, which Natasha knew so well, the deacon brought out the little footstool on which the priest kneels when he reads the prayers on Trinity Sunday, and set it before the holy gates leading into the sanctuary. The priest came out in his purple velvet calotte, adjusted his hair, and with an effort dropped on his knees. All the congregation knelt with him, looking at one another in perplexity. There followed the prayer just received from the Synod – the prayer for the deliverance of Russia from enemy invasion.

'Lord God of might, God of our salvation!' began the priest in the clear, mild, unemphatic tones peculiar to the Slav clergy, which act so irresistibly on a Russian heart.

Lord God of might, God of our salvation, in Thy mercy and bounty look this day on Thy humble people, and graciously hear us, and spare us, and have mercy upon us. Behold the enemy, which is confounding

Thy land and would fain lay waste the universe, has risen against us. Behold these lawless men are gathered together to overthrow Thy kingdom, to destroy Thy holy Jerusalem, Thy beloved Russia: to defile Thy temples, to overturn Thine altars and profane our sanctuaries. How long, O Lord, how long shall the wicked triumph? How long shall they wield their unlawful power?

Almighty God, hear us when we pray to Thee: strengthen with Thy might our most gracious Sovereign Lord the Emperor Alexander Pavlovich; forget not his virtue and meekness, reward him according to his righteousness and let it preserve us, Thy chosen Israel! Bless his counsels, his undertakings and his deeds; fortify his kingdom by Thine Almighty Hand, and vouchsafe him victory over his enemy, even as Thou didst give Moses victory over Amalek, Gideon over Midian, and David over Goliath. Preserve his armies, put weapons of brass in the hands of those who go forth in Thy name, and gird their loins with strength for the battle. Take up Thy sword and Thy buckler, and arise and help us: confound and put to shame them that devise evil against us, and let them be scattered before the face of Thy faithful armament as dust before the wind, and may Thy mighty Angel chastise and defeat them. May they be ensnared in the net that they know not of, and their designs which they have hatched in secret be turned against them. Let them go down before the feet of Thy servants, and be laid low by our hosts. Lord, Thou art able to save both great things and small. Thou art God, and man cannot prevail against Thee.

O God of our fathers, remember Thy bounteous mercy and lovingkindness that Thou hast shown of old! Cast us not from Thy presence, nor let Thy wrath be kindled against our iniquities, but according to Thy lovingkindness, according unto the multitude of Thy tender mercies heed not our transgressions and iniquities. Create in us a clean heart, and renew a right spirit within us. Fortify us everyone by faith in Thee, confirm us with hope, breathe into us true love one for another, arm us with unity of spirit in the righteous defence of the inheritance which Thou gavest to us and to our forefathers, and let not the sceptre of the unrighteous be exalted over the destinies of those whom Thou hast sanctified.

O Lord our God, in Whom we believe and in Whom we put our trust, let us not be confounded as we look for Thy mercy, and vouchsafe us a sign for our blessing that they that hate us and our holy Orthodox faith may see and be put to shame and perish; and may all the nations know that Thou art the Lord and we are Thy people. Show Thy mercy upon us this day, O Lord, and grant us Thy salvation; make the hearts of Thy servants to rejoice in Thy mercy; strike down our enemies and be swift to vanquish them beneath the feet of Thy faithful servants. For Thou art the defence, the succour and the victory of them that put their trust in Thee, and to Thee be all glory, to Father, Son and Holy Spirit, as it was in the beginning, is now and ever shall be, world without end. Amen.

In Natasha's receptive condition this prayer had a deep effect on her. She listened to every word about Moses' victory over Amalek, and Gideon's over Midian, and David's over Goliath, and about the destruction of Thy Jerusalem, and she prayed to God with all the feeling and fervour with which her heart was overflowing, though she was not really clear what she was asking of God in the prayer. With all her soul she joined in the petition for a right spirit, for the strengthening of her heart by faith and hope and the breathing into them of love. But she could not pray that her enemies might be trampled underfoot when but a few minutes before she had been wishing she had more of them to love and pray for. Yet neither could she doubt the propriety of the prayer that was being read by the priest on his knees. Her heart knew a thrill of awe and horror at the punishment that overtakes men for their sins, and especially for her own sins, and she prayed to God to forgive them all, and her too, and grant them all, and her too, peace and happiness. And it seemed to her that God heard her prayer.

19

EVER since the day when Pierre, on his way home from the Rostovs' with Natasha's grateful look fresh in his mind, had gazed at the comet in the sky and felt as though something new was opening before him – from that day the haunting problem of the vanity and folly of all earthly things had ceased to torment him. That terrible question 'Why? Wherefore?', which till then had appeared to trouble him in the midst of every occupation, was now replaced not by another question or by the answer to the former question, but by *her* image. Whether he listened to or himself took part in trivial conversations, whether he read or heard tell of some instance of human baseness or stupidity, he was not horrified as of old: he did not ask himself why people fussed, when all was so transient and uncertain, but he pictured her to himself as he had last seen her, and all his doubts vanished – not because she was the answer to the questions that met him at every turn but because his image of her instantly lifted him into another world, a serene realm of spiritual activity, where there could be neither right nor wrong – a realm of beauty and love which it was worth living for. Whatever worldly infamy came to his notice, he would say to himself:

'Well, what does it matter if So-and-so who has robbed the country and the Tsar has honours conferred on him by the State and the Tsar, since yesterday she smiled on me, and begged me to come, and I love her, and no one will ever know.'

Pierre still went into society, drank as much as before, and led the same idle and dissipated life, because besides the hours he spent at the Rostovs' he had to get through the rest of his time somehow, and the habits and the acquaintances he had made in Moscow formed a current that bore him along irresistibly. But of late, when the news from the theatre of war daily became more alarming, and Natasha's health had begun to improve and she had ceased to call for the same tender pity, he fell more and more prey to a restlessness which he could not explain. He felt that the position in which he found himself could not go on much longer, that a catastrophe was coming which would change the whole course of his life, and he sought impatiently and everywhere for signs of this approaching disaster. One of his brother freemasons had revealed to Pierre the following prophecy concerning Napoleon, drawn from the Revelation of St John the Divine.

Chapter xiii, verse 18 of Revelations says:

Here is wisdom. Let him that hath understanding count the number of the beast: for it is the number of a man; and his number is Six hundred threescore and six.

And the fifth verse of the same chapter:

And there was given unto him a mouth speaking great things and blasphemies; and power was given unto him to continue forty and two months.

If the French alphabet is written out and given the same numerical values as the Hebrew, in which the first nine letters denote units and the next the tens and so on, we get the following:

a	b	c	d	e	f	g	h	i	k	l	m	n	o	p	q	r	s
1	2	3	4	5	6	7	8	9	10	20	30	40	50	60	70	80	90

t	u	v	w	x	y	z
100	110	120	130	140	150	160

Turning the words *l'empereur Napoléon* into numbers on this system, it appears that the sum of them equals 666 (including a 5 for the letter *e* dropped by elision from the *le* before *empereur*), and Napoleon is seen to be the beast prophesied in the Apocalypse. Moreover, by applying the same system to the words *quarante-deux* (forty-two), that is, the term allowed to the beast that spoke 'great things and blasphemies', the same number 666 obtains; from which it follows that the limit fixed for Napoleon's power had come in the year 1812, when the French Emperor reached his forty-second year. This prophecy made a great impression on Pierre, and he frequently asked himself what would put an end to the power of the beast, that is, of Napoleon, and tried by the same system of turning letters into figures and reckoning them up to find an answer to the question that engrossed him. He wrote the words *l'empereur Alexandre, la nation russe* and added up their numbers, but the sums came to far more or far less than the 666. Once when he was engaged with these calculations he wrote down his own name in French – *Comte Pierre Besouhoff*, but again the total did not come out right. He changed the spelling, substituting *z* for *s* and adding *de* and the article *le*, and still he failed to obtain the desired result. Then it occurred to him that if the answer he sought were contained in his name, it would certainly include his nationality too. So he tried *Le russe Besuhof*, and reckoning up the numbers got 671. This was only five too much, and five corresponded to *e*, the very letter elided from the article before the word *empereur*. Dropping the *e*, though of course incorrectly, gave Pierre the answer he was after: *l'russe Besuhof* – exactly 666. This discovery excited him greatly. How, and by what means, he was connected with the great event foretold in the Apocalypse he did not know, but he did not for a moment doubt that connexion. His love for Natasha, Antichrist, Napoleon's invasion, the comet, 666, *l'empereur Napoléon* and *l'russe Besuhof* – all these taken together had to mature and burst forth, and lift him out of that bewitched, futile round of Moscow habits to which he felt himself held captive, and lead him to some mighty exploit and great happiness.

*

On the eve of the Sunday on which the special prayer was read, Pierre had promised the Rostovs to bring them, from Count Rostopchin whom he knew well, both the appeal to the nation and the latest military news. In the morning, when he went to call at Count Rostopchin's, Pierre met there a courier fresh from the army. This courier was an acquaintance of Pierre's, a regular *habitué* of the Moscow ball-rooms.

'For heaven's sake, can't you relieve me of something ?' said the courier. 'I have a whole sackful of letters to parents.'

Among these letters was one from Nikolai Rostov to his father. Pierre took charge of that letter, and Count Rostopchin also gave him a copy of the Sovereign's appeal to Moscow which had just come from the press, the latest army orders and his own most recent bulletin. Glancing through the army orders, Pierre found in one of them, in the lists of killed, wounded and decorated, the name of Nikolai Rostov, awarded a St George's Cross of the fourth class for bravery displayed in the Ostrovna affair, and in the same announcement the appointment of Prince Andrei Bolkonsky to the command of a regiment of Chasseurs. Though he did not want to remind the Rostovs of Bolkonsky, Pierre could not resist the inclination to rejoice their hearts with the news of their son's decoration, so, keeping the Tsar's appeal, the bulletin and the other announcements to take with him when he went to dinner, he sent the printed army order and Nikolai's letter to the Rostovs.

His conversation with Count Rostopchin and the latter's hurried, preoccupied air, the meeting with the courier who had casually alluded to the disastrous way things were going in the army, the rumours of the discovery of spies in Moscow and of a broadsheet circulating in the city stating that Napoleon had sworn to be in both Russian capitals by the autumn, and talk of the Tsar's expected arrival next day – all combined to revive in Pierre with fresh intensity that feeling of agitation and suspense which he had been conscious of ever since the appearance of the comet, and especially since the beginning of the war.

The idea of entering the army had, for some time, been much in his mind, and he would assuredly have done so had he not been deterred, first, by his membership of the Order of Freemasonry, to which he was bound by oath and which preached eternal peace and the abolition of war, and, secondly, by the fact that when he saw the great mass of Moscovites who had donned uniform and sang the praises of patriotism, he felt somehow ashamed to take the same step. But the chief reason which kept him from carrying out his design to enter upon military service lay in the obscure conception that he, *l'russe Besuhof*, who had the number of the beast, 666, was predestined from eternity to take some part in setting a limit to the power of the beast 'speaking great things and blasphemies', and that therefore he ought not to undertake anything but wait for what was bound to come to pass.

20

A FEW intimate friends were, as usual on Sundays, dining with the Rostovs.

Pierre went early so as to find them alone.

He had grown so stout that year that he would have been grotesque had he not been so tall and had such powerful limbs, and been so strong that he carried his bulk with evident ease.

Puffing and muttering something to himself, he went up the stairs. His coachman did not even ask whether he should wait. He knew that when the count was at the Rostovs' he stayed till near midnight. The Rostovs' footmen rushed eagerly forward to help him off with his cloak and take his stick and hat. Pierre, from club habit, always left both stick and hat in the ante-room.

The first person he saw at the Rostovs' was Natasha. Even before he saw her, while taking off his cloak, he heard her. She was practising sol-fa exercises in the music-room. He knew that she had not sung since her illness, and so the sound of her voice surprised and delighted him. He opened the door softly and saw her in the lilac dress she had worn at church, walking about the room singing. She had her back to him when he opened the door, but when she turned quickly and saw his broad, surprised face, she blushed and came swiftly up to him.

'I want to try and sing again,' she said. 'At least it's something to do,' she added as if by way of excuse.

'Quite right too!'

'How glad I am you have come! I am so happy today,' she said with the old animation Pierre had not seen in her for a long time. 'You know, Nicolas has got the St George's Cross? I'm so proud of him.'

'Oh yes, I sent you the announcement. Well, I don't want to interrupt you,' he added, and would have gone on to the drawing-room.

Natasha stopped him.

'Count, is it wrong of me to sing?' she said, blushing, but still keeping her eyes fixed inquiringly on Pierre.

'No. ... Why should it be? On the contrary. ... But why do you ask me?'

'I don't know myself,' replied Natasha quickly, 'but I shouldn't like to do anything you disapproved of. I have such complete faith in you. You don't know how important you are to me, and how much you have done for me! ...' She spoke rapidly and did not notice how Pierre flushed at these words of hers. 'I saw in the same announcement, *he*, Bolkonsky' (she uttered the name in a hurried whisper), 'he is in Russia, and in the army again. What do you think,' she said hastily, evidently hurrying for fear her strength might fail her, 'will he ever forgive me? Will he not always bear me ill will? What do you think? What do you think?'

'I think ...' said Pierre. 'He has nothing to forgive. ... If I were in his place ...'

Association of ideas carried Pierre back in imagination to the time when he had tried to comfort her and said that if instead of being himself he were the best man in the world and free he would beg on his knees for her hand, and the same feeling of pity, tenderness and love took possession of him and the same words rose to his lips. But she did not give him time to utter them.

'Yes, you – you ...' she said, rapturously pronouncing the word *you* – 'that's a different matter. Anyone kinder, more generous or better than you I have never known, and nobody could be! If it had not been for you then, and now too, I don't know what would have become of me, because ...'

Her eyes suddenly filled with tears; she turned away, lifted her music before her face, and began singing and walking up and down the room again.

At that moment Petya ran in from the drawing-room.

Petya was now a handsome ruddy lad of fifteen, with full red lips, very like Natasha. He was preparing for the university, but lately he and his friend Obolensky had secretly made up their minds to join the hussars.

Petya came rushing up to talk to his namesake of this important matter. He had asked Pierre to find out whether he would be accepted in the hussars.

Pierre walked about the drawing-room not listening to what Petya was saying.

The boy pulled him by the arm to attract his attention.

'Well, what about my business – please tell me, for mercy's sake! You are my only hope!' said Petya.

'Oh yes, your affairs. You want to join the hussars? I'll speak about it. This very day I'll tell them all about it.'

'Well, *mon cher*, did you get the manifesto?' asked the old count. 'My little countess was at the service in the Razumovskys' chapel and heard the new prayer. Very fine it was, she tells me.'

'Yes, I've got it,' replied Pierre. 'The Emperor will be here tomorrow ... there's to be an extraordinary meeting of the nobility, and a levy, so they say, of ten men per thousand. Oh yes, let me congratulate you!'

'Yes, indeed, praise God! Well, and what news from the army?'

'We have retreated again. I'm told we're already back nearly to Smolensk,' answered Pierre.

'Mercy on us, mercy on us!' exclaimed the count. 'Where's the manifesto?'

'The Emperor's appeal? Ah, yes!'

Pierre began feeling in his pockets for the papers and could not find them. Still slapping his pockets, he kissed the countess's hand as she came in, and then looked round uneasily, evidently expecting Natasha, who had left off singing now but had not yet appeared in the drawing-room.

'Upon my word, I don't know what I've done with it,' he said.

'There he is, always losing everything,' remarked the countess.

Natasha entered with a softened and agitated expression, and sat down looking mutely at Pierre. As soon as she came into the room Pierre's face, which had been overcast, suddenly lighted up, and while still searching for the papers he glanced at her intently several times.

'By heaven, I'll drive home, I must have left them there. Most certainly. ...'

'But you'll be late for dinner.'

'Oh, and my coachman has gone.'

But Sonya, who had gone to look for the papers in the ante-room, had found them in Pierre's hat, where he had carefully tucked them under the lining. Pierre wanted to begin reading them immediately.

'No, after dinner,' said the old count, obviously anticipating much enjoyment from the reading.

At dinner they drank champagne to the health of the new chevalier of St George, and Shinshin told them the gossip of the town about the illness of the old Georgian princess, Métivier's disappearance from Moscow, and how some German fellow had been brought before Rostopchin and accused of being a *champignon* – a French spy – (so Count Rostopchin had told the story), and how Rostopchin let him go, assuring the people that he was not a *champignon* but simply an old German toadstool.

'Yes, they keep arresting people,' said the count. 'I tell the countess she should not speak French so much. This is not the time for it.'

'And have you heard ?' said Shinshin. 'Prince Golitsyn has engaged a tutor to teach him Russian. It is becoming dangerous to speak French in the streets.'

'And how about you, Count Piotr Kirillich ? If there's a general call-up, you too will have to mount a horse, eh ?' remarked the old count, addressing Pierre.

Pierre had been silent and preoccupied all through dinner. He looked at the count as though not understanding.

'Oh yes, the war,' he said. 'No ! A fine soldier I should make ! And yet the whole business is so strange – so extraordinary – I am quite at sea. I don't know, I am far from having military tastes, but in these days no one can answer for himself.'

After dinner the count settled himself comfortably in an easy-chair, and with a serious face asked Sonya, who enjoyed the reputation of being an excellent reader, to read the appeal.

To Moscow, our chief capital:
The enemy has entered the confines of Russia with immense forces. He comes to lay waste our beloved country,

Sonya carefully read aloud in her thin treble. The count listened with closed eyes, heaving abrupt sighs at certain passages.

Natasha sat bolt upright, gazing with searching looks, now at her father, now at Pierre.

Pierre felt her eyes on him and tried not to look round. The countess shook her head disapprovingly and wrathfully at every solemn expression in the manifesto. In all these words she saw only one thing: that the danger menacing her son would not soon be over. Shinshin, pursing lips into a sardonic smile, was clearly preparing to make fun at the first opportunity – of Sonya's reading, of the count's next remark, or even of the very manifesto should no better pretext present itself.

After reading about the perils threatening Russia, the hopes the Emperor placed on Moscow and especially on its illustrious Nobility, Sonya, with a quiver in her voice due principally to the attention with which they were listening to her, came to the last words:

We shall not be slow to appear among our people in the capital, and in other parts of our dominion, for consultation and for the guidance of all our militia levies, both those now barring the enemy's path and those newly formed to overthrow him wherever he may show himself. May the ruin and destruction which he would precipitate on us recoil on his own head, and may Europe, delivered from bondage, glorify the name of Russia!

'That's the way!' cried the count, opening his moist eyes and sniffing repeatedly as if a strong vinaigrette had been held to his nose. 'Let our Sovereign but say the word and we will sacrifice everything, begrudging nothing.'

Before Shinshin had time to utter the joke he was ready to make at the expense of the count's patriotism Natasha sprang up from her seat and ran to her father.

'What a darling our Papa is!' she cried, kissing him, and then she glanced at Pierre again with the unconscious coquetry which had come back to her with the return of better spirits.

'Bravo, what a patriot you are!' said Shinshin.

'Not at all, but simply ...' Natasha began, offended. 'You think everything funny, but this is no laughing matter. ...'

'Laughing matter indeed!' put in the count. 'Let him but say the word and we'll all go. ... We're not a set of Germans. ...'

'But did you notice,' said Pierre, 'that it spoke about "consultation"?'

'Well, whatever it's for. ...'

At that moment Petya, to whom nobody was paying any attention, came up to his father and, with a very red face, said in a voice which was now breaking and so was alternately deep and shrill:

'Well, Papa, now is the time to tell you – and Mamma, too, please – to say to you that you positively must let me enter the army, because I cannot .., well, that's all. ...'

The countess, in dismay, raised her eyes to heaven, clasped her hands and turned angrily to her husband.

'There, that's what comes of your talking!'

But the count had already recovered from his excitement.

'What next!' said he. 'A pretty soldier you'd make! No – nonsense! You have your studies to attend to.'

'It's not nonsense, Papa! Fedya Obolensky is younger than me, and he's going too. Besides, I couldn't study now anyhow, when ...' Petya stopped short, flushed till his face perspired, yet stoutly went on '... when our Fatherland is in danger.'

'That'll do, that'll do – enough of this nonsense. ...'

'But you said yourself that we would sacrifice everything.'

'Petya! Be quiet, I tell you!' cried the count with a glance at his wife, who had gone pale and was staring fixedly at her young son.

'And I say – Piotr Kirillich here will tell you too. ...'

'I tell you it's nonsense. The milk's hardly dry on his lips and he wants to go into the army! Really, I must say!' And the count, taking the papers, moved to go out of the room, probably to read them once more before having a nap.

'Piotr Kirillich, what about it? – let's go and have a smoke. ...'

Pierre felt embarrassed and hesitating. Natasha's unwontedly brilliant and eager eyes, continually turned upon him with a more than cordial look, had reduced him to this condition.

'No, I think I'll go home.'

'Go home? Why, you meant to spend the evening with us. ... You don't often come nowadays as it is. And this girl of mine,' said the count good-humouredly, pointing to Natasha, 'only brightens up when you are here.'

'Yes, I had forgotten. ... I really must go home. ... Business ...' said Pierre hurriedly.

'Well, then, *au revoir!*' said the count and went out of the room.

'Why are you going? What are you upset for? What is it?' Natasha asked Pierre, looking challengingly into his eyes.

'Because I love you!' was what he wanted to say, but he did not say it, and only crimsoned till the tears came, and lowered his eyes.

'Because it is better for me not to be here so much. ... Because ... No, simply I have business. ...'

'Why? No, tell me!' Natasha was beginning resolutely, and suddenly stopped.

The two looked at each other in dismay and confusion. He tried to smile but could not: his smile expressed suffering, and he silently kissed her hand and left.

Pierre made up his mind not to go to the Rostovs' any more.

21

AFTER the uncompromising refusal he had received, Petya went to his room and, locking himself in, wept bitterly. When he came in to tea, silent, morose and with tear-stained face, everybody pretended not to notice anything.

Next day the Emperor arrived in Moscow, and several of the Rostovs' house-servants begged permission to go and see the Tsar. That morning Petya was a long time dressing and doing his hair and arranging his collar to look like a grown-up man. He frowned before the looking-glass, gesticulated, shrugged his shoulders and finally, without a word to anyone, took his cap and went out of the house by the back door, trying not to be observed. Petya had decided to go straight to where the Emperor was and to explain frankly to some gentleman-in-waiting (Petya imagined that the Emperor was always surrounded by gentlemen-in-waiting) that he, Count Rostov, in spite of his youth, wished to serve his country, that youth could be no hindrance to devotion, and that he was ready to ... Petya, while dressing, had prepared a great many fine speeches to make to the gentleman-in-waiting.

Petya relied for success in reaching the Emperor on the very fact of being so young – he even thought how surprised everyone would be at his youth – and at the same time by the arrangement of his collar and his hair and by the sedate, deliberate way he would walk he meant to give the impression of being a grown-up man. But the farther he went and the more his attention was diverted by the ever-increasing crowds round the Kremlin, the less he remembered to keep up the sedateness and deliberation characteristic of grown-up people. As he approached the Kremlin he had to struggle to avoid being crushed, and with a resolute and threatening mien stuck his elbows out on each side of him. But at Trinity Gate, in spite of his determined air, the throng of people, probably unaware of the patriotic intentions bringing him to the Kremlin, so pressed him against the wall that he was obliged to give in and stop while carriages rumbled in beneath the archway. Near Petya stood a peasant woman, a footman, two tradesmen and a discharged soldier. After standing for some time in the gateway Petya tried to push forward in front of the others, without waiting for all the carriages to pass, and began vigorously working his way with his elbows, but the peasant woman standing beside him, who was the first to be poked, shouted at him angrily:

'Here, my young gentleman, what are you shoving for? Can't you see we're all standing still? What do you want to push for?'

'That's a game everyone can play,' said the footman, and he, too, set to work with his elbows and squeezed Petya into a very ill-smelling corner of the gateway.

Petya wiped his perspiring face with his hands, and pulled up the damp collar which at home he had arranged so carefully to look like a man's.

He felt that he no longer offered a presentable appearance, and feared that if he showed himself in this guise to the gentlemen-in-waiting they would not admit him to the Emperor. But the crush made it impossible to tidy himself up or move to another place. One of the generals who drove by was an acquaintance of the Rostovs', and Petya wanted to ask his help but came to the conclusion that this would not be a manly thing to do. When all the carriages had passed in, the crowd, carrying Petya with it, streamed forward into the square, which was already full of people. Not only in the square but on the slopes and the roofs – everywhere were people. As soon as Petya found himself in the square he heard the bells ringing and the joyous hum of the crowd flooding the whole Kremlin.

For a while the crush was less in the square, but all at once heads were bared and there was another surge forward. Petya was so squashed that he could hardly breathe, and everybody shouted 'Hurrah! hurrah! hurrah!'

Petya stood on tiptoe, and pushed and pinched, but he could see nothing except the people about him.

Every face wore the same expression of excitement and enthusiasm. A shopkeeper's wife standing next to Petya sobbed and the tears ran down her cheeks.

'Father! Angel! Little father!' she kept repeating, wiping away her tears with her fingers.

'Hurrah!' shouted the crowd on all sides.

For a moment the mass of people stood still; then they rushed forward again.

Beside himself with excitement, Petya, clenching his teeth and rolling his eyes ferociously, plunged forward, elbowing his way and shouting 'Hurrah!' as though he were ready and willing that moment to kill himself and everyone else, but on either side of him equally fierce faces pushed and shoved, and everybody yelled 'Hurrah!'

'So this is what the Emperor is!' thought Petya. 'No, I could never petition him myself – that would be too presumptuous!'

Nevertheless, he continued to force his way desperately forward, and just beyond the backs in front of him he caught glimpses of an open space spread with a strip of red carpet; but just at that instant the crowd swayed and receded – the police in front were driving back those who had pressed too close to the procession: the Emperor was passing from the palace to the cathedral of the Assumption – and Petya received such a sudden blow in the ribs, and was squeezed so hard, that all at once everything went dim before his eyes and he lost consciousness. When he came to himself a man of clerical appearance with the long grey hair hanging down at the back and wearing a shabby blue cassock – probably a church clerk and chanter – was supporting him under the arm with one hand, while warding off the pressure of the crowd with the other.

'A young gentleman's been crushed!' the deacon was saying. 'Mind there! ... Gently. ... You're crushing him, you're crushing him!'

The Emperor had entered the cathedral of the Assumption. The crowd fanned out again more evenly, and the clerk got Petya, pale and breathless, to the big cannon. Several people felt sorry for Petya, and suddenly a whole crowd turned and milled round him. Those who were standing near tended him, unbuttoned his coat, seated him on the raised platform of the cannon, and showered abuse on whoever it was had squashed him.

'Anyone could get crushed to death like that! What next! Killing people! Why, the poor dear's as white as a sheet!' various voices were heard saying.

Petya soon recovered, the colour returned to his cheeks, the pain passed off, and at the cost of that temporary discomfort he had obtained a place on the cannon, from which he hoped to see the Emperor who was to walk back that way. Petya no longer thought of preferring his request. If only he could just see the Emperor he would be happy!

While the service was proceeding in the cathedral of the Assumption – it was a combined service of prayer on the occasion of the Emperor's arrival and of thanksgiving for the conclusion of peace with the Turks – the crowd dispersed about the square outside, and hawkers appeared, selling kvass, gingerbread and poppy-seed sweets (of which Petya was particularly fond), and ordinary conversation was heard again. One tradesman's wife was showing her torn shawl, and saying how much she had paid for it; another observed that all silk goods were very dear nowadays. The deacon who had rescued Petya was talking to a functionary about the different priests who were officiating that day with the bishop. The clerk several times used the words 'and chapter', which Petya did not understand. Two young workmen were jesting with some servant-girls cracking nuts. All these exchanges, especially the jokes with the servant-girls, which at any other time would have fascinated Petya at his age, did not interest him now. He sat on his high perch on the cannon, as much agitated as before by the thought of the Emperor and his love for him. The combination of the feeling of pain and terror when he was being crushed and that of rapture still further intensified his sense of the solemnity of the occasion.

Suddenly the roar of cannon was heard from the embankment (the firing was in celebration of the signing of peace with the Turks), and the crowd made a dash for the embankment to watch. Petya would have run off there too, but the deacon who had taken the young gentleman under his protection would not let him. The guns were still firing when officers, generals and gentlemen-in-waiting came running out of the cathedral, followed by others in less haste. Caps were lifted again, and those who had run to look at the cannon ran back. At last four men wearing uniforms and decorations emerged from the portals of the cathedral. 'Hurrah! hurrah!' shouted the crowd again.

'Which one is he? Which one?' asked Petya in a tearful voice of those around him, but no one answered; everybody was too excited and Petya, picking out one of the four, and hardly able to see him for the tears of joy that started to his eyes, concentrated all his enthusiasm on him – though it happened not to be the Emperor – frantically yelled 'Hurrah!' and vowed that tomorrow, come what might, he would join the army.

The crowd rushed after the Emperor, accompanied him to the palace and began to disperse. By this time it was late, and Petya had had nothing to eat and was drenched with perspiration; however, he did not go home but stood with a smaller though still considerable crowd before the palace while the Emperor dined. He gazed up at the palace windows, expecting he knew not what, and envying alike the grand personages who drove up to the entrance to dine with the Emperor and the footmen waiting at table, glimpses of whom could be seen through the windows.

While the Emperor was dining Valuyev, looking out of the window, said:

'The people are still hoping for another sight of your Majesty.'

They had nearly finished dinner, and the Emperor, munching a biscuit, got up and went out on to the balcony. The crowd, with Petya in the middle, rushed towards the balcony.

'Angel! Little father! Hurrah! Father!' ... cried the crowd, and Petya with it, and again the women and some of the men of weaker stuff, including Petya, wept for joy.

A fair-sized piece of the biscuit the Emperor was holding in his hand broke off, fell on the balcony railing, and from the railing to the ground. A coachman in a jerkin, who stood nearest, pounced on the piece of biscuit and snatched it up. Several people rushed at the coachman. Seeing this, the Emperor had a plateful of biscuits brought, and began throwing them from the balcony. Petya's eyes almost started out of his head; more keyed up than ever by the danger of being crushed, he flung himself on the biscuits. He did not know why, but he had to have a biscuit from the Tsar's hand and felt that he must stand his ground. He made a dash and upset an old woman who was just about to seize a biscuit. But the old woman refused to consider herself defeated, though she was lying on the ground – she grabbed at some biscuits but her hand did not reach them. Petya pushed her hand away with his knee, seized a biscuit and, as though afraid of being late, shouted 'Hurrah!' again in a hoarse voice.

The Emperor went in, and after that the greater part of the crowd began to disperse.

'There, I said if only we waited – and so it was!' said one and another delightedly among the throng.

Happy as Petya was, he felt sad at having to go home knowing that all the enjoyment of that day was over. He did not go straight back from the Kremlin but called in on his friend Obolensky, who was fifteen and also entering the regiment. When he got home Petya announced resolutely and firmly that if they would not give their permission, then he would run away. And next day Count Ilya Rostov, though he had not yet quite yielded, went to inquire how he could arrange for Petya to serve somewhere where it would be as safe as possible.

22

Two days later, on the morning of July the 15th, an immense number of carriages were drawn up outside the Slobodskoy Palace.

The great halls were full. In the first were the Nobility and gentry in their uniforms; in the second bearded merchants in full-skirted coats of blue cloth and wearing medals. The room where the nobles were gathered was all bustle and movement. The chief magnates sat on high-backed chairs round a large table under the portrait of the Emperor, but the majority of the gentry were strolling about the room.

All the nobles, whom Pierre saw every day either at the club or in their own houses, were in uniform – some in the uniform of Catherine's day, others in that of the Emperor Paul, others again in the new uniforms of Alexander's time, or the ordinary uniform of the Nobility, and the general guise of being in uniform imparted a certain strange and fantastic character to these diverse and familiar personalities, both old and young. Particularly striking were the old men, dim-eyed, toothless, bald, sallow and bloated, or gaunt and wrinkled. For the most part they sat quietly in their places, or if they walked about and talked attached themselves to someone younger. Just like the faces of the crowd Petya had seen in the Kremlin square, all these faces in general expectation of some solemn event offered a conspicuous contrast to their usual everyday – yesterday's – expression when interest was centred on a game of boston, Petrushka the cook, Zinaida Dmitrievna's health.

Pierre was there too, uncomfortably buttoned up since early morning in a nobleman's uniform that had become too tight for him. He was in a high state of agitation: this extraordinary assembly not only of nobles but also of the merchant class – les États généraux (States-General) – revived in his mind a whole series of ideas he had long laid aside but which were deeply imprinted in his soul: thoughts of the Contrat social and the French Revolution. The words that had struck him in the Emperor's manifesto – that the Sovereign was coming to the capital for consultation with his people – confirmed him in this chain of thought. And supposing that something of importance in that direction was at hand, the something which he had long been looking for, he wandered about, watching and listening but nowhere finding any echo of the ideas that engrossed him.

The Emperor's manifesto was read, evoking enthusiasm, and then the assembly broke up into groups to discuss matters. Besides the ordinary topics of conversation Pierre heard men debating where the marshals of the Nobility were to stand when the Emperor came in, when the ball should be given in the Emperor's honour, whether they should group themselves according to districts or the whole province together ... and so on; but as soon as the war and the whole object of convening the Nobility was mentioned the talk became uncertain and hesitating. Everyone seemed to prefer listening to speaking.

One middle-aged man, handsome and virile, in the uniform of a retired naval officer, was speaking in one of the rooms, and a little knot of people pressed about him. Pierre went up to the circle that had formed round the speaker, and began to listen. Count Ilya Rostov, in his uniform of Catherine's reign, was sauntering about with a pleasant smile among the crowd, with all of whom he was acquainted. He too approached this group and paused to listen, smiling kindly, as he always did, and nodding his head in approbation of what the speaker was saying. The retired naval officer was speaking very boldly (this could be seen from the expression on the faces of the listeners and from the fact that some persons whom Pierre knew for the meekest and most timid of men walked away disapprovingly, or expressed their disagreement). Pierre pushed his way into the middle of the group, listened, and convinced himself that the speaker was indeed a liberal but with views quite different from his own. The naval officer spoke in the peculiarly mellow, sing-song baritone characteristic of the Russian Nobility, agreeably slurring his r's and clipping his consonants – the voice of a man who calls to his servants, 'Heah! Bwing me my pipe!' It was a voice that betrayed familiarity with the pleasures of the table, and a note of authority.

'What if the inhabitants of Smolensk have offahd to waise militia for the Empewah? Is Smolensk to lay down the law fo' us? If the noble awistocwacy of the pwovince of Moscow thinks fit, it can show its loyalty to our Sov'weign the Empewah in othah ways. Have we fo'gotten the waising of the militia in the yeah 'seven? All that did was to enwich the pwiests' sons, and thieves and wobbahs. ...'

Count Ilya Rostov smiled blandly, and nodded his head in approval.

'And was our militia of any use to the Empia? Not the slightest! They only wuined our farming intewests. Bettah have another conscwiption ... o' owah men will weturn to us neithah soldier no' peasants but simply spoiled and good fo' nothing. The Nobility don't gwudge theah lives – evewy man jack of us will go and bwing wecwuits, and the Sov'weign need only say the word and we will all die fo' him!' added the orator, warming up.

Count Rostov's mouth watered with satisfaction and he nudged Pierre, but Pierre wanted to speak himself. He moved forward, feeling stirred though not yet sure why he was stirred or what he would say. He was just opening his mouth when one of the senators, a toothless old man with a shrewd, choleric face, standing near the first speaker, interrupted him. Evidently accustomed to managing debates and keeping up an argument, he began in low but distinct tones:

'I imagine, sir,' said he, mumbling with his toothless mouth, 'that we are summoned here not for the purpose of discussing whether at the present moment it would be in the best interests of the Empire to levy recruits or call out the militia. We have been summoned to reply to the appeal which our Sovereign the Emperor graciously deigns to make to us. We may leave it to the supreme authority to judge between conscription or the militia. ...'

Pierre suddenly found the right outlet for his excitement. He felt exasperated with the senator who was introducing this conventional and narrow attitude towards the duties that lay before the Nobility. Pierre stepped forward and cut him short. He himself did not yet know what he was going to say, but he began eagerly, expressing himself in bookish Russian and occasionally lapsing into French.

'Excuse me, your Excellency,' he began. (Pierre was well acquainted with the senator but he thought it necessary on this occasion to address him formally.) 'Though I cannot agree with the gentleman ...' (he hesitated: he would have liked to say with *mon très honorable préopinant* – the honorable gentleman who has just spoken), 'with the gentleman ... whom I have not the honour of knowing; still I imagine that the Nobility have been called together not merely to express their sympathy and enthusiasm but also to deliberate upon the measures by which we may assist our Fatherland! I imagine,' he went on, warming to his subject, 'that the Emperor himself would be ill-pleased to find in us merely owners of peasants whom we are willing to devote to his service, together with our own persons, as *chair à canon* – cannon fodder – instead of obtaining from us any co-co-counsel.'

Several of those listening withdrew from the circle, when they noticed the senator's sardonic smile and the freedom of Pierre's remarks. Count Rostov was the only person who approved of Pierre's speech, just as he had approved of what the naval officer had said, and the senator, and in general agreed with whatever he heard last.

'Before discussing these questions,' Pierre continued, 'I consider we should do well to ask the Emperor – most respectfully to ask his Majesty – to inform us of the exact number of the troops we have, and the position in which our armies and our forces now find themselves, and then. ...'

But scarcely had Pierre uttered these words before he was attacked from three sides at once. The most violent onslaught came from an old acquaintance, a boston player who had always been very well disposed towards him, Stepan Stepanovich Adraksin. Adraksin was in uniform, and whether it was due to the uniform or to other causes, Pierre saw before him quite a different man. With an expression of senile wrath suddenly flushing his face, Adraksin screamed out at Pierre:

'In the first place, I tell you we have no right to put such questions to the Emperor; and secondly, if the Russian Nobility had any such right the Emperor could make us no answer. The movements of the troops depend on the movements of the enemy – the numbers rise and fall. ...'

Another voice, that of a nobleman of medium height, some forty years of age, whom Pierre had seen in days gone by at the gipsies' entertainments and knew as a wretched card-player, interrupted Adraksin. But he too was quite transformed by his uniform, as he moved up to Pierre.

'Yes, and this is not the time for deliberation,' said this nobleman. 'The time has come for action: the war is in Russia. The enemy is advancing to destroy Russia, to desecrate the tombs of our fathers, to carry off our wives and children.' The speaker smote his breast. 'We will arise, we will go to war as one man for our father the Tsar!' he cried, rolling his bloodshot eyes. Several approving voices were heard in the throng. 'We are Russians and will not grudge our blood for the defence of our faith, the throne and the Fatherland! We must leave off our idle dreaming if we are sons of our Fatherland! We will show Europe how Russia rises to the defence of Russia!'

Pierre tried to reply but could not get a word in. He was conscious that the sound of his words, apart from any meaning they conveyed, was less audible than the sound of his adversary's excited voice.

Count Rostov at the back of the little group was nodding approval. Several of the audience turned their shoulders briskly to the orator at the conclusion of a phrase and said:

'Hear, hear!'

Pierre was anxious to say that he was by no means averse to sacrificing his money, his peasants or himself, only one ought to know the state of affairs in order to be able to apply the remedy, but it was impossible. A number of voices were shouting and talking together, so that Count Rostov had not time to signify agreement with all of them, and the group grew in size, split up, re-formed again and moved off, all talking at once, into the largest hall, to the big table there. Not only was Pierre prevented from speaking but he was rudely interrupted, pushed aside, and backs were turned to him as though he were the common enemy. This happened not because they disliked the tenor of his speech, which was already forgotten after all the subsequent speeches; but to animate it the crowd needed some tangible object for its love and a similar object for its hate. Pierre furnished it with the latter. Many orators spoke after the excited nobleman, and all in the same tone, a number of them eloquently and with originality. Glinka, the editor of the *Russian Messenger*, who was recognized and greeted with cries of 'Author! Author!', said that hell must be repulsed by hell, that he had watched a child smiling at the flash of lightning and the clap of thunder, 'but we will not be like that child'.

'Hear, hear! Smiling at the clap of thunder!' was echoed approvingly at the back of the assembly.

The throng drifted up to the large table, where grey or bald-headed old noblemen of seventy were sitting, wearing uniforms and decorations. Almost all of them Pierre had seen in their own homes with their private jesters, or playing boston at the club. With an incessant hum of voices the crowd advanced to the table. The orators, pressed against the high chair-backs by the surging mass, spoke one after another and sometimes two at once. Those who stood further back noticed what the speaker omitted to say and hastened to supply the gap. Others were busy in the heat and crush ransacking their brains to find some idea and hurriedly utter it. The old grandees, whom Pierre knew, sat looking first at one and then at another, and their expressions for the most part betrayed nothing but the fact that they found the room very hot. Pierre, however, felt painfully agitated, and the general desire to show that they were ready to go to all lengths – which found expression in tones and looks rather than in the tenor of the speeches – infected him too. He did not renounce his opinions but somehow felt himself in the wrong and anxious to justify himself.

'I only said that we could make sacrifices to better purpose when we know what is needed!' he cried, trying to be heard above the other voices.

One little old man close by him looked round but his attention was immediately diverted by an exclamation at the opposite side of the table.

'Yes, Moscow will be surrendered! She will be our expiation!' one man was shouting.

'He is the enemy of mankind!' cried another.

'Allow me to speak. ...'

'Gentlemen, you are crushing me! ...'

23

AT that moment Count Rostopchin with his protruding chin and alert eyes strode into the room, wearing the uniform of a general with sash over his shoulder. The crowd parted before him.

'Our Sovereign the Emperor will be here immediately,' announced Rostopchin. 'I am straight from the palace. I presume that in the position we are in there is little need for discussion. The Emperor has deigned to summon us and the merchants. They will pour out their millions' (he pointed to the merchants' hall), 'while it is our business to raise men and not spare ourselves. ... That is the least we can do!'

A consultation took place confined to the grandees sitting at the table. Their whole conference was more than subdued, and the old voices saying one after another, 'I agree,' or, for the sake of variety, 'I am of the same opinion,' and so on, even sounded mournful after all the hubbub that had gone before.

The secretary was told to write down the resolution adopted by the Moscow Nobility and Gentry, that they would furnish a levy of ten men in every thousand of their serfs, fully equipped, as Smolensk had done. Their chairs made a scraping noise as the gentlemen who had been conferring rose with an air of relief, and began walking about to stretch their legs, taking their friends' arms and chatting in couples.

'The Emperor! The Emperor!' was the cry that suddenly resounded through the various halls, and the whole throng hurried to the entrance.

The Emperor entered through a broad lane between two walls of noblemen. Every face expressed reverent and awe-struck curiosity. Pierre was standing rather far off, and could not quite catch all the Emperor said. From what he did hear he understood that his Majesty was speaking of the peril threatening the Empire, and of the hopes he placed on the Moscow Nobility. The Emperor was answered by a voice informing him of the resolution just arrived at by the Nobility.

'Gentlemen!' said the Tsar in a trembling voice.

A ripple of excitement ran through the crowd, which then fell quiet again, so that Pierre distinctly heard the pleasantly warm and human voice of the Emperor saying with emotion:

'I never doubted the devotion of the Russian nobles. But this day it has surpassed my expectations. I thank you in the name of the Fatherland. Gentlemen, let us act! Time is more precious than anything. ...'

The Emperor ceased speaking, the crowd began pressing round him, and rapturous exclamations were heard on all sides.

'Yes, more precious than anything ... spoken royally,' said the voice of Count Rostov with a sob. He had heard nothing but understood everything in his own way.

From the hall of the Nobility the Emperor went into the merchants' room, where he remained for about ten minutes. Pierre was among those who saw him come back with tears of emotion in his eyes. As became known later, the Emperor had scarcely begun to address the merchants before the tears gushed from his eyes and he continued in a trembling voice. When Pierre saw the Emperor he was coming out accompanied by two merchants, one of whom Pierre knew, a stout contractor. The other was the mayor, a man with a thin sallow face and narrow beard. Both were weeping. Tears filled the thin man's eyes but the stout contractor was sobbing outright like a child, while he kept repeating:

'Take life and property too, your Majesty!'

Pierre's one feeling at that moment was a desire to show that he was ready to go to all lengths and make any sacrifice. The constitutional tendency of his speech weighed on his conscience: he sought an opportunity of glossing it over. On learning that Count Mamonov was furnishing a regiment, Bezuhov at once informed Count Rostopchin that he would provide and maintain one thousand men.

Old Rostov could not tell his wife of what had passed without tears, and there and then granted Petya's request, and went himself to enter his name.

Next day the Emperor left Moscow. All the assembly of nobles took off their uniforms and settled down again in their homes and clubs, and not without some groans gave orders to their stewards about the levy, wondering at what they had done.

PART TWO

I

NAPOLEON began the war with Russia because he could not resist going to Dresden, could not help his head being turned by the homage he received, could not help donning Polish uniform and yielding to the stimulating influence of a June morning, and could not refrain from giving way to outbursts of fury in the presence of Kurakin and afterwards of Balashev.

Alexander refused all negotiations because he felt himself personally insulted. Barclay de Tolly did his utmost to command the army in the best way possible because he wished to fulfil his duty and win the renown of being a great general. Rostov charged the French because he could not restrain his longing for a gallop across the level plain. And in the same fashion all the innumerable individuals who took part in the war acted in accordance with their natural dispositions, habits, circumstances and aims. They were moved by fear or vanity, they rejoiced or were indignant, they argued and supposed that they knew what they were doing and did it of their own free will, whereas they were all the involuntary tools of history, working out a process concealed from them but intelligible to us. Such is the inevitable lot of men of action, and the higher they stand in the social hierarchy the less free they are.

Now those who took part in the events of the year 1812 have long ago passed from the scene, their personal interests have vanished, leaving no trace, and nothing remains of that time save its historical results.

Providence compelled all these men, striving for the attainment of their own private ends, to combine for the accomplishment of a single stupendous result, of which no one man (neither Napoleon, nor Alexander, still less any of those who did the actual fighting) had the slightest inkling.

It is plain to us now what caused the destruction of the French army in 1812. No one will dispute that the cause of the loss of Napoleon's French forces was, on the one hand, their advance into the heart of Russia late in the season without any preparation for a winter campaign; and, on the other, the character given to the war by the burning of Russian towns and the hatred aroused among the Russian people for the enemy. But no one at the time foresaw (what now seems so obvious) that this was the only way an army of eight hundred thousand men – the best army in the world led by the best general – could be defeated in conflict with a raw army of half its numerical strength, led by inexperienced commanders as the Russian army was. *Not only did no one see this* but *on the Russian side* every effort was systematically directed towards preventing the only thing that could save Russia, while *on the French side*, despite Napoleon's experience and so-called military genius, every exertion was made to push on to Moscow at the end of the summer, that is, to do the very thing that was bound to lead to destruction.

In historical works on the year 1812 French writers are very fond of saying that Napoleon was aware of the danger of extending his line, that he sought to give battle and that his marshals advised him to halt at Smolensk; and of making similar statements to show that, even at the time, the perils of the campaign were understood. Russian authors are still fonder of telling us that from the commencement of the campaign there existed a plan to lure Napoleon into the depths of Russia – after the manner of the Scythians – and this plan some of them attribute to Pfuhl, others to some Frenchman, others to Toll, and others again to Alexander, in support of which they cite memoirs, projects and letters containing hints of such a course of action. But all these suggestions of foresight concerning what happened, on the part of French and Russians alike, stand out now only because they fit in with what befell. Had the event not occurred these intimations would have been neglected, as hundreds of thousands of contrary intimations and surmises are forgotten which were current at the period but are now consigned to oblivion because the event falsified them. There are always so many conjectures as to the issue of any event that, however the matter may end, there will invariably be people to declare: 'I said so at the time', entirely forgetting that among their numerous hypotheses were some in favour of quite the opposite.

The notion that Napoleon was aware of the danger of extending his line, and that the Russians had a scheme for luring the enemy into the depths of Russia, obviously belong to this category; and only by much straining can historians ascribe such reflections to Napoleon and his marshals, or such plans to the Russian generals. All the facts are in flat contradiction to such suppositions. During the whole period of the war not only was there no desire on the part of the Russians to decoy the French into the heart of the country but from the moment they crossed the frontier everything was done to stop them. And far from dreading the extension of his line of communications, Napoleon welcomed every step forward as a triumph, and did not seek pitched battles at all as eagerly as he had done in his previous military operations.

At the very beginning of the campaign our armies were broken up, and our sole aim was to unite them, though uniting the armies presented no advantage if our object was to retire and draw the enemy into the depths of the country. Our Emperor was with the troops to inspire them to dispute every inch of Russian soil and on no account to retreat. An immense camp was fortified at Drissa in accordance with Pfuhl's plan, and there was no intention to withdraw further. The Emperor reproached the commanders-in-chief for every yard they retreated. The Emperor could never have imagined letting the enemy reach Smolensk, still less could he have contemplated the burning of Moscow, and when our armies did unite he was indignant that Smolensk had been taken and burnt without a general engagement having been fought before its walls.

Thus it was with the Emperor, and the Russian commanders and the people as a whole were even more incensed at the thought that our forces were retreating far inside our borders.

Napoleon, having divided our armies, advanced deep into the interior, letting slip several opportunities of forcing an engagement. In August he was in Smolensk and thinking only of how to advance further, though, as we see now, that advance meant inevitable ruin.

The facts show perfectly clearly that Napoleon did not foresee the danger of an advance on Moscow, and that Alexander and the Russian generals had no idea at that time of luring Napoleon on but were bent on stopping him. Napoleon was enticed into the heart of the country not as the result of any plan, the possibility of which no one believed in, but in consequence of a most complex interplay of the intrigues, desires and ambitions of those who took part in the war, who had no perception whatever of what was to come or of the sole means of saving Russia. Everything happens fortuitously. The army is split up early in the campaign. We try to effect a junction between the different sections with the apparent intention of giving battle and checking the enemy's advance, but by this effort to unite, while avoiding battle with a far stronger enemy, we are forced to retreat at an acute angle, and so lead the French on to Smolensk. But it is not enough to say that we withdrew at an acute angle because the French were advancing between our two armies: the angle became still more acute and we retired still further because Barclay de Tolly was an unpopular foreigner detested by Bagration (who would come under his command), and Bagration, as leader of the second army, did his utmost to delay joining forces and coming under Barclay's command as long as he could. Bagration was slow in effecting the junction (though this was the chief aim of all at Headquarters) because it seemed to him he would be exposing his army to danger on this march, and that it would be better for him to retire more to the left and south, harassing the enemy's flank and rear, and securing recruits for the army from the Ukraine. Whereas it looks as if he thought this up because he did not want to come under the command of the detested foreigner Barclay, who was his junior in the Service.

The Emperor was with the army to encourage it, but his presence, and his ignorance of what steps to take, and the enormous number of advisers and plans, paralysed the first army and it retired.

In the Drissa camp the intention was to make a stand; but Paulucci, with ambitions to become commander-in-chief, unexpectedly employed his energy to influence Alexander, and Pfuhl's whole scheme was abandoned and the matter entrusted to Barclay. But as Barclay did not inspire complete confidence his power was limited.

The armies were split up, there was no unity of command and Barclay was not liked; but this confusion and division and the unpopularity of the foreign commander-in-chief resulted on the one hand in vacillation and the avoidance of a battle (which would have been inevitable had the armies been united and someone other than Barclay been in command) and, on the other, growing indignation against the foreigners and an increase of patriotic fervour.

At last the Emperor left the army, on the pretext – the most convenient and indeed the only one that could be found for his departure – that it was necessary for him to fan the enthusiasm of the inhabitants of the capitals to wage war on a national scale, and this visit of the Emperor to Moscow did in fact treble Russian armed might.

The Emperor left the army in order not to obstruct the commander-in-chief's undivided control, and hoping that more decisive action would then be taken; but the commander's position became still more difficult and impaired. Bennigsen, the Tsarevich and a swarm of adjutants-general remained with the army to keep the commander-in-chief under observation and urge him to greater activity, and Barclay, feeling less free than ever under the surveillance of all these 'eyes of the Emperor', waxed still more chary of undertaking any decisive operation, and avoided giving battle.

Barclay stood for prudence. The Tsarevich hinted at treachery and demanded a general engagement. Lubomirsky, Bronnitsky, Wlocki, and others of the same mind swelled the clamour to such a point that Barclay, using the excuse of sending papers to the Emperor, despatched these Polish adjutants-general to Petersburg, and plunged into an open struggle with Bennigsen and the Tsarevich.

At Smolensk, in spite of Bagration's wishes to the contrary, the armies at last united.

Bagration drove up in a carriage to the house occupied by Barclay. Barclay donned his official sash and came out to greet and present his report to his senior officer, Bagration. Bagration, not to be outdone in this contest of magnanimity, places himself under Barclay's command, despite his own seniority in rank, but, having assumed a subordinate position, agreed with him less than ever. By the Emperor's express order Bagration made his reports direct to him, and wrote to Arakcheyev:

My Sovereign's will is law but I cannot work with the *minister* [so he called Barclay]. For mercy's sake send me somewhere else, if only in command of a regiment, for I cannot stand it here. Headquarters are so crammed full of Germans that a Russian cannot breathe and there is no making head or tail of anything. I thought I was serving my Sovereign and the Fatherland but it turns out that I am really serving Barclay, which I confess I have no mind for.

The swarm of Bronnitskys and Wintzingerodes and their like still further poisoned relations between the commanders-in-chief, and resulted in even less unity. Preparations were made to attack the French before Smolensk. A general was sent to inspect the position. This general, detesting Barclay, rode off to visit a friend of his own, a corps-commander, and having spent the day with him, returned to Barclay and roundly condemned a proposed battleground which he had never seen.

While all this intriguing and argument over the battlefield was going on, and while we were looking for the French – having lost touch with them – the French stumbled upon Nevyerovsky's division and reached the walls of Smolensk.

We were surprised into having to fight at Smolensk to save our lines of communication. The battle was fought, and thousands were slain on both sides.

Smolensk was abandoned contrary to the wishes of the Emperor and of the whole people. But Smolensk was set fire to by its own inhabitants, who had been betrayed by their governor. And these ruined inhabitants, offering an example to other Russians, fled to Moscow, full of their losses and kindling hatred of the foe. Napoleon advances further; we retreat; and so the very thing is attained that is destined to overthrow Napoleon.

2

THE day after his son's departure Prince Nikolai Bolkonsky summoned Princess Maria to his study.

'Well, now are you satisfied?' he demanded. 'You have made me quarrel with my son! Are you satisfied? That was all you wanted! Satisfied? ... This is painful to me, painful. I am old and infirm, and this was your wish. Well, gloat over it, gloat over it! ...'

And after that Princess Maria did not see her father again for a week. He was ill and did not leave his study.

Princess Maria noticed to her surprise that during this illness the old prince excluded Mademoiselle Bourienne too from his room. Tikhon alone attended him.

At the end of the week the prince reappeared and resumed his former way of life, devoting himself with special zeal to the laying out of his farm buildings and gardens, and completely breaking off all relations with Mademoiselle Bourienne. His frigid tone and air with Princess Maria seemed to say: 'There, you see? You plotted against me, told lies to Prince Andrei about my relations with that Frenchwoman and made me quarrel with him, but you see I can do without you, and without that Frenchwoman either!'

One half of the day Princess Maria spent with little Nikolai, supervising his lessons, teaching him Russian and music herself, and talking to Dessalles. The rest of the time she spent over her books, or with her old nurse or the 'God's folk', who sometimes came up by the back stairs to visit her.

Princess Maria's attitude to the war was the general attitude of women when there is a war. She feared for her brother who was in it, was horrified and amazed at the strange cruelty that impels men to slaughter one another; but she had no notion of the significance of this war, which seemed to her exactly like all those of the past. She did not realize the import of the war, although Dessalles, with whom she was always talking, was passionately interested in its progress and tried to explain to her his views about it, and although her 'God's folk' who came to see her all with terror reported, in their own way, the popular rumours about the invasion by Antichrist, and although Julie (now Princess Drubetskoy), who had renewed her correspondence with her, sent patriotic letters from Moscow – written in her curious Frenchified Russian.

I write to you in Russian, my good friend [wrote Julie], because I have a detestation towards all the French, and their language equally, which I cannot support to hear spoken. ... We in Moscow are all elated with enthusiasm for our adored Emperor.

My poor husband is enduring pains and hunger in miserable Jewish taverns; but the news which I have inspires me yet more.

You have without doubt heard of the heroic exploit of Raevsky, embracing his two sons and saying: 'I will perish with them but we will not budge!' And indeed, though the enemy was twice stronger than we, we were unshakeable. We pass the time as best we can, but in war as in war! Princess Aline and Sophie spend whole days with me, and we, unhappy widows of live husbands, have beautiful conversations while we scrape cloth to make lint. Only you, my friend, are wanting ...

and so on.

The principal reason why Princess Maria failed to grasp the significance of the war was because the old prince never spoke of it, ignored its existence and laughed at Dessalles when he mentioned the war at dinner. The prince's tone was so calm and confident that Princess Maria accepted it without question.

All that July the old prince was exceedingly active and even lively. He planned another garden and began a new building for the domestic serfs. The only thing that made Princess Maria anxious about him was that he slept very little and instead of having his bed in his study changed his sleeping-place every day. One day he would order his camp-bedstead to be set up in the gallery, another time he would remain on the couch or in a tall-backed chair in the drawing-room and doze there without undressing, while Petrushka, the lad who had replaced Mademoiselle Bourienne, read to him. Then he would try spending a night in the dining-room.

On the 1st of August a second letter came from Prince Andrei. In his first, received shortly after he had left home, Prince Andrei had dutifully asked his father's forgiveness for what he had allowed himself to say, and begged to be restored to his favour. To this letter the old prince had replied affectionately, and from that time had kept the Frenchwoman at a distance. Prince Andrei's second letter, written near Vitebsk after the French had occupied that town, contained a brief account of the whole campaign, with a sketch-map to illustrate it, and his reflections as to the further progress of the war. In this letter Prince Andrei pointed out to his father the inadvisability of staying at Bald Hills, so close to the theatre of war and in the direct line of the enemy's advance, and counselled him to move to Moscow.

At dinner that day, on Dessalles's observing that the French were said to have already entered Vitebsk, the old prince remembered his son's letter.

'Had a letter from Prince Andrei today,' he said to Princess Maria. 'Haven't you read it?'

'No, father,' the princess replied timidly. She could not possibly have read the letter, of whose arrival she had not even heard.

'He writes about this war,' said the prince, with the ironic smile that had become habitual to him in speaking of the present war.

'That must be very interesting,' said Dessalles. 'Prince Andrei is in a position to know. ...'

'Oh, most interesting!' said Mademoiselle Bourienne.

'Go and fetch it for me,' said the old prince to Mademoiselle Bourienne. 'You know – under the paper-weight on the little table.'

Mademoiselle Bourienne jumped up with alacrity.

'No, don't!' he exclaimed with a frown. 'You go, Mihail Ivanich.'

Mihail Ivanich rose and went to the study. But he had hardly left the room before the old prince, looking about him nervously, threw down his dinner-napkin and went himself.

'No one can do anything ... they always make some muddle,' he muttered.

While he was away Princess Maria, Dessalles, Mademoiselle Bourienne and even little Nikolai looked at one another without speaking. The old prince came hurrying back, accompanied by Mihail Ivanich and bringing the letter and a plan, which he laid beside him, not letting anyone read them at dinner.

When they had moved into the drawing-room he handed the letter to Princess Maria and, spreading out before him the plan of his new building and fixing his eyes upon it, told her to read the letter aloud. After she had done so Princess Maria looked inquiringly at her father. He was studying the plan, apparently absorbed in his own thoughts.

'What do you think about it, prince?' Dessalles ventured to ask.

'I? I? ...' said the prince, seeming to rouse himself with a painful effort and not taking his eyes from the plan of the building.

'Very possibly the theatre of war will move so near to us that ...'

'Ha-ha-ha! The theatre of war!' said the prince. 'I have always said, and I say still, that the theatre of war is Poland and the enemy will never get beyond the Niemen.'

Dessalles looked in amazement at the prince, who was talking of the Niemen when the enemy were already at the Dnieper; but Princess Maria, forgetting the geographical position of the Niemen, supposed that what her father said was true.

'When the snow melts they'll be swallowed up in the Polish swamps. It's only they who can't see that,' the old prince continued, evidently thinking of the campaign of 1807 which seemed to him so recent. 'Bennigsen ought to have entered Prussia earlier, then things would have taken a different turn. ...'

'But, prince,' Dessalles began timidly, 'the letter speaks of Vitebsk. ...'

'Ah, the letter? Yes ...' replied the prince peevishly. 'Yes ... yes ...' His face suddenly took on a morose expression. He paused. 'Yes, he writes that the French were beaten at ... at ... what river was it?'

Dessalles dropped his eyes.

'The prince says nothing about that,' he remarked gently.

'Doesn't he? Well, I didn't invent it, that's quite certain.'

A long silence ensued.

'Yes ... yes ... Well, Mihail Ivanich,' he said suddenly, raising his

818

head and pointing to the plan of the building, 'tell me how you propose to make that alteration. ...'

Mihail Ivanich went up to the plan, and the prince, after talking to him about the new building, cast a wrathful glance at Princess Maria and Dessalles and departed to his room.

Princess Maria saw Dessalles's embarrassed, wondering look fixed on her father, noticed his silence and was struck by the fact that her father had forgotten his son's letter on the drawing-room table; but she was not only afraid to speak of it and ask Dessalles why he sat disconcerted and silent: she was afraid even to think about it.

In the evening Mihail Ivanich, sent by the prince, came to Princess Maria for Prince Andrei's letter which had been forgotten in the drawing-room. Princess Maria gave him the letter, and then, much as she disliked asking, ventured to inquire what her father was doing.

'Very busy as usual,' replied Mihail Ivanich with a politely ironic smile which caused Princess Maria to turn pale. 'He worries a good deal over the new building. He has been reading a little, but now' – Mihail Ivanich lowered his voice – 'now he's at his bureau, engaged on his will, I expect.' (Of late one of the prince's favourite occupations had been the preparation of some documents he meant to leave at his death and which he called his 'will'.)

'And is Alpatych being sent to Smolensk?' asked Princess Maria.

'Oh yes, to be sure. He has been waiting to start for some time.'

3

WHEN Mihail Ivanich returned to the study with the letter the old prince, spectacles on and a shade over his eyes, was sitting at his open bureau with screened candles, holding a paper at arm's length, and in a somewhat dramatic attitude was reading over his manuscript – his 'Remarks' as he called it – which were to be delivered into the hands of the Emperor after his death.

When Mihail Ivanich went in there were tears in the prince's eyes evoked by the memory of the time when the paper he was now reading had been written. He took the letter from Mihail Ivanich, put it in his pocket, folded up his papers and called in Alpatych, who had long been waiting.

The prince had a list of things he wanted done in Smolensk, and walking up and down the room past Alpatych, who stood by the door, he gave his instructions.

'First, writing-paper – do you hear? Eight quires, like this sample, gilt-edged ... it must be exactly like the sample. Varnish, sealing-wax – according to Mihail Ivanich's list.'

He paced backwards and forwards for a while and glanced at his memorandum.

'Then deliver the letter about the deed to the governor in person.'

Next bolts for the doors of the new building were required and had to be of a special pattern the prince had himself designed. After that a box bound with iron must be ordered to keep his 'will' in.

The instructions to Alpatych took over two hours and still the prince did not let him go. He sat down, sank into thought and, closing his eyes, dropped into a doze. Alpatych made a slight movement.

'Get you gone, now, get you gone! If there is anything else I'll send after you.'

Alpatych went out. The prince returned to his bureau, glanced into it, fingered his papers, shut the bureau again and sat down to the table to write to the governor.

It was late when he got to his feet after sealing the letter. He was tired and wanted to sleep but he knew he would not be able to, and that the most melancholy thoughts came to him in bed. He called Tikhon and went through the rooms with him, to show him where to set up his bed for that night. He walked about, measuring every corner.

There was no place that seemed satisfactory, but worst of all was his customary couch in the study. That couch had become an object of dread to him, no doubt because of the oppressive thoughts he had had when lying on it. Nowhere was quite right, but the corner behind the piano in the sitting-room pleased him best of all: he had never slept there yet.

With the help of a footman Tikhon brought in the bedstead and began putting it up.

'Not like that, not like that!' cried the prince, and himself pushed the bed a few inches further from the corner and then closer to it again.

'Well, at last I have finished! Now I shall rest,' thought the prince, and he let Tikhon undress him.

Frowning with vexation at the exertion necessary to divest himself of his coat and trousers, the prince undressed, dropped heavily down on the bed and appeared to sink into thought, staring contemptuously at his withered yellow legs. He was not really thinking but only deferring the moment of making the effort to lift his legs and heave himself over on the bed. 'Ugh, what a trial! Oh, that these toils might end and *you* release me!' he mused. Pressing his lips together he made the effort for the twenty-thousandth time and lay down. But hardly had he done so before he felt the bed rocking evenly to and fro beneath him as though it were breathing heavily and jolting. He had this sensation almost every night. He opened his eyes just as they were closing.

'No peace, damn them!' he grumbled in fury at some unknown person. 'Ah yes, there was something else of importance – something of great importance that I was keeping to think of in bed. The bolts? No, I told him about them. No, it was something, something in the drawing-room. Princess Maria talked some nonsense. Dessalles – that fool – said something. Something in my pocket – can't remember.'

'Tikhon, what were we talking about at dinner?'

'About Prince Andrei. ...'

'Quiet, be quiet!' The prince slapped his hand down on the table. 'Yes, I know, Prince Andrei's letter! Princess Maria read it. Dessalles said something about Vitebsk. Now I'll read it.'

He bade Tikhon fetch the letter from his pocket and move the little table with the lemonade and a spiral wax candle on it closer to the bed, and putting on his spectacles he began reading. Only now for the first time, as he read the letter in the stillness of the night, by the feeble light under the green shade, did he grasp its meaning for a moment.

'The French at Vitebsk! Four days' march and they could reach Smolensk – perhaps they are there already! Tikhon!' Tikhon started up. 'No, never mind, never mind!' he cried.

He slipped the letter under the candlestick and closed his eyes. And the Danube rose before his mind – a brilliant noonday, the reeds, the Russian camp and himself a young general without a wrinkle on his face, hale and hearty and ruddy, going into Potemkin's gaily-coloured tent, and the burning sensation of jealousy of the favourite agitates him as violently now as it had done then. And he recalls every word uttered at that first interview with Potemkin. And then he sees a rather short, stout woman with a sallow, greasy skin, the Dowager-Empress, with her smile and the words she spoke at her first gracious reception of him, and then that same face on the catafalque, and the brush with Zubov by the coffin over his right to kiss her hand.

'Oh, to make haste, to make haste back to that time and have done with all the present. Oh, if only they would leave me in peace!'

4

BALD HILLS, Prince Nikolai Bolkonsky's estate, lay forty miles east of Smolensk and a couple of miles from the main road to Moscow.

The same evening that the prince gave Alpatych his instructions, Dessalles asked to see Princess Maria and told her that, since the prince was not very well and was taking no steps to secure his safety, though from Prince Andrei's letter it was clear that to remain at Bald Hills might be dangerous, he respectfully advised her to send a letter by Alpatych to the provincial governor at Smolensk, asking him to let her know the state of affairs and the degree of risk to which Bald Hills was exposed. Dessalles wrote the letter to the governor for Princess Maria, and she signed it and gave it to Alpatych with instructions to hand it to the governor and in the case of danger to come back as quickly as possible.

Having received all his orders Alpatych, wearing a white beaver hat – a present from the prince – and carrying a walking-stick as the prince did, went out, escorted by his family, to get into the leather gig with its three sleek roan horses.

The large bell was muffled and the little harness bells were stuffed with paper. The prince allowed no one at Bald Hills to drive with ringing bells. But Alpatych loved to have bells ringing when he went on a long journey. His satellites – the head clerk, a counting-house clerk, the cook and the cook's assistant, two old women, a boy footman in Cossack dress, the coachman and various other servants – were seeing him off.

His daughter placed chintz-covered down cushions under him and behind his back. His old sister-in-law popped in a small bundle, and one of the coachmen helped him into the vehicle.

'There, there, women's fuss! Oh, females, females!' said Alpatych, puffing and speaking rapidly just as the prince did, and he climbed into the trap.

After giving the head clerk parting instructions about the work to be done, Alpatych, now certainly no longer imitating the prince, lifted his hat from his bald head and crossed himself three times.

'If anything should ... you come back, Yakov Alpatych. For Christ's sake think of us!' his wife called to him, alluding to the rumours of the war and the enemy.

'Ah, these women and their fuss!' Alpatych muttered to himself as he drove off, looking about him at the fields of rye turning yellow, at the thickly growing oats still green, and at other quite black fields where they were only just beginning the second ploughing. Alpatych continued his journey, admiring the crop of corn that was singularly fine that season, staring at the rye fields in which here and there reaping was already in progress, meditating like a true husbandman on the sowing and the harvest, and asking himself whether he had not forgotten any of the prince's instructions.

Having stopped twice on the way to feed his horses, he reached the city towards evening on the 4th of August.

On the road Alpatych kept meeting and overtaking baggage-trains and troops. As he approached Smolensk he heard the sounds of distant firing, but these did not impress him. What struck him most was the sight, on the outskirts of Smolensk, of a splendid field of oats in which a camp had been pitched and which was being mown down by some soldiers, evidently for fodder. This did make an impression on Alpatych but he soon forgot it in thinking over his own business.

All the interests of Alpatych's life for upwards of thirty years had been bounded by the will of the prince, and he never stepped outside that limit. Anything not connected with the execution of the prince's orders had no interest, had in fact no existence, for Alpatych.

On reaching Smolensk on the evening of the 4th of August Alpatych put up in the suburb of Gachen, across the Dnieper, at the inn kept by Ferapontov, where he had been in the habit of stopping for the last thirty years. Twelve years before, Ferapontov, through Alpatych's good offices, had bought a wood from the prince and begun to trade, and now he had a house, an inn and a corn-chandler's shop in the same province. Ferapontov was a stout, dark, red-faced peasant in the forties, with thick lips, a broad knob of a nose, similar knobs over his black, knitted brows, and a round belly.

Wearing a waistcoat over his calico shirt, Ferapontov was standing outside his shop which opened on to the street. Catching sight of Alpatych, he went up to him.

'You're right welcome, Yakov Alpatych. Folks be all leaving town, but here you are arriving,' said he.

'Leaving town – how's that?' asked Alpatych.

'To be sure, I always say folks is foolish! All scared now of a Frenchman!'

'Old wives' gossip, old wives' gossip!' said Alpatych.

'That's just what I think, Yakov Alpatych. I tell 'em there's orders not to let *him* in, so it's all right. And the peasants charging as much as three roubles for the use of a horse and cart – they've no conscience!'

Yakov Alpatych listened without hearing. He asked for a samovar, and hay for his horses, and after he had sipped his tea he went to bed.

All night long troops tramped past the inn. Next day Alpatych donned a jacket which he kept for wearing in town, and set forth to do his errands. It was a sunny morning, and by eight o'clock already hot. 'A good day for harvesting,' thought Alpatych.

Beyond the city the sounds of firing had been audible since daybreak. At eight o'clock the boom of cannon mingled with the rattle of musketry. The streets were thronged with hurrying people, and there were many soldiers, but drivers still plied for hire, the shopkeepers stood at their doors and morning service was going on as usual in the churches. Alpatych bought the things he had to buy, called in at the government offices, went to the post and to the governor's. In the offices and shops and at the post office everyone was talking of the troops, and of the enemy who was already attacking the town: everybody was asking everybody else what was to be done, and trying to calm each other's fears.

Outside the governor's house Alpatych found a large gathering, and saw Cossacks and a travelling carriage belonging to the governor. On the steps he met two of the landed gentry, one of whom he knew. This gentleman, an ex-captain of the police, was exclaiming vehemently:

'But I tell you this is no joke! It's all very well if you're single – "One man though undone is but one", as the proverb says, but with a family of thirteen, and all the goods and chattels. ... Things have come to such a pass that we shall all be ruined – what do the authorities amount to if they allow that? They ought to be hanged, the brigands! ...'

'Come, come, hush now,' said the other.

'What do I care? Let him hear! We're not dogs,' said the ex-captain of police, and looking round he noticed Alpatych.

'Ah, Yakov Alpatych, what brings you here?'

'I'm come to see the governor, by command of his Excellency,' answered Alpatych, lifting his head proudly and thrusting his hand into the bosom of his coat as he always did when he mentioned the prince. ... 'His Excellency bid me inquire into the position of affairs,' he added.

'Well, you may as well know, then,' cried the gentleman, 'they've brought things to such a pretty state that there are no carts or anything! ... There, hear that?' said he, pointing in the direction from which the sounds of firing came.

'They've led us all to ruin ... the brigands!' he repeated, and descended the porch steps.

Alpatych shook his head, and went upstairs. The waiting-room was full of tradesmen, women and functionaries, looking dumbly at one another. The door of the governor's room opened and they all stood up and moved forward. A clerk ran out, said something to a merchant, beckoned to a stout official with a cross hanging round his neck to follow him, and vanished again, obviously anxious to avoid the inquiring looks and queries directed to him. Alpatych moved forward and the next time the clerk emerged, placing his hand in the breast of his buttoned coat he addressed him and held out the two letters.

'For his Honour the Baron Asch, from General-in-chief Prince Bolkonsky,' he announced with such solemnity and so portentously that the clerk turned to him and took the letters.

A few minutes later the governor received Alpatych and hurriedly said to him:

'Inform the prince and princess that I knew nothing: I acted on the highest instructions – here ...' he held out a printed paper to Alpatych. 'Still, as the prince is not well, my advice to them is to go to Moscow. I am just setting off there myself. Tell them. ...'

But the governor did not finish: a begrimed and perspiring officer ran into the room and began to say something in French. A look of dismay came over the governor's face.

'You can go,' he said, nodding to Alpatych, and fell to interrogating the officer.

Searching, panic-stricken, helpless glances were turned on Alpatych when he came out of the governor's room. He hurried back to the inn, unable to help listening now to the firing, which was closer and getting hotter all the time.

The document the governor had given to Alpatych ran as follows:

I assure you that the city of Smolensk is not in the slightest danger as yet, and it is unlikely that it will be so threatened. I from the one side and Prince Bagration from the other are marching to unite our forces before Smolensk, which junction will be effected on the 22nd instant, and the combined armies will proceed with their joint forces to defend their compatriots of the province entrusted to your care until their efforts shall have beaten back the enemies of our Fatherland, or until the last warrior in our valiant ranks has perished. From this you will see that you have a perfect right to reassure the inhabitants of Smolensk, for those defended by two such brave armies may well be confident that victory will be theirs. (Order of the day from Barclay de Tolly to the Civil Governor of Smolensk, Baron Asch, 1812.)

People were roaming uneasily about the streets.

Carts piled high with household utensils, chairs and clothes-presses kept emerging from the gates of houses and proceeding through the town. Carts were standing at the house next to Ferapontov's, and women were wailing and lamenting as they exchanged good-byes. A small yard-dog was frisking about in front of the harnessed horses, barking.

Alpatych's step was more hurried than usual as he entered the inn yard and went straight to the shed where his horses and trap were. The coachman was asleep. He woke him up, told him to get ready, and crossed to the house. From the private room of the family came the sounds of a child crying, the heartrending sobs of a woman, and the furious, husky shouting of Ferapontov. The cook, fluttering about the passage like a frightened hen, cried as soon as she saw Alpatych:

'He's been thrashing the life out of her – beating the mistress to death. ... Beat and beat her, he did, and knocked her about!'

'What for?' asked Alpatych.

'She kept begging to go away. She's a woman! "Take me away," says she, "don't let me perish with my little children. Folks," says she, "are all gone, so why," says she, "don't we go?" And so he began to thrash her and drag her round the room!'

At these words Alpatych nodded his head as if in approval, and not caring to hear more he went towards the door of the room opposite the innkeeper's, where he had left his purchases.

'You brute, you murderer!' screamed a thin, pale woman, bursting out of the door at that moment with a baby in her arms and her kerchief torn from her head. She ran down the steps into the yard. Ferapontov came out after her, but seeing Alpatych he pulled down his waistcoat, smoothed his hair, yawned and followed Alpatych into the other room.

'Going already, be you?' he asked.

Without answering the question, or looking round at the innkeeper, Alpatych sorted his packages and asked how much he owed.

'We'll reckon up! Well, been at the governor's, eh?' inquired Ferapontov. 'What did you hear?'

Alpatych replied that the governor had told him nothing definite.

'How can the likes of us with our business pack up and go?' said Ferapontov. 'Why, it'd be seven roubles a cartload as far as Dorogobuzh, and I tell 'em it's not Christian to ask it. Selivanov, now, made a good thing Thursday – sold flour to the army at nine roubles a sack. What do you say to some tea?' he added.

While the horses were being harnessed Alpatych and Ferapontov over their tea discussed the price of corn, the crops and the splendid harvesting weather.

'Well, it seems to be getting quieter,' remarked Ferapontov, finishing his third cup and getting up. 'Our men must have got the best of it. They said they wouldn't let 'em in. I suppose we're in force all right. I heard tell Matvey Ivanych Platov pitched eighteen thousand of 'em into the Marina t'other day, and drowned the lot.'

Alpatych gathered together his parcels, handed them over to the coachman who had come in, and settled up with the innkeeper. The noise of wheels, hooves and bells was heard from the gateway as a little trap passed out.

It was by now not long after midday. Half the street lay in shadow, while the other half was in brilliant sunshine. Alpatych glanced out of the window and went to the door. All of a sudden there came a strange sound of a far-away hiss and thump followed by the boom of cannon blending into a dull roar that set the windows rattling.

Alpatych went out into the street. Two men were running past towards the bridge. From different sides came the whistle and crashing of round-shot and the bursting of shells falling on the town. But these sounds attracted little attention among the inhabitants compared with the noise of firing beyond the walls. Napoleon had ordered a hundred and thirty guns to open up on the town after four o'clock. The people did not at first grasp the meaning of this bombardment, and the crash of falling grenades and cannon-balls only excited curiosity. Ferapontov's wife, who till then had kept up a steady whimpering in the barn, became quiet and, with the baby in her arms, went out to the gate and stood silently staring at the people and listening to the noise.

The cook and a shopkeeper came to the gate. With lively interest they all tried to get a glimpse of the projectiles as they flew over their heads. Several people came round the corner talking eagerly.

'What force!' remarked one. 'Smashed the roof and ceiling to splinters!'

'Rooted up the earth like a pig!' said another.

'Capital business, makes one look alive!' laughed the first. 'Lucky you skipped aside or you'd have been no more!'

The crowd stopped them, and they described how a cannon-ball had fallen on a house close to them. Meanwhile other missiles, now a cannon-ball with a swift sinister hiss, now a grenade with its agreeable intermittent whistle, flew incessantly over the people's heads; but not one fell near them, they all flew over. Alpatych took his seat in the trap. The innkeeper stood at the gate.

'Will you never have done gaping?' he shouted to a kitchen-woman, who in her red petticoat, with sleeves rolled up and her bare elbows swinging, had stepped to the corner to listen to what was being said.

'There's a marvel for you!' she was saying, but hearing her master's voice she turned back, pulling down her skirt which had been tucked up.

Once more, but very close this time, something whistled, swooping down like a small bird. There was a flash of fire in the middle of the street, the sound of an explosion, and the street was shrouded in smoke.

'Scoundrel, what did you do that for?' shouted the innkeeper, rushing to the kitchen-woman.

At the same instant the piteous wailing of women rose from all sides, the terrified baby began to scream, and in silence, with pale faces, the people crowded round the cook. Above all the clamour rose the groans and exclamations of the kitchen-woman.

'Oh-h-h, good kind souls! Dear friends, don't let me die! Good kind souls! ...'

Five minutes later no one was left in the street. The cook, with her thigh broken by a fragment of the grenade, had been carried into the kitchen. Alpatych, his coachman, Ferapontov's wife and children, and the yard-man were all sitting in the cellar listening. The thunder of cannon, the hiss of projectiles and the piteous moaning of the cook, which prevailed over all else, never ceased for a single instant. Ferapontov's wife alternately rocked and hushed her baby, and when anyone came into the cellar asked in a pathetic whisper what had become of her husband who had stayed in the street. A shopman told her the master had gone with the crowd to the cathedral to fetch the wonder-working icon of Smolensk.

Towards dusk the cannonade began to subside. Alpatych left the cellar and stood in the doorway. The evening sky that had been so clear was overcast with smoke, through which the sickle of the new moon shone strangely, high up in the sky. After the terrible roar of the guns a hush seemed to hang over the city, broken only by the rustle of footsteps far and wide, the sound of groans and distant shouts, and the crackle of fires. The cook's moaning had now ceased. In two directions clouds of black smoke curled up from fires and drifted away. Soldiers in various uniforms walked or ran confusedly about the streets, like ants from a demolished ant-hill. Several of them slipped into Ferapontov's yard before Alpatych's eyes. Alpatych went out to the gate. A retreating regiment, the men jostling each other in their hurry, blocked the street.

Noticing him, an officer said: 'The town is being abandoned, get away, get away!' and turning immediately to the soldiers, he shouted: 'I'll teach you to keep out of the yards!'

Alpatych went back to the house, called the coachman and bade him set off. Ferapontov's whole household followed Alpatych and the driver out. The women, who had been silent till then, broke into sudden lamentations when they saw the smoke – and there were flames too – now visible in the twilight. As though echoing them, similar wails rose up in other parts of the street. Under the penthouse Alpatych and the coachman arranged the tangled reins and traces of their horses with trembling fingers.

As Alpatych drove out of the gate he saw some ten soldiers in

Ferapontov's open shop, talking loudly and filling their bags and knapsacks with wheaten flour and sunflower seeds. Just then Ferapontov returned and went into the shop. On seeing the soldiers he was about to shout at them but suddenly stopped short and, clutching at his hair, burst into a sobbing laugh.

'Carry it all away, lads! Don't leave it for those devils!' he cried, himself snatching up some sacks of flour and pitching them into the street. Some of the soldiers were frightened and ran away, others went on stuffing their bags. Catching sight of Alpatych, Ferapontov turned to him.

'Russia is done for!' he shouted. 'Alpatych, it's all over! I'll set fire to the place myself. We're done for! ...' and Ferapontov ran into the yard.

An unbroken stream of soldiers was blocking up the whole street, so that Alpatych could not get out and was obliged to wait. Ferapontov's wife and children were also sitting in a cart, waiting till it was possible to drive away.

Night had fallen now. There were stars in the sky and from time to time the new moon shone through the veil of smoke. On the slope down towards the Dnieper, Alpatych's cart and that of the inn-keeper's wife, which had been slowly moving forward amid the rows of soldiers and other vehicles, were brought to a halt. In a side street not far from the cross-roads where the traffic had come to a full stop a house and some shops were burning. The fire was already dying down. The flames now sank down and were lost in the black smoke, then suddenly flared up to illumine with strange distinctness the faces of the people crowding at the cross-roads. Black figures flitted to and fro before the fire, and cries and shouts were heard above the incessant crackling of the flames. Seeing that it would be some time before his gig could proceed, Alpatych got down and turned into the side street to look at the fire. Soldiers were scurrying back-wards and forwards, and he saw a couple of them and a man in a frieze coat dragging burning beams into another yard across the street, while others carried armfuls of hay.

Alpatych joined a great crowd of people standing before a high barn which was blazing briskly. The walls were all in flames and the back wall had fallen in; the wooden roof was collapsing and the rafters were alight. The crowd was obviously waiting to see the roof fall in, and Alpatych watched too.

'Alpatych!' a familiar voice suddenly hailed the old man.

'Mercy on us, your Excellency!' answered Alpatych, immediately recognizing the voice of the young prince.

Prince Andrei in his riding-cloak and mounted on a black horse, was looking at Alpatych from the back of the crowd.

'What are you doing here?' he asked.

'Your ... your Excellency,' stammered Alpatych, and broke into sobs. 'Your ... your ... Is it really all over with us? Your father. ...'

'What are you doing here?' Prince Andrei repeated.

The flames blazed up again at that moment, and Alpatych saw his young master's pale, worn face. He described how he had been sent to the town and had difficulty in getting away.

'What do you say, your Excellency – is it all over with us?' he asked again.

Prince Andrei, making no reply, took out a note-book and, raising his knee, began scribbling in pencil on a page he tore out. He wrote to his sister:

Smolensk has surrendered. Bald Hills will be occupied by the enemy within a week. Leave at once for Moscow. Let me know as soon as you start – send by special messenger to Usvyazh.

Having written this and handed the sheet of paper to Alpatych, he gave him verbal instructions about the arrangements for the departure of the prince, the princess, his son and the boy's tutor, and told him how and where to communicate with him immediately. Before he had time to finish, a staff-officer accompanied by a suite, galloped up to him.

'You a colonel!' shouted the staff-officer with a German accent, in a voice Prince Andrei knew. 'Under your very eyes houses are being set on fire and you stand by! What do you mean by it? You will have to answer for this!' shouted Berg, who was now assistant to the chief-of-staff of the commander of the left flank of the infantry of the First Army, a very agreeable and prominent position, as Berg said.

Prince Andrei glanced at him and, without replying, went on with his instructions to Alpatych.

'So tell them that I shall wait till the 10th for an answer, and if by that time I do not get word that they have all got away I shall be obliged to throw up everything and go myself to Bald Hills'.

'Prince,' said Berg, recognizing Prince Andrei, 'I only spoke as I did because it is my duty to carry out my orders, and I am always most scrupulous in carrying out ... You must excuse me, please,' Berg tried to apologize.

There was a crash in the burning building. The fire died down for a moment and wreaths of black smoke rolled from under the roof. There was another fearful crash, followed by the collapse of something huge.

'Oooo!' yelled the crowd, as the ceiling of the granary fell in and the burning grain wafted a smell as of cakes baking. The flames flared up again, lighting the animated, delighted, harassed faces of the spectators.

The man in the frieze coat brandished his arms in the air and shouted:

'Hurrah, lads! Now she's raging! Well done!'

'That's the owner himself,' several voices were heard saying.

'So then,' continued Prince Andrei to Alpatych, 'tell them just what I have said.' And without a word to Berg, who stood mute beside him, he put spurs to his horse and rode down the side street.

5

FROM Smolensk the troops continued to retreat, with the enemy close on their heels. On the 10th of August the regiment Prince Andrei commanded was marching along the high road past the avenue that led to Bald Hills. The heat and drought had gone on for more than three weeks. Every day fleecy clouds floated across the sky, occasionally shutting out the sun, but towards evening the sky would clear again and the sun set in a sombre red haze. Only the heavy night-dews refreshed the earth. The wheat left in the fields was burnt up and dropping out of the ear. The marshes dried up. The cattle lowed from hunger, finding nothing to graze on in the sun-baked meadows. Only at night and in the forests while the dew lasted was it ever cool. But on the road, the high road along which the troops marched, there was no coolness even at night or where the road passed through the forest: the dew made no impression on the sandy dust inches deep. As soon as it was daylight the soldiers began to move. The artillery and baggage-wagons ploughed along noiselessly, buried almost to their axles, and the infantry sank ankle-deep in the soft, choking, burning dust that never cooled even at night. Sandy dust clung to their legs and to the wheels, rose and hung like a cloud overhead, and got into eyes, ears, hair and nostrils, and, worst of all, settled in the lungs of the men and beasts that moved along the road. The higher the sun rose, the higher rose that cloud of dust, and through the screen of tiny fiery particles one could look with naked eye at the sun, which showed like a huge crimson ball in the cloudless sky. There was not a breath of wind, and the men suffocated in the stagnant atmosphere. They marched with handkerchiefs tied over their noses and mouths. When they reached a village there was a rush for the wells. They fought over the water, and drank it down to the mud.

Prince Andrei was in command of a regiment, and deeply concerned with its organization, the welfare of the men and the necessity of receiving and giving orders. The burning and evacuation of Smolensk marked an epoch in his life. A novel feeling of intense indignation with the enemy made him forget his personal sorrow. He was devoted heart and soul to the interests of his regiment, and was considerate and kind to his men and his officers. In the regiment they called him 'our Prince', were proud of him and loved him. But he was kind and gentle only with those of his own regiment, with Timohin and his like – people quite new to him, belonging to a different world, who could have no notion of his past. So soon as chance threw him in the way of any of his old acquaintances, or any one from the Staff, he bristled up immediately, and was vindictive, ironical and scornful. Everything that was reminiscent of the past was repugnant to him, and so in his relations with that former world he confined himself to trying to do his duty and not to be unfair.

In truth, everything appeared to Prince Andrei in a dark and gloomy light, especially after Smolensk had been abandoned on the 6th of August (he considered that the town could and should have been defended), and after his ailing father had been forced, as he supposed, to flee to Moscow, leaving his beloved Bald Hills, which he had built and peopled, to be plundered. But despite this, thanks to his position, Prince Andrei had something to think about entirely apart from general matters – his regiment. On the 10th of August the column of which his unit formed part reached the turning leading off to Bald Hills. Two days previously he had received news that his father, his son and his sister had left for Moscow. Though there was nothing for Prince Andrei to do at Bald Hills, he decided, with a characteristic desire to aggravate his own sufferings, that he must ride over there.

He ordered his horse to be saddled and, leaving his regiment on the march, rode off to his father's estate, where he had been born and had spent his childhood. Riding past the pond, where there always used to be dozens of peasant women chattering away as they rinsed their linen or beat it with wooden beetles, Prince Andrei noticed that there was not a soul about, and that the little washing-platform had been torn away and was floating on its side in the middle of the pond, half under water. He rode to the keeper's lodge. There was no one to be seen at the stone gates of the drive and the door was unlocked. Grass had already begun to grow over the garden paths, and calves and horses were straying about in the English park. Prince Andrei went up to the hot-house: some of the glass panes were smashed, and of the trees in tubs several were overturned and others dried up. He shouted for Taras, the gardener. No one answered. Going round the hot-house to the ornamental garden, he saw that the carved wooden fence was broken and branches of the plum-trees had been torn off with the fruit. An old peasant, whom Prince Andrei could remember seeing as a boy at the gate, was sitting on a green garden-seat plaiting a bast shoe.

He was deaf and did not hear Prince Andrei's approach. He was sitting on the old prince's favourite bench, and beside him strips of bast were hanging on the broken and withered branches of a magnolia.

Prince Andrei rode up to the house. Several lime-trees in the old garden had been cut down and a piebald mare and her foal were wandering about among the rose bushes in front of the house. The shutters were all up, except at one window downstairs which was open. A little serf-boy, catching sight of Prince Andrei, ran into the house.

Alpatych, having got his family away, remained alone at Bald Hills: he was sitting indoors reading the *Lives of the Saints*. On learning that Prince Andrei was there, he came out, with his spectacles on his nose and buttoning his coat; he hurried up to the prince, and without a word began weeping and kissing his young master's knee.

Then, vexed at his own weakness, he turned away and began to give an account of the position of affairs. Everything precious and valuable had been moved to Bogucharovo. Up to eight hundred bushels of grain had also been carted away. The hay and the spring corn, which, according to Alpatych, had been wonderful that year, had been commandeered by the troops and cut while still green. The peasants were ruined; some of them, too, had gone to Bogucharovo; a small number remained.

Without waiting to hear him out, Prince Andrei asked:

'When did my father and sister leave?' – meaning when had they left for Moscow.

Alpatych, supposing the question to refer to their departure for Bogucharovo, replied that they had set off on the 7th, and again went into details concerning arrangements for the estate, asking for instructions.

'Is it your Honour's orders that I let the oats go, on getting a receipt from the officers?' he inquired. 'We still have six hundred quarters left.'

'What am I to say to him?' Prince Andrei wondered, looking down on the old man's bald head shining in the sun, and seeing by the expression on his face that Alpatych himself realized the untimeliness of such questions, and only asked them to deaden his own grief.

'Yes, let it go,' he said.

'In case your Excellency noticed some disorder in the garden,' pursued Alpatych, 'it could not be prevented. Three regiments were here and camped for the night. The dragoons especially behaved ... I took down the name and rank of their commanding officer to lodge a complaint.'

'Well, and what are you going to do? Shall you stay, if the enemy occupies the place?' Prince Andrei asked him.

Alpatych turned his face to Prince Andrei and looked at him; then suddenly, with a solemn gesture, he lifted his arm upwards.

'He is my refuge, and His will be done!' he exclaimed.

A group of peasants and indoor servants were coming across the meadow, uncovering their heads as they drew near Prince Andrei.

'Well, good-bye!' said Prince Andrei, bending over to Alpatych. 'You must go away too. Take what you can; and tell the peasants to make their way to the Ryazan estate, or the property near Moscow.'

Alpatych clung to Prince Andrei's leg and broke into sobs. Gently disengaging himself, Prince Andrei spurred his horse and rode down the avenue at a gallop.

He passed the old man again, still sitting in the ornamental garden, as impassive as a fly on the face of a loved one who is dead, tapping on the last on which he was making the bast shoe. Two little girls came running out from the hot-house, their skirts full of plums picked from the trees there, and stopped short on meeting Prince Andrei. When she saw the young master the elder girl, with a look of alarm on her face, clutched her younger companion by the hand and hid with her behind a birch-tree, not stopping to gather up the green plums they dropped.

Prince Andrei turned away with startled haste, unwilling to let them see that they had been observed. A feeling of pity welled up in him for the pretty, frightened child. He was afraid to look at her, yet at the same time had an overwhelming desire to do so. Looking at these children, he was seized by a new, comforting sense of relief as he became aware of the existence of other interests in life, quite remote from his own and just as legitimate. These little persons were evidently possessed by the one passionate idea – to carry off and devour those green plums without being caught – and Prince Andrei shared their hope for success in their enterprise. He could not resist another glance at them. Fancying that the danger was over, they had darted out of their hiding-place and, chirruping something in their shrill little voices and holding up their skirts, they were scampering merrily across the meadow as fast as their bare, sunburned little legs would carry them.

Prince Andrei was somewhat refreshed by his ride away from the dusty high road along which the troops were marching. But not far from Bald Hills he came out on the road again and overtook his regiment at its halting-place by the dam of a small lake. It was towards two o'clock in the afternoon. The sun, a red ball through the dust, baked and scorched his back intolerably through his black coat. The dust hung motionless as ever above the buzz of talk that came from the resting troops. There was not a breath of wind. As he rode along the embankment Prince Andrei smelt the fresh, muddy smell of the lake. He longed to take a dive into the water, however dirty it might be. He glanced round at the pool from which came shrieks and laughter. The small lake, thickly covered with green slime, was visibly half a yard higher and overflowing the dam, being full of white, naked human bodies with brick-red hands, faces and necks, splashing about in it. All this bare white human flesh, laughing and shrieking, was floundering about in that dirty pool like carp crammed into a water-pot. There was a ring of merriment in that splashing, and that was what made it especially pathetic.

One fair-haired young soldier of the third company, whom Prince

Andrei knew and who had a strap round the calf of his leg, crossed himself, stepped back to get a good run, and plunged into the water. Another, a swarthy non-commissioned officer who always looked shaggy, stood up to his waist in the water wriggling his muscular form and snorting with satisfaction as he poured the water over his head with hands black to the wrists. There was a noise of slapping, yelling and puffing.

Everywhere, on the bank, on the dam and in the lake, there was white, healthy, muscular flesh. The officer, Timohin, with his little red nose, was rubbing himself down on the embankment. He felt rather abashed at seeing the prince but decided to address him nevertheless.

'It's really pretty good, your Excellency! Wouldn't you like to try?' said he.

'Too dirty,' replied Prince Andrei, making a grimace.

'We'll clear it out for you in a jiffy,' said Timohin, and, not stopping to put his clothes on, ran to get the men out of the lake.

'The prince wants to bathe.'

'What prince? Ours?' cried various voices, and the men were all in such haste to make way for him that Prince Andrei hardly had time to deter them. He thought that he would far rather souse himself with water in the barn.

'Flesh, bodies, *chair à canon!*' he reflected, looking at his own naked body and shuddering, not so much with cold as with aversion and horror, incomprehensible even to himself, aroused by the sight of that immense multitude of bodies splashing about in the dirty lake.

*

On the 7th of August Prince Bagration wrote as follows from his quarters at Mihalovka on the Smolensk road:

Dear Count Alexei Andreyevich [he was writing to Arakcheyev but knew that his letter would be read by the Emperor, and therefore weighed every word to the best of his ability].

I presume that the *minister* – [as he called Barclay] de Tolly – has already reported the abandonment to the enemy of Smolensk. It is painful, it is sad, and the whole army is in despair that this most important place should have been wantonly relinquished. I, for my part, personally entreated him most urgently, and finally even by letter; but nothing would persuade him. Upon my honour I swear to you that

Napoleon was in a greater fix than he has ever been, and might have lost half his army but he could not have taken Smolensk. Our troops fought and are fighting as never before. With fifteen thousand men I kept the enemy at bay for thirty-five hours and beat them; but *he* was not willing to hold out for a mere fourteen hours. It is a blot and a disgrace on our armies, and as for him – methinks he ought not to be alive.

If he reports that our losses were heavy, it is not true: perhaps around four thousand, not that; but even had it been ten thousand, that's war! The enemy, on the other hand, lost untold numbers. ...

What would it have cost him to hold out for a couple of days longer? In any case the French would have had to retire of their own accord, for they hadn't a drop of water for their men or their horses. He gave me his word he would not retreat, and then all of a sudden sends a message that he is withdrawing that very night. We cannot wage war in this way, or we may soon bring the enemy to Moscow. ...

There is a rumour that you are thinking of making peace. God forbid! To make peace after our sacrifices, after such insane retreats – you would be setting all Russia against you and everyone of us would feel ashamed of wearing the Russian uniform. If it has come to that, we must fight so long so Russia can and so long as there are men able to stand. ...

One man ought to be in command, not two. Your minister may be all right in the ministry but as a general he is not merely bad but execrable, yet the fate of the whole Fatherland has been entrusted to his hands! ... I am, I assure you, nearly beside myself with vexation: forgive me for writing so boldly. It is plain that anyone who can advocate the conclusion of a peace, and approves of confiding the command of the army to the minister, is no friend to the Sovereign and hopes for the ruin of us all. And so I write frankly: call out the militia. For the minister is leading our visitors after him to the capital in the most masterly fashion. Wolzogen, the Imperial aide-de-camp, is held in great suspicion by the whole army. He is said to be more Napoleon's man than ours, and he is the minister's prime counsellor. I am not merely civil to him but as obedient as a corporal, although I am his senior. This is painful, but, as I am devoted to my Sovereign and Benefactor, I submit. Only I grieve for the Emperor that he should entrust our valiant army to such as he. Consider – in the course of this retreat we have lost, through fatigue or left sick in hospital, over fifteen thousand men; whereas had we attacked this would not have happened. Tell me for God's sake what will Russia – our mother Russia – say to such cowardice, and why are we abandoning our good and gallant country to such rabble and implanting feelings of hate and shame in every Russian?

What is there to fear? Whom are we afraid of? It is no fault of mine if the minister shilly-shallies, is a coward, is dense and dilatory, and has all the worst defects. The whole army bewails it and calls down every sort of curse upon him. ...

6

ALL the innumerable sub-divisions into which it is possible to classify the phenomena of life may be assembled into two categories: the one, where matter predominates; the other, where form is the prevailing factor. In the latter group – by contrast with life in the village, in the country, in the provincial town, or even in Moscow – may be placed the life of Petersburg, and especially the life of its *salons*. The life of the fashionable drawing-room continues unvarying.

Since 1805 we had been quarrelling and being reconciled with Napoleon, making constitutions and unmaking them again; but the *salons* of Anna Pavlovna and Hélène were the same as they had been – the former seven, the latter five years – before. At Anna Pavlovna's everybody was as perplexed as ever by Napoleon's successes, and saw in them and in the subservience of the sovereigns of Europe a malicious conspiracy, intended solely to cause unpleasantness and anxiety to the Court circle of which Anna Pavlovna was the representative. In Hélène's house, which Rumyantsev himself honoured with his visits, regarding Hélène as a remarkably intelligent woman, the same enthusiasm prevailed in 1812 as in 1808 for the 'great nation' and the 'great man', together with regret for the breach with France, which, in the opinion of those who gathered at Hélène's, ought without delay to be terminated by peace.

Of late, since the Emperor's return from the army, there had been some excitement in these rival *salons*, accompanied by demonstrations of mutual hostility, but the bias of each circle remained unaffected. Except for the most unimpeachable legitimists, Anna Pavlovna's set refused to receive anyone who was French, and patriotic views were expressed that one ought not to go to the French theatre, and that to maintain the French troupe there was costing the government as much as the maintenance of a whole army corps. The progress of the war was eagerly followed, and the most flattering reports of our army were circulated. In the Hélène-Rumyantsev-French circle the rumours of the barbarities of the enemy and of the war were discredited and every conciliatory effort on the part of Napoleon was discussed in full. This set upbraided the premature counsels of those who advised speedy preparations for the removal to Kazan of the Court and the girls' educational establishments under the patronage of the Dowager-Empress. In general, the whole war was looked on in Hélène's drawing-room as a series of formal demonstrations which would very soon end in peace, and Bilibin's view prevailed – Bilibin was now in Petersburg and constantly at Hélène's (where it behoved every sensible man to be seen) – that gunpowder would not mend matters but those who invented it. Moscow's patriotic fervour, tidings of which reached Petersburg with the return of the Emperor, they derided ironically, with much wit though with equal circumspection.

In Anna Pavlovna's circle, on the contrary, these patriotic demonstrations roused the greatest enthusiasm, and were spoken of as Plutarch speaks of the deeds of the heroes of antiquity. Prince Vasili, who still occupied his former important posts, constituted the connecting link between the two sets. He visited 'my good friend Anna Pavlovna' and was likewise to be seen in 'my daughter's diplomatic *salon*', and often in his constant comings and goings between the two camps became confused and said at Hélène's what he should have said at Anna Pavlovna's, and vice versa.

Soon after the Emperor's return Prince Vasili, in a conversation about the progress of the war at Anna Pavlovna's, sharply criticized Barclay de Tolly, but was undecided as to who ought to be appointed commander-in-chief. One of the visitors, usually spoken of as '*un homme de beaucoup de mérite*', described how he had that day seen Kutuzov, the newly elected chief of the Petersburg militia, presiding over the enrolment of recruits at the Treasury, and cautiously ventured to suggest that Kutuzov would be the man to satisfy all requirements.

Anna Pavlovna remarked with a melancholy smile that Kutuzov had done nothing but cause the Emperor annoyance.

'I told them so over and over again at the Assembly of the Nobility,' interposed Prince Vasili, 'but they wouldn't listen to me. I told them his election as chief of the militia would not please the Emperor. They would not listen.

'It's all this mania for opposition,' he went on. 'And what public are they playing to, I should like to know ? It's all because we want to ape the silly enthusiasm of those Moscovites,' Prince Vasili continued, forgetting for a moment that it was at Hélène's one had to jeer at Moscow's fervour, while at Anna Pavlovna's it was as well to admire it. But he retrieved his mistake at once. 'Now is it suitable for Kutuzov, the oldest general in Russia, to be presiding at that tribunal? And he'll get nothing by that move! How could they possibly appoint a man commander-in-chief who cannot sit a horse, who drops asleep at a council – a man, too, of the lowest morals! A pretty reputation he gained for himself in Bucharest! I don't speak of his capacity as a general, but at a time like this how could we nominate a decrepit, blind old man, yes, positively blind? A fine idea to have a blind general! He can't see a thing. To play at blindman's-buff? ... He doesn't see at all!'

No one made any rejoinder to this.

On the 24th of July this was a perfectly correct view. But on the 29th of July Kutuzov received the title of prince. This mark of favour might indicate a desire to shelve him, and therefore Prince Vasili's way of thinking continued to be correct though now he was not in any hurry to express it. But on the 8th of August a committee, consisting of Field-marshal Saltykov, Arakcheyev, Vyazmitinov, Lopuhin and Kochubey, met to consider the progress of the war. This committee came to the conclusion that our failures were due to a lack of unity in the command, and, though the members of the committee were aware of the Emperor's dislike of Kutuzov, after a brief deliberation they agreed to advise his appointment as commander-in-chief. And that same day Kutuzov was appointed commander-in-chief with full powers over the armies and over the whole region occupied by them.

On the 9th of August Prince Vasili once more met the man 'de beaucoup de mérite'. The latter was very attentive to Anna Pavlovna, in the hope of getting himself appointed director of one of the educational establishments for young ladies. Prince Vasili strode into the room with an air of happy triumph, like a man who has attained the object of his desires.

'Well, have you heard the great news? Prince Kutuzov is field-marshal! All differences are settled. I am so glad, so delighted! At last we have a man!' said he, glancing sternly and significantly round at the whole company.

L'homme de beaucoup de mérite, in spite of his anxiety to obtain the post he coveted, could not refrain from reminding Prince Vasili of his former opinion. (This was a breach of manners to Prince Vasili in

Anna Pavlovna's drawing-room, and also to Anna Pavlovna herself, who had likewise received the tidings with eager satisfaction, but he could not resist the temptation.)

'But, prince, they say he is blind!' he observed, quoting Prince Vasili's own words.

'What next! He sees well enough,' said Prince Vasili quickly, in a deep voice and with a slight cough – the voice and cough with which he was wont to dispose of all difficulties. 'He sees well enough,' he repeated. 'And what I am particularly pleased about,' he went on, 'is that the Emperor has given him full powers over all the armies and the whole region – powers no commander-in-chief has ever had before. He is a second autocrat,' he concluded with a victorious smile.

'God grant it, God grant it!' said Anna Pavlovna.

L'homme de beaucoup de mérite, who was still a novice in Court society, wishing to flatter Anna Pavlovna by upholding her first opinion on this subject, observed:

'They say the Emperor was reluctant to give Kutuzov such authority. I hear that Kutuzov coloured like a young girl having La Fontaine's *Contes* read to her, when he said: "Your Sovereign and the Fatherland award you this honour".'

'Perhaps his heart was not altogether in it,' said Anna Pavlovna.

'Oh no, no!' protested Prince Vasili warmly. 'He would not now put Kutuzov second to anyone.' In Prince Vasili's opinion, not only was Kutuzov the best of men but everybody worshipped him. 'No, that is impossible,' said he, 'for our Sovereign has always appreciated him highly.'

'Only God grant that Prince Kutuzov assumes real power and does not allow *anyone* to put a spoke in his wheel – *des batons dans les roues*,' remarked Anna Pavlovna.

Prince Vasili understood at once who was meant by that *anyone*, and he said in a whisper:

'I know for a fact that Kutuzov made it an express condition that the Tsarevich should not be with the army. Do you know what he said to the Emperor?'

And Prince Vasili repeated the words supposed to have been spoken by Kutuzov to the Emperor: '"I can neither punish him if he does wrong nor reward him if he does well." Oh, a very shrewd fellow is Prince Kutuzov! I have known him this many a day.'

'They even say,' remarked *l'homme de beaucoup de mérite*, who did not yet possess a courtier's tact, 'that his Excellency made it an express condition that the Emperor himself should not be with the army.'

At these words Prince Vasili and Anna Pavlovna simultaneously turned their backs on him and looked mournfully at one another, with a sigh of pity for his *naïveté*.

7

WHILE all this was happening in Petersburg the French, having already left Smolensk behind them, were steadily approaching nearer and nearer to Moscow. Napoleon's historian, Thiers, like others of his historians, tries to justify his hero by saying that Napoleon was drawn on to the walls of Moscow against his will. He is as right as any of his kind who look for the explanation of historic events in the will of one man; he is as right as his Russian *confrères* who maintain that Napoleon was lured to Moscow by the skilful strategy of the Russian generals. Here, besides the law of 'retrospectiveness', which makes all the past appear a preparation for events that occur subsequently, reciprocity comes in, confusing the whole matter. A good chess player who has lost a game is genuinely convinced that his failure resulted from a false move on his part, and tries to see the mistake he made at the beginning of the game, forgetting that at each stage of play there were similar blunders, so that no single move was perfect. The mistake on which he concentrates attention attracts his notice simply because his opponent took advantage of it. How much more complex is the game of war, which must be played within certain limits of time and where it is a question not of one will manipulating inanimate objects but of something resulting from the innumerable *collisions* of diverse wills!

After Smolensk Napoleon sought a battle beyond Dorogobuzh, at Vyazma, and then at Tsarevo-Zaimishche; but it turned out that owing to a combination of circumstances without number the Russians could not give battle before they reached Borodino, seventy miles from Moscow. From Vyazma Napoleon issued the order to advance direct upon Moscow. *Moscow, the Asiatic capital of this great Empire, the sacred city of the peoples of Alexander; Moscow, with its countless churches looking like Chinese pagodas* – this Moscow allowed Napoleon's imagination no rest. On the march from Vyazma to Tsarevo-Zaimishche Napoleon rode his bob-tailed light bay ambling horse, accompanied by his Guards, his bodyguard, his pages and aides-de-camp. Berthier, his chief-of-staff, had dropped behind to interrogate a Russian prisoner taken by the cavalry. Followed by Lelorme d'Ideville, an interpreter, he overtook Napoleon at a gallop and pulled up with an amused expression.

'Well?' asked Napoleon.

'One of Platov's Cossacks – says that Platov is joining up with the main army, and that Kutuzov has been appointed commander-in-chief. A very shrewd rascal, with a long tongue!'

Napoleon smiled and bade them give the Cossack a horse and bring the man to him. He wanted to have a talk with him himself. Several adjutants galloped off, and an hour later Lavrushka, the serf Denisov had turned over to Rostov, rode up to Napoleon, wearing an orderly's short jacket and sitting on a French cavalry saddle, looking sly, tipsy and mirthful. Napoleon told him to ride by his side, and began questioning him.

'You are a Cossack?'

'Yes, a Cossack, your Honour.'

The Cossack, says Thiers, relating this episode, *ignorant in whose company he found himself, for there was nothing in Napoleon's plain appearance to suggest to the Oriental mind the presence of a monarch, talked in the most free-and-easy manner of the incidents of the war.* In reality, Lavrushka, having got drunk the day before and left his master dinnerless, had been thrashed for it and sent to the village in quest of fowls, where he engaged in looting till the French caught and took him prisoner. Lavrushka was one of those coarse, impudent lackeys who have seen a good deal of life, who consider it imperative to employ trickery and cunning whatever they do, are ready to render any sort of service to their master and can always smell out his baser impulses, especially those prompted by vanity and pettiness.

Finding himself in the society of Napoleon, whose identity he easily and confidently recognized, Lavrushka was not in the least abashed but merely set to work to win the favour of his new master.

He knew very well that this was Napoleon, and Napoleon's presence intimidated him no more than Rostov's or the sergeant-major's with his knout, for the simple reason that there was nothing which either the sergeant-major or Napoleon could deprive him of.

So he rattled on, repeating all the gossip he had heard among the orderlies. Much of it was true. But when Napoleon asked him whether the Russians thought they would beat Bonaparte or not Lavrushka screwed up his eyes and considered.

He detected a sharp piece of cunning in the question, as men of his type see cunning in everything, so he frowned and did not answer immediately.

'This is the size of it,' he said thoughtfully, 'if there's a battle pretty soon, yours will win. That's a fact. But let three days go by, and it's likely to be a long job.'

Lelorme d'Ideville smilingly interpreted this to Napoleon as follows: 'If a battle takes place within the next three days the French will win, but if it were postponed after that God knows what would be the outcome.' Napoleon did not smile, though he was obviously in high good humour, and ordered these words to be repeated.

Lavrushka noticed this and to entertain him further added (affecting ignorance of Napoleon's identity):

'We know, you've got your Bonaparte, aye, and he's beaten everybody in the world; but we're of different kidney ...' hardly aware how or why this boastful bit of patriotism slipped out at the end. The interpreter translated these words without the conclusion, and Bonaparte smiled.

The young Cossack brought a smile to the lips of his august interlocutor, says Thiers.

After riding a few paces in silence Napoleon turned to Berthier and said that he would like to see the effect on *this child of the Don* of learning that the man he was addressing was the Emperor himself, the very Emperor who had carved his immortally victorious name on the Pyramids.

The fact was accordingly communicated to Lavrushka.

Realizing that this was meant to disconcert him and that Napoleon expected him to be panic-stricken, Lavrushka for the gratification of his new masters promptly pretended to be astounded, aghast. He opened round eyes and made the sort of face he put on when he was being led off to be whipped. *As soon as Napoleon's interpreter had spoken,* says Thiers, *the Cossack was dumbfounded. He did not utter another word, and rode with his eyes fixed on the conqueror whose fame had reached him across the steppes of the East. All his loquacity was suddenly arrested and gave place to a naïve and silent awe. Napoleon, having rewarded him, ordered him to be set free like a bird one restores to its native fields.*

Napoleon continued on, dreaming of the Moscow that filled his imagination, while the 'bird one restores to its native fields' galloped back to our outposts, inventing on the way the tale he would tell his comrades. What had really taken place he had no mind to relate, simply because it seemed to him not worth the telling. He found the Cossacks, inquired for the regiment operating with Platov's detachment, and by evening located his master, Nikolai Rostov, quartered at Yankovo. Rostov was just mounting his horse to ride round the neighbouring villages with Ilyin. He let Lavrushka have another horse and took him along with him.

8

PRINCESS MARIA was not in Moscow and out of harm's way as Prince Andrei supposed.

After Alpatych's return from Smolensk the old prince suddenly seemed to awake as from a dream. He gave orders for the militiamen to be called up from the villages and armed, and wrote a letter to the commander-in-chief informing him of his intention to stay at Bald Hills and defend himself to the last, leaving it to the commander-in-chief's discretion whether or not to take measures for the defence of Bald Hills, where one of Russia's oldest generals was preparing to be captured or killed. At the same time he announced to his household that he would remain at Bald Hills.

But, while determined himself not to leave, he made arrangements for sending the princess with Dessalles and the little prince to Bogucharovo, and from there to Moscow. Princess Maria, alarmed by her father's feverish, sleepless activity following on his previous apathy, could not bring herself to desert him, and for the first time in her life ventured to disobey. She refused to go, and a fearful tempest of wrath broke over her. The prince repeated every injustice he had ever inflicted on his daughter. Trying to put her in the wrong, he told her she had worn him out, estranged him from his son, had harboured the vilest suspicions of him and made it the object of her life to poison his existence; and he drove her from his study, declaring that he did not care if she did not go away. He said that he did not wish to be reminded of her existence, and warned her not to let him set eyes on her again. The fact that he did not, as she had feared, order her to be removed from Bald Hills by main force, but only forbade her to show herself to him, was a comfort to Princess Maria. She knew it meant that in the secret depths of his soul he was glad she was remaining at home and had not gone away.

The morning after little Nikolai had left, the old prince donned full uniform and prepared to visit the commander-in-chief. The calèche was ready at the door. Princess Maria saw him walk out of the house in uniform with all his orders, and go down the garden to inspect his armed peasants and domestic serfs. She sat by the window listening to his voice which reached her from the garden. Suddenly several men came running up the avenue with frightened faces.

Princess Maria ran out on to the steps, down the flower-bordered path and into the avenue. She was met by a crowd of militiamen and servants moving towards her, and in the centre of this throng several men were half supporting half dragging along a little old man in a uniform and decorations. She ran up to him and, in the play of the tiny rings of sunlight that filtered through the shade of the lime-tree avenue, could not be sure what change there was in his face. All she could see was that his former stern, determined expression had altered to one of timidity and submission. When he caught sight of his daughter he moved his helpless lips and uttered a hoarse sound. It was impossible to understand what he meant. He was lifted up, carried to his study and laid on the couch he had so dreaded of late.

The doctor, who was fetched that same night, bled him and announced that the prince had had a stroke, paralysing his right side.

To remain at Bald Hills was becoming more and more dangerous, and the next day they moved the prince to Bogucharovo, the doctor travelling with him.

By the time they reached Bogucharovo, Dessalles and the little prince had already left for Moscow.

For three weeks the old prince lay stricken with paralysis, getting neither better nor worse, in the new house Prince Andrei had built at Bogucharovo. His mind had gone; he lay like a twisted corpse. He muttered without cease, twitching his eyebrows and lips, and it was impossible to tell whether he was aware of his surroundings or not. Only one thing was certain – that he was suffering and wished to say something. But what it was, no one could divine: was it some whim of a sick and semi-delirious brain, did it relate to public affairs, or had it to do with family matters?

The doctor maintained that this restlessness meant nothing and was due to physical causes; but Princess Maria believed (and the fact that her presence always intensified his agitation confirmed her supposition) that he wanted to tell her something.

He was obviously suffering both physically and mentally. There was no hope of recovery. It was impossible to move him – what if he were to die on the road? 'Wouldn't it be better if the end did come, if it were all over?' Princess Maria thought sometimes. Night and day, hardly sleeping at all, she watched over him, and, terrible to say, often watched, not in the hope of finding signs of improvement but looking for symptoms of the approach of the end.

Strange as it was to her to acknowledge this feeling in herself, yet there it was. And what was still more horrible to Princess Maria was the fact that since her father's illness (if not even before, when she elected to stay with him, vaguely anticipating that something would happen) all the aspirations and hopes that had been forgotten or slumbering within her came to life again. Thoughts that had not entered her head for years – dreams of a life free from the fear of her father, even of the possibility of love and a happy married life – haunted her imagination like temptations of the devil. No matter how strenuously she tried to set them aside she returned to them again and again, and often caught herself thinking how she would order her life now, after *this* was over. It was temptation of the devil and Princess Maria knew it. She knew that the sole weapon against *him* was prayer, and she tried to pray. She put herself into the attitude of prayer, gazed at the icons, repeated the words of a prayer, but she could not pray. She felt that a different world had now taken possession of her – the world of activity, arduous and free – completely the opposite of the spiritual world which had enclosed her till now and in which her greatest comfort had been prayer. She could not pray and could not weep, and practical cares absorbed her mind.

To remain at Bogucharovo was becoming unsafe. From all sides came news of the approach of the French, and in one village, a dozen miles from Bogucharovo, a homestead had been sacked by French marauders.

The doctor insisted on the necessity of moving the prince; the Marshal of the Province sent an official to Princess Maria to persuade her to get away as quickly as possible; and the head of the rural police visited Bogucharovo and urged the same thing, saying that the French were only some twenty-five miles away, that French proclamations were circulating in the villages, and that if the princess did not take her father away before the 15th he could not answer for the consequences.

The princess decided to go on the 15th. The whole of the 14th she was busy making preparations and giving instructions, for which everyone applied to her. That night she spent as usual, without undressing, in the room next to the one where the old prince lay. Several times she woke to hear his groans and muttering, the creak of his bed, and the steps of Tikhon and the doctor when they turned him over. Several times she listened at the door, and it seemed to her that his mutterings were louder than usual and that he was more restless. She could not sleep, and several times went to the door and listened: she wanted to go in but hesitated. Though he could not speak, Princess Maria saw and knew how he disliked any sign of anxiety on his account. She had noticed how he always looked away in displeasure when he saw her anxious eyes involuntarily fixed on him. She knew that her intrusion in the middle of the night, at an unusual hour, would irritate him.

But never had she felt so grieved for him, never had she so dreaded to lose him. She went over their lives together, and in every word of his, every action, found a manifestation of his love for her. Occasionally these recollections were interrupted by those promptings of the devil, the thoughts of what would happen after his death, and how she would arrange her new life of freedom. But she drove away such imaginings with loathing. Towards morning he became quieter and she fell asleep.

She woke late. The clear-sightedness which often accompanies the moment of waking showed her unmistakably what it was that was of most interest to her in her father's illness. She woke, listened to what was going on behind the door and, hearing him groan, said to herself with a sigh that things were still the same.

'But what change could there be? What did I hope for? I hope for his death!' she cried, revolted with herself.

She washed, dressed, said her prayers and went out to the porch. In front of the steps the carriages into which their things were being packed were standing without horses.

It was a warm, grey morning. Princess Maria lingered in the porch, still horrified at her own spiritual infamy and trying to arrange her thoughts before going in to see her father.

The doctor came downstairs and out to her.

'He is a little better today,' said he. 'I was looking for you. One can make out something of what he says. His head is clearer. Come in – he is asking for you. ...'

Princess Maria's heart beat so violently at this news that she turned pale and leaned against the door to keep from falling. To see him, to talk to him – feel his eyes on her now that her whole soul was overflowing with those dreadful, wicked thoughts – was a torment of joy and terror.

'Come along,' said the doctor.

Princess Maria entered her father's room and went up to the bed. He was lying on his back propped up high, and his small bony hands with their knotted purple veins rested on the quilt. His left eye gazed straight before him, his right eye was awry and his lips and eyebrows were motionless. He looked so thin, so small and pathetic. His face seemed to have shrivelled or fallen away, so that his features appeared smaller. Princess Maria went up and kissed his hand. His left hand pressed hers in a way that showed he had long been waiting for her to come. He twitched her hand, and his eyebrows and lips quivered angrily.

She looked at him in dismay, trying to fathom what he wanted of her. When she changed her position so that his left eye could see her face he was calmer at once, not taking his eyes off her for some seconds. Then his lips and tongue moved, sounds came and he tried to speak, gazing at her timidly and imploringly, evidently afraid that she might not understand him.

Straining all her faculties, Princess Maria looked at him. The grotesque effort it cost him to manage his tongue made her drop her eyes and with difficulty repress the sobs that rose in her throat. He said something, repeating the same words several times. She could not understand them but tried to guess what he was saying and inquiringly repeated the syllables he uttered.

'S–s ... tr–d ... tr–d ...' he got out two or three times. It was impossible to make any sense of the sounds. The doctor thought he had guessed their meaning, and suggested 'The princess is afraid?' The prince shook his head, and again repeated the same words.

'My soul is troubled?' asked Princess Maria.

He uttered a sort of bellow in confirmation of this, took her hand and began clasping it to different parts of his breast as if trying to find the right place for it.

'Always thinking ... about you ... thinking ...' he then articulated far more intelligibly than before, now that he was persuaded of being understood.

Princess Maria pressed her head against his hand to hide her sobs and tears.

He moved his hand over her hair.

'I have been calling for you all night ...' he brought out.

'If only I had known ...' she said through her tears. 'I was afraid to come in.'

He squeezed her hand.

'Weren't you asleep?'

'No, I could not sleep,' said Princess Maria, shaking her head.

Unconsciously imitating her father, she now spoke like him, using signs as much as possible, and almost had the same difficulty with her tongue.

'Dear heart ...' or was it 'Dearest ...'? – Princess Maria could not tell; but from the look in his eyes she knew that he had called her something tender and affectionate, which he had never done before. 'Why didn't you come in?'

'And I – I was wishing for his death!' thought Princess Maria.

He was silent for a space.

'Thank you ... daughter dear ... for all the, for all ... forgive ... thank you ... forgive ... thank you! ...' and the tears trickled from his eyes. 'Call my Andrei,' he said suddenly, and a shy, childlike look of uncertainty showed itself in his face. It was as if he himself were aware that there was something out of the way about his request. So at least it seemed to Princess Maria.

'I have had a letter from him,' she replied.

He glanced at her with timid surprise.

'Where is he?'

'He's with the army, *mon père*, at Smolensk.'

He lay silent for a long time, his eyes shut. Presently, as if in answer to his doubts and as much as to say that now he understood and re-membered everything, he nodded his head and opened his eyes again.

'Yes,' he said, softly and distinctly. 'Russia is lost! They have destroyed her!'

And once more he began to sob, and the tears flowed from his eyes. Princess Maria could contain herself no longer, and wept too as she gazed at his face.

He closed his eyes again. His sobs ceased. He pointed to his eyes, and Tikhon, understanding what he meant, wiped away the tears.

Then he opened his eyes and said something which none of them could understand, until at last Tikhon made out what it was and repeated it. Princess Maria tried to connect the sense of his words with what he had just been speaking about. First she thought he was referring to Russia – or perhaps to Prince Andrei, or herself, or his grandson, or his own death – and so she could not divine what it was he was saying.

'Put on your white dress. I like it,' he had said.

When she understood, Princess Maria sobbed louder than ever, and the doctor, taking her arm, led her out to the verandah, trying to persuade her to calm herself and go on with the preparations for the journey. After she had left the room the prince again began speaking about his son, about the war, about the Emperor, angrily twitching his eyebrows and raising his hoarse voice, and then came the second and final stroke.

Princess Maria stayed on the verandah. The day had cleared, and it was hot and sunny. She could not realize anything, could think of nothing and feel nothing except passionate love for her father, love which it seemed to her she had never felt until that moment. She ran sobbing into the garden, towards the pond, along the avenues of young lime-trees Prince Andrei had planted.

'Yes ... I ... I ... I wished him dead. Yes, I wanted it to end quickly ... that I might be at peace. ... But what will become of me ? What use will peace be to me when he is gone ?' Princess Maria murmured, walking round the park with hurried steps and pressing her hands to her bosom, which heaved with convulsive sobs.

When she had completed the tour of the garden, which brought her back to the house again, she saw Mademoiselle Bourienne (who had remained at Bogucharovo, refusing to leave) coming towards her with a stranger. It was the District Marshal, who had called in person to impress upon the princess the need for a prompt departure. Princess Maria listened but his words held no meaning for her. She took him into the house, offered him lunch, and sat down with him. Then, excusing herself, she went to the old prince's door. The doctor came out with an agitated face and told her she could not enter.

'Go away, princess! Go away, go away!'

She returned to the garden and sat on the grass by the pond at the foot of the slope, where no one could see her. She did not know how long she stayed there. A woman's footsteps running along the path roused her. She got up and saw Dunyasha, her maid, who had evidently been sent to look for her, stop short, as though in alarm, at the sight of her mistress.

'Please, princess. ... The prince ...' said Dunyasha in a breaking voice.

'Coming, here I am, coming!' the princess cried quickly, not giving Dunyasha time to finish what she was saying; and, trying to avoid seeing the girl, she ran towards the house.

'Princess, it is God's will! You must be prepared for the worst,' said the Marshal, meeting her at the door into the house.

'Leave me alone! It's not true!' she cried angrily.

The doctor tried to stop her. She pushed him aside and ran to her father's door. 'Why do they all look so frightened and try to stop me? I don't need them. And what are they doing here?' she thought. She opened the door and the bright daylight in that previously darkened room startled her. Her old nurse and some other women were in the room. They all drew back from the bed, making way for her. He was still lying on the bed as before, but the stern expression on his calm face arrested Princess Maria on the threshold.

'No, he is not dead – it cannot be!' Princess Maria said to herself. She approached, and struggling with the terror that seized her pressed her lips to his cheek. But she instantly recoiled. In a flash all the deep tenderness she had been feeling for him vanished before the horror and dread of what lay there on the bed before her. 'No, he is no more! He is no more, but here, in the place where he was, is something unfamiliar and sinister, some fearful, terrifying and loathsome mystery!' And covering her face with her hands Princess Maria sank into the arms of the doctor, who held her up.

*

Watched by Tikhon and the doctor, the women washed what had been the prince, bound a kerchief round the head that the jaw should not stiffen with the mouth open, and with another kerchief tied his legs together. Then they dressed him in his uniform, with his decorations, and laid the shrivelled little body on a table. Heaven only knows under whose direction and when all this was accomplished, but it all got done as if of its own accord. By nightfall candles were burning round the coffin, a pall was spread over it, the floor was strewn with sprays of juniper, a printed prayer scroll was tucked in under the wrinkled head, and a deacon sat in the corner of the room reading aloud the Psalter.

A concourse of members of the household and people from outside crowded about the coffin in the drawing-room – for all the world like horses who jostle, shying and snorting, round a dead horse. The Marshal was there, and the village elder, and peasant women, all staring with round, awe-stricken eyes, crossing themselves and bowing before they kissed the cold, stiff hand of the old prince.

9

UNTIL Prince Andrei went to live at Bogucharovo the estate had always been owned by absentee landlords, and so the Bogucharovo peasants were of quite a different character from those of Bald Hills, from whom they differed in speech, dress and disposition. They were steppe-peasants. The old prince would commend their industry and endurance when they came to Bald Hills to help with the harvest or to dig ponds and ditches; but he had never liked them because of their dourness.

Prince Andrei's most recent stay at Bogucharovo, when he introduced hospitals and schools and reduced the quit-rent the peasants had to pay, instead of softening them, had, on the contrary, only intensified the traits which made up what the old prince called their churlishness. Strange, obscure rumours were always finding credence among them: now they were all going to be enrolled as Cossacks, or forcibly converted to some new religion; or there was talk about some supposed proclamation of the Tsar's; or they got the notion that their freedom had been granted them when they took the oath of allegiance to the Tsar Paul in 1797 – only the gentry had denied them afterwards; then they expected Piotr Fiodorovich's return to the throne in seven years' time, when there would be freedom for all and everything would be so simple and easy that there would be no laws at all. Rumours of the war and of Bonaparte and his invasion were connected in their minds with the same sort of obscure notions of Antichrist, the end of the world and perfect freedom.

In the vicinity of Bogucharovo were a number of large villages belonging to the Crown or to proprietors whose serfs paid quit-rent and could work where they pleased. There were very few resident landowners in the neighbourhood, and consequently very few domestic or literate serfs and the lives of the peasantry of those parts were more noticeably and powerfully affected than elsewhere by the mysterious undercurrents in the life-stream of the Russian people, the causes and significance of which are so baffling to contemporaries. One such phenomenon had occurred some twenty years before, when the peasants took it into their heads to emigrate to some unknown 'hot rivers'. Hundreds of families, among them the Bogucharovo folk, suddenly began selling their cattle and moving towards the south-east. Like birds flying somewhere beyond the sea, so these men with their wives and children poured south-eastwards, to parts where none of them had ever been before. They set off in caravans, bought their freedom one by one, ran and drove and walked towards the 'hot rivers'. Many were caught and punished, sent to Siberia; many perished of cold and starvation on the road; many returned of their own accord; and the movement died down of itself, just as it had sprung up, without apparent reason. But such undercurrents still flowed among the people, and were gathering impetus for some new outbreak, likely to prove just as perplexing, as unexpected and, at the same time, as simple, natural and violent. Now, in 1812, to anyone living in close contact with the peasants it was patent that these hidden currents were working with extraordinary energy, and that an outbreak of some kind was at hand.

Alpatych, who had arrived at Bogucharovo shortly before the old prince's demise, noticed that there was considerable excitement among the peasantry; and that, unlike the Bald Hills district, where over a radius of forty miles all the peasants were moving away, abandoning their villages to be devastated by the Cossacks, here in the steppe region round Bogucharovo the peasants, so the report ran, were in communication with the French, received certain leaflets from them which passed from hand to hand, and had no thought of leaving their homes. He learned through domestic serfs loyal to him that a muzhik named Karp, who possessed great influence in the village commune and had recently been away driving a government transport, had returned with the news that the Cossacks were destroying deserted villages, but the French did not touch them. Alpatych also knew that on the previous day another peasant had even brought from the village of Vislouhovo, which was occupied by the French, a proclamation from the French general that no harm would be done to the inhabitants, and that everything taken from them would be paid for, provided they remained where they were. As proof of this the peasant brought from Vislouhovo a hundred roubles in notes (he did not know that they were forgeries) paid him in advance for hay.

And last, and most important of all, Alpatych knew that on the morning of the very day he gave the village elder orders to collect carts to convey the princess's luggage from Bogucharovo there had been a meeting in the village at which it had been decided not to move but to wait. Yet there was no time to lose. On the 15th, the day of the old prince's death, the Marshal had insisted that Princess Maria should leave at once, as it was becoming dangerous. He had told her that after the 16th he could not answer for what might happen. On the evening of the day the old prince died the Marshal departed, promising to return on the morrow for the funeral. But this he was unable to do, for he received tidings that the French had unexpectedly advanced, and he had barely time to get his own family and valuables away.

For thirty years or so Bogucharovo had been managed by the village elder, Dron, whom the old prince used to call by the affectionate diminutive 'Dronushka'.

Dron was one of those peasants – physically and mentally vigorous – who grow patriarchal beards as soon as they reach man's estate, and go on unchanged till they are sixty or seventy years old, without a grey hair or the loss of a tooth, as straight and strong at sixty as at thirty.

Soon after the exodus to the 'hot rivers', in which he had taken part with the rest, Dron was made village elder and overseer of Bogucharovo, and had now filled those positions irreproachably for three and twenty years. The peasants were more afraid of him than they were of their master. Both the old prince and the young prince and the steward respected and jestingly called him 'the minister'. During all this time Dron had never once been drunk or ill, or shown the slightest sign of fatigue after nights without sleep or the most exhausting labour, and though he could not read or write he had never forgotten a single item of money, or the number of quarters of flour in any of the endless cartloads he sold for the prince, or missed a single shock of wheat on an acre of the Bogucharovo fields.

It was this peasant Dron whom Alpatych summoned on the day of the prince's funeral, after his arrival from the plundered estate of Bald Hills. He told him to have a dozen horses got ready for the princess's carriages, and eighteen carts for the luggage which she was to take with her from Bogucharovo. Though the peasants paid rent instead of working as serfs, Alpatych never dreamed there would be any difficulty in having this order carried out, since the village contained two hundred and thirty taxable households and the peasants were well-to-do. But on hearing the order Dron lowered his eyes and stood silent. Alpatych named certain peasants he knew, and told him to requisition carts from them.

Dron replied that the horses of these peasants were away on hire. Alpatych mentioned the names of others, but they too, according to Dron, had no horses available: some of their horses were with the government transport trains, others were out of condition, still others had died for lack of forage. In Dron's opinion there was no hope of collecting horses enough for the carriages, much less for the carting of baggage.

Alpatych looked sharply at Dron and frowned. In the same way as Dron was a pattern of what a village elder should be, so Alpatych had not managed the prince's estates for nothing all those twenty years, and was a model overseer, possessing in the highest degree the faculty of divining the needs and instincts of those with whom he had to deal, and this made him an excellent steward. One glance at Dron was enough to tell him that his answers were not the expression of his personal views but the general mood of the Bogucharovo commune, by which the elder had already been carried away. But at the same time he knew that Dron, who had saved money and was detested by the village, must be hesitating between the two camps – the masters' and the peasants'. This wavering he detected in his eyes, and so Alpatych frowned and moved closer to Dron.

'Now, Dron, my friend, you listen to me!' he said. 'Don't tell me any more of this nonsense. His Excellency Prince Andrei himself gave me orders to move all the folk away and not leave them behind with the enemy, and those are the Tsar's orders too. Anyone who stays is a traitor to the Tsar. Do you hear?'

'I hear,' answered Dron without lifting his eyes.

Alpatych was not satisfied with this reply.

'Aye, Dron, there'll be trouble!' he said, shaking his head.

'It's for you to command,' said Dron dejectedly.

'Aye, Dron, have done!' Alpatych repeated, withdrawing his hand from his bosom and solemnly pointing to the floor at Dron's feet. 'I can see right through you, and not only that – I can see three yards into the ground under you,' he continued, gazing at the floor by Dron's feet.

Dron was disconcerted. He glanced furtively at Alpatych and lowered his eyes again.

'You drop this nonsense, and tell the people to pack up their chattels and go to Moscow, and to have the teams ready tomorrow morning for the princess's things. And don't you go attending the meeting, do your hear?'

Dron suddenly fell on his knees.

'Yakov Alpatych, discharge me! Take the keys from me and discharge me, for Christ's sake!'

'Stop that!' cried Alpatych sternly. 'I can see into the earth three yards under your feet,' he repeated, knowing that his skill in beekeeping, his knowledge of the right time to sow the oats, and the fact that he had been able to retain the old prince's favour for a score of years had long ago gained him the reputation of being a sorcerer, and that the power of seeing three yards under a man is considered an attribute of wizards.

Dron got up and was about to say something but Alpatych interrupted him.

'What is it you've all got into your heads, eh? … What are you thinking of? Eh?'

'What am I to do with the people?' said Dron. 'They're all in a ferment. And I've already told them. …'

'"Told them," I dare say!' exclaimed Alpatych. 'Are they drinking?' he asked abruptly.

'In a ferment they are, Yakov Alpatych. They have got hold of another barrel.'

'Then you listen to me. I'll go to the captain of police, and you let them know, and tell them they must stop all this and see about getting the teams ready.'

'Very good,' answered Dron.

Alpatych did not insist further. He had managed peasants too long not to be aware that the best way to make them obey was not to show the slightest suspicion that they might disobey. Having wrung a submissive 'Very good' from Dron, Alpatych contented himself with that, though he not only suspected but was practically certain in his own mind that without the intervention of the military authorities the carts would not be forthcoming.

And so it turned out: the evening came but no carts. In the village, outside the tavern, another meeting had been held which voted to drive the horses out into the forest and not provide carts. Without saying a word of all this to the princess, Alpatych had his own belongings unloaded from the wagons which had come from Bald Hills and those horses put to the princess's carriages, while he went off to the governor.

10

AFTER her father's funeral Princess Maria shut herself up in her room and would admit no one. A maid came to the door to say that Alpatych was there asking for instructions about their departure. (This was before his talk with Dron.) Princess Maria sat up on the sofa where she had been lying, and replied through the closed door that she would never go away anywhere, and begged to be left in peace.

The windows of the room in which she was lying looked to the west. She lay on the sofa with her face to the wall, picking with her fingers at the buttons on the leather cushion and seeing nothing but that cushion, while her confused thoughts were concentrated on one subject – the irrevocability of death and her own spiritual baseness, of which she had had no idea till it showed itself during her father's illness. She wanted to pray but did not dare to – in her present state of mind she dared not address herself to God. For a long time she lay thus.

The sun had reached the other side of the house, and its slanting rays shone in through the open window, lighting up the room and part of the morocco cushion at which Princess Maria was looking. The current of her thoughts was suddenly arrested. Unconsciously she sat up, smoothed her hair, got to her feet and walked over to the window, instinctively drawing into her lungs the freshness of the clear but windy evening.

'Yes, now you can enjoy your fill of the evening! He is gone, and there is no one to hinder you,' she said to herself, and sinking into a chair she let her head fall on the window-sill.

Someone spoke her name in a gentle tender voice from the garden, and kissed her on the head. She looked up. It was Mademoiselle Bourienne in a black dress and weepers. She softly approached Princess Maria, kissed her with a sigh and promptly burst into tears. Princess Maria looked at her. All the times they had been at loggerheads and her jealousy of the Frenchwoman came back to her; but she remembered too how *he* had changed of late towards Mademoiselle Bourienne, and could not bear the sight of her, thereby showing how unjust had been the strictures Princess Maria had heaped on her in her heart. 'Besides, is it for me, for me who wished he would die, to pass judgement on anyone ?' she thought.

A vivid picture presented itself to Princess Maria of Mademoiselle Bourienne's position, kept at a distance of late and at the same time dependent on her and living in her house. And she began to feel sorry for her. She gave her a mild inquiring look and held out her hand. Mademoiselle Bourienne at once started crying again and kissing her hand, speaking of the affliction that had descended on the princess and claiming to participate in it. She declared that her only consolation in her own grief was the fact that the princess permitted her to share it with her. All their old misunderstandings, she said, must sink into nothing before this great sorrow, and she felt that her conscience was clear in regard to everyone, and that *he* from above saw her affection and gratitude. The princess heard her without taking in what she was saying, but occasionally glancing at her and listening to the sound of her voice.

'Your position is doubly terrible, dear princess,' said Mademoiselle Bourienne after a pause. 'I understand that you could not – that you cannot – think of yourself, but with my love for you I am bound to do so. ... Has Alpatych been to you ? Has he spoken to you about going away ?' she asked.

Princess Maria made no reply. She did not understand who was to go, and where to. 'Is it possible to plan or think of anything now ? What does it matter ?' she thought, and did not reply.

'You know, *chère Marie*,' said Mademoiselle Bourienne, 'that we are not safe; we are surrounded by the French. It would be dangerous to move now. If we go, we are almost certain to be taken prisoner, and God knows ...'

Princess Maria looked blankly at her companion.

'Oh, if anyone knew how nothing makes any difference to me now, nothing,' she said. 'Of course I would not on any account move away from *him*. ... Alpatych did say something about going. ... Speak to him. I will have nothing to say to it, and I don't want ...'

'I have been talking to him. He hopes to get us away tomorrow; but in my opinion it would be better now to remain here,' said Mademoiselle Bourienne. 'Because, you will agree, *chère Marie*, to fall into the hands of the soldiers or of rioting peasants on the road would be dreadful.'

Mademoiselle Bourienne drew forth from her reticule a proclamation (not printed on ordinary Russian paper) issued by the French General Rameau, telling people not to leave their homes and that the French authorities would afford them proper protection. She handed the document to the princess.

'I think the best thing would be to appeal to this general,' she continued, 'and I am sure all due respect would be shown you.'

Princess Maria read the paper, and her face worked spasmodically with dry sobs.

'How did you get this?' she asked.

'They probably realized I was French by my name,' replied Mademoiselle Bourienne, flushing.

Holding the proclamation in her hand, Princess Maria got up from the window, and with a pale face walked out of the room into Prince Andrei's old study.

'Dunyasha – send Alpatych to me, or Dron. Anyone!' she said. 'And tell Mademoiselle Bourienne that I want to be alone,' she added, hearing Mademoiselle Bourienne's voice. 'We must get off at once! At once!' she said, appalled at the idea of being left in the hands of the French.

'What if Prince Andrei were to know that she was in the power of the French! That she, the daughter of Prince Nikolai Bolkonsky, had asked General Rameau for protection and accepted his good offices!' The mere suggestion of such a thing filled her with horror, made her shudder, turn crimson and experience such a rush of anger and pride as she had never felt before. All the bitterness, and still more the humiliation, of her position rose keenly to her imagination. 'They, the French, would take up their quarters in this house; *Monsieur le général* Rameau would occupy Prince Andrei's study and amuse himself by looking through and reading his letters and papers. Mademoiselle Bourienne would do the honours of Bogucharovo. I should be given some small room as a favour, the soldiers would violate my father's newly-dug grave to steal his crosses and decorations, they would tell me of their victories over the Russians, would pretend to sympathize with my grief ...' thought Princess Maria, not thinking her own thoughts but feeling bound to think as her father and brother would have done. For herself she did not care where she stayed or what happened to her, but at the same time she felt that she was the representative of her dead father and of Prince Andrei. Unconsciously she thought their thoughts and felt their feelings. Whatever they would have said, whatever they would have done, it was now incumbent on her to do. She went into Prince Andrei's study, and trying to identify herself with his ideas she reviewed her position.

The exigencies of life, which her father's death had seemed to sweep away, all at once rushed back upon her with a new and hitherto unknown force, and took possession of her.

Agitated and flushed, she walked about the room, summoning now Mihail Ivanich, now Tikhon or Dron. Dunyasha, the old nurse and the maids could none of them say how far Mademoiselle Bourienne's statement was correct. Alpatych was not at home: he had gone to the police authorities. Neither could the architect, Mihail Ivanich, who came in with sleepy eyes on being sent for, tell Princess Maria anything. With precisely the same smile of acquiescence with which he had been accustomed during the course of fifteen years to meet the old prince's remarks without committing himself, he now replied to Princess Maria, so that there was no getting anything definite out of him. The old valet, Tikhon, whose wan and sunken face bore the stamp of inconsolable grief, answered, 'Yes, princess' to all Princess Maria's questions, and could scarcely refrain from sobbing as he looked at her.

At length the village elder, Dron, came into the room and with a deep bow to the princess stood near the door.

Princess Maria walked up and down the room and stopped facing him.

'Dear Dron,' she said, seeing in him a staunch friend – the same kind Dron who every year had brought home a special kind of gingerbread from the fair at Vyazma which he presented to her with a smile. 'Dear Dron, since our sad loss ...' she began, and paused, unable to continue.

'We are all in God's hands,' he said, with a sigh.

They were silent for a moment.

'Dron, Alpatych has gone off somewhere. I have no one to turn to. Is it true, as they tell me, that I can't even get away?'

'Why shouldn't you get away, your Excellency? Of course you can,' said Dron.

'I was told it would be dangerous because of the enemy. Dear friend, I am helpless, I do not understand, I am entirely alone. I want to leave without fail tonight or early tomorrow morning.'

Dron did not speak. He looked up from under his brows at Princess Maria.

'There are no horses,' he said. 'I told Yakov Alpatych so.'

'How is that?' asked the princess.

'It's all the visitation of the Lord,' said Dron. 'What horses we had have been taken for the army, or else they died – that's the way it is this year. It's not a case of feeding horses – we may perish of hunger ourselves! As it is, some go three days without a bite. We've nothing; we're ruined.'

Princess Maria listened attentively to what he told her.

'The peasants are ruined? They have no bread?' she asked.

'They're dying of hunger,' said Dron. 'It's no use talking of horses and carts.'

'But why didn't you tell me, Dron? Isn't it possible to help them? I'll do all I can. ...'

It seemed strange to Princess Maria that at a time when her heart was overflowing with sorrow there could be rich people and poor people, and the rich do nothing to succour the poor. She had heard vaguely that there was such a thing as 'seignorial corn' and that it was sometimes given to the peasants. She knew, too, that neither her brother nor her father would refuse the peasants in their need; she was only afraid of making some mistake in the wording of the instructions she meant to give for this distribution. She was glad that she had an excuse for doing something in which she could, without scruple, forget her own grief. She proceeded to inquire from Dron about the peasants' needs, asking him whether there was a reserve store of corn at Bogucharovo.

'I suppose we have grain belonging to my brother?' she asked.

'The master's grain has not been touched,' replied Dron proudly. 'The prince gave no orders about selling it.'

'Give it to the peasants, let them have all they need. I authorize you to do so in my brother's name,' said Princess Maria.

Dron was silent, except for a deep sigh.

'You distribute that corn among them, if it will be enough. Distribute it all. This is an order in my brother's name; and tell them that what is ours is theirs. We grudge them nothing. Tell them so.'

Dron gazed intently at the princess while she was speaking.

'Discharge me, ma'am, for God's sake! Bid me give up the keys,' said he. 'Twenty-three years I've served and done no wrong. Discharge me, for God's sake!'

Princess Maria had no notion what he wanted of her, or why he was asking to be discharged. She replied that she had never doubted his devotion and that she was ready to do anything for him and for the peasants.

II

AN hour later Dunyasha came in to tell the princess that Dron had returned, and all the peasants were assembled at the granary by the princess's orders and wished to speak with their mistress.

'But I did not send for them,' said Princess Maria. 'I only told Dron to let them have the grain.'

'For the love of God, princess dear, have them sent away, and don't you go out to them. It's all a plot,' said Dunyasha, 'and as soon as Yakov Alpatych is back we will start ... and please don't ...'

'What do you mean – a plot?' asked Princess Maria in amazement.

'I am sure of it – please listen to me, for God's sake! Ask old nurse too. They say they won't agree to move away at your orders.'

'You are making some mistake. Why, I never ordered them to leave,' said Princess Maria. 'Fetch Dron.'

Dron came and confirmed what Dunyasha had said: the peasants were there by the princess's instructions.

'But I never sent for them,' declared the princess. 'You must have given my message wrong. I only said that you were to give them the grain.'

Dron only sighed in reply.

'If you order it, they will go away,' he said.

'No, no. I'll go out to them,' said Princess Maria.

In spite of Dunyasha's and the old nurse's attempts to dissuade her, Princess Maria went out on to the steps. Dron, Dunyasha, the old nurse and Mihail Ivanich followed.

'They probably think I am offering them the grain to keep them here, while I go away myself, leaving them at the mercy of the French,' reflected Princess Maria. 'I will promise them monthly provisions and housing on the Moscow estate. I am sure André would do more still for them in my place,' she thought, as she went out in the twilight towards the crowd waiting on the pasture by the barn.

There was a stir in the gathering as the men moved closer together and rapidly took off their hats. Princess Maria, with downcast eyes and her feet tripping over her skirt, went up to them. So many different eyes, old and young, were fixed on her, and there were so many different faces that she could not distinguish any one of them, and, feeling that she must speak to them all at once, did not know how to set about it. But again the sense that she was the representative of her father and her brother gave her courage, and she boldly began her speech.

'I am very glad you have come,' she said, not raising her eyes and conscious of the hurried, violent beating of her heart. 'My good Dron tells me that the war has ruined you. That is our common misfortune and I shall grudge nothing to help you. I am myself going away because it is not safe here … and the enemy is near … because … I am giving you everything, my friends, and I beg you to take everything, all our grain, that you may not suffer want. But if you have been told that I am giving you the corn to keep you here – that is not true. On the contrary, I ask you to move with all your belongings to our Moscow estate, and there I promise you I will see to it that you shall not be in need. You shall be given housing and food.'

The princess paused. In the crowd sighs were heard, and that was all.

'I am not doing this on my own account,' she continued. 'I do it in the name of my dead father, who was a good master to you, and for my brother and his son.'

Again she stopped. No one broke the silence.

'This is our common misfortune and we will share it together. All that is mine is yours,' she concluded, scanning the faces before her.

All eyes were gazing at her with one and the same expression, the meaning of which she could not fathom. Whether it was curiosity, devotion, gratitude, or apprehension and distrust, the expression on all the faces was identical.

'We're very thankful for your bounty, but it won't do for us to take the master's grain,' said a voice from the back of the crowd.

'But why not?' asked the princess.

No one answered, and Princess Maria, looking round at the crowd, noticed that every eye dropped at once on meeting hers.

'But why won't you take it?' she asked again.

There was no reply.

The silence began to oppress the princess and she tried to catch somebody's eye.

'Why don't you speak?' she said, addressing a very old man who stood just in front of her, leaning on his stick. 'If you think something more is wanted, tell me! I will do anything,' she said, catching his eye.

But as if this angered him he hung his head and muttered:

'Why should we? We don't want the grain.'

'What – us abandon everything? We don't agree to it! ... Don't agree. ... We are sorry for you, but we're not willing. Go away yourself, on your own ...' rang out from the mob on different sides.

And again all the faces in the crowd wore the same expression, and now it was certainly not an expression of curiosity or gratitude but of angry determination.

'But you can't have understood me,' said Princess Maria with a sad smile. 'Why don't you want to go? I promise to give you new homes and provide for you, while here the enemy would rob and plunder you. ...'

But her voice was drowned by the voices of the crowd.

'We're not willing! Let them plunder us! We won't take your grain. We won't agree to it!'

Again Princess Maria tried to catch someone's eye, but not a single one was turned to her: evidently they were all trying to avoid her look. She felt strange and ill at ease.

'Oh yes, an artful tale!' – 'Follow her into slavery!' – 'Pull down your houses and go into bondage! I dare say!' – '"I'll give you grain," says she!' – voices in the crowd were exclaiming.

With drooping head Princess Maria left the crowd and went back to the house. Reiterating her orders to Dron to have the horses ready against their departure the next morning, she went away to her room and remained alone with her thoughts.

12

FOR a long while that night Princess Maria sat by the open window of her room, hearing the sound of the peasants' voices floating across from the village, but she was not thinking of them. She felt that she could not understand them, however long she thought. Her mind was concentrated on one thing: her affliction, which now, after the interruption caused by anxieties to do with the present, seemed already to belong to the past. Now she could remember, could weep and pray.

With the setting of the sun the breeze had dropped. The night was still and cool. Towards midnight the voices began to die down, a cock crowed, the full moon began to rise from behind the lime-trees, a fresh, white, dewy mist rose from the ground and quiet reigned over the village and the house.

One after another, pictures of the recent past – of her father's illness and last moments – came into her mind. With melancholy pleasure she dwelt on these images, repelling with horror only the last one, the vision of his death, which she felt she had not the courage to contemplate even in imagination at this still and mystic hour of the night. And these pictures presented themselves to her so clearly and in such detail that they seemed now in the actual present, now from the past, and now in the future.

She had a vivid picture of the moment when he had his first stroke and was being dragged in, held under the armpits, from the garden at Bald Hills, muttering something with his helpless tongue, twitching his grey eyebrows and looking anxiously and timidly at her.

'Even then he wanted to tell me what he told me the day he died,' she thought. 'What he said to me then was all the time in his mind.'

And then she recalled in every detail the night at Bald Hills before the stroke, when with a foreboding of disaster she had remained at home with him against his will. She had not slept and in the small hours had stolen downstairs on tiptoe and gone to the door of the conservatory, where his bed had been put that night, and listened at the door. He was saying something to Tikhon in a weary, exhausted voice. Evidently he wanted to talk. 'And why didn't he call me ? Why didn't he let me be there instead of Tikhon ?' Princess Maria had asked herself then and wondered again now. 'Now he will never tell anyone all that was in his heart. Now the moment will never return for him or for me when he might have said all he longed to say, and I and not Tikhon might have heard and understood him. Why didn't I go in then?' she thought. 'Perhaps he would have said to me then what he said the day he died. Twice he asked about me while he was talking to Tikhon. He wanted to see me, and I was standing there outside the door. It was sad and not easy for him to talk to Tikhon, who did not understand him. I remember how he began speaking to him about Lise as if she were alive – he had forgotten she was dead – and Tikhon reminded him that she was no more, and he shouted "Fool!" He was heavy-hearted. As I stood outside I heard him groan and lie down on the bed and cry: "Oh God!" Why didn't I go in then? What could he have done to me? What could I have lost by it? Perhaps he would have been comforted and called me then – what he did.' And Princess Maria repeated aloud the caressing word he had used to her on the day of his death. 'Dear-est!' she repeated, and burst into tears which relieved her aching soul. She could see his face before her now. And not the face she had known ever since she could remember and had always seen at a distance, but the timid frail face she had seen that last day when she bent close to catch what he was saying, close enough for the first time to see all the lines and wrinkles on it.

'Dear-est!' she repeated again.

'What was he thinking when he uttered that word? What is he thinking now?' she wondered suddenly. And in answer she saw him with the expression she had seen on the face bound up with a white kerchief as he lay in his coffin. And the horror which had seized her then, when she had touched him and known that *that* was not *he* but something ghastly and mysterious, seized her again. She tried to think of something else, tried to pray, but could do neither. With staring eyes she gazed at the moonlight and the shadows, every instant expecting to see his dead face, and she felt that the silence that reigned without and within the house held her fast.

'Dunyasha!' she whispered. 'Dunyasha!' she screamed wildly, and tearing herself from the spell she rushed to the servants' room, running into the old nurse and the maids who came hurrying towards her.

13

ON the 17th of August Rostov and Ilyin, accompanied only by Lavrushka, just back from his brief captivity, and an hussar on orderly duty, set forth from their quarters at Yankovo, ten miles or so from Boguccharovo, to try out a new horse Ilyin had bought and discover whether there was any hay to be had in the villages.

For the last three days Boguccharovo had been half-way between the two hostile armies, so that it was as easy for the Russian rearguard to get to it as for the French vanguard. Consequently Rostov, like the careful squadron-commander he was, wanted to be the first to lay hands on such provisions as might be left there.

Rostov and Ilyin were in the highest of spirits. On the way to Boguccharovo, an estate which belonged to some prince and had a manor-house and farm where they hoped to find a large domestic staff with some pretty servant-girls, they questioned Lavrushka about Napoleon and laughed at his stories, and raced one another to try Ilyin's new horse.

Rostov had no idea that the village they were going to was the property of that very Bolkonsky who had been betrothed to his sister.

Rostov and Ilyin gave rein to their horses for a last race along the incline before reaching Boguccharovo, and Rostov, outstripping Ilyin, was the first to gallop into the village street.

'You win,' cried Ilyin, flushed.

'Yes, I'm always first, not only on grass-land but here too,' answered Rostov, patting his foaming Don horse.

'And I'd have won on my Frenchy, your Excellency,' said Lavrushka from behind, alluding to the wretched cart-horse he was riding, 'only I didn't want to put you to shame.'

They rode at a foot-pace to the barn, where a large crowd of peasants was standing.

Some of the men bared their heads, others stared at the new-comers without doffing their caps. Two lank old peasants with wrinkled faces and scanty beards emerged from the tavern, reeling and singing a tuneless song, and approached the officers with smiles.

'Fine fellows!' said Rostov, laughing. 'Is there any hay here?'

'And like as two peas,' said Ilyin.

'A me-r-r-y me-r-r-y c-o-o-m-pan ...!' sang one of the peasants with a blissful smile.

A peasant came out of the crowd and went up to Rostov.

'Which side will you be from?' he asked.

'The French,' replied Ilyin jestingly, 'and this is Napoleon himself' – and he pointed to Lavrushka.

'So you're Russians, are you?' the peasant inquired again.

'And is there a large force of you here?' asked another, a short man, advancing to them.

'Very large,' answered Rostov. 'But what brings you all together here?' he added. 'Is it a holiday?'

'The old men are met about village business,' answered the peasant, moving away.

At that moment two women and a man in a white hat made their appearance, on the road leading from the big house, coming towards the officers.

'The one in pink is mine, so keep off!' said Ilyin, catching sight of Dunyasha running resolutely towards him.

'She'll be the girl for us!' said Lavrushka, winking.

'What is it you want, my pretty?' asked Ilyin with a smile.

'The princess sent me to ask your regiment and your name.'

'This is Count Rostov, squadron-commander, and I am your humble servant.'

'Co-o-om-pa-ny!' roared the tipsy peasant with a beatific smile as he looked at Ilyin talking to the girl. Alpatych followed Dunyasha, taking off his hat to Rostov as he approached.

'I make bold to trouble your Honour,' said he respectfully but with a shade of contempt for the youthfulness of the officer, and with a hand thrust in his bosom. 'My mistress, the daughter of General-in-chief Prince Nikolai Bolkonsky, who died on the 15th of this month, finding herself in difficulties on account of the outlandishness of these people here' – he pointed to the peasants – 'asks you to come up to the house. ... If your Honour will be so good as to ride a few yards further on,' said Alpatych with a melancholy smile, 'as it is not seemly in the presence of ...' He indicated the two peasants who were hovering about him like gadflies about a horse.

'Hey! ... Alpatych. ... Yakov Alpatych. ... Ser'ous shing! 'Schuse us, for mershy's shake, eh?' said the peasants, smiling gleefully at him.

Rostov looked at the tipsy muzhiks and smiled.

'Or perhaps they amuse your Honour?' remarked Alpatych with a sedate look, as he pointed at the old men with his free hand.

'No, there's nothing very entertaining here,' said Rostov, and he rode on a little way. 'What is the matter?' he inquired.

'I make bold to inform your Honour that these coarse peasants here are unwilling to let the mistress leave the estate, and threaten to unharness her horses, so that though everything has been ready packed since morning her Excellency cannot get away.'

'Impossible!' cried Rostov.

'I have the honour to be reporting to you the actual truth,' said Alpatych.

Rostov dismounted, gave his horse to the orderly and walked with Alpatych to the house, questioning him further about the state of affairs. It appeared that the princess's offer of corn to the peasants the previous day, and her talk with Dron and with the peasants at the meeting, had made matters so much worse that Dron had finally given up the keys of office, joined the peasants, and refused to come when Alpatych sent for him; and that in the morning when the princess ordered the horses to be put in for her journey the peasants had flocked in a great crowd to the barn and despatched a messenger to say they would not let the princess leave the village: that there was an edict that people were not to move from their homes and that they would unharness the horses. Alpatych had gone out to reason with them but was told (it was Karp who did most of the talking, Dron kept in the background of the crowd) that the princess could not be allowed to go since it was contrary to orders, but that if she stayed they would serve and obey her in everything as they had always done.

At the moment when Rostov and Ilyin were galloping along the road Princess Maria, in spite of the arguments of Alpatych, her old nurse and the maids, had given orders to have the horses put in, and had made up her mind to start, but seeing the horsemen cantering up the coachmen took them for the French and ran away, and the women of the household set up a wail.

'Kind sir! Our blessed protector! God has sent you!' cried deeply affected voices as Rostov crossed the vestibule.

Princess Maria was sitting, helpless and distraught, in the large sitting-room when Rostov was shown in. She had no idea who he was and why he was there, or what was going to become of her. When she saw his Russian face, and recognized by his manner and the first words he uttered that he was a man of her own walk in life, she looked up at him with her deep, starry eyes and began speaking in a voice that faltered and trembled with emotion. Rostov found something very romantic in this meeting. 'A defenceless girl, overcome with grief, alone, abandoned to the mercy of coarse, rebellious peasants! And what strange destiny has brought me here!' thought

Rostov as he watched her and listened to her story. 'And what sweetness and nobility there is in her features and expression!'

When she began to tell him that all this had happened the day after her father's funeral her voice shook. She turned away, and then, as though afraid Rostov might ascribe her words to a desire to work on his pity, she glanced at him with an apprehensive look of inquiry. There were tears in Rostov's eyes. Princess Maria noticed it, and looked gratefully at him with the luminous eyes which made one forget the plainness of her face.

'I cannot express how glad I am, princess, that I happened to come riding this way and now have the occasion to put myself entirely at your service,' said Rostov, rising. 'You can start immediately, and I pledge you my word of honour that no one shall dare to cause you the slightest unpleasantness if only you will allow me to act as your escort.' And bowing respectfully, as if to a lady of royal blood, he moved towards the door.

Rostov's deferential tone implied that though he would consider it a happiness to be acquainted with her he did not wish to take advantage of her misfortune to intrude.

Princess Maria understood and appreciated his delicacy.

'I am very, very grateful to you,' she said in French, 'but I hope it was all only a misunderstanding and that no one is to blame for it.' She suddenly began to cry.

'Excuse me!' she said.

Rostov, knitting his brows, made another low bow and left the room.

14

'WELL, is she pretty? Ah, my boy – my pink girl's delicious; her name's Dunyasha. ...'

But a glance at Rostov's face silenced Ilyin. He saw that his hero and captain had come back in quite a different frame of mind.

Rostov cast Ilyin a wrathful look and, without replying, strode off towards the village.

'I'll show them! I'll pay them, the ruffians!' he muttered to himself.

Alpatych followed Rostov at a quick trot just short of a run, catching up with him with difficulty.

'What decision has your Honour come to?' said he, overtaking him.

Rostov halted and, doubling his fists, suddenly made a threatening movement towards Alpatych.

'Decision? What decision? You old dotard! ...' he shouted. 'What have you been thinking about? Eh? The peasants are unruly and you stand gaping at them! You're a traitor yourself! I know you. I'll flay the skin off the lot of you!' ... And as if afraid of wasting his store of anger he left Alpatych and hastened on. Alpatych, swallowing his wounded pride, sailed after Rostov, keeping pace as best he could and continuing to impart his views. He said the peasants had got themselves into such a refractory state that at the present moment it would be imprudent to 'contrary' them without the support of an armed force, so that would it not be better first to send for the military?

'I'll give them armed force. ... I'll "contrary" them!' growled Rostov mechanically, choking with irrational animal fury and the need to vent it. With no definite plan of action, without considering, he strode impetuously towards the crowd. And the nearer he drew to it the more Alpatych felt that this rashness might lead to good results. The peasants in the crowd were similarly impressed when they saw Rostov's swift, unswerving steps and resolute, scowling face.

After the hussars had ridden into the village and Rostov had gone to see the princess a certain hesitation and difference of opinion had arisen among the gathering. Some of the peasants said that the horsemen were Russians and might take it amiss that the mistress was being detained. Dron was of this way of thinking, but as soon as he expressed his view Karp and others attacked their ex-elder.

'How many years have you been fattening on the village?' Karp shouted at him. 'It's all one to you! You'll dig up the pot of money you've buried and be off! ... What do you care whether they burn up our homes or not?'

'We've been told to keep order, and no one to leave their places or take away a single grain – and there she goes with all she's got!' cried another.

''Twas your son's turn to be conscripted, but no fear! Not your noodle of a son!' a little old man suddenly burst out, pouncing on Dron. 'So they took my Vanka and shaved him for a soldier! But we all have to die.'

'To be sure, we all have to die!'

'I'm not against the commune,' said Dron.

'Not you! You've filled your belly. ...'

The two lanky peasants had their say. As soon as Rostov, followed by Ilyin, Lavrushka and Alpatych, came up to the crowd Karp, thrusting his fingers into his belt and smiling slightly, walked to the front. Dron, on the contrary, retired to the rear, and the crowd huddled closer together.

'Hey! Who is your elder here?' shouted Rostov, striding up to the mob.

'The elder? What do you want with him?' ... asked Karp.

But before the words were well out of his mouth his cap flew off and a fierce blow jerked his head to one side.

'Caps off, traitors!' thundered Rostov. 'Where's the elder?' he cried furiously.

'The elder. ... He's asking for the elder! ... Mr Dron, he wants you!' said one and another in meek flustered tones, while one by one caps were removed.

'We should never think of mutiny, we're observing orders,' insisted Karp, and at that moment several voices began speaking together.

'It's as the elders settle – there's too many of you be giving orders. ...'

'Argue, would you? ... Mutiny! ... Scoundrels! Traitors!' roared Rostov recklessly, in a voice not his own, while he gripped Karp by the collar. 'Bind him, bind him!' he roared, though there was no one to bind him but Lavrushka and Alpatych.

Lavrushka, however, ran up to Karp and seized his arms from behind.

'Shall I call our fellows from below the hill, your Honour?' he shouted.

Alpatych turned to the peasants and called upon two of them by name to come and bind Karp. The peasants obediently stepped out of the crowd and began undoing their belts.

'Where's the village elder?' demanded Rostov in a loud voice.

With a pale and frowning face Dron moved to the front.

'Are you the elder! Bind him, Lavrushka!' shouted Rostov, as if that order, too, could not possibly meet with any opposition. And in fact two more peasants began binding Dron, who took off his own belt and handed it to them as though to assist in the operation.

'And now all of you listen to me!' Rostov turned to the peasants. 'Back to your homes this instant – and don't let me hear another word from you!'

'Why, we ain't done no harm!' – 'We just acted silly, that's all!' – 'Only made fools of ourselves!' ... 'Didn't I say it wasn't right?' murmured several voices at once, bickering with one another.

'There, what did I tell you?' said Alpatych, coming into his own again. ''Twas wrong of you, lads!'

'We bin foolish, Yakov Alpatych,' replied the men, and the crowd began to break up and disperse through the village.

The two men with their arms bound were led off to the main yard. The two drunken peasants followed them.

'Aye, now look at you!' said one of them to Karp.

'Fancy speaking to your betters like that! What on earth were you thinking of? An idiot you are, a downright idiot!' added the other.

Inside a couple of hours the teams were standing in the courtyard of the Bogucharovo house. The peasants were briskly carrying out the Bolkonsky belongings and packing them on to the carts, super-intended by Dron, who at Princess Maria's desire had been released from the lumber-room where he had been locked up.

'Mind, be careful – not like that!' said one of the peasants, a tall man with a round, smiling face, taking a casket out of a housemaid's hands. 'That cost money, that did. Why, if you chuck it in like that, or shove it under the rope, it'll get scratched. I don't like to see things done like that. Do everything properly, in the right way, I say. There, look – put it under the matting and cover it with hay – that's the way of it.'

'Oh these books, these books!' said another peasant, bringing out Prince Andrei's library cupboards. 'Mind you don't stumble! Mercy, what a weight, boys – they're a healthy lot of books!'

'Yes, that man kept his pen busy and didn't hop about,' remarked the tall, round-faced peasant gravely, pointing with a significant wink to the dictionaries lying on top.

*

Unwilling to obtrude himself on the princess, Rostov did not go back to the house but remained in the village, waiting for her to drive out. When the carriages started he mounted and escorted her as far as the road occupied by our troops, eight miles from Bogucharovo. At the inn at Yankovo he respectfully took his leave, for the first time permitting himself to kiss her hand.

'But it was nothing – nothing!' he blushingly replied to Princess

Maria's expressions of gratitude for having saved her life (as she called it). 'Any police-officer would have done as much. If we had only peasants to fight, we should not have let the enemy advance so far,' said he, trying with a sort of bashfulness to change the subject. 'I am only happy to have had the opportunity of making your acquaintance. Good-bye, princess. I wish you good fortune and consolation, and hope I may meet you again in happier circumstances. If you want to spare my blushes, please do not thank me!'

But the princess, if she did not thank him further in words, thanked him with the whole expression of her face, which shone with gratitude and warmth. She could not believe that there was nothing to thank him for. On the contrary, she had no doubt that had it not been for him she must inevitably have fallen a victim to the rebellious peasants and the French; that to save her *he* had exposed himself to obvious and terrible danger; and even more certain was the fact that he was a man of lofty and noble soul, able to sympathize with her position and her grief. His kindly, honest eyes, which had filled with tears when she herself had wept as she spoke of her loss, haunted her imagination.

When she had said good-bye to him and was left alone Princess Maria suddenly felt tears starting to her eyes, and then, not for the first time, the strange question occurred to her: 'Had she fallen in love with him?'

During the rest of the journey to Moscow, though the princess's position was not a cheerful one Dunayasha, who was in the carriage with her, more than once observed that her mistress's face wore a pensive, half-happy smile as she leaned to look out of the window.

'Well, supposing I do love him?' thought Princess Maria.

Ashamed as she was of acknowledging to herself that she had fallen in love with a man who would perhaps never care for her, she comforted herself with the reflection that no one would ever know, and that it could not be reprehensible if, without ever speaking of it to anyone, she continued to the end of her days to love the first and last love of her life.

Sometimes when she recalled the way he had looked at her, his sympathy and what he had said, happiness did not appear impossible to her. And then it was that Dunayasha would notice her smiling as she looked out of the carriage window.

'And to think that he should come to Bogucharovo and at that very moment too!' mused Princess Maria. 'And that his sister should have refused Andrei!'* And in all this Princess Maria saw the hand of Providence.

The impression made on Rostov by Princess Maria was a very agreeable one. To think of her gave him pleasure, and when his comrades, hearing of his adventure at Bogucharovo, rallied him on having gone to look for hay and picked up one of the richest heiresses in Russia he lost his temper. He lost his temper precisely because the idea of marrying the gentle Princess Maria, who had impressed him so pleasantly and who possessed such enormous means, had more than once, against his will, occurred to him. So far as he personally was concerned, Nikolai could not wish to find a better wife: by marrying her he would make the countess, his mother, happy, and would repair his father's broken fortunes; and would even – Nikolai felt it – be for the happiness of Princess Maria.

But what of Sonya? And his plighted word? And that was why it made Rostov angry to be rallied about the Princess Bolkonsky.

15

On receiving the command of the armies Kutuzov remembered Prince Andrei and sent word to him to report at Headquarters.

Prince Andrei arrived at Tsarevo-Zaimishche on the very day and at the very hour when Kutuzov was making his first inspection of the troops. He stopped in the village at the priest's house, in front of which the commander-in-chief's carriage was standing, and sat down on the bench at the gate to await his 'Serene Highness', as everyone now called Kutuzov. From the field beyond the village came the strains of regimental music interrupted by the roar of a vast multitude shouting 'Hurrah!' to the new commander-in-chief. A couple of orderlies, a courier and a major-domo stood by the gate, some ten paces from Prince Andrei, taking advantage of their master's absence to enjoy the fine weather. A swarthy little lieutenant-colonel of hussars, with a portentous growth of moustache and side-whiskers, rode up to the gate and, glancing at Prince Andrei, inquired whether

* A woman might not marry with her brother's or sister's brother-in-law. Therefore, a marriage between Natasha and Prince Andrei would have brought Princess Maria and Nikolai Rostov within the proscribed degrees of affinity. – Tr.

his Serene Highness was lodging there and whether he would soon be back.

Prince Andrei replied that he was not on his Serene Highness's staff and had likewise only just arrived. The lieutenant-colonel turned to one of the spruce-looking orderlies, who answered him with the peculiar disdain with which a commander-in-chief's orderly speaks to an ordinary officer:

'What? His Serene Highness? I expect he will be here before long. What do you want?'

The lieutenant-colonel of hussars grinned beneath his moustache at the orderly's tone, dismounted, gave his horse to a despatch-runner and approached Bolkonsky with a slight bow. Bolkonsky made room for him on the bench, and the lieutenant-colonel sat down beside him.

'You waiting for the commander-in-chief, too?' he began. 'They say he weceives evewyone, thank God! It was a vewy diffewent matter with those pork-butchers! Yermolov was not far out when he asked to be pwomoted a German. Now p'waps Wussians will get a look in. As it was, devil only knows what they were up to. Always wetweating and wetweating. Did you take part in the campaign?' he asked.

'I had the pleasure,' said Prince Andrei, 'not only of taking part in the retreat but of losing everything I valued in that retreat – not to speak of the estates and the home of my birth ... my father, who died broken-hearted. I am a Smolensk man.'

'Ah? ... Are you Pwince Bolkonsky? Vewy glad to make your acquaintance! I am Lieutenant-Colonel Denisov, better known as Vasska,' said Denisov, pressing Prince Andrei's hand and looking into his face with a particularly kindly interest. 'Yes, I heard about it,' he went on sympathetically, and after a short pause added: 'Yes, this is Scythian warfare all wight. All vewy well – only not for those who get a dwubbing. So you are Pwince Andwei Bolkonsky?' He nodded his head. 'Vewy pleased, pwince, vewy pleased to make your acquaintance!' he repeated with a melancholy smile, and again pressed Prince Andrei's hand.

Prince Andrei knew about Denisov from Natasha's stories of her first suitor. This recollection, at once sweet and bitter, carried him back to those painful sensations over which he had not lingered lately but which still found place in his soul. Of recent times he had been visited by so many other very grave impressions – like the evacuation of Smolensk, his visit to Bald Hills, the news of his father's death – and had experienced so many emotions that for a long while now those memories had left him alone, and when they returned did not affect him nearly so violently. And for Denisov, too, the associations awakened by the name of Bolkonsky belonged to a far-away, romantic past when one evening after supper and Natasha's singing he had proposed to a little girl of fifteen without realizing what he was doing. He smiled at the remembrance of that time and of his love for Natasha, and immediately passed on to what now interested him passionately and to the exclusion of everything else. This was a plan of campaign which he had developed while serving at the outposts during the retreat. He had laid the plan before Barclay de Tolly, and was now bent on putting it to Kutuzov. The plan was based on the fact that the French line of operations was too extended, and his idea was that, instead of or concurrently with a frontal attack to bar the advance of the French, we should harass their communications. He began explaining his plan to Prince Andrei.

'They can't hold all that line. It's impossible. I will undertake to bweak thwough. Give me five hundwed men and I will cut their communications, that's certain! There's only one way – guewilla warfare!'

Denisov had got to his feet as he expounded his plan to Bolkonsky. In the middle of his commentary they heard the acclamations of the army, growing more incoherent and widespread, mingling with music and song, and coming from the parade-ground. There were sounds of horses' hooves and cheering at the end of the village street.

'He's coming! He's coming!' shouted a Cossack standing at the gate.

Bolkonsky and Denisov moved up to the gate, at which a knot of soldiers (a guard of honour) was standing, and they saw Kutuzov coming down the street, mounted on a rather small bay horse. An immense suite of generals followed. Barclay was riding almost beside him, and a crowd of officers ran after and around them shouting 'Hurrah!'

His adjutants galloped on ahead into the yard. Kutuzov impatiently kicked his heels into his horse, which ambled slowly along under his weight, and continually nodded his head and raised his hand to his white Horse Guard's cap with a red band and no peak. When he reached the guard of honour, a stalwart set of Grenadiers, most of them wearing decorations, who were saluting him, he considered them for a minute in silence, with the steady intent gaze of a commander, and then turned to the crowd of generals and officers surrounding him. His face suddenly assumed an ambiguous expression, and he shrugged his shoulders with an air of perplexity.

'And to think that with fine fellows like these we retreat and retreat!' he said. 'Well, good-bye, general,' he added, and rode into the yard past Prince Andrei and Denisov.

'Hurrah! hurrah! hurrah!' The shouts rent the air behind him.

Since Prince Andrei had last seen him Kutuzov had grown still more corpulent, flabby and bloated with fat. But the familiar bleached eyeball, the scar and the expression of weariness in his face were still the same. He was wearing the white Horse Guard's cap and a military greatcoat with a whip on a narrow strap hanging over his shoulder. He sat slumped and swaying on his sturdy little horse.

'Whew! ... whew! ... whew!' he whistled almost distinctly as he rode into the courtyard. His face expressed the relief of a man who looks forward to resting after a performance. He drew his left foot out of the stirrup and with a lurch of his whole body, frowning with the exertion, brought it up on to the saddle, leaned on his knee, and with a groan let himself drop into the arms of the Cossacks and adjutants who stood ready to support him.

He pulled himself together, looked round with half-shut eyes, glanced at Prince Andrei and, evidently not recognizing him, moved with his shambling gait towards the porch. 'Whew ... whew ... whew!' he whistled, and shot another look at Prince Andrei. As is often the case with old men, it was only after a few seconds that he connected Prince Andrei's face with the personality he remembered.

'Ah, how are you, prince? How are you, my dear boy? Come along ...' he said wearily, and, glancing round, stepped heavily on to the porch which creaked under his weight. He unbuttoned his coat and sat down on a bench in the porch.

'Well, how's your father?'

'I received news of his death yesterday,' said Prince Andrei abruptly.

Kutuzov looked at him with eyes wide with dismay, and then took off his cap and crossed himself. 'God rest his soul! May the Lord's will be done with all of us!' He sighed deeply and was silent. 'I loved and respected him, and I sympathize with you with all my heart.'

He embraced Prince Andrei, holding him to his fat breast and for some time did not let him go. When he released him Prince Andrei saw that Kutuzov's flabby lips were trembling and there were tears in his eyes. He sighed and pressed with both hands on the bench to raise himself.

'Come – come to my room and we'll have a chat,' said he.

But at that moment Denisov, no more intimidated by his superiors than by the enemy, walked confidently up, his spurs clanking on the steps, regardless of the indignant whispers of the adjutants who tried to prevent him. Kutuzov, his hands still pressed on the seat, looked at him with displeasure. Denisov, introducing himself, announced that he had to communicate to his Highness a matter of great importance for the welfare of the Fatherland. Kutuzov bent his weary eyes on Denisov, and lifting his hands with a gesture of annoyance folded them across his stomach and repeated: 'For the welfare of the Fatherland? Well, what is it? Speak up!' Denisov blushed like a girl (it was strange to see the colour rise on that whiskered, time-worn, hard-drinking face) and began boldly expounding his plan of cutting the enemy's lines of communication between Smolensk and Vyazma. Denisov's home was in those parts and he knew every inch of the country. His plan seemed unquestionably a good one, especially with the energy of conviction he threw into his words. Kutuzov sat staring at his own legs, occasionally looking over into the yard of the adjoining cottage, as though expecting something unpleasant to appear from there. From the cottage there did in fact emerge, while Denisov was speaking, a general with a portfolio under his arm.

'What?' exclaimed Kutuzov in the middle of Denisov's exposition. 'Ready so soon?'

'Ready, your Highness,' said the general.

Kutuzov shook his head, as much as to say: 'How is one man to get through it all?' and gave his attention again to Denisov.

'I give you my word of honour as a Wussian officer,' Denisov was saying, 'that I can bweak Napoleon's line of communication!'

'What relation are you to Intendant-General Kirill Andreyevich Denisov?' asked Kutuzov, interrupting him.

'He is my uncle, your Highness.'

'Ah, we were very good friends,' said Kutuzov cheerfully. 'Right, right, my dear boy. You stay here at Headquarters, and tomorrow we'll have a talk.'

With a nod to Denisov he turned away and stretched out his hand for the papers Konovnitsyn had brought him.

'Would not your Highness find it more comfortable indoors?' suggested the general on duty in a disgruntled voice. 'There are plans to be examined and several papers to sign.'

An adjutant appeared at the door and announced that everything was in readiness within. But apparently Kutuzov preferred to be rid of business before going into the house. He scowled. ...

'No, have a table brought here, my dear boy. I'll look through them here,' said he. 'Don't go away,' he added, turning to Prince Andrei. Prince Andrei remained in the porch and listened to the general on duty.

While the report was being read, Prince Andrei heard the murmur of a woman's voice and the rustle of a silk dress through the half-open door of the house. Several times as he glanced that way he caught sight behind the door of a plump, rosy-faced, handsome woman in a pink dress with a lilac silk kerchief on her head. She was holding a dish in her hand and evidently waiting for the commander-in-chief to come in. Kutuzov's adjutant whispered to Prince Andrei that this was the wife of the priest whose home it was, who intended to offer his Highness the bread and salt of hospitality. 'Her husband met his Serene Highness with the Cross at the church, and she means to welcome him to the house. ... She's a pretty little thing,' added the adjutant with a smile. Kutuzov looked round at these words. He was listening to the general's report (which consisted chiefly of an appraisal of the position at Tsarevo-Zaimishche), just as he had listened to Denisov and, seven years before that, to the discussion at the council of war on the eve of Austerlitz. He was evidently listening merely because he had ears, which, in spite of the bit of tarred hemp* in one of them, could not help hearing; but it was plain that nothing the general could say would surprise or even interest him, that he knew beforehand all that would be said, and listened only because he must, just as he might have sat through a service in church. All that Denisov had said was sensible and to the point. What the general was saying was even more sensible and to the point, but Kutuzov made it clear that he despised knowledge and wisdom and knew of something else that would decide the matter – something that had nothing to do with cleverness and knowledge. Prince Andrei watched the commander-in-chief's face attentively, and the only expression he could detect was a mixture of boredom, curiosity as to the meaning of the

* A popular remedy in Russia against earache. – Tr.

feminine whispering behind the door, and a desire to observe propriety. It was obvious that Kutuzov scorned intellect and learning, and even the patriotic feeling shown by Denisov, but scorned them not because of his own intellect or sentiment or knowledge (for he made no effort to display anything of the kind), but because of something else. He despised them because he was old and had seen too much of life. The only clause of his own that Kutuzov inserted in the report related to looting by the Russian troops. At the end of the report the general put before him a document for signature concerning the recovery of payment from army-commanders, upon receipt of an application by the landowner, for the loss of standing oats.

Kutuzov smacked his lips together and shook his head when he was told about this.

'Into the stove with it ... burn it! And I tell you once for all, my dear fellow,' said he, 'throw all such things into the fire. Let 'em cut the crops and burn wood to their hearts' content. I don't order it, and it's not with my permission, but I can't pursue the matter either. It can't be helped. One must take life as it comes.' He glanced once more at the paper. 'Oh, this German punctilio!' he muttered, shaking his head.

16

'WELL, that's all!' said Kutuzov as he signed the last of the documents; and, rising clumsily and straightening the folds in his fat white neck, he moved towards the door with a more cheerful expression.

The priest's wife, flushing rosy red, snatched up the dish which, though she had been so long preparing, she did not succeed in presenting at the right moment after all. With a low bow she offered it to Kutuzov.

Kutuzov screwed up his eyes, smiled, chucked her under the chin and said:

'Ah, what a pretty face! Thanks, sweetheart!'

He took some gold coins from his trouser pocket and put them on the dish for her. 'Well, and how are things here?' he asked, moving to the door of the room that had been made ready for him. The priest's wife, with every dimple in her rosy cheeks smiling, followed him into the room. The adjutant came out to Prince Andrei in the porch and invited him to lunch. Half an hour later Prince Andrei was again called to Kutuzov. He found him reclining in an arm-chair, still in the same unbuttoned military coat. He had a French novel in his hand, which he laid aside as Prince Andrei came in, marking the place with a paper-knife. It was *Les Chevaliers du Cygne* by Madame de Genlis, as Prince Andrei saw by the cover.

'Well, sit down, sit down here. Let's have a little talk,' said Kutuzov. 'It's sad, very sad. But remember, my dear fellow, that I am a father to you, a second father. ...'

Prince Andrei told Kutuzov all he knew about his father's death, and what he had seen at Bald Hills when he had ridden that way.

'What a pass they have brought us to!' Kutuzov exclaimed suddenly in an agitated voice, evidently seeing from Prince Andrei's story a clear picture of the state Russia was in. 'But give me time, give me time!' he added with a grim look, and apparently unwilling to dwell on a subject that stirred him too deeply he said: 'I sent for you to keep you with me.'

'I thank your Highness,' answered Prince Andrei, 'but I am afraid I am no longer any good for staff work,' he explained with a smile which Kutuzov noticed.

Kutuzov glanced at him inquiringly.

'But above all,' added Prince Andrei, 'I have grown used to my regiment. I am fond of the officers, and I fancy the men have come to like me. I should be sorry to leave the regiment. If I decline the honour of being in attendance on you, believe me ...'

A shrewd, kindly and at the same time subtly ironic twinkle lit up Kutuzov's podgy face. He cut Bolkonsky short.

'I am sorry, for you would have been useful to me. But you are right, you are right! It is not here that *men* are wanted. Advisers are always plentiful but men are scarce. The regiments would be very different if all the advice-givers would serve with them as you do. I remember you at Austerlitz. ... I remember – yes, I remember you with the standard!' said Kutuzov, and a flush of pleasure suffused Prince Andrei's face at this recollection.

Kutuzov held out his hand and drew him close, offering him his cheek to kiss, and again Prince Andrei saw tears in the old man's eyes. Though Prince Andrei knew that Kutuzov's tears came easily and that he was being particularly affectionate and tender with him from a wish to show sympathy with his loss, still this reminder of Austerlitz pleased and gratified him.

'Go your own way, and God bless you. I know your path is the path of honour.' He paused. 'I missed you at Bucharest: I wanted someone to send …' And changing the topic Kutuzov began talking of the Turkish war and the peace that had been concluded. 'Yes, I have been roundly abused,' he said, 'both for the war and the peace … but it all chanced opportune. *Tout vient à point à celui qui sait attendre.* And there were as many counsellors there as here …' he went on, returning to the subject he was evidently full of. 'Ugh, those advisers, those advisers!' said he. 'If we had listened to all of them we should be in Turkey now – peace would not have been signed, and the war would not be over yet. It's all hurry, hurry – but more haste less speed! Kamensky would have come to grief there if he hadn't died first. He went storming fortresses with thirty thousand men. It's easy enough to take fortresses but not so easy to win a campaign. To do that, it's not storming fortresses and attacking but *patience and time* that are needed. Kamensky sent his soldiers to take Rustchuk, but I trusted to these two alone – patience and time – and took more fortresses than Kamensky ever did, and made the Turks eat horse-flesh!' He nodded his head. 'And the French shall too, you mark my words,' he went on, growing more vehement and pounding his chest. 'It'll be horse-flesh for them with me!' And again there was a glisten of tears in his eyes.

'But we shall have to accept battle, shan't we?' remarked Prince Andrei.

'Of course, if everybody insists on it, there's no help for it. … But believe me, my dear boy, the two most powerful warriors are *patience and time*: they will do everything. Only our wise counsellors don't see it that way, that's the trouble. Some are in favour, others aren't. What's one to do?' he asked, evidently expecting an answer. 'Well, what would you have me do?' he repeated, and his eyes shone with a deep, knowing look. 'I'll tell you what to do,' he pursued, since Prince Andrei still did not reply. 'I'll tell you what to do, and what I do. *Dans le doute, mon cher,*' he paused, '*abstiens-toi.*' He spoke the words with slow emphasis. 'When in doubt, my dear fellow, do nothing.

'Well, good-bye, my dear fellow. Remember, with all my heart I feel for you in your sorrow, and that for you I'm not his Serene Highness, or prince, or commander-in-chief, but a father. If ever you want anything, come straight to me. Good-bye, my dear boy.'

Again he embraced and kissed Prince Andrei. And then, before

Prince Andrei had time to close the door after him, Kutuzov gave a sigh of relief and settled down with the novel he was reading, *Les Chevaliers du Cygne*, by Madame de Genlis.

Prince Andrei could not have explained how or why it was, but after this interview with Kutuzov he went back to his regiment feeling reassured as to the course of affairs generally and as to the man to whom it had been entrusted. The more he realized the complete absence of self-interest in the old man – who had as it were outlived the fire of his passions, leaving only the habit of them, and whose intellect (which co-ordinates events and draws conclusions) had resolved itself into the single faculty for quietly contemplating the progress of events – the more confident he felt that everything would turn out as it should. 'He will not introduce anything of his own. He will not scheme or start anything,' thought Prince Andrei, 'but he will listen, bear in mind all that he hears, put everything in its rightful place. He will not stand in the way of anything expedient or permit what might be injurious. He knows that there is something stronger and more important than his own will – the inevitable march of events, and he has the brains to see them and grasp their significance, and seeing that significance can abstain from meddling, from following his personal desires and aiming at something else. And above all,' thought Prince Andrei, 'one believes in him because he's Russian, in spite of the novel by Genlis and his French proverbs, and because his voice shook when he exclaimed "What a pass they have brought us to!" and had a sob in it when he said he would "make 'em eat horse-flesh!" '

It was this feeling, more or less unconsciously shared by all, that was behind the unanimous approval which accompanied the appointment of Kutuzov to the chief command, harmonizing, as it did, with national sentiment, and overriding every intrigue at Court.

17

AFTER the Emperor's departure from Moscow life in the capital flowed on in its ordinary channels, resuming its normal course to such an extent that it was difficult to recall those few days of patriotic fervour and enthusiasm, hard to believe that Russia was really in danger and that the members of the English Club were at the same time sons of the Fatherland prepared for any sacrifice. The one thing that brought back the universal uprush of patriotism that had swept Moscow during the Emperor's stay was the call for contributions of men and money – promises, once offered, and quickly invested in legal, official form, had to be complied with.

Though the enemy was nearing Moscow, Moscovites were not inclined to regard their situation with any greater degree of seriousness: on the contrary they became even more frivolous, as is always the case with people who see a great catastrophe approaching. At the advent of danger there are always two voices that speak with equal force in the human heart: one very reasonably invites a man to consider the nature of the peril and the means of escaping it; the other, with a still greater show of reason, argues that it is too depressing and painful to think of the danger since it is not in man's power to foresee everything and avert the general march of events, and it is better therefore to shut one's eyes to the disagreeable until it actually comes, and to think instead of what is pleasant. When a man is alone he generally listens to the first voice; in the company of his fellow-men, to the second. So it was now with the inhabitants of Moscow. It was a long time since Moscow had seen so much gaiety as there was that year.

Rostopchin's broadsheets, headed by woodcuts of a drinking-shop, a tapster and a Moscow burgher called Karpushka Tchigirin – *an old soldier having had a drop too much at the inn, who flies into a great rage and abuses the French in the most colourful language when he hears that Bonaparte means to march on Moscow, comes out of the drink-shop and harangues the crowd collected under the Imperial sign of the eagle* – were as much read and discussed as the latest *bouts-rimés* of Vasili Lvovich Pushkin.

In the corner room at the club, members gathered to peruse these broadsheets, and some approved of the way Karpushka was made to jeer at the French, saying that *Russian cabbages will blow them up like balloons, Russian porridge burst their bellies and cabbage-soup finish them off. They are all dwarfs, and one peasant-woman will toss three of them at a time with a hay-fork*. Others did not like the tone, declaring that it was stupid and vulgar. People said that Rostopchin had expelled all Frenchmen, and, indeed, all foreigners, from Moscow, and that there had been some spies and agents of Napoleon among them, but this story was told chiefly for the sake of being able to introduce Rostopchin's witty remark *à propos* of the occasion. The foreigners were put on a boat bound for Nizhni, and Rostopchin had said to them in

French: 'Keep yourselves to yourselves. Get into the boat and take care not to turn it into Charon's ferry.' There was talk of all the government offices having already removed from Moscow, and here Shinshin's *bon mot* was brought in – to the effect that for this, at least, Moscow ought to be grateful to Napoleon. It was said that Mamonov's regiment would cost him eight hundred thousand roubles; that Bezuhov had spent even more on his, but that the best thing of all was that the count himself was going to don a uniform and ride at the head of his regiment without charging anything for the spectacle.

'You have no mercy on anyone,' said Julie Drubetskoy as she picked up and pressed together a bunch of ravelled lint with her slender, beringed fingers.

Julie was about to leave Moscow next day and was giving a farewell *soirée*.

'*Bezuhov est ridicule*, but he is so kind and good-natured. What pleasure is there to be so *caustique*?'

'A forfeit!' cried a young man in a militiaman's uniform, whom Julie called '*mon chevalier*', and who was going with her to Nizhni.

In Julie's set, as in many other circles in Moscow, it had been agreed to speak nothing but Russian, and those who forgot and spoke French paid a fine to the Committee for Voluntary Contributions.

'A double forfeit for a Gallicism,' said a Russian author who was present. '"What pleasure is there to be" is not Russian.'

'You show no mercy on anyone,' pursued Julie to the young man, paying no heed to the author's criticism. '*Caustique*, I admit,' she said, 'and I'll pay, and I am prepared to pay again for the pleasure of telling you the truth. For Gallicisms I refuse to be answerable,' she remarked, turning to the writer. 'I have neither the money nor the time to engage a tutor to teach me Russian, like Prince Golitsyn. Ah, here he is!' she added. '*Quand on* ... No, no,' she protested to the militiaman, 'you're not going to catch me. Talk of the sun and out it comes!' and she smiled amiably at Pierre. 'We were just speaking about you, and saying that your regiment was sure to be better than Mamonov's,' she told him, with the society woman's natural facility for making free with the truth.

'Oh, don't talk to me of my regiment,' replied Pierre, kissing his hostess's hand and taking a seat beside her. 'I am sick to death of it.'

'You will lead it in person, of course?' said Julie, exchanging a derisive, knowing look with the militiaman.

The militiaman in Pierre's presence was by no means so ready to be caustic, and his countenance betokened perplexity as to what Julie's smile could mean. In spite of his absent-mindedness and good nature, Pierre's personality never failed to cut short any attempt to ridicule him to his face.

'No,' laughed Pierre, glancing down at his huge, bulky figure. 'I should make too good a target for the French; besides, I doubt whether I could hoist myself on to a horse's back. ...'

Among those whom Julie's guests picked upon as a subject for their gossip were the Rostovs.

'I hear that their affairs are in a very bad way,' said Julie. 'And he is so unreasonable – the count, I mean. The Razumovskys wanted to buy the house and estate near Moscow, but it drags on and on. He will ask too much.'

'No, I fancy the sale will come off in a few days now,' said someone. 'Though it is madness to buy anything in Moscow in these times.'

'Why?' asked Julie. 'Surely you don't think Moscow is in danger?'

'Why are you leaving then?'

'I? What a question! I am going because ... well, because everybody else is; and besides – I am not a Joan of Arc or an Amazon.'

'Yes, yes, of course. Give me some more strips of linen.'

'If he manages the business properly he ought to be able to pay off all his debts,' said the militiaman, speaking of Rostov.

'He's a nice old man, but a very *pauvre sire*. And why are they staying on in town so long? They meant to leave for the country ages ago. Natalie is quite well again now, isn't she?' Julie asked Pierre with a sly smile.

'They are waiting for their younger son,' Pierre replied. 'He joined Obolensky's Cossacks and was sent off to Belaya Tserkov. The regiment is being formed there. But now they have had him transferred to my regiment and he is expected every day. The count would have gone long ago but nothing would induce the countess to leave Moscow before her son arrived.'

'I met them the day before yesterday at the Arharovs'. Natalie has quite recovered her looks and her spirits. She sang a song. How easily some people get over everything!'

'Get over what?' inquired Pierre, looking displeased.

Julie smiled. 'You know, count, such chivalrous knights as you are only to be found in Madame de Souza's novels!'

'Knights? What do you mean?' demanded Pierre, blushing.

'Oh come, my dear count. All Moscow knows. Really, I am surprised at you,' said Julie, speaking in French again.

'A fine, a fine!' cried the militiaman.

'Oh, all right. One can't open one's mouth nowadays – what a bore it is!'

'What does all Moscow know?' Pierre asked angrily, rising to his feet.

'Oh fie, count, you know!'

'I do not,' said Pierre.

'I know what great friends you have always been with Natalie, and so ... But I was always more friendly with Vera – that dear Vera!'

'*Non, madame,*' Pierre continued in a tone of annoyance. 'I have certainly not taken upon myself the role of Natalie Rostov's knight. Indeed, it is almost a month since I was at their house. But I cannot understand the cruelty. ...'

'*Qui s'excuse – s'accuse,*' said Julie, smiling and waving the lint triumphantly, and to have the last word she promptly changed the subject. 'By the way, I heard that poor Marie Bolkonsky arrived in Moscow yesterday. You know she lost her father?'

'Really? Where is she? I should very much like to see her,' said Pierre.

'I spent the evening with her yesterday. She is going on today or tomorrow morning to their estate near Moscow, taking her little nephew.'

'Tell me, and how is she?' asked Pierre.

'All right, but sad. But do you know who rescued her? It is quite a romance. Nikolai Rostov. She was surrounded, and they wanted to kill her and some of her servants were wounded. He rushed in and saved her. ...'

'Another romance,' said the militiaman. 'Really this general stampede has been got up expressly to marry off all our old maids. Katishe is one, Princess Bolkonsky another.'

'Do you know, I verily believe she is *un petit peu amoureuse du jeune homme?*'

'Forfeit, forfeit, forfeit!'

'But how could I say that in Russian?'

18

WHEN Pierre returned home he was handed two of Rostopchin's broadsheets that had been brought that day.

The first denied the report that Count Rostopchin had forbidden people to leave Moscow: on the contrary, he was glad that ladies and merchants' wives were leaving the city. 'There will be less panic and less gossip,' ran the broadsheet, 'but I will stake my life on it that the scoundrel will never set foot in Moscow.' These words showed Pierre clearly for the first time that the French would set foot in Moscow. In the second broadsheet it was announced that our Headquarters were at Vyazma, that Count Wittgenstein had defeated the French but that, as many of the inhabitants of the capital were desirous of arming themselves, weapons were ready for them at the arsenal; sabres, pistols and muskets could be had at low prices. The tone of this proclamation was not as jocose as those which had been attributed to the tapster Tchigirin. Pierre pondered over these broadsheets. Evidently the terrible storm-cloud which his soul longed for with all its might, though it excited an involuntary thrill of horror, was drawing near.

'Shall I join the army and enter the Service, or shall I wait?' he asked himself for the hundredth time. He took up a pack of cards that lay on the table and began to spread them out for a game of patience.

'If this game comes out,' he said to himself, shuffling the cards, holding them in his hand and lifting his head, 'if it comes out, it means ... what does it mean?'

Before he had time to decide what it would mean he heard the voice of the eldest princess at the door of his study, asking whether she might come in.

'Then it will mean that I must go to the army,' Pierre told himself. 'Come in, come in!' he called to the princess.

Only the eldest princess, the one with the long waist and the stony face, was still living in Pierre's house. The two younger sisters had both married.

'Forgive me, *mon cousin*, for disturbing you,' said she in an accusing and agitated voice. 'You know it is high time to come to a decision. What is going to happen? Everyone has left Moscow and the people are rioting. Why do we stay?'

'On the contrary, everything looks satisfactory, *ma cousine*,' said Pierre in the bantering tone he habitually adopted towards her, to carry off his embarrassment at being in the position of a benefactor to her.

'Satisfactory – oh yes! Very satisfactory! Only this morning Varvara Ivanovna was telling me how our troops are distinguishing themselves. It certainly does them credit! And the people, too, are in a complete state of revolt and will listen to no one – even my maid has begun to be insolent. At this rate they will soon be slaughtering us. It isn't safe to walk in the streets. But, above all, the French will be here any day now, so what are we waiting for? I ask just one favour of you, *mon cousin*,' pleaded the princess, 'arrange for me to be taken to Petersburg. Whatever I may be, I couldn't live under Bonaparte's rule.'

'Oh come, *ma cousine*! Where do you get your information from? On the contrary ...'

'I tell you I won't submit to your Napoleon! Others may if they please. ... If you won't do this for me ...'

'But I will, I'll give the order at once.'

The princess, obviously provoked at having no one to quarrel with, sat on the very edge of her chair, muttering to herself.

'But you have been misinformed,' said Pierre. 'Everything is quiet in the city and there is not the slightest danger. See, I've just been reading ...' He showed her the broadsheet. 'Count Rostopchin writes that he will stake his life on it that the enemy will not set foot in Moscow.'

'Oh, that count of yours!' the princess began spitefully. 'He's a hypocrite, a rascal, who has himself been exciting the people to sedition. Didn't he write in those idiotic broadsheets promising honour and glory to whoever should drag anyone – no matter whom – by the hair of his head to the lock-up? (How silly?) This is what his cajolery has brought us to. Varvara Ivanovna told me the mob nearly killed her because she started to say something in French.'

'Ah well, that is the way of things. ... You take matters too much to heart,' said Pierre, and he began laying out his cards for patience.

Although his game of patience came out, Pierre did not join the army but stayed on in Moscow, now much depopulated, in the same fever of uncertainty and alarm and yet eagerly looking forward to something awful.

Towards evening of the following day the princess took her departure, and Pierre's head steward came to inform him that the money needed for the equipment of his regiment could not possibly be raised except by selling one of the estates. The steward impressed on Pierre generally that such expensive caprices as fitting out a regiment would be his ruin. Pierre listened, scarcely able to repress a smile.

'Well, then, sell,' said he. 'There's no help for it, I can't draw back now!'

The worse the position of affairs, and in particular of his own affairs, the better pleased Pierre felt, and the more apparent was it that the catastrophe he expected was at hand. Hardly anyone he knew was left in town. Julie had gone, Princess Maria had gone. Of his intimate friends only the Rostovs were still there, but he did not go to see them.

To distract his thoughts he drove out that day to the village of Vorontsovo to see the great balloon Leppich was constructing to use against the enemy, and a trial balloon that was to go up next day. The balloon was not yet ready; but Pierre learnt that it was being constructed by the Emperor's desire. The Emperor had written to Count Rostopchin about it as follows:

As soon as Leppich is ready, get together a crew of reliable and intelligent men for his car, and send a courier to General Kutuzov to let him know. I have informed him of the matter.

Impress upon Leppich, please, to be very careful where he descends for the first time, that he may not make any mistake and fall into the hands of the enemy. It is essential that he should co-ordinate his movements with those of the commander-in-chief.

On his way home from Vorontsovo, as he was driving through Bolotny square Pierre saw a great crowd collected round the place of execution. He stopped and got out of his trap. A French cook, accused of being a spy, had just been flogged. The executioner was untying from the flogging-bench a stout man with red whiskers, in blue stockings and a green jacket, who was groaning piteously. Another offender, thin and pale, stood near. Both, to judge by their faces, were French. Looking as sick with dread as the lean Frenchman, Pierre elbowed his way through the crowd.

'What does this mean? Who are they? What have they done?' he kept asking.

But the attention of the throng – clerks, burghers, shopkeepers, peasants and women in mantles and cloaks – was so intently riveted on what was happening on the place of execution that no one answered him. The stout man got up, shrugged his shoulders with a scowl, and clearly anxious to show fortitude began to pull on his jacket without looking about him; but suddenly his lips trembled and to his own rage he started to cry, in the way grown men of sanguine temperament do cry. The crowd fell to passing loud remarks, to stifle their feelings of pity, as it seemed to Pierre.

'Cook to some prince ...'

'Eh, mounseer, Russian sauce would appear a bit strong for French taste ... sets the teeth on edge, eh?' said a wrinkled chancery clerk standing near Pierre, just as the Frenchman broke into tears. The clerk glanced round, obviously hoping for signs of appreciation for his joke. Several people laughed, others continued to gaze in dismay at the executioner who was undressing the second Frenchman.

Pierre choked, and knitting his brows turned hastily away, went back to his trap, muttering to himself, and took his seat. As they drove along he shuddered, and exclaimed several times so audibly that the coachman inquired:

'Yes, sir?'

'Where on earth are you going?' shouted Pierre as the coachman turned down Lubyanka street.

'You told me to drive to the Governor-general's,' answered the coachman.

'Idiot! Ass!' shouted Pierre, berating his coachman – a thing he rarely did. 'Home, I said! And make haste, blockhead!' And then:

'I must get away this very day,' he murmured to himself.

At the sight of the tortured Frenchman and the crowd round the place of execution Pierre had so definitely made up his mind that he could no longer remain in Moscow, and must leave that very day for the army, that it seemed to him either that he had told the coachman so or that the man ought to have known it of himself.

On reaching home Pierre instructed his omniscient and omnipotent head-coachman, who was known to all Moscow, that he would leave that night for the army at Mozhaisk, and to have his saddle-horses sent there. All this could not be arranged in one day, so on Yevstafievich's representations Pierre delayed his departure for another twenty-four hours to allow time for the relay horses to be sent on ahead.

On the 24th the weather cleared up after a spell of rain, and after dinner Pierre left Moscow. Stopping to change horses in the night at Perhushkovo, he learned that a great battle had been fought that evening. (This was the battle of Shevardino.) He was told that the firing had made the earth tremble there at Perhushkovo; but when he inquired who had been victorious, no one could give him any information. By dawn the following morning Pierre was approaching Mozhaisk.

Every house in Mozhaisk had soldiers quartered in it, and at the hostel where Pierre was met by his groom and coachman there was not a room to be had. The whole place was full of officers.

Everywhere, in the town and on the outskirts, troops were stationed or on the march. On all sides were Cossacks, foot- and horse-soldiers, wagons, caissons and cannon. Pierre pushed forward as fast as he could, and the farther he went from Moscow and the deeper he plunged into this sea of troops the more he was overcome by anxiety and a new, pleasurable sensation which he had never experienced before. It was somewhat akin to the feeling he had felt at the Slobod-skoy Palace at the time of the Emperor's visit – a sense of the urgent necessity for taking some step and making some sacrifice. He was conscious at this moment of a glad conviction that everything which constitutes the happiness of men – the comforts of life, wealth, even life itself – was rubbish which it was a joy to fling away, when one thought of. ... Thought of what, Pierre could not say, and indeed he did not attempt to analyse for whom or for what he found such peculiar delight in sacrificing everything. He was not interested in knowing the object of the sacrifice: the mere fact of sacrificing in itself afforded him a new and joyous sensation.

19

ON the 24th of August the battle of the Shevardino Redoubt was fought; on the 25th not a shot was fired by either side; on the 26th came the battle of Borodino.

How and with what object were the battles of Shevardino and Borodino given and accepted? Why was the battle of Borodino fought? There was not the least sense in it, either for the French or the Russians. Its immediate result for the Russians was, and was bound to be, that we were brought a step further towards the destruction of

Moscow (the very thing we dreaded above all else in the world); and for the French, that they were brought nearer to the destruction of their whole army (which they, too, dreaded above everything in the world). What the result must be was perfectly obvious, and yet Napoleon offered and Kutuzov accepted the battle.

If military leaders were guided by reason it would seem that it must have been clear to Napoleon that in advancing thirteen hundred miles and giving battle with a probability of losing a quarter of his men, he was marching to certain destruction; and that it must have been equally clear to Kutuzov that by accepting battle and risking the loss of a quarter of his army, he would certainly lose Moscow. For Kutuzov this was a mathematical certainty, just as in a game of draughts if I have one man less and go on exchanging I am bound to lose, and so I mustn't exchange. When my opponent has sixteen men and I have fourteen I am only one-eighth weaker than he, but when I have exchanged thirteen more men he will be three times as strong as I am.

Up to the battle of Borodino our forces were to the French in the approximate proportion of five to six, but after the battle, of one to two. In other words, before the battle we had a hundred thousand as against their one hundred and twenty thousand, and after the battle it was our fifty thousand to a hundred thousand of them. Yet the shrewd and experienced Kutuzov accepted battle, while Napoleon, an acknowledged military genius, offered battle, losing a quarter of his army and lengthening his lines of communication further than ever. If we are told that he expected the occupation of Moscow to complete the campaign, as the taking of Vienna had closed a previous campaign, we may say that there are many evidences to the contrary. Napoleon's historians themselves relate that from Smolensk onwards he was anxious to call a halt; that he was fully aware of the danger of his extended position, and knew that the capture of Moscow would not see the end of the campaign, for Smolensk had shown him the state in which Russian towns were left, and he had not received a single reply to the repeated expressions of his desire to open negotiations.

In giving and accepting battle at Borodino, Kutuzov and Napoleon acted contrary to their intentions and their good sense. But later on, to fit the accomplished facts, the historians provided cunningly devised proofs of the foresight and genius of the generals, who of all the blind instruments of history were the most enslaved and involuntary.

The ancients have passed down to us examples of epic poems in which the heroes furnish the whole interest of the story, and to this day we are unable to accustom our minds to the idea that history of that kind is meaningless for our epoch.

As to the other question: how the battle of Borodino and the preceding battle of Shevardino came to be fought, there exists an explanation just as positive and well known but absolutely fallacious. All the historians describe the affair thus:

The Russian army, they say, *in its retreat from Smolensk sought for itself the most favourable position for a general engagement, and such a position they found at Borodino.*

The Russians, they say, *fortified this position in advance on the left of the high road (from Moscow to Smolensk) and almost at right angles to it, from Borodino to Utitsa, at the very place where the battle was fought.*

In front of this position, they tell us, *a fortified earthwork was thrown up on the Shevardino Redoubt as an outpost for observation of the enemy's movements. On the 24th*, we are told, *Napoleon attacked this advanced post and took it, and on the 26th he fell on the whole Russian army, which had taken up its position on the field of Borodino.*

So the histories say, and it is all quite wrong, as anyone may see who cares to investigate the facts.

The Russians did not seek out the most favourable position but, on the contrary, during their retreat passed by several positions superior to Borodino. They did not halt at any one of these positions because Kutuzov would not occupy a position he had not himself selected, because the popular clamour for an engagement had not yet expressed itself forcefully enough, and because Miloradovich had not yet arrived with the militia, and for countless other reasons. The fact is that there were stronger positions on the road the Russian army had passed along, and that the position at Borodino (where the battle was fought), far from being strong was no more a *position* than any other spot one might find in the Russian Empire by haphazardly sticking a pin in the map.

The Russians not only did not fortify the position on the field of Borodino to the left of and at a right angle to the high road (that is, the spot on which the battle was fought) – until the 25th of August 1812 they never dreamed of the possibility of the battle taking place there. This is shown, first by the fact that before the 25th there were no entrenchments there, and that the earthworks begun on the 25th were not completed by the 26th; and secondly, the evidence of the Shevardino Redoubt itself: situated in front of the position where battle was accepted it had no meaning. Why was it more strongly fortified than any other post? And why were all efforts exhausted and six thousand men sacrificed to defend it till late at night on the 24th? A picket of Cossacks would have sufficed to keep watch on the enemy. And as a third proof that the position of the battlefield was not foreseen and that the Shevardino Redoubt was not an advanced post of that position, we have the fact that up to the 25th Barclay de Tolly and Bagration were under the impression that the Shevardino Redoubt was the *left flank* of the position, and that Kutuzov himself in his report written in hot haste after the battle speaks of the Shevardino Redoubt as the *left flank* of the position. It was only much later, when detailed accounts of the battle of Borodino were penned at leisure, that the inaccurate and extraordinary statement was invented (probably to cover up the blunders of the commander-in-chief who had to be represented as infallible) that the Shevardino Redoubt was an *advanced* post – when in reality it was simply the fortified point of the left flank – and that the battle of Borodino was fought by us on an entrenched position previously selected, whereas it was fought on a position quite unforeseen and almost unfortified.

The affair obviously took place in this way: a position was selected on the river Kolocha – which intersects the high road not at a right but at an acute angle – so that the left flank was at Shevardino, the right flank near the village of Novoe and the centre at Borodino, at the confluence of the rivers Kolocha and Voina. To anyone who looks at the field of Borodino without thinking of how the battle was actually fought, this position, protected by the Kolocha, presents itself as an obvious choice for an army whose object was to check the advance of an enemy marching along the Smolensk road to Moscow.

Napoleon, riding up to Valuevo on the 24th, did not (we are told in the history books) discover the Russians in their position between Utitsa and Borodino (he could not have seen that position because it did not exist), and did not see the advanced post of the Russian army. It was only when in pursuit of the Russian rearguard that he stumbled upon the left flank of the Russian position – at the Shevardino Redoubt – and, to the surprise of the Russians, moved his troops across the Kolocha. And the Russians, since it was too late for a general engagement, withdrew their left wing from the position they had intended to occupy, and took up a new position which had not been foreseen and was not fortified. By crossing to the other side of the Kolocha to the left of the high road, Napoleon shifted the whole forthcoming battle from right to left (looking from the Russian side) and transferred it to the plain between Utitsa, Semeonovsk and Borodino – a plain no more advantageous as a position than any other plain in Russia – and there the whole battle of the 26th of August took place.

Had Napoleon not ridden out on the evening of the 24th to Kolocha, and had he not then ordered an immediate attack on the redoubt but had begun the attack next morning, no one could have felt any uncertainty as to the Shevardino Redoubt being the left flank of our position; and the battle would have been fought where we expected it. In that case we should probably have defended the Shevardino Redoubt – our left flank – still more obstinately; we should have attacked Napoleon in the centre or on the right, and the general engagement would have taken place on the 25th, on the position prepared and fortified for it. But as the attack on our left flank was made in the evening after the retreat of our rearguard (that is, immediately after the action at Gridneva), and as the Russian commanders would not or could not begin a general engagement then on the evening of the 24th, the first and most important operation of the battle of Borodino was already lost on the 24th, and that loss clearly led to the loss of the one fought on the 26th.

After the loss of the Shevardino Redoubt we found ourselves, on the morning of the 25th, without a position for our left flank, and were forced to draw in this left wing and hastily entrench it where it chanced to be.

But not only was the Russian army on the 26th of August defended by weak, unfinished earthworks, but the disadvantage of that position was aggravated by the fact that the Russian generals, not having fully realized what had happened (i.e. the loss of our position on the left flank and the shifting of the whole field of the forthcoming battle from right to left), maintained their extended formation from the village of Novoe to Utitsa, and consequently had to transfer their forces from right to left during the engagement. So it happened that throughout the entire operation the Russians had to face the whole French army launched against our left flank with but half as many men. (Poniatowski's action against Utitsa and Uvarov's on the right flank against the French were quite independent of the main course of the fighting.)

And so the battle of Borodino was not fought at all as the historians describe, in their efforts to gloss over the mistakes of our leaders even at the cost of diminishing the glory due to the Russian army and people. The battle of Borodino was not fought on a carefully picked and fortified position with forces only slightly weaker on the Russian side. As a result of the loss of the Shevardino Redoubt the Russians fought the battle of Borodino on an open and almost unentrenched position, with forces only half as numerous as the French; that is to say, under conditions in which it was not merely unthinkable to fight for ten hours and still leave the contest in doubt, but unthinkable to preserve an army for even three hours from complete disintegration and flight.

20

ON the morning of the 25th Pierre was driving out of Mozhaisk. On the winding slope of the monstrously steep hill leading out of the town, just beyond the cathedral that crowns the hill on the right, where a service was being held and the bells were pealing, Pierre got out of his carriage and proceeded on foot. A cavalry regiment followed him down the hill, the singers of the regiment in front. A train of carts came up the hill towards him filled with casualties from the previous day's engagement. The peasant drivers, shouting and lashing their horses, kept crossing from side to side. The carts, in each of which three or four wounded soldiers were lying or sitting, jolted over the stones that had been flung on the steep incline to make it something like a road. The wounded men, bandaged with rags, and with pale cheeks, compressed lips and knitted brows, clung to the sides of the carts as they were shaken and thrown against one another. Almost all of them stared with naïve, childlike curiosity at Pierre's white hat and green swallow-tail coat.

Pierre's coachman shouted angrily at the convoy of wounded to keep to one side of the road. The cavalry regiment, coming down the hill with its singers, overran Pierre's carriage and blocked the way. Pierre halted, finding himself squeezed to the edge of the road that had been hollowed out in the hill. The sun did not reach over the side of the hill into the cutting, and there it felt cold and damp, but overhead it was a bright August morning and the chimes rang out merrily.

One team with its load of wounded drew up at the side of the road close to Pierre. The driver in his bast shoes ran panting up to his cart, shoved a stone under one of the back wheels, which had no tyres, and began arranging the breeching on his worn-out horse, which had stopped.

One of the wounded, an old soldier with his arm in a sling, walking behind the cart, caught hold of it with his sound arm and turned to look at Pierre.

'Well, fellow-countryman, are we to be put down here or will they take us on to Moscow?' he asked.

Pierre was so deep in thought that he did not hear the question. He was staring now at the cavalry regiment, which had met face to face with the convoy of wounded, now at the cart he stood by, in which two wounded men were sitting and one was lying. One of the pair sitting up in the cart had apparently been wounded in the cheek. His whole head was bound up with rags and one side of his face was swollen as big as a child's head. His nose and mouth were twisted to one side. This soldier was looking at the cathedral and crossing himself. The other, a young lad, a fair-haired recruit as white as though there was not a drop of blood in his thin face, gazed at Pierre with a fixed, good-natured smile. The third soldier lay prone so that his face was not visible. The cavalry singers were now abreast of the cart.

> Ah, my head's all mazed
> In foreign parts ...

they sang the military dance tune.

As if in response, but with a different strain of merriment, the metallic notes of the bells reverberated from the heights above, while the hot rays of the sun bathed the top of the opposite slope with still another sort of gaiety. But where Pierre stood under the hillside, by the cart full of wounded soldiers and the panting little nag, it was damp, sombre and dismal.

The soldier with the swollen cheek looked angrily at the cavalry-singers.

'Ah, the swells!' he muttered reproachfully.

'It's not soldiers only but peasants too I've seen today! The peasants – even they have to go,' said the soldier who was leaning against the cart, addressing Pierre with a melancholy smile. 'They're not so particular nowadays. ... They mean to throw the whole nation against them – in a word, it's Moscow. They want to make an end of it.'

In spite of the incoherence of this statement Pierre understood what the soldier wanted to say and nodded agreement.

The road was clear again. Pierre walked down the hill and got into his carriage. As he drove on he looked, first to one side and then to the other, for someone he knew, but encountered everywhere only unfamiliar faces belonging to all sorts of regiments, and all staring with the same astonishment at his white hat and green tail-coat.

He had gone nearly three miles before he met his first acquaintance, and hailed him eagerly. This was a doctor, one of the heads of the army medical service. He was driving towards Pierre in a covered gig, sitting beside a young doctor, and on recognizing Pierre he called to the Cossack on the driver's seat to pull up.

'Count! Your Excellency – how do you come to be here?' asked the doctor.

'Oh, I wanted to have a look. ...'

'Yes, there'll be plenty to see. ...'

Pierre got out to talk to the doctor, confiding to him his intention of taking part in the battle.

The doctor advised Bezuhov to apply direct to Kutuzov.

'Why should you hang about God knows where during the battle, unable to see a thing?' said he, exchanging glances with his young colleague. 'And his Serene Highness knows you, anyway, and will receive you gladly. Yes, you do that, my friend.'

The doctor seemed tired and in a hurry.

'So you think ... Oh yes, I was going to ask you – where exactly is our position?' said Pierre.

'Our position?' repeated the doctor. 'Well, that is something that is not in my line. Take the route through Tatarinova; there's a lot of digging going on there. Climb up on to the barrow: you can get a good view from the top.'

'Can one see from there? ... If you would ...'

But the doctor interrupted him and moved towards the gig.

'I would go with you but so help me God I'm up to here' – and he indicated his throat. 'I am racing to the commander of the corps. How do matters stand? ... You know, count, there'll be a battle tomorrow. Out of an army of a hundred thousand we must expect at least twenty thousand casualties; and we haven't stretchers or pallets or dressers or surgeons enough for six thousand. To be sure, we've got ten thousand carts, but we need other things as well. We shall have to do the best we can.'

The strange thought that of those thousands of men, alive and well, young and old, who had stared with such light-hearted amusement at his hat (perhaps the very men he had noticed), twenty thousand were inevitably doomed to suffer wounds and death – made a deep impression on Pierre.

'They may be dead tomorrow. How is it then they can think of anything but death?' And suddenly, by some mysterious association of ideas, he saw a vivid picture of the steep descent from Mozhaisk – the carts with the wounded, the jangling chimes, the slanting rays of the sun and the chorus of the cavalrymen.

'The cavalry ride into battle and meet the wounded on the way, and never for a moment do they think of what is in store for them. They ride by winking at their wounded comrades. Yet of those men twenty thousand are doomed to die, and they can still find it in them to wonder at my hat! Strange!' thought Pierre, as he went on towards Tatarinova.

Outside a gentleman's house on the left of the road stood carriages, wagons, and a crowd of orderlies and sentinels. This was where the commander-in-chief was putting up, but when Pierre arrived he found that his Serene Highness and almost all the staff were out – they had gone to a service of intercession. Pierre pushed on in the direction of Gorky.

Driving up the hill into the little village street he saw for the first time the peasants of the militia in their white shirts, with the badge of the cross on their caps. Shouting and laughing together, eager and perspiring, they were at work on a huge knoll overgrown with grass, to the right of the road.

Some were digging, others wheeling barrow-loads of earth along planks, while a third lot stood about doing nothing.

Two officers were standing on the knoll directing the men. Seeing these peasants evidently still amused by the novelty of finding themselves soldiers reminded Pierre of the wounded men at Mozhaisk again, and he understood what the soldier had tried to express when he said: 'They mean to throw the whole nation at the enemy's head.' The sight of these bearded peasants toiling on the field of battle, with their queer, clumsy boots, their perspiring necks, and here and there with shirts unbuttoned obliquely across their chests, exposing their sunburnt collar-bones, impressed Pierre more strongly than anything he had yet seen or heard with the solemnity and gravity of the moment.

21

PIERRE got out of his carriage and walking past the toiling militia-men climbed on to the knoll from which the doctor had told him he could get a view of the field of battle. It was around eleven o'clock in the morning. The sun was a little to the left and behind him, and in the clear rarefied atmosphere the huge panorama that stretched like an amphitheatre before him lay bathed in brilliant light.

The Smolensk high road ran winding through this amphitheatre, intersecting it towards the left at the top, and passing through a village with a white church some five hundred yards in front of and below the knoll. This was Borodino. Below the village the road crossed the river by a bridge and winding up and down rose higher and higher to the hamlet of Valuevo, visible about four miles away, where Napoleon now was. Beyond Valuevo the road disappeared into a yellowing forest on the horizon. Far away in the distance in that birch and fir forest to the right of the road the cross and belfry of the Kolotsky monastery gleamed in the sun. Here and there over the whole of that blue expanse, to right and to left of the forest and the road, smoking camp-fires could be seen, and blurred masses of troops – ours and the enemy's. The country to the right – along the course of the two rivers Kolocha and Moskva – was broken and hilly. Through the gaps between the hills the villages of Bezzubovo and Zaharino showed in the distance. On the left the ground was more level; there were fields of grain and the smoking ruins of the village of Semeonovsk that had been set on fire were visible.

All that Pierre saw to right and left of him was so negative that no part of the scene before his eyes answered his expectations. Nowhere was there a field of battle such as his imagination had pictured: there were only fields, clearings, troops, woods, the smoke of camp-fires, villages, mounds and streams; and try as he would he could descry no military 'position' in this landscape teeming with life. He could not even distinguish our troops from the enemy's.

'I must ask someone who knows,' he thought, and addressed himself to an officer who was looking with curiosity at his huge un-military figure.

'Would you have the goodness to tell me,' said Pierre, 'the name of the village opposite?'

'Burdino, isn't it called?' said the officer, turning inquiringly to his companion.

'Borodino,' corrected the other.

The officer, evidently glad of an opportunity for a talk, moved nearer to Pierre.

'Are those our men there?' asked Pierre.

'Yes, the others farther away are the French,' said the officer. 'There they are, there you can see them.'

'Where? Where?' asked Pierre.

'You can see them with the naked eye. ... Look there!'

The officer pointed to the smoke rising on the left beyond the river, and the same stern and serious expression came into his face that Pierre had noticed on many of the faces he had met.

'Ah, so those are the French! And there? ...' Pierre indicated a mound on the left, near which some troops could be seen.

'Those are ours.'

'Ours, are they? And over there? ...' Pierre waved his hand in the direction of another knoll in the distance, with a big tree on it, not far from a village that lay in a hollow where more camp-fires were smoking and something black was visible.

'That's *his* too,' said the officer. (It was the Shevardino Redoubt.) 'It was ours yesterday, but now it's *his.*'

'Then how about our position?'

'Our position?' replied the officer with a smile of satisfaction. 'I can tell you all about that because I had to do with the construction of practically all our entrenchments. There, do you see – that's our centre, at Borodino, just over there,' and he pointed to the village with the white church directly in front of them. 'There's where we cross the Kolocha. You see down there where the rows of hay are lying in the hollow – that's the bridge. That is our centre. Our right flank is over yonder' – he pointed sharply to the right, far away in the broken ground. 'That's where the river Moskva is, and we have thrown up three redoubts there, very strong ones. Our left flank ...' here the officer paused. 'Well, this is a bit difficult to explain. ... Yesterday our left flank was there at Shevardino – look, where that oak is – but now we have withdrawn our left wing. Now it's over there – do you see that village and the smoke? That's Semeonovsk, yes, there,' he pointed to Raevsky's Redoubt. 'But the battle will hardly be there. *His* having moved his troops there is only a blind. *He* will probably pass round to the right of the Moskva. However, at all events there'll be a lot of us missing at roll-call tomorrow!' he ended.

An elderly sergeant who came up during the officer's speech had waited in silence for him to finish speaking, but at this point, evidently not liking the last remark, he interrupted him.

'We must fetch up some gabions,' he said severely.

The officer looked disconcerted, as though he realized that though one might think of how many men would be missing next day one ought not to talk about it.

'Very well, send No. 3 Company again,' he replied hurriedly. 'And who are you? Are you one of the doctors?'

'No, I was just having a look round on my own,' answered Pierre, and he descended the hill again, passing the peasant militiamen.

'Oh, those damned fellows!' muttered the officer, who followed him holding his nose as he hurried past the men at work.

'Here they come! ... They've got her. ... There she is. ... They'll be here in a minute ...' voices were suddenly heard saying; and officers, soldiers and militiamen began running forward along the road.

A church procession was coming up the hill from Borodino. First along the dusty road marched a company of infantry with their shakos off and trailing arms. From behind them came the sound of chanting.

Soldiers and militiamen ran bareheaded past Pierre to meet the procession.

'They are bringing her, our Holy Mother, our Protectress! ... The Iberian icon of the Mother of God!'

'The Holy Mother of Smolensk! ...' someone corrected.

The militiamen, both those who had been in the village and those who had been at work on the battery, threw down their spades and ran to meet the procession. Behind the battalion which came marching along the dusty road walked the priests in their vestments – one little old man in a hood, with attendant deacons and choristers. Behind them soldiers and officers bore a huge icon with a blackened face and silver mountings. This was the icon that had been brought away from Smolensk and had since accompanied the army. Behind, before and all around walked or ran crowds of soldiers with bared heads, making obeisances to the very ground.

At the top of the hill the procession stopped. The men who had been holding the icon aloft by the linen bands attached to it were relieved by others, the chanters relit their censers and the service began. The scorching rays of the sun beat down vertically; a faint fresh breeze played with the hair on bared heads and fluttered the ribbons trimming the icon; the singing sounded subdued under the open sky. A huge bare-headed crowd of officers, soldiers and militiamen stood round the icon. In a space apart, behind the priest and a chanter, were gathered the personages of rank. A bald general with the order of St George hanging from his neck stood directly at the priest's back, and not crossing himself (he was evidently a German) patiently waited for the end of the service, which he thought it necessary to listen to, probably so as to arouse the patriotism of the Russian people. Another general stood in a martial pose, looking about him and making swift little signs of the cross in front of his chest. Standing among the crowd of peasants, Pierre recognized several persons he knew in the circle of officials, but he did not look at them – his whole attention was absorbed in watching the serious expression on the faces of the throng of soldiers and militiamen, who were all gazing raptly at the icon. As soon as the weary chanters, who were singing the service for the twentieth time that day, began languidly and mechanically to sing: 'O Mother of God, save thy servants from all adversities,' and the priest and deacon came in with: 'For to thee under God every man doth flee as to a steadfast bulwark and defence,' all those faces were fired with the same consciousness of the solemnity of the approaching moment which Pierre had seen on the faces at the foot of the hill at Mozhaisk, and by fits and starts on many faces he had met that morning. And heads were bowed more frequently and hair tossed back, and there was the sound of sighing and beating the breast as men crossed themselves.

The crowd round the icon suddenly parted and pressed against Pierre. Someone, a very important personage to judge by the haste with which they made way for him, was going up to the icon.

It was Kutuzov, who had been reconnoitring the position and on his way back to Tatarinova had stopped to join in the service. Pierre recognized him at once by his peculiar figure, which distinguished him from everybody else.

In a long overcoat over his enormously stout, round-shouldered body, with his white head uncovered and his puffy face showing the white ball of the eye he had lost, Kutuzov advanced with his lunging, staggering gait into the ring and stopped behind the priest. He crossed himself with an accustomed movement, bent till he touched the ground with his hand, and sighing heavily bowed his grey head. Behind Kutuzov was Bennigsen and the suite. Despite the presence of the commander-in-chief, which drew the attention of all the superior officers, the militiamen and soldiers continued their prayers without looking at him.

When the service was over Kutuzov stepped up to the icon, dropped ponderously on his knees, touched the earth with his forehead, and then for a long time struggled to rise to his feet but he was too heavy and feeble. His grey head twitched with the effort. At last he got himself up, and naïvely thrusting out his lips as children do kissed the icon and again bowed and touched the ground with his hand. The other generals followed his example; then the officers, and after them the soldiers and militiamen, came up with excited faces, pushing each other and shoving breathlessly forward.

22

CAUGHT in the thick of the crowd and staggering in the crush, Pierre looked about him.

'Count – Count Bezuhov! How did you get here?' said a voice.

Pierre looked round. Boris Drubetskoy, brushing his knees with his hand (he had probably made them dusty kneeling before the icon like the others), came up to him smiling. Boris was elegantly attired, with just a suggestion of the wear and tear appropriate on active service. He wore a long coat, and like Kutuzov had a riding-whip slung across his shoulder.

Kutuzov, meanwhile, reached the village, where he seated himself in the shade of the nearest house, on a bench which one Cossack ran to fetch and another hastily covered with a rug. An immense and magnificent retinue surrounded the commander-in-chief.

The icon had gone farther on its way, accompanied by the throng. Pierre stopped some thirty paces from Kutuzov, talking to Boris, explaining his desire to be present at the battle and inspect the position.

'I tell you what you had better do,' said Boris. 'I will offer you the hospitality of the camp. You will see everything best from where Count Bennigsen is to be. I am in attendance on him, you know. I'll mention it to him. But if you would like to ride round the position, come along with us. We are just going to the left flank. And then when we get back, do spend the night with me and we'll arrange a game of cards. Of course you know Dmitri Sergeich? He lodges there,' and he pointed to the third house in Gorky.

'But I should have liked to see the right flank. I'm told it is very strong,' said Pierre. 'I should have liked to start from the Moskva river and ride round the whole position.'

'Well, that you can do later, but the great thing is – the left flank. ...'

'Oh yes. And where is Prince Bolkonsky's regiment? Can you point it out to me?' asked Pierre.

'Prince Andrei's? We shall pass it and I'll take you to him.'

'What were you saying about the left flank?' asked Pierre.

'To tell you the truth, between ourselves, there's no making out how things stand with our left flank,' said Boris, confidentially lowering his voice. 'Count Bennigsen intended something quite different. He meant to fortify that knoll over there, and not ... but' – Boris shrugged his shoulders – 'his Serene Highness would not hear of it, or else he was talked round. You see ...' But Boris did not finish, for at that moment, Kaisarov, Kutuzov's adjutant, came up to Pierre. 'Ah, Kaisarov,' said Boris with a free and easy smile, 'I was just trying to explain our position to the count. It is amazing how his Serene Highness was able to foresee the enemy's intentions so accurately!'

'You mean about the left flank?' asked Kaisarov.

'Yes, exactly. That left flank of ours is now extremely strong.'

Although Kutuzov had dismissed all superfluous personnel from the staff, Boris had contrived to remain at Headquarters after the changes. He had established himself with Count Bennigsen, who, like everyone on whom Boris had been in attendance, considered young Prince Drubetskoy invaluable.

In the higher command there were two sharply defined parties: Kutuzov's party and that of Bennigsen, the chief of staff. Boris belonged to the latter faction, and no one else was quite so skilful at insinuating – while at the same time showing servile respect to Kutuzov – that the old fellow was not much good and that it was Bennigsen who managed everything. Now the resolutive moment of battle had come which would mean either the downfall of Kutuzov and the transfer of power to Bennigsen, or if Kutuzov won the battle it could be made to seem that the credit was Bennigsen's. In either case many important rewards were bound to be distributed after the morrow's engagement, and new men would be brought to the fore. And all that day the anticipation of this put Boris in a state of nervous stimulation.

After Kaisarov, others of his acquaintance came up to Pierre, and he had not time to reply to all the questions about Moscow that were showered upon him, or to listen to all they had to tell him. Exhilaration and anxiety were written on every face. But it seemed to Pierre that the cause of the excitement which some of the faces betrayed could be traced more to preoccupation with their own individual advancement, and he could not help remembering the expression he had seen on other faces, which spoke of concern not with personal matters but with the universal questions of life and death. Kutuzov caught sight of Pierre's figure and the group gathered round him.

'Call him to me,' said Kutuzov.

An adjutant communicated his Serene Highness's message, and Pierre went towards the bench. But a militiaman was there before him. It was Dolohov.

'How did that fellow get here?' asked Pierre.

'Oh, he's such a sly dog, he pokes himself in everywhere!' was the answer. 'He was degraded to the ranks, you know. Now he wants to bob up again. He's been proposing some scheme or other, and at night goes crawling up to the enemy's picket line. ... There's no denying he's plucky!'

Pierre took off his hat and bowed respectfully to Kutuzov.

'I decided that if I laid the matter before your Highness, you would either dismiss me, or say you already knew what I had to tell you, and in that case I shouldn't be any the worse off ...' Dolohov was saying.

'Very true, very true.'

'But if I were right, I should be rendering a service to my Fatherland, for which I am ready to die.'

'Very true ... very true. ...'

'And should your Highness require a man who is not particular whether he keeps his skin whole or not, I beg you will remember me. ... Perhaps I might be of use to your Highness.'

'Very true ... very true,' Kutuzov repeated, looking with a laughing, narrowing eye at Pierre.

Meanwhile Boris, with the finesse of the courtier, stepped up to Pierre's side near Kutuzov, and in the most natural manner, without raising his voice, said to Pierre as though continuing an interrupted conversation:

'The militiamen have got themselves into clean white shirts to be ready to die. There's heroism for you, count!'

Boris said this to Pierre with the evident intention of being overheard by his Serene Highness. He knew Kutuzov's attention would be caught by those words, and so it was.

'What are you saying about the militiamen?' he asked Boris.

'They're preparing for tomorrow, your Highness – they've put on clean shirts to be ready for death.'

'Ah! ... A wonderful, unique people!' said Kutuzov, and closing his eyes he nodded his head. 'A unique people!' he repeated with a sigh.

'So you want to smell gunpowder?' he said to Pierre. 'Yes, it's a pleasant smell. I have the honour to be one of your wife's admirers. Is she well? My quarters are at your service.'

And, as old people often do, Kutuzov began looking abstractedly about him, as though forgetting all he wanted to say or do.

Then, apparently recollecting the object of his search, he beckoned to Andrei Sergeich Kaisarov, the brother of his adjutant.

'Those verses ... those verses of Marin's ... how do they go, eh? The lines he wrote about Gerakov? "To the corps, Preceptor shalt thou be ..." Recite them, recite them!' said he, relaxing his features in readiness to laugh.

Kaisarov recited the lines. ... Kutuzov smilingly nodded his head to the rhythm of the verses.

When Pierre left Kutuzov, Dolohov approached and took his hand.

'I am very glad to meet you here, count,' he said in a loud tone, disregarding the presence of strangers, and speaking with marked determination and solemnity. 'On the eve of a day which God alone knows who of us is fated to survive, I am glad to have the opportunity of telling you how sorry I am for the misunderstandings which existed between us, and I should like you to have no ill-feelings against me. I beg you to forgive me.'

Pierre looked at Dolohov with a smile, not knowing what to say to him. With tears in his eyes Dolohov embraced Pierre and kissed him.

Boris had said something to his general, and Count Bennigsen turned to Pierre and proposed that he should join him in a ride along the lines.

'You will find it interesting,' said he.

'Yes, indeed,' replied Pierre.

Half an hour later Kutuzov had left for Tatarinova, and Bennigsen and his suite, with Pierre among them, set out on their tour of inspection.

23

FROM Gorky, Bennigsen descended the high road to the bridge which the officer on the knoll had pointed out to Pierre as the centre of our position, and where rows of fragrant new-mown hay lay by the riverside. They crossed the bridge into the village of Borodino, then switched to the left and, passing immense numbers of men and guns, came to a high knoll where militiamen were digging. This was the redoubt, as yet unnamed, which afterwards became known as the Raevsky Redoubt or the Knoll-battery.

Pierre paid no special attention to this mound. He did not know that it was to be the most memorable spot for him on the whole plain of Borodino. Then they rode through the ravine to Semeonovsk, where soldiers were dragging away the last beams and timbers left to the huts and barns. After that they continued downhill and uphill, across a field of rye (trampled and laid flat as though by hail), along a track newly made by the artillery over the furrows of the ploughed land, until they reached some flèches, at which men were still at work.

Bennigsen drew up at the earthworks and began looking at the Shevardino Redoubt opposite (which had been ours the day before), where several horsemen could be descried. The officers said that either Napoleon or Murat was there, and all gazed eagerly at the little group of horsemen. Pierre too stared at them, trying to guess which of the scarcely discernible figures was Napoleon. At last the little band rode away from the mound and disappeared from sight.

Bennigsen, addressing a general who approached him, began explaining the whole position of our troops. Pierre listened, straining every faculty to grasp the essential points of the impending battle, but to his mortification he felt that his mental capacity was not equal to the task. He could make nothing of it. Bennigsen stopped speaking, and noticing that Pierre was listening, suddenly said to him:

'This doesn't interest you, I'm afraid?'

'Oh, on the contrary, it is most interesting!' replied Pierre, not quite truthfully.

From the flèches they rode still farther to the left, along a road which wound through a thick, low-growing birch-wood. In the middle of the wood a brown hare with white paws sprang out and, scared by the trampling of so many horses, grew so confused that it leapt along the road in front of them for a long while, exciting general attention and amusement, and only when several voices shouted at it did it dart to one side and vanish in the thicket. After about a mile and a half of woodland they came out on a clearing where troops of Tuchkov's corps were stationed to defend the left flank.

Here, at the very extremity of the left flank, Bennigsen talked a great deal and with much heat, and made, as it seemed to Pierre, dispositions of great military importance. In front of Tuchkov's forces was some high ground not occupied by troops. Bennigsen was loud in his criticism of this oversight, declaring that it was madness to leave a height which commanded the surrounding country unoccupied, and to be satisfied with placing troops below it. Several of the generals expressed the same opinion, one in particular maintained with martial heat that they were put there to be slaughtered. Bennigsen, on his own responsibility, ordered the corps to be moved to the height.

This disposition on the left flank made Pierre more than ever doubtful of his capacity to understand military matters. As he listened to Bennigsen and the other generals criticizing the position of the troops at the foot of the hill, he grasped their opinion perfectly and agreed with them; but for that very reason he could not imagine how the man who had placed them there on the low ground could have made so gross and palpable a blunder.

Pierre did not know that these troops were not, as Bennigsen supposed, put there to defend the position, but had been stationed in that concealed spot to lie in ambush, unobserved, and strike an approaching enemy without warning. Bennigsen did not know this, and moved the troops forward according to his own ideas, without saying anything about the change to the commander-in-chief.

24

On this bright evening of August the 25th Prince Andrei lay leaning on his elbow in a tumble-down shed in the village of Knyazkovo, at the farther end of the encampment of his regiment. Through a gap in the broken wall he could see, beside the wooden fence, a row of thirty-year-old birches with their lower branches lopped off, a field with shocks of oats lying about it, and some bushes near which rose the smoke of camp-fires – the soldiers' kitchens.

Narrow and burdensome and of no use to anyone as his life now seemed to Prince Andrei, he felt disturbed and irritable on the eve of action, just as he had done seven years before at Austerlitz.

He had received and issued the orders for next day's battle, and had nothing more to do. But his thoughts – the most straightforward, clearest and therefore most terrible thoughts – would give him no peace. He was aware that tomorrow's engagement would be the most dreadful of all he had taken part in, and for the first time in his life the possibility of death presented itself to him – not in relation to his earthly life, or to any consideration of the effect his death might have on others, but simply in relation to himself, to his own soul – and rose before him plainly and awfully with a vividness that made it seem almost a concrete reality. And from the height of this vision all that had hitherto tormented and preoccupied him suddenly became illumined by a cold white light, having no shadows, without perspective, without distinction of outline. His whole life appeared to him like a series of magic-lantern pictures which he had been staring at by artificial light through a glass. Now he suddenly saw those badly-daubed pictures, without the glass, in the clear light of day. 'Yes, yes! There they are, those lying images that agitated, enthralled and tormented me,' he said to himself, passing in review the principal pictures of the magic-lantern of his life and looking at them now in the cold white daylight of his clear perception of death. 'There they are, those rudely painted figures that once seemed splendid and mysterious. Honour and glory, the good of society, love for a woman, the Fatherland itself – what grand pictures they used to seem to me, with what profound meaning they seemed to be filled! And it is all so simple, so colourless and crude in the cold white light of the morning which I feel is dawning for me.' The three great sorrows of his life held his attention especially; his love for a woman, his father's death, and the French invasion which had overrun half Russia. 'Love! ... that little girl who seemed to me brimming over with mystic forces. How I loved her! I dreamed romantic dreams of love, of happiness with her! Oh, how naïve and callow I was!' he groaned aloud. 'Why, I believed in some ideal love which was to keep her faithful to me for the whole twelve months of my absence! Like the tender dove of the fable she was to pine away, parted from me! But it was all vastly more simple ... it was all horribly simple and loathsome!

'My father, too, laid out Bald Hills, and thought the place was his – that it was his land, his air, his peasants. But Napoleon came along and swept him aside, unconscious of his existence, as he might brush a chip of wood from his path, and his Bald Hills and his whole life fell to pieces. Princess Maria says that it is a trial sent from above. What is the trial for, since he is no more and never will be? He will never come back again! He is no more! So for whom is the trial intended? The Fatherland, the destruction of Moscow! And tomorrow I shall be killed, perhaps not even by a Frenchman but by one of our own side, by a soldier discharging a musket close to my ear, as one of them did yesterday; and the French will come along and take me by my head and my heels and pitch me into a hole that I may not stink under their noses; and life generally will go on under new conditions, just as natural in their turn as the old ones, and I shall not know about them, for I shall be no more.'

He gazed at the row of birch-trees with their motionless green and yellow foliage and the white bark, shining in the sun. 'To die ... to be killed tomorrow ... to be no more. ... That all this should still be, but no me. ...'

He pictured the world without himself. And the birches with their light and shade, the curly clouds and the smoke of the camp-fires – everything around him suddenly underwent a transformation into something sinister and threatening. A cold shiver ran down his spine. He started to his feet, went out of the shed and began walking up and down.

Returning indoors, he heard voices outside the shed.

'Who's there?' he called.

The red-nosed Captain Timohin, Dolohov's old squadron-commander but now from lack of officers promoted to the command of a battalion, shyly entered the shed, followed by an adjutant and the paymaster of the regiment.

Prince Andrei got up hurriedly, listened to the business they had come about, gave a few further instructions and was about to dismiss them when he heard a familiar, lisping voice outside the shed.

'Devil take it!' exclaimed this voice as its owner stumbled over something.

Prince Andrei looked out of the shed and saw Pierre, who had tripped and almost fallen flat over a pole lying on the ground. As a rule Prince Andrei disliked seeing people of his own set, and especially Pierre, who reminded him of all the painful moments of his last visit to Moscow.

'You? What a surprise!' he cried. 'What brings you here? I didn't expect to see you!'

As he said this his eyes and face expressed more than coldness – they expressed hostility, which Pierre noticed at once. He had approached the shed with the greatest eagerness but when he saw Prince Andrei's face he felt constrained and ill at ease.

'I came – well – you know – I came ... it was interesting to me,' stammered Pierre, who had so often that day stupidly repeated the word 'interesting'. 'I wanted to see the battle.'

'Oh yes, and what do your freemason brethren say about war? How would they prevent it?' said Prince Andrei ironically. 'Well, and how's Moscow? How are my folks? Have they got to Moscow at last?' he asked more seriously.

'Yes, they have. Julie Drubetskoy told me so. I went to call, but missed them. They had gone on to your estate near Moscow.'

25

THE officers would have retired but Prince Andrei, apparently reluctant to be left alone with his friend, invited them to stay and have tea. Benches were brought in, and tea. With some amazement the officers gazed at Pierre's huge, bulky figure, and listened to his talk of Moscow and the position of our army, round which he had ridden. Prince Andrei sat silent, and his expression was so forbidding that Pierre addressed himself chiefly to Timohin, the kindly battalion-commander.

'So you understand the whole disposition of our troops?' Prince Andrei interrupted him.

'Yes – that is, how do you mean?' said Pierre. 'Not being a military man I can't say I do fully; but still I understand the general arrangement.'

'Well, then, you know more than anyone else,' said Prince Andrei in French.

'Oh!' said Pierre incredulously, looking through his spectacles at Prince Andrei. 'Well, and what do you think of the appointment of Kutuzov?' he asked.

'I welcomed it. That is all I can say,' replied Prince Andrei.

'And tell me your opinion of Barclay de Tolly? In Moscow they are saying heaven knows what about him. ... What do you think of him?'

'Ask these gentlemen,' said Prince Andrei, indicating the officers.

Pierre looked at Timohin with the condescendingly doubtful smile with which everybody involuntarily addressed that officer.

'It was a gleam of *serene* light in the dark, your Excellency, when his *Serene* Highness took over,' said Timohin, stealing shy glances continually at his colonel.

'Why so?' asked Pierre.

'Well, to mention only firewood and fodder – let me tell you. You see, when we were retreating from Swienciany we dared not touch a stick or a wisp of hay or anything. We were going away so *he* would get it all – wasn't that the way of it, your Excellency?' he said, turning to his prince. 'And woe to us if we so much as laid a finger on anything! In our regiment two officers were court-martialled for that sort of offence. Well, since his *Serene* Highness took command everything became perfectly straightforward. We see the matter *serene* as daylight. ...'

'Then why did the other forbid it?'

Timohin looked about in confusion, at a loss to know how and what to reply to such a question. Pierre turned to Prince Andrei with the same inquiry.

'Why, so as not to lay waste the country we were abandoning to the enemy,' said Prince Andrei with angry sarcasm. 'It's a sound principle: never allow pillage, never let your men get accustomed to marauding. Well now, at Smolensk, too, Barclay de Tolly was quite right when he argued that the French might outflank us, since they outnumbered us. But he could not understand this,' cried Prince Andrei in shrill tones, as though he had suddenly lost control of his voice: 'he could not understand that for the first time we were fighting on Russian soil, that there was a spirit in the men such as I had never seen before, that we had held the French for two days and that that success had multiplied our strength tenfold. He ordered us to retreat, and all our efforts and losses went for nothing. Of course he did not mean to betray us, he tried to do everything for the best, he thought everything out beforehand; and that is why he is no good. He is no good at the present juncture just because he plans it all out in advance, very judiciously and accurately, as every German has to. How can I explain? ... Well, say your father has a German valet, and he's an excellent valet and satisfies your father's requirements better than you could, and all's well and good. But if your father is mortally ill you'll send away the valet and attend to your father with your own unpractised, awkward hands, and be more comfort to him than a skilled man who is a stranger could. That's what happened with Barclay de Tolly. While Russia was well, a foreigner could serve her and be a splendid minister; but so soon as she is in danger she needs one of her own kin. But in your club they go and make him out to be a traitor! The sole result of traducing him as a traitor will be that later on, ashamed of their false accusations, they will suddenly turn him into a hero or a genius, which would be still more unfair to him. He's an honest and conscientious German. ...'

'They say he's an able general, though,' remarked Pierre.

'I don't know what is meant by "an able general",' replied Prince Andrei ironically.

'An able general,' said Pierre, 'well, it's one who leaves nothing to chance ... who foresees the adversary's intentions.'

'But that's impossible,' cried Prince Andrei, as if this were a point that had been settled long ago.

Pierre looked at him in surprise.

'And yet,' he observed, 'don't they say war is like a game of chess?'

'Yes,' replied Prince Andrei, 'but with this little difference, that in chess you may think over each move as long as you please, taking your time, and with this further difference that a knight is always stronger than a pawn and two pawns are always stronger than one, while in war a battalion is sometimes stronger than a division and sometimes weaker than a company. The relative strength of opposing armies can never be predicted. You may be quite sure,' he went on, 'that if things depended on arrangements made by the staff, I should be there helping to make those arrangements, but instead of that I have the honour to serve here in the regiment with these gentlemen, and I consider that the issue of tomorrow's engagement will rest with us rather than with them. ... Success never has and never will depend on position, or equipment, or even on numbers – least of all on position.'

'What does it depend on, then?'

'On the feeling that is in me and in him' – he pointed to Timohin, 'and in every soldier.'

Prince Andrei glanced at Timohin, who was staring at his colonel in alarm and bewilderment. In contrast to his former silent reserve Prince Andrei seemed excited now. Apparently he could not refrain from expressing the thoughts that had suddenly occurred to him.

'A battle is won by the side that has firmly resolved to win. Why did we lose the battle of Austerlitz? The number of French casualties was almost equal to ours, but very early in the day we said to ourselves that we were losing the battle, and we did lose it. And we said so because we had nothing to fight for then: we wanted to get away from the battlefield as soon as we could. "We're defeated, so let us run!" And we ran. If we had not said that till the evening, heaven knows what might not have happened. But tomorrow we shan't say that. You talk about our position, of the left flank being weak and the right flank too extended,' he went on. 'All that's nonsense. It doesn't come into it at all. But what awaits us tomorrow? A hundred million incalculable contingencies, which will be determined on the instant by whether they run or we do, whether this man or that man is killed; but all that is being done at this moment is mere pastime. The fact is, the people with whom you rode round inspecting the position not only do not help matters but are a positive hindrance. They are concerned with their own petty interests, and nothing else.'

'At such a moment?' said Pierre reproachfully.

'*At such a moment*,' repeated Prince Andrei. 'For them it is simply a propitious moment to oust a rival and win an extra cross or ribbon. To my mind tomorrow means this: a hundred thousand Russian and a hundred thousand French soldiers have met to fight, and the thing is that these two hundred thousand men *will* fight and the side that fights the more savagely and spares itself least will win. And if you like I will tell you that whatever happens, and whatever mess those at the top may make, we shall win tomorrow's battle. Tomorrow, happen what may, the day will be ours!'

'You are right there, your Excellency! That's the whole truth of it!' cut in Timohin. 'Who would spare himself now? The soldiers in my battalion, would you believe it, wouldn't touch their vodka! "It's not a time for that", they say.'

All were silent.

The officers rose. Prince Andrei went out of the shed with them, giving final orders to the adjutant. After the officers had gone Pierre moved nearer to Prince Andrei, and was about to start a conversation when they heard the clatter of three horses on the road not far from the shed, and looking in that direction Prince Andrei recognized Wolzogen and Clausewitz, accompanied by a Cossack. Still talking, they passed so close that Pierre and Prince Andrei could not help overhearing the following, in German:

'The war must be extended over a wider area. That is a conviction which I cannot advocate too highly,' one of them was saying.

'Oh, undoubtedly,' replied the other, 'since the aim is to wear out the enemy, one cannot, of course, take into account damage and injury suffered by private persons.'

'Certainly not,' confirmed the first voice.

'Oh yes, spread the war!' said Prince Andrei with an angry snort, when they had ridden by. 'In that "wider area" I had a father and a son and a sister at Bald Hills. He doesn't care about that. That's what I was just saying to you – those German gentlemen won't win the battle tomorrow, they will only make a mess of it, so far as they are able, because they have nothing in their German heads but theories not worth an empty egg-shell, while their hearts are void of the one thing that's needed for tomorrow, which Timohin has. They have handed all Europe over to *him*, and now they come here to teach us. Fine teachers, I must say!' and again his voice grew shrill.

'So you think that we shall win a victory tomorrow?' asked Pierre.

'Yes, yes,' answered Prince Andrei absently. 'One thing I would do if I had the power,' he began again. 'I would not take prisoners. What sense is there in taking prisoners? It's playing knights of old. The French have destroyed my home and are on their way to destroy Moscow; they have outraged and are outraging me every moment. They are my enemies. In my opinion they are all criminals and that expresses the feeling of Timohin and the whole army with him. They must be put to death. Since they are my enemies, they cannot be my friends, whatever was said at Tilsit.'

'Oh yes,' murmured Pierre, looking with shining eyes at Prince Andrei. 'I entirely agree with you!'

The question that had worried Pierre on the Mozhaisk hill and all that day now seemed to him quite clear and fully solved. He now realized all the import and all the gravity of this war and the impending battle. All he had seen that day, all the significant, stern expressions on the faces he had seen in passing, appeared to him in a new light now. The latent heat (as they say in physics) of patriotism which was present in all these men he had seen was now intelligible to him, and explained the composure and almost light-heartedness with which they were all preparing for death.

'Not to take prisoners,' Prince Andrei continued. 'That by itself would transform the whole aspect of war and make it less cruel. As it is we have been playing at war – that's what's vile! We play at being magnanimous and all the rest of it. Such magnanimity and sensibility are like the magnanimity and sensibility of the lady who faints at the sight of a calf being killed: she is so tender-hearted that she can't look at blood – but fricassée of veal she will eat with gusto. They prate about the rules of warfare, of chivalry, of flags of truce and humanity to the wounded, and so on. All fiddle-sticks. I saw chivalry and flags of truce in 1805: they humbugged us and we humbugged them. They plunder people's homes, circulate false paper money, and worst of all they kill our children and our fathers, and then talk of the rules of warfare and generosity to a fallen foe. No quarter, I say, but kill and be killed! Anyone who has reached this conclusion through the same suffering as I have ...'

Prince Andrei, who had believed it was a matter of indifference to him whether they took Moscow as they had taken Smolensk, was unexpectedly pulled up in his argument by a sudden cramp in his throat. He walked to and fro a few times in silence, but his eyes glittered feverishly and his lips quivered as he began to speak again.

'If there were none of this magnanimity business in warfare, we should never go to war, except for something worth facing certain death for, as now. Then there would not be wars because Paul Ivanich had given offence to Mihail Ivanich. And when there was a war, like this present one, it would be war! And then the spirit and determination of the fighting men would be something quite different. All these Westphalians and Hessians that Napoleon has dragged at his heels would never have come to Russia, and we should not have gone fighting in Austria and Prussia without knowing why. War is not a polite recreation but the vilest thing in life, and we ought to understand that and not play at war. Our attitude towards the fearful necessity of war ought to be stern and serious. It boils down to this: we should have done with humbug, and let war be war and not a game. Otherwise, war is a favourite pastime of the idle and frivolous … there is no profession held in higher esteem than the military. And what is war? What makes for success in warfare? What are the morals of the military world? The aim and end of war is murder; the weapons employed in war are espionage, treachery and the encouragement of treachery, the ruining of a country, the plundering and robbing of its inhabitants for the maintenance of the army, and trickery and lying which all appear under the heading of the art of war. The military world is characterized by the absence of freedom – in other words, a rigorous discipline – enforced inactivity, ignorance, cruelty, debauchery and drunkenness. And yet this is the highest caste in society, respected by all. Every monarch in the world, except the Emperor of China, wears a military uniform, and bestows the greatest rewards on the man who kills the greatest number of his fellow-creatures. Tens of thousands of men meet – as they will tomorrow – to massacre one another: to kill and maim, and then they will offer up thanksgiving services for having slain such vast numbers (they even exaggerate the number) and proclaim a victory, supposing that the more men they have slaughtered the more credit to them. Think of God looking down and listening to them!' cried Prince Andrei in a shrill, piercing voice. 'Ah, my friend, life has become a burden to me of late. I see that I have begun to understand too much. And it doesn't do for man to taste of the tree of the knowledge of good and evil. … Ah well, it's not for long!' he added. 'However, you're sleepy, and it's time I turned in, too. Get back to Gorky,' said Prince Andrei suddenly.

'Oh no!' Pierre replied, looking at Prince Andrei with eyes full of scared sympathy.

'Yes, you ought to be off: before a battle one needs a good night's rest,' repeated Prince Andrei. He went quickly up to Pierre and embraced and kissed him. 'Good-bye, be off with you!' he cried.

'Whether we meet again – no …' and hastily turning away he entered the shed.

It was already dark, and Pierre could not make out whether the expression of Prince Andrei's face was angry or tender.

For some time he stood in silence, deliberating whether to follow him or go away. 'No, he does not want me!' Pierre decided, 'and I know that this is our last meeting!' He heaved a deep sigh and rode back to Gorky.

In the shed Prince Andrei stretched himself on a rug but he could not sleep.

He closed his eyes. One set of images succeeded another in his imagination. There was one picture on which he dwelt long and joyfully. It was an evening in Petersburg, and with an eager, excited face Natasha was telling him how she had gone to look for mushrooms the previous summer and had lost her way in the big forest. Incoherently she described the still depths of the forest, and her sensations, and her talk with a bee-keeper she met, and every minute she broke off to say: 'No, I can't, I'm not telling it properly; no, you won't understand,' although Prince Andrei tried to reassure and persuade her that he did understand, and he really had understood all she wanted to express. But Natasha had been dissatisfied with her own words – she felt that they did not give an idea of the passionately poetic feeling she had known that day and which she wanted to convey. 'He was such a delightful old man, and it was so dark in the forest … and he had such a kind… No, I can't describe it,' she had said, flushed and agitated. Prince Andrei smiled now the same happy smile he had smiled then as he looked into her eyes. 'I understood her,' he thought. 'Not only did I understand her but it was just that inner, spiritual force, that sincerity, that ingenuousness – the very soul of her which seemed to be pinioned by her body – it was that soul I loved in her … loved so intensely, so happily. …' And suddenly he recalled what it was that had put an end to his love. '*He* cared nothing for all that. *He* did not see or understand anything of that kind. All he saw was a pretty, *fresh* young creature, with whom he did not deign to link his destiny. And I? … And he is still alive and enjoying life!'

Prince Andrei jumped up as though he had been scalded, and began pacing to and fro in front of the shed again.

26

On the 25th of August, the eve of the battle of Borodino, M. de Beausset, prefect of the French Emperor's palace, and Colonel Fabvier arrived, the former from Paris and the latter from Madrid, at Napoleon's quarters at Valuevo.

Changing into court uniform, M. de Beausset ordered a box he had brought for the Emperor to be carried before him, and walked into the outer compartment of Napoleon's tent, where he busied himself in unpacking the box while conversing with Napoleon's aides-de-camp who crowded round him.

Fabvier remained at the entrance of the tent, talking to some generals of his acquaintance.

The Emperor Napoleon had not yet left his bedroom and was finishing his toilet. Uttering little snorts and grunts, he presented now his stout back, now his plump hairy chest to the flesh-brush with which a valet was rubbing him down. Another valet, with his finger over the mouth of a bottle, was sprinkling eau-de-Cologne on the Emperor's pampered person with an expression which seemed to say that he alone knew where and how much eau-de-Cologne should be applied. Napoleon's short hair was wet and matted on the forehead, but his face, though puffy and yellow, expressed physical satisfaction. 'Go on, harder, go on! ...' he said, slightly tensing himself and giving a grunt, to the valet who was rubbing him. An aide-de-camp, who had come into the bedroom to report the number of prisoners taken in the previous day's engagement, was standing at the door, having accomplished his errand, awaiting permission to withdraw. Napoleon, scowling, glared at the aide-de-camp under his brows.

'No prisoners!' said he, repeating the aide-de-camp's words. 'They are compelling us to annihilate them. So much the worse for the Russian army. ... Go on ... harder – put more energy into it!' he muttered, hunching his fat shoulders before the valet. 'All right. Show in Monsieur de Beausset, and Fabvier too,' he said, nodding to the aide-de-camp.

'Very good, sire,' and the aide-de-camp disappeared through the door of the tent.

The two valets quickly got his Majesty into the blue uniform of the Guards and he entered the reception-room with firm, swift steps.

Beausset meanwhile had been busily engaged in arranging the present he had brought from the Empress, on two chairs directly in front of the door the Emperor must come in by. But Napoleon had dressed and emerged with such unexpected promptness that he had not time to finish setting up the surprise.

Napoleon at once noticed what they were about and guessed they were not ready. He did not want to deprive them of the pleasure of preparing a surprise for him, so he pretended not to see Monsieur de Beausset and beckoned Fabvier to him. With a deep frown, and without speaking, Napoleon listened to what Fabvier was saying about the heroism and devotion of his army fighting before Salamanca, at the other end of Europe, and who had but one thought – to be worthy of their Emperor – and but one fear – to fail to please him. The result of that battle had been deplorable. Napoleon made ironic remarks during Fabvier's account, making it understood that he had not expected matters could go otherwise in his absence.

'I must make up for that in Moscow,' said Napoleon. 'I will see you later,' he added, and summoned de Beausset, who had by this time succeeded in preparing his effect, having placed some object on the chairs and covered it with a piece of drapery.

De Beausset made a courtier's low bow, such as only the old retainers of the Bourbons knew how to make, and stepped forward, presenting an envelope.

Napoleon turned to him gaily and pulled his ear.

'You have been quick, I am very glad to see you. Well, what is Paris saying?' he asked, his look of severity suddenly changing to one of friendliness.

'Sire, all Paris regrets your absence,' replied de Beausset, as was proper.

But though Napoleon knew de Beausset had to say this, or something of the kind, and though in his lucid moments he knew it was untrue, it pleased him to hear de Beausset say it. He honoured him with another touch on the ear.

'I am sorry to have given you such a long journey,' said he.

'Sire, I expected nothing less than to find you at the gates of Moscow,' replied de Beausset.

Napoleon smiled, and lifting his head absently looked round to the right. An aide-de-camp glided forward with a gold snuff-box and offered it. Napoleon took it.

'Yes, it has turned out luckily for you,' he said, lifting the open snuff-box to his nose. 'You are fond of travel, and in three days you will see Moscow. I am sure you did not expect to see the Asiatic capital. You will have a pleasant excursion.'

De Beausset bowed in gratitude at this regard for his taste for travel (of which he had not till then been aware).

'Ha, what have we here?' asked Napoleon, observing that all the suite kept glancing at something concealed under a cloth.

With courtly agility, not turning his back on his Sovereign, de Beausset retired two steps, swung half round and whipped off the covering, saying as he did so:

'A present to your Majesty from the Empress.'

It was a portrait, painted in vivid colours by Gérard, of the son born to Napoleon and the Austrian Emperor's daughter – the child whom for some reason everyone called the 'King of Rome'.

An exceedingly pretty curly-headed little boy with eyes like those of the Infant Christ in the Sistine Madonna was depicted playing stick and ball. The ball represented the terrestrial globe and the stick in his other hand was the sceptre.

Though it was not altogether clear what the artist had intended to express by painting the so-called King of Rome impaling the earth on a stick, the allegory apparently seemed to Napoleon, as it had to everyone who had seen it in Paris, perfectly intelligible and enchanting.

'The King of Rome!' he exclaimed, pointing to the portrait with a graceful gesture. 'Admirable!'

With the natural facility of an Italian for altering the expression of his face at will he approached the portrait and assumed a look of pensive tenderness. He felt that what he said and did at that moment would be history, and it occurred to him that the best line he could take now, when his great glory enabled his son to play stick and ball with the terrestrial globe, would be to display, in contrast to that grandeur, the simplest paternal affection. His eyes dimmed with emotion, he moved forward, looked round for a chair (a chair sprang up under him) and sat down in front of the painting. At a single gesture from him everyone withdrew on tiptoe, leaving the great man to himself and his sentiments.

Having sat for a little while and passed his fingers – he could not have said why – over the rough texture of the high lights, he got up and recalled de Beausset and the officer on duty. He commanded the portrait to be carried out in front of his tent, so that the Old Guard, stationed round about, might not be deprived of the happiness of seeing the King of Rome, the son and heir of their adored Monarch.

And as he anticipated, at breakfast, to which he had honoured M. de Beausset with an invitation, they heard the rapturous cries of the officers and men of the Old Guard who had run up to see the picture.

'*Vive l'Empereur! Vive le roi de Rome! Vive l'Empereur!*' came the ecstatic shouts.

After breakfast Napoleon, in Beausset's presence, dictated his order of the day to the army.

'Short and to the point!' he remarked, when he had read over the proclamation he had dictated straight off without corrections. It ran as follows:

Soldiers! The battle you have so longed for is at hand. Victory depends on you. It is essential for us; it will give us everything we need – comfortable quarters and a speedy return to our own country. Acquit yourselves as you acquitted yourselves at Austerlitz, Friedland, Vitebsk and Smolensk. Let posterity far down the ages recall with pride your achievements this day. May it be said of each man among you: 'He was in the great battle before Moscow!'

'Before Moscow!' repeated Napoleon, and inviting M. de Beausset, who was so fond of travel, to accompany him on his ride he went out of the tent to where the horses stood saddled.

'Your Majesty is too kind!' said Beausset in response to the invitation to accompany the Emperor: he wanted to sleep, he did not ride well and was afraid of horses.

But Napoleon nodded to the traveller and de Beausset was obliged to mount. When Napoleon came out of the tent the acclamations of the Guards before his son's portrait redoubled. Napoleon frowned.

'Take him away,' he said, pointing with a gracefully majestic gesture to the portrait. 'It is too early yet for him to look upon a field of battle.'

De Beausset lowered his eyelids and bent his head with a deep sigh, testifying thereby how profoundly he appreciated and comprehended the Emperor's words.

27

THE whole of that day of the 25th of August, so his historians tell us, Napoleon spent on horseback inspecting the locality, considering the plans submitted to him by his marshals and giving commands in person to his generals.

The original line of the Russian disposition along the river Kolocha had been dislocated by the capture of the Shevardino Redoubt on the 24th, and part of the line – the left flank – had been drawn farther back. That portion of the line was not entrenched, nor was it protected any longer by the river, and the ground in front was more open and level than elsewhere. It was evident to anyone, whether soldier or civilian, that it was here the French should attack. One would have thought that no great deliberation would be necessary to reach this conclusion, nor any particular care or trouble on the part of the Emperor and his marshal; nor would there be any need of that high degree of talent called genius, which people are so fond of attributing to Napoleon. Yet the historians who described the battle afterwards and the men who surrounded Napoleon at the time, and Napoleon himself, thought otherwise.

Napoleon rode over the plain, surveying the countryside with a sagacious air, wagging his head approvingly or dubiously to himself, and without communicating to the generals around him the profound chain of reasoning which guided him in his decisions conveyed to them merely the final conclusions in the form of commands. When Davoust, now styled Duke of Eckmühl, suggested turning the Russian left wing Napoleon replied, without explaining, that it would not be necessary. On the other hand to a proposal made by General Campan (who was to attack the flèches) to lead his division through the woods Napoleon signified his assent, although the so-called Duke of Elchingen (Ney) ventured to remark that moving through woodland was risky and might break up the formation of the division.

After examining the ground over against the Shevardino Redoubt Napoleon pondered a little in silence and then indicated two points where he wished batteries to be set up by the morrow to bombard the Russian entrenchments, and the positions where, in line with them, the field-artillery should be placed.

Having given these and other commands, he returned to his tent, and the dispositions for the battle were written down from his dictation.

These dispositions, of which French historians speak with rapture and other historians with deep respect, were as follows:

At daybreak the two new batteries established during the night on the plateau occupied by the Prince of Eckmühl will open fire on the two opposing batteries of the enemy.

At the same time the commander of the artillery of the 1st Corps, General Pernetti, with thirty cannon of Campan's division and all the howitzers of Dessaix's and Friant's division will move forward, open fire and shower shells on the enemy's battery, which will thus have in action against it:

> 24 guns of the artillery of the Guards
> 30 guns of Campan's division
> 8 guns of Friant's and Dessaix's division
> —
> a total of 62 guns.

The commander of the artillery of the 3rd Corps, General Fouché, will place the howitzers of the 3rd and 8th Corps, sixteen in all, on the flanks of the battery that is to shell the entrenchment on the left, thus giving this battery an effective of some 40 pieces.

General Sorbier is to be in readiness to advance, at the first word of command, with all the howitzers of the Guards' artillery against one or other of the entrenchments.

During the cannonade Prince Poniatowski is to advance through the wood on the village and turn the enemy's position.

General Campan will move through the wood to seize the first fortification.

With the action fairly started on these lines subsequent commands will be issued in accordance with the enemy's movements.

The cannonade on the left flank will begin as soon as the guns of the right wing are heard. The sharpshooters of Morand's division and of the Viceroy's division will open a heavy fire the moment they see that the attack on the right wing has begun.

The Viceroy will occupy the village* and debouch by its three bridges, keeping on a level with Morand's and Gérard's divisions, which under his leadership will march on the redoubt and come into line with the rest of the forces of the army.

* Borodino.

All this must be done in good order (*le tout se fera avec ordre et méthode*), taking care to keep troops in reserve so far as possible.

The Imperial Camp near Mozhaisk,

6th September, 1812.*

These dispositions – which are seen to be exceedingly obscure and confused if one ventures to discard superstitious awe for Napoleon's genius and analyse them – contain four points, four different orders, not one of which could be, or was, carried out.

In the dispositions it is said, first, *that the batteries placed on the spot selected by Napoleon, with the guns of Pernetti and Fouché which were to come in line with them, in all 102 cannons, were to open fire and shell the Russian flèches and redoubts.* This could not be done, since from the spots chosen by Napoleon the projectiles did not carry to the Russian works; and those 102 guns shot into the air until the nearest commander, contrary to Napoleon's instructions, moved them forward.

The second instruction given was that *Poniatowski, advancing to the village through the wood, should turn the Russian left flank.* This could not be done, and was not done, because Poniatowski, advancing on the village through the wood, met Tuchkov there barring his way, and could not and did not turn the Russian position.

The third order was: *General Campan will move through the wood to seize the first fortification.* Campan's division did not seize the first fortification, but was driven back, for on emerging from the wood it was obliged to re-form under a hail of Russian grapeshot, of which Napoleon knew nothing.

The fourth instruction was that *the Viceroy will occupy the village (Borodino) and debouch by its three bridges, keeping on a level with Morand's and Gérard's divisions* (for whose movements no directions are given), *which under his leadership will march on the redoubt and come into line with the rest of the forces.*

As far as one can make out – not so much from the unintelligible phraseology as from the Viceroy's attempts to execute the orders he received – it seemed he was to move through Borodino from the left to the redoubt, while the divisions of Morand and Gérard were to advance simultaneously from the front.

All this, like the other paragraphs of the disposition, was impossible to carry out. After getting through Borodino the Viceroy was driven

* The date of the French proclamation is new style, corresponding to August 25th, old style. – *Tr.*

back to the Kolocha and could advance no farther; while the divisions of Morand and Gérard did not take the redoubt but were beaten off, and the redoubt was only taken at the end of the battle by the cavalry (a thing probably unforeseen and not heard of by Napoleon). So not one of the orders in the disposition was, or could be, executed. But the disposition stated that *after the action has begun on these lines subsequent commands will be issued in accordance with the enemy's movements,* and therefore it might be inferred that Napoleon would take all necessary measures during the progress of the engagement. But this was not, and could not be, the case because during the whole battle Napoleon was so far from the scene of action that (as it appeared later) the course of the battle could not have been known to him, and not a single instruction given by him during the fight could be executed.

28

MANY historians contend that the French failed at Borodino because Napoleon had a cold in the head, and that if it had not been for this cold the orders he gave before and during the battle would have been still more full of genius, and Russia would have been annihilated and the face of the world would have been changed. To historians who believe that Russia was shaped by the will of one man – Peter the Great – and that France was transformed from a republic into an empire and French armies marched into Russia at the will of one man – Napoleon – the argument that Russia remained a power because Napoleon had a bad cold on the 26th of August may seem logical and convincing.

If it had depended on Napoleon's will whether to fight or not to fight the battle of Borodino, or had it depended on his will whether he gave this order or that, it is evident that a cold affecting the functioning of his will might have saved Russia, and consequently the valet who forgot to bring Napoleon his waterproof boots on the 24th would be the saviour of Russia. On that method of reasoning such a corollary is irrefutable, as irrefutable as Voltaire's verdict pronounced in jest (he did not realize what he was jesting about) that the Massacre of St Bartholomew was due to Charles IX's dyspepsia. But for minds which cannot admit that Russia was fashioned by the will of one man, Peter I, or that the French Empire was created and the war with Russia begun by the will of one man, Napoleon, such reasoning will seem not merely unsound and preposterous but contrary to the whole nature of human reality. The question, What causes historic events? will suggest another answer, namely, that the course of earthly happenings is predetermined from on high, and depends on the combined volition of all who participate in those events, and that the influence of a Napoleon on the course of those events is purely superficial and imaginary.

Strange as the proposition may seem at first sight that the Night of St Bartholomew, for which Charles IX gave the order, was not the outcome of his will, and that he only thought he had decreed it; or that the slaughter of eighty thousand men at Borodino was not due to Napoleon's will (though he gave the orders for the opening stages and the general conduct of the battle), and that he only fancied it was his doing – strange as this proposition appears, yet human dignity, which tells me that each one of us is, if not more, at least not less a man than the great Napoleon, demands the acceptance of this interpretation of the question, and historical research abundantly confirms it.

At the battle of Borodino Napoleon did not fire a shot nor kill anyone. All that was done by the soldiers. Therefore he did not do any killing himself.

The soldiers of the French army went out to slay Russian soldiers on the field of Borodino not because of Napoleon's orders but in answer to their own impulse. The whole army – French, Italians, Germans, Poles – famished, ragged and weary of the campaign, felt at the sight of an army barring the road to Moscow that the wine was drawn and must be drunk. Had Napoleon then forbidden them to fight the Russians they would have killed him and fought with the Russians because they had to.

When they heard Napoleon's proclamation offering them as compensation for crippling wounds and death the thought that posterity would say that they too had been in the battle before Moscow they shouted 'Vive l'Empereur!' just as they had cried 'Vive l'Empereur!' at the portrait of the little boy piercing the terrestrial globe with a toy stick, and just as they would have cried 'Vive l'Empereur!' to any absurdity that might be told them. There was nothing left for them to do but shout 'Vive l'Empereur!' and go into battle to get food and rest as conquerors in Moscow. So it was not because of Napoleon's commands that they killed their fellow-men.

And it was not Napoleon who ordained the course of the battle, for no part of his plan was executed and during the engagement he did not know what was going on before him. Therefore the way in which these men slaughtered one another was not decided by Napoleon's will but occurred independently of him, in accord with the will of the hundreds of thousands of individuals who took part in the common action. It *only seemed* to Napoleon that it was all happening because he willed it so. Hence the question whether Napoleon had or had not a cold in the head is of no more interest to history than whether the least of the transport soldiers had a cold or not.

Napoleon's cold on the 26th of August becomes of still less account in that the assertions made by various writers – that because of this cold his dispositions before, and orders during, the battle were not as skilful as on previous occasions – are completely wrong.

The dispositions cited above are by no means inferior, are indeed superior, to previous dispositions which had won him victories in the past. His supposed orders during the battle were also no worse than the commands he had given in the course of other actions, but were much the same as usual. But these dispositions and commands seem less fortunate only because the battle of Borodino was the first battle in which Napoleon was not victorious. The profoundest and most splendid dispositions and orders look wretched, and every military expert can criticize them with a consequential air, when they have not resulted in victory, and the feeblest dispositions and orders seem excellent, and learned people devote entire volumes to demonstrating their merits, when they relate to a battle that has been won.

The dispositions drawn up by Weierother at Austerlitz were a model of perfection of their kind but still they have been condemned – condemned for their very perfection, for their excessive minuteness.

Napoleon played his part as representative of authority quite as well at Borodino as at his other battles – perhaps better. He did nothing harmful to the progress of the battle; he inclined to the more reasonable opinions; he made no confusion, did not contradict himself, did not lose his head or run away from the field of battle, but with his sound judgement and great military experience calmly and with dignity performed his role of appearing to be in supreme control.

29

ON returning from a second careful inspection of the lines, Napoleon remarked:

'The chess-board is set, tomorrow we begin the game.'

Calling for some punch and summoning de Beausset, he began to talk to him about Paris, discussing various changes he intended to make in the Empress's household, and surprising the prefect by his memory for the minutest details relating to the Court.

He showed interest in trifles, joked about de Beausset's love of travel, and chatted carelessly, as a famous surgeon confident that he knows his job will often chat while he tucks up his sleeves and puts on his apron, and the patient is being strapped to the operating-table. 'I have the whole business at my finger-tips, and it's all clear and definite in my head. When the time comes to set to work I shall do it as no one else could, but now I can jest, and the more I jest and the cooler I am the more hopeful and reassured you ought to feel, and the more you may wonder at my genius.'

Having finished his second glass of punch, Napoleon went to rest before the serious business which, as he imagined, lay before him next day.

He was too much interested in the task that awaited him to sleep, and in spite of his cold, which had got worse with the evening damp, he got up at three o'clock in the morning and went into the other and larger division of the tent, noisily blowing his nose. He asked whether the Russians had not withdrawn. He was told that the enemy's lines were still in the same places. He nodded approval.

The adjutant on duty came into the tent.

'Well, Rapp, do you think we shall do good business today?' Napoleon asked him.

'Without doubt, sire,' answered Rapp.

Napoleon looked at him.

'Do you remember, sire, the remark you were pleased to make to me at Smolensk?' continued Rapp. 'The wine is drawn and must be drunk.'

Napoleon frowned, and sat for a long while in silence, his head resting on his hand.

'This poor army,' he said suddenly, 'it has greatly diminished since

Smolensk. Fortune is a fickle jade, Rapp. I have always said so and I am beginning to know it by experience. But the Guards, Rapp, the Guards are intact, are they not?' he inquired.

'Yes, sire,' replied Rapp.

Napoleon took a lozenge, put it in his mouth and glanced at his watch. He was not sleepy and it was still not nearly morning. There were no further orders to give for the sake of killing time, for they had all been given and were even now being executed.

'Have the biscuits and rice been served out to the regiments of the Guards?' asked Napoleon sternly.

'Yes, sire.'

'The rice too?'

Rapp replied that he had issued the Emperor's orders in regard to the rice, but Napoleon shook his head with a dissatisfied air, as though he doubted whether his instructions had been carried out. An attendant came in with punch. Napoleon called for another glass for Rapp and took a few sips from his own in silence.

'I have no taste or smell,' he remarked, sniffing at the glass. 'This cold is a nuisance. They talk about medicine – what is the good of medicine when they can't cure a cold! Corvisart gave me these lozenges but they do no good. What do the doctors know? They can't cure anything. Our body is a machine for living. That is what it is made for, and that is its nature. Leave life to take care of itself, and don't interfere: it will fight its own battles a great deal better than if you paralyse its powers by encumbering it with remedies. Our body is like a perfect watch meant to go for a certain time; the watchmaker cannot open it – he can only adjust it by fumbling his way blindfold. Yes, our body is a machine for living, that is all.'

And having as it were started making definitions, which he had a weakness for doing, Napoleon suddenly hazarded one on a fresh subject. 'Do you know, Rapp, what military art is?' he asked. 'It is the art of being stronger than the enemy at a given moment. *Voilà tout.*'

Rapp made no reply.

'Tomorrow we shall have Kutuzov to deal with!' said Napoleon. 'We shall see! Do you remember, at Braunau he was in command of an army for three weeks and never once mounted a horse to inspect his entrenchments? We shall see!'

He looked at his watch. It was still only four o'clock. He still had no desire for sleep, the punch was finished and there was still nothing to do. He got up, walked to and fro, put on a warm overcoat and a hat and went out of the tent. The night was dark and damp: one could almost hear the moisture falling. Nearby, the camp-fires of the French Guards burned dimly, and in the distance those of the Russian line glimmered through the smoke. All was still, and the rustle and tramp of the French troops already moving to take up their positions sounded distinctly.

Napoleon walked up and down in front of his tent, stared at the fires and listened to the stamping, and, as he was passing a tall guardsman in a shaggy cap who was on sentry duty before his tent and who had drawn himself up like a black pillar at sight of the Emperor, Napoleon stood still facing him.

'What year did you enter the Service?' he asked with that affectation of military bluntness and geniality with which he always addressed the soldiers.

The man answered.

'Ah, one of the veterans. Has your regiment had its rice?'

'It has, your Majesty.'

Napoleon nodded and walked away.

*

At half past five Napoleon rode to the village of Shevardino.

It was growing light, the sky was clearing, a single cloud lay in the east. The deserted camp-fires were burning themselves out in the pale light of the morning.

A solitary deep cannon-shot boomed out on the right, echoed and then died away in the prevailing silence. Several minutes passed. A second and a third report shook the air; a fourth and fifth boomed solemnly near by on the right.

The first shots had not ceased to reverberate before others rang out, and still others, mingling and overtaking one another in a continuous roar.

Napoleon and his suite made their way to the Shevardino Redoubt and there dismounted. Play had begun.

30

WHEN Pierre returned to Gorky after seeing Prince Andrei he directed his groom to get the horses ready and to call him early in the morning, and then immediately fell fast asleep behind a screen in the corner which Boris had given up to him.

Before Pierre was properly awake next morning there was not a soul left in the hut. The panes were rattling in the little windows. His groom was standing at his side shaking him.

'Your Excellency! Your Excellency! Your Excellency! ...' the groom kept repeating persistently while he shook Pierre by the shoulder without looking at him, having apparently lost hope of ever rousing him.

'Eh? Has it begun? Is it time?' Pierre asked, opening his eyes.

'Hark at the firing, sir,' said the groom, an old soldier. 'All the gentlemen have gone already, and his Serene Highness himself rode past long ago.'

Pierre dressed in haste and ran out into the porch. Outside it was bright, fresh, dewy and cheerful. The sun, just bursting forth from behind a cloud that had obscured it, splashed its rays through the rifts in the clouds, over the roofs of the street opposite, on the dew-besprinkled dust of the road, on to the walls of the houses, through the gaps in the wooden palings and on Pierre's horses standing before the hut. The roar of guns sounded more distinct in the open air. An adjutant accompanied by his Cossack passed by at a sharp trot.

'It's time, count, it's time!' called the adjutant.

Telling his groom to follow with a horse, Pierre walked down the street to the knoll from which he had surveyed the field of battle the day before. A crowd of military was collected there, the staff-officers could be heard talking French, and Pierre saw Kutuzov's grey head in a white cap with the red band, the grey nape of his neck sunk between his shoulders. Kutuzov was looking through a field-glass along the high road before him.

As he mounted the steps to the knoll Pierre glanced at the scene spread beneath his eyes and was spell-bound at the beauty of it. It was the same panorama which he had admired from the mound the day before, but now the whole prospect swarmed with troops, smoke-clouds from the guns hung overhead and the slanting rays of the bright sun, rising slightly to the left behind Pierre, filled the clear morning air with rosy golden light and long dark shadows. The distant forest which bound the horizon might have been carved out of some greeny-yellow precious stone, its undulating outline being pierced beyond Valuevo by the Smolensk high road thick with troops.

In the foreground glittered golden cornfields and copses. Everywhere, to right, to left and in front were soldiers. The whole scene was animated, majestic and unexpected; but what struck Pierre most of all was the view of the battlefield itself, of Borodino and the hollows on both sides of the Kolocha.

Over the Kolocha, over Borodino and on both sides of it, especially to the left where the Volna flowing through marshy ground falls into the Kolocha, a mist had spread, melting, parting, shimmering with light in the brilliant sunshine, magically colouring and outlining everything. The smoke of the guns mingled with this mist, and over the whole landscape, through the mist and smoke, sparkled the morning sun, gleaming on the water, on the dew, on the bayonets of the infantry congregated along the river banks and in Borodino. Through this transparent veil could be seen the white church, and here and there a cottage roof in Borodino, or thick clumps of soldiers, green ammunition-chests or cannon. And the whole scene moved, or seemed to move, as the mist and smoke trailed over the wide plain. Just as the mist wreathed about the hollows of Borodino, so beyond and above, and in particular farther to the left, along the entire line, over the woods, over the fields, in the valleys, on the ridges of the high ground curling clouds of powder-smoke continually formed out of nothing, here a solitary puff, now a bevy together, at longer intervals or in quick succession, swelling, thickening, swirling round, merging and fading away.

These puffs of smoke and the reports that accompanied them were, strange to say, what gave the chief beauty to the spectacle.

'Pooff!' – suddenly a round compact ball of smoke flew up, turning from violet to grey to a milky-white, and 'boom!' followed the report a second later.

'Pooff-pooff!' – and two clouds rose up, pushing one another and merging together; and 'boom-boom!' came the sounds confirming what the eye had seen.

Pierre glanced over at the first puff of smoke which an instant before had been a round compact ball, and in its place he saw balloons of smoke drifting sideways, and pooff ... (a pause) pooff-pooff rose three others, then four more, each one answered at the same interval by a beautiful, firm, precise boom ... boom-boom-boom. Sometimes the smoke-clouds seemed to scud across the sky, sometimes they hung still while woods, fields and glittering bayonets ran past them. From the left, over fields and bushes, these great balls of smoke were constantly rising, followed by their solemn reports, while nearer still, over the lowlands and the woods, burst little cloudlets of musket-smoke which had no time to form into balls but had their little echoes in just the same way. '*Trak-ta-ta-tak!*' crackled the musketry, but it sounded thin and irregular in comparison with the roar of artillery.

Pierre longed to be there in the midst of the smoke, the glittering bayonets, the movement and the noise. He looked round at Kutuzov and his suite, to compare his impressions with those of others. They were all gazing at the field of battle, as he had done, and, he fancied, with the same feelings. Every face now shone with that *latent heat* of excitement which Pierre had noticed the day before and understood perfectly after his talk with Prince Andrei.

'Go, my dear fellow, go ... and Christ be with you!' Kutuzov was saying to a general standing beside him, but he kept his eyes fixed on the battlefield.

Having got this order, the general went past Pierre on his way down the knoll.

'To the crossing!' replied the general coldly and sternly, in reply to one of the staff who asked where he was going.

'So will I. I'll go there too,' thought Pierre, and followed in the same direction.

The general mounted a horse which his Cossack led forward. Pierre went to his groom who was holding the horses. Asking which was the quietest, Pierre clambered up, clutched at the horse's mane, pressed his heels into the animal's belly and, feeling that his spectacles were slipping but unable to let go of the mane and the reins, he galloped after the general, causing the staff-officers to smile as they watched from the knoll.

31

AT the bottom of the hill the general after whom Pierre was galloping turned sharply to the left, and Pierre, losing sight of him, rode into the back of some ranks of infantry marching ahead of him. He tried to pass either to the front of them or to the right or left; but there were soldiers everywhere, all with the same preoccupied expression, intent on some mysterious but evidently important matter. They all cast the same annoyed look of inquiry at this stout man in the white hat who for some unknown reason was trampling them under his horse's hooves.

'What do you want to ride into the middle of a battalion for ?' one man shouted at him.

Another gave the horse a prod with the butt-end of a musket and Pierre, leaning over his saddle-bow and scarcely able to control the plunging animal, galloped ahead of the soldiers to where there was an open space.

In front of him he saw a bridge and other soldiers stood there firing. Pierre rode up to them. Though he was unaware of it, he had come to the bridge over the Kolocha between Gorky and Borodino, which the French (having occupied Borodino) were attacking in the first phase of the battle. Pierre saw there was a bridge in front of him and that soldiers were doing something in the smoke on both sides of it and in the meadow, among the rows of new-mown hay he had noticed the day before; but despite the incessant firing going on there it never occurred to him that this was the very heart of the battle. He did not hear the bullets whistling from every side, or the projectiles flying over his head, did not see the enemy on the other side of the river, and it was a long time before he saw the dead and wounded, though many fell not far from him. With a smile that did not leave his lips he gazed about him.

'What's that fellow doing in front of the line ?' somebody shouted at him again.

'To the left !' ... 'Keep to the right !' the men called to him.

Pierre went to the right and unexpectedly encountered one of General Raevksy's adjutants whom he knew. The adjutant looked furiously at him, evidently also intending to shout at him, but recognizing him he nodded.

'How did you come here ?' he said, and galloped on.

Feeling out of place and useless there, and afraid of getting in the way again, Pierre galloped after the adjutant.

'What's happening here ? May I come with you ?' he asked.

'Just a moment, just a moment !' replied the adjutant, and riding up to a stout colonel who was standing in the meadow he gave him some message, and then turned to Pierre.

'What brings you here, count ?' he asked with a smile. 'Still curious, are you ?'

'Yes, yes,' said Pierre.

But the adjutant wheeled his horse about and rode on.

'Here it's tolerable,' remarked the adjutant, 'but on the left flank where Bagration is they're getting it frightfully hot.'

'Really?' said Pierre. 'Where is that?'

'Come along with me to our knoll. We can get a view from there, and it's not too bad with our battery,' said the adjutant. 'Will you come?'

'After you,' replied Pierre, looking round for his groom.

It was only then for the first time that Pierre noticed the wounded, staggering along or being carried on stretchers. In the very meadow with the rows of fragrant hay through which he had ridden the day before the motionless form of a soldier was lying crosswise, his head thrown awkwardly back and his shako off.

'Why have they left that poor fellow?' Pierre was about to ask, but seeing the adjutant's stern face looking in the same direction he checked himself.

Pierre did not find his groom and rode along the hollow with the adjutant towards Raevsky's Redoubt. His horse lagged behind the adjutant's and jolted him at every step.

'You're not used to riding, count, I fancy?' remarked the adjutant.

'No, it's not that, but her action seems so jerky,' said Pierre in a perplexed tone.

'Why ... she's wounded!' cried the adjutant. 'The off foreleg above the knee. A bullet, no doubt. Congratulations, count, on your baptism of fire!'

Making their way in the smoke past the 6th Corps, behind the artillery which had been moved forward and was keeping up a deafening cannonade, they came to a small wood. There it was cool and quiet and smelt of autumn. Pierre and the adjutant got off their horses and walked up the hill on foot.

'Is the general here?' asked the adjutant, on reaching the redoubt.

'He was here a minute ago – he went that way,' someone answered, pointing to the right.

The adjutant looked round at Pierre as if puzzled to know what to do with him now.

'Don't trouble about me,' said Pierre. 'I'll go up on the mound if I may?'

'Yes, do. You'll see everything from there and it's not so dangerous. And I'll come back for you.'

Pierre went up to the battery and the adjutant rode on. They did not meet again, and only much later did Pierre learn that he lost an arm that day.

The mound – afterwards known to the Russians as the Knoll-battery or Raevsky's Redoubt, and to the French as *la grande redoute, la fatale redoute, la redoute du centre* – was the famous spot around which tens of thousands fell and which the French regarded as the key to the whole position.

This redoubt consisted of a knoll, on three sides of which trenches had been dug. Within the entrenchment stood ten guns which fired through the gaps left in the earthwork.

In line with the knoll cannon were stationed on either side, and these too kept up an incessant fire. A little to the rear of the guns stood the infantry. Climbing the knoll, Pierre had no suspicions that this little space, dug with some not very big trenches and from which a few guns were firing, was the most important point of the battle.

He fancied indeed (simply because he happened to be there) that it was one of the least significant places in the field.

Having reached the knoll, Pierre sat down at one end of a trench which enclosed the battery, and gazed at what was happening around him, with an unconscious smile of happiness. Occasionally he rose to his feet and walked about the battery, still with the same smile, trying not to get in the way of the soldiers who were loading and hauling the guns and continually running past him with bags and charges. The guns of this battery never stopped firing, one after another, with a deafening roar, enveloping the whole neighbourhood in powder-smoke.

In contrast to the painful anxiety felt by the infantry soldiers of the covering force, here in the battery, where a limited number of gunners busy at their work were separated from the rest by a trench, there was a general feeling of eager excitement, a sort of family feeling shared by all alike.

At first the intrusion of Pierre's unmilitary figure in a white hat made an unpleasant impression. The soldiers cast sidelong glances of surprise and even alarm at him as they ran by. The senior artillery-officer, a tall, long-legged, pock-marked man, on the pretence of examining the action of the cannon at the far end, moved over to Pierre and stared at him inquisitively.

A boyish, round-faced little officer, still a mere lad and evidently only just out of the Cadet College, who was very diligently commanding the two guns entrusted to him, addressed Pierre sternly.

'Permit me to ask you to stand aside, sir,' he said. 'You cannot stay here.'

The soldiers shook their heads disapprovingly as they looked at Pierre. But when they satisfied themselves that this man in the white hat was not only doing no harm as he sat quietly on the slope of the trench, or with a shy courteous smile made way for the soldiers, but walked about the battery as calmly as though he were strolling along a boulevard, their feeling of hostile ill-will was gradually transformed into a playful tenderness like the affection soldiers feel for the dogs, cocks, goats and animals in general which share the fortunes of the regiment. The men soon accepted Pierre in their own minds as one of their family, adopted him, gave him a nickname ('our gentleman') and made kindly fun of him among themselves.

A shell tore up the earth a couple of paces from Pierre. Brushing off the dirt which the missile had scattered over his clothes, he glanced around him with a smile.

'How is it you baint feared, sir?' a red-faced, broad-shouldered soldier asked Pierre with a grin that disclosed a set of sound, white teeth.

'Are you afraid, then?' said Pierre.

'What else d'ye expect?' answered the soldier. 'She don't have no mercy, you know. Down she crashes and out fly your guts. A man can't help being feared,' he said, laughing.

Several of the soldiers stopped beside Pierre with amused, friendly faces. They somehow had not expected him to talk like anybody else, and the discovery that he did so delighted them.

'It's our job – we're soldiers. But it's a wonderful thing in a gentleman. There's a gentleman for you!'

'To your places!' cried the young officer to the men gathered round Pierre.

The young officer was evidently for the first or perhaps the second time on duty of this kind, and accordingly treated his superiors and the men with extravagant punctilio and formality.

The thunder of cannon and the rattle of musketry was growing fiercer all over the field, particularly on the left where Bagration's flèches were, but from where Pierre was hardly anything could be distinguished for the smoke. Moreover, his whole attention was taken up with watching the little family circle of men shut off from the rest of the world on the battery. His first unconscious delight in the sights and sounds of the battlefield had now given place to another feeling, especially since he had seen that soldier lying alone in the hayfield. Seated on the slope of the earthwork he observed the faces of those around him.

By ten o'clock a score of men had been carried away; a couple of cannon had been disabled and shells fell thicker and faster on the battery, while bullets hummed and whistled from out of the distance. But the men serving the battery did not seem to pay any heed: merry voices and joking were heard on all sides.

'Here's a beauty!' shouted a soldier as a grenade came hissing towards them.

'Not this way, my pretty – try the infantry!' added another with a chuckle as the shell flew across and fell among the ranks of the covering forces.

'Hallo! Bowing to a friend of yours?' laughed a third to a peasant who ducked as a cannon-ball sped past.

A few soldiers collected by the wall of the trench, trying to make out what was happening in front.

'They've drawn the line back, look. They've given way,' said they, pointing across the earthwork.

'Mind your own business,' an old sergeant shouted at them. 'If they've retired it's because there's work for them to do farther back.'

And taking one of the men by the shoulder the sergeant gave him a shove with his knee. They all laughed.

'Serve No. 5! Forward!' rang the command from the other end.

'Now then, a good pull, all together,' chorused the cheerful voices of the men shifting the cannon.

'That one nearly had our gentleman's hat off!' cried the red-faced humorist, showing his teeth and chaffing Pierre. 'Oh, you hussy!' he added reproachfully to a ball which hit a cannon-wheel and carried off a man's leg.

'Now, you foxes there!' laughed another to the militiamen who were creeping in and out among the guns after the wounded man. 'Don't care much for this gruel, do you? Oh, you crows! that pulls you up!' they shouted at the militiamen who stood hesitating before the soldier whose leg had been torn off.

'Oo ... oo ... lad,' they cried, mocking the peasants. 'They don't like it at all, they don't.'

Pierre noticed that every ball that hit the redoubt, every man that fell, increased the general elation.

The gleams of a hidden burning fire flashed like lightning from an approaching thunder-cloud, brighter and brighter, more and more often in the faces of all these men (as though in defiance of what was taking place).

Pierre did not look out at the battlefield and was not concerned to know what was happening there. He was entirely absorbed in the contemplation of that fire which blazed more fiercely with every moment, and which (so he felt) was flaming in his own soul too.

At ten o'clock the infantry that had been in the thickets and along the Kamenka streamlet in front of the battery retreated. From the battery they could be seen running back past it, bearing their wounded on their muskets. A general with his suite came on to the redoubt and after speaking to the colonel and giving Pierre an angry look went away again, having ordered the infantry supports behind the battery to lie down, so as to be less exposed to fire. Immediately after this, from the ranks of the infantry more to the right of the battery came the sound of a drum and shouts of command, and the men with the battery saw the ranks of infantry move forward.

Pierre looked over the breastworks. One face particularly caught his eye, belonging to a pale young officer who was walking backwards, letting his sword hang down and looking uneasily around.

The ranks of the infantry disappeared in the smoke but prolonged cheering and rapid musketry fire could still be heard. A few minutes later multitudes of wounded men and stretcher-bearers came back from that direction. Faster and faster the shells rained down on the battery. A number of casualties lay about unattended. The men round the cannon bustled more busily than ever. No one paid any attention to Pierre now. Once or twice he was furiously shouted at for being in the way. The senior officer strode with long swift steps from gun to gun, a scowl on his face. The officer-lad, his cheeks still more flushed, gave the men their orders more punctiliously than ever. The soldiers handed up the charges, turned, loaded and performed their work with strained smartness, giving little jumps as they walked, as though they were on springs.

The storm-cloud was close overhead, and the fire which Pierre had watched kindling flashed in every face. He was standing beside the commanding officer. The young little lieutenant, his hand to his shako, ran up to his superior.

'I have the honour to report, sir, that only eight rounds are left. Are we to continue firing?' he asked.

'Grapeshot!' the senior officer cried, looking over the wall of the trench without answering.

Suddenly something happened: the young officer gave a gasp and bending double collapsed sitting on the ground, like a bird shot on the wing. Everything went strange, confused and overcast before Pierre's eyes.

Cannon-ball after cannon-ball whistled by, striking the earthwork, the soldiers or a gun. Pierre, who had scarcely heard these sounds before, could now hear nothing else. On the right of the battery soldiers shouting 'Hurrah!' were running, not forward, it seemed to Pierre, but back.

A cannon-ball struck the very edge of the breastwork by which he was standing, sending earth flying; a black ball flashed before his eyes and at the same instant smacked into something. Some militiamen who were entering the battery ran back.

'All with grapeshot!' shouted the officer.

The sergeant hurried up to the officer and in a frightened whisper (like a butler informing his master at a dinner-party that there is no more of the wine he asked for), said that the charges were finished.

'The scoundrels! What are they about?' fulminated the officer, turning to Pierre.

The officer was perspiring and red in the face and his eyes glittered beneath the frowning brow.

'Run to the reserves and bring up the ammunition-boxes!' he yelled, angrily avoiding Pierre with his eyes and addressing the soldier.

'I'll go,' said Pierre.

Making no reply, the officer strode across to the other side.

'Cease firing. ... Wait!' he bellowed.

The man who had been ordered to go for ammunition stumbled against Pierre.

'Ah, sir, it's no place for you here,' he said, and ran down the slope.

Pierre hastened after him, steering away from the spot where the young officer was sitting.

One cannon-ball, a second and a third flew over him, hitting the ground in front, beside and behind him. Pierre ran down the slope.

'Where am I going?' he suddenly wondered just as he came up to the green ammunition-boxes. He halted irresolutely, uncertain whether to return or go on. Suddenly a fearful concussion flung him backwards to the ground. At the same instant he was dazzled by a great flash of flame, and a deafening roar, a hiss and crash set his ears ringing.

When he came to himself he was sitting on the ground leaning on his hands; the ammunition-box which had been beside him was gone – only a few charred green boards and rags littered the scorched grass – and a horse, dragging fragments of its shafts, galloped past, while another horse was lying, like Pierre, on the ground and screaming long and piercingly.

32

BESIDE himself with terror, Pierre jumped up and ran back to the battery as to the one refuge from the horrors encompassing him.

As he entered the earthwork he noticed that there was no sound of firing from the battery but that men were doing something there. He had no time to make out who these men were. He saw the senior officer leaning over the breastwork with his back to him, as if he were examining something below and that one of the soldiers he had remarked before was struggling to tear free from some men who had got him by the arm, and crying 'Help! Help!' He also saw something else that was strange.

But he had not time to realize that the colonel had been killed, that the soldier shouting 'Help!' was a prisoner, and that another man had been bayoneted in the back before his eyes, for hardly had he set foot in the redoubt when a lean, sallow-faced, perspiring man in a blue uniform rushed on him sword in hand, shouting something. Instinctively guarding against the shock – as they had been running full tilt against each other without seeing – Pierre put out his hands and clutched the man (it was a French officer) by the shoulder with one hand and by the throat with the other. The officer, dropping his sword, seized Pierre by the collar.

For several seconds they gazed with startled eyes at one another's unfamiliar-looking faces, and both were bewildered at what they had done and what they were to do next. 'Am I taken prisoner or am I taking him prisoner?' each of them was wondering. But evidently the French officer was more inclined to believe that he had been taken prisoner because Pierre's powerful hand, impelled by instinctive fear, was tightening its grip on his throat. The Frenchman was about to say something when just above their heads a cannon-ball whistled, terrible and low, and it seemed to Pierre that the Frenchman's head had been torn off, so swiftly had he ducked it.

Pierre also ducked his head and let go with his hands. Giving no further thought to the question who had taken whom prisoner, the Frenchman ran back to the battery, while Pierre dashed downhill, stumbling over the dead and wounded, who it seemed to him were catching at his feet. But before he reached the foot of the knoll he was met by a dense crowd of Russian soldiers who, floundering, tripping up and cheering, were rushing in wild merriment towards the battery. (This was the charge for which Yermolov claimed the credit, declaring that it was only his gallantry and good fortune that made such a feat possible – the attack in which he is supposed to have flung on to the redoubt some St George Crosses he had in his pocket, for the first soldiers who got there.)

The French, who had captured the battery, fled. Our men shouting 'Hurrah!' pursued them so far beyond the guns that they were with difficulty called back.

The prisoners were brought down from the battery, among them a wounded French general whom the officers surrounded. Crowds of wounded, both Russians and French (Pierre recognized some of the Russians), walked or crawled or were carried on stretchers from the battery, their faces distorted with agony. Pierre went up on the knoll again where he had spent over an hour, and of that little family circle which had, as it were, adopted him, he found not one. There were many dead whom he did not know but some he recognized. The young officer was still sitting huddled up in a pool of blood at the edge of the earth wall. The red-faced soldier was still twitching convulsively, but they did not carry him away.

Pierre ran down the slope.

'They must surely leave off now. Now they will be horrified at what they have done!' he thought, aimlessly following in the wake of a procession of stretcher-bearers moving from the battlefield.

But behind the veil of smoke the sun still stood high, and in front, and especially on the left around Semeonovsk, a turmoil still seethed in the smoke, and the thunder of cannon and musketry, far from slackening, grew louder and more desperate, like a man who puts all his remaining strength into one final cry.

33

THE principal action of the battle of Borodino was fought on a seven-thousand-foot space between Borodino and Bagration's flèches. (Outside this radius the Russians had made a brief diversion in the middle of the day with Uvarov's cavalry, on the one side, and on the other, beyond Utitsa, there had been the skirmish between Poniatowski and Tuchkov; but these were isolated and relatively trifling episodes in comparison with what took place in the centre of the battlefield.) It was on the open tract of ground visible from both sides, between Borodino and the flèches beside the wood, that the real engagement was fought in the simplest and most artless manner imaginable.

The battle began with a cannonade from both sides of several hundred guns.

Then, when the whole field was shrouded in smoke, two divisions, Dessaix's and Campan's, advanced from the French right, while Murat's troops moved on Borodino from the left. It was about two-thirds of a mile from Bagration's flèches to the Shevardino Redoubt where Napoleon was standing; and nearly a mile and a half, as the crow flies, from Napoleon's post to Borodino, and therefore Napoleon could not see what was happening there, especially as the smoke mingling with the mist entirely hid that part of the plain. The soldiers of Dessaix's division advancing upon the flèches were visible only until they began to descend the ravine which separated them from the earthworks. As soon as they dropped into the hollow the smoke of the guns and musketry on the flèches grew so dense that it curtained off the whole of the farther slope. Now and then it was possible to catch a glimpse through the fog of some black object – probably men – or the glint of bayonets. But whether they were moving or stationary, whether they were French or Russian, was impossible to distinguish from the Shevardino Redoubt.

The sun had risen bright and its slanting rays shone full on Napoleon's face as, shading his eyes with his hand, he looked at the flèches. The smoke hung low before the flèches and sometimes it looked as if the smoke were stirring, at others as if the troops moved. Occasionally shouts were heard through the firing but there was no knowing what was being done there.

Napoleon, standing on the knoll, gazed through a field-glass, and in the tiny circlet of glass saw smoke and men, sometimes his own, sometimes Russians, but when he looked again with the naked eye he could not find what he had been looking at.

He descended the knoll and began to pace up and down in front of it.

Occasionally he paused to listen to the firing and strain his eyes towards the battlefield.

But not only was it impossible to make out what was happening from where he stood down below, or from the knoll above on which some of his generals had taken their stand, but even from the flèches themselves, where Russian and French soldiers now found themselves together or alternately – dead, wounded and alive, frightened or panic-stricken – it was impossible to make out what was taking place. For several hours in succession, amid incessant cannon- and musketry-fire, now only Russians were seen there, now only French, now infantry, now cavalry: they showed themselves, fell, fired, struggled hand to hand, not knowing what to do with one another, shouted and ran back again.

From the battlefield adjutants he had sent out and orderlies from his marshals were continually galloping up to Napoleon with reports of the progress of the action; but all these reports were deceptive, both because in the heat of the fray it was impossible to say what was happening at any given moment, and because many of the adjutants did not go to the actual place of conflict but simply repeated what they had heard from others; and also because while an adjutant was riding the couple of miles to Napoleon circumstances changed and the news he brought was already ceasing to be accurate. Thus an adjutant came galloping up from Murat with tidings that Borodino had been occupied and the bridge over the Kalocha was in the hands of the French. The adjutant asked whether Napoleon wished the troops to cross the bridge. Napoleon gave orders for the troops to form up on the farther side and wait. But before that command was given – almost as soon in fact as the adjutant had left Borodino – the bridge had been retaken by the Russians and burnt, in the very skirmish with which Pierre had got mixed up at the beginning of the day.

Another adjutant rushed up from the flèches with a pale and frightened face and reported to Napoleon that their attack had been repulsed, Campan wounded and Davoust killed; while in fact the entrenchments had been recaptured by other French troops (at the very time when the adjutant was told that the French had been driven back), and Davoust was alive and well except for slight bruising. On the basis of such inevitably untrustworthy reports Napoleon gave his orders, which had either been executed before he gave them, or else could not be, and never were, executed.

The marshals and generals who were closer to the scene of action but, like Napoleon, not actually taking part in the fighting and only occasionally went within bullet range made their own dispositions without referring to Napoleon, and themselves directed from where and in what direction to fire, and decided where the cavalry should gallop and the infantry should run. But even their orders, like Napoleon's, were seldom carried out, and then only partially. For the most part the opposite happened to what they enjoined. Soldiers ordered to advance fell back on meeting grape-shot; soldiers ordered to remain where they were, suddenly seeing an unexpected body of the enemy before them, would either turn tail or rush forward, and the cavalry dashed unbidden in pursuit of the flying Russians. In this way two cavalry regiments galloped through the Semeonovsk hollow and as soon as they reached the top of the incline faced about and bolted headlong back again. The infantry likewise often went flying about in directions quite contrary to those they had been told to take. All decisions as to where and when to bring up the guns, when to send infantry to fire or horsemen to ride down the Russian infantry – all such decisions were made by the officers on the spot nearest to the units concerned, without consulting Ney, Davoust or Murat, much less Napoleon. They had no fear of getting into trouble for not fulfilling orders or for acting on their own initiative, for in battle the issue at stake is man's most precious possession – his own life – and it sometimes seems that safety lies in running back, sometimes in running forward, and these men who were right in the thick of the fray acted in accordance with the temper of the moment. In reality, however, all these movements back and forth did not improve or affect the position of the troops. All their onslaughts on one another did little harm: the harm, the death and disablement was the work of the cannon-balls and bullets that were flying all about the open space where these men were floundering to and fro. As soon as they got out of range of the shot and the shell their superior officers located in the background promptly restored order and discipline, and under the influence of that discipline led them back to the zone of fire, where order fell victim to terror of death and a blind stampede in all directions.

34

NAPOLEON's generals – Davoust, Ney and Murat, who were near that region of fire and sometimes even entered it – more than once led huge masses of orderly troops that way. But, contrary to what had invariably happened in all their former battles, instead of the news they expected of the enemy's flight, these disciplined masses returned as disorganized, panic-stricken mobs. The generals re-formed them but their number was steadily dwindling. In the middle of the day Murat sent his adjutant to Napoleon to request reinforcements.

Napoleon was sitting at the foot of the knoll, drinking punch, when Murat's adjutant galloped up with the assurance that the Russians would be routed if his Majesty would let them have another division.

'Reinforcements?' exclaimed Napoleon in grim amazement, staring, as though failing to comprehend his words, at the handsome boyish adjutant who wore his black hair in floating curls (like Murat). 'Reinforcements,' thought Napoleon to himself. 'How can they require reinforcements when they already have half the army concentrated against one weak, unentrenched Russian wing?'

'Tell the King of Naples,' said Napoleon sternly, 'that it is not noon yet, and I do not yet see my chess-board clearly. Go. ....'

The handsome young adjutant with the long hair sighed deeply, without removing his hand from his hat, and galloped back to the slaughter.

Napoleon got up and, summoning Caulaincourt and Berthier, began talking to them about matters unconnected with the battle.

In the midst of this conversation, which was beginning to interest Napoleon, Berthier's eyes were attracted to a general who was galloping towards the knoll on a lathering horse, followed by his suite. It was Belliard. Dismounting, he strode rapidly up to the Emperor and boldly, in a loud voice, started to explain the absolute necessity of reinforcements. He swore on his honour that the Russians were lost if the Emperor would release one more division.

Napoleon shrugged his shoulders and continued to pace up and down without answering. Belliard began to talk noisily and vehemently to the generals of the suite gathered round him.

'You are very fiery, Belliard,' said Napoleon, turning to the general again. 'It is easy to make a mistake in the heat of the battle. Go and have another look and then come back to me.'

Belliard had hardly disappeared before a fresh messenger from another part of the field galloped up.

'Well, what is it now?' asked Napoleon in the tone of a man irritated at being continually disturbed.

'*Sire, le Prince ...*' began the adjutant.

'Wants reinforcements?' said Napoleon with an angry gesture.

The adjutant bowed his head affirmatively and began to deliver his report, but the Emperor turned from him, took a couple of steps, stopped, came back and beckoned to Berthier.

'We must give them the reserves,' he said, with a slight upward gesture of his hands. 'Who do you think should go?' he asked of Berthier ('that gosling I hatched into an eagle,' as he called him afterwards).

'Sire, send Claparède's division,' replied Berthier, who knew all the divisions, regiments and battalions by heart.

Napoleon nodded assent.

The adjutant galloped off to Claparède's division, and a few minutes later the Young Guards, who were drawn up behind the knoll, moved forward. Napoleon watched in silence.

'No!' he cried suddenly to Berthier. 'I can't send Claparède. Send Friant's division.'

Though there was no advantage of any kind in dispatching Friant's division rather than Claparède's, and even obvious inconvenience and delay now in recalling Claparède and sending Friant, the order was carried out to the letter. Napoleon did not observe that in relation to his army he played the part of the doctor, whose action in hindering the course of nature with his nostrums he so truly gauged and condemned.

Friant's division vanished like the rest into the smoke of the battle-field. From every side adjutants continued to arrive at a gallop, all with the same story to tell, as if they had conspired beforehand. They all asked for reinforcements, declaring that the Russians were standing firm and maintaining a hellish fire under which the French troops were melting away.

Napoleon sat on a camp-stool deep in thought.

Monsieur de Beausset, who was so fond of travelling and had eaten nothing that morning, came up to the Emperor and respectfully ventured to suggest lunch to his Majesty.

'I hope I may already congratulate your Majesty on a victory?' he said.

Napoleon shook his head. Monsieur de Beausset, supposing the negative referred to the assumed victory and not to lunch, took the liberty of remarking, in a half-jesting tone, that there could be no mortal reason for not having lunch when lunch was available.

'Go away ...' Napoleon jerked out morosely, and turned his back on him.

An Olympian smile of pity, regret and unction beamed on Monsieur de Beausset's face, and he glided away to the other generals.

Napoleon was in the grip of the depression which descends on the gambler who, after a long run of luck during which he recklessly flung his money about and won every time, suddenly finds, just when he has carefully calculated all the chances of the game, that the more he considers his play the more surely he loses.

His troops were the same, his generals the same, there had been the same preparations, the same dispositions, the same proclamation *court et énergique*, he himself was the same – he knew that and knew that he was vastly more experienced and skilful even than he had been before. The enemy too was the same as at Austerlitz and Friedland – yet the crushing weight of his arm fell impotent as though spellbound.

All the old methods that had invariably been crowned with success had already been employed. Today as usual he had concentrated his batteries on a single point, had thrown forward his reserves to break the enemy's line, had ordered a cavalry attack by 'the men of iron'; yet not only was there no victory but from all sides poured in the same tidings of generals killed and wounded, of reinforcements needed, of the impossibility of beating back the Russians, and of the disarray of his own troops.

Hitherto, after he had given two or three orders and uttered a couple of sentences, marshals and adjutants had come galloping up with congratulations and happy faces, announcing trophies in the shape of the capture of whole corps of prisoners, of sheaves of enemy eagles and standards, of cannon and stores, and Murat had begged leave only to loose the cavalry to gather in the baggage-trains. Thus it had been at Lodi, Marengo, Arcola, Jena, Austerlitz, Wagram and so on, and so on. But now something strange was happening to his armies.

Notwithstanding news of the capture of the flèches, Napoleon saw that things were not going the same way – not at all the same way – as they had in his other battles. He saw too that what he was feeling all the men about him, with their military experience, were feeling too. There was gloom on every face: each man avoided his neighbour's eye. Only a de Beausset could fail to grasp the import of what was happening. Napoleon, of course, with his extensive knowledge of war, well knew what it meant for the attacking side still not to be in sight of victory after straining every effort for eight hours on end. He knew that this was equivalent to defeat and that the least accident might now – at the critical point the battle had reached – involve him and his army in ruin.

When he ran his mind from the beginning over this strange Russian campaign, in which not a single victory had been won, in which not a flag, nor a cannon, nor an army corps had been captured in two months; when he looked at the underlying dejection in the faces round him and listened to reports of the Russians still holding their ground – a terrible nightmare feeling seized him, and all the ill-starred eventualities occurred to him that might seal his doom. The Russians might fall on his left wing, might break through his centre; he himself might be killed by a stray cannon-ball. All this was possible. In former battles he had only considered the chances of success, but now an infinite number of possible disasters presented themselves and he expected them all. Yes, it was like a dream in which a man imagines a murderer advancing to attack him. He raises his arm to strike his assailant a terrible blow which he knows should demolish him, and then feels his arm drop powerless and limp as a rag, and the horror of inevitable annihilation seizes him in his helplessness.

The news that the Russians were attacking the left flank of the French army filled Napoleon with just such horror. He sat in silence on a camp-stool below the knoll, with bowed head and elbows on his knees. Berthier approached and suggested that they should ride along the line to ascertain the position of affairs.

'What? What did you say?' asked Napoleon. 'Yes, tell them to bring my horse.'

He mounted and rode towards Semeonovsk.

In the slowly dispersing powder-smoke, over the whole plain through which Napoleon rode, horses and men were lying in pools of blood, singly or in heaps. Neither Napoleon nor any of his generals had ever before seen such a frightful sight or so many slain in so small an area. The roar of guns, that had not ceased for ten hours, wearied the ear and gave a peculiar character to the spectacle (like music accompanying *tableaux vivants*). Napoleon rode up to the high ground at Semeonovsk and through the haze he saw ranks of soldiers in uniforms of unfamiliar hues. They were the Russians.

The Russians stood in serried ranks behind Semeonovsk village and its mound, and their guns thundered unremittingly all along the line, filling the air with smoke. It was no longer a battle: it was a prolonged massacre, equally fruitless to the French and the Russians. Napoleon reined in his horse, and again sank into that brown study from which Berthier had roused him. He could not stop what was going on before and around him, and which he was supposed to be directing and which was apparently dependent on him, and for the first time, because of its ill success, the thing struck him as unnecessary and horrible.

One of the generals riding up to Napoleon ventured to offer to lead the Old Guard into action. Ney and Berthier, standing near Napoleon, exchanged looks and smiled contemptuously at so preposterous a suggestion.

Napoleon let his head sink on his breast and was long silent.

'At eight hundred leagues from France I am not going to have my Guard destroyed!' he said, and turning his horse, rode back to Shevardino.

35

KUTUZOV, his grey head bent and his heavy body slumped, was sitting on the same rug-covered bench where Pierre had seen him that morning. He issued no orders but simply gave or withheld his assent to what was proposed to him.

'Yes, yes, do so,' he would answer to the various proposals. 'Yes, yes, my dear boy, go and have a look,' he would say to this one or that of those about him; or, 'No, better not – better wait a little.' He listened to the dispatches that were brought him, and gave directions when his subordinates demanded that of him; but when listening to the dispatches he did not seem to be interested in the import of the words spoken but rather in something else – in the expression of the face and the tone of voice of those who were reporting. Long experience in war had taught him, and the wisdom of age had made him realize, that it was impossible for one man to direct hundreds of thousands of others waging a struggle with death, and he knew that the outcome of a battle is determined not by the dispositions of the commander-in-chief, nor the place where the troops are stationed, nor the number of cannon or the multitude of the slain, but by that intangible force called the spirit of the army, and he kept an eye on that force and guided it as far as lay within his power.

Kutuzov's general expression was one of concentrated, quiet attention. His face wore a strained look as if he found it difficult to master the fatigue suffered by his old and feeble frame.

At eleven o'clock they brought him news that the flèches captured by the French had been retaken but that Prince Bagration was wounded. Kutuzov groaned and shook his head.

'Ride over to Prince Bagration and find out the details,' he said to one of the adjutants, and then turned to the Duke of Württemberg, who was standing behind him.

'Would your Highness please take command of the 2nd Army?'

Soon after the duke's departure – before he could possibly have reached Semeonovsk – his adjutant came back with a message from him asking Kutuzov for more troops.

Kutuzov frowned and sent an order to Dokhturov to take over command of the 2nd Army, and a request to the duke – whom he said he could not spare at such a moment – to return to him. When news was brought that Murat had been taken prisoner, and the staff-officers congratulated him, Kutuzov smiled.

'Wait a little, gentlemen,' said he. 'The battle is ours, and there is nothing extraordinary in the capture of Murat. Still, we must not crow too soon.'

Nevertheless, he sent an adjutant to make the fact known to the troops.

When Shcherbinin came spurring up from the left flank with the report that the French had got possession of the flèches and the village of Semeonovsk, Kutuzov, judging by the sounds on the battlefield and by the look on Shcherbinin's face that he brought bad news, got up as though to stretch his legs and, taking Shcherbinin by the arm, led him to one side.

'Go, my dear fellow,' he said to Yermolov, 'and see whether something can't be done.'

Kutuzov was in Gorky, the centre of the Russian position. The assault directed by Napoleon against our left flank had been several times repulsed. In the centre the French had not got beyond Borodino, and on their left flank Uvarov's cavalry had put the enemy to flight.

Towards three o'clock the French attacks ceased. On the faces of all who came from the field of battle, and of those who stood around him, Kutuzov read an expression of extreme tension. He was satisfied with the day's success – a success exceeding his expectation – but the old man's strength was failing him. Several times his head sank forward, as though falling, and he dozed off. They brought him some dinner.

Adjutant-General Wolzogen, the man whom Prince Andrei had overheard saying the war 'must be extended over a wider area' as he rode by, and whom Bagration so detested, rode up while Kutuzov was at dinner. Wolzogen had come from Barclay de Tolly to report on the progress of affairs on the left flank. The sagacious Barclay de Tolly, seeing crowds of wounded men running back, and the rear ranks of the army in disorder, weighed all the circumstances, concluded that the battle was lost and sent his favourite officer to the commander-in-chief with this news.

Kutuzov was laboriously chewing roast chicken and he looked up at Wolzogen with narrowed, twinkling eyes.

Wolzogen, nonchalantly stretching his legs, approached Kutuzov with a half-contemptuous smile on his lips, scarcely touching the peak of his cap.

He behaved to his Serene Highness with a certain affectation of indifference intended to show that as a highly trained military man he left it to the Russians to make an idol of this useless old dotard but that *he* knew whom he was dealing with. '*Der alte Herr*' (the Germans among themselves always spoke of Kutuzov as 'the old gentleman') 'is taking things very easy,' thought Wolzogen, and glancing severely at the dishes set in front of Kutuzov he proceeded to report to 'the old gentleman' the position of affairs on the left flank as Barclay had told him to and as he himself had seen and interpreted it.

'All the points of our position are in the enemy's hands and they cannot be driven back because there are not the troops to do it; the men are running away and it is impossible to stop them,' he submitted.

Kutuzov ceased chewing and stared at Wolzogen in amazement, as though not comprehending what was said to him. Wolzogen, observing the effect produced on *der alte Herr*, said with a smile:

'I do not consider I should be justified in concealing from your Highness what I have seen. ... The troops are completely routed. ...'

'You have seen? You have seen? ...' shouted Kutuzov with a fierce frown, and rising quickly to his feet he went up to Wolzogen.

'How ... how dare you! ...' he shouted, choking and making a threatening gesture with his trembling arms. 'How dare you, sir, say that to *me*? You know nothing about it. Tell General Barclay from me that his information is incorrect and that the real course of the battle is better known to me, the commander-in-chief, than to him.'

Wolzogen was about to make a rejoinder but Kutuzov interrupted him.

'The enemy has been repulsed on the left and defeated on the right flank. If you have seen amiss, sir, do not allow yourself to speak of what you do not know. Be so good as to return to General Barclay and inform him of my fixed intention to attack the enemy tomorrow,' said Kutuzov sternly.

All were silent and the only sound was the heavy breathing of the panting old commander-in-chief.

'They are repulsed everywhere, for which I thank God and our brave army. The enemy is defeated and tomorrow we shall drive him from the sacred soil of Russia,' said Kutuzov, crossing himself, and he suddenly ended with a sob as his eyes filled with tears.

Wolzogen, shrugging his shoulders and curling his lips, walked away in silence, marvelling at 'the old gentleman's conceited stupidity'.

'Ah, here he is, my hero!' said Kutuzov to a portly, handsome, black-haired general who at this moment approached the knoll.

This was Raevsky, who had spent the whole day at the most critical part of the field of Borodino.

Raevsky reported that the troops were standing their ground firmly and that the French were not venturing a further attack.

After hearing him, Kutuzov said in French:

'Then you do not think *like some others* that we must retreat?'

'On the contrary, your Highness, where the issue is undecided it is always the most stubborn who come out victorious,' replied Raevsky, 'and in my opinion ...'

'Kaisarov!' Kutuzov called to his adjutant. 'Sit down and write out the order of the day for tomorrow. And you,' he turned to another, 'ride along the line and announce that tomorrow we attack.'

While Kutuzov was talking to Raevksy and dictating the order of the day, Wolzogen returned from Barclay and announced that General Barclay de Tolly would be glad to have written confirmation of the order the field-marshal had given.

Kutuzov, without looking at Wolzogen, gave directions for the order to be written out which the former commander-in-chief very prudently desired to have to relieve himself of all responsibility.

And through the mysterious indefinable bond which maintains throughout an army one and the same temper, known as 'the spirit of the troops', and which constitutes the chief sinew of war, Kutuzov's words, his order for renewing the battle on the following day, immediately became known from one end of the army to the other.

The words – the exact form of the order – were by no means the same when they reached the farthest links in the chain. In fact there was not a syllable in the accounts passing from mouth to mouth at different ends of the lines that resembled what Kutuzov had actually said; but the drift of his words spread everywhere because what he had said was not the result of shrewd calculations but the outflow of a feeling that lay deep in the heart of the commander-in-chief and deep in the heart of every Russian.

And when they were told that tomorrow they were to attack the enemy, and from the highest quarters heard confirmation of what they wanted to believe, the exhausted, wavering men took comfort and courage again.

36

PRINCE ANDREI'S regiment was among the reserves which until after one o'clock were stationed inactive behind Semeonovsk, under heavy artillery fire. Towards two o'clock the regiment, having already lost more than two hundred men, was moved forward into a trampled oat-field in the gap between Semeonovsk and the Knoll-battery where thousands of men perished that day and on which an intense, concentrated fire from several hundred enemy guns was directed between one and two o'clock.

Without stirring an inch or firing a shot the regiment here lost another third of its effectives. In front, and especially on the right, the guns boomed amid perpetual smoke, and out of that mysterious domain of smoke which shrouded the whole space in front swift hissing cannon-balls and slow whistling shells flew unceasingly. Now and then, as if to allow them a respite, a quarter of an hour would pass during which the cannon-balls and shells all flew overhead, but at other times several men would be torn from the regiment in the course of a single minute, and the slain were continually being dragged away and the wounded carried off.

Each new explosion diminished the chances of life for the survivors. The regiment was drawn up in battalion-columns three hundred paces apart but, in spite of that, one and the same mood prevailed everywhere. All alike were taciturn and morose. At rare intervals talk was heard in the ranks but it was hushed at each thud of a successful shot followed by the cry of 'Stretchers!' Most of the time, by their officers' orders, the men sat on the ground. One, taking off his shako, carefully loosened the gathers of the lining and drew them tight again; another, crumbling some dry clay in his hands, polished his bayonet; another fingered the strap and altered the buckle of his bandolier; while still another carefully smoothed and rewound his leg-bands and pulled his boots on again. Some built little houses of the clods of the ploughed field, or plaited straws of stubble. All seemed entirely absorbed in their occupations. When anyone was killed or wounded, when the stretchers trailed by, when our troops were forced back, when the smoke opened a little and disclosed great masses of the enemy, no one paid any attention to these circumstances. But when our artillery or cavalry advanced, or some of our infantry were seen to move forward, approving remarks were heard on all sides. But quite extraneous incidents that had nothing to do with the battle were what attracted most notice; as though the minds of these mortally exhausted men found relief in the ordinary trifles of everyday life. A battery of artillery passed in front of the regiment. One of the horses of an ammunition-cart put its leg over a trace. 'Hey, look at that trace-horse! ... Get her leg out! She'll be down. ... Hey, haven't they any eyes?' Such were the comments shouted all along the line. Another time general attention was attracted by a small brown dog, come from heaven knows where, which trotted busily in front of the ranks with tail stiffly erect, till suddenly a shell fell close by, when it squealed and dashed away with its tail between its legs. Yells and shrieks of laughter rang out from the whole regiment. But distractions of this kind did not last more than a moment, and for eight hours the men had been without food or occupation, in constant fear of death, and their pale and haggard faces grew paler and more haggard.

Prince Andrei, pale and haggard like everyone else in the regiment, paced to and fro in the meadow next to the oat-field from one boundary-line to the other, with his hands clasped behind his back and his eyes fixed on the ground. There was nothing for him to do and no orders to be given. Everything was done of itself. The slain were dragged behind the line, the wounded carried away and the ranks closed up. If any soldiers ran to the rear they made haste to return at once. At first Prince Andrei, thinking it his duty to keep up the spirits of his men and to set them an example, had walked about among the ranks, but he soon became convinced that this was unnecessary and that there was nothing they could learn from him. All his energies, like those of every soldier, were unconsciously bent on keeping his mind off the horrors of their situation. He wandered about the meadow, dragging his feet, making the grass rustle, and contemplating the dust which covered his boots. Then he strode along trying to step in the tracks left by the mowers when they had scythed the meadow; or, counting his steps, calculated how many times he would have to walk from one boundary to another to make a mile; or he would strip the flowers from the wormwood that grew along the edge of the field, rub them in his palms and sniff their bittersweet, pungent scent. Nothing remained of the fabric of thought which he had so painfully elaborated the day before. He thought of nothing at all. He listened with weary ears to the ever-repeating sounds, distinguishing the whistle of flying projectiles from the booming of cannon-shot, looked from time to time at the faces of the men of the first battalion which he had looked at over and over again, and waited. 'Here it comes ... this one's coming our way again!' he would say to himself as he listened to the approaching screech of something flying out of that smoke-hidden realm. 'One! Another! More still! That one's down. ...' He paused and looked along the ranks. 'No, it's gone over. But that one struck!' and once more he would take to pacing up and down, trying to reach the boundary strip in sixteen strides.

A whizz and a thud! Five paces from him a cannon-ball tore up the dry soil and disappeared into the earth. A chill ran down his back. Again he glanced at the ranks. Probably a number of men had been hit – a large crowd had collected near the second battalion.

'Adjutant!' he shouted. 'Tell those men not to stand so close together.'

The adjutant, having obeyed the instruction, approached Prince Andrei. From the other side a battalion commander rode up on horseback.

'Look out!' cried a soldier in a terrified voice, and like a bird dropping to the ground with a swift whirr of wings a shell plopped down with a dull thud within a couple of yards from Prince Andrei and close to the battalion-commander's horse. The horse, heedless of whether it were right or wrong to manifest fear, snorted, reared and, almost unseating the major, galloped off. The horse's terror infected the men.

'Lie down!' yelled the adjutant, throwing himself flat on the ground.

Prince Andrei hesitated. The smoking shell spun like a top between him and the prostrate adjutant, near a clump of wormwood between the ploughed land and the meadow.

'Can this be death?' Prince Andrei wondered, casting a fleeting glance of quite unwonted envy at the grass, the wormwood and the thread of smoke that curled upward from the whistling black ball. 'I can't die, I don't want to die. I love life – I love this grass, this earth, this air. ...' These were the thoughts in his mind, and at the same time he remembered that people were looking at him.

'For shame, sir!' he said to the adjutant. 'What sort of ...'

He did not finish. Simultaneously there was an explosion, a splintering sound like a window-frame being smashed, a suffocating smell of powder, and Prince Andrei was jerked to one side and, flinging up his arm, fell on his face.

Several officers ran up to him. Blood was welling out from the right side of his abdomen, making a great stain on the grass.

The militiamen were called with the stretchers and stood behind the officers. Prince Andrei lay on his chest with his face in the grass, gasping painfully.

'Well, what are you waiting for? Come along!'

The peasants came close and took him by the shoulders and legs but he groaned piteously and the men, exchanging looks, set him down again.

'Pick him up, up with him, it must be done!' cried someone.

They lifted him by the shoulders again and laid him on the stretcher.

'Ah, my God, my God! –'

'What is it?' – 'In the belly? That means it's all over with him then!' – voices among the officers were heard saying.

'It practically grazed my ear,' said the adjutant.

The peasants, adjusting the stretcher to their shoulders, hastily directed their steps along the path they had trodden to the dressing-station.

'Keep in step! ... Ah! ... these peasants!' cried an officer, putting a hand on their shoulders and checking them as they jogged unevenly along, jolting the stretcher.

'In step there, Fiodr, can't you! Hey, Fiodr!' said the foremost peasant.

'That's got it!' said the one behind cheerfully when he had fallen into step.

'Your Excellency! Prince – Prince!' said the trembling voice of Timohin, who had run up and was looking down on the stretcher.

Prince Andrei opened his eyes and looked up at the speaker from the depths of the stretcher where his head had sunk back, and closed his eyelids again.

The militiamen carried Prince Andrei to the dressing-station by the wood, where the vans waited. The ambulance-station consisted of three tents with flaps turned back, pitched at the edge of the birch-grove. In the wood stood the ambulance-vans and horses. The horses were munching their oats from portable troughs and the sparrows flew down and pecked the scattered grains. Some crows, scenting blood, flew about among the birch-trees, cawing impatiently. All round the tents, over an area of more than five acres, blood-stained men variously attired stood, sat or lay. Crowds of stretcher-bearers, staring with dejected faces, hung about the wounded: the officers in charge kept trying to drive them away but to no avail. Deaf to the commands of their officers, the soldiers stood leaning against their stretchers and gazed steadily, as though trying to grasp the meaning of the terrible spectacle before their eyes. From the tents came the sound of loud, angry wailing mingled with plaintive moans. At intervals dressers ran out for water or to point out those who were to be brought in next. The wounded waiting their turn outside the tents groaned, sighed, wept, screamed, swore or begged for vodka. Some were delirious. Prince Andrei's bearers, stepping over the crowd of wounded who had not yet been seen to, carried him, as a regimental commander, close to one of the tents, where they halted, awaiting instructions. Prince Andrei opened his eyes and for a long while could not make out what was going on around him. He remembered the meadow, the wormwood, the ploughed field, the black whirling ball and his sudden passionate upsurge of love of life. A couple of steps from him stood a tall, handsome, black-haired non-commissioned officer with a bandaged head, leaning against a branch. He had bullet-wounds in the head and leg, and was talking loudly, attracting general attention. A crowd of wounded men and stretcher-bearers had gathered round him in an eager audience.

'We gave him such a dose of it that he chucked everything and we grabbed the king himself!' cried this sergeant, looking about him with feverishly glittering black eyes. 'If only them reserves 'ad come up right, lads, there wouldn't 'ave been a smell of him left, for I can tell you. ...'

Like all the others near the speaker. Prince Andrei gazed at him with bright eyes and felt a sense of comfort. 'But isn't it all the same now ?' he thought. 'And what will it be like there, and what has there been here ? What made me so reluctant to part with life ? There was something in this life I did not and don't understand.'

37

ONE of the doctors came out of the tent in a blood-soaked apron, holding a cigar between the thumb and little finger of one of his blood-stained hands, so as not to besmear it. He threw his head back and looked about him, but beyond the wounded men. He evidently wanted a short respite. After turning his head this way and that, he sighed and looked down.

'All right, come along,' he said in reply to a dresser who called his attention to Prince Andrei, and he told them to carry him into the tent.

Murmurs arose among the wounded who were waiting.

'The quality only, it seems, in the next world too,' remarked one.

Prince Andrei was carried in and laid on a table that had only just been cleared, and which a dresser was washing down. He could not make out distinctly what was in the tent. The pitiful groans on all sides and the agonizing pain in his thigh and stomach distracted him. Everything he saw about him merged into a single general impression of naked, bleeding human bodies which seemed to fill the whole of the low tent, just as a few weeks before, on that hot August day, bodies had filled the dirty pond beside the Smolensk road. Yes, it was the same flesh, the same *chair à canon*, the sight of which had excited in him then a sort of horror prophetic of what he felt now.

There were three operating-tables in the tent. Two were occupied, on the third they had placed Prince Andrei. For a little while he was left alone, an involuntary witness of what was being done at the other tables. On the nearest one sat a Tartar, probably a Cossack judging by the uniform thrown down beside him. Four soldiers were holding him while a doctor in spectacles was cutting into his muscular brown back. 'Ugh, ugh, ugh!' grunted the Tartar, and suddenly lifting his swarthy, snub-nosed face with its high cheek-bones, and baring his white teeth, he began to wriggle and twitch his body, and set up a long, shrill, piercing screech. The other table was surrounded with people. A big stout man was stretched upon it, his head thrown back, and there was something strangely familiar to Prince Andrei in the curly hair, its colour and the shape of the head. Several dressers were pressing on his chest to hold him down. One large white plump leg kept twitching with a regular spasmodic jerk. The man was sobbing and choking convulsively. Two surgeons – one of whom was pale and trembling – were silently doing something to the man's other gory leg. When he had finished with the Tartar, over whom a great-coat was thrown, the spectacled doctor came across to Prince Andrei, wiping his hands.

He glanced at Prince Andrei's face and quickly turned away.

'Get his clothes off! What are you waiting for?' he cried angrily to the dressers.

His earliest, most distant childhood came back to Prince Andrei when the dresser with sleeves rolled up began hastily unbuttoning and taking off his clothes. The doctor bent close over the wound, probed it and sighed deeply. Then he made a sign to someone, and the ex-cruciating pain in his abdomen made Prince Andrei lose consciousness. When he came to himself the splintered portions of his thigh-bone had been extracted, the torn flesh cut away and the wound bandaged. Water was being sprinkled on his face. As soon as Prince Andrei opened his eyes the doctor bent down, kissed him on the lips without a word and hurried away.

After the agony he had borne Prince Andrei was conscious of a well-being such as he had not experienced for a long time. His imagination reverted to all the best and happiest moments of his life, especially his earliest childhood when he used to be undressed and put to bed, when his nurse had sung lullabies over him, and burying his head in the pillows he had felt happy in the mere feeling of being alive. All this rose to his mind, not like the past even, but as though it were the actual present.

The doctors were busily engaged with the wounded man, the shape of whose head had seemed familiar to Prince Andrei: they were lifting him up and trying to quiet him.

'Show it to me ... Oh, ooh ... ooooh!' his frightened moans could be heard, abject with suffering and broken by sobs.

Hearing those groans, Prince Andrei wanted to weep. Whether because he was dying a death without glory, or because he was sorry to part with life, or because of those memories of a childhood that could never return, or because he was in pain and others were in pain and that man near him was moaning so piteously – at any rate he felt like weeping childlike, good, almost happy tears.

The wounded man was shown his amputated leg stained with clotted blood and with the boot still on.

'Oh! O-oo-h!' he sobbed like a woman.

The doctor who had been standing beside him, in the way of his face being seen, moved aside.

'My God! What is this? Why is he here?' said Prince Andrei to himself.

In the miserable, sobbing, shattered creature whose leg had just been amputated he recognized Anatole Kuragin. It was Anatole they were supporting in their arms and offering a glass of water but his trembling, swollen lips could not grasp the rim. Anatole drew a sobbing, convulsive breath. 'Yes, it is he! Yes, that man is somehow closely and painfully connected with me,' thought Prince Andrei, not yet quite taking in what he was looking at. 'What is that man's connexion with my childhood, with my life?' he asked himself, and could not find the answer. And all at once a new unexpected recollection from that childlike world of purity and love presented itself to Prince Andrei. He remembered Natasha as he had seen her for the first time at the ball in 1810, with her slender neck and arms, with her timid, happy face prepared for ecstasy, and his soul awoke to a love and tenderness for her which were stronger and more pulsing with life than they had ever been. Now he remembered the link between himself and this man who was gazing vaguely at him through the tears that filled his swollen eyes. Prince Andrei remembered everything, and a passionate pity and love for this man welled up in his happy heart.

Prince Andrei could no longer restrain himself, and wept tender compassionate tears for his fellow-men, for himself and for their errors and his own.

'Sympathy, love of our brothers, for those who love us and for those who hate us, love of our enemies – yes, the love that God preached on earth, that Princess Maria tried to teach me and I did not understand – that is what made me sorry to part with life, that is what remained for me had I lived. But now it is too late. I know it!'

38

THE fearful spectacle of the battlefield heaped with dead and wounded, in conjunction with the heaviness of his head and the news that some twenty generals he knew personally were among the killed or wounded, and the sense of the impotence of his once mighty arm, produced an unexpected impression on Napoleon, who usually liked to contemplate the killed and wounded, thereby (as he thought) testing his strength of mind. On this day the horrible appearance of the battlefield was too much for this dauntless spirit, which he regarded as the source of his worth and greatness. He hastened away from the scene of action and returned to the Shevardino knoll, where he sat on his camp-stool, his sallow face bloated and downcast, his eyes dim, his nose red and his voice hoarse, looking down and involuntarily listening to the sounds of the firing. In sickly dejection he awaited the end of the business in which he considered himself the prime mover but which he was powerless to arrest. A natural, human sentiment for a brief moment gained the ascendant over the mirage that he had served so long. He felt in his own person the sufferings and death he had seen on the battlefield. The heavy feeling in his head and chest brought home the possibility for him too of agony and death. At that moment he did not desire Moscow, or victory, or glory (what need had he of more glory?). The one thing he wished for was rest, tranquillity and release. But when he had been on the Semeonovsk heights the officer in command of the artillery had proposed to him to bring several batteries up on to that high ground to increase the fire on the Russian troops massed in front of Knyaz-kovo. Napoleon had assented, and given orders that he should be informed of the effect those batteries produced.

An adjutant came now to report that, in obedience to the Emperor's bidding, two hundred guns had been concentrated on the Russians but that they still held their ground.

'Our fire mows them down in rows but they hang on,' said the adjutant.

'They want more! ...' said Napoleon in a husky voice.

'Sire?' asked the adjutant, who had not caught the words.

'They want more!' Napoleon croaked hoarsely, frowning. 'Well, give it them!'

Already, without orders from him, the thing he wanted, and for which he only gave the order because he thought it was expected of him, was being done. And he fell back into his old artificial realm of fantasies of grandeur, and again (as a horse walking a treadmill may imagine it is doing something for itself) he meekly resumed the cruel, mournful, irksome and inhuman rôle which was his destiny.

And not for that day and hour alone were the mind and conscience of this man darkened, on whom the burden of all that was happening weighed more heavily than on all the others who took part in it. Never to the end of his life had he the least comprehension of goodness, beauty or truth, or of the significance of his actions, which were too contrary to goodness and truth, too remote from everything human for him ever to be able to grasp their import. He could not disavow his deeds, lauded as they were by half the world, and so he was obliged to repudiate truth and beauty and all humanity.

Not on that day alone, as he rode over the battlefield strewn with men killed and maimed (the work, he supposed, of his will) did he reckon as he looked at them how many Russians lay there for each Frenchman and, beguiling himself, find reason for rejoicing in the calculation that there were five Russians for every Frenchman. This was not the only time he wrote to Paris that 'the field of battle was a superb sight' because of the fifty thousand corpses lying there: even on the island of St Helena, in the peaceful solitude where he said he intended to devote his leisure to an account of the mighty deeds he had accomplished, he wrote:

The Russian war should have been the most popular war of modern times: it was a war on the side of good sense and sound interests, to bring peace and security to all. It was purely pacific and conservative.

It was a war for a great cause, the end of uncertainties and the beginning of security. A new horizon, new labours would have opened out, full of well-being and prosperity for all. The European system was established: all that remained was to organize it.

Satisfied on these great points, and at peace with all the world, I too should have had my *Congress* and my *Holy Alliance*. These are ideas stolen from me. In that assembly of great sovereigns we could have discussed our interests like one family and have rendered account to the peoples as clerk to master.

In this way Europe would soon have become in reality but a single people and every man travelling anywhere would have found himself in the common fatherland. I would have insisted on all navigable rivers being free to all, required that the seas should be common to all and that the great standing armies be reduced henceforth to mere bodyguards for sovereigns.

On my return to France, to the bosom of the great, strong, magnificent, serene and glorious Fatherland, I would have proclaimed her frontiers immutable; all future wars purely *defensive*; all fresh aggrandizement *anti-national*. I would have made my son my partner in the Empire; my *dictatorship* would have been over, and his constitutional reign would have begun. . . .

Paris would have been the capital of the world, and the French the envy of the nations! . . .

My time then and my old age would have been devoted, in company with the Empress and during the royal apprenticeship of my son, to visiting in leisurely fashion, with our own horses like a genuine country couple, every corner of the Empire, receiving complaints, redressing wrongs and scattering public buildings and benefactions wherever we went.

Yes, he, foreordained by Providence to the sad, dependent role of executioner of the peoples, persuaded himself that the motive of his actions had been the welfare of the peoples, and that he could control the destinies of millions and confer benefits by the exercise of his power!

Of the four hundred thousand men who crossed the Vistula [he wrote further concerning the Russian war], half were Austrians, Prussians, Saxons, Poles, Bavarians, Wurttembergers, Mecklenburgers, Spaniards, Italians, Neapolitans. A third of the Imperial army, strictly speaking, consisted of Dutch, Belgians, inhabitants of the Rhineland, Piedmontese, Swiss, Genevese, Tuscans, Romans, inhabitants of the Thirty-second Military Division, of Bremen, of Hamburg, and so on; it included scarcely a hundred and forty thousand who spoke French. The Russian expedition actually cost France less than fifty thousand men; the Russian army in the retreat from Vilna to Moscow lost in various battles four times as many men as the French army; the burning of Moscow cost the lives of a hundred thousand Russians who perished of cold and starvation in the forests; finally, in its march from Moscow to the Oder, the Russian army also suffered from the inclemency of the season; so that by the time it reached Vilna it numbered only fifty thousand, and less than eighteen thousand at Kalisch.

He imagined that the war with Russia came about by his volition, and the horror of what was done made no impression on his soul. He boldly assumed full responsibility for what happened, and his darkened mind found justification in the fact that among the hundreds of thousands who met their deaths there were fewer Frenchmen than Hessians and Bavarians.

39

SEVERAL tens of thousands of men lay dead in various attitudes and uniforms on the fields and meadows belonging to the Davydov family and certain Crown serfs – those fields and meadows where for centuries the peasants of Borodino, Gorky, Shevardino and Semeonovsk had harvested their crops and grazed their cattle. For nearly three acres round the dressing-stations the grass and earth were soaked with blood. Soldiers of different arms, wounded and unwounded, with scared faces, dragged themselves back to Mozhaisk from the one army and Valuevo from the other. Other crowds, exhausted and hungry, went forward led by their officers. Still others held their ground and continued to fire.

Over all the plain, which had been so gay and beautiful with bayonets glittering and little puffs of smoke in the morning sun, there now hung a fog of damp and smoke, and the air was foul with a strange, sour smell of saltpetre and blood. Clouds had gathered and drops of rain began to fall on the dead and wounded, on the panic-stricken and the weary, and on those who were filled with misgiving. 'Enough, enough!' the rain seemed to be saying. 'Stop! ... Bethink yourselves! What are you doing?'

A flicker of doubt began to creep into the minds of the tired and hungry men on both sides – were they to go on slaughtering one another? Hesitation could be read on every face, and every heart was occupied with the question: 'Why – for whom – must I kill and be killed? ... Let the others get on with it and do what they like, but I've had enough!' By the evening this thought had ripened in every soul. Horror at what they were doing was near the surface and all these men were in a condition at any moment to throw everything up and run away anywhere.

But though towards the end of the struggle the men were conscious of the nightmare of their actions, though they would have been glad to leave off, some mysterious, inexplicable power continued to control them, and the surviving gunners – one out of every three – soaked with sweat, grimed with powder and blood, still brought up the charges, loaded, aimed and applied the match, though they stumbled and panted with fatigue. The cannon-balls flew just as swiftly and cruelly from each side, smashing human bodies, and still the fearful work went on, not by the will of individual men but at the will of Him who governs men and worlds.

Anyone looking at the disorder in the rear of the Russian army would have said that the French had only to make one further slight effort and the Russian army would have disappeared into nothing; and anyone seeing behind the French lines would have said that one last little effort on the part of the Russians would be the end of the French. But neither the French nor the Russians put forth that last effort, and the flame of battle burnt slowly out.

The Russians did not make that effort because they were not attacking the French. At the beginning of the battle they merely stood on the road to Moscow, barring it to the enemy, and at the conclusion of the engagement they still stood there exactly as they had at the beginning. But even had the aim of the Russians been to drive the French from their positions they could not have made this final effort, because all the Russian forces had been routed: there was not a single section of the army that had not suffered in the battle, and the Russians in merely holding their positions lost ONE HALF of their effectives.

The French, with the thought of their fifteen years of victories, with their confidence in Napoleon's invincibility, with the knowledge that they had got possession of part of the battlefield and had lost only a quarter of their men and still had their Guards intact – twenty thousand strong – might easily have made that effort. The French, who had attacked the Russian army with the object of driving it from its position, ought to have made that effort, for so long as the Russians continued to bar the way to Moscow, as before, the aim of the French had not been attained, and all their exertions and losses had been in vain. But the French did not make that effort. Some historians declare that if only Napoleon had used his Old Guards, who were intact, the battle would have been won. To speak of what would have happened had Napoleon sent forward his Guards is like talking of what would happen if spring came in autumn. It could not be. Napoleon did not sacrifice his Guards, not because he did not want to, but because it could not be done. All the generals, officers and soldiers of the French army knew that this was out of the question, because the flagging spirit of the troops did not allow of it.

It was not Napoleon alone who experienced that nightmare feeling of the mighty arm being stricken powerless: all the generals and soldiers of his army, whether they had taken part in the battle or not, after all their experience of previous battles – when a tenth of such pressure had started the enemy fleeing – knew a similar feeling of awe and dread before this foe who, after losing ONE HALF of his men, still stood as formidable at the end as at the beginning of the battle. The moral force of the French, the attacking army, was exhausted. The Russians at Borodino won – not the sort of victory which is specified by the capture of scraps of material on the end of sticks, called standards, or of the ground on which the troops had stood and were standing – but a moral victory, the kind of victory which compels the enemy to recognize the moral superiority of his opponent and his own impotence. The French invaders, like a maddened wild beast that in its onslaught receives a mortal wound, became conscious that it was doomed, but could not call a halt, any more than the Russian army, of half its strength, could help giving way. By the impetus it had been given the French army was still able to roll forward to Moscow; but there, without further effort on the part of the Russians, it was bound to perish, bleeding to death from the wound received at Borodino. The direct consequence of the battle of Borodino was Napoleon's causeless flight from Moscow, his return along the old Smolensk road by which he had come, the destruction of the invading army of five hundred thousand men and the downfall of Napoleonic France, on which at Borodino for the first time the hand of an adversary of stronger spirit had been laid.

PART THREE

I

IT is impossible for the human intellect to grasp the idea of absolute continuity of motion. Laws of motion of any kind only become comprehensible to man when he can examine arbitrarily selected units of that motion. But at the same time it is this arbitrary division of continuous motion into discontinuous units which gives rise to a large proportion of human error.

Take, for instance, the well-known sophism of the ancients which set out to prove that Achilles would never catch up with a tortoise that had the start of him, even though Achilles travelled ten times as fast as the tortoise: by the time Achilles has covered the distance that separated him from the tortoise, the tortoise has advanced one-tenth of that distance ahead of him. While Achilles does this tenth the tortoise gains a hundredth, and so on *ad infinitum*. This problem appeared to the ancients insoluble. The absurdity of the finding (that Achilles could never overtake the tortoise) follows from arbitrarily dividing motion into separate units, whereas the movement both of Achilles and the tortoise was continuous.

By adopting smaller and smaller units of motion we only approach the solution of the problem but never reach it. It is only by admitting infinitesimal quantities and their progression up to a tenth, and taking the sum of that geometrical progression, that we can arrive at the solution of the problem. A new branch of mathematics, having attained the art of reckoning with infinitesimals, can now yield solutions in other more complex problems of motion which before seemed insoluble.

This new branch of mathematics, which was unknown to the ancients, by admitting the conception, when dealing with problems of motion, of the infinitely small and thus conforming to the chief condition of motion (absolute continuity), corrects the inevitable error which the human intellect cannot but make if it considers separate units of motion instead of continuous motion.

In the investigation of the laws of historical movement precisely the same principle operates.

The march of humanity, springing as it does from an infinite multitude of individual wills, is continuous.

The discovery of the laws of this continuous movement is the aim of history. But to arrive at these laws of continuous motion resulting from the sum of all those human volitions human reason postulates arbitrary, separated units. The first proceeding of the historian is to select at random a series of successive events and examine them apart from others, though there is and can be no *beginning* to any event, for one event flows without any break in continuity from another. The second method is to study the actions of some one man – a king or a commander – as though their actions represented the sum of many individual wills; whereas the sum of individual wills never finds expression in the activity of a single historical personage.

Historical science in its endeavour to approximate the truth is constantly isolating smaller and smaller units for examination. But, however small the units it takes, we feel that to postulate any disconnected unit, or to assume a *beginning* to any phenomenon, or to say that the volitions of all men are expressed in the actions of any one historical character, is false *per se*.

The critic has only to select some larger or smaller unit as the subject of observation – as criticism has every right to do, seeing that whatever unit history observes must always be arbitrarily selected – for any deduction drawn from history to disintegrate into small particles like dust, without the slightest exertion on his part.

Only by assuming an infinitesimally small unit for observation – a differential of history (that is, the common tendencies of men) – and arriving at the art of integration (finding the sum of the infinitesimals) can we hope to discover the laws of history.

*

The first fifteen years of the nineteenth century in Europe present an extraordinary movement of millions of people. Men leave their customary pursuits, tear from one end of Europe to the other, plunder and slaughter one another, triumph and despair, and for some years the whole flow of life is transformed into a powerful current which at first runs higher and higher and then subsides. What was the cause of this activity, by what laws was it governed ? – asks the human intellect.

The historians, replying to this question, lay before us the sayings and doings of a few dozen men in a building in the city of Paris, calling these sayings and doings 'the Revolution'. Then they give us an elaborate biography of Napoleon and of certain persons favourably or hostilely disposed to him; talk of the influence some of these people had upon others; and say: 'That is what was at the back of this movement and those are the laws it followed.'

But the human intellect not only refuses to believe in their explanation but flatly declares that this method of interpreting is not sound, because in it a smaller phenomenon is taken as the cause of a greater one. The sum of men's individual wills produced both the Revolution and Napoleon, and only the sum of those wills first tolerated and then destroyed them.

'But whenever there has been conquest there has been a conqueror, and every subversion of an empire brings forth great men,' says history. 'Yes indeed, in every case where conquerors appear there have been wars,' human reason replies, 'but this does not prove that the conquerors were the cause of the wars, or that it is possible to discover the factors leading to warfare in the personal activity of a single man.' Whenever I look at my watch and see the hand pointing to ten I hear the bells beginning to ring in the church close by; but I have no right to assume that because the bells start ringing when the watch hand reaches ten the movement of the bells is caused by the position of the hands of my watch.

When I see a steam-engine move I hear the whistle, I see the valves opening and the wheels turning; but I have no right to conclude that the whistle and the turning of wheels cause the movement of the engine.

Peasants say that a cold wind blows in late spring because the oaks are budding, and it is a fact that a cold wind does blow every spring when the oak is coming out. But though I do not know what causes the cold winds to blow when the oak-buds unfold, I cannot agree with the peasants that the unfolding of the oak-buds is the cause of the cold wind, for the force of the wind is altogether outside the influence of the buds. I see only a coincidence of occurrences such as happens with all the phenomena of life, and I see that however long and however carefully I study the hands of the watch, the valve and the wheels of the engine, and the oak-bud, I shall never find out what makes the bells ring, the locomotive move and the wind blow in spring. To do that I must completely change my point of observation and consider the laws regulating steam, bells and the wind. The historians must do likewise. And experiments in this direction have already been made.

To elicit the laws of history we must leave aside kings, ministers and generals, and select for study the homogeneous, infinitesimal elements which influence the masses. No one can say how far it is possible for man to advance in this way towards an understanding of the laws of history; but it is obvious that this is the only path to that end, and that the human intellect has not, so far, applied in this direction one-millionth of the energy which historians have devoted to describing the deeds of various kings, generals and ministers, and propounding reflections of their own concerning those deeds.

2

THE forces of a dozen different European nations burst into Russia. The Russian army and people fall back, avoiding a clash, to Smolensk, and again from Smolensk to Borodino. The French army flows on to Moscow, its goal, with gathering impetus. As it approaches the goal, momentum increases, just as the velocity of a falling body increases as it nears the earth. Behind it lie hundreds of miles of devastated, hostile country; ahead, only a dozen or so miles separate it from its goal. Every soldier in Napoleon's army is conscious of this, and the invasion is propelled onward by its own momentum.

The more the Russian army retreats the more fiercely burns the spirit of fury against the enemy: every step back adds fuel to the flames. At Borodino the collision takes place. Neither army is destroyed, but the Russian army, immediately after the collision, retreats as inevitably as a ball rebounds after colliding with another flying with greater impetus to meet it; and just as inevitably the ball of invasion that has advanced with such momentum rolls on for some distance (though the collision has deprived it of all vigour).

The Russians retire eighty miles – to the other side of Moscow; the French reach Moscow and there come to a halt. For five weeks after this there is not a single battle. The French do not stir. Like a mortally wounded beast, bleeding and licking its wounds, they remain inert in Moscow for five weeks, and then suddenly, without any new reason, they turn tail; they make a dash for the Kaluga road and (after a victory, too, since the field of Malo-Yaroslavets is still theirs after the engagement) flee back, without risking a single serious action, faster and faster, to Smolensk, beyond Smolensk, beyond Vilna, beyond the Berezina, on and on.

On the evening of the 26th of August Kutuzov and the whole Russian army were convinced that the battle of Borodino was a victory. Kutuzov reported to that effect to the Emperor. He gave orders to prepare for a fresh assault to finish off the enemy, not because he wanted to deceive anybody but because he knew, as everyone who had taken part in the battle knew, that the enemy was beaten.

But all that evening and next day reports kept coming in, one after another, of unprecedented losses – of the loss of half the army – and another battle proved physically impossible.

It was out of the question to give battle before information had been collected, the wounded gathered in, the supplies of ammunition replenished, the dead counted, new officers appointed to replace those who had been killed, and before the men had had food and sleep. And meanwhile, the very next morning after the battle, the French army advanced of itself upon the Russians, carried forward by the force of its own impetus, accelerated now in inverse ratio to the square of the distance from its goal. Kutuzov wanted to renew the attack on the following day, and the whole army was with him. But the desire to make an attack is not enough: there must also be the possibility of doing so, and that possibility did not exist. It was impossible not to fall back one day's march, and then in the same way it was impossible not to retreat a second and a third day's march, and finally, on the 1st of September when the army drew near Moscow – despite the strength of the feeling that had arisen in all ranks – the force of circumstances compelled it to retire beyond Moscow. And the troops retreated one more last day's march, and abandoned Moscow to the enemy.

To those who are wont to suppose that plans of campaigns and battles are made by generals in the same way as any of us sitting over a map in our study may imagine how we would have arranged things in this or that battle the questions present themselves: Why did Kutuzov, if he had to retreat, do this or that? – Why did he not take up a position before reaching Fili? – Why did he not fall back at once by the Kaluga road, leaving Moscow to itself? – and so on. People accustomed to reason in this way forget, or do not know, the inevitable conditions which always limit the action of any commander-in-chief.

The conditions in which a commander-in-chief operates in the field have no sort of resemblance to the conditions we imagine to ourselves sitting at our ease in our studies and going over some campaign on the map, with a certain given number of soldiers on the one side and the other, in a certain known locality, and starting our plan from some given moment. A commander-in-chief never finds himself at the *beginning* of an event – the position from which we always contemplate it. The general is always in the midst of a series of shifting events and so he can never at any point deliberate on the whole import of what is going on. Imperceptibly, moment by moment, an event takes shape in all its bearings, and at every instant of this uninterrupted, consecutive shaping of events the commander-in-chief is at the heart of a most complex play of intrigues, cares, contingencies, authorities, projects, counsels, threats and deceits, and is continually obliged to reply to innumerable, often mutually contradictory questions.

Learned military critics assure us quite seriously that Kutuzov should have moved his army to the Kaluga road long before reaching Fili, and that somebody actually submitted such a proposal to him. But the commander of an army, especially at a critical moment, has not one but dozens of schemes proposed to him, each based on the rules of strategy and tactics and contradicting all the rest. A commander-in-chief's business, it would seem, is merely to select one of these projects. But even this he cannot do. Events and time will not wait. It is suggested to him, let us suppose, on the 28th to cross on to the Kaluga road, but just then an adjutant gallops up from Miloradovich asking whether he is to engage the French or retire. An order must be given him immediately, on the instant. And the order to retreat carries us past the turn to the Kaluga road. And after the adjutant comes the commissariat officer to inquire where the stores are to be taken; the chief medical officer wants to know where the wounded are to go; a courier from Petersburg brings a letter from the Sovereign, refusing to admit the possibility of abandoning Moscow; while the commander-in-chief's rival, who is trying to cut the ground from under his feet (and there are always not one but several such), presents a new project diametrically opposed to the plan of retreating along the Kaluga road. Added to all this, the commander-in-chief's own energies require sleep and refreshment; a worthy general who has been overlooked when decorations were bestowed arrives to complain; the inhabitants of the district implore protection; an officer sent to inspect the locality returns with a report flatly contradicting what the officer sent out before him has said; and a spy, a prisoner and a general who has been on reconnaissance all describe the position of the enemy's army quite differently. People who do not understand or who forget these inevitable conditions in which a commander-in-chief has to operate show us, for instance, the position of the troops at Fili and take for granted that the commander-in-chief could, on the 1st of September, with complete freedom decide whether to abandon Moscow or defend the city; whereas, with the Russian army less than four miles from Moscow, no such option existed. When, then, was this question decided? It was decided at Drissa, at Smolensk, and most palpably of all it was decided on the 24th of August at Shevardino, on the 26th at Borodino and each day and hour and minute of the retreat from Borodino to Fili.

3

THE Russian army, having retreated from Borodino, paused at Fili. Yermolov, who had been sent to reconnoitre the position, rode up to the field-marshal.

'There is no possibility of fighting in this position,' he said.

Kutuzov looked at him in wonder and made him repeat what he had said. When he had done so, Kutuzov reached towards him.

'Give me your hand,' said he, and turning it over so as to feel the pulse, remarked: 'You are not well, my dear fellow. Think what you are saying.'

On the Poklonny hill, four miles from Moscow's Dorogomilov gate, Kutuzov got out of his carriage and sat down on a bench by the roadside. A great cluster of generals gathered round him, and Count Rostopchin, who had come out from Moscow, joined them. This brilliant company separated into several groups and discussed among themselves the advantages and disadvantages of the position, the state of the army, the various plans proposed, the situation of Moscow and military matters generally. Though they had not been summoned for the purpose, and though it was not so called, they all felt that this was really a council of war. Conversation was confined to matters of public interest. If anyone did repeat or inquire any piece of personal news, it was done in a whisper, and such digressions were immediately followed by a return to topics of general concern. Not a jest, not a laugh, not even a smile was exchanged among all these men. They were all making an obvious effort to rise to the occasion. And all the groups, while talking among themselves, tried to keep near the commander-in-chief (whose bench formed the centre of the whole crowd) and to speak so that he might hear them. The commander-in-chief listened, occasionally asking for something to be repeated, but did not himself enter into conversation or express any opinion. For the most part, after listening to the talk of some group, he turned away with an air of disappointment, as though at not hearing anything of what he hoped to hear. Some were commenting on the position that had been chosen, criticizing not so much the position itself as the intellectual qualifications of those who had selected it. Others argued that a blunder had been made earlier and that a battle should have been fought two days before. Others again were discussing the battle of Salamanca, which a Frenchman named Crosart, who had just arrived in a Spanish uniform, was describing to them. (This Frenchman and one of the German princes serving with the Russian army were analysing the siege of Saragossa with a view to the possibility of defending Moscow in a similar manner.) Count Rostopchin was telling a fourth little coterie that he was prepared to die with the city militia under the walls of the capital but that he still could not help regretting having been left in ignorance of what was happening, and that had he known it sooner things would have been different. . . . A fifth group, parading the profundity of their strategic insight, discussed the direction the troops would now have to take. A sixth talked sheer nonsense. Kutuzov's expression grew more and more preoccupied and gloomy. From all these conversations he drew one conclusion: that to defend Moscow was a *physical impossibility* in the fullest sense of the words. It was so utterly impossible that even if some insane commander were to give orders to fight confusion would ensue but no battle would take place. No battle would take place because all the officers of the high command not merely recognized the position to be impossible but had got to the point of discussing what was to be done after the inevitable abandonment of that position. How could generals lead their men to a field of battle which they regarded as untenable? The junior officers and even the soldiers themselves (they, too, form their conclusions) likewise thought that the position could not be held, and therefore could not march out to fight when they were morally sure of defeat. That Bennigsen continued to urge the defence of this position, and others still deliberated it, no longer had significance in itself: the only significance was the excuse it offered for dissension and intrigue. This Kutuzov was well aware of.

Bennigsen, who had chosen the position, was making a passionate display of his Russian patriotism (Kutuzov could not listen to him without wincing) by insisting that Moscow must be defended. His purpose was as clear as daylight to Kutuzov: if the defence failed, to throw the blame on Kutuzov who had brought the army as far as the Sparrow Hills without giving battle; if it succeeded, to claim the credit for himself; or if battle were not given, to clear himself of the crime of abandoning Moscow. But this intriguing did not occupy the old man's mind now. One single, terrible question absorbed him. And to that question he heard no reply from anyone. The question for him now was: 'Can I really have allowed Napoleon to reach Moscow, and when did I do it? What decided it? Was it yesterday when I ordered Platov to retreat, or was it the evening before when I had a nap and left Bennigsen in charge? Or was it earlier still? ... When, when was this fearful business set in motion? Moscow must be abandoned. The army must retire, and I must give the order for it.' To give that dreadful order seemed to him tantamount to resigning the command of the army. And apart from the fact that he loved power to which he was accustomed (the honours awarded to Prince Prozorovsky, under whom he had served when he was in Turkey, galled him), he was convinced that he was destined to save Russia and that was why, against the Emperor's wish and by the will of the people, he had been placed in supreme command. He was persuaded that in these critical circumstances he was the one man who could remain at the head of the army, that he was the only man in the world capable of facing the invincible Napoleon undismayed; and he was filled with consternation at the thought of the order he must issue. But it was essential to come to some decision, and these discussions around him, which were beginning to assume altogether too free a character, must be cut short.

He beckoned the senior generals to him.

'For good or for evil I must trust my own judgement,' he said in French, getting up from the bench, and he rode off to Fili, where his carriages were waiting.

4

A COUNCIL OF WAR assembled at two in the afternoon in the better, larger part of the cottage belonging to a man named Andrei Savostyanov. The men, women and children of the big peasant family crowded into the back room across the passage. Only Malasha, Andrei's six-year-old granddaughter, whom his Serene Highness had petted, giving her a lump of sugar while he drank his tea, stayed behind on top of the stove in the front room. Malasha peeped down from the stove with shy delight at the faces, the uniforms and the decorations of the generals, who one after another came into the room and sat down on the broad benches in the corner under the icons. 'Grandad' himself, as Malasha in her own mind called Kutuzov, was sitting apart from the rest in a dark corner behind the stove. He sat slumped in a folding armchair and continually cleared his throat and pulled at the collar of his coat, which, though it was unbuttoned, still seemed to rub his neck. The officers, as they came in one after another, walked up to the field-marshal: he shook hands with some, to others he merely nodded. His adjutant, Kaisarov, was about to draw back the curtain from the window facing Kutuzov but the latter waved his hand angrily and Kaisarov understood that his Serene Highness did not wish his face to be seen.

Round the peasant's deal table, on which lay maps, plans, pencils and papers, there was such a crowd that the orderlies brought in another bench and put it near the table. Yermolov, Kaisarov and Toll, who had all just arrived, seated themselves on this bench. Immediately under the icons, in the place of honour, sat Barclay de Tolly, his high forehead merging into his bald crown. He had a St George Cross round his neck and looked pale and ill. For two days now he had been suffering from an attack of ague, and at this very moment was shivering feverishly. Beside him sat Uvarov, telling him something in low tones (they all spoke quietly) accompanied by rapid gesticulation. Chubby little Dokhturov was listening attentively with eyebrows raised and hands clasped over his stomach. On the other side, resting his broad head with its bold features and brilliant eyes on his hand, sat Count Ostermann-Tolstoy, apparently immersed in his own thoughts. Raevsky, as usual twisting his black hair forward into curls on his temples, glanced now at Kutuzov, now at the door with a look of impatience. Konovnitsyn's firm, handsome, kindly face was lighted by a tender, shrewd smile. He caught Malasha's eye and winked at her in a way that set the little girl smiling.

They were all waiting for Bennigsen, who, on the pretext of examining the position afresh, was taking his time over a tasty dinner. They waited for him from four o'clock till six and all that time did not enter on their deliberations but talked of extraneous matters in subdued tones.

Only when Bennigsen came into the hut did Kutuzov leave his corner and approach the table but still so as to avoid placing himself in the light of the candles that had been put there.

Bennigsen opened the proceedings with the question: 'Shall we abandon the sacred and ancient capital of Russia without a struggle, or shall we defend it?' A prolonged silence followed. Every face was overcast and only Kutuzov's angry grunts and occasional cough broke the stillness. All eyes were fixed on him. Malasha too gazed at 'Grandad'. She was nearer to him than any of the others and saw that his face was working: he seemed to be going to cry. But this did not last long.

'*The sacred and ancient capital of Russia!*' he cried suddenly, repeating Bennigsen's words in an irate voice and thereby underlining the false note in them. 'Allow me to tell your Excellency that that phrase has no meaning for a Russian.' (He lurched his heavy body forward.) 'That is not the way to formulate the question which I have invited these gentlemen here to discuss. It is a military problem, to be stated as follows: Since the safety of Russia depends on the army, would it be more to our advantage to risk the loss of the army and of Moscow by accepting battle or to give up Moscow without a battle? That is the question on which I want your opinion,' and he sank back in his chair.

A debate began. Bennigsen did not yet consider his game lost. Agreeing with the view of Barclay and others that it was impossible to make a stand at Fili, he aired his Russian patriotism and devotion to Moscow by proposing to move troops from the right to the left flank during the night, and strike at the French right wing next day. Opinions were divided, and arguments were advanced for and against this project. Yermolov, Dokhturov and Raevsky sided with Bennigsen. Whether they were dominated by a sense that some sacrifice was called for before abandoning the capital, or were influenced by other, personal considerations, these generals seemed not to realize that their present deliberations could not alter the inevitable course of events and that Moscow was to all intents already abandoned. The other generals understood this and, setting aside the question of Moscow, turned their attention to the direction the army should take in its retreat. Malasha, looking on, wide-eyed, interpreted the proceedings of the council differently. To her it was a private tussle between 'Grandad' and 'Long-coat' as she christened Bennigsen. She saw that they were spiteful to each other, and secretly she took 'Grandad's' part. In the middle of the conversation she caught the quick, sly glance 'Grandad' cast Bennigsen, and then immediately after she noted with glee that 'Grandad' said something to 'Long-coat' which settled him. Bennigsen suddenly reddened, and strode angrily up and down the room. What had so gone home was Kutuzov's quiet, softly-uttered comment on the advisability or inadvisability of Bennigsen's proposal to move troops by night from the right to the left flank to attack the French right wing.

'Gentlemen,' said Kutuzov, 'I could not give my consent to the count's plan. Moving troops in close proximity to the enemy is always risky, and military history supports that conviction. For instance' – Kutuzov paused, as though to reflect, searching for an example, and then with a bright, naïve glance at Bennigsen – 'well, take the battle of Friedland, which, as the count no doubt well remembers, was not ... completely successful, only because our troops were rearranged while too near the enemy. ...'

A silence, lasting perhaps a minute but which felt never-ending, hung over the meeting.

The discussion was renewed but frequent lulls occurred and the feeling was general that nothing more could be said.

During one of those pauses Kutuzov heaved a deep sigh, as though preparing to speak. They all looked at him.

'Eh bien, messieurs! I see that it is I who will have to bear the brunt of it,' he said, and rising slowly he moved to the table. 'Gentlemen, I have heard your views. Some of you will not agree with me. But I' (he stopped), 'on the authority entrusted to me by my Sovereign and my country, give the order to retreat.'

After that the generals began to disperse with the solemnity and silent circumspection which people observe when they separate after a funeral.

Certain of the generals in low tones, in an entirely different key from that in which they had spoken during the council, made some communication to the commander-in-chief.

Malasha, who ought to have been at supper long ago, cautiously let herself down from her perch, clinging with her little bare feet to the projections of the stove, and, slipping between the legs of the generals, she darted out of the room.

After he had dismissed the assembly Kutuzov sat for a long while with his elbows on the table, pondering the terrible question: 'When, at what point had it become inevitable that Moscow must be abandoned? When was the thing done that made it inevitable? And who is to blame for it?'

'I did not expect this – not this,' he said to his adjutant, Schneider, when the latter came in late that night. 'I did not expect this! I did not think this would happen!'

'Your Highness must get some rest,' said Schneider.

'But it's not over yet! They shall devour horse-flesh yet, like the Turks!' cried Kutuzov, not heeding him and bringing his podgy fist down on the table. 'They too ... if only ...'

5

MEANWHILE, in circumstances of even greater importance than the retreat of the army without a battle – namely, the evacuation and burning of Moscow – Rostopchin, who is generally represented as dictating this step, was acting in a very different manner from Kutuzov.

This event – the abandonment and burning of Moscow – was as inevitable after the battle of Borodino as the retreat of the army beyond Moscow without fighting.

Every Russian might have predicted it, not by reasoning things out but by hearkening to the sentiment inherent in each of us and in our forefathers.

In every town and village on Russian soil, from Smolensk onwards, without the assistance of Count Rostopchin and his broadsheets, the same thing took place as happened in Moscow. The nation awaited the enemy with indifference: there was no rioting, no excitement, no one was torn to pieces. People calmly awaited their fate, feeling that when the time came they would know what they must do. And as soon as the enemy drew near, the well-to-do elements of the population departed, abandoning their possessions, while the poorer classes remained and burnt and destroyed what was left.

The conviction that this must and always will be the way of things was, and is, deeply implanted in every Russian heart. And this consciousness – nay, more, the presentiment that Moscow would be taken – pervaded Russian society in Moscow in that year 1812. Those who started quitting Moscow as early as July and the beginning of August showed that this was what they expected. Those who went away, taking what they could and abandoning their houses and half their property, did so in obedience to that latent patriotism which expresses itself not in phrases, not in sacrificing one's children to save the Fatherland, and such-like unnatural exploits, but unobtrusively, simply, organically and so in the way that always produces the most powerful results.

'It is disgraceful to run away from danger; only cowards are deserting Moscow,' they were told. In his broadsheets Rostopchin urged that it was ignominious to leave Moscow. They were ashamed at being branded as cowards, ashamed of going away, but still they left, knowing that it must be so. Why did they go? It is impossible to suppose that Rostopchin had scared them with his tales of atrocities perpetrated by Napoleon in the countries he conquered. The first to leave were the wealthy, educated people, who knew quite well that Vienna and Berlin had remained intact, and that during Napoleon's occupation the inhabitants of those cities had spent their time pleasantly in the company of the bewitching Frenchmen whom the Russians, and especially the Russian ladies, at that time liked so much.

They went because for Russians the question was not whether they would be comfortable or not under French rule in Moscow. To live under French administration was out of the question: it would be worse than anything. They were going away even before the battle of Borodino, and still more rapidly after Borodino, regardless of appeals to defend the capital, regardless of the proclamations of the governor of Moscow announcing his intention to take the wonder-working icon of the Iberian Mother of God and sally forth to combat, or the air-balloons that were to destroy the French, and regardless of all the nonsense Rostopchin wrote in his broadsheets. They knew that it was for the army to fight, and that if the army could not it would be no use for them to rush out with young ladies and house-serfs to do battle with Napoleon on the Three Hills, and so they must make haste and get away, sorry as they were to abandon their property to destruction. They drove away with never a thought of the sublime import of forsaking this immense, flourishing city and thereby consigning it to the flames (for a great city of wooden buildings abandoned by its inhabitants was certain to burn). They drove away, each on his own account, and yet it was only in consequence of their departure that the illustrious event was accomplished which will for ever remain the crowning glory of the Russian people. The lady who as early as June set off from Moscow with her Negroes and her buffoons for her Saratov estates, with a vague feeling that she was not going to be a subject of Bonaparte's, and in fear of being stopped by Count Rostopchin's orders, was simply and genuinely helping in the great work which saved Russia. And Count Rostopchin himself, who now cried shame on those who were leaving and now had the government offices transferred; now distributed quite useless weapons to the drunken rabble; ordered a procession of icons one day and the next forbade Father Augustin to bring out the icons and holy relics; now seized all the private conveyances in Moscow and on one hundred and thirty-six of them removed the air-balloon that was being constructed by Leppich; now hinted that he would burn Moscow and related how he had set fire to his own house, and now wrote a proclamation to the French solemnly upbraiding them for having razed the home of his childhood; now claimed the glory for Moscow in flames, now repudiated it; now commanded the people to capture all spies and bring them to him, then blamed them for doing so; now expelled all the French residents from Moscow and then allowed Madame Aubert-Chalmé (the centre of the whole French colony in Moscow) to remain, but ordered the respected old postmaster, Klucharov, to be arrested and banished for no particular offence; now assembled the people on the Three Hills to fight the French and then, to get rid of them, handed a man over to them to murder and himself drove away by a back gate; now vowed that he would not survive the fall of Moscow, and later on wrote French verses in albums concerning his share in the affair* – this man had no inkling of the mean-

*Je suis né Tartare.   (I was born a Tartar.
  Je voulais être Romain.   I wanted to be a Roman.
  Les Français m'appelèrent barbare. The French called me a barbarian,
  Les Russes – Georges Dandin.   The Russians – George Dandin.)

ing of what was happening. All he wanted was to do something himself, to startle people, to perform some heroic feat of patriotism; and
like a child he frolicked in the face of the momentous and inescapable
circumstance of the abandonment and burning of Moscow, and tried
with his puny hand now to speed and now to stay the prodigious tide
of popular feeling that was bearing him along with it.

6

HÉLÈNE, having returned with the Court from Vilna to Petersburg,
found herself in a difficult situation.

In Petersburg she had enjoyed the special patronage of a grandee
who occupied one of the highest positions in the Empire. In Vilna she
had formed a liaison with a young foreign prince. When she returned
to Petersburg both the prince and the magnate were there, both
claiming their rights, and Hélène was confronted with a new problem in her career – how to preserve her intimacy with both without
offending either.

What might have seemed difficult, if not impossible, to another
woman caused never a thought to the Countess Bezuhov, who plainly
deserved her reputation of a most intelligent woman. Had she attempted concealment, or tried subterfuge to extricate herself from her
awkward position, she would have spoilt her case by acknowledging
herself guilty. But Hélène, like a truly great man who can do anything he pleases, at once put herself in the right, as she really believed,
and placed the blame on everyone else.

The first time the young foreign prince ventured to reproach
her she lifted her beautiful head and, half turning to him, said
firmly:

'That's just like a man – selfish and cruel! I might have expected it.
Woman sacrifices herself for you; she suffers, and this is her reward!
What right have you, *monseigneur*, to demand an account of my
friendships, of my attachments? He is a man who has been more than
a father to me!'

The prince was about to say something but Hélène interrupted
him.

'*Eh bien, oui*,' said she, 'it may be that he has other sentiments for
me than those of a father but that is no reason why I should shut my

door on him. I am not a man that I should repay kindness with ingratitude! Know, *monseigneur*, that in all that relates to my private feelings I render account only to God and my conscience,' she concluded, laying her hand on her lovely fully expanded bosom as she glanced up to heaven.

'But for God's sake listen to me!'

'Marry me, and I will be your slave!'

'But that is impossible.'

'You would not stoop to marriage with me, you ...' said Hélène, bursting into tears.

The prince made to comfort her, but Hélène (as if quite distraught) said through her tears that there was nothing to prevent her marrying, that there were precedents (there were up to that time very few but she mentioned the cases of Napoleon and some other exalted personages), that she had never been a wife to her husband, that she had been dragged an unwilling victim to the altar.

'But the law, religion ...' murmured the prince, already yielding.

'Laws, religion. ... What were they invented for, if they can't arrange that?' said Hélène.

The foreign prince was astonished that so simple a reflection had never occurred to him, and he applied for advice to the holy brethren of the Society of Jesus, with whom he was in close relations.

A few days later, at one of those enchanting fêtes which Hélène was in the habit of giving at her summer villa on Stone Island, a certain charming Monsieur de Jobert was presented to her: a man no longer young, with snow-white hair and brilliant black eyes, *un Jésuite à robe courte* – a lay member of the Society – who in the garden by the light of the illuminations and to the strains of music conversed long with her of love for God, for Christ, for the Heart of the Mother of God, and of the consolations the one true Catholic faith afforded in this world and the next. Hélène was touched, and more than once tears rose to her eyes and to Monsieur de Jobert's, and her voice trembled. A dance, for which her partner came to fetch her, cut short this conversation with her future *directeur de conscience*; but the next evening Monsieur de Jobert came alone to see Hélène, and after that he was a frequent visitor.

One day he took the countess to a Roman Catholic church, where she fell on her knees before the altar to which she was conducted. The fascinating, middle-aged Frenchman laid his hands on her head and, as she herself afterwards described it, she felt something like the wafting of a fresh breeze into her soul. It was explained to her that this was *la grâce*.

Next, a long-frocked *abbé* – *un abbé à robe longue* – was brought to her. He heard her confession and absolved her from her sins. The following day she received a little casket containing the Sacred Host, which was left at her house for her to partake of. A few days later Hélène learned to her satisfaction that she had now been admitted into the true Catholic Church, and that very shortly the Pope himself would hear of her case and would send her a certain document.

All that was done around her and with her at this time, all the attention devoted to her by so many clever men and expressed in such agreeable, refined ways, and the state of dovelike purity she was now in (she wore only white dresses and white ribbons all these days) afforded her gratification; but her gratification never for a moment caused her to lose sight of her objective. And as it always happens in contests of cunning that a stupid person gets the better of cleverer ones, Hélène – realizing that the real end of all these fine words and manoeuvres was to obtain money from her, having converted her to Catholicism, for the benefit of Jesuit institutions (concerning which she received several hints) – before parting with her money demanded that the various formalities should be carried out which were necessary to free her from her husband. According to her understanding, the whole point of any religion was merely to provide recognized forms of propriety as a background for the satisfaction of human desires. And with this idea in mind she insisted, in one of her conversations with her spiritual director, on getting an answer to the question how far her marriage was binding.

They were sitting in the twilight by a window in the drawing-room. Through the window came the scent of flowers. Hélène was wearing a white dress, transparent over the bosom and shoulders. The sleek, well-fed *abbé*, with his plump, clean-shaven chin, his pleasant, firm mouth, and his white hands meekly folded on his knees, sat close to Hélène and with a subtle smile on his lips and a discreet glance of admiration for her beauty gazed from time to time at her face as he expounded his opinion on the subject. Hélène, with a restless smile, looked at his curly hair and his full, smooth-shaven, dark-shaded cheeks, and every moment expected the conversation to take a fresh turn. But the *abbé*, though unmistakably enjoying his companion's beauty, was carried away by his own skilful handling of the question.

The course of the father confessor's arguments ran as follows:

'In your ignorance of the import of what you were undertaking you made a vow of conjugal fidelity to a man who on his part, by entering into matrimony without recognizing the religious solemnity of marriage, was guilty of an act of sacrilege. This marriage lacked the dual significance it should have had. Yet in spite of this your vow was binding upon you. You have deviated from it. What sin did you commit by so doing? *Péché véniel ou péché mortel* – a venial sin or a mortal sin? A venial sin, for you acted without evil intention. If now, with the object of bearing children, you married again your sin might be forgiven. But the question again becomes a twofold one: firstly …'

'But I imagine,' Hélène, who was getting bored, said suddenly with one of her bewitching smiles, 'that having espoused the true faith I cannot be bound by any obligations laid upon me by a false religion.'

Her spiritual adviser was astounded at having the problem presented to him with all the simplicity of Columbus's egg. He was delighted at the unexpected rapidity of his pupil's progress but could not abandon the edifice of intellectual argument which he had constructed with so much pains.

'Let us understand one another, countess,' he said with a smile, and proceeded to do what he could to refute his spiritual daughter's contention.

7

HÉLÈNE perceived that the matter was very simple and easy from the ecclesiastical point of view, and that her spiritual counsellors were raising difficulties only because they were apprehensive as to how the secular authorities might regard the matter.

So she made up her mind that society must be prepared to look at the matter in the right light. She provoked the jealousy of the elderly grandee, and said the same thing to him as she had to her other suitor – that is, gave him to understand that the sole means of obtaining exclusive rights over her was to marry her.

The elderly magnate was at first just as much taken aback by this suggestion that he should marry a woman whose husband was alive as the younger man had been; but Hélène's imperturbable conviction that it was as simple and natural as marrying a young girl had its effect on him too. Had Hélène herself betrayed the least trace of hesitation, shame or dissembling, her cause would undoubtedly have been lost; but not only did she show no sign of reserve or shame – on the contrary, with frank and simple-hearted naïveté she told her intimate friends (and this meant all Petersburg) that both the prince and the magnate had proposed to her, and that she loved both and was afraid of grieving either.

The rumour instantly spread about Petersburg, not that Hélène desired a divorce from her husband (had this been the report very many persons would have protested strongly against so illegal an intention), but that the unhappy and interesting Hélène was in doubt which of her two suitors to marry. The question now was not how far any marriage was possible but which party would be the better match, and how the Court would look on it. There were, it is true, some rigid individuals unable to rise to the heights of the occasion who saw in the project a desecration of the sacrament of marriage; but such people were few and far between, and they held their peace, while the majority were interested in Hélène's happiness and which would be the better match for her. As to whether it were right or wrong for a woman to marry whose husband was alive, nothing was said – that question had evidently already been settled by persons 'wiser than you and I', and to express any doubts as to the regularity of the solution arrived at would be to risk exposing one's stupidity and lack of *savoir faire*.

Only Maria Dmitrievna Ahrosimov, who had come to Petersburg that summer to see one of her sons, allowed herself to express an opinion flatly contrary to the general point of view. Meeting Hélène at a ball, she stopped her in the middle of the room and amid widespread silence said in her gruff voice:

'So wives have now started marrying while their husbands are alive! I dare say you think you've discovered something new. But you have been forestalled, madam. That was thought of a long time ago. They do the same in all the broth ...', and with these words Maria Dmitrievna turned back her wide sleeves with her characteristic threatening gesture, glanced round sternly and walked across the ball-room.

Though people were afraid of Maria Dmitrievna, she was looked upon in Petersburg as an eccentric, and so of what she said they seized on only the one coarse word at the end, repeating it in a whisper and supposing the whole point of her remark to lie there.

Prince Vasili, whose memory of late was failing so that he often repeated himself a hundred times, said to his daughter whenever he chanced to see her:

'Hélène, I have a word to say to you,' and he would lead her aside, drawing her hand downwards. 'Rumours have come to my ears of certain projects concerning ... you know what. Well, my dear child, you know that my paternal heart would rejoice to feel. ... You have had so much to bear. ... But, *chère enfant* ... you must consult only your own heart. That is all I have to say,' and concealing an emotion identical on each occasion, he would press his cheek against his daughter's and move away.

Bilibin, who had in no wise lost his reputation for possessing a ready wit and was a friend of Hélène's – one of those disinterested allies such as a brilliant woman always manages to attach to herself, men who may be relied upon never to change from friend to lover – one day at a 'small and intimate gathering' gave her his view on the whole subject.

'Listen, Bilibin,' said Hélène (she always called friends of the category to which Bilibin belonged by their surnames), and she touched his coat-sleeve with her white, beringed fingers. 'Tell me, as you would a sister, what ought I to do? Which of the two?'

Bilibin wrinkled up the skin over his eyebrows and pondered, a smile on his lips.

'You do not take me aback, you know,' said he. 'As a true friend I have thought and thought about this business. You see, if you marry the prince' (the younger suitor) and he crooked a finger, 'you lose for ever the chance of marrying the other, and you displease the Court into the bargain. (There is some sort of blood-relationship there, as you are aware.) But if you take the old count you will make his *last* days happy, and afterwards as the widow of the great lord ... the prince would no longer be making a *mésalliance* in contracting a marriage with you.' And Bilibin unwrinkled his forehead.

'You are a true friend!' cried Hélène radiantly, and again touching Bilibin's sleeve. 'But the fact is I love them both, and I don't want to hurt either of them. I would give my life for the happiness of both,' she declared.

Bilibin shrugged his shoulders, as much as to say that not even he could help in that quandary.

'*Une maîtresse-femme!*' thought Bilibin. 'That is what is called putting things squarely. She would like to be married to all three at once.'

'But tell me, how is your husband going to look upon this matter?' he asked, the security of his reputation preserving him from all fear of discrediting himself by so naïve a question. 'Will he agree?'

'Oh, he is so fond of me!' said Hélène, who for some reason fancied that Pierre too adored her. 'He will do anything for me.'

Bilibin puckered his forehead to give intimation of the coming *mot*.

'Even divorce you?' he said.

Hélène laughed.

Among those who ventured to doubt the equity of the proposed marriage was Hélène's mother, Princess Kuragin. She was constantly gnawed by envy of her daughter, and now that the ground for her jealousy was the one nearest to her own heart she could not reconcile herself to the idea. She consulted a Russian priest as to the feasibility of divorce and re-marriage during the husband's lifetime. The priest assured her that this was impossible and, to her delight, referred her to a text in the Gospel which (so it seemed to him) plainly forbids re-marriage while the husband is alive.

Armed with these arguments, which appeared to her irrefutable, the princess drove round to her daughter's early one morning to be sure of finding her alone.

Hélène listened to her mother's objections and then smiled with gentle irony.

'Here, it says in so many words that whoso marrieth her which is divorced ...' said the old princess.

'Ah, *maman*, don't talk nonsense. You don't understand. In my position I have obligations,' began Hélène, speaking in French, which she felt suited her case better – Russian made it sound somehow dubious.

'But my dear ...'

'Ah, *maman*, how is it you don't understand that the Holy Father, who has the power to grant dispensations ...'

At this point the lady companion who lived with Hélène came in to announce that his Highness was in the drawing-room and wished to see her.

'No, tell him I don't wish to see him, that I am furious with him for not keeping his word.'

'*Comtesse*, there is mercy for every sin,' said a fair-haired young man with a long face and long nose, entering the room.

The old princess rose respectfully and curtsied. The young man took no notice of her. Princess Kuragin nodded to her daughter and sailed to the door.

'Yes, she is right,' mused the old princess, all her convictions dissipated by the appearance of his Highness. 'She is right; but how was it in our youth – gone now for ever – we knew nothing of this? Yet it is so simple,' she thought as she got into her carriage.

*

By the beginning of August Hélène's affairs were settled and she wrote to her husband (who, so she imagined, was deeply attached to her), making known to him her intention of marrying N.N. and telling him that she had embraced the one true faith. She requested him to execute all the formalities necessary for a divorce, in regard to which the bearer of her letter would give him due particulars.

'Whereupon, my dear, I pray God to have you in His holy and powerful keeping – Your friend Hélène.'

This letter was brought to Pierre's house in Moscow while he was away on the field of Borodino.

8

TOWARDS the end of the battle of Borodino Pierre fled for a second time from Raevsky's battery and joined a throng of soldiers hastening along the ravine to Knyazkovo, reached the dressing-station and, seeing blood and hearing cries and groans, hurried on, caught up in the mob of soldiers.

The one thing Pierre desired now with his whole soul was to get away quickly from the terrible scenes through which he had lived that day and return to ordinary conditions of life, and go to sleep quietly in his own room in his own bed. He felt that only in the ordinary conditions of life would he be able to understand himself and all that he had seen and experienced. But such ordinary conditions of life were nowhere to be found.

Though shells and bullets did not whistle over the road along which he travelled, still he saw here on all sides the same sights he had seen on the field of battle. There were the same suffering, exhausted and sometimes strangely indifferent faces; everywhere the same blood, the same military greatcoats, the same sound of firing, which though distant now still aroused horror. And in addition there was the suffocating heat and dust.

Having walked a couple of miles along the Mozhaisk highway, Pierre sat down by the roadside.

Dusk had fallen and the roar of guns had died away. Pierre lay leaning on his elbow for a long time, watching the shadowy figures that filed past him in the dark. He was continually fancying that a cannon-ball was sweeping down on him with a terrible screech, and then he started and half rose. He had no idea how long he had been there. In the middle of the night three soldiers, dragging some brushwood after them, settled themselves near him and began making a fire.

Casting sidelong glances at Pierre, the soldiers got the fire to burn and placed an iron pot on it into which they broke some biscuits and added a little fat. The appetizing odour of frying food mingled with the smell of smoke. Pierre sat up and sighed. The soldiers (there were three of them) were eating and talking among themselves, paying no heed to Pierre.

'And who are you?' one of them suddenly asked Pierre, evidently meaning by that, and Pierre understood it so, that they would give him a share of their food if he were hungry and could prove he were an honest man.

'I?...' said Pierre, feeling it necessary to minimize his social position as far as possible, so as to be closer to the soldiers and more within their comprehension. 'Actually I am a militia officer but my men are not here. I went into the battle and got separated from them.'

'That so?' said one of the soldiers.

Another shook his head.

'Well, you can have some of our mash if you like!' said the first, and licking clean a wooden spoon he handed it to Pierre.

Pierre squatted by the fire and fell to eating the mixture in the pot which he thought more delicious than any food he had ever tasted. As he sat bending over the pot, helping himself to large spoonfuls and greedily swallowing them down one after another, his face was lit up by the fire, and the soldiers studied him in silence.

'Where've you to go to, tell us that?' asked one of them.

'To Mozhaisk.'

'You're gentry then?'

'Yes.'

'And what's yer name?'

'Piotr Kirillovich.'

'Well, Piotr Kirillovich, you come along of us, we'll take you there.'

In the pitch dark the soldiers walked with Pierre to Mozhaisk.

By the time they got as far as Mozhaisk and were climbing the steep hill into the town the cocks were already crowing. Pierre continued on with the trio, quite forgetting that his inn was at the bottom of the hill and he had passed it. He might not have remembered it at all (so generally bewildered was he), had he not chanced halfway up the hill to stumble on his groom, who had been to look for him in the town and was now returning to the inn. The groom recognized Pierre in the darkness by his white hat.

'Your Excellency!' he cried. 'Why, we had quite given you up! How is it you are on foot? And, mercy on us, where are you going?'

'Oh yes!' said Pierre.

The soldiers stood still.

'Found your own folks then?' said one of them. 'Well, good-bye – Piotr Kirillovich, wasn't it?'

'Good-bye, Piotr Kirillovich!' repeated the other voices.

'Good-bye!' said Pierre, and he started back with his groom towards the inn.

'I ought to give them something!' he thought, feeling in his pocket. 'No, better not,' some inner voice prompted him.

There was not a room to be had at the hostelry, they were all occupied. Pierre went out into the yard, and muffling himself up from head to foot lay down in his carriage.

9

PIERRE had scarcely laid his head on the cushion before he felt himself dropping asleep; but all of a sudden, with a vividness that was almost real, he heard the *boom-boom-boom* of the cannon, the slapping sound of falling shells, the groans and cries, smelt the blood and powder, and a feeling of horror and the dread of death took possession of him. He opened his eyes in panic and put his head out from the cloak. All was tranquil in the yard. There was only someone's orderly talking at the gate and splashing through the mud. Above Pierre's head some pigeons, disturbed by the movement he had made in sitting up, fluttered under the dark eaves of the penthouse. The peaceful strong smell of stables, which at that instant delighted Pierre's heart, pervaded the whole courtyard – a smell of hay, of manure and of birchwood tar. Between the dark roofs of two penthouses he could see the clear, starry sky.

'Thank God, that is all over!' he thought, covering his head up again. 'Oh, what an awful thing fear is, and how disgracefully I gave way to it! Whereas they – *they* were steady and cool all the time, to the very end …' thought he. *They* in Pierre's mind were the soldiers, those who had been on the battery, those who had given him food and those who had prayed before the icon. *They* – those strange people of whom he had known nothing hitherto – *they* stood out clearly and sharply from everyone else.

'To be a soldier, an ordinary soldier!' thought Pierre as he dropped off to sleep. 'To throw oneself heart and soul into that common life, to learn the secret of what makes them what they are. But how cast off all the superfluous, devilish burden of the outer man ? There was a time when I could have done it. I could have run away from my father, as I wanted to. I might even after the duel with Dolohov have been sent to serve as a soldier.' And his thoughts flashed back to the dinner at the English Club when he had challenged Dolohov, and his meeting with his benefactor at Torzhok. And here a picture of a solemn assembly of the Lodge at the English Club arose before his mind, with someone he knew, someone near and dear to him sitting at the end of the table. 'Why, it is he! It is my benefactor. But surely he died ?' mused Pierre. 'Yes, he died; and I did not know he was alive. How sorry I am that he died, and how glad I am that he is alive again!' On one side of the table sat Anatole, Dolohov, Nesvitsky, Denisov and others like them (in Pierre's dream the category to which these men belonged was as defined as the category of those he termed *they*), and those people, Anatole and Dolohov, were shouting and singing at the tops of their voices; but through their clamour the voice of his benefactor was heard speaking all the while, and the sound of his words was as weighty and uninterrupted as the din of the battlefield, but pleasant and comforting. Pierre did not understand what his benefactor was saying, but he knew (species of thought were also quite distinct in his dream) that he was talking of goodness and the possibility of being like *them*. And *they* with their simple, kind, steadfast faces surrounded his benefactor on all sides. But though they were kindly they did not look at Pierre, did not know him. Pierre wanted to attract their attention and speak to them. He sat up but in that second became aware that his legs were bare and chill.

He felt ashamed and put an arm over his legs, from which the cloak had in fact slipped off. For a moment, as he rearranged his cloak, Pierre opened his eyes and saw the same penthouse roofs, posts and yard, but now everything was enveloped in a bluish light and sparkling with dew or frost.

'Dawn already!' thought Pierre. 'But that's not the point. I want to hear and understand my benefactor's words.' He muffled himself in the cloak again, but now neither the masonic dinner nor his benefactor was there. All that remained were ideas clearly expressed in words, ideas that someone was uttering or that he himself was formulating.

Afterwards when he recalled those thoughts Pierre was convinced that someone outside himself had spoken them, though they had been evoked by the impressions of that day. He had never, it seemed to him, been capable of thinking such thoughts and expressing them like that when awake.

'War,' the voice had said, 'is the most painful act of subjection to the laws of God that can be required of the human will. Single-heartedness consists in submission to the will of God; there is no escaping Him. And *they* are single-hearted. *They* do not talk, they act. Speech is silver but silence is golden. Man can be master of nothing while he is afraid of death. But he who does not fear death is lord of all. If it were not for suffering, man would not know his limitations, would not know himself. The hardest thing' (Pierre went on to think or hear in his dream) 'is to know how to unite in your soul the significance of the whole. To unite the whole?' he asked himself. 'No, not to unite. Thoughts cannot be united, but to *harness* all these ideas together – that's what's needed! Yes, we *must harness* them, *must harness* them!' Pierre repeated to himself with a thrill of ecstasy, feeling that these words and they alone expressed what he wanted to say and solved the problem that tormented him.

'Yes, we must harness together, it is time to harness.'

'Time to harness, time to harness, your Excellency! Your Excellency!' some voice was echoing. 'We must harness, it is time to harness. ...'

It was the groom waking Pierre. The sun was shining full in Pierre's face. He glanced at the dirty inn-yard in the middle of which soldiers were watering their lean horses at the well, while carts were moving out of the gate. Pierre turned away with repugnance and, closing his eyes, made haste to roll over again on the carriage-seat. 'No, I don't want any part of that - I don't want to see and understand that. I want to follow out the things revealed to me in my dream. Another second and I should have understood it all. But what am I to do? Harness it all, but how can I harness everything?' And Pierre found to his dismay that the meaning of all he had seen and thought in his dream had slipped away.

The groom, the coachman and the innkeeper told Pierre that an officer had come with information that the French were nearing Mozhaisk and that our troops were moving on.

Pierre got up and, having given orders for them to harness his horses and catch him up, he went through the town on foot.

The troops were marching out, leaving nearly ten thousand wounded behind them, who could be seen in the yards, at the windows of the houses and in the streets, where they crowded round the carts that were to take some of them away, shouting, cursing and exchanging blows. Pierre offered a seat in his carriage, which had overtaken him, to a wounded general he knew, and drove with him to Moscow. On the road he was told of the death of his brother-in-law, Anatole, and of Prince Andrei.

10

On the 30th of August Pierre reached Moscow. Almost at the city gates he was met by Count Rostopchin's adjutant.

'Well we have been searching for you everywhere,' said the adjutant. 'The count wants to see you urgently. He begs that you will come to him immediately on a very important matter.'

Without going home, Pierre hailed a conveyance and drove to the governor-general's.

Count Rostopchin had only that morning returned from his summer villa at Sokolniky. The ante-room and reception-room of the count's residence were full of officials who had been summoned or had come for instructions. Vasilchikov and Platov had already seen the count and explained to him that the defence of Moscow was out of the question, and the city would have to be surrendered. Though this news was being concealed from the inhabitants, the officials – the heads of the various government departments – knew that Moscow would soon be in the hands of the enemy, just as Count Rostopchin himself knew it; and to escape personal responsibility they had all come to the governor to inquire how they were to act with their respective departments.

As Pierre entered the waiting-room a courier from the army emerged from an interview with the count.

The courier made a despairing gesture in answer to the questions directed to him, and passed through the room.

While he waited, Pierre watched with weary eyes the different functionaries, old and young, military and civilian, important and unimportant, who were gathered there. They all had long faces and seemed agitated. Pierre went up to one group among whom he recognized an acquaintance. After greeting Pierre, they continued with their conversation.

'If they're evacuated and brought back again later on it will do no harm, but as things are now one can't answer for anything.'

'But look here, what he writes,' said another, pointing to a printed sheet he held in his hand.

'That's another matter. That's necessary for the populace.'

'What is it?' asked Pierre.

'Oh, a new broadsheet.'

Pierre took it and began to read.

His Serene Highness Prince Kutuzov, in order to effect an early junction with the troops moving towards him, has passed through Mozhaisk and occupied a strong position where the enemy will not find it easy to attack him. Forty-eight cannon with ammunition have been sent him from here, and his Serene Highness declares that he will defend Moscow to the last drop of his blood and is ready to fight even in the streets of the city. My friends, do not let the closing of the Courts of Law occasion any alarm: it was necessary to remove them but we will give the evil-doer a taste of our law, you may be sure! When the time comes I shall want some gallant lads from the town and the country too. I shall utter my call a day or two beforehand but it is not necessary yet, so I hold my peace. An axe is a good weapon, a hunting-spear is not bad, but best of all would be a three-pronged fork: a Frenchman is no heavier than a sheaf of rye. Tomorrow after dinner I shall take the Iberian icon of the Mother of God to the wounded in St Catherine's hospital. There we will have some water blessed: that will help them to get well quicker. I am all right now. I had a bad eye but now I can see out of both.

'Why, military authorities have assured me that there could be no fighting in the city itself,' said Pierre, 'and that the position ...'

'To be sure, that's just what we were saying,' replied the first speaker.

'And what does he mean by "I had a bad eye but now I can see out of both"?' asked Pierre.

'The count had a sty,' explained the adjutant, smiling, 'and was very much put out when I told him people had called to ask what was the matter with him. By the way, count,' he added suddenly, addressing Pierre with a smile, 'we heard that you are having domestic difficulties and that the countess, that your wife ...'

'I don't know anything,' said Pierre indifferently. 'What is it you have heard?'

'Oh well, you know how people so often invent things. I only say what I heard.'

'But what did you hear?'

'Oh, they say,' observed the adjutant with the same smile, 'that the countess, your wife, is preparing to go abroad. I expect it's nonsense. ...'

'It may be,' said Pierre, looking about him absentmindedly. 'And who is that?' he asked, indicating a short old man in a clean blue peasant-overcoat, with a big snow-white beard and eyebrows and a ruddy face.

'That? Oh, he's a certain tradesman – I mean, he's the eating-house-keeper, Vereshchagin. You have heard the story of the proclamation, I dare say?'

'Oh, so that's Vereshchagin!' said Pierre, scrutinizing the calm, self-reliant face of the old man and seeking for signs in it to denote a traitor.

'That's not the man himself – that's the father of the fellow who wrote the proclamation,' said the adjutant. 'The son is in custody, and I fancy it will go hardly with him.'

A little old gentleman wearing a star, and another official, a German with a cross round his neck, joined the group.

'You see,' proceeded the adjutant, 'it is a puzzling business. The proclamation appeared a couple of months back. The count was informed of it. He ordered an inquiry to be made. Gavrilo Ivanich here started to investigate and found that the proclamation had passed through exactly sixty-three hands. He goes to one man and asks: "How did you come by it?" – "Had it from So-and-so." He tried the next. "Where did you get it?" and so on until he reaches Vereshchagin, an ignorant merchant – you know, one of those self-made men,' said the adjutant, smiling. 'He is asked: "Who gave you this?" And the point is, we knew perfectly well where he got it. He could only have had it from the Postmaster. But evidently they had some secret understanding. "No one," says he. "I made it up myself." He was threatened and coaxed but he stuck to it that he wrote it himself. And so it was reported to the count, who sent for the man. "From whom did you get this proclamation?" – "I wrote it myself." Well, you know the count,' said the adjutant cheerfully, with a smile of pride. 'He flared up like anything – and just think of the fellow's audacity, his stubborn lying! ...'

'And the count wanted him to implicate Klucharov? I understand,' said Pierre.

'Not at all,' rejoined the adjutant in dismay. 'Klucharov had sins enough to answer for without that, and that is why he was banished. But this is the point: the count was furious. "How could you have written it yourself?" says he, and he picked up the *Hamburg Gazette* that was lying on the table. "Here it is! You did not write it yourself but translated it, and translated it atrociously too, because even in French you are an idiot!" And what do you think? "No," says he, "I didn't read any gazettes, I made it up myself." – "Well, if that's so, you're a traitor, and I'll have you tried and hanged! Confess now, who did you get it from?" – "I never seen any newspapers, I made it up myself." And there the matter stuck. The count summoned the father too but the fellow held out. He was sent for trial and sentenced to penal servitude, I believe. Now the father is here to intercede for him. But he's a worthless young scamp! You know the kind – tradesman's son, dandy, lady-killer. Picked up a bit of learning somewhere and now thinks himself a cut above everybody else. That's the sort he is. His father keeps a cookshop here on the Kamenny bridge – and you remember in the parlour there was a large icon of God the Father painted with a sceptre in one hand and an orb in the other? Well, he takes it home with him for a few days, and what do you suppose he does? Found some scoundrel of a painter. ...'

II

In the middle of this new anecdote Pierre was called in to the governor-general.

When he entered the private room Count Rostopchin, scowling, was rubbing his forehead and eyes with his hand. A short man was saying something but as soon as Pierre appeared he stopped and left the room.

'Ah, good-day, doughty warrior!' said Rostopchin immediately the other man had gone. 'We have been hearing about your *prouesses*! But that's not what I want to talk about just now. Between ourselves, *mon cher*, are you a freemason?' he asked in a severe tone, as though that were a crime but one which he intended to pardon. Pierre remained silent. 'I am well informed, my friend, but I know that there are masons and masons, and I hope that you are not one of those who, by way of regenerating the human race, are doing their best to ruin Russia.'

'Yes, I am a mason,' Pierre replied.

'There you are, you see, my dear fellow! I don't expect you are ignorant of the fact that Messrs Speransky and Magnitsky have been put in their proper places, as also has Klucharov. Others likewise, who under the guise of building up the temple of Solomon have been trying to destroy the temple of their Fatherland. You may take it for granted there are good reasons for what has been done, and that I could not have banished the Postmaster had he not been a dangerous person. It has now come to my knowledge that you lent him your carriage to take him from the city, and that you have even accepted papers from him for safe custody. I like you, and wish you no harm, and as you are half my age I advise you, as a father would, to break with men of that stamp and take yourself off from here as fast as you possibly can.'

'But what was Klucharov's crime?' asked Pierre.

'That is my business, and it's not yours to question me,' cried Rostopchin.

'If he is accused of having circulated Napoleon's proclamation it is not proved that he did so,' said Pierre (not looking at Rostopchin), 'and Vereshchagin ...'

'Now we have it!' Rostopchin shouted at Pierre louder than before, frowning suddenly. 'Vereshchagin is a renegade and a traitor who will be punished as he deserves,' he said with the vindictiveness with which people speak at the recollection of an insult. 'But I did not send for you to discuss my actions but to give you advice – or an order if you prefer that term. I request you to break off all connexion with Klucharov and his like, and to leave town. And I will knock the nonsense out of any and everybody' – but, probably realizing that he was railing at Bezuhov, who so far was guilty of no offence, he added in French, cordially seizing Pierre's hand: 'We are on the eve of a public disaster and I haven't time to say civil things to everyone who has business with me. My brain's often in a perfect whirl. Well, *mon cher*, what are you personally going to do?'

'Why, nothing,' answered Pierre, without raising his eyes and with no change in the thoughtful expression on his face.

The count frowned.

'A friendly word of advice, *mon cher*. Be off as soon as you can: that's all I have to say to you. Happy he who has ears to hear. Good-bye, my dear boy. Oh yes!' he called through the door after Pierre, 'is it true the countess has fallen into the clutches of the holy fathers of the Society of Jesus?'

Pierre did not answer, and walked out of Rostopchin's more angry and out of humour than he had ever been known to look before.

★

By the time he reached home it was already growing dark. About eight different people came to see him that evening: the secretary of some committee, the colonel of his battalion of militia, his steward, his major-domo, and various other persons with petitions. They all had business with Pierre and wanted decisions from him. Pierre did not understand and was not interested in any of the questions, and only answered in order to get rid of these people. When at last he was left alone he opened and read his wife's letter.

'*They* – the soldiers in the battery; Prince Andrei killed ... the old man. ... Single-heartedness is submission to God. Suffering is necessary ... the significance of everything ... one must harness ... my

wife is going to be married. ... One must forget and understand. ...'
And, without undressing, he threw himself on his bed and fell asleep
immediately.

When he awoke next morning the major-domo came in to inform
him that a special messenger, a police officer, had come from Count
Rostopchin to find out whether Count Bezuhov had left or was
leaving town.

A dozen people were waiting in the drawing-room to see Pierre on
business. He dressed hurriedly and, instead of going down to see
them, went to the back porch and out through the gate.

From that moment until after the devastation of Moscow, in spite
of every effort to trace him, no one of Bezuhov's household saw
Pierre again, or could discover his whereabouts.

12

THE Rostovs remained in Moscow till the 1st of September, the day
before the enemy entered the city.

After Petya had joined Obolensky's regiment of Cossacks and had
gone away to Byelaya Tserkov, where the regiment was being enrolled, the countess was seized with panic. The thought that both her
sons were at the war, that they had both gone from under her wing,
that today or tomorrow either or both of them might be killed, like
the three sons of a lady of her acquaintance, struck her that summer
for the first time with cruel explicitness. She tried to get Nikolai back,
wanted to go after Petya herself, place him somewhere in Petersburg,
but none of these ideas proved practicable. Petya could not return
unless his regiment did so, or unless he was transferred to another
regiment on active service. Nikolai was somewhere with the army
and nothing had been heard from him since his last letter in which he
had given a detailed account of his meeting with Princess Maria. The
countess could not sleep at nights, and when she did drop off dreamed
that both her sons had been killed. After many consultations and discussions the count at last hit on a plan to relieve the countess's anxiety.
He got Petya transferred from Obolensky's regiment to Bezuhov's,
which was in training outside Moscow. Though Petya would still
remain in the Service the transfer would give the countess the consolation of seeing at least one of her sons under her wing, and she hoped
to arrange matters for her Petya so as not to let him go again but

always get him appointed to places where there was no risk of his finding himself in a battle. While Nikolai had been the only one in danger the countess had fancied (and had suffered pangs of remorse over it) that she loved her first-born better than all her other children; but when her younger boy, the scapegrace who had been bad at his lessons, was always breaking things in the house and making himself a nuisance to everybody, that snub-nosed Petya with his merry black eyes and fresh rosy cheeks where soft down was just beginning to show, slipped away into the company of those big, dreadful, cruel men who were fighting somewhere about something and apparently finding pleasure in it – then his mother thought she loved him more, far more, than all her other children. The nearer the time came for the return of her longed-for Petya, the more restless grew the countess. She began to think she would never live to see such happiness. Not only Sonya's presence but her beloved Natasha's too, and even her husband's, irritated her. 'What do I want with them? I want no one but Petya,' she thought.

One day towards the end of August the Rostovs received another letter from Nikolai. He wrote from the province of Voronezh where he had been sent to procure remounts, but this letter did not soothe the countess's apprehensions. Knowing that one son was out of danger made her the more anxious about Petya.

Although by the 20th of August almost all the Rostovs' acquaintances had left Moscow, and although everybody tried to persuade the countess to get away as quickly as possible, she would not hear of leaving until her treasure, her adored Petya, had come back. On the 28th of August Petya arrived. The morbidly-passionate affection with which his mother received him did not please the sixteen-year-old officer. Though she concealed her intention of keeping him under her wing, Petya guessed her designs and, instinctively fearing that he might melt when he was with her and 'go soft' (as he expressed it in his own mind), he treated her coldly, avoided her and during his stay in Moscow attached himself exclusively to Natasha, for whom he had always cherished a peculiarly tender, brotherly affection, almost amounting to adoration.

Thanks to the count's characteristic carelessness, nothing was ready for their departure by the 28th of August, and the wagons that were to come from their Ryazan and Moscow estates to remove their household belongings only appeared on the 30th.

From the 28th to the 31st, Moscow was all bustle and commotion. Every day thousands of casualties wounded at Borodino were brought in by the Dorogomilov gate and deposited in various parts of Moscow, and thousands of carts conveyed the inhabitants and their possessions out by the other gates. In spite of Rostopchin's broadsheets, or because of them or independently of them, the strangest and most contradictory rumours circulated about the town. Some said that no one was to be allowed to depart; others, on the contrary, declared that all the icons had been taken out of the churches and everybody was to be forced to go. Some said there had been another battle after Borodino, at which the French had been routed, while others reported that the whole Russian army had been annihilated. Some asserted that the Moscow militia, with the clergy at their head, were going to the Three Hills; others whispered that Archbishop Augustin had been forbidden to leave, that traitors had been seized, that the peasants were rioting and plundering people on their way from Moscow, and so on. But all this was only talk, while in reality (though the council at Fili at which it was decided to abandon Moscow had not yet been held) both those who left and those who remained all felt that Moscow would assuredly be surrendered, though they did not say so freely, and that they must make all haste to get away and save their belongings. There was a feeling that everything was about to collapse, and that a sudden change was imminent, but up to the 1st of September things still continued the same. Like a criminal being led to the gallows, who knows that in a minute he must die but yet stares about him and straightens the cap sitting awry on his head, so Moscow automatically carried on with the routine of daily life, though aware that the hour of destruction was at hand when all the conventional conditions of existence would be torn asunder.

During the three days preceding the occupation of Moscow the whole Rostov family was absorbed in various activities. The head of the family, Count Rostov, continually drove about the city collecting all the rumours that were in circulation, and when at home gave superficial and hasty directions concerning the preparations for their departure.

The countess superintended the packing, was out of humour with everything, and kept in continual pursuit of Petya, who was always running away from her and exciting her jealousy by spending all his time with Natasha. Sonya was the only person who really saw to the practical business of getting things packed. But Sonya had been particularly silent and melancholy of late. Nicolas' letter in which he mentioned Princess Maria had occasioned, in her presence, the most joyful auguries from the countess, who saw in Nicolas' encounter with Princess Maria a direct dispensation of Providence.

'I never really felt happy about Bolkonsky's engagement to Natasha,' said the countess, 'but I always longed for Nikolai to marry the princess, and I have a presentiment that he will. And what a good thing it would be!'

Sonya felt this was true; that the only possibility of retrieving the fortunes of the Rostovs was for Nicolas to marry an heiress, and that the princess would be an excellent match. But this was a very bitter reflection for her. In spite, or perhaps in consequence, of her grief she took on herself all the difficult work of seeing after the storing and packing of the household goods, and was busy for whole days together. The count and countess referred to her when they had any orders to give. Petya and Natasha, on the contrary, far from helping their parents got in everybody's way and were a general nuisance. Almost from morning till night the house resounded with their flying footsteps, their cries and spontaneous laughter. They laughed and were gay, not because there was any reason for laughter but because gaiety and mirth were in their hearts and so everything that happened seemed to them a cause for rejoicing and laughter. Petya was in high spirits because he had left home a boy and returned (so everyone told him) a fine young man, because he was at home, because he had left Byelaya Tserkov, where there was no prospect of taking part in an early battle, and come to Moscow where any day there might be fighting, and above all because Natasha, whose lead he always followed, was in high spirits. Natasha was gay because for too long she had been sad and now nothing reminded her of the cause of her sadness, and she was feeling well again. She was happy too because she had someone to adore her – the adoration of others was the lubricant necessary if the wheels of her mechanism were to run quite smoothly – and Petya adored her. But above all they were gay because there was war at the very gates of Moscow, because there would be fighting at the barriers, arms were being distributed, everybody was rushing here and there, and altogether something extraordinary was happening, and that is always exciting, especially for the young.

ON Saturday the 31st of August everything in the Rostovs' house seemed at sixes and sevens. All the doors stood wide open, all the furniture had been carried out or put somewhere else, looking-glasses and pictures had been taken down. The rooms were littered with trunks, bits of straw, wrapping-paper and cord. Peasants and house-serfs trod heavily over the parquet floors carrying out baggage. The courtyard was crowded with carts, some loaded high and already roped up, others still empty.

The voices and steps of the army of servants and peasants who had come with their carts rang through the courtyard and the house. The count had been out since morning. The countess had a headache, brought on by all the noise and turmoil, and was lying down in the new sitting-room with a vinegar compress on her head. Petya was not at home: he had gone to see a friend with whom he was planning to obtain a transfer from the militia to a regiment on active service. Sonya was in the ball-room superintending the packing of the glass and china. Natasha was sitting on the floor of her dismantled room with dresses, ribbons and scarves strewn about her, staring at the floor and holding in her hands an old ball-dress, the very one (quite out of date now) which she had worn at her first Petersburg ball.

Natasha's conscience had pricked her for being idle when everyone else was so busy, and several times in the course of the morning she had tried to do something to help, but her heart was not in it and she had always been incapable of doing any kind of work that did not captivate her completely. For a time she had stood beside Sonya while the china was being packed, with the idea of lending a hand, but she soon gave that up and went to her room to pack her own things. At first she had found it amusing to give away dresses and ribbons to the maids, but when it came to packing what was left she found it a wearisome task.

'Dunyasha, you pack! You will, won't you, dear ?'

And when Dunyasha willingly agreed to do it all for her Natasha sat down on the floor with the old ball-dress in her hands and fell to dreaming of things far removed from what should then have been occupying her mind. She was roused from her reverie by the chatter of the maids in the next room (which was theirs) and the sound of their hurried footsteps going to the back porch. Natasha got up and looked out of the window. An enormous train of wounded men had come to a halt outside in the street.

The maids, the footmen, the housekeeper, the old nurse, the cooks, coachmen, post-boys and scullions were all at the gate, staring at the wounded.

Natasha flung a white pocket-handkerchief over her hair and holding the ends in both hands went out into the street.

The old housekeeper, Mavra Kuzminishna, had stepped out of the crowd by the gate and gone up to a cart with a hood constructed of bast mats, and was talking to a pale young officer who lay inside. Natasha moved a few steps forward and stopped shyly, still holding her handkerchief on, and listened to what the housekeeper was saying.

'So haven't you any kith or kin in Moscow, then?' she was asking. 'You'd be more comfortable in a house somewhere ... in ours for instance ... the family are leaving.'

'I don't know if they'd let me,' replied the officer in a weak voice. 'There's our commanding officer ... ask him,' and he pointed to a stout major who was walking back along the street past the row of carts.

Natasha glanced with frightened eyes into the face of the wounded man, and at once went to meet the major.

'Can some of the wounded stay in our house?' she asked.

The major raised his hand to his cap with a smile.

'Which one do you want, mam'selle?' he said, screwing up his eyes and smiling.

Natasha quietly repeated her question, and her face and her whole manner were so serious, though she was still holding on to the ends of her handkerchief, that the major ceased smiling and after some reflection – as if considering how far it were possible – replied in the affirmative.

'Oh yes, why not? Certainly they can,' he said.

Giving him a slight bow, Natasha stepped back quickly to Mavra Kuzminishna, who was still talking to the wounded officer, full of pity and sympathy.

'They may. He says they may!' whispered Natasha.

The cart in which the officer lay turned into the Rostovs' courtyard, and dozens of carts with wounded men began at the invitation of the townsfolk to draw up at the steps of the houses in Povarsky street.

Natasha was evidently pleased at having to do with strange people and circumstances. She and Mavra Kuzminishna tried to get as many of the wounded as possible into their yard.

'We must tell your papa, though,' said Mavra Kuzminishna.

'Never mind, never mind, what does it matter? For one day we can move into the drawing-room. They can have all our part of the house.'

'What an idea, young lady! Even if we give them the wing, the men's room and old nurse's room, we must still ask permission.'

'All right, I'll go and ask.'

Natasha ran into the house and tip-toed through the half-open door into the sitting-room where there was a strong smell of vinegar and Hoffman's drops.

'Are you asleep, mamma?'

'How can I sleep?' said the countess, waking up just as she was dropping into a doze.

'Mamma, darling!' said Natasha, kneeling by her mother and laying her cheek against hers. 'I am sorry, forgive me, I'll never do it again: I woke you up! Mavra Kuzminishna sent me: they have brought some wounded here – officers. Will you have them? They've nowhere to go. I knew you would ...' she said quickly all in one breath.

'What officers? Who has been brought here? I don't understand at all?' said the countess.

Natasha laughed, the countess too smiled faintly.

'I knew you'd give permission ... so I'll tell them,' and kissing her mother Natasha jumped up and darted to the door.

In the hall she met her father, who had come home with bad news.

'We have lingered on too long!' said the count with involuntary vexation. 'The club's closed and the police are leaving too.'

'Papa, you don't mind, I've invited some of the wounded into the house?' said Natasha.

'Of course not,' answered the count absently. 'That's not the point. I beg of you now to have done with trifling, and help to pack and get off – tomorrow we must go. ...'

And the count proceeded to give similar instructions to the major-domo and the servants.

Petya came back at dinner-time and told them the news he had heard. He said the people were fetching weapons from the Kremlin, and though Rostopchin had said in his broadsheet that he would sound the alarm a couple of days beforehand it was known in the town that tomorrow everyone was to go armed to the Three Hills, where a great battle would be fought.

The countess looked with nervous horror at her son's eager, excited face while he was saying this. She realized that if she uttered a word to dissuade him from going to this battle (she knew how delighted he was with the prospect) he would say something about *men* and *honour* and the *Fatherland* – some extravagant masculine absurdity which there would be no denying and that would be fatal to her plans; and so, hoping to arrange to leave before then and take Petya with them as their defender and protector, she said nothing to her son, but after dinner called the count aside and implored him with tears in her eyes to take her away quickly, that very night if possible. With the instinctive cunning of a woman where her affections are concerned she, who till then had not shown the slightest trace of alarm, declared that she would die of fright if they did not leave that very night. There was no pretence about it: she was now afraid of everything.

14

MADAME SCHOSS, who had been out to visit her daughter, increased the countess's terrors still further by describing the scenes she had witnessed outside a spirit-store in Myasnitsky street. She had taken that street on her way home but had been held up by a drunken mob rioting in front of the shop. She had hailed a cab and returned by a roundabout route and the driver had told her that the crowd had been breaking open the casks of spirit, having received orders to that effect.

After dinner the entire Rostov household set to work with eager haste to pack their belongings and prepare for departure. The old count, suddenly rousing himself to the task, kept trotting to and fro between the courtyard and the house, shouting confused instructions to the scurrying servants and urging them to still greater haste. Petya directed operations in the courtyard. Sonya was completely bewildered by the count's contradictory orders and did not know what to be at. The servants raced about the house and yard, shouting, quarrelling and making a din. Natasha too, with the ardour characteristic of her in all she did, suddenly threw herself into the fray. At first her intervention in the business of packing was received sceptically. No one expected anything but pranks from her, and they ignored her instructions; but her demands to be obeyed were so passionately earnest, and she grew angry and came so near weeping because they would not pay attention, that she at last succeeded in making them believe in her. Her first achievement, which cost her immense effort and established her authority, was the packing of the carpets. The count had a number of valuable Gobelin tapestries and Persian rugs in the house. When Natasha fell to work two large chests stood open in the ball-room, one almost full of china, the other of carpets. There was a great deal more china left waiting on the tables, and still more was coming from the pantry. There was nothing for it but to start on a third chest and the men had gone to fetch one.

'Sonya, wait, we can pack everything into these two,' said Natasha.

'Impossible, miss, we've already tried,' said the butler.

'No, wait a moment, please.'

And Natasha began taking out of the packing-case the plates and dishes wrapped in paper.

'We must put the dishes in here with the rugs,' said she.

'Why, it'll be a mercy if we get the carpets alone into three chests,' said the butler.

'Oh wait, please!' And Natasha rapidly and deftly began sorting out the things. 'These we won't want,' she said of some plates of Kiev ware. 'These, yes – these must go in among the rugs,' she decided, fishing out the Saxony dishes.

'Do stop, Natasha. Leave it alone, we can manage it all without you,' pleaded Sonya disparagingly.

'What a young lady!' exclaimed the major-domo.

But Natasha would not give in. She pulled everything out and quickly proceeded to repack, deciding that there was no need at all to take the ordinary cheaper carpets or the everyday crockery. When everything was out of the chests, they started again. And in fact, by rejecting almost everything which was not worth taking, all that was of value really did go into the two chests. Only the lid of the case containing the rugs would not shut. They could have taken out one or two things but Natasha was determined not to be beaten. She arranged and rearranged the contents, squeezed them down, made the butler and Petya – whose help she had enlisted – press on the lid, and added her own desperate efforts.

'There, that's enough, Natasha,' said Sonya. 'I see you were right, but now just take out the top one.'

'I won't!' cried Natasha, with one hand holding back the hair that hung over her perspiring face while with the other she pushed at the rugs. 'Now press, Petya! Press, Vasilich! Hard!' she cried.

The rugs yielded and the lid closed. Natasha, clapping her hands, squealed with delight, and tears gushed from her eyes. But this only lasted a second. She immediately applied herself to a new job, and now the servants put complete faith in her. The count did not take it amiss when they told him that Natasha had countermanded some order of his, or the servants went to her to ask whether a cart was sufficiently loaded and could it be roped up! Thanks to Natasha's supervision progress was swift now: everything of little account was left out and the most valuable things were packed as compactly as possible.

Still, in spite of their united efforts far into the night, they could not get everything done. The countess fell asleep and the count, deferring their departure till morning, went to bed.

Sonya and Natasha slept in the sitting-room without undressing.

That night another wounded man was driven along Povarsky street, and Mavra Kuzminishna, who was standing at the gate, had him brought into the Rostovs' courtyard. She supposed, she said, that he must be a very important personage. He was in a calèche with the hood raised, and was quite covered by the apron. On the box beside the driver sat a venerable-looking old valet. A doctor and two soldiers followed in a cart.

'Come into our house, come in. The family are all going, the whole house will be empty,' said the old woman, addressing the aged valet.

'Well, perhaps,' said he with a sigh. 'We don't expect to get him home alive! We've a house of our own in Moscow, but it's a long way from here, and there's no one living in it either.'

'This way, please, you are very welcome. There's plenty of everything in the master's house. Come in,' said Mavra Kuzminishna. 'Is the gentleman very bad, then?' she asked.

The valet made a hopeless gesture.

'There's no hope! We must ask the doctor.'

And the old servant got down from the box and went up to the cart behind.

'Very good,' said the doctor.

The valet returned to the calèche, peeped in, shook his head, bade the coachman turn into the yard, and stopped beside Mavra Kuzminishna.

'Merciful Saviour!' she murmured.

She invited them to take the wounded man into the house.

'The family won't object ...' she said.

But it was necessary to avoid carrying the wounded man upstairs, and so they took him into the wing and put him in the room that had been Madame Schoss's.

The wounded man was Prince Andrei Bolkonsky.

15

MOSCOW's last day had dawned. It was a clear, bright autumn morning, a Sunday. Just as on ordinary Sundays the church bells everywhere were ringing for service. It seemed that no one yet was able to realize what awaited the city.

Only two indications marked the crisis in which Moscow found herself: the rabble – that is, the unusual number of the poorer classes wandering the streets – and the price of commodities. Factory hands, house-serfs and peasants flocked out early that morning to the Three Hills in immense crowds, which were swelled by clerks, divinity students and gentry. After waiting there for Rostopchin, who did not turn up, and convinced now that Moscow would be surrendered, they dispersed about the town to the public-houses and cookshops. Prices, too, on that day indicated the state of affairs. Weapons, gold coin, carts and horses rose steadily, while the value of paper money and luxury goods for town use kept falling, so that by midday there were instances of carters, in lieu of payment, keeping for themselves half of any expensive goods, such as cloth, which they were delivering, and of peasant horses fetching five hundred roubles each, while furniture, mirrors and bronzes went begging.

In the Rostovs' staid old-fashioned house the collapse of all the usual conditions of life was scarcely noticeable. True, three out of their immense retinue of servants vanished during the night, but nothing was stolen; and as to the value of their possessions – the thirty peasant carts brought in from their estates in the country were in themselves worth a fortune and were the envy of many, people offering enormous sums of money for them. Not only were the

Rostovs offered huge sums for the horses and carts but all the previous evening and from early morning on the 1st of September orderlies and servants sent by wounded officers came to their courtyard, and wounded men dragged themselves out from the house and from neighbouring houses where they were accommodated, imploring the servants to try to get them a lift out of Moscow. The major-domo, to whom these entreaties were addressed, though he was sorry for the wounded, resolutely refused, saying that he would never even dare to hint at such a thing to the count. However hard it was to leave the wounded behind, it was self-evident that if one gave up one cart to them, why not another, and so on, until it came to putting one's own carriage too at their service? Thirty teams would not save all the wounded, and in the general catastrophe it was impossible not to think of oneself and one's own family first. So reasoned the major-domo on his master's behalf.

On waking up that morning Count Ilya Rostov slipped quietly from his bedroom, so as not to wake the countess who had only fallen asleep towards morning, and came out to the porch in his lilac silk dressing-gown. The loaded wagons were standing in the courtyard. The carriages were drawn up at the steps. The major-domo stood at the street-door talking to an elderly orderly and a pale young officer with his arm in a sling. Seeing his master, the major-domo made a significant and peremptory sign to them both that they should go.

'Well, Vasilich, is everything ready?' asked the count, rubbing his bald head; and looking benignly at the officer and the orderly he nodded to them. (The count liked new faces.)

'We can harness at once, your Excellency.'

'Well, that's capital. As soon as the countess wakes we'll be off, God willing! What is it, gentlemen?' he added, turning to the officer. 'Are you staying in my house?'

The officer came nearer. His pale face suddenly flushed crimson.

'Count ... for God's sake ... let me find a corner in one of your carts! I have nothing here with me. ... I could quite well travel with the luggage. ...'

Before the officer had finished speaking the orderly made the same request on behalf of his master.

'Of course, of course, only too glad!' said the count hastily. 'Vasilich, you see to it. Have a wagon or two cleared, that one there, say ... or ... well, whatever's needed ...' he added, muttering some vague order. But the glowing look of gratitude on the officer's face instantly set the seal on the order. The count glanced about him: everywhere – in the yard, at the gates, at the windows of the 'wing' – he saw wounded men and orderlies. They were all gazing at him and moving towards the porch.

'Please step into the gallery, your Excellency,' said the major-domo. 'What are your Excellency's instructions about the pictures?'

The count went into the house with him, repeating his injunctions not to refuse any of the wounded who asked for a lift.

'After all, we can always take some of the things out, you know,' he added in a low, confidential whisper, as though afraid of being overheard.

At nine o'clock the countess woke, and Matriona Timofyevna, who had been her lady's maid before her marriage and now performed the duties of a sort of chief gendarme for her, came to say that Madame Schoss was greatly incensed, and that the young ladies' summer dresses could not possibly be left behind. On the countess inquiring the cause of Madame Schoss's resentment, it appeared that her trunk had been taken off its cart, and that all the loads were being uncorded and the luggage removed to make room for wounded men, whom the count in the simplicity of his heart had said were to come with them. The countess sent for her husband.

'What's this, my dear? I hear the luggage is being unloaded.'

'You know, love, I wanted to tell you. ... Little countess, my dear ... an officer came up to me – they begged me to let them have a few carts for the wounded. After all, those things of ours are only things but think what it would mean for them to be left behind! ... Here they are in our very yard – we invited them ourselves, some of them are officers. ... You know, I really think, *ma chère* ... let them come with us ... what is the hurry anyway?'

The count said this timidly, in the way he spoke whenever the subject was in any way connected with money. The countess well knew this tone, which always ushered in some project prejudicial to her children's interests, such as the building of a new gallery or conservatory, the inauguration of a private theatre or orchestra, and she made it a habit and regarded it as a duty to oppose anything that was announced in that timid manner.

She assumed her air of tearful resignation and said to her husband:

'Listen to me, count, you have mismanaged things so that we are getting nothing for the house, and now you want to throw away all our – all *the children's* – property! Why, you told me yourself that we have a hundred thousand roubles' worth of valuables in the house. I don't agree, my dear, I don't agree. You must do as you please! It's the government's business to look after the wounded. They know that. Look at the Lopuhins opposite – every stick of theirs they cleared out two days ago. That's what other people do. It's only we who are such fools. If you have no consideration for me, do at least think of the children.'

Flourishing his arms in despair, the count left the room without a word.

'Papa, what is the matter?' asked Natasha, who had followed him to her mother's room.

'Nothing! Nothing that concerns you!' muttered the count testily.

'But I heard,' said Natasha. 'Why does mamma object?'

'What business is it of yours?' cried her father.

Natasha walked away to the window and pondered.

'Papa, here's Berg come to see us!' she said, looking out of the window.

16

BERG, the Rostovs' son-in-law, was by now a colonel wearing the orders of Vladimir and Anna, and he still filled the same pleasant, comfortable post of assistant to the chief of staff of the lieutenant-general of the 1st division of the Second Corps.

On the 1st of September he had come to Moscow from the army.

He had nothing to do in Moscow, but he had noticed that every-one in the army was asking for leave to go to Moscow and had some business there. So he considered it necessary to request leave of ab-sence for family and domestic reasons.

Berg drove up to his father-in-law's house in his spruce little trap drawn by a pair of sleek roans, exactly like those of a certain prince. He looked closely at the carts in the yard and as he went up the steps took out a clean pocket-handkerchief and tied a knot in it.

From the ante-room Berg ran with smooth though impatient steps into the drawing-room, where he embraced the count, kissed Na-tasha's hand and Sonya's, and hastened to inquire after 'Mamma's' health.

'Health, at a time like this?' said the count. 'Come, tell us the news.

How about the army? Are they retreating, or will there be another battle?'

'Only the Eternal One can tell what will be the fate of our Fatherland, papa,' said Berg. 'The army is afire with the spirit of heroism, and even now its chieftains, so to speak, are assembled in council. No one knows what is coming. But in general I can tell you, papa, that no words can do justice to the heroic spirit, the truly "antique" valour of the Russian army, which they – which it' (he corrected himself) 'showed, or rather, displayed in the battle of the 26th. I can assure you, papa' (he smote himself on the chest as he had seen a general do who had made much the same speech, but Berg was a trifle late – he should have struck his breast at the words 'Russian army'), 'I can assure you that we officers, far from having to urge the men on, or anything of that sort, had much ado to restrain those … those … yes, those exploits recalling the valour of antiquity,' he rattled off. 'General Barclay de Tolly risked his life everywhere at the head of the troops, I can assure you. Our corps was posted on a hill-side. You can imagine!' And Berg proceeded to relate all that he had picked up from hearsay since the engagement. Natasha watched Berg with a persistent stare that disconcerted him, as if she were trying to find in his face the answer to some problem.

'Altogether such heroism as was displayed by our Russian fighting men is beyond description and beyond praise!' said Berg, glancing round at Natasha and, as though anxious to conciliate her, replying to her intent look with a smile. '"Russia is not in Moscow, she lives in the hearts of her sons!" Isn't that so, Papa?' said he.

At this point the countess came in from the sitting-room, looking tired and cross. Berg jumped to his feet, kissed her hand, inquired after her health and remained standing by her, shaking his head from side to side to express sympathy.

'Yes, mamma, to tell the truth these are hard and sorrowful times for every Russian. But why are you so worried? You have still time to get away. …'

'I can't make out what the servants are up to,' said the countess, turning to her husband. 'They've just told me nothing is ready yet. You see how necessary it is for someone to take charge. This is where we miss Mitenka. There won't be any end to it.'

The count was about to say something but with a visible effort restrained himself. He got up from his chair and went to the door.

Berg, meanwhile, had taken out his handkerchief as though to blow his nose, and, seeing the knot in it, pondered, shaking his head sadly and meaningly.

'Do you know, I have a great favour to ask of you, papa,' said he.

'H'm?' said the count, and stopped.

'I was driving past Yusupov's house just now,' said Berg with a laugh, 'when the steward, a man I know, ran out and asked me whether I wouldn't care to buy any of their things. I went in out of curiosity, you know, and there is a little chiffonier and a dressing-table. You remember how dear Vera wanted one and we quarrelled about it.' (At the mention of the chiffonier Berg unconsciously slipped into a tone expressive of his pleasure in his admirable domestic establishment.) 'And it's such a charming piece! The drawers pull out and there's one with a secret English lock, you know! Dear Vera's been wanting one for a long time. I should so like to make her a surprise. I saw what a number of peasant carts you have in the yard. Spare me one of them; I will pay the man well, and …'

The count frowned and cleared his throat.

'Ask the countess; I don't give the orders.'

'If it's troublesome, pray don't,' said Berg. 'Only I should so have liked it on dear Vera's account.'

'Oh, to the devil with all of you! To the devil, the devil, the devil! …' roared the old count. 'My head's in a whirl!'

And he left the room.

The countess began to cry.

'Yes, indeed, mamma, these are very trying times!' said Berg.

Natasha went out of the room with her father and, as though unable to make up her mind on some difficult point, at first followed him and then turned and ran downstairs.

Petya was in the porch, engaged in distributing weapons to the servants who were to leave Moscow. The loaded carts were still standing in the courtyard. Two of them had been uncorded, and a wounded officer was climbing into one, helped by an orderly.

'Do you know what it's about?' Petya asked Natasha.

Natasha knew that he meant what their father and mother had been quarrelling about. She did not answer.

'It's because papa wanted to give up all the carts to the wounded,' said Petya. 'Vasilich told me. In my opinion …'

'In my opinion,' Natasha suddenly almost shrieked, turning a furious face on Petya, 'in my opinion, this is so horrid, so abominable, so. ... I don't know what. Are we a lot of wretched Germans?'

Her throat quivered with convulsive sobs and, afraid of weakening and letting the force of her anger run to waste, she turned and dashed headlong up the stairs.

Berg was sitting beside the countess, trying with filial duty to console her. The count, pipe in hand, was striding about the room, when Natasha, her face distorted with indignation, burst in like a hurricane and walked quickly up to her mother.

'It's horrible, disgraceful!' she screamed. 'It can't be true that it's by your orders!'

Berg and the countess gazed at her in alarm and bewilderment. The count stood still in the window, listening.

'Mamma, it's impossible: look what's happening in the courtyard!' she cried. 'They are being left! ...'

'What's the matter with you? Who are "they"? What do you want?'

'Why, the wounded! You can't do it, mamma! It's all wrong. ... No, mamma darling, it's not right. Forgive me, dearest. ... Mamma, what do we want with all those things? You only look at what's going on in the courtyard. ... Mamma! We can't ...!'

The count stood in the window and listened to Natasha without turning his head. Suddenly he gave a sort of gulp and put his face closer to the casement.

The countess glanced at her daughter, saw her face full of shame for her mother, saw her agitation, and understood why her husband kept his eyes averted, and she looked about her with a distracted air.

'Oh, do as you please! Am I interfering with anyone?' she said, not giving way all at once.

'Mamma, darling, forgive me.'

But the countess pushed her daughter away and went up to the count.

'*Mon cher*, you arrange what is right. ... You know I don't understand about it,' she said, with downcast eyes.

'Out of the mouth of babes ...' murmured the count through tears of joy, and he embraced his wife, who was glad to hide her ashamed face against his breast.

'Papa! Mamma! May I see to it? May I? ...' asked Natasha. 'And we'll take all that we really need.'

The count nodded, and Natasha was gone, darting through the ball-room to the ante-room and downstairs into the courtyard, her foot as light as when she used to play tag as a child.

The servants gathered round Natasha but could not believe the strange order she brought them until the count himself, in his wife's name, confirmed the instructions to give up all the carts to the wounded and take the trunks back to the store-rooms. When they understood, the servants set to work with a will at this new task. It no longer seemed strange to them but, on the contrary, no other course seemed possible, just as a quarter of an hour before not only had no one thought it strange that the wounded should be left behind while the furniture was taken: it was the natural thing.

The entire household, as if to atone for not having done it sooner, eagerly lent a hand with getting the wounded into the wagons. The wounded men crawled out of their rooms and crowded round the carts with pale, happy faces. The news spread that places were to be had in the Rostovs' carts, and wounded men began coming into the courtyard from other neighbouring houses. Many of the wounded begged them not to take out the chests but simply to let them sit on top of the luggage. But once the work of unloading had begun there was no stopping it. It seemed not to matter whether all or only half the things were left behind. Cases full of china, bronzes, pictures and mirrors that had been so carefully packed the night before now lay about the yard, and still they sought and found possibilities of taking out this or that and letting the wounded have another and yet another cart.

'There's room for four more here,' said the steward. 'They can have my trap, otherwise what is to become of them?'

'Give them my wardrobe cart,' said the countess. 'Dunyasha can come with me in the carriage.'

They cleared the wardrobe cart and sent it to fetch wounded men from two doors off. The whole household, servants included, were full of happy excitement. Natasha was worked up to a pitch of enthusiasm such as she had not known for a long time.

'What can we tie this to?' asked the servants, trying to fix a trunk on the narrow footboard at the back of the carriage. 'We must keep at least one cart.'

'What's in it?' asked Natasha.

'The master's books.'

'Leave it. Vasilich will take care of it. It's not wanted.'

The phaeton was full of passengers, and there was a doubt as to where Count Petya was to sit.

'On the box. You'll go on the box, won't you, Petya?' cried Natasha.

Sonya, too, was busy all this time; but the object of her efforts was quite different from Natasha's. She was putting away the things that had to be left behind and making a list of them by the countess's desire, and doing her best to get as much taken with them as possible.

17

WELL before two o'clock in the afternoon the Rostovs' four carriages, packed full and ready to start, stood at the front door. One by one the wagons with the wounded filed out of the courtyard.

The calèche in which Prince Andrei was lying attracted Sonya's attention as it drove past the porch just as she and a maid were arranging a comfortable seat for the countess in the huge, lofty coach standing at the steps.

'Whose calèche is that?' she inquired, leaning out of the carriage window.

'Why, haven't you heard, miss?' replied the maid. 'It's the wounded prince: he spent the night in our house and is going on with us.'

'But who is it? What is his name?'

'It's our intended that was – Prince Bolkonsky!' sighed the maid. 'They say he is dying.'

Sonya jumped out of the coach and ran to the countess. The countess, ready dressed for the journey in shawl and bonnet, was wearily wandering up and down the drawing-room waiting for the rest of the party to assemble and sit for a moment with closed doors for the usual silent prayer before starting out. Natasha was not in the room.

'*Maman*,' said Sonya. 'Prince Andrei is here, wounded and dying. He is going with us.'

The countess opened her eyes in dismay and, clutching Sonya's arm, glanced about her.

'Natasha?' she whispered.

At that first moment this news had but one significance for both of them. They knew their Natasha, and alarm as to what might be the effect on her outweighed all sympathy for the man whom they both liked.

'Natasha does not know yet, but he is going with us,' said Sonya.

'You say he is dying?'

Sonya nodded.

The countess threw her arms around Sonya and burst into tears.

'The ways of the Lord are past finding out!' she thought, feeling that the omnipotent hand of Providence, hitherto unseen, was becoming manifest in all that was now taking place.

'Well, mamma, we're all ready. What's the matter? ...' asked Natasha with animated face, running into the room.

'Nothing,' answered the countess. 'If we're ready, then let us be off.'

And the countess bent over her reticule to hide her agitated face. Sonya hugged Natasha and kissed her.

Natasha looked inquisitively at her.

'What is it? What has happened?'

'Nothing – noth ...'

'Something very bad, concerning me? ... What is it?' persisted the intuitive Natasha.

Sonya sighed and made no reply. The count, Petya, Madame Schoss, Mavra Kuzminishna and Vasilich came into the drawing-room, and having closed the doors they all sat down and remained for several moments silently seated without looking at one another.

The count was the first to rise, and with a loud sigh crossed himself before the icon. All the others did the same. Then the count proceeded to embrace Mavra Kuzminishna and Vasilich, who were to stay behind in Moscow, and while they caught at his hand and kissed his shoulder he patted their backs, muttering some vaguely affectionate and reassuring words. The countess went off to the little prayer-room where Sonya found her on her knees before the icons that had been left here and there hanging on the wall. (The most precious ones, which were counted as family heirlooms, they were taking with them.)

In the porch and in the yard the servants who were going – all of whom had been armed with swords and daggers by Petya – with their trousers tucked inside their high boots, and belts and girdles tightened, were exchanging farewells with those who were to be left behind.

As is invariably the case at a departure, several things had been forgotten or packed in the wrong place, and two grooms were kept a long time standing one each side of the open carriage-door, waiting to help the countess up the carriage-steps, while maids bringing cushions and bundles flew backwards and forwards between the house, the carriages, the calèche and the phaeton.

'They always will forget everything as long as they live!' said the countess. 'You know that I can't sit like that.'

And Dunyasha, clenching her teeth to keep silent, but with an aggrieved look on her face, hastily got into the coach to rearrange the cushions.

'Ah, servants, servants!' muttered the count, shaking his head.

Yefim, the old coachman, who was the only one the countess trusted to drive her, sat perched up on the box and never so much as glanced round at what was going on behind him. His thirty years' experience had taught him that it would be some time yet before they would say, 'Off now, and God be with us!'; and that even after that he would be stopped at least twice while they sent back for some forgotten article; and then once more for the countess herself to lean out of the window and beg him in heaven's name to be careful driving downhill. He knew all this and therefore awaited what was to come with more patience than his horses, especially the near one, the chestnut Falcon, who was pawing the ground and champing the bit. At last all were seated, the carriage-steps pulled up, the door was shut with a bang, a forgotten travelling-case sent for, and the countess had popped her head out and said what was expected of her. Then Yefim slowly doffed his hat and began crossing himself. The postilion and all the other servants did the same.

'God be with us!' cried Yefim, putting on his hat. 'Off now!'

The postilion cracked his whip. The right shaft-horse tugged at his collar, the high springs creaked and the body of the coach swayed. The footman sprang on to the box as the coach jolted out of the courtyard and over the uneven pavement; the other vehicles bumped along behind, and the procession started up the street. The occupants of the carriages, the calèche and the phaeton all crossed themselves as they passed the church opposite. The servants who were remaining in Moscow walked on either side of the vehicles to see the travellers off.

Natasha had rarely experienced such keen delight as she felt at that moment sitting in the carriage beside the countess and gazing at the slowly receding walls of forsaken, agitated Moscow. Now and then she put her head out of the carriage-window and looked back, and then in front at the long train of wounded preceding them. Almost at the head of the line she could see the raised hood of Prince Andrei's calèche. She did not know who was in it but each time she took stock of the procession her eyes sought that calèche. She knew it would be right in front.

In Kudrino, from Nikitsky street, Presny and Podnovinskoy street emerged several other trains of vehicles similar to the Rostovs' and by the time they reached Sadovoy street the carriages and carts were two abreast all along the road.

As they were going round the Suharev water-tower Natasha, who was inquisitively and alertly scrutinizing the people driving or walking by, exclaimed with joyful surprise:

'My goodness! Mamma, Sonya, look, it's he!'

'Who? Who?'

'Look, do look! It *is* Bezuhov!' cried Natasha, putting her head out of the carriage-window and staring at a tall, stout man in a coachman's long coat, whose gait and the way he held himself made it obvious that he was a gentleman in disguise. He was passing under the arch of the Suharev tower accompanied by a sallow-faced, beardless little old man in a frieze coat.

'Yes, it really is Bezuhov in a coachman's coat, with a queer-looking old boy,' said Natasha. 'Do look, do look!'

'Of course it isn't. How can you talk such nonsense!'

'Mamma,' screamed Natasha, 'I'll stake my head it's he. I assure you! Stop, stop!' she cried to the coachman.

But the coachman could not stop, because more carts and carriages were filing out of Meshchansky street and the Rostovs were being shouted at to move on and not hold up the traffic.

However, though now at a much greater distance, all the Rostovs did indeed see Pierre – or someone extraordinarily like him – wearing a coachman's coat and going along the street with bent head and a serious face beside a small, beardless old man who looked like a footman. This old man noticed a face thrust out of the carriage-window staring at them, and respectfully touching Pierre's elbow said something to him, pointing to the carriage. Pierre appeared to be sunk in thought and it was some time before he understood what was being said to him. At length, when he realized, he looked in the direction indicated and, recognizing Natasha, immediately yielded to his first impulse and took a quick step towards the coach. But having gone a dozen paces he seemed to remember something and stopped short.

Natasha's face, leaning out of the window, beamed with mischievous affection.

'Piotr Kirillich, come here! You see, we recognized you! This is wonderful!' she cried, stretching out a hand to him. 'What are you doing? Why are you dressed like that?'

Pierre took the outstretched hand and kissed it awkwardly as he walked beside the carriage (which continued moving).

'What has happened, count?' asked the countess in an astonished, commiserating tone.

'I – I – Why? Don't ask me,' said Pierre, and he looked round at Natasha whose radiant, happy expression – which he felt without looking at her – flooded him with enchantment.

'What are you doing – or are you going to stay in Moscow?'

Pierre hesitated.

'In Moscow?' he said doubtfully. 'Yes, in Moscow. Good-bye.'

'Oh, how I wish I were a man, I'd stay with you! How splendid!' said Natasha. 'Mamma, do let me.'

Pierre glanced absently at Natasha and was about to say something but the countess interrupted him.

'We heard you were at the battle?'

'Yes, I was,' answered Pierre. 'Tomorrow there will be another battle ...' he was beginning, but Natasha broke in.

'But what is the matter, count? You are not like yourself. ...'

'Oh, don't ask me, don't ask me! I don't know. Tomorrow. ... But no! Good-bye, good-bye!' he muttered. 'Terrible times!' and dropping behind the carriage he stepped on to the pavement.

Natasha for a long while still kept her head out of the window, beaming at him with her fond, slightly quizzical, joyous smile.

18

FROM the time he had disappeared from home, two days before, Pierre had been living in the empty abode of his deceased benefactor, Osip Bazdeyev. This is how it happened.

When he woke on the morning after his return to Moscow and his interview with Count Rostopchin, he could not at first make out where he was and what was required of him. When his major-domo mentioned among the names of those who were waiting to see him that of the Frenchman who had brought the letter from his wife, the Countess Hélène, one of the fits of bewilderment and despair to which he was so liable suddenly came over him. He felt all at once that everything was now at an end, everything was in confusion and crumbling to pieces, that no one was right or wrong, the future held nothing and there was no escape from this coil of troubles. With an unnatural smile on his lips and muttering to himself, he now sat down on the sofa in an attitude of helplessness, now rose, went to the door and peeped through the crack into the ante-room, then turned back with a fierce gesture and took up a book. His major-domo came in for the second time to say that the Frenchman who had brought the letter from the countess was very anxious to see him if only for a minute, and that someone from Bazdeyev's widow had called to ask Pierre to take charge of her husband's books, as she herself was leaving for the country.

'Oh yes, at once – wait. ... No, no, go and say I will be along directly,' Pierre replied to the major-domo.

But as soon as the man had left the room Pierre snatched up his hat which was lying on the table and left his study by the other door. There was no one in the passage. Pierre walked the whole length of the corridor to the stairs and, frowning and rubbing his forehead with both hands, went down as far as the first landing. The hall-porter was standing at the front door. From the landing where Pierre stood there was a second staircase leading to the back entrance. He ran down this staircase and out into the yard. No one had seen him. But as soon as he turned out of the gates into the street the coachmen waiting by their carriages, and the gate-porter, caught sight of him and took off their caps. Aware of their eyes fixed on him, Pierre behaved like an ostrich which hides its head in the shrub to avoid being seen: he hung his head and, quickening his pace hurried down the street.

Of all the business awaiting Pierre that morning the task of sorting Bazdeyev's books and papers appeared to him the most urgent.

He hailed the first conveyance he met and told the driver to go to Patriarch's Ponds, where the widow Bazdeyev's house was.

He kept turning to look about him at the long lines of loaded carts that were making their way out of Moscow from all sides, and, balancing his bulky person so as not to be tipped out of the rickety old chaise, Pierre knew the light-hearted sensation of a runaway school-boy, as he chatted with the driver.

The man told him that arms were being distributed that day in the Kremlin and that next day everyone would be sent out beyond the Three Hills gate, where a great battle was to be fought.

When they reached Patriarch's Ponds Pierre had some difficulty in recognizing the house, where he had not been for some time. He went up to the garden-gate. Gerasim, the sallow, beardless old man Pierre had seen with Bazdeyev five years before at Torzhok, came out in answer to his knock.

'Anyone at home?' asked Pierre.

'Owing to present circumstances my mistress and the children have gone to their house in the country at Torzhok, your Excellency.'

'I'll come in all the same: I want to look through the books,' said Pierre.

'Be so good as to step this way. Makar Alexeyevich, the brother of my late master – God rest his soul! – has stayed behind; but as your Honour is aware he is in feeble health.'

Pierre knew that Makar Alexeyevich was Bazdeyev's half-witted brother, who was given to tippling.

'Yes, yes. Let us go in …' said Pierre, and he walked into the house.

A tall, bald-headed, red-nosed old man wearing a dressing-gown and with goloshes on his bare feet was standing in the vestibule. When he saw Pierre he muttered something angrily and shuffled off along the passage.

'He was a very clever man once but now, as your Honour can see, he has quite declined,' said Gerasim. 'Will you come this way into the study?' Pierre nodded. 'It has not been disturbed since it was sealed up. The mistress gave orders that if anyone should come from you they were to have the books.'

Pierre went into the gloomy study which he had entered with such trepidation in his benefactor's lifetime. Now thick with dust and un-touched since Bazdeyev's death, the room was gloomier than ever.

Gerasim opened one of the shutters and crept away on tiptoe. Pierre walked round the room, went up to the bookcase in which the manuscripts were kept and took out what had once been one of the most important and sacred documents of the Order. This consisted of some of the original acts of the Scottish Lodges, with Bazdeyev's notes and commentaries. He sat down at the dusty writing-table and, spreading the manuscripts before him, opened them out, then closed them and finally pushed them away, and resting his head on his hand fell to musing.

Gerasim peeped in cautiously several times and saw Pierre always sitting in the same atittude.

More than two hours passed. Gerasim ventured to make a slight noise at the door to attract Pierre's attention. Pierre did not hear him.

'Is the driver to be discharged, your Honour ?'

'Oh, yes!' said Pierre, rousing himself and hastily getting to his feet. 'Listen,' he added, taking Gerasim by the button of his coat and looking down at the old man with moist, shining eyes full of exaltation. 'I say, you know that tomorrow there is to be a battle ... ?'

'So they've been saying,' replied Gerasim.

'I beg you not to tell anyone who I am, and to do what I ask you. ...'

'Certainly, sir,' said Gerasim. 'Would your Honour like something to eat ?'

'No, but I want something else. I want peasant clothes and a pistol,' said Pierre, unexpectedly blushing.

'Certainly, your Excellency,' said Gerasim, after thinking for a moment.

All the rest of that day Pierre spent alone in his benefactor's study, and Gerasim heard him pacing restlessly from one corner of the room to the other and talking to himself, and he spent the night on a bed made up for him there.

Gerasim, with the equanimity of a servant who has seen many things in his time, accepted Pierre's installation in the house without surprise, and he seemed, indeed, pleased to have someone to wait on. That same evening – without even permitting himself to wonder what they were wanted for – he procured a coachman's coat and cap for Pierre, and promised to get him the pistol next day. Twice that evening Makar Alexeyevich shuffled along to the door in his goloshes, and stood there gazing ingratiatingly at Pierre. But as soon as Pierre turned to him he wrapped his dressing-gown round him with a shamefaced, irate look and hurried away. It was when Pierre, wearing the coachman's coat obtained and fumigated for him by Gerasim, was on his way with the old man to buy a pistol at the Suharev market that he met the Rostovs.

19

Kutuzov's order to fall back across Moscow to the Ryazan road was issued on the night of the 1st of September.

The vanguard started at once, marched slowly by night, without haste and in good order; but at daybreak the retiring troops nearing the city at the Dorogomilov bridge saw ahead of them masses of soldiers crowding and pushing across the bridge, toiling up the opposite side and blocking the streets and alleys, while endless multitudes of fighting-men were bearing down on them from behind; and they were seized with unreasoning hurry and alarm. There was a general surge forward on to the bridge, to the fords and to the boats. Kutuzov had himself driven round by the back streets to the other side of Moscow.

By ten o'clock on the morning of the 2nd of September the only troops left in the Dorogomilov suburbs were the regiments of the rearguard, and the crush was over. The main army was already on the far side of Moscow or beyond.

At this same time – ten in the morning of the 2nd of September – Napoleon was standing in the midst of his troops on the Poklonny hill gazing at the panorama spread out before him. From the 26th of August to the 2nd of September, that is from the battle of Borodino to the entry of the French into Moscow, all that agitating, memorable week, there had been that extraordinary autumn weather which always comes as a surprise, when the sun hangs low and shines more warmly than in spring; when everything sparkles so brightly in the pure, limpid atmosphere that the eyes are dazzled while the lungs are braced and refreshed by breathing in fragrant autumn air; when even the nights are warm and when in those dark mild nights golden stars slip from the skies, startling and delighting us.

At ten in the morning of the 2nd of September this weather still held. The early light was magical. Moscow, seen from the Poklonny hill, stretched far and wide with her river, her gardens and her churches, and seemed to be living a life of her own, her cupolas twinkling like stars in the sunlight.

The sight of the strange city with its peculiar architecture such as he had never seen before filled Napoleon with the rather envious and uneasy curiosity men feel when they contemplate an alien form of life which ignores their presence. This city appeared to be instinct with life. By those indefinable tokens by which one can infallibly distinguish, even at a distance, a living body from a dead one, Napoleon from the Poklonny hill could detect the throb of life in the town and felt, as it were, the breathing of that great and beautiful being.

'That Asiatic city of the innumerable churches, holy Moscow! Here it is at last – here is the famous city! It was high time,' said Napoleon, and dismounting from his horse, he bade them open the plan of Moscow before him, and he summoned his interpreter, Lelorme d'Ideville.

'A town occupied by the enemy is like a maid who has lost her honour,' he thought (a remark he had already made to Tuchkov at Smolensk). And from that point of view he gazed at the oriental beauty before his eyes for the first time. Even to himself it seemed strange that the desire he had so long cherished, and thought so attainable, had at last been realized. In the clear morning light he gazed from the city to the map, from the map to the city, verifying details, and the certainty of possessing it agitated and awed him.

'But how could it be otherwise?' he thought. 'Here is this capital at my feet, awaiting her fate. Where is Alexander now, and what must he be feeling? Strange, beautiful, majestic city! And a strange and majestic moment! In what light do I appear to them now?' he mused, thinking of his soldiers. 'Here is this city – the reward for all those faint-hearted men,' he reflected, glancing at those near him and at the troops coming up and forming into line. 'One word from me, one wave of my arm, and the ancient capital of the Tsars would be no more. But my clemency is ever prompt to descend upon the vanquished. I must be magnanimous and truly great. ... But no,' he thought suddenly, 'it can't be true that I am in Moscow. Yet here she is lying at my feet, her golden domes and crosses flashing and scintillating in the sun. But I will spare her. On the ancient monuments of barbarism and despotism I will inscribe great words of justice and mercy. ... Alexander will feel that most painfully of all: I know him.' (It seemed to Napoleon that the principal significance of what was taking place lay in the personal contest between himself and Alexander.) 'From the heights of the Kremlin – yes, there is the Kremlin, yes – I will give them the laws of justice, I will teach them the meaning of true civilization, I will make generations of boyars remember with affection the name of their conqueror. I will tell the deputation that I did not and do not seek war, that I have waged war only against the false policy of their Court, that I love and respect Alexander and that in Moscow I will accept terms of peace worthy of myself and of my peoples. I have no wish to take advantage of the fortunes of war to humiliate an esteemed monarch. "Boyars," I will say to them, "I do not desire war. I desire peace and prosperity for all my subjects." In any case, I know their presence will inspire me, and I shall speak to them as I always do: clearly, impressively and magnanimously. But can it be true that I am in Moscow? Yes, there she lies!'

'Let the boyars be brought to me,' he said, addressing his suite.

A general with a brilliant following of adjutants galloped off at once to fetch the boyars.

Two hours passed. Napoleon had lunched and was again standing on the same spot on the Poklonny hill awaiting the deputation. His speech to the boyars had now taken definite shape in his mind. It was a speech full of dignity and majesty as Napoleon understood it.

Napoleon himself was carried away by the tone of great-hearted chivalry he intended to adopt towards Moscow. In imagination he appointed days for *une réunion dans le palais des Czars*, at which Russian grandees would mingle with the courtiers of the French Emperor. He mentally named a governor, one who would win over the population. Having heard that there were many charitable institutions in Moscow, he decided in his mind that he would shower his bounty on all of them. He thought that just as in Africa he had had to put on a burnous and sit in a mosque, so in Moscow he must be open-handed after the manner of the tsars. And in order conclusively to touch the hearts of the Russians – and being like all Frenchman unable to imagine anything affecting without a reference to '*ma chère, ma tendre, ma pauvre mère*' – he resolved to have an inscription on all these charitable foundations in large letters: THIS ESTABLISHMENT IS DEDICATED TO MY DEAR MOTHER. Or no, it should be simply: MAISON DE MA MÈRE. 'But am I really in Moscow? Yes, there she is before me, but why is the deputation from the city so long in appearing?' he wondered.

Meanwhile an agitated consultation was being carried on in whispers among his generals and marshals in the rear of the suite. The adjutants sent to fetch the deputation had returned with the news that Moscow was empty, that everyone had left the city, many on foot. The faces of those conferring together were pale and perturbed. It was not the fact that Moscow had been abandoned by its inhabitants (grave as that might seem) that alarmed them: the problem that dismayed them was how to tell the Emperor – without putting his Majesty in the terrible position of appearing what the French call *ridicule* – that he had been waiting for the boyars all this time in vain, that there were drunken mobs in Moscow but no one else. Some said that a deputation of some sort must be scraped together somehow; others opposed this idea, insisting that the Emperor, after being carefully and skilfully prepared for it, ought to hear the truth.

'He will have to be told, all the same,' said some gentlemen of the suite. *'Mais messieurs ...'*

The position was the more awkward because the Emperor, pondering on his magnanimous plans, was walking patiently up and down before the outspread map, shading his eyes to look from time to time along the road to Moscow, with a proud and happy smile.

'But it's impossible ...' the gentlemen-in-waiting kept repeating, shrugging their shoulders and unable to bring themselves to pronounce the terrible word which was in all their minds: *le ridicule*. ...

Meanwhile the Emperor, weary of his futile wait, his actor's instinct suggesting to him that the sublime moment by being too drawn out was losing its grandeur, made a sign with his hand. A single report of a signalling-gun followed, and the troops, already assembled outside the city, moved into Moscow through the Tver, Kaluga and Dorogomilov gates. Faster and faster, vying with one another, they advanced at the double or at a trot, concealed in the clouds of dust they raised and making the air ring with their deafening shouts.

Caught up in their enthusiasm, Napoleon rode with his army as far as the Dorogomilov gate, but there he halted again and, dismounting from his horse, for some considerable time strode about the Kamer-Kollezhsky rampart, waiting for the deputation.

20

MOSCOW meanwhile was empty. There were still people in the city – perhaps a fiftieth part of its former inhabitants still remained – but it was empty. It was empty in the sense that a dying, queenless hive is empty.

In a queenless hive no life is left, though to a superficial glance it seems as much alive as other hives.

The bees circle about a queenless hive in the heat of the midday sun as gaily as about other living hives; from a distance it smells of honey like the others, and the bees fly in and out just the same. But one has only to give a careful look to realize that there is no longer any life in the hive. The bees do not fly in and out in the same way, the smell and sound that meet the bee-keeper are different. A tap on the wall of the sick hive and, instead of the instant, unanimous response, the buzzing of tens of thousands of bees threateningly lifting their stings and by the swift fanning of wings producing that whirring, living hum, the bee-keeper is greeted by an incoherent buzzing from odd corners of the deserted hive. From the alighting-board, instead of the former winy fragrance of honey and venom, and the breath of warmth from the multitudes within, comes an odour of emptiness and decay mingling with the scent of honey. No sentinels watch there, curling up their stings and trumpeting the alarm, ready to die in defence of the community. Gone is the low, even hum, the throb of activity, like the singing of boiling water, and in its place is the fitful, discordant uproar of disorder. Black oblong robber-bees smeared with honey fly timidly, furtively, in and out of the hive: they do not sting but crawl away at the sign of danger. Before, only bees laden with honey flew into the hive, and flew out empty; now they fly out laden. The bee-keeper opens the lower chamber and peers into the bottom of the hive. Instead of black, glossy bees tamed by toil, that used to hang down, clinging to each other's legs, in long clusters to the floor of the hive, drawing out the wax with a ceaseless murmur of labour – now drowsy shrivelled bees wander listlessly about the floor and walls of the hive. Instead of a neatly glued floor, swept by winnowing wings, the bee-keeper sees a floor littered with bits of wax, excrement, dying bees feebly kicking their legs and dead bees that have not been cleared away.

The bee-keeper opens the upper compartment and examines the top super of the hive. Instead of serried rows of insects sealing up every gap in the combs and keeping the hive warm, he sees the skilful, complex edifice of combs, but even here the virginal purity of old is gone. All is neglected and befouled. Black robber-bees prowl swiftly and stealthily about the combs in search of plunder; while the short-bodied, dried up home-bees, looking withered and old, languidly creep about, doing nothing to hinder the robbers, having lost all desire and all sense of life. Drones, hornets, wasps and butterflies flutter about, knocking awkwardly against the walls of the hive. From here and there among the cells containing dead brood and honey comes an occasional angry buzz; here and there a couple of workers, faithful to old habits, are cleaning out the brood-cells, a task beyond their strength, laboriously dragging away dead bees or drones, without knowing why they do it. In another corner two old bees indolently fight, or clean themselves, or feed one another, themselves unaware whether with friendly or hostile intent. Elsewhere a crowd of bees, squashing one another, fall on some victim, attack and smother it. And the debilitated or dead bee drops slowly, light as a feather, among the heap of corpses. The keeper parts the two centre frames to look at the brood-cells. In place of the close dark circles of bees in their thousands sitting back to back and guarding the lofty mysteries of the work of generation he sees dejected, half-dead and drowsy shells of bees in hundreds only. They have almost all of them died unawares, sitting in the sanctuary they had guarded and which is now no more. They reek of decay and corruption. Only a few of them stir, rise up and idly fly to settle on the enemy's hand, lacking the spirit to die stinging him: the rest are dead and spill down as light as fish-scales. The bee-keeper closes the hive, chalks a mark on it and presently, when he has time, breaks it open and burns it clean.

So in the same way was Moscow empty when Napoleon, weary, uneasy and morose, paced up and down by the Kamer-Kollezhsky rampart, awaiting what to his mind was an essential if but formal observance of the proprieties – a deputation.

In various odd corners of Moscow a few people still remained aimlessly moving about, following their old habits, with no understanding of what they were doing.

When with due circumlocution Napoleon was apprised that Moscow was deserted he scowled furiously at his informant and, turning away, continued his silent promenade.

'My carriage!' he said.

He took his seat beside the aide-de-camp on duty and drove into the suburbs.

'Moscow deserted!' he said to himself. 'What an incredible climax!'

He did not drive into the town, but put up at an inn in the Dorogomilov suburb.

The *coup de théâtre* had not come off.

21

THE Russian troops poured through Moscow from two in the morning till two in the afternoon, bearing away with them the last departing inhabitants and the wounded.

The greatest crush during the movement of the troops took place at the Kamenny, Moskva and Yauza bridges.

While the troops, dividing into two streams to pass round the Kremlin were thronging the Moskva and Kamenny bridges a great mob of soldiers, taking advantage of the delay and congestion, turned back from the bridges and slipped stealthily and noiselessly past the church of Vasili Blazhenny and through the Borovitsky gate, back up the hill to Red Square, where some instinct told them that without much difficulty they could lay their hands on what did not belong to them. Crowds of the kind seen at cheap sales filled all the passages and alleys of the Bazaar. But there were no wheedling, honeyed voices inviting customers to enter, no hawkers, no brightly coloured press of women purchasers – only soldiers in uniforms and overcoats who had laid down their arms and were going into the rows of shops empty-handed to emerge silently, loaded with spoil. Tradesmen and their assistants (of whom there were but few) moved about among the soldiers quite bewildered. They unlocked their shops and locked them up again, and themselves helped the gallant soldier-lads to carry away their wares. On the square in front of the Bazaar drums were beating the roll-call. But the drums, instead of bringing the looting ranks rushing back, on the contrary set them running farther and farther from its signal. Among the soldiers in the shops and passages were men in grey coats, with the shaven heads of convicts. Two officers, one with a scarf over his uniform and mounted on a lean, iron-grey horse, the other in a cloak and on foot, stood talking at the corner of Ilyinka street. A third officer galloped up to them.

'The general's orders are that they are all to be driven out at once, without fail. Why, this is outrageous! Half the men have scattered. You, where are you off to? ... And you there?' he shouted to three infantrymen without muskets who were slipping past him into the Bazaar, holding up the skirts of their greatcoats.

'Yes, you try collecting them together!' replied another officer.

'It can't be done! The only hope is to push on quickly before the rest bolt. There's nothing else for it.'

'But how? They are stuck there, wedged on the bridge, without moving. Shouldn't we put a cordon round to prevent the remaining few from breaking ranks?'

'Forward and drive them out!' shouted the senior officer.

The officer wearing the scarf dismounted, called up a drummer and went with him into the arcade. A number of soldiers started to make off together. A shopkeeper with red pimples on his cheeks about his nose, and a quietly persistent, calculating expression on his bloated face, hurried ostentatiously up to the officer, gesticulating.

'Your Honour!' said he. 'Be so good as to grant us protection. We are not close-fisted – any trifle now ... you are welcome. Wait now, I'll fetch out a piece of cloth – a couple of pieces now for a gentleman like yourself, 'twould be a pleasure. For we know how things are – but this is sheer robbery! Pray, your Honour, guards should be posted, if only to give us a chance to put up the shutters. ...'

Several shopkeepers gathered round the officer.

'Eh, it's no use whining!' said one of them, a thin man with a stern face. When one's head is gone one doesn't weep over one's hair! Let 'em take what they like!' And with a vigorous sweep of his arm he turned sideways, away from the officer.

'It's all very well for you to talk, Ivan Sidorich!' said the first tradesman angrily. 'Please step inside, your Honour!'

'Talk indeed!' shouted the thin man. 'In my three shops here I have a hundred thousand roubles' worth of goods. Can they be saved when the army has gone? Ah, my brethren, God's will is not in men's hands!'

'If you please, your Honour!' repeated the first shopkeeper, bowing.

The officer hesitated, and his face betrayed uncertainty.

'Why, what business is it of mine!' he exclaimed suddenly, and strode on rapidly down the arcade. From one open shop came the sound of blows and vituperation, and just as the officer was going up to it a man in a grey coat, with a shaven head, was flung violently out of the door.

The man doubled himself up and bounded past the tradesmen and the officer. The officer pounced on the soldiers who were in the shop. But at this point fearful screams reached them from the huge crowd on the Moskva bridge, and the officer ran out into the square.

'What is it? What is it?' he asked, but his comrade was already galloping off past Vasili Blazhenny in the direction of the outcry. The officer mounted his horse and followed. As he neared the bridge he saw two cannon unlimbered, the infantry marching across the bridge, several overturned carts, a few frightened faces and the soldiers laughing. Next to the cannon stood a wagon with a pair of horses harnessed to it. Behind, close to the wheels, huddled four greyhounds in collars. The wagon was piled high with a mountain of goods, and on the very top, beside a child's chair with its legs in the air, sat a peasant woman uttering shrill, despairing shrieks. He was told by his fellow-officers that the screams of the crowd and the woman's squeals arose from the fact that General Yermolov, riding up to the mob and learning that soldiers were straying away to the shops while civilians blocked the bridge, had ordered two guns to be unlimbered and a show made of firing at the bridge. The crowd, squashing together, upsetting carts, trampling one another and yelling desperately, had cleared off the bridge, and the troops had moved forward.

22

MEANWHILE the city proper was deserted. There was scarcely a soul in the streets. Gates and shops were all locked; only here and there a solitary shout or drunken song echoed near the taverns. Nobody ventured abroad in a carriage and the sound of footsteps was rare. Povarsky street was silent and deserted. The immense courtyard of the Rostovs' house was littered with wisps of straw and dung from the horses, and no one was about. In the great drawing-room of the house – abandoned with all its contents – were two human beings: the yard-porter Ignat and the page-boy Mishka, Vasilich's grandson, who had stayed in Moscow with his grandfather. Mishka had opened the clavichord and was drumming on it with one finger. The yard-porter, his arms akimbo, stood smiling with satisfaction before the large looking-glass.

'Isn't this fine, eh, Uncle Ignat?' said the boy, beginning to bang on the keyboard with both hands at once.

'Ay, ay!' answered Ignat, wondering at the broadening grin on his face in the mirror.

'Oh, you shameless creatures! Right down shameless!' exclaimed the voice of Mavra Kuzminishna, who had come noiselessly in behind them. 'Look at you grinning at yourself, you fat mug! Is that what you're here for? There's nothing put away downstairs and Vasilich is fair worn out. Just you wait!'

Ignat left off smiling and, hitching up his belt, went out of the room with meekly downcast eyes.

'Auntie, I was only just touching ...' said the boy.

'I'll give you "just touching", you young scamp you!' cried Mavra Kuzminishna, shaking her fist at him. 'Go and get the samovar to boil for your grandad.'

Mavra Kuzminishna flicked the dust off the clavichord and closed it, and with a deep sigh left the drawing-room and locked the door.

Going out into the yard, she paused to consider where she should take herself next – to drink tea in the servants' hall with Vasilich, or into the store-room to put away the things that still lay about.

Quick footsteps sounded in the quiet street. Someone stopped at the gate and a hand rattled the latch, trying to open it.

Mavra Kuzminishna went to the gate.

'Who is it you want?'

'The count – Count Ilya Rostov.'

'And who are you?'

'An officer. I should very much like to see him,' came the reply in a pleasant, well-bred Russian voice.

Mavra Kuzminishna unlocked the gate and a round-faced lad of eighteen with a strong family resemblance to the Rostovs walked into the courtyard.

'They have gone away, sir. Set off yesterday evening at vesper-time,' said Mavra Kuzminishna cordially.

The young officer standing by the gateway as though hesitating whether to enter or not clicked his tongue.

'Ah, how annoying!' he muttered. 'I ought to have come yesterday. ... Oh, what a pity! ...'

Mavra Kuzminishna meanwhile was intently and sympathetically scrutinizing the familiar Rostov features of the young man's face, his tattered cloak and downtrodden boots.

'What did you want to see the count for?' she asked.

'Oh, well ... it can't be helped!' exclaimed the lad in a tone of vexation, and he placed his hand on the gate as if intending to go away. He paused again, undecided.

'It's like this,' he said all at once, 'I am a kinsman of the count's, and he has always been very kind to me. And as you can see' (he glanced down at his cloak and boots with a frank, merry smile), 'I am in rags and haven't a farthing, so I was going to ask the count ...'

Mavra Kuzminishna did not let him finish.

'Just you wait a wee minute, sir. Only a minute now,' said she.

And as soon as the officer let go of the latch she turned about and hurrying away on her old legs went through the back-yard to the servants' quarters.

While Mavra Kuzminishna was trotting to her room the officer walked up and down the courtyard, gazing at his tattered boots with lowered head and a faint smile on his lips. 'What a pity I have missed uncle! What a nice old body! Where has she run off to? I must ask her the shortest way to pick up my regiment: they must have got to the Rogozhsky gate by this time,' he reflected. Just then Mavra Kuzminishna appeared round the corner of the house, looking scared and at the same time determined. She carried a check kerchief in her hand, tied in a knot. A few steps from the officer she undid the kerchief and took out of it a white twenty-five rouble note and thrust it at him.

'If his Excellency had been at home ... of course he would ... for a kinsman, but with times what they are ... perhaps ...'

Mavra Kuzminishna faltered in confusion. But the officer did not refuse, and showed no haste, but took the note and thanked her.

'If the count had been home ...' Mavra Kuzminishna murmured apologetically. 'Christ be with you, sir! God keep you safe!' she said, bowing and showing him out.

The officer, smiling and shaking his head as if amused at himself, ran almost at a trot through the deserted streets towards the Yauza bridge to overtake his regiment.

But Mavra Kuzminishna stayed on at the closed gate for some time with moist eyes, pensively nodding her head and feeling a sudden rush of motherly tenderness and pity for the young unknown soldier.

23

FROM an unfinished house in Varvarka, the ground floor of which was a dram-shop, came the sounds of drunken brawling and singing.

Some ten factory hands were sitting on benches at tables in a dirty little room. Tipsy, sweating, bleary-eyed, with wide gaping mouths, they were singing some sort of song. They sang discordantly, laboriously, with effort – not, plainly, because they felt like singing but simply to show they were drunk and out to enjoy themselves. One, a tall, fair-haired fellow in a clean blue coat, was standing over the others. His face with its fine, straight nose would have been handsome but for the thin, compressed, twitching lips and lustreless, frowning, fixed eyes. He stood over the singers and, apparently possessed by some notion, solemnly beat time above their heads with stiff jerks of his white arm, its sleeve rolled back to the elbow, while he tried to spread his dirty fingers out unnaturally wide. The sleeve of his coat kept slipping down and he always carefully tucked it up again with his left hand, as if it were of particular importance that the sinewy white arm he was flourishing should be bare. In the middle of the song scuffling and blows were heard in the passage and the porch. The tall lad waved his arm.

'That'll do!' he cried peremptorily. 'There's a fight outside, boys!' And still tucking up his sleeve he went out to the porch.

The factory hands followed him. They had been drinking under the leadership of the tall young man, having brought the tavern-keeper some skins from the factory that morning and been treated to drinks for their trouble. Some blacksmiths working in a smithy near by, hearing sounds of revelry in the tavern and supposing it to have been broken into, thought that they also would like to take a hand, and a fight had ensued in the porch.

The publican was exchanging blows with a blacksmith in the doorway and just as the factory hands arrived on the scene the smith, wrenching himself free from the tavern-keeper, fell flat on his face on the pavement.

Another smith plunged in at the door, shoving with his chest against the publican.

The young fellow with the sleeve rolled up dealt the intruding blacksmith a blow in the face and uttered a wild yell:

'Up, lads! We're being attacked!'

At that moment the first smith got to his feet and scratching his bruised face to make it bleed lifted up his voice and wailed:

'Police! Murder! ... Man killed! Help! ...'

'Lord have mercy, killed dead, a man killed dead!' screamed a woman running out of the gates next door. A crowd gathered round the blood-stained smith.

'Haven't you ruined folks enough, stripping the shirts off their backs?' said a voice, addressing the publican. 'And now you've killed a man, have you? Cut-throat!'

The tall lad, standing on the steps, turned his bleared eyes from the publican to the smiths and back again, as if considering which of them he ought to fight.

'Murderer!' he shouted suddenly to the publican. 'Tie him up, lads!'

'Tie me up, would you? You tie me up?' roared the publican, shaking off the men advancing on him, and snatching his cap from his head he flung it on the ground. As though this action had some mysterious, ominous significance, the factory hands who had surrounded the publican paused irresolute.

'I know the law, me boy, like the back of me hand. I'll take the matter to the captain of police. You think I won't get to him? No one can't commit robbery and violence these days!' shouted the publican, picking up his cap.

'Let's step along then! ...' 'Let's step along then!' the publican and the tall young fellow repeated one after the other, and they moved up the street together. The blood-stained blacksmith fell in beside them. The factory hands and others followed behind, talking and shouting.

At the corner of Maroseyka, opposite a large house with closed shutters and bootmaker's sign-board, stood a group of some twenty bootmakers, thin, spent, dismal-faced men wearing overalls and tattered coats.

'Why don't he give us our wages we're entitled to?' a lean boot hand with a scanty beard and knitted brows was saying. 'He sucks our life-blood out of us, and then he thinks he's quit of us! Fooled us the whole week, and now he's brought us to this pass he's skipped it.'

Seeing the mob and the blood-bespattered smith, the man paused and all the bootmakers with eager curiosity joined the moving crowd.

'Where you folks be going to?'

'Why, to the police, to be sure!'

'Say, is it true our side's beaten?'

'What do you think? Look at what folks is saying!'

Questions and answers were exchanged. The publican, taking advantage of the increased numbers of the rabble, dropped behind and returned to his tavern.

The tall youth, not noticing the disappearance of his enemy, and waving his bare arm, went on talking vociferously, attracting general attention to himself. The people pressed round him in the main, expecting to get from him some explanation of the problems that filled their minds.

'"Show me order," he says. "Show me the law." "That's what the government's for!" Isn't it the truth I'm telling you, good Christians?' said the tall young man, almost perceptibly smiling. 'Does he think there's no government? How could we do without a government? Otherwise there'd be plenty willing to rob us!'

'Stuff and nonsense!' said a voice from the crowd. 'Do you suppose they'd give up Moscow like that? Someone's been codding you and you swallowed it hook, line and sinker! Aren't there troops in plenty about? Let *him* in, indeed! That's what the authorities are for. You'd better listen to what people are saying,' said some of the mob, pointing to the tall fellow.

Near the wall of China-town a little knot of people were gathered round a man in a frieze coat who held a paper in his hand.

'An edict – they're reading an edict!' cried various voices, and the crowd rushed towards the reader.

The man in the frieze coat was reading the broadsheet of August the 31st. When the mob pressed round he seemed disconcerted but, at the demand of the tall lad who had pushed his way up to him, in a rather tremulous voice he began to read the notice from the beginning.

'I am going early tomorrow morning to see his Serene Highness the Prince,' he read – ('Serin Highness,' repeated the tall fellow solemnly, with a smile on his lips and a frown on his forehead) – 'to consult with him, to act and to aid the army to exterminate the scoundrels. We, too, will take a hand ...' the reader went on and then paused – ('See,' shouted the youth triumphantly, 'he's going to put everything straight for you ...') – 'in rooting up and sending these visitors to the devil. I shall be back by dinner-time and we'll put our shoulders to the wheel, make a job of it and have done with the miscreants.'

The last words were received in complete silence. The tall lad hung his head gloomily. It was evident that no one had understood the end part. The words 'I shall be back by dinner-time' in particular plainly offended both reader and audience. The mood of the people was tuned to a high pitch and this was too simple and unnecessarily commonplace: it was exactly what anyone of them might have said, and therefore what an announcement emanating from the supreme authority had no business to say.

They all stood in despondent silence. The tall youth moved his lips and swayed slightly.

'Why don't we ask him? ... That's him himself! ... How'd it be to ask him? ... Why not? He'll explain ...' voices in the back rows of the crowd were suddenly heard saying, and the general attention turned to the police-superintendent's trap which drove into the square, escorted by two mounted dragoons.

The chief of police, who had driven out that morning by Count Rostopchin's orders to set fire to the barks in the river and had in connexion with that errand acquired a large sum of money which was at that moment in his pocket, on seeing a crowd bearing down upon him, told his coachman to stop.

'Who are these people?' he shouted to the men who were moving separately and timidly in the direction of his trap. 'Who are these people I should like to know?' he repeated, receiving no reply.

'Your Honour, they ...' said the clerk in the frieze coat, 'your Honour, in accordance with the proclamation of his most illustrious Excellency, the Count, they desire to serve, not sparing their lives, and it is not any kind of riot but as his most illustrious Excellency, the Count, said ...'

'The count has not gone. He is here and arrangements will be made for you,' said the chief of police. 'Drive on!' he cried to his coachman.

The crowd stood still, pressing round those who had heard what the representative of power had said, and staring after the departing trap.

Just then the superintendent of police looked back in alarm, said something to his coachman, and his horses trotted faster.

'We've been cheated, mates! Let us go to the count himself!' shouted the tall youth. 'Don't let him escape, lads! Let him answer us! Hold him!' cried different voices, and the mob dashed in pursuit of the trap.

Shouting noisily, the crowd set off after the chief of police, in the direction of Lubyanka street.

'Look at that – the gentry and the tradespeople have all gone away and left us to perish. Do they think we're dogs?' voices in the crowd caught up one after another.

24

ON the evening of the 1st of September, after his interview with Kutuzov, Count Rostopchin had returned to Moscow mortified and offended at not having been invited to attend the Council of War, and because Kutuzov had paid no attention to his offer to take part in the defence of the city, amazed also at the novel discovery he had made at the camp, which treated the tranquillity of the capital and its patriotic fervour not only as matters of quite secondary importance but as altogether irrelevant and trivial. Chagrined, affronted and amazed by all this, Count Rostopchin had returned to Moscow. After supper he lay down on a sofa without undressing, and between midnight and one in the morning was awakened by a courier with a letter from Kutuzov. The letter requested the count to be good enough to dispatch police officers to conduct the troops across the city, as the army was to retire beyond Moscow on to the Ryazan highway. This was no news to Rostopchin. He had known that Moscow would be abandoned not merely since his interview the previous day with Kutuzov on the Poklonny hill but ever since the battle of Borodino, for all the generals who had come to Moscow after that battle had with one voice declared that another pitched battle was out of the question, and with Rostopchin's sanction government property had been removed by night, and half the inhabitants had left. Nevertheless this information, conveyed in the form of a simple note with a command from Kutuzov and received at night, rousing him out of his first sleep, astonished and irritated the count.

Afterwards, in his memoirs explaining his actions at this time, Count Rostopchin reiterates that his two great aims were: to maintain good order in Moscow and to expedite the departure of the public. If one accepts this twofold aim, everything Rostopchin did appears irreproachable. But if so, why were the holy relics, the arms, ammunition, gunpowder and stores of grain not removed? Why were thousands of the inhabitants deceived into a belief that Moscow would not be given up – and thereby ruined? 'To preserve the tranquillity of the city,' explains Count Rostopchin. Then why were masses of worthless documents from government offices, and Leppich's balloon, and other articles sent out? 'To leave the town empty,' says Count Rostopchin's explanation. One need only admit the premise that public peace of mind is in danger and any action finds justification.

All the horrors of the Reign of Terror in France were based entirely on solicitude for public tranquillity.

What foundation was there for Count Rostopchin's dread of popular disturbance in Moscow in 1812? What reason was there for assuming any probability of an uprising in the city? The inhabitants were leaving Moscow, their place being filled by the retreating troops. Why should that cause the masses to riot?

Neither in Moscow nor anywhere in Russia did anything resembling an insurrection ever occur at the approach of the enemy. On the 1st and 2nd of September more than ten thousand people were still in Moscow and, except for a mob which collected in the governor's courtyard – and that at his own instigation – there was no trouble. It is obvious there would have been still less reason to anticipate a disturbance among the people if after the battle of Borodino, when the surrender of Moscow became a certainty, or at least a probability, Rostopchin, instead of exciting the public by distributing arms and posting up broadsheets, had taken steps for the removal of the holy relics, the gunpowder, munitions and money, and had told the population plainly that the town would be abandoned.

Rostopchin, an impulsive, sanguine man who had always moved in the highest spheres of the administration, though he had patriotic sentiments had no understanding whatsoever of the people he supposed himself to be controlling. Ever since the enemy's entry into Smolensk, in imagination he had been seeing himself playing the part of directing national feeling – guiding the heart of Russia. He did not merely fancy – as every governing official always does fancy – that he was managing the external behaviour of the citizens of Moscow, but he also thought he was shaping their mental attitude by means of his broadsheets and placards composed in the vulgar, slangy jargon which the people despise in their own class and do not understand from those in authority. The picturesque rôle of leader of popular feeling was so much to Rostopchin's taste, he had grown so used to it, that the necessity of relinquishing it and surrendering Moscow with no heroic display of any kind took him unawares: the ground was suddenly cut from under his feet and he was utterly at a loss what to do. Though he knew it was coming, he could not really bring himself to believe till the last minute that Moscow must be sacrificed, and did nothing to prepare for it. The inhabitants left against his wishes. If the government offices were removed, it was only due to the insistence of the officials, to whom the count reluctantly yielded. He was entirely absorbed in the rôle he had created for himself. As is often the case with those endowed with a spirited imagination, though he had long known that Moscow would be abandoned he had known it only with his intellect: he was not convinced of it in his heart and did not mentally adapt himself to the new situation.

All his painstaking and energetic activity – how far it was useful or had any effect on the people is another question – had been directed simply towards arousing in the masses his own feeling of patriotic hatred of the French and confidence in himself.

But when the catastrophe began to assume its true historic proportions; when expressing hatred for the French in words was plainly insufficient; when it was not even possible to give expression to that hatred by fighting a battle; when self-confidence was of no avail in relation to the one question before Moscow; when the whole population streamed out of Moscow as one man, abandoning their belongings and proving by this negative gesture the strength of their patriotic fervour – then the part Rostopchin had chosen suddenly became meaningless. All at once he found himself alone, weak and ridiculous, with no ground to stand on.

Wakened from his sleep to receive that cold, peremptory note from Kutuzov, Rostopchin felt the more irritated the more he felt himself to be guilty. Everything that had been expressly entrusted to him, the state property which he should have removed, was still in Moscow. There was no possibility of getting it all away.

'Who is to blame for this? Who has let things come to such a pass?' he ruminated. 'Not I, of course. I had everything in readiness. I had Moscow firmly in hand. And now see what a pretty plight they have led us to! Villains! Traitors!' he thought, not exactly identifying the villains and traitors but feeling it necessary to pour hatred on those, whoever they might be, who were to blame for the false and ludicrous position in which he found himself.

All that night Count Rostopchin issued orders, for which people were continually coming to him from all parts of Moscow. His intimates had never seen the count so gloomy and irritable.

'Your Excellency, there's a messenger from the director of the Registrar's Department asking for instructions. ... From the Consistory, from the Senate, from the University, from the Foundling Hospital. ... The suffragan has sent to. ... So-and-so wants to know. ... What are your orders about the Fire Brigade? The governor of the prison asks ... The superintendent of the lunatic asylum is here. ...' And so it went on all night long.

To all these inquiries the count's replies were short and severe, their drift being that instructions from him were not needed now, that somebody had spoilt all his careful preparations, and that that somebody would have to shoulder full responsibility for anything that might happen from now on.

'Oh, tell the idiot,' he said in answer to the inquiry from the Registrar's Department, 'to stay and look after his archives. What is this nonsense about the Fire Brigade? Let 'em get on their horses and be off to Vladimir, and not leave them to the French.'

'Your Excellency, the superintendent of the lunatic asylum has come: what does your Excellency wish him to do?'

'Wish him to do? Leave, that's all. And turn the lunatics loose in the town. When we have madmen in command of our armies God evidently means these others to be at large too.'

When asked what was to be done about the convicts in the gaol the count shouted furiously at the governor:

'Do you expect me to provide you with a couple of battalions – which we have not got – for a convoy? Release 'em, and that settles it!'

'Your Excellency, some of them are political prisoners – Meshkov, Vereshchagin. ...'

'Vereshchagin! Hasn't he been hanged yet?' roared Rostopchin. 'Bring him to me!'

25

By about nine o'clock in the morning, with the troops already moving through Moscow, the count had ceased to be importuned for instructions. Those who were able to get away were going of their own accord; those who had stayed behind were deciding for themselves what they had better do.

The count ordered his carriage round to take him to Sokolniky, and sat waiting in his study with folded hands, morose, sallow and taciturn.

In quiet, untroubled times every administrator believes that it is only by his efforts that the whole population under his charge is kept going; and in this consciousness of being indispensable lies the chief reward of his pains and exertions. So long as the calm lasts, the administrator-pilot holding on to the ship of the people with a boat-hook from his frail bark, and himself gliding along, naturally imagines that his efforts move the ship he is clinging to. But let a storm spring up, let the sea begin to heave and the great vessel toss about of itself, and any such illusion becomes impossible. The ship rides on in mighty independence, the boat-hook no longer reaches to the moving vessel and the pilot, from being the arbiter, the source of power, finds himself an insignificant, feeble, useless person.

Rostopchin felt this, and it riled him.

The chief of police, who had been stopped by the crowd, arrived to see him at the same time as an adjutant to say that the horses were ready. Both were pale, and the superintendent of police, after reporting the accomplishment of his mission, informed the count that a vast assembly had collected in the courtyard wanting to see him.

Without a word Rostopchin got up and walked with rapid steps to his light, luxuriously furnished drawing-room, crossed to the balcony door, laid his hand on the latch, let go of it and went to the window from which he could get a better view of the crowd. The tall young lad was standing in front, waving his arm and saying something with a dour look. The blood-stained smith stood beside him with a sombre air.

'Is my carriage ready?' asked Rostopchin, stepping back from the window.

'It is, your Excellency,' replied the adjutant.

Rostopchin went to the balcony door again.

'But what is it they want?' he asked the superintendent of police.

'Your Excellency, they say they have rallied, in accordance with your orders, to go against the French, and they were shouting something about treachery. But it is a turbulent mob, your Excellency. I had much ado to get away. Your Excellency, if I may venture to suggest ...'

'Have the goodness to retire! I know what to do without your assistance,' cried Rostopchin angrily. He stood by the balcony door looking at the crowd. 'This is what they have done with Russia! This is what they have done with me!' he brooded, irrepressible fury welling up within him against the someone to whom what was happening might be attributed. As is often the case with hot-tempered people he was overcome with rage, but had still to find a scapegoat on which to vent it. 'There they are – the mob, the dregs of the populace,' he said to himself in French as he gazed at the crowd. 'The rabble they have stirred up by their folly! They want a victim,' he thought as he watched the waving arm of the tall fellow in front. And this idea came into his head precisely because he, too, wanted a scapegoat, an object for his wrath.

'Is the carriage ready?' he asked again.

'Yes, your Excellency. What orders do you wish to give concerning Vereshchagin? He is waiting at the porch,' said the adjutant.

'Ah!' exclaimed Rostopchin, as though struck by some sudden recollection.

And quickly throwing open the door he strode resolutely out on to the balcony. The buzz of talk was instantly hushed, caps and hats were doffed and all eyes raised to the count.

'Good-day, lads!' said the count briskly and loudly. 'Thanks for coming. I'll be out with you in a moment but first we have to settle accounts with a miscreant. We must punish the blackguard who has been the undoing of Moscow. Wait for me!'

And the count stepped as briskly back into the room, slamming the door behind him.

An approving murmur of satisfaction ran through the crowd. 'He'll deal with all the villains, you'll see! And you said the French. ... He'll show us the rights and wrongs of it all!' the mob were saying, as if reproving one another for their lack of faith.

A few minutes later an officer hurried out of the front door, gave an order, and the dragoons formed up in line. The crowd pressed eagerly from the balcony towards the porch. Rostopchin, coming out with swift, irate, steps, looked quickly about him as if seeking someone.

'Where is he?' he demanded, and as he spoke he saw a young man with a long thin neck, and half of his head that had been shaven covered with short hair, appearing round the corner of the house between two dragoons. He was dressed in a threadbare blue cloth coat lined with fox fur, that had once been stylish, and filthy convict trousers of fustian, thrust into thin, dirty, down-at-heel boots. Heavy iron shackles dragged on his weak, thin legs, hampering his uncertain gait.

'Ah!' said Rostopchin, hastily averting his eyes from the young man in the fur-lined coat and pointing to the bottom step of the porch. 'Stand him there!'

With a clank of fetters the young man lurched clumsily to the spot indicated, putting a finger in the tight collar of his coat which rubbed his skin, twisted his long neck twice this way and that, and, sighing submissively, folded before him a pair of hands which were too delicate to belong to a workman.

For several seconds, while the young fellow was taking up his position on the step, there was complete silence. Only from the rear of the crowd, where the people were all trying to push forward to the one spot, came grunts and groans, jostling and the shuffling of feet.

Rostopchin stood frowning and passing his hand over his face while he waited for the young man to get to the step.

'My friends!' he said, with a metallic ring in his voice. 'This man, Vereshchagin, is the scoundrel who has lost us Moscow.'

The young man in the fur-lined coat, stooping a little, stood in a resigned attitude, his wrists crossed over his stomach. His emaciated young face, with its expression of hopelessness and the hideous disfigurement of the half-shaven head, hung down. At the count's first words he raised it slowly and stared up at him as though he wanted to say something, or at least catch his eye. But Rostopchin did not look at him. Like a cord, a vein behind the young man's ear swelled livid on his long thin neck, and suddenly his face flushed.

All eyes were fixed on him. He returned the gaze of the crowd and, as though made hopeful by the expression he read on their faces, he gave a timid, pitiful smile, and lowering his head again shifted his feet on the step.

'He has betrayed his Tsar and his country, he has sold himself to Bonaparte. He is the only man of us all to have disgraced the name of Russia. It is because of him that Moscow is meeting her end,' said Rostopchin in a harsh, monotonous voice, but all at once he glanced down at Vereshchagin, who continued to stand in the same meek attitude. As though what he saw drove him to frenzy, he raised his arm and almost yelled to the people:

'Take the law into your own hands! I pass him over to you!'

The crowd made no answer and merely packed closer and closer. The press was intolerable; to breathe in that stifling, infected atmosphere, to be unable to stir and to be expecting something unknown, uncomprehended and terrible was becoming an agony. Those standing in front, who saw and heard what was taking place before them, all stood, with wide, startled eyes and gaping mouths, straining all their strength to resist the forward thrust on their backs from behind.

'Slay him! ... Let the traitor perish and not bring shame on the name of Russia!' screamed Rostopchin. 'Cut him down! It is my command!'

Hearing not so much Rostopchin's actual words as their venomous tone, the mob groaned and heaved forward, but stopped again.

'Count! ...' the timid yet theatrical voice of Vereshchagin broke in upon the momentary lull that followed. 'Count! There is one God judges us. ...' He lifted his head and again the thick vein in his thin neck filled with blood and the colour rapidly came and went in his face. He did not finish what he was trying to say.

'Cut him down! It is my command! ...' shouted Rostopchin, suddenly growing as white as Vereshchagin.

'Draw sabres!' cried the officer to the dragoons, unsheathing his own sword.

Another still more violent wave surged through the crowd, and reaching the front ranks carried them forward and threw them staggering against the very steps of the porch. The tall young fellow, with petrified face and his hand arrested in mid-air, stood beside Vereshchagin.

'Cut at him!' the officer almost whispered to the dragoons, and one of the soldiers, his face suddenly convulsed with fury, struck Vereshchagin on the head with the flat of his sword.

Vereshchagin, uttering a sharp cry of surprise, looked round in alarm, as though not knowing why this was done to him. A like moan of surprise and horror ran through the crowd.

'Merciful Lord!' exclaimed someone compassionately.

But after the exclamation of surprise that had escaped from Vereshchagin he uttered a piteous cry of pain, and that cry was his undoing. The barrier of human feeling that had held the mob in check, strained to its utmost limit, suddenly snapped. The crime was begun, its consummation now inevitable. The plaintive groan of reproach was swallowed up in the fierce and maddened roar of the crowd. Like the seventh and last roller which wrecks a ship, that final irresistible wave lifted at the back of the concourse, surged through to the front ranks, sweeping them off their feet and engulfing everything. The dragoon prepared to strike again. Vereshchagin with a scream of terror, covering his head with his hands, flung himself into the crowd. The tall youth, against whom he stumbled, gripped him by the throat and with a wild cry fell with him under the feet of the shoving, frenzied mass.

Some hit and tore at Vereshchagin, others at the tall youth. The shrieks of those who were being trampled on and of those who were trying to rescue the tall lad only increased the virulence of the mob. It was long before the dragoons could extricate the bleeding, half-murdered factory hand, And in spite of the feverish haste with which the mob strove to finish off the work that had been begun, it was a long time before those who were hitting, throttling and mangling Vereschchagin were able to beat the life out of him: the crowd pushed on them from all sides, heaving to and fro like one man with them in the middle and making it impossible for them either to kill or release him.

'Hit him with an axe, eh ? ... They've trampled him to death.... Traitor, he sold Christ! ... Still alive, is he ? ... He's a tough one... serve him right! What about a hatchet ? ... Isn't he dead yet ?'

Only when the victim ceased to struggle and his shrieks had given way to a long-drawn, rhythmic death-rattle did the mob around the prostrate, bleeding corpse hurriedly begin to change places. Everyone came up, glanced at what had been done, and pushed back again, aghast, remorseful and astonished.

'O Lord, the people are like wild beasts! It's a wonder anyone was spared!' exclaimed some voice in the crowd. 'Quite a young fellow, too ... must have been a merchant's son, to be sure the people... They do say he's not the right one. ... What d'you mean – not the right one ? ... Merciful Lord! ... And there's another got butchered too – they say he's nearly done for. ... Oh, what a people! There's no sin they're afraid of ...' said the same mob now as they stared with rueful pity at the dead body with its long, thin neck half-severed and the livid face fouled with blood and dust.

A punctilious police official, considering the presence of a corpse in his Excellency's courtyard unseemly, bade the dragoons drag it away into the street. Two dragoons took hold of the mangled legs and hauled the body along the ground. The dead, shaven head, gory and grimed, was trailed along, rolling from side to side on the long neck. The crowd shrank away from the corpse.

When Vereshchagin fell and the crowd burst forward with savage yells and heaved about him, Rostopchin suddenly turned pale and, instead of making for the back where his horses were waiting, strode rapidly along the passage leading to the rooms on the ground floor, looking down and not knowing where he was going or why. The count's face was white and he could not control the feverish twitching of his lower jaw.

'Your Excellency, this way. ... Where would your Excellency be going? ... This way, please ...' said a trembling, frightened voice behind him.

Count Rostopchin was incapable of making any reply. Turning obediently he went in the direction indicated. At the back entrance stood his calèche. The distant roar of the howling mob was audible even there. He hastily took his seat and told the coachman to drive to his country house at Sokolniky. When they reached Myasnitsky street and could no longer hear the shouting the count began to repent. He recalled with dissatisfaction the excitement and fear he had betrayed before his subordinates. 'The hoi polloi is dreadful – hideous,' he said to himself in French. 'They are like wolves, only to be appeased with flesh. "Count, there is one God judges us!"' – Vereshchagin's words suddenly recurred to him, and a disagreeable chill ran down his spine. But this was only a momentary feeling and Count Rostopchin smiled disdainfully at himself. 'I had other duties,' thought he. 'The people had to be mollified. Many another victim has perished and is perishing for the public good' – and he began reflecting on the social obligations he had towards his family and towards the city entrusted to his care, and on himself – not himself as Fiodr Vasilyevich Rostopchin (he fancied that Fiodr Vasilyevich Rostopchin was sacrificing himself for *le bien public*), but himself as governor of Moscow, as the representative of authority invested with full powers by the Tsar. 'Had I been simply Fiodr Vasilyevich my course of action would have been quite different; but it was my duty to safeguard my life and dignity as governor.'

Lightly swayed on the easy springs of the carriage and no longer hearing the terrible sounds of the crowd, Rostopchin grew calmer physically and, as always happens, simultaneously with physical relief his reason suggested arguments to salve his conscience. The thought which reassured Rostopchin was not a new one. Ever since the world was created and men began killing one another no man has ever committed a crime of this character against his fellow without comforting himself with this same idea – *le bien public*, the hypothetical welfare of other people.

The man not actuated by passion never knows what this good is; but the man who has committed a crime is always very sure where that welfare lies. And Rostopchin now knew it.

Not only did he not reproach himself in his deliberations for what he had done but he even found grounds for self-complacency in having so successfully made use of a convenient opportunity at once to punish a criminal and satisfy the rabble.

'Vereshchagin had been tried and condemned to death,' Rostopchin argued to himself (though the Senate had only sentenced Vereshchagin to hard labour). 'He was a traitor and a spy. I could not let him go unpunished, and thus I slew two birds with one stone: I appeased the mob by presenting them with a victim and I punished a miscreant.'

By the time he had reached his country house and begun to busy himself with private affairs the count had completely regained his composure.

Half an hour later he was driving behind swift horses across the Sokolniky plain, his mind no longer dwelling on past events but turned to the future and what was to come. He was off to the Yauza bridge where he had been told Kutuzov was. Count Rostopchin was rehearsing to himself the angry, biting reproaches he meant to address to Kutuzov for his deception. He would make that foxy old courtier feel that the responsibility for all the calamities bound to follow the surrender of the capital and the annihilation (as Rostopchin regarded it) of Russia would redound entirely on his doting old grey head. Thinking over beforehand what he would say to Kutuzov, Rostopchin twisted about on the seat of the calèche and angrily surveyed the landscape on either side.

The Sokolniky plain was deserted. Only at one end, in front of the alms-house and the lunatic asylum, little knots of people in white could be seen, and a few others like them were wandering separately about the field, shouting and gesticulating.

One of these was running across the path of Count Rostopchin's carriage, and the count himself, his coachman and escort of dragoons watched with a vague mixture of consternation and curiosity these mad creatures who had just been turned loose, and especially the one running towards them. His long thin legs catching in his dressing-gown, he reeled along at breakneck speed, his eyes fixed on Rostopchin, shouting something in a hoarse voice and signalling for the carriage to stop. The lunatic's sombre, impassioned face, overgrown with uneven tufts of beard, was haggard and yellow. His dark agate eyes with their saffron whites rolled frenziedly.

'Wait! Stop, I tell you!' he cried piercingly, and again fell to shouting breathlessly with emphatic gestures and intonations.

He reached the calèche and ran beside it.

'Thrice have they slain me, thrice have I risen from the dead. They stoned me, crucified me. ... I shall rise again ... shall rise again ... shall rise again. They tore my body to pieces. The Kingdom of God will be overthrown. ... Thrice will I overthrow it and thrice set it up again,' he shrieked, his voice growing shriller and shriller.

Count Rostopchin suddenly paled as he had done when the crowd closed in on Vereshchagin. He turned away. 'Dri-drive faster!' he called to the coachman in a quaking voice.

The calèche flew over the ground as fast as the horses could go, but for a long time Count Rostopchin still heard the insane, despairing scream echoing away in the distance, while his eyes saw nothing but the wondering, frightened, bleeding face of the 'traitor' in the fur-lined coat.

Recent as that image was, Rostopchin felt that it had already cut deep into his heart, etching its imprint there. He knew now that time would never dim the bloody trace of that recollection: on the contrary, the longer he lived the more cruelly, the more vindictively would that fearful memory lacerate his heart. It seemed to him that he could hear now the ring of his own words: 'Cut him down! If you don't, you shall answer for it with your heads!'

'Why did I utter those words? They came out somehow by accident. ... I need not have said them,' he thought. 'Then nothing would have happened.' He saw the frightened face of the dragoon who had struck the first blow – his expression had suddenly changed to one of ferocity – and the look of silent, timid reproach that boy in the fur-lined coat had cast on him. ... 'But I did not do it on my own account. I had no choice. ... The mob, the traitor ... public welfare,' he mused.

Troops were still crowding the bridge over the Yauza. It was hot.

Kutuzov, beetle-browed and dejected, was sitting on a bench·by the bridge tracing patterns with his whip in the sand, when a calèche dashed up noisily. A man in the uniform of a general, with plumes in his hat, approached Kutuzov and addressed him in French, half hesitatingly, half wrathfully, his eyes shifting uneasily. It was Count Rostopchin. He told Kutuzov that he had come because Moscow, the capital, was no more and there was nothing left but the army.

'Things might have been very different if your Highness had not assured me you would not abandon Moscow without a battle: none of this would have happened,' he said.

Kutuzov stared at Rostopchin as though, not grasping the significance of what was said, he was exerting all his energies to read the special meaning at that moment written on the face of the man addressing him. Rostopchin, disconcerted, fell silent. Kutuzov quietly nodded and, still keeping his searching eyes on Rostopchin's face, murmured softly:

'No, I shall not give up Moscow without a battle!'

Whether Kutuzov was thinking of something else entirely when he pronounced those words, or spoke them purposely, knowing them to be meaningless, at all events Rostopchin made no reply and hastily withdrew. And – wonder of wonders! – the governor-general of Moscow, the haughty Count Rostopchin, taking a Cossack whip in his hand, went to the bridge, and began to shout and hurry along the carts that were blocked together there.

26

TOWARDS four o'clock in the afternoon Murat's troops were entering Moscow. In front rode a detachment of Württemberg hussars, and behind them the King of Naples in person, accompanied by a numerous suite.

Near the centre of Arbat, not far from the church of St Nikolai of the Miraculous Apparition, Murat halted to await information from the advanced detachment as to the condition of the 'citadel,' *le Kremlin*.

A little group of the inhabitants left in Moscow gathered round Murat. They all stared with shy perplexity at this strange, long-haired commander decked in feathers and gold.

'I say, is that their tsar? He's not bad,' queried low voices.

An interpreter approached the knot of onlookers.

'Caps ... caps off!' they muttered to each other. The interpreter picked out an old porter and asked if it were far to the Kremlin. Puzzled by the unfamiliar Polish accent and not realizing that the interpreter was speaking Russian, the porter had no notion what was being said to him and took refuge behind the others.

Murat approached the interpreter and told him to ask where the Russian army was. One of the Russians understood this question and several voices began answering the interpreter simultaneously. A French officer from the advance detachment rode up to Murat and reported that the gates into the citadel had been barricaded and that probably there was an ambush there.

'Right,' said Murat, and turning to one of the gentlemen of his suite he commanded four light cannon to be moved forward and the gates to be shelled.

The artillery emerged at a trot from the column following Murat and advanced up Arbat. When they reached the end of Vozdvizhenky street they halted and drew up in the square. Several French officers superintended the placing of the guns and examined the Kremlin through field-glasses.

The bells in the Kremlin were ringing for vespers, and this sound troubled the French. They imagined it to be a call to arms. A few infantrymen ran to the Kutafyev gate. Beams and barriers made of planks lay across the gateway. Two musket-shots rang out as soon as an officer with some men began running towards it. A general standing by the guns shouted words of command to the officer, and the latter and his men ran back again.

Three more shots came from the direction of the gate.

One shot grazed the leg of a French soldier and from behind the barricade a few voices were heard uttering a strange cry. Immediately, as though at a word of command, the expression of quiet good humour on the faces of the French general, officers and men was replaced by a look of stubborn, concentrated preparedness for action and suffering. To all of them, from the marshal to the humblest private, this was not a particular street in Moscow, not the Troitsa gate, but a new battlefield likely to be the scene of a bloody conflict. And all were ready for that conflict. The cries from behind the gates ceased. The guns were brought forward. The artillery men blew the ash off their linstocks. An officer shouted 'Fire!' and two whistling sounds of canister-shot rent the air one after another. The shot rattled against the stone of the gateway, on the wooden beams and barriers, and two wavering clouds of smoke fluttered up over the square.

A second or two after the echoes of the shots had died away over the stone Kremlin the French heard a curious sound above their heads. Thousands of jackdaws flew up from the walls and circled in the air, cawing and noisily flapping their wings. At the same instant a solitary human cry rose from the gateway, and amid the smoke appeared the figure of a man, bare-headed and wearing a long peasant coat. Grasping his musket, he took aim at the French. 'Fire!' repeated the artillery officer, the crack of a rifle rang out simultaneously with the roar of two cannon. The gate was again hidden in smoke.

Nothing more stirred behind the barricade, and the French infantry with their officers advanced to the gate. In the gateway lay three wounded and four dead. Two men in peasant coats were in full flight along the foot of the walls towards Znamenka street.

'Clear this lot away!' said the officer, pointing to the beams and the corpses, and the French soldiers, after dispatching the wounded, threw the bodies over the parapet.

Who those men were nobody knew. 'Clear this lot away!' was all that was said of them, and they were flung aside and later on removed that they might not stink. Thiers alone dedicates a few eloquent lines to their memory: 'These wretches had invaded the sacred citadel, supplied themselves with fire-arms from the arsenal and fired (the wretches) on the French. Some of them were hacked down with the sword, and the Kremlin was purged of their presence.'

Murat was informed that the way was clear. The French entered the gates and began pitching their camp in the Senate square. The soldiers hurled chairs out of the windows of the Senate House into the square to use as fuel for the fires they lit there.

Other detachments marched through the Kremlin and encamped along Moroseyka, Lubyanka and Pokrovka streets. Others bivouacked in Vozdvizhenka, Nikolsky and Tverskoy streets. Not finding citizens to entertain them, the French instead of billeting themselves on the inhabitants, as was the usual practice in a town, lived in the city as if it were a camp.

Their uniforms were tattered, they were famished, worn-out and reduced to a third of their original strength, but the French troops nevertheless entered Moscow in good order. It was a harassed and exhausted yet still active and menacing army. But it was an army only up to the moment when the soldiers of that army scattered to their different quarters. As soon as the units of the various regiments started to disperse among the wealthy and deserted mansions the army *qua* army ceased to exist and something nondescript came into being that was neither citizen nor soldier but what is known as marauder. Five weeks later, when these same men left Moscow, they no longer formed an army. They were a mob of marauders, each dragging away with him a quantity of articles which seemed to him valuable or useful. The aim of each of these men when he left Moscow was not, as it had been, to conquer but simply to keep the booty he had acquired. Like the monkey which slips its paw into the narrow neck of a pitcher to grasp a handful of nuts and will not open its fist for fear of losing its plunder, and is thereby the undoing of itself, so the French when they left Moscow were doomed to perish because they lugged their loot with them, yet to relinquish what they had stolen was as impossible for them as for the monkey to let go of its handful of nuts. Ten minutes after each regiment had made its entry into any given quarter of Moscow not a soldier, not an officer was to be found. Through the windows of the houses men could be seen in military uniforms and Hessian boots, laughing and strolling through the rooms. In cellars and store-rooms other men were busy among the provisions; in the yards they were unlocking or breaking open coach-house and stable doors; they kindled fires in kitchens, rolled up their sleeves and kneaded, baked and cooked while frightening, amusing or wheedling women and children. Men such as these there were in plenty everywhere, in all the shops and houses; but the army was no more.

The very first day order after order was issued by the French command forbidding the troops to disperse about the town, severely prohibiting violence to the inhabitants, or looting, and announcing a general roll-call for that same evening. But in spite of all such measures the men, who only yesterday had still constituted an army, poured over the opulent, deserted city with its comforts and copious supplies. Like a hungry herd of cattle that keeps together over a barren plain but which there is no holding as soon as it reaches rich pastures, so did the army stray far and wide about the wealthy city.

Moscow was without its inhabitants, and the soldiers were sucked into her like water into sand, radiating out in all directions from the

Kremlin which they had entered first. Cavalrymen would go into a merchant's house which had been abandoned, find stabling and to spare for their horses – yet move on, all the same, and take possession of the house next door which looked better to them. Many appropriated several houses, chalking their names on them, and quarrelled and even came to blows with other companies for them. Soldiers had no sooner settled into their quarters than they ran out into the streets to see the city, and hearing that everything had been abandoned hurried off to where objects of value were to be had for the taking. The officers followed to try and control the soldiers, and were involuntarily lured into behaving in the same fashion. In Carriage Row shops had been left full of vehicles, and generals flocked there to select calèches and coaches for themselves. The few remaining citizens invited senior officers into their houses, hoping thereby to secure themselves against being plundered. Wealth there was in abundance: there seemed no end to it. The parts occupied by the French were surrounded by other regions still unexplored and unoccupied where, they thought, still greater treasure was to be found. And Moscow engulfed the army deeper and deeper into herself. Just as when water is spilt on dry ground both water and dry ground disappear into mud, so when the famished army marched into the luxurious deserted city, it was the destruction of army and wealthy city alike, and filth, conflagrations and marauding bands sprang up in their place.

*

The French attributed the burning of Moscow *au patriotisme féroce de Rostopchine*; the Russians to the barbarity of the French. In reality, however, responsibility for the burning of Moscow was not due and cannot be ascribed to any one person or number of persons. Moscow burned, as any city must have burned which was built of wood – quite apart from the question whether there were or were not one hundred and thirty inefficient fire-engines in the town. Deserted Moscow had to burn, as inevitably as a heap of shavings is sure to burn if sparks are scattered on it for several days in succession. A wooden city, which has its conflagrations almost every day in spite of the presence of householders careful of their property, and a watchful police, could not fail to burn when its inhabitants were gone and their places taken by soldiers who smoked their pipes, made campfires of the Senate chairs in the Senate square, and cooked themselves meals twice a day. In peace-time it is only necessary to billet troops in the villages of any district for the number of fires in that district to increase immediately. How much then must the probability of fire increase in an abandoned timber-constructed town occupied by a foreign army! *Le patriotisme féroce de Rostopchine* and the barbarity of the French do not enter in. Moscow was set on fire through soldiers smoking pipes, through cook-stoves and camp-fires, through the carelessness of enemy soldiers living in houses that were not their own. Even if there was any arson (which is very doubtful, for no one had any reason for starting fires – in any case a troublesome and dangerous proceeding), arson cannot be regarded as responsible, for the same thing would have happened without any incendiarism.

However tempting it might be for the French to blame Rostopchin's savage patriotism and for the Russians to throw the blame on the scoundrel Bonaparte, or, in after years, to place the heroic torch in the hands of their own people, it is impossible not to see that there could be no such direct cause of the fire, since Moscow was as certain to be burned as any village, factory or house forsaken by its owners for strangers to take possession of and cook their porridge in. Moscow was burned by its inhabitants – that is true; but by those who had left her and gone away, not by those who stayed behind. Moscow under enemy occupation was not treated with respect like Berlin, Vienna and other towns simply because her citizens, instead of welcoming the French with the bread and salt of hospitality and the keys of the gates, preferred to abandon her.

27

IT was not till the evening of the 2nd of September that the tide of invasion, spreading out starwise as it did, reached the quarter where Pierre was staying.

After the last two days spent in solitude and in such unusual circumstances, Pierre was in a state bordering on insanity. One insistent train of thought wholly obsessed him. He could not have told how or when it had first come but now it had such complete possession of him that he remembered nothing of the past, realized nothing of the present; and all he saw and heard about him seemed like a dream.

Pierre had left home solely to escape from the intricate tangle of life's daily demands which held him fast, and which in his present condition he was incapable of unravelling. On the pretext of sorting the deceased's books and papers he had gone to Bazdeyev's house in search of relief from the turmoil of life, for in his mind Bazdeyev was connected with a world of eternal, quiet, solemn thoughts, the very opposite of the restless confusion into which he felt himself being dragged. He sought a peaceful refuge, and in Bazdeyev's study did indeed find it. As he sat leaning his elbows on the dust-covered writing-table in the deathlike stillness of the library impressions and recollections of the last few days began to rise before him in calm and significant succession, among them memories of the battle of Borodino in particular and of that overwhelming sense of his own unimportance and spuriousness compared with the truth, simplicity and strength of character of those whose image was stamped on his soul and whom he thought of as *they*. When he was roused from his reverie by Gerasim the idea occurred to him of taking part in the popular defence of Moscow which he knew was projected. And with this end in view he had asked Gerasim to procure him a peasant coat and a pistol, confiding to him his intention of keeping his identity secret and remaining in Bazdeyev's house. Then during the first day of solitude and idleness (Pierre tried several times to fix his attention on the masonic manuscripts but in vain), his mind more than once reverted vaguely to something that had struck him before – the cabalistic significance of his name in connexion with Bonaparte's. But the notion that he, *L'russe Besuhov*, was destined to set a term to the power of *the Beast* came to him as yet only as one of those fancies which flit idly through the brain, leaving no trace behind.

When, following the purchase of the peasant coat simply with the object of taking part in the defence of Moscow by the people, Pierre had met the Rostovs and Natasha had said to him: 'Are you going to stay in Moscow? Oh, how splendid!' the thought flashed into his mind that it really might be splendid, even if Moscow were taken, to remain and do what he was predestined to do.

Next day, full of the idea of not sparing himself and not lagging in any way behind *them*, Pierre went to the Three Hills gate. But back in the house again, convinced that Moscow would not be defended, he suddenly felt that what before had only occurred to him as a possibility had now become absolutely necessary and inevitable. He must remain in Moscow, *incognito*, must meet Napoleon and kill him –

and either perish or deliver all Europe from her misery, which it seemed to him was entirely due to Napoleon.

Pierre knew all the details of the attempt on Bonaparte's life by a German student in Vienna in 1809, and knew that the student had been shot. And the risk to which he would be exposing his life in carrying out his design excited him still more.

Two sentiments of equal intensity attracted Pierre irresistibly to this purpose. The first was the feeling that sacrifice and suffering were demanded from him in view of his consciousness of the common calamity, the feeling that had impelled him to go to Mozhaisk on the 25th and to place himself in the very thick of the battle, and had now caused him to run away from his own house, to give up the luxury and comfort to which he was accustomed, and sleep in his clothes on a hard sofa and eat the same food as Gerasim. The other was that vague and typically Russian contempt for everything conventional, artificial and accepted – for everything the majority of mankind regards as the highest good in the world. Pierre had first experienced this strange and fascinating feeling in the Slobodskoy Palace, when he had suddenly seen that wealth and power and life – all that men so painstakingly acquire and cherish – if they are worth anything at all are only worth the measure of joy afforded by renouncing them.

It was the same impulse that induces a volunteer-recruit to spend his last farthing on drink, the drunken man to smash looking-glasses and windows for no apparent reason, although he knows he will have to empty his purse to pay for the damage; the urge which impels a man to commit actions which from an ordinary point of view are insane, to essay, as it were, his personal power and strength and testify to the existence of a higher criterion of life outside mere human limitations.

Ever since the day Pierre experienced this sensation for the first time in the Slobodskoy Palace he had been continuously under its influence but only now found full satisfaction for it. Moreover at this present moment Pierre was supported in his design and prevented from abandoning it by the steps he had already taken in that direction. If he were now to leave Moscow like everyone else, his flight from home, the peasant coat, the pistol and his announcement to the Rostovs that he would be staying in Moscow would lose all meaning and appear laughable and ridiculous (a point on which Pierre was very sensitive).

Pierre's physical condition, as is always the case, corresponded to his mental state. The coarse fare to which he was unused, the vodka he drank during those days, the absence of wine and cigars, his dirty unchanged linen, two almost sleepless nights spent on a short couch without bedding – all this helped to keep him in a state of nervous excitement bordering on madness.

*

It was two o'clock in the afternoon. The French had already entered Moscow. Pierre knew this but instead of acting he only brooded on his scheme, going over it in the minutest detail. Pierre in his imaginings never clearly pictured to himself the striking of the blow or the death of Napoleon, but with extraordinary vividness and melancholy enjoyment dwelt on his own destruction and heroic fortitude.

'Yes, alone, for the sake of all, I must accomplish this deed or perish!' he mused. 'Yes, I will go up to him ... and then suddenly ... Shall it be with a pistol or a dagger? But no matter. "Not I but the hand of Providence punishes thee," I shall tell him,' thought Pierre, pondering the words he would say as he killed Napoleon. 'Well, then, take me and execute me!' he went on, murmuring to himself and bowing his head with a sad but firm expression on his face.

While Pierre was standing in the middle of the room reflecting in this fashion the study door opened and the figure of Makar Alexeyevich appeared on the threshold, his usual timid self transformed out of all recognition. His dressing-gown hung open. His face was red and distorted. He was unmistakably drunk. At first he was disconcerted at seeing Pierre, but observing embarrassment on Pierre's countenance too he was at once emboldened and, staggering on his thin legs, advanced into the middle of the room.

'They're scared,' he exclaimed in a husky, confidential voice. 'I say, I won't surrender, I say ... Am I not right, sir?'

He deliberated for a moment; then, suddenly catching sight of the pistol on the table, seized it with surprising rapidity and ran out into the corridor.

Gerasim and the porter, who had followed at Makar Alexeyevich's heels, stopped him in the vestibule and tried to take the pistol from him. Pierre, coming out into the corridor, looked with pity and repugnance at the half-crazy old man. Makar Alexeyevich, scowling with exertion, clung to the pistol and screamed in his hoarse voice something that he evidently considered very exalted.

'To arms! Board them! No, you shan't have it!' he yelled.

'There now, that'll do, thank'ee. Pray let go, sir. Come along, sir, please! ...' pleaded Gerasim, cautiously trying to steer Makar Alexeyevich by his elbows towards the door.

'Who are you? Bonaparte! ...' shouted Makar Alexeyevich.

'It ain't right of you, sir. You come along to your room now, and have a lie down. Let me have the pistol please.'

'Off with you, scurvy knave! Touch me not! Do you see this?' shrieked Makar Alexeyevich, brandishing the pistol. 'Board 'em!'

'Catch hold!' whispered Gerasim to the porter.

They seized Makar Alexeyevich by the arms and dragged him to the door.

The vestibule was filled with an unseemly noise of scuffling and drunken, husky gasping.

Suddenly a new sound, a shrill, feminine scream, reverberated from the porch, and the cook came running into the vestibule.

'It's them! Oh heavens above! ... O Lord, they're here! Four on 'em, on horseback!' she cried.

Gerasim and the porter let go of Makar Alexeyevich and in the hush that followed in the passage several hands were heard banging at the front door.

28

PIERRE, having decided that until the time came for him to carry out his project it would be best not to disclose his identity or his knowledge of French, stood at the half-open door into the passage, intending to conceal himself as soon as the French entered. But the French entered and still Pierre did not retire – an irresistible curiosity kept him riveted there.

There were two of them. One, an officer – a tall, handsome, soldierly figure; the other evidently a private or an orderly, a squat, thin, sunburnt man with sunken cheeks and a dull expression. The officer walked in front, leaning on a stick and limping a little. When he had advanced a few steps he stopped, having apparently made up his mind that these were good quarters, turned round and shouted in a loud, peremptory voice to the soldiers standing in the doorway to put up the horses. Having done this, the officer with a jaunty gesture, crooking his elbow high in the air, stroked his moustaches and lightly touched his hat.

'Good-day, everybody!' said he gaily, smiling and looking about him.

No one made any reply.

'Are you the master here?' the officer asked Gerasim.

Gerasim gazed at the officer with anxious inquiry.

'Quarters, quarters, lodgings!' exclaimed the officer, looking down at the little man with a condescending and good-natured smile. 'The French are good fellows. What the devil! Don't let us get touchy, *mon vieux*!' he went on, clapping the scared and silent Gerasim on the shoulder. 'Well, does no one speak French in this establishment?' he asked (still speaking in French), glancing round and meeting Pierre's eyes. Pierre moved away from the door.

The officer addressed himself to Gerasim again, asking to see the rooms in the house.

'Master not here – me no understand … my – your …' said Gerasim, striving to render his words more comprehensible by speaking in broken Russian.

Still smiling, the French officer spread his hands out before Gerasim's nose, intimating that he did not understand him either, and limped towards the door where Pierre was standing. Pierre was about to retreat in order to go and hide but at that very second he caught sight of Makar Alexeyevich appearing at the open kitchen door with the pistol in his hand. With a madman's cunning Makar Alexeyevich eyed the Frenchman, raised the pistol and took aim.

'Board 'em!' yelled the tipsy man, pressing his finger on the trigger.

The Frenchman, hearing the shout, turned round and at that instant Pierre flung himself on the drunkard. Just as Pierre snatched at the pistol and jerked it up Makar Alexeyevich at last succeeded in pressing the trigger. There was a deafening report and all were enveloped in a cloud of smoke. The Frenchman went pale and rushed to the door.

Forgetting his intention of concealing his knowledge of French, Pierre, snatching away the pistol and throwing it on the floor, ran to the officer and addressed him in French.

'You are not wounded?' he asked.

'I think not,' answered the officer, examining himself, 'but I had a narrow escape that time,' he added, pointing to the damaged plaster on the wall. 'Who is that man?' he demanded, looking sternly at Pierre.

'Oh, I am really in despair at what has happened,' said Pierre quickly, quite forgetting the part he had intended to play. 'He is mad, an unfortunate wretch who did not know what he was doing.'

The officer went up to Makar Alexeyevich and took him by the collar.

Makar Alexeyevich, pouting his lips, stood swaying and leaning against the wall as though dropping asleep.

'Brigand! You shall pay for this,' said the Frenchman, letting go of him. 'We French are merciful after victory but we do not pardon traitors,' he continued, with a look of morose dignity and a graceful, vigorous gesture.

Pierre in French pleaded further with the officer not to be too hard on the drunken imbecile. The Frenchman listened in silence, with the same gloomy air, and then suddenly turned to Pierre with a smile. For a second or two he scrutinized him without speaking. His handsome face assumed a melodramatically sentimental expression, and he held out his hand.

'You saved my life. You must be French,' said he.

For a Frenchman the deduction was axiomatic. Only a Frenchman could perform an heroic action, and to save the life of Monsieur Ramballe, a captain of the 13th Light Brigade, was undoubtedly a most heroic action.

But however impeccable this logic, however well-grounded the conviction the officer based upon it, Pierre felt it necessary to disillusion him.

'I am Russian,' he said shortly.

'Tut-tut-tut! Tell that to others,' said the Frenchman, waving his finger before his nose and smiling. 'You shall let me hear all about that presently. I am delighted to meet a compatriot. Well, what are we to do with this man?' he added, applying to Pierre now as to a brother. Even if Pierre were not a Frenchman, having once received that loftiest of appellations the officer's tone and look suggested that he did not care to disavow it. In reply to his last question Pierre again explained who Makar Alexeyevich was, and how just before his arrival the drunken imbecile had carried off the loaded pistol which they had not had time to recover from him, and begged the officer not to punish him.

'You saved my life. You are French. You ask me to pardon him? I grant your request. Take this man away!' he exclaimed with rapidity and energy, and linking his arm in Pierre's, whom he had promoted Frenchman for saving his life, he went with him into the room.

The soldiers in the yard, hearing the shot, came into the passage asking what had happened and proclaiming their readiness to punish the offenders but the officer stopped them sternly.

'You will be called when you are wanted,' he said.

The men withdrew. The orderly, who had meanwhile explored the kitchen, came up to his officer.

'Captain, there is soup and a leg of mutton in the kitchen,' said he. 'Shall I serve them up?'

'Yes, and bring some wine,' answered the captain.

29

When the Frenchman went into the room with Pierre the latter thought it his duty to assure him once more that he was not French and wished to retire, but the officer would not hear of it. He was so extremely courteous, amiable, good-natured and genuinely grateful to Pierre for saving his life that Pierre had not the heart to refuse, and sat down with him in the parlour – the first room they entered. To Pierre's asseverations that he was not French the captain, plainly at a loss to understand how anyone could refuse so flattering a title, shrugged his shoulders and said that if Pierre absolutely insisted on passing for a Russian, so be it, but for all that he would be bound in eternal gratitude to Pierre for saving his life.

Had this man been endowed with even the slightest capacity for perceiving the feelings of others, and had he had the faintest inkling of Pierre's feelings, the latter would probably have left him; but his lively insensibility to everything other than himself disarmed Pierre.

'Frenchman or Russian prince *incognito*,' said the French officer, eyeing Pierre's fine though soiled linen and the ring on his finger, 'I owe my life to you, and offer you my friendship. A Frenchman never forgets an insult or a service. I offer you my friendship. That is all I can say.'

There was so much good nature and nobility (in the French sense of the word) in the officer's voice, in the expression of his face and in his gestures that Pierre unconsciously responded with a smile to his smile and pressed the hand held out to him.

'Captain Ramballe, of the 13th Light Brigade, Chevalier of the *Légion d'Honneur* for the affair of the 7th' (this was Borodino), he introduced himself, an irrepressible smile of complacency curling the lips under his moustache. 'Will you be so good as to tell me now with whom I have the honour of conversing so agreeably instead of lying in an ambulance with that maniac's bullet in my body ?'

Pierre replied that he could not give his name, and coloured up while he tried to invent a name and some plausible excuse for not revealing it, but the Frenchman hastily interrupted him.

'I beg of you!' said he. 'I appreciate your reasons. You are an officer ... a staff-officer, perhaps. You have borne arms against us. It is no concern of mine. I owe you my life. That is enough for me. I am wholly at your service. You are a nobleman ?' he concluded with a shade of inquiry in his voice. Pierre bent his head. 'Your Christian name ? I ask nothing more. Monsieur Pierre, you say ? ... Excellent. That is all I want to know.'

When the mutton and an omelette, a samovar, vodka and some wine which the French had taken from a Russian cellar were brought in Ramballe invited Pierre to share his dinner, and himself immediately fell to, greedily and without delay attacking the viands like a healthy, hungry man, munching vigorously with his strong teeth, constantly smacking his lips and exclaiming, 'Excellent! Delicious!' His face flushed and perspired. Pierre was hungry and glad to share the repast. Morel, the orderly, appeared with some hot water in a saucepan and placed a bottle of claret in it. He also fetched a bottle of kvass from the kitchen for them to try. The French called it *limonade de cochon*, and Morel spoke well of the 'pig's lemonade' he had found in the kitchen. But as the captain had the wine they had looted on their way across Moscow he left the kvass to Morel and devoted himself to a bottle of Bordeaux. He wrapped a table-napkin round the neck of the bottle and poured out wine for himself and Pierre. Hunger appeased and the wine made the captain even more lively and he chatted non-stop all through dinner.

'Yes, my dear Monsieur Pierre, I must offer up a fine votive candle for you for having saved me from that – that madman. ... You see, I have bullets enough in my body already. Here is one I got at Wagram' (he touched his side) 'and this was Smolensk' – he indicated the scar on his cheek. 'And there's this leg, which, as you have noticed, is reluctant to walk: that happened at the great battle of *la Moskowa*' (which was the French name for the battle of Borodino) 'on the 7th. Ye gods, that was something tremendous! You should have seen it – a deluge of fire. A tough job you set us there, upon my word! That is something you can be proud of all right. And, *ma parole*, in spite of the nasty smack I received there I should be ready to begin all over again. I pity those who missed it.'

'I was there,' said Pierre.

'No, really? So much the better!' pursued the Frenchman. 'You certainly are brave enemies, though. The big redoubt held out well, *nom d'une pipe*. And you made us pay dear for it. I was at it three times – sure as I sit here. Three times we were right on the cannon and three times we were knocked back like cardboard soldiers. Beautiful it was, Monsieur Pierre! Your grenadiers were superb, by Jove! Half a dozen times in succession I saw them close up their ranks and march as though on parade. Fine fellows! Our King of Naples, who knows what's what, cried "Bravo!" Well, well, so you're one of us soldiers!' he smiled after a momentary pause. 'So much the better, so much the better, Monsieur Pierre! Terrible in battle … gallant … with the fair' (he winked and smiled), 'that's your Frenchman for you, eh, Monsieur Pierre?'

The captain was so naïvely and good-naturedly gay, so obtuse and self-satisfied that Pierre almost winked back as he looked at him cheerfully. Probably the word 'gallant' led the captain to reflect on the state of things in Moscow.

'*À propos*, tell me, is it true all the women have left Moscow? What a queer idea! What had they to be afraid of?'

'Would not the French ladies leave Paris if the Russians were to enter?' asked Pierre.

'Ha, ha, ha!' The Frenchman gave vent to a merry, hearty chuckle, and slapped Pierre on the shoulder. 'That's a good one, that is!' he exclaimed. 'Paris? … Why Paris – Paris is …'

'Paris is the capital of the world …' Pierre finished for him.

The captain looked at Pierre. He had a habit of stopping short in the middle of a sentence and staring intently with his laughing, genial eyes.

'Well, if you hadn't told me you were Russian, I would have wagered you were a Parisian. You have that … I don't know what, that ...' and having pronounced this compliment he again gazed at him mutely.

'I have been in Paris. I spent some years there,' said Pierre.

'Oh yes, one can see that quite plainly. Paris! ... The man who doesn't know Paris is a barbarian. You can tell a Parisian two leagues off. Paris is Talma, la Duschénois, Potier, the Sorbonne, the boulevards,' and, perceiving that this conclusion was somewhat of an anticlimax, he added quickly: 'There is only one Paris in the world. You have been in Paris and you remain Russian. Well, I don't esteem you the less for that.'

Under the influence of the wine, and after the days spent in solitude with his sombre thoughts, Pierre could not help taking pleasure in talking to this jolly and good-tempered person.

'To return to your ladies – I hear they are lovely. What a wretched idea to go and bury themselves in the steppes when the French army is in Moscow. What a chance those girls have missed. Your peasants now – that's another thing; but you are civilized beings, you ought to know us better than that. We have occupied Vienna, Berlin, Madrid, Naples, Rome, Warsaw – all the capitals of the world. We are feared, but we are loved. We are worth knowing. And then the Emperor ...' he began, but Pierre interrupted him.

'The Emperor?' echoed Pierre, and his face suddenly wore a mournful and embarrassed look. 'Is the Emperor ...?'

'The Emperor? He is generosity, clemency, justice, order, genius themselves – that's what the Emperor is! It is I, Ramballe, who tell you so ... I, the Ramballe you see before you, was his enemy eight years ago. My father was an émigré count. ... But that man was too much for me. He has taken hold of me. I could not resist the spectacle of the grandeur and glory with which he was covering France. When I realized what he was aiming at, when I saw that he was preparing a bed of laurels for us, you know, I said to myself: "This is something like a monarch!" and I gave myself up to him. Oh yes, *mon cher*, he is the greatest man of the ages, past or future.'

'Is he in Moscow?' Pierre stammered with a guilty look.

The Frenchman glanced at Pierre's guilty face and smiled.

'No, he will make his entry tomorrow,' he replied, and went on with his talk.

Their conversation was interrupted by several voices shouting at the gate and Morel coming in to inform the captain that some

Württemberg hussars had appeared and wanted to put up their horses in the yard where the captain's horses were. This difficulty had arisen chiefly because the hussars did not understand what was said to them in French.

Ramballe had their senior N.C.O. called in, and in a stern voice asked to what regiment he belonged, who was his commanding officer and by what right he allowed himself to claim quarters that were already occupied. The German, who knew very little French, answered the first two questions and gave the names of his regiment and of his commanding officer, but in reply to the third, which he did not understand, he began to explain in German interlarded with a few words of broken French that he was the quartermaster of his regiment and his colonel had ordered him to occupy all the houses in the row. Pierre, who knew German, interpreted for the captain what the quartermaster said and translated the captain's reply into German for the Württemberg hussar. When he grasped what was being said to him the German gave in, and took his men elsewhere. The captain went out into the porch and shouted some orders.

When he returned to the room Pierre was sitting in the same place as before, with his hands clasped on his head. His face expressed suffering. He really was suffering at that moment. As soon as the captain had gone out and he was left alone he suddenly came to himself and realized the position he was in. It was not that Moscow had been taken, not that these happy conquerors were making themselves at home there and patronizing him. Painful as that was, it was not that which tortured Pierre at that moment. He was tortured by the consciousness of his own weakness. A few glasses of wine and a chat with this good-natured fellow had been enough to dissipate the black and determined mood in which he had spent the last few days and which was essential for the execution of his design. Pistol and dagger and peasant coat were ready. Napoleon was to make his entrée tomorrow. Pierre was still just as convinced that it would be a praiseworthy and public-spirited act to slay the malefactor; but he felt now that he would not do it. Why? – he did not know but he had a sort of presentiment that he would not carry out his intention. He struggled against this recognition of his own weakness but was dimly aware that he could not overcome it, that his former dark thoughts of vengeance, assassination and self-sacrifice had been blown away like dust by contact with the first human being.

The captain came into the room, limping slightly and whistling a tune.

The Frenchman's chatter, which had previously amused Pierre, now repelled him. The tune he was whistling, his gait and the gesture with which he twirled his moustache, now all seemed offensive. 'I will go away at once. I won't say another word to him,' thought Pierre. He thought this but still sat on in the same place. Some strange feeling of impotence tied him to the spot; he longed to get up and go but could not.

The captain, on the contrary, appeared to be in high spirits. He walked a couple of times up and down the room. His eyes sparkled and his moustaches twitched as if he were smiling to himself at some amusing fancy.

'Charming fellow, the colonel of those Württembergers,' he said suddenly. 'He's a German but a good chap if ever there was one. But – a German.' He sat down facing Pierre. 'By the way, you know German, then?'

Pierre looked at him in silence.

'What is the German for "*shelter*"?'

'*Shelter?*' repeated Pierre. '*Shelter* in German is *Unterkunft.*'

'How do you pronounce it?' the captain asked quickly, with a shade of distrust in his voice.

'*Unterkunft,*' Pierre repeated.

'*Onterkoff,*' said the captain, and looked at Pierre for several seconds with mischievous eyes. 'Awful fools, these Germans, don't you think so, Monsieur Pierre?' he concluded.

'Well, another bottle of this Moscow claret, eh? Morel will warm us up another little bottle – Morel!' he called out gaily.

Morel brought candles and a bottle of wine. The captain studied Pierre in the candlelight and was obviously struck by his companion's troubled expression. With genuine concern and sympathy in his face, Ramballe went up to Pierre and bent over him.

'Down in the mouth, are we, eh?' he said, touching Pierre's hand. 'Have I upset you? No, tell me the truth, have you anything against me?' he asked Pierre. 'Perhaps it's the state of affairs?'

Pierre did not answer but looked cordially into the Frenchman's eyes. He found the sympathy he read in them pleasing.

'*Parole d'honneur*, to say nothing of what I owe you, I feel real liking for you. Can I do anything for you? You have only to command me.

For life and death. I say it with my hand on my heart!' he declared, slapping himself on the chest.

'Thank you,' said Pierre.

The captain gazed at Pierre as he had done when he learnt the German word for 'shelter,' and his face suddenly brightened.

'Well, in that case, I drink to our friendship!' he cried gaily, filling two glasses with wine.

Pierre took one of the glasses and emptied it. Ramballe drained his too, pressed Pierre's hand again and leaned his elbow on the table in a pose of pensive melancholy.

'Yes, my dear friend,' he began, 'such are the caprices of fortune. Who would have thought I should be a soldier and captain of the dragoons in the service of Bonaparte, as we used to call him? And yet here I am in Moscow with him. I must tell you, *mon cher*,' he continued in the sad, measured tones of a man about to embark on a long story, 'our name is one of the most ancient in France.'

And with the easy-going, naïve frankness of a Frenchman the captain told Pierre the history of his forefathers, his childhood, boyhood and youth, and all about his relations, and his financial and family affairs, *ma pauvre mère* playing, of course, a prominent part in the recital.

'But all that is only the stage-setting of life; the real thing is love – love! Am I not right, Monsieur Pierre?' said he, warming up. 'Another glass?'

Pierre again emptied his glass and poured himself out a third.

'Oh! *les femmes, les femmes!*' and the captain, gazing at Pierre with liquid eyes, began talking of love and his adventures with the fair sex, which were very numerous, as might readily be believed, seeing the officer's handsome, self-satisfied face and the eager enthusiasm with which he spoke of women. Although all Ramballe's accounts of his love-affairs had that sensual character in which the French find the unique charm and poetry of love, yet he told his story with such honest conviction that he was the only man who had ever tasted and known all the sweets of love, and he gave such alluring descriptions of women, that Pierre listened to him with curiosity.

It was evident that *l'amour* which the Frenchman was so fond of was not that low and simple sensual passion Pierre had at one time felt for his wife, nor was it the romantic sentiment which he had kindled in himself for Natasha. (Ramballe held both these kinds of love in equal contempt – the one was all very well for clodhoppers,

.the other for nincompoops.) *L'amour* which the Frenchman worshipped consisted pre-eminently in an unnatural relation to the woman
and in a combination of monstrous circumstances which lent the chief
charm to the emotion.

Thus the captain related the touching story of his love for a fascinating marquise of five-and-thirty and at the same time for a delightful, innocent child of seventeen, the daughter of the bewitching marquise. Mother and daughter had vied with each other in generosity,
and the rivalry which ended in the mother sacrificing herself and
offering her daughter in marriage to her lover even now, though it
was a memory of a distant past, moved the captain deeply. Then he
narrated an episode in which the husband played the part of the lover,
while he – the lover – assumed the rôle of husband, as well as several
comic incidents from his reminiscences of Germany, where *Unterkunft* means *shelter* and husbands eat sauerkraut and the young girls
are 'too blonde'.

Finally he came to his latest adventure, in Poland, still fresh in the
captain's memory and described by him with rapid gestures and
glowing face: the story of how he had saved the life of a Pole (on the
whole saving life featured strongly in the captain's recitals) and the
Pole had entrusted to him his enchanting wife (*parisienne de cœur*)
while he himself entered the French service. The captain was fortunate, the enchanting Polish lady had wanted to elope with him, but
prompted by a magnanimous impulse the captain had restored the
wife to the husband, remarking as he did so: 'I saved your life, and
now I save your honour!' As he repeated these words the captain
wiped his eyes and gave himself a shake as though to shake off the
weakness which assailed him at this touching memory.

As men often do at a late hour, and under the influence of wine,
Pierre listened to the captain's tales, and while he followed and took
in all that was told him he was also following a train of personal
recollections which for some reason suddenly flooded his imagination.
Hearing these stories of love, his own love for Natasha suddenly rose
before him in a succession of pictures which he mentally compared
with Ramballe's descriptions. When the captain enlarged on the
struggle between love and duty Pierre was reminded in every detail
of his last meeting with the object of his love at the Suharev water-
tower. At the time, that meeting had not made much impression on
him – he had not once thought of it since. But now it seemed to him

that there was something very significant and poetic in the encounter.

'Piotr Kirillich, come here! You see, we recognized you!' He could hear her words now, could see her smile, her travelling hood and the curl straying out from beneath it ... and there seemed to him something pathetic and touching in it all.

Having finished his account of the bewitching Polish lady, the captain turned to Pierre with the inquiry whether he had experienced a similar impulse to sacrifice himself for love, or known a feeling of envy of the legitimate husband.

Pierre, thus challenged, raised his head and felt an urgent craving to give vent to the thoughts that filled his mind. He began to explain that he looked upon love for women somewhat differently. He said that in all his life he had loved and still loved only one woman, and that she could never be his.

'*Tiens!*' exclaimed the captain.

Pierre then confided that he had loved this woman from his earliest youth but had not dared to think of her because she was too young, and because he had been an illegitimate son without a name. Afterwards, when he had received a name and a fortune he had not dared think of her because he loved her too well, setting her high above all the world and especially, therefore, above himself.

When he reached this point Pierre asked the captain whether he could understand that.

The captain made a gesture signifying that even if he did not understand it he begged Pierre to proceed.

'Platonic love. Moonshine! ...' he muttered to himself.

Whether it was the wine he had drunk, or a necessity to pour out his heart, or the certainty that this man did not know and would never know any of the persons concerned in his tale, or whether it was all these things together, something loosened Pierre's tongue. Speaking thickly, and with a far-away look in his shining eyes, he told the whole story of his life: his marriage, Natasha's love for his best friend, her perfidy, and all his own simple relations with her. Impelled on by Ramballe's questions, he told him too what he had at first kept secret—his position in society and even his name.

What impressed the captain more than anything else in Pierre's account was the fact that Pierre was very wealthy, owned two palatial mansions in Moscow and had abandoned everything and not left the capital but was staying on, concealing his name and rank.

It was a very late hour when they went out into the street together. The night was mild and light. To the left of the house, in Petrovsky street, was the glow of the first fire to break out in Moscow. On the right a young crescent moon hung high in the sky, and in the opposite quarter of the heavens blazed the comet which was connected in Pierre's heart with his love. Gerasim, the cook and two Frenchmen stood laughing and talking by the gate, in two mutually incomprehensible languages. They were looking at the glow of the fire burning in the town.

There was nothing alarming in a small remote fire in the immense city.

Gazing at the high starry sky, at the moon, at the comet and at the glare from the fire, Pierre felt a thrill of joyous and tender emotion. 'How lovely it all is – what more could one want?' he thought. And suddenly remembering his intention he grew dizzy and faint, and must have fallen had he not leaned against the fence to save himself.

Without taking leave of his new friend Pierre moved away from the gate with unsteady steps and returning to his room lay down on the sofa and instantly fell asleep.

30

THE glow of the first fire that broke out on the 2nd of September was watched from various roads and with various feelings by the fugitive Moscovites and the retreating troops.

The Rostovs spent that night at Mytishchy, fourteen miles from Moscow. They had started so late on the 1st of September, the road had been so encumbered by vehicles and troops, so many things had been forgotten and servants sent back for them, that they had decided to halt for the first night at a place three miles out of Moscow. The next morning they woke late and there were again so many delays that they got no farther than Great Mytishchy. At ten o'clock that evening the Rostov family and the wounded travelling with them were all distributed in the yards and huts of that large village. After settling their masters for the night the Rostovs' servants and coachmen and the orderlies of the wounded officers had supper, fed their horses and came out into the porches.

In a hut nearby lay Raevsky's adjutant with a fractured wrist, and the dreadful pain he was in made him groan piteously and incessantly, and his moaning had a gruesome sound in the darkness of the autumn night. He had spent the previous night in the same yard as the Rostovs. The countess declared she had been unable to close her eyes on account of his groaning, and at Mytishchy she moved into a less comfortable hut simply to be farther away from the wounded man.

One of the servants suddenly noticed against the dark sky beyond the high body of the coach standing before the porch the small glow of another fire. One such glow had long been visible and everybody knew it was the village of Little Mytishchy burning – set on fire by Mamonov's Cossacks.

'Look over there, boys! Another fire!' remarked the orderly.

They all looked round.

'Yes, they said as how them Cossacks of Mamonov's had fired Little Mytishchy.'

'Nay, that's not Mytishchy! 'Tis too far off.'

'It must be Moscow!'

Two of the men went round to the other side of the coach and squatted on the step.

'That there fire's too far to the left – why, Mytishchy lies yonder and this be way round on t'other side.'

Several more men joined the first.

'I say, it's flaring up right enough,' said one. 'That's a fire in Moscow, my friends – in Sushchevsky or mebbe Rogozhsky.'

No one made any comment and for some time they all stared in silence at the flames of this new conflagration spreading in the distance.

Old Danilo Terentyich, the count's valet (as he was called) came up to the group and shouted at Mishka.

'What are you standing there gaping at, fat-head? ... The count will be callin' and no one about. Go and tidy up the master's clothes.'

'I only just run out for some water,' said Mishka.

'What's your opinion, Danilo Terentyich? Isn't that there fire in Moscow?' asked one of the footmen.

Danilo Terentyich made no reply, and again for a long while they all watched dumbly. The glow spread, rising and falling, wider and wider.

'God have mercy! The wind and this dry weather ...' said another voice.

'Look'ee! See how far it's gone! O Lord above! Why, you can

1082

even see the crows flying. Lord have mercy on us poor sinners!'

'They'll put it out, never fear!'

'Who's to put it out?' cried Danilo Terentyich, who had hitherto been silent. His voice was quiet and deliberate. ''Tis Moscow sure enough, lads,' said he. 'Our white-walled Mother Mosc ...' His voice faltered and broke into an old man's sob.

And it seemed as though they had all only been waiting for this to make them realize the meaning of the red glare they were watching. There were sighs, the murmur of prayer and the sobbing of the count's old valet.

31

THE valet returned to the count and told his master that Moscow was burning. The count put on his dressing-gown and went out to look. Sonya and Madame Schoss, who had not yet undressed, went with him. Natasha and the countess were left alone indoors. (Petya was no longer with the family, having gone on ahead with his regiment, which was making for Troitsa.)

The countess burst into tears when she heard the news that Moscow was in flames. Natasha, pale, with staring eyes, was sitting on the bench under the icons (in the same spot she had dropped into when they arrived), and had paid no attention to her father's words. She was listening to the ceaseless moaning of the adjutant, three houses off.

'Oh, how awful!' exclaimed Sonya, returning from the yard, chilled and frightened. 'I do believe all Moscow will burn, there's a dreadful glow! Natasha, do look! You can see it now from the window,' she said to her cousin, obviously trying to distract her mind. But Natasha gazed at her as though not understanding what was asked of her, and again fixed her eyes on the corner of the stove. She had been in this condition of stupor since early that morning, when Sonya, to the surprise and annoyance of the countess, had for some unaccountable reason found it necessary to tell Natasha that Prince Andrei was among the wounded travelling with them. The countess had seldom been so angry with anyone as she was with Sonya. Sonya had cried and begged to be forgiven, and now, as though striving to atone for her fault, continued doubly attentive to her cousin.

'Look, Natasha, what a frightful fire it is!' said she.

'What is?' asked Natasha. 'Oh yes, Moscow.'

And as though not to offend Sonya, and to get rid of her, she turned her head to the window and looked out in such a way that it was evident she could see nothing, and then resumed her former attitude.

'But you didn't see?'

'Yes, really I did,' Natasha declared in a voice that pleaded to be left in peace.

And it was plain both to the countess and Sonya that in the nature of things neither Moscow nor the burning of Moscow nor anything else could be of any interest to Natasha.

The count returned and lay down behind the partition. The countess went up to her daughter and rested the back of her hand on her head as she was wont to do when Natasha was ill, then pressed her lips to her forehead to feel whether she was feverish, and finally kissed her.

'Are you cold? You are trembling all over. You'd better lie down,' said the countess.

'Lie down? All right, I will. I'll lie down at once,' answered Natasha.

When Natasha had been told that morning that Prince Andrei was seriously wounded and was travelling with them she had at first asked endless questions: Where was he going? How had he been wounded? Was it serious? And could she see him? But after she had been told that she could not see him, that he was gravely wounded but his life was not in danger, she gave up asking questions or speaking at all, obviously having no faith in what they said and convinced that whatever she tried she would get the same answers. All the way she had sat motionless in a corner of the coach with those wide eyes, the expression in which the countess knew so well and dreaded so much, and now she was sitting in just the same way on the bench in the hut. She was planning something, was either coming or had come to some decision – this the countess knew but what the decision might be she did not know, and that alarmed and worried her.

'Natasha, undress, darling. Come and lie on my bed.'

(The countess was the only one for whom a bed had been made up on a bedstead. Madame Schoss and the two girls were to sleep on some hay on the floor.)

'No, mamma, I'll lie here on the floor,' Natasha replied irritably, and she went to the window and opened it. Through the opened window the moans of the adjutant came more distinctly. She leaned her head out into the damp night air, and the countess saw her slender neck shaking with sobs and throbbing against the window-frame. Natasha knew it was not Prince Andrei moaning. She knew Prince Andrei was in the same courtyard as themselves, that he was in the next hut across the passage; but these terrible incessant groans made her sob. The countess exchanged a look with Sonya.

'Come to bed, darling; come to bed, my pet,' said the countess, gently touching Natasha's shoulder. 'Come along now and lie down.'

'Yes, yes, all right. ... I'll lie down at once,' said Natasha, hurriedly undressing and tugging at the strings of her petticoat.

When she had thrown off her dress and put on a dressing-jacket she sat down with her feet tucked under her, on the bed that had been made up on the floor, jerked her short braid of fine hair to the front and began re-plaiting it. Her long, thin, practised fingers rapidly and deftly parted, plaited and tied up the braid. Natasha's head moved from side to side from habit but her eyes, feverishly wide, stared straight before her with the same fixed intensity. When her toilet for the night was finished she sank quietly on to the sheet spread over the hay on the side nearest the door.

'Natasha, you lie in the middle,' said Sonya.

'No, I shall stay here,' muttered Natasha. 'And do go to bed,' she added crossly, and buried her face in the pillow.

The countess, Madame Schoss and Sonya hurriedly undressed and went to bed. The small lamp in front of the icons was the only light left in the room. But out in the yard there was the glare from the fire at Little Mytishchy a mile and a half away, and the noisy clamour of peasants shouting in the tavern across the street, which Mamonov's Cossacks had broken into, and the adjutant's uninterrupted moaning.

For a long time Natasha lay listening to the sounds that reached her from within and without, and did not stir. First she heard her mother praying and sighing, and the creaking of her bed under her, Madame Schoss's familiar whistling snore and Sonya's soft breathing. Then the countess called to Natasha. Natasha did not answer.

'I think she's asleep, mamma,' whispered Sonya.

After a brief silence the countess spoke again but this time no one answered her.

Soon after that Natasha heard her mother's even breathing. Natasha did not move, though her little bare foot poking out from under the quilt felt frozen against the uncovered floor.

A cricket chirped in a crack in the wall, as though celebrating a victory over all the world. Far away a cock crowed, and another responded near by. The shouts had died down in the tavern; only the moaning of the adjutant was heard. Natasha sat up.

'Sonya, are you asleep? Mamma?' she whispered.

No one answered. Slowly and carefully Natasha got up, crossed herself and stepped cautiously on to the cold, dirty floor with her slim, supple bare feet. The boards creaked. Tripping lightly from one foot to the other she ran like a kitten the few steps to the door and took hold of the cold door-handle.

It seemed to her that something was banging on the walls of the hut with heavy, rhythmical strokes: it was the beating of her own heart, torn with dread, with love and terror.

She opened the door, stepped across the threshold and on to the chill damp earth of the passage outside. The cold all about her refreshed her. Her bare foot touched a sleeping man; she stepped over him and opened the door of the hut in which Prince Andrei was lying. It was dark in the hut. In the far corner, on a bench beside the bed where something lay, stood a tallow candle with a great smouldering wick.

From the moment she had been told that morning of Prince Andrei's wound and his presence there, Natasha had resolved that she must see him. She did not know why she had to: she knew the meeting would be painful and felt the more certain that it was essential.

All day long she had lived in the hope of seeing him that night. But now when the moment had come she was filled with dread of what she might see. How was he disfigured? What was left of him? Was he like that unceasing moan of the adjutant's? Yes, he was all that. In her imagination he was that terrible moaning personified. When she caught sight of an indistinct shape in the corner and mistook his knees raised under the counterpane for his shoulders she pictured some fearful body there, and stood still in terror. But an irresistible force drew her forward. She made one cautious step, then another, and found herself in the middle of a small room cumbered with baggage. Another man – Timohin – was lying in a corner on the benches beneath the icons, and two others – the doctor and a valet – lay on the floor.

The valet sat up and whispered something. Timohin, in pain from a wound in his leg, was not asleep and gazed wide-eyed at this strange apparition of a girl in a white chemise, dressing-jacket and night-cap. The valet's sleepy, frightened exclamation, 'What is it? What do you want?' only made Natasha hasten to the figure lying in the corner. Horribly unlike a human being as that body looked, she must see him. She slipped past the valet, the snuff fell from the candle-wick and she saw Prince Andrei quite clearly with his arms stretched out on the quilt, looking just as she had always seen him.

He was the same as ever; but the feverish flush on his face, his glittering eyes directed rapturously towards her, and especially his neck, soft as a child's, showing above the turn-down collar of his nightshirt, gave him a peculiarly innocent, boyish look which was quite new to her in Prince Andrei. She went up to him and with a swift, supple, youthful movement dropped on her knees.

He smiled and held out his hand to her.

32

SEVEN days had passed since Prince Andrei had come to himself in the ambulance-station on the field of Borodino. All that time he had been in a state of almost continuous unconsciousness. His feverish condition and the inflammation of his intestines, which were injured, were in the doctor's opinion certain to carry him off. But on the seventh day he ate with relish a slice of bread and drank some tea, and the doctor noticed that his temperature was lower. Prince Andrei had regained consciousness in the morning. The first night after they left Moscow had been fairly warm and he had remained in the calèche, but at Mytishchy the wounded man had himself asked to be carried indoors and given some tea. The pain caused by moving him into the hut had made him groan aloud and lose consciousness again. When he had been stretched on his camp bedstead he lay for a long while motionless with closed eyes. Then he opened them and murmured softly: 'How about the tea?' The doctor was amazed by this ability to remember such a small everyday thing. He felt Prince Andrei's pulse, and to his surprise and regret found that it had improved. He was regretful because he knew by experience that his patient could not live and that if he did not die now he would do so a little later with greater suffering. With Prince Andrei was the red-nosed major of his regiment, Timohin, who had joined him in Moscow with a wound in the leg received at the same battle of Borodino.

They were accompanied by the surgeon, Prince Andrei's valet, his coachman and two orderlies.

They gave Prince Andrei some tea. He drank it eagerly, looking with feverish eyes at the door in front of him, as though trying to understand and remember something.

'I don't want any more. Is Timohin here?' he asked.

Timohin edged along the bench towards him.

'I'm here, your Excellency.'

'How's the wound?'

'Mine? All right, sir. But how are you?'

Prince Andrei pondered again, apparently in an effort to recollect.

'Couldn't they get me the book?' he asked.

'What book?'

'A New Testament. I haven't one.'

The doctor promised to procure it for him, and began to inquire of the prince how he was feeling. Prince Andrei answered all his questions reluctantly, though rationally, and then said he would like a bolster placed under him as he was uncomfortable and in great pain. The doctor and the valet lifted the cloak with which he was covered, and making wry faces at the noisome smell of putrefying flesh that came from the wound began to examine the fearful place. The doctor was deeply troubled over something, made some slight change in the dressings and turned the wounded man over so that he groaned and lost consciousness again and grew delirious with the pain. He kept asking them to be quick and get him the book and put it 'just here'.

'What trouble would it be to you?' he said. 'I haven't one – please get one for me. Put it under me just for a minute,' he pleaded in a piteous voice.

The doctor went into the passage to wash his hands.

'You fellows have no conscience,' said he to the valet who was pouring water over his hands. 'I take my eyes off you for half a second. ... He's in such agony, I wonder how he lives through it.'

'I thought we had put something under him, as Christ is my witness I did!' said the valet.

The first time Prince Andrei realized where he was and what was the matter with him, and remembered being wounded and how, was when the calèche stopped at Mytishchy and he asked to be carried into the hut. Pain clouded his senses again until he came to himself inside the hut, and while he was drinking tea he went over in his mind all that had happened to him, remembering most vividly the moment in the ambulance station when at the sight of the sufferings of a man he disliked those new thoughts had come to him with such promise of happiness. And those thoughts – though vague now and cloudy – again possessed his soul. He remembered that he had a new source of happiness now, and that this happiness was somehow connected with the New Testament. That was why he had asked for the New Testament. But the uncomfortable position in which they had laid him, without support for his wound, and being turned over, confused his mind and it was only in the complete stillness of the night that he came to himself for the third time. Everybody around him was sleep. A cricket chirped across the passage; someone was shouting and singing in the street; cockroaches rustled over the table, the icons and the walls, and a big fly flopped on his pillow and fluttered about the tallow candle beside him, the wick of which was charred into a shape like a mushroom.

His mind was not in a normal state. A man in good health usually thinks of, feels and remembers an immense number of different things simultaneously but has the power and resolution to select one series of ideas or phenomena on which to concentrate his whole attention. A man who is not ill can break away from the profoundest of meditations to say a civil word to anyone who comes in, and then return again to his own thoughts. But Prince Andrei's mind was not in a normal condition in this respect. All the powers of his mind were more active and clearer than ever but they acted apart from his will. The most heterogeneous notions and visions occupied him at one and the same moment. Sometimes his brain suddenly began to work with a vigour, clarity and depth it had never attained when he was in health. And then, just as suddenly, in the midst of its work it would switch to some unexpected obsession, and he lacked the strength to turn it back again.

'Yes, a new happiness was revealed to me – a happiness which is man's imprescriptible right,' he said to himself as he lay in the semi-darkness of the quiet hut gazing fixedly before him with feverish, wide-open eyes. 'A happiness beyond the reach of material forces, unaffected by the external material influences which touch man – a happiness of the soul alone, the happiness of loving! To feel it is in every man's power but only God can conceive and enjoin it. But how did God ordain this law? Why was the Son ...?' The thread of these ideas was suddenly broken, and Prince Andrei heard (though he could not tell whether it was delirium or reality) a low, lisping voice repeating over and over in measured rhythm: '*I piti-piti-piti*' and then again '*i ti-ti*' and '*i piti-piti-piti*' and '*i ti-ti*' once more. At the same time he felt as though a strange, ethereal edifice of delicate needles or splinters was rising over his face, from the very centre of it, to the sound of this whispered music. He felt that he must balance carefully (though it was difficult) so that the airy structure should not collapse; but nevertheless it kept collapsing and then slowly rising again to the rhythmic murmur of the music. 'It is stretching out, stretching out, spreading and growing!' said Prince Andrei to himself. And while he listened to the whispering beat, and felt the edifice of needles drawing out and lifting, the red halo of light round the candle caught his eye by fits and starts, and he heard the rustle of cockroaches and the buzzing of the fly that flopped against his pillow and his face. Each time the fly brushed his cheek it burnt him like a hot iron; and yet to his surprise, though it struck the very spot where the strange fabric of needles was rising from his face, it did not demolish it. But apart from all this there was one other thing of importance. That something white by the door – the statue of a sphinx – which weighed on him too.

'But perhaps it's my shirt on the table,' thought Prince Andrei, 'and those are my legs, and that is the door, but why is it always stretching and expanding – and that *piti-piti-piti* and *ti-ti* and *piti-piti-piti*. ... That's enough, please leave off – stop!' Prince Andrei besought someone wearily. And all at once his mind cleared again, and thought and feeling floated to the surface, having extraordinary clarity and force.

'Yes – love' (he reflected again, quite lucidly). 'But not that love which loves for something, to gain something or because of something, but the love I knew for the first time when, dying, I saw my enemy and yet loved him. I experienced the love which is the very essence of the soul, the love which requires no object. And I feel that blessed feeling now too. To love one's neighbours, to love one's enemies, to love everything – to love God in all His manifestations. Human love serves to love those dear to us but to love one's enemies we need divine love. And that is why I knew such joy when I felt I loved that man. What became of him? Is he alive? ... Human love may turn to hatred but divine love cannot change. Nothing, not even death, can destroy it. It is the very nature of the soul. Yet how many people have I hated in my life? And of them all none did I love and hate as much as her.' And he vividly pictured Natasha to himself, not as he had pictured her in the past with her charms only, which gave him such delight, but for the first time imagining her soul. And he understood her feelings, her suffering, her shame and remorse. Now, for the first time, he realized all the cruelty of his rejection of her, the cruelty of breaking with her. 'If only I might see her once more. Just once to look into those eyes and say ...'

Piti-piti-piti and *ti-ti*, and *piti-piti – boom!* flopped the fly. ... And his attention was suddenly transported into the other mixed world of reality and hallucination in which something peculiar was taking place. The edifice was still rising, unbroken, something was still stretching out and the candle with its red halo was still burning, and the same shirt which looked like a sphinx lying by the door; but in addition to all this there was a creaking sound and a whiff of fresh air, and a new white sphinx appeared, standing in the doorway. And that sphinx had the white face and shining eyes of the very Natasha of whom he had just been thinking.

'Oh, how wearisome this everlasting delirium is!' thought Prince Andrei, trying to expel that face from his imagination. But the vision stayed before his eyes with all the strength of reality, was coming nearer. ... Prince Andrei tried to return to the world of pure thought but he could not, and delirium drew him back into its domain. The soft murmuring voice kept up its rhythmic whisper, something was squeezing, stretching out, and the strange face was before him. Prince Andrei summoned all his might in an effort to recover his senses, he moved slightly, and suddenly there was a humming in his ears, a dimness in his eyes, and like a man sinking under water he lost consciousness. When he came to himself Natasha, the veritable living Natasha, whom of all people he most longed to love with the new, pure, divine love that had been revealed to him, was on her knees before him. He recognized that it was the real living Natasha, and did not wonder but was quietly happy. Natasha knelt rooted to the ground (she could not have stirred), gazing at him with frightened eyes and restraining her sobs. Her face was pale and rigid. Only her lips and chin quivered a little.

Prince Andrei fetched a sigh of relief, smiled and held out his hand.

'You?' he said. 'What happiness!'

With a swift but circumspect movement Natasha came nearer, still on her knees, and cautiously taking his hand she bent her face over it and began kissing it, just touching it lightly with her lips.

'Forgive me!' she said in a whisper, lifting her head and glancing at him. 'Forgive me!'

'I love you,' said Prince Andrei.

'Forgive ...'

'Forgive what?' he asked.

'Forgive me for what I di – d!' faltered Natasha in a scarcely audible, broken whisper, and again began quickly covering his hand with kisses, softly brushing her lips against it.

'I love you more, better than before,' said Prince Andrei, raising her face with his hand so as to look into her eyes.

Those eyes, swimming with happy tears, gazed at him with timid commiseration and joyous love. Natasha's thin, white face with its swollen lips was more than plain – it looked ghastly. But Prince Andrei did not see her face, he saw the shining eyes which were beautiful. They heard the sound of voices behind them.

Piotr, the valet, wide awake by now, had roused the doctor. Timohin, who had not slept at all for the pain in his leg, had long been watching all that was going on, carefully covering his bare body with the sheet as he huddled up on his bench.

'What does this mean?' said the doctor, getting up from his bed on the floor. 'Please to be gone, madam!'

At that moment a maid sent by the countess, who had noticed her daughter's absence, knocked at the door.

Like a somnambulist awakened in the middle of a trance Natasha walked out of the room, and returning to her hut sank sobbing on her bed.

*

From that day, during all the remainder of the Rostovs' journey, at every halting-place and wherever they spent a night, Natasha never left the wounded Bolkonsky's side, and the doctor was obliged to admit that he had never expected to see in a young girl such constancy or such skill in nursing a wounded man.

Terrible as it seemed to the countess to think that Prince Andrei might (and very probably would, too, from what the doctor said) die on the road in her daughter's arms, she had not the heart to oppose

Natasha. Although the idea did occur that, with the renewal of affectionate relations between the wounded Prince Andrei and Natasha, should he recover, their engagement might be renewed, no one – least of all Natasha and Prince Andrei – spoke of this. The open question concerning life or death which hung not only over Bolkonsky but over the whole of Russia shut out all other considerations.

33

ON the 3rd of September Pierre awoke late. His head ached, the clothes in which he had slept without undressing chafed his body and he was oppressed by a vague sense of having done something shameful the day before. That something shameful was his talk the previous evening with Captain Ramballe.

It was eleven o'clock by his watch but it seemed peculiarly dark out of doors. Pierre got up, rubbed his eyes and, seeing the pistol with an engraved stock which Gerasim had put back on the writing-table, remembered where he was and what lay before him that day.

'But am I not too late already?' he wondered. 'No, *he* will surely not make his entry into Moscow before noon.'

Pierre did not allow himself to reflect on what lay ahead of him but made haste to act.

Straightening his clothes, Pierre took up the pistol and was about to set out. But then for the first time it occurred to him that he certainly could not carry the weapon in his hand through the streets. It would be difficult to conceal such a big pistol even under his full coat. He could not put it in his belt or carry it under his arm without its being noticeable. Moreover, the pistol had been discharged and he had not had time to reload it. 'No matter, the dagger will do,' he said to himself, though when planning the execution of his purpose he had more than once come to the conclusion that the great mistake made by the student in 1809 was that he had tried to kill Napoleon with a dagger. But as Pierre's chief aim seemed to be not so much to succeed in his project as to prove to himself that he was not renouncing his intention but was doing all he could to achieve it, he hurriedly took the blunt jagged dagger in a green sheath which he had bought together with the pistol at the Suharev market, and hid it under his waistcoat.

Tying the sash round his peasant's coat and pulling his cap forward,

Pierre walked along the corridor, trying not to make a noise and to avoid meeting the captain, and stepped out into the street.

The conflagration he had looked at so indifferently the evening before had grown sensibly bigger during the night. Moscow was on fire at various points. The buildings in Carriage Row, across the river, in the Bazaar and Povarsky street, as well as the barges on the Moskva river and the timber yards by the Dorogomilov bridge were all ablaze.

Pierre's route took him through side streets to Povarsky street, and from there along Arbat to the church of St Nikolai: this was the spot which he had long since fixed upon for the deed he was meditating. The gates of most of the houses were locked and the shutters up. The streets and alleys were deserted. The air was full of smoke and the smell of burning. From time to time he met a few scared and anxious Russians, and Frenchmen with a look not of the city but of the camp about them, walking in the middle of the road. Both Russians and French looked inquisitively at Pierre. Apart from his height and breadth, and the queer suggestion of morose and concentrated suffering in his face and whole figure, the Russians stared at him because they could not make out to what class he could belong. The French looked back at him with puzzled eyes mainly because Pierre, unlike other Russians who all gazed at the French in trepidation or curiosity, paid no attention to them. At the gates of one house three Frenchmen, who were trying to explain something to some Russians who did not understand them, stopped Pierre and asked him if he knew French.

Pierre shook his head and walked on. In another side street a sentinel on guard beside a green caisson shouted at him but it was only when the shout was threateningly repeated and he heard the click of the musket which the sentinel took up that he realized he ought to have taken the opposite pavement. He heard and saw nothing around him. With a sense of nervous haste and horror he carried his resolution within him like something terrible and alien, fearful – after his experience of the previous night – of losing it. But he was not destined to arrive with his mood intact at the place to which he was bending his steps. Moreover, even if nothing had happened to hinder him *en route*, his design could not now have been carried out, for the reason that Napoleon had passed Arbat more than four hours earlier on his way from the Dorogomilov suburb to the Kremlin, and was at that moment seated in the Imperial study in the Palace, in the worst of humours, giving precise and detailed orders in regard to the urgent measures to be taken for extinguishing the fire, preventing looting and reassuring the inhabitants. But Pierre did not know this; entirely absorbed in what lay before him, he was suffering the anguish men go through when they persist in undertaking a task impossible for them – not because of its inherent difficulties but because of its incompatibility with their own nature. He was tortured by the dread of weakening at the decisive moment and so forfeiting his self-respect.

Though he saw and heard nothing around him he found his way by instinct and did not go wrong in the lanes that led to Povarsky street.

The nearer he approached Povarsky street, the thicker was the smoke everywhere, and the atmosphere was positively warm from the heat of the conflagration. Tongues of flame curled up here and there behind the house-tops. He met more people in the streets, and these people were more agitated. But Pierre, though he was conscious that something unusual was happening around him, did not grasp the fact that he was getting near the fire. As he followed a foot-path across the large open space skirting Povarsky street on one side and the gardens of Prince Gruzinsky's house on the other, Pierre suddenly heard the desperate weeping of a woman close to him. He stopped as if awakening from a dream, and lifted his head.

On the parched dusty grass on one side of the path all sorts of household goods lay in a heap: feather-beds, a samovar, icons and boxes. On the ground, near the trunks, sat a thin woman no longer young, with long, projecting upper teeth, wearing a black cloak and cap. This woman, swaying to and fro and muttering something, was crying convulsively. Two little girls between ten and twelve years old, dressed in dirty short frocks and cloaks, were staring at their mother with a look of stupefaction on their pale, frightened faces. The youngest child, a boy of about seven, who wore an overcoat and a huge cap evidently not his own, was sobbing in the arms of an old nurse. A dirty, bare-legged servant-girl was sitting on a trunk, and having let down her flaxen tresses was tidying her plait and sniffing at the singed hair. The husband, a short, stooping man in a uniform, with sausage-shaped whiskers, and smooth locks of hair showing under his square-set cap, with expressionless face was sorting the trunks piled one on top of the other, and dragging some garments from under them.

As soon as she saw Pierre the woman almost flung herself at his feet.

'Merciful heavens – good Christian folk – save us, help me, kind sir! Help us, somebody,' she articulated through her sobs. 'My baby. ... My little daughter. ... My youngest girl left behind! ... Burnt to death! ... Oh-oh-oh, why did I give suck. ... Oh-oh-oh!'

'There, that'll do, Maria Nikolayevna,' expostulated her husband in a mild voice, evidently only to exonerate himself before the stranger. 'Sister must have taken care of her. Otherwise where else can she be?' he added.

'Monster! Villain!' screeched the woman furiously, her tears suddenly ceasing. 'There's no heart in you, you don't feel for your own child! Any other man would have rescued her from the fire. But he is a monster, not a man, not a father. You, honoured sir, are a well-born person,' she continued, addressing Pierre rapidly between her sobs. 'The place caught fire next door and blew our way. The girl screamed "Fire!" and we rushed to get our things out, and escaped with what we laid our hands on. ... This is all we could snatch up ... the holy icons, and my dowry bed. All the rest is gone. We caught up the children. But not little Katya. Ooh! O Lord! ...' and again she fell to sobbing. 'My baby, my little one, burnt to death, burnt to death!'

'But where – where was she left?' asked Pierre.

The sympathetic, interested expression on his face told the woman that this man might help her.

'Good, kind sir!' she cried, clutching at his legs. 'Benefactor! Put me out of my misery. ... Aniska, go, you hussy, show him the way!' she screamed to the servant-girl, angrily opening her mouth and exposing her long teeth still more.

'Show me the way, show me, I ... I'll go,' Pierre gasped out quickly.

The dirty servant-girl stepped from behind the trunk, put up her plait and, sighing, walked in front along the path on her stumpy bare legs. Pierre felt as if he had suddenly come back to life after a heavy swoon. He held his head higher, his eyes shone with the light of life, and with swift strides he followed and overtook the girl, and came out on Povarsky street. The whole street was shrouded in black smoke. Here and there tongues of flame broke through the screen. A huge crowd had gathered in front of the conflagration. In the middle of the street stood a French general, saying something to those about him. Pierre, accompanied by the servant-girl, was advancing to the spot where the French general was standing, but the French soldiers stopped him.

'Not this way!' a voice shouted to him.

'Here, master,' cried the girl. 'We'll cut across the Nikulins and go by the alley.'

Pierre turned back, giving a spring now and then to keep up with her. The girl ran across the street, scurried down a side alley on the left and, passing three houses, dived into a yard on the right.

'It's just here,' she said, and running across the yard opened a gate in a wooden fence and, stopping short, pointed out to Pierre a small timber-built 'wing', which was blazing away fiercely. One wall had fallen in, the other was on fire, and bright flames issued from the openings of the windows and under the roof.

As Pierre went in at the little gate he was met by a rush of hot air and instinctively drew back.

'Which is it? Which is your house?' he asked.

'Oooh!' wailed the girl, pointing to the annexe. 'That's it. That's where we lived. Sure, you're burnt to death, our treasure, our little Katya, my precious little missy! Oooh!' lamented Aniska, feeling at the sight of the fire that she too must give expression to her emotions.

Pierre darted up to the 'wing' but the heat was so great that he found himself obliged to skirt round it, and came upon a large house, which so far was only burning at one end, just below the roof. A mob of Frenchmen swarmed round it. At first Pierre did not understand what these men, who were dragging something out of the house, were about; but seeing a French soldier in front of him hit at a peasant with the flat of his sabre, in an effort to get from him a coat lined with fox-fur, he became vaguely aware that looting was in progress here – but he had no time to dwell on the thought.

The crackling and rumble of falling walls and ceilings, the hiss and sizzle of the flames, and the excited shouts of the crowd; the sight of the swaying smoke, now belching out thick and black, now shooting upwards, glittering with sparks, with here and there dense red sheaves of flame (or little golden fish-scales licking the walls); the heat and smoke, the sense of urgent movement everywhere, produced in Pierre the exalted feeling of excitement which fires commonly cause. The effect on Pierre was particularly strong because all at once, at the sight of the fire, he felt himself suddenly liberated from the ideas weighing upon him. He felt young, gay, ready and resolute. He ran round to the other side of the annexe and was about to dash into the part which was still standing when he heard several voices shouting just above his head, followed by a cracking sound and the crash of something heavy falling close beside him.

Pierre looked up and saw at the windows of the house some Frenchmen who had just dropped the drawer of a chest filled with metal articles. Other French soldiers standing below went up to the drawer.

'What does that fellow there want?' shouted one of them, referring to Pierre.

'There's a child in that house,' cried Pierre in French. 'Haven't you seen a child?'

'What's he talking about? Get out!' several voices replied, and one of the soldiers, evidently afraid that Pierre might want to rob them of the silver and bronzes that were in the drawer, moved menacingly towards him.

'A child?' shouted a Frenchman from above. 'I did hear something squealing in the garden. Perhaps it's the brat the fellow's looking for. Got to help one another, you know. ...'

'Where is it? Where is it?' asked Pierre.

'Over there, that way!' called the Frenchman from the window, pointing to the garden at the back of the house. 'Wait, I'll come down.'

And in a minute the Frenchman, a black-eyed fellow with a patch on his cheek, in his shirt-sleeves, did in fact jump out of a window on the ground floor, and slapping Pierre on the shoulder ran with him into the garden. 'Look sharp, you there!' he cried to his comrades. 'It's warming up.'

Running behind the house to a gravel path, the Frenchman pulled Pierre by the arm and pointed to a circular space where a little girl of three in a pink frock was lying under a garden seat.

'There's your bratling for you. Oh, it's a girl, so much the better!' said the Frenchman. 'G'bye, old man. Got to help one another, we're all brothers, you know,' and the Frenchman with the patch on his cheek ran back to his comrades.

Pierre, breathless with joy, started up to the little girl and would have taken her in his arms. But seeing a stranger the sickly, scrofulous-looking child, unattractively like her mother, screamed and began to run away. Pierre grabbed her, however, and lifted her in his arms. She screeched in desperate fury, and struggled with her thin little fists to pull Pierre's hands away and to bite them with her slobbering

1098

mouth. Pierre was seized with horror and revulsion such as he might have had at contact with some small animal, and he had to make an effort not to throw the child down. He ran back with her to the big house. By now, however, it was impossible to return by the way he had come: the maid, Aniska, was nowhere to be seen, and Pierre with a feeling of pity and disgust pressed the wet, pitifully howling baby to himself as tenderly as he could and hurried across the garden in search of some other exit.

34

WHEN Pierre, after running across courtyards and down by-lanes, got back with his little burden to the Gruzinsky garden at the corner of Povarsky street he did not at first recognize the place from which he had set out to look for the child, so packed was it with people and goods that had been dragged out of the houses. Besides the Russian families with their belongings saved from the fire, there were a good many French soldiers about in a variety of clothing. Pierre took no notice of them. He was in a hurry to find that civil servant's family, in order to restore the daughter to her mother and go back and rescue someone else. Pierre felt that he had a great deal more to do, and to do quickly. Hot from the heat, and from running, the sense of youth, energy and determination which had come upon him when he ran off to save the baby glowed within him more strongly than ever. The child was quiet now and, clinging to Pierre's coat with her little hands, sat on his arm gazing about her like some small wild animal. He glanced down at her occasionally, with a half smile. He fancied he saw something pathetically innocent in the frightened, sickly little face.

Neither the civil servant nor his wife were in the place where he had left them. Pierre walked among the crowd with rapid steps, scanning the various faces he met. Unconsciously he noticed a Georgian or Armenian family consisting of a very old man with beautiful Oriental features, wearing a new, cloth-faced sheepskin and new boots, an old woman of similar type and a young woman. The latter – a very young woman – struck Pierre as the perfection of Oriental beauty with her sharply-outlined, arched, black eyebrows, her extraordinarily soft bright colour and lovely, impassive oval face. Amid the chattels scattered about in the crowd on the open space, with her rich satin mantle and the bright lilac kerchief on her head, she suggested a delicate, exotic plant thrown down in the snow. She was sitting on some bundles a little behind the old woman, her big black almond eyes under the long lashes fixed on the ground before her. Evidently she was aware of her beauty and it made her fearful. Her face impressed Pierre and he looked round at her several times as he scurried along by the fence. When he had reached the end, still without finding the people he was seeking, he stopped and surveyed the scene about him.

Pierre's figure with the baby in his arms was now more conspicuous than before, and a group of Russians, both men and women, gathered round him.

'Have you lost someone, good sir?' – 'You're gentry, aren't you?' – 'Whose child is it?' they asked him.

Pierre explained that the baby belonged to a woman in a black cloak who had been sitting at this spot with her other children, and asked whether anyone knew her and where she had gone.

'Why, that must be the Anferovs,' said an old deacon, addressing a pock-marked peasant woman. 'Lord have mercy, Lord have mercy!' he added in his professional bass.

'The Anferovs? No,' said the woman. 'Why, the Anferovs went early this morning. It'll either be Maria Nikolayevna's child, or the Ivanovs'.'

'He says a woman, and Maria Nikolayevna's a lady,' remarked a house-serf.

'Surely you know her – a thin woman with long teeth,' said Pierre.

'That's Maria Nikolayevna all right. They moved off into the garden when these wolves swooped down,' said the woman, pointing to the French soldiers.

'O Lord, have mercy on us!' ejaculated the deacon again.

'Go over that way, they're yonder. That's where she is. Beside herself and crying her eyes out,' continued the woman. 'She's there. You'll find her all right.'

But Pierre was not listening to the women. For some seconds he had been intent on what was happening a few yards away. He was watching the Armenian family and two French soldiers who had approached them. One of these, a nimble little man, was wearing a blue coat with a piece of rope tied round his waist for a belt. He had a night-cap on his head and his feet were bare. The other, whose appearance struck Pierre particularly, was a long, lank, round-shouldered, fair-haired man with slow movements and an idiotic expression. He was clad in a frieze tunic, blue trousers and big torn Hessian boots. The little barefooted Frenchman in the blue coat went up to the Armenians, said something and grabbed at the old man's legs, and the old man at once began pulling off his boots as fast as he could. The other soldier, in the tunic, stopped in front of the beautiful Armenian girl and with his hands in his pockets stood staring at her, without speaking or moving.

'Here, take the child!' exclaimed Pierre peremptorily, handing the little girl to the peasant woman. 'You give her back to them – give her back!' he almost shouted, putting the child, who had started to scream, on the ground and turning to look at the Frenchmen and the Armenian family again. The old man was by now sitting barefoot. The little Frenchman had appropriated his second boot and was slapping one boot against the other. The old man was saying something in a voice broken by sobs, but all this Pierre only saw in a passing glimpse: his whole attention was directed to the Frenchman in the frieze tunic who had meanwhile swaggered leisurely up to the young woman and, taking his hands out of his pocket, caught hold of her neck.

The beautiful Armenian continued to sit motionless, in the same attitude, with her long lashes drooping, as if she did not see or feel what the soldier was doing to her.

By the time Pierre had run the few steps that separated him from the Frenchmen the tall marauder in the tunic was already tearing the necklace from the Armenian beauty's neck, and the young woman, clutching at her throat, uttered a piercing shriek.

'Let that woman alone!' cried Pierre in a husky, furious voice, seizing the lank soldier by his round shoulders and hurling him aside.

The soldier fell, scrambled to his feet and made off. But his comrade, throwing down the boots and drawing his sword, moved threateningly towards Pierre.

'Look here, no monkey tricks!' he shouted.

Pierre was in such a transport of rage that he was oblivious of everything and his strength increased tenfold. He rushed at the barefooted Frenchman and, before the latter could draw his sabre, knocked him off his feet and was hammering him with his fists. The crowd roared its approval, and at the same moment a patrol of French Uhlans came round the corner. The Uhlans rode up at a trot and surrounded Pierre and the Frenchman. Pierre remembered nothing of what happened after that. He only knew that he was hitting someone and being hit, until in the end he found that his hands were bound and that a group of French soldiers were standing round and searching him.

'Lieutenant, he has a dagger,' were the first words that meant anything to Pierre.

'Aha, a weapon,' said the officer, and he turned to the barefooted soldier who had been arrested with Pierre. 'All right, you can tell your story at the court-martial.' And then he addressed Pierre: 'Do you speak French?'

Pierre glared about him with bloodshot eyes and did not reply. Evidently his face must have looked frightful, for the officer said something in a whisper and four more Uhlans left the rest and stationed themselves on either side of Pierre.

'Do you speak French?' the officer asked again, keeping at a distance from Pierre. 'Call the interpreter.'

A little man in Russian civilian dress rode out from the ranks. By his clothes and speech Pierre immediately recognized him for a French salesman from one of the Moscow shops.

'He doesn't look like a man of the people,' pronounced the interpreter, eyeing Pierre narrowly.

'Oho! He looks very much like an incendiary to me,' remarked the officer. 'Ask him who he is,' he added.

'Who are yeou?' demanded the interpreter. 'Yeou must answer the officer.'

'I shall not tell you who I am. I am your prisoner. Take me away,' Pierre suddenly replied in French.

'Ah-ha!' muttered the officer with a frown. 'Right then, quick march!'

A crowd had collected round the Uhlans. Nearest to Pierre stood the pock-marked peasant woman with the child. When the patrol set off she stepped forward.

'Where be they taking 'ee, you poor dear you?' said she. 'And the little lass, the little lass – what am I to do wi' 'er if she ain't theirs?' she cried.

'What does that woman want?' asked the officer.

Pierre was like one intoxicated. His elation increased at the sight of the little girl he had rescued.

'What does she want?' he exclaimed. 'She has got my daughter there, whom I just saved from the flames,' he declared. '*Adieu!*' And without in the least knowing what had possessed him to tell this aimless lie he strode triumphantly off between the French soldiers.

The patrol of Uhlans was one of those sent out on Durosnel's orders into the various streets of Moscow to put a stop to pillage and, still more, to capture the incendiaries who, according to the general impression prevalent that day among the French High Command, were the cause of the conflagrations. After riding up and down a number of streets the patrol arrested five more Russian suspects: a small shopkeeper, two divinity students, a peasant and a house-serf – and a few marauders. But of all these suspicious characters Pierre seemed the most suspect of all. When they had all been brought for the night to a big house on the Zubov rampart, which was being used as a guardhouse, Pierre was separated from the others and placed under strict surveillance.

WAR AND PEACE

*

BOOK FOUR

PART ONE

I

IN Petersburg all this time an intricate battle was raging in the highest circles, with greater violence than ever, between the parties of Rumyantsev, the French, Maria Feodorovna, the Tsarevich and others, overlaid as usual by the buzzing of the Court drones. But Petersburg's daily round – tranquil, luxurious, concerned only with phantoms and reflections of life – continued as before, so that it was not easy, and needed a determined effort, to form any true idea of the peril and the difficulty in which the Russian nation was placed. There were the same levées and balls, the same French theatre, the same activities at Court, the same interests and intrigues in the government service. It was only in the very highest circles that attempts were made to keep in mind the critical nature of the actual situation. The different behaviour of the two Empresses in these trying circumstances was commented upon in whispers. While the Dowager-Empress Maria Feodorovna, anxious for the welfare of the charitable and educational institutions under her patronage, had all the necessary steps taken for their transfer to Kazan (and the effects belonging to these institutions were already packed), the Empress Elizaveta Alexeyevna, when asked what instructions she was graciously pleased to give, with her wonted Russian patriotism had vouchsafed that she could issue no commands about State institutions, since that was the province of the Sovereign, but in so far as she personally was affected she declared that she would be the last to quit Petersburg.

At Anna Pavlovna's on the 26th of August, the very day of the battle of Borodino, there was a *soirée*, the crowning attraction of which was to be the reading of a letter from His Eminence the Metropolitan of Moscow to accompany a present to the Emperor of an icon of St Sergii. This letter was regarded as a model of ecclesiastical, patriotic eloquence. Prince Vasili himself, famed for his elocution, was to read it aloud. (He had even read more than once at the Empress's.) His 'art' consisted in pouring out the words, quite independently of their meaning, in a loud, resonant voice alternating between a despairing wail and a tender murmur, so that it was wholly a matter of chance whether the wail or the murmur fell on one word or another. This reading, as was always the case with Anna Pavlovna's entertainments, had a political significance. On this particular evening she was expecting several important personages who were to be made to feel ashamed of frequenting the French theatre, and roused to a patriotic frame of mind. Already a considerable number of her guests had arrived but Anna Pavlovna, not yet seeing in her drawing-room all whose presence she deemed necessary, delayed the reading and kept the conversation on general topics.

The news of the day in Petersburg was the serious indisposition of Countess Bezuhov. She had fallen ill unexpectedly a few days previously, had missed several gatherings of which she would have been the ornament, and was said to be receiving no one and, instead of the celebrated Petersburg physicians who usually attended her, had put herself in the hands of some Italian medico who was treating her by some new and extraordinary method.

Everyone was very well aware that the lovely countess's illness arose from the complications of marrying two husbands at the same time, and that the Italian doctor's cure lay in the removal of this difficulty; but at Anna Pavlovna's no one ventured to think of this or even, as it were, to know what they did know.

'The poor countess is very ill, I hear. The doctor talks of angina pectoris.'

'Angina? Oh, that's a dreadful malady!'

'They say the rivals are reconciled, thanks to this angina. ...' The word *angina* was repeated with much relish.

'I hear the old count is very pathetic. He cried like a child when the doctor told him how serious it was.'

'Oh, it would be a terrible loss. She's such a bewitching creature.'

'Are you speaking of the poor countess?' said Anna Pavlovna, joining the group. 'I sent to ask how she was, and am informed that she is a little better. Oh, there's no doubt of it, she's the most delightful woman on earth,' she went on, with a smile at her own enthusiasm. 'We belong to different camps but that does not prevent me from appreciating her as she deserves. And she is so unhappy!' added Anna Pavlovna.

Supposing that by this last remark Anna Pavlovna was slightly lifting the veil of mystery that hung over the countess's illness, one unwary young man went so far as to express surprise that no well-known doctor had been called in and that the countess should be treated by a quack who might administer dangerous remedies to his patient.

'Your information may be better than mine,' retorted Anna Pavlovna suddenly, letting fly very venomously at the inexperienced young man, 'but I have it on good authority that this doctor is a most learned, able man. He is private physician to the Queen of Spain.'

And having thus annihilated the young man Anna Pavlovna turned to another little group where Bilibin was discoursing on the Austrians: he had wrinkled up the skin on his forehead and was evidently on the point of letting it smooth out again with the utterance of one of his *mots*.

'I find it quite charming,' he was saying, referring to a diplomatic note that had been sent to Vienna with some Austrian banners captured from the French by Wittgenstein, 'the hero of Petropol,' as he was called in Petersburg.

'What is that?' inquired Anna Pavlovna, securing silence for the witticism which she had heard before.

And Bilibin repeated the precise words of the diplomatic dispatch concocted by him.

'The Emperor returns these Austrian banners,' quoted Bilibin, 'friendly banners gone astray and found off their right way,' letting the wrinkles run off his brow.

'Charming, charming!' observed Prince Vasili.

'The road to Warsaw, perhaps,' Prince Hippolyte suddenly remarked in a loud voice. Everybody looked at him, at a loss to understand what he wanted to convey by this. Prince Hippolyte himself glanced about him in amused wonder. He knew no more than the others what his words meant. In the course of his diplomatic career he had more than once noticed that a few words thus unexpectedly thrown in passed for being very witty, and at every opportunity he thus uttered the first words that entered his head. 'They may turn out lucky,' he would think, 'but if not, someone is sure to arrange matters.' And the awkward silence that ensued was in fact broken by the appearance of the insufficiently patriotic individual whom Anna Pavlovna was waiting for and hoping to convert, and, smiling and shaking a finger at Hippolyte, she invited Prince Vasili to the table and setting two candles and the manuscript before him begged him to begin. There was a general hush.

'Most gracious Sovereign the Emperor!' declaimed Prince Vasili severely, looking round at his audience as much as to inquire whether anyone had anything to say to the contrary. But nobody breathed a word. 'Moscow, our ancient capital, the New Jerusalem, receives *her* Messiah' – he hurled a sudden emphasis on the '*her*' – 'even as a mother embraces in her arms her zealous sons, and through the gathering mists, foreseeing the dazzling glory of thy dominion, sings aloud in exultation, "Hosanna! Blessed is he that cometh!"'

Prince Vasili pronounced these last words in a tearful voice.

Bilibin attentively examined his nails, and many of the audience appeared abashed, as though wondering what they had done wrong. Anna Pavlovna whispered the next words in advance, like an old woman muttering the prayer to come at communion: 'Let the insolent and brazen Goliath ...' she murmured.

Prince Vasili continued:

'Let the insolent and brazen Goliath from the borders of France encompass the realm of Russia with the murderous terrors of death; lowly faith, the sling of the Russian David, shall be swift to smite at the head of his pride that thirsteth for blood. This icon of St Sergii, the ancient zealot of our country's weal, comes to your Imperial Majesty. I grieve that my failing strength prevents my rejoicing in the sight of your most gracious countenance. I send up fervent prayers to Heaven that the Almighty may exalt the generation of the righteous and in His mercy fulfil the hopes of your Majesty.'

'*Quelle force! Quel style!*' cried one and another, in praise of reader and author alike.

Animated by this oration, Anna Pavlovna's guests discussed for a long time the state of the Fatherland, and made various conjectures as to the issue of the battle to be fought in the next few days.

'You will see,' said Anna Pavlovna, 'tomorrow, on the Emperor's birthday, we shall get news. I have a happy presentiment.'

2

ANNA PAVLOVNA'S presentiment was in fact realized. Next day, during a Te Deum at the Palace chapel on the occasion of the Emperor's birthday, Prince Volkonsky was called out of church to receive a dispatch from Prince Kutuzov. This was Kutuzov's report penned from Tatarinova on the day of the battle. Kutuzov wrote that the Russians had not fallen back a single step, that the French losses were much heavier than ours, and that he was writing in haste from the field of battle before he had had time to collect the latest intelligence. So apparently there must have been a victory. And immediately, without leaving the church, thanks were offered up to the Creator for His succour, and for the victory.

Anna Pavlovna's presentiment was realized, and all that morning a joyous high-day and holiday mood reigned in the city. Everyone believed our success to have been complete, and some people even went so far as to talk of Napoleon having been taken prisoner, of his deposition and of the selection of a new ruler for France.

It is very difficult for events to be reflected in their true force and perspective so far from the scene of action and amid the conditions of Court life. Public events inevitably group themselves round some personal circumstance. So now in the present instance the joy of the Court sprang as much from the fact that the news had arrived on the Emperor's birthday as from the victory itself. It was like a success-fully arranged surprise. Kutuzov's report also made mention of the Russian losses, naming among the killed Tuchkov, Bagration and Kutaissov. Here again the world of Petersburg centred its grief on one happening – the death of Kutaissov. Everybody knew him, the Emperor liked him, he was young and interesting. That day every-one met with the words:

'What a wonderful coincidence! To come just during the Te Deum! But Kutaissov – what a loss! Ah, what a pity!'

'What did I tell you about Kutuzov?' Prince Vasili kept repeating now with a prophet's pride. 'I always said he was the only man cap-able of beating Napoleon.'

But on the following day no news arrived from the army and the public voice began to waver. The courtiers suffered agonies over the agonies of suspense which the Emperor was suffering.

'Just think of the Emperor's position!' said those at Court, and instead of singing Kutuzov's praises as they had the day before they began to pass judgement on him as the cause of the Emperor's anxiety. Prince Vasili no longer boasted of his protégé Kutuzov, but remained silent when the commander-in-chief was spoken of. Moreover, towards the evening of that day, as if everything were conspiring to alarm and disquiet Petersburg society, a terrible piece of news was announced. Countess Hélène Bezuhov had suddenly died of that fearful malady, the name of which it had been so agreeable to pronounce. At large gatherings the official story was accepted that Countess Bezuhov had died of a terrible attack of angina pectoris, but in select circles details were forthcoming of how the private physician of the Queen of Spain had prescribed small doses of a certain drug to bring about a certain effect; but that Hélène, worried by the old count's suspicions of her and by the fact that her husband to whom she had written (that wretched, profligate Pierre) had not replied, had suddenly swallowed an enormous dose of the drug and died in agony before assistance could be given. It was said that Prince Vasili and the old count had at first turned on the Italian; but the latter had produced notes from the unfortunate deceased of such a character that they quickly let the matter drop.

Conversation in general centred round three melancholy circumstances: the Emperor's lack of news, the loss of Kutaissov and the death of Hélène.

On the third day after Kutuzov's dispatch a country gentleman arrived from Moscow, and the news of the surrender of that capital to the French was all over the town. This was awful! What a position for the Emperor to be in! Kutuzov was a traitor, and Prince Vasili assured those who came to condole with him on his daughter's death that nothing else was to be expected of a blind and depraved old man (whose praises he had once sung so loudly – but it was pardonable that in his grief he should forget what he had said before).

'I am only amazed that the fate of Russia could have been entrusted to such a man.'

So long as the news was not official it was still possible to doubt it, but twenty-four hours later the following communication came from Count Rostopchin.

Prince Kutuzov's adjutant has brought me a letter in which he demands that I should furnish police officers to escort the army to the Ryazan road. He writes that he is regretfully abandoning Moscow. Sire, Kutuzov's action decides the fate of the capital and of your Empire! The nation will shudder to learn that the city which represents the greatness of Russia, and in which lie the ashes of your ancestors, is in the hands of the enemy. I am following the army. I have had everything removed, and it only remains for me to weep over the lot of my Fatherland.

On receiving this dispatch the Emperor sent Prince Volkonsky to Kutuzov with the following rescript:

Prince Mihail Ilarionovich! No communication has come to hand from you since the 29th of August. Meanwhile I have received, by way of Yaroslavl, under date of September 1st, from the Governor-general of Moscow, the sad tidings that you, with the army, have decided to abandon Moscow. You may imagine the effect this news has had upon me, and your silence adds to my amazement. I send Adjutant-general Prince Volkonsky with this, to ascertain from you the situation of the army and the reasons which have impelled you to so melancholy a decision.

3

NINE days after the abandonment of Moscow a courier from Kutuzov reached Petersburg with the official announcement of the surrender of the city. This courier was a Frenchman, Michaud, who did not know Russian. But, though a foreigner, he was, as he himself was wont to declare, 'Russian in heart and soul'.

The Emperor at once received the messenger in his study in the Palace on Kamenny Island. Michaud, who had never seen Moscow before the campaign, and who did not speak a word of Russian, yet felt deeply moved (as he wrote) when he appeared before '*notre très gracieux souverain*' with the news of the burning of Moscow, the flames of which had lighted up his route.

Though the source of Monsieur Michaud's chagrin must indeed have been different from that to which the grief of the Russian people was due, he had such a melancholy face when he was shown into the Emperor's study that the Tsar at once asked:

'Do you bring me sad news, colonel?'

'Very sad, sire,' replied Michaud, casting his eyes down with a sigh. '*L'abandon de Moscou*.'

'Can they have surrendered my ancient capital without a battle?' exclaimed the Emperor quickly, the angry colour mounting to his cheek.

Michaud respectfully delivered the message Kutuzov had entrusted to him, to the effect that it had been impossible to fight before Moscow, and, seeing that the choice lay between losing the army as well as Moscow or losing Moscow alone, the field-marshal had been obliged to choose the latter.

The Emperor listened in silence, not looking at Michaud.

'Has the enemy entered the city?' he asked.

'Yes, sire, and by now Moscow is in ashes. I left it a blaze of flames,' replied Michaud in a decided tone, but glancing at the Emperor he was appalled at what he had said. The Tsar was breathing heavily and rapidly, his lower lip twitched and the tears gushed to his fine blue eyes.

But this lasted only a moment. The Emperor suddenly frowned, as though vexed with himself for his own weakness, and raising his head addressed Michaud in a firm voice:

'I see, colonel, from all that is happening to us, that Providence requires great sacrifices of us. ... I am ready to submit myself in all things to His will; but tell me, Michaud, how was my army when you left – when it saw my ancient capital abandoned without a blow struck. Did you perceive signs of discouragement?'

Observing that his *très gracieux souverain* had regained his composure, Michaud too recovered himself but was not immediately ready to reply to the Emperor's direct and relevant question, which called for a direct answer.

'Sire, have I your Majesty's permission to speak frankly as befits a plain, honest soldier?' he asked, to gain time.

'Colonel, that is what I always demand,' said the Tsar. 'Conceal nothing from me; I want to know exactly how matters stand.'

'Sire!' said Michaud with the faintest suggestion of a smile on his lips, having now managed to think of an answer in the form of a light and respectful quibble – 'Sire, I left the whole army, from the commanders to the lowest soldier, in a state of extreme and desperate terror. ...'

'How so?' the Emperor interrupted him, frowning severely. 'Are my Russians cast down by misfortune? ... Never!'

This was just what Michaud was waiting for to get in his *jeu de mots*.

'Sire,' he said with a respectful playfulness of expression, 'their only fear is lest your Majesty, out of goodness of heart, should be persuaded to make peace. They are burning for the combat,' declared this representative of the Russian people, 'and to prove to your Majesty by the sacrifice of their lives how devoted they are. ...'

'Ah!' said the Emperor, reassured, and with a friendly light in his eyes he patted Michaud on the shoulder. 'You set me at ease, colonel.'

He bent his head and was silent for some time.

'Well, then, go back to the army,' he said, drawing himself up to his full height and addressing Michaud with a genial and majestic gesture, 'and tell our brave fellows – tell all my loyal subjects wherever you may go – that when I have not a soldier left I shall put myself at the head of my beloved Nobility, of my worthy peasants, and so use the last resources of my Empire. I have more at my command than my enemies suspect,' he added, growing more and more animated. 'But if it should be written in the decrees of Divine Providence,' he continued, raising to heaven his beautiful, mild eyes, shining with emotion, 'that my dynasty should cease to reign on the throne of my ancestors, then, after exhausting every means in my power, I shall let my beard grow to here' (the Emperor put his hand halfway down his chest) 'and go and eat potatoes with the meanest of my peasants rather than sign the shame of my country and of my dearly loved people, whose sacrifices I know how to appreciate.'

Uttering these words in a voice full of feeling, the Emperor suddenly turned away, as if to hide from Michaud the tears that rose to his eyes, and walked to the farther end of his study. After standing there a few moments he strode back to Michaud and gave his arm a powerful squeeze below the elbow. His gentle, handsome face was flushed and his eyes gleamed with determination and anger.

'Colonel Michaud, do not forget what I say to you here; perhaps one day we may recall it with satisfaction. ... Napoleon or I,' said the Emperor, touching his breast. 'We can no longer both reign. I have learned to know him, he will not deceive me again. ...'

And the Emperor paused, with a frown.

Hearing these words and seeing the steadfast look of resolve in the Emperor's eyes, Michaud – 'a foreigner but Russian in heart and soul' – at that solemn moment felt himself *enthousiasmé* by all that he had heard (as he used to recount later), and gave expression to his own feelings and those of the Russian people, whose representative he considered himself to be, in the following exclamation:

'Sire!' said he, 'your Majesty is at this moment signing the glory of the nation and the salvation of Europe!'

With an inclination of his head the Emperor dismissed Michaud.

WITH half of Russia in enemy hands, and the inhabitants of Moscow fleeing to distant provinces, with one levy after another being raised for the defence of the Fatherland, we, who were not living in those times, cannot help imagining that all Russians, great and small, were solely engaged in immolating themselves, in trying to save their country or in weeping over its downfall. All the stories and descriptions of those years, without exception, tell of nothing but the self-sacrifice, the patriotic devotion, the despair, the anguish and the heroism of the Russian people. Actually, it was not at all like that. It appears so to us because we see only the general historic interest of the period, and not all the minor personal interests that men had. Yet, in reality, private interests of the immediate present are always so much more important than the wider issues that they prevent the wider issues which concern the public as a whole from ever being felt – from being noticed at all, indeed. The majority of the people of that time paid no attention to the broad trend of the nation's affairs, and were only influenced by their private concerns. And it was these very people who played the most useful part in the history of their day.

Those who were striving to understand the general course of events, and trying by self-sacrifice and heroism to take a hand in it, were the most useless members of society; they saw everything upside down, and all they did for the common good proved to be futile and absurd – like Pierre's regiment, and Mamonov's, which looted Russian villages, and the lint scraped by the ladies, that never reached the wounded, and so on. Even the amateur dialecticians, who in their fondness for subtilties and the expression of their feelings endlessly discussed Russia's situation, unconsciously introduced into their speeches an impress of hypocrisy or falsity, or else of profitless fault-finding and animosity directed against persons who were blamed for what no one could help. The interdiction anent tasting the fruit of the tree of knowledge comes out more conspicuously in historical events than anywhere. It is only subconscious activity that bears fruit, and a man who plays a part in an historic event never understands its import. As soon as he tries to realize its significance his actions become sterile.

The more closely a man was engaged in the events then taking place in Russia the less did he perceive their meaning. In Petersburg and in the provinces remote from Moscow, ladies, and gentlemen in militia uniforms, mourned over the fate of Russia and her ancient capital, and talked of self-sacrifice and so forth; but in the army, which was withdrawing beyond Moscow, almost nothing was said or thought about Moscow, and looking back at the scene of the fire, no one swore to be avenged on the French: their minds were on the coming pay-day, the next halt, Matrioshka the *vivandière*, and the like. ...

Nikolai Rostov, without any idea of self-sacrifice but casually, because the war had caught him in the Service, took a real and continuous part in the defence of his country, and consequently he looked upon what was happening in Russia without despair or sombre syllogizing. Had he been asked what he thought of the state of affairs in Russia he would have replied that it wasn't for him to think about it, that Kutuzov and others were there for that purpose, but that he had heard that the regiments were to be made up to their full strength, that fighting would probably go on for a good while yet, and that things being so, it was quite likely he might be in command of a regiment in a couple of years' time.

Since he regarded the matter in this light he took the announcement that he was being sent to Voronezh to buy remounts for his division not only without regret at being deprived of participation in the coming engagement but with the greatest satisfaction – which he did not conceal and which his comrades fully sympathized with.

A few days before the battle of Borodino Nikolai received the necessary money and official warrants, and sending some hussars on in advance he set out with post-horses for Voronezh.

Only those who know what it is to spend several months on end in the atmosphere of an army on active service can appreciate how blissfully happy Nikolai felt when he got beyond the region overrun with troops and their foraging parties, provision-trains and field hospitals – when, instead of soldiers, army wagons and the filth which betrays the presence of a military camp, he found himself among villages of peasant men and women, gentlemen's country houses, fields with grazing cattle, and post-houses with their sleepy masters. He was so happy that he might have been seeing everything for the first time. The sight of wholesome young women without a dozen officers hanging round each of them was a particular wonder and delight – women, too, who were pleased and flattered that a passing officer should joke with them.

Enchanted alike with himself and his fate, Nikolai arrived at night at an hotel in Voronezh, ordered all the things he had over so long a period missed in camp, and next day, after an extra careful shave, in full-dress uniform which he had not worn for some time past, went to present himself to the authorities.

The commander of the local militia was a civilian general, an old man who was evidently enjoying his military status and rank. He gave Nikolai a brusque reception (imagining this to be the proper military manner) and interrogated him importantly, as though he had a right to do so, approving and disapproving and apparently deliberating on the course of events generally. Nikolai was in such good spirits that this only amused him.

From the commander of the militia he drove to the governor. The governor was a brisk little man, very affable and unpretentious. He told Nikolai of the stud-farms where he might find horses, recommended him to a horse-dealer in the town and a landed proprietor fourteen miles out of town who had the best horses, and promised him every assistance.

'You are Count Ilya Rostov's son? My wife was a great friend of your dear mother's. We are at home on Thursdays – today is Thursday, so please come and see us, without ceremony,' said the governor as Nikolai took his leave.

Nikolai hired post-horses and making his quartermaster get in beside him set off at a gallop straight from the governor's to the gentleman with the stud fourteen miles away. Everything seemed pleasant and easy to Nikolai during that first part of his stay in Voronezh, and, as happens when a man is in a happy frame of mind, everything went well and without difficulty.

The country gentleman turned out to be an old cavalry officer, a bachelor, a great horse-fancier, a sportsman, the possessor of some century-old brandy, besides some old Hungarian wine, who had a den where he smoked, and some superb horses.

In a very few words Nikolai came to terms with him, acquiring seventeen picked stallions for six thousand roubles – to serve (as he explained) as show specimens of his remounts. After dining and doing rather more than ample justice to the Hungarian wine, Nikolai –

having exchanged embraces with the country gentleman with whom he was already on the friendliest of footings – drove back in the gayest of moods at a furious pace over the most abominable road, continually urging the driver on, so as to be in time for the governor's *soirée*.

When he had changed, sluiced cold water over his head and scented himself, Nikolai appeared at the governor's, a little late but with the adage 'Better late than never' ready on the tip of his tongue.

It was not a ball, and nothing had been said about dancing, but everyone knew that Katerina Petrovna would play walses and *écossaises* on the clavichord and that there would be dancing, and so everyone had come dressed as for a ball.

Provincial life in 1812 went on very much as usual, the only difference being that there was more stir in the towns, owing to the advent of numerous wealthy families from Moscow, and in the air a marked devil-may-care, in for a penny, in for a pound spirit noticeable in everything all over Russia at that time, while the inevitable small talk, instead of being concerned with the weather and mutual acquaintances, now turned on Moscow, the army and Napoleon.

The gathering at the governor's consisted of the cream of Voronezh society.

There were any number of ladies, there were several of Nikolai's Moscow acquaintances; but of the men there was not one who could even begin to rival the chevalier of St George, the hussar remount-officer, the good-natured, well-bred Count Rostov. Among the men was an Italian prisoner, an officer of the French army, and Nikolai felt that the presence of this prisoner – a living trophy, as it were – enhanced his own importance as a Russian hero. It seemed to him that everyone shared this sentiment, and he treated the Italian cordially but with a certain dignity and reserve.

The moment Nikolai entered the room in his hussar uniform, diffusing about him a fragrance of perfume and wine, and had uttered and heard others repeat his 'Better late than never', people clustered round him. All eyes were turned on him, and he felt at once that he had stepped into his proper position in the province – that of universal favourite – always a pleasant position to be in, and intoxicatingly so after long deprivation. Not only at the posting-stations, at inns and in the country landowner's smoking-room had servant-girls been flattered by his notice, but here too at the governor's party it seemed to Nikolai there was an inexhaustible array of young married ladies and pretty girls impatient for a share of his attention. The ladies and the young girls flirted with him, the old people concerned themselves from the first day to get this gallant young rake of a hussar married and settled down. Among these was the governor's wife herself, who welcomed Rostov as a near relative and called him 'Nicolas'.

Katerina Petrovna did in fact proceed to play waltzes and *écossaises*, and dancing began, in which Nikolai still further captivated provincial society by his mastery. He even surprised them all by his exaggeratedly free-and-easy style. Nikolai wondered a little himself at the way he danced that evening. He had never danced like that in Moscow and would indeed have considered such an extremely lax manner indecorous and bad form; but here he felt it incumbent on him to astonish them all by something extraordinary, something they would be compelled to accept as the regular thing in the capitals though new to them in the provinces.

All the evening Nikolai devoted most of his attentions to a blue-eyed, plump and pleasing little blonde, the wife of a local official. With the naïve conviction of young men who are enjoying themselves that other men's wives were created for their especial benefit Rostov never left this lady's side, and treated her husband with a friendly air, almost as though there was a private understanding between them and they knew without putting it into words how excellently they, that is, Nikolai and the other man's wife, would get on together. The husband, however, appeared to think otherwise, and tried to take a lowering tone with Rostov. But the latter's frank good humour was so boundless that more than once the husband was obliged, in spite of himself, to yield before Nikolai's good cheer. But towards the end of the evening, as the wife's face grew more flushed and animated the husband's became more stolid and melancholy, as though they had only a modicum of vivacity between them and when it rose in the wife it declined in the husband.

5

WITH a smile that never left his lips Nikolai sat leaning slightly forward in an arm-chair, bending closely over the pretty blonde and paying her mythological compliments.

Jauntily shifting the position of his legs in their tight riding-breeches, diffusing a smell of perfume, and admiring his fair companion, himself and the handsome shape of his legs in their well-fitting Hessian boots, Nikolai was telling the little blonde that he meant to carry off a certain lady here in Voronezh.

'What is she like?'

'Charming, divine. Her eyes' (Nikolai gazed at his companion) 'are blue, her mouth is coral and ivory; her figure' (he glanced at her shoulders) 'like Diana's. ...'

The husband came up and asked his wife darkly what she was talking about.

'Ah, Nikita Ivanych!' cried Nikolai, rising courteously. And as though anxious for Nikita Ivanych to share in the fun he began to tell him, too, of his intention of running off with a blonde lady.

The husband smiled grimly, the wife gaily. The governor's kindly wife came up with a disapproving look on her face.

'Anna Ignatyevna wants to see you, Nicolas,' said she, pronouncing the name in such a way that Rostov was at once aware that Anna Ignatyevna was a very important person. 'Come with me, Nicolas. You said I could call you that, didn't you?'

'Oh yes, *ma tante*. But who is she?'

'Anna Ignatyevna Malvintsev. She has heard about you from her niece whom you rescued. ... Can you guess?'

'I rescued such a lot of people!' said Nikolai.

'Her niece, Princess Bolkonsky. She is here in Voronezh with her aunt. Oho! He blushes! Why, are ...?'

'Not a bit of it – I assure you, *ma tante*.'

'Very well, very well! Oh, what a boy it is!'

The governor's wife led him up to a tall and very stout old lady in a sky-blue toque, who had just finished a game of cards with the most eminent personages of the town. This was Madame Malvintsev, Princess Maria's aunt on her mother's side, a wealthy, childless widow who had always lived in Voronezh. When Rostov approached she was standing and paying her debts after the game. Sternly and importantly screwing up her eyes, she glanced at him and went on berating the general who had won from her.

'Very glad to see you, my dear,' she then said, holding out her hand to Nikolai. 'Pray come and see me.'

After a few words about Princess Maria and her late father, whom

Madame Malvintsev had evidently not cared for, and inquiring what news Nikolai had of Prince Andrei, who was apparently no favourite of hers either, the dignified old lady dismissed him with a renewal of her invitation to come and see her.

Nikolai promised to do so and blushed again as he bowed. At the mention of Princess Maria he experienced a sensation of shyness, even of fear, which he himself could not understand.

Having left Madame Malvintsev, Nikolai started back to the dancing but the governor's little wife laid a plump hand on his sleeve and, saying that she wanted to have a talk with him, led him to her sitting-room, from which those who were there immediately withdrew so as not to be in her way.

'Do you know, *mon cher*,' began the governor's wife with a serious expression on her kind little face, 'that really would be the match for you: would you like me to arrange it?'

'Whom do you mean, *ma tante*?' asked Nikolai.

'I will make a match for you with the princess. Katerina Petrovna suggests Lili but I say, no – the princess. I am sure your mother will be grateful to me. Really, she's a charming girl! And by no means so plain as all that.'

'Indeed, she isn't!' exclaimed Nikolai, as though offended at the idea. 'For my part, *ma tante*, as befits a soldier I never force myself on anyone, nor do I refuse anything that turns up,' he said, without stopping to consider what he was saying.

'But you must remember: this is no light matter.'

'Of course not!'

'Yes, yes,' said the governor's wife, as though talking to herself. 'But listen, *mon cher*, just one thing, you are too attentive by far to that other lady – *la blonde*. The husband cuts a sorry figure, true ...'

'Oh no, he and I are good friends,' exclaimed Nikolai in the simplicity of his heart: it had never occurred to him that a pastime which he found so agreeable could be other than agreeable to anyone else.

'What a lot of nonsense I said to the governor's wife, though!' thought Nikolai suddenly at supper. 'Now she really will start arranging a match for me, and what about Sonya? ...' And when he was bidding the governor's wife good-night, and she said to him with a smile, 'Well, remember then,' he drew her aside.

'*Ma tante*, listen, to tell you the truth ...'

'What is it, my dear? Come and sit down here.'

Nikolai suddenly felt a desire, an irresistible impulse to confide his most private thoughts (which he would never have told his mother, his sister or an intimate friend) to this woman who was almost a stranger. Afterwards, when he recalled this unsolicited, inexplicable fit of candour, which nevertheless had very important consequences for him, it seemed – as it always does seem in such instances – that he had merely been seized by some silly whim; yet that burst of frankness, together with other trivial events, had immense consequences for him and for all his family.

'It's like this, *ma tante*. For a long time *Maman* has been bent on marrying me to an heiress, but the very idea of marrying for money is repugnant to me.'

'Oh yes, I can quite understand that,' said the governor's wife.

'But Princess Bolkonsky – that's a different matter. I will tell you the truth: in the first place, I like her very much, I feel drawn to her; and then, after I met her in such circumstances – so strangely – it has often struck me that it was fate. Especially if you remember that *Maman* has had it in mind for a long time, only I never happened to meet her before – it always happened somehow that we did not meet. And then as long as my sister, Natasha, was betrothed to her brother of course it was out of the question for me to think of marrying her. And just when Natasha's engagement had been broken off it must needs happen that I meet her ... well, and then everything. ... You see, it's like this. ... I have never spoken to anyone about this, and I never will. Only to you. ...'

The governor's wife pressed his elbow gratefully.

'You know Sonya, my cousin? I love her, and I promised to marry her, and I mean to marry her. ... So you see there can be no question ever about –' concluded Nikolai incoherently, flushing crimson.

'My dear boy, my dear boy, what a way to look at things! Why, Sonya hasn't a farthing, and you said yourself that your papa's affairs are in a very bad way. And what about your mamma? It would kill her, for one thing. Then Sonya, if she's a girl with a heart – what sort of life would it be for her? Your mother in despair, you all ruined. ... No, *mon cher*, you and Sonya must realize that.'

Nikolai did not speak. It was a comfort for him to hear these arguments.

'All the same, *ma tante*, it cannot be,' he said with a sigh, after a brief silence. 'And besides, would the princess have me? And another thing, she is in mourning. Why, it's not to be thought of!'

'But you don't suppose I'm going to take you by the throat and get you married out of hand, do you? There are ways of doing everything,' said the governor's wife.

'What a match-maker you are, *ma tante* ...' said Nikolai, kissing her plump little hand.

6

ON reaching Moscow after her meeting with Rostov, Princess Maria had found her nephew there with his tutor, and a letter from Prince Andrei telling her how to get to her aunt, Madame Malvintsev, at Voronezh. The arrangements for the journey, anxiety about her brother, the organization of her life in a new home, fresh faces, the - education of her nephew – all this deadened the voice as it were of temptation which had tormented her during her father's illness and after his death, and especially since her encounter with Rostov. She was sad. Now, after a month passed in quiet surroundings, she felt more and more deeply the loss of her father, which was associated in her heart with the downfall of Russia. She was restless and agitated: the thought of the perils to which her brother, the only near relation left to her, was exposed was a continual torture. She worried too about the upbringing of her nephew, for which she constantly felt herself unfitted; but in the depths of her soul she was at peace with herself because she was conscious of having suppressed the dreams and hopes of happiness that had been on the point of springing up within her in connexion with Rostov's appearance on the scene.

When the governor's wife called on Madame Malvintsev the day after the party and, after discussing her plans with the aunt (and remarking that, though in present circumstances a formal courtship was of course not to be thought of, still the young people might be brought together and allowed to get to know one another), and Madame Malvintsev having expressed approval, began to speak of Rostov in Princess Maria's presence, singing his praises and describing how he had blushed on hearing Princess Maria's name mentioned, her emotion was not one of joy but of pain: her inner harmony was destroyed, and desires, doubts, self-reproach and hope rose up again.

During the two days that elapsed before Rostov called, Princess Maria never stopped pondering what her behaviour to him should be. First she decided not to go down to the drawing-room when he called to see her aunt – that it would not be proper, in her deep mourning, to receive visitors; then she thought this would be rude after what he had done for her; then it occurred to her that her aunt and the governor's wife had intentions concerning herself and Rostov (the glances they gave and some of the words they let fall seemed to confirm this surmise); then she told herself that only she with her inborn depravity could think such things of them: they could not fail to realize that in her position, while she was still wearing the heaviest mourning, such match-making would be an insult both to her and to her father's memory. Assuming for a moment that she did go down to see him, Princess Maria would start imagining the words he would say to her and what she would say to him, and at one moment they seemed to her unwarrantably frigid, at the next they struck her as carrying too much meaning. Above all, she dreaded the embarrassment which she felt sure would overwhelm and betray her as soon as she saw him.

But when on Sunday morning after church the footman came to the drawing-room to announce that Count Rostov had called, only a faint flush suffused her cheeks and her eyes lit up with a new and radiant light.

'You have met him, Aunt?' said Princess Maria in a composed voice, not knowing herself how she could be outwardly so calm and natural.

When Rostov entered the room the princess looked down for an instant, as though to give the visitor time to greet her aunt, and then just as Nikolai turned to her she raised her head and met his gaze with shining eyes. With a movement full of dignity and grace she half rose with a smile of delight, held out her slender, delicate hand to him, and began to speak in a voice in which for the first time new deep, womanly notes vibrated. Mademoiselle Bourienne, who was in the drawing-room, stared at Princess Maria in bewildered surprise. Herself a most accomplished coquette, she could not have manoeuvred better on meeting a man whom she wanted to attract.

'Either black suits her wonderfully, or she really has grown better-looking without my noticing it. And, above all, what *savoir faire* and grace!' thought Mademoiselle Bourienne.

Had Princess Maria been capable of reflection at that moment she would have been even more astonished than Mademoiselle Bourienne at the change that had taken place in herself. From the moment she set eyes on that dear, loved face, some new vital force took possession of her and compelled her to speak and act irrespective of her own volition. From the time Rostov entered the room her face was transformed. Just as when a light is lit inside a carved and painted lantern, suddenly revealing in unexpected, breath-taking beauty of detail the fine, intricate tracery of its panels, which till then had seemed coarse, dark and meaningless, so was Princess Maria's face suddenly transfigured. For the first time all the pure, spiritual, inward travail in which she had lived till then came out into the open. All her inner searchings of spirit, her sufferings, her striving after goodness, her resignation, her love and self-sacrifice – all this now shone forth in those radiant eyes, in her sweet smile, in every feature of her tender face.

Rostov saw all this as clearly as though he had known her whole life. He felt that the being before him was utterly different from and better than anyone he had met before, and, above all, better than himself.

Their conversation was very simple and ordinary. They talked of the war, like everyone else unconsciously exaggerating their sorrow over it; they spoke of their last meeting – Nikolai trying to change the subject; they talked of the governor's kindly wife, of Nikolai's relatives and of Princess Maria's.

Princess Maria did not allude to her brother, diverting the conversation as soon as her aunt mentioned Andrei. It was evident that while there might be some pretence about her grief over the misfortunes of Russia her brother was too near her heart and she neither could nor would speak superficially of him. Nikolai noticed this, as he noticed every shade of Princess Maria's character, with a keenness of insight not at all typical of him, and everything confirmed his conviction that she was an altogether rare and unusual being. Nikolai, exactly like Princess Maria in her turn, blushed and was embarrassed when people spoke to him about the princess, and even when he thought of her, but in her presence he felt perfectly at ease, and by no means confined himself to the set speeches which he had prepared in advance but said what, always quite appropriately, came into his head at the moment.

When a pause occurred during his short visit Nikolai, as people always do where there are children, turned to Prince Andrei's little son, caressing him and asking him whether he would like to be a hussar. He took the child on his knee, played with him and looked round at Princess Maria. With a softened, happy, shy look she was watching the little lad she loved in the arms of the man she loved. Nikolai caught that look, and as though he divined its significance flushed with pleasure and fell to kissing the child with simple-hearted gaiety.

On account of her mourning Princess Maria was not going into society at all, and Nikolai did not think it the proper thing to visit her again; but the governor's wife still persisted in her match-making, passing on to Nikolai the flattering things Princess Maria said of him, and *vice versa*, and pressing him to declare himself to Princess Maria. For this purpose she arranged a meeting between the young people at the bishop's house before morning service.

Though Rostov told the governor's wife that he was not going to make any declaration to Princess Maria, he promised to be there.

Just as at Tilsit Rostov had not allowed himself to doubt that what everybody accepted as right was right, so now, after a brief but genuine struggle between his efforts to order his life as he felt it should be ordered and a humble submission to circumstances, he chose the latter alternative and surrendered to the power which, he felt, was irresistibly carrying him away. He was aware that to declare his feelings to Princess Maria after his promise to Sonya would be what he would call dastardly. And he knew that he would never behave in a dastardly fashion. But he also knew (or rather felt at the bottom of his heart) that in resigning himself now to the force of circumstances and of the people guiding him he was not only doing nothing wrong but was doing something very, very important – more important than anything he had ever done in his life.

After his visit to Princess Maria, though his manner of life remained externally the same, all his former amusements lost their charm for him and he often found himself thinking of her. But he never thought about her as he had thought of all the young girls, without exception, whom he had met in society, nor as he had over a long period, and sometimes rapturously, thought about Sonya. Like almost every up-right, honest young man he had pictured each of these young ladies as a possible future wife, setting her in his imagination against a back-ground of married life – the white morning wrapper, his wife behind the samovar, his wife's carriage, the little ones, *maman* and papa, their attitude to his wife, and so on and so forth; and these pictures of the future he found enjoyable. But when he thought of Princess Maria, to whom they were trying to get him betrothed, he could never see the two of them together as man and wife. If he tried to do so, everything seemed incongruous and false, and only filled him with dread.

7

THE dreadful news of the battle of Borodino, of our casualties in killed and wounded, and the even more terrible tidings of the loss of Moscow reached Voronezh in the middle of September. Princess Maria, having learnt of her brother's wound only from the newspapers and having no definite information, prepared to go in search of him (so Nikolai was told, though he had not seen her again himself).

When he heard the news of the battle of Borodino and the abandonment of Moscow Rostov was not seized with despair, rage, a desire for vengeance, or the like, but everything in Voronezh suddenly seemed to him dreary and irksome: his conscience almost reproached him, and he was ill at ease. All the talk that he listened to rang false in his ear; he did not know what to think of events and felt that only back in the regiment would everything become clear to him again. He made haste to conclude his purchase of horses, and was often without cause ill-tempered with his servant and quartermaster.

A few days before his departure a solemn Te Deum, at which Nikolai was present, was held in the cathedral in thanksgiving for the victory gained by the Russian armies. He stood a little behind the governor, and held himself with befitting decorum throughout the service, meditating the while on a great variety of subjects. When the ceremony was over, the governor's wife beckoned him to her.

'Did you see the princess?' she asked, with a motion of her head towards a lady in black standing behind the choir.

Nikolai immediately recognized Princess Maria, not so much by the profile he saw under her hat as by the feeling of shyness, awe and pity which instantly came over him. Princess Maria, evidently absorbed in her thoughts, was crossing herself for the last time before leaving the church.

Nikolai gazed at her in wonder. It was the same face he had seen before; there was the same general look of refined, inner, spiritual travail, but now there was an utterly different light in it. It had a pathetic expression of sorrow, prayer and hope. As he had done before when she was present, Nikolai went up to her without waiting to be prompted by the governor's wife, or asking himself whether or not it were right and proper to address her here in church, and told her that he had heard of her trouble and sympathized with all his heart. She no sooner heard his voice than a vivid glow suffused her face, lighting up at once her sorrow and her joy.

'One thing I wanted to tell you, princess,' said Rostov. 'If Prince Andrei were not alive, it would have been announced in the gazettes, since he is a colonel.'

The princess looked at him, not grasping what he was saying but comforted by the expression of sympathetic concern on his face.

'And I know so many cases of a splinter-wound (the papers said it was a shell) either proving fatal at once or else very slight,' continued Nikolai. 'We must hope for the best, and I am sure ...'

Princess Maria interrupted him.

'Oh, it would be so aw ...' she exclaimed, and agitation preventing her from finishing, she bent her head with a graceful movement (all her gestures were graceful in his presence) and glancing gratefully up at him she followed after her aunt.

That evening Nikolai did not go out anywhere but stayed in his lodgings in order to square up certain accounts with the horse-dealers. By the time he was through with the business it was too late for paying visits but still too early to go to bed, and for a long while he paced up and down the room reflecting on his life, a thing he rarely did.

Princess Maria had made an agreeable impression on him when he met her near Smolensk. The fact of having encountered her in such unusual circumstances, and of his mother having at one time pointed her out to him as a good match, had caused him to regard her with especial interest. When he came on her again in Voronezh the impression she made on him was not merely pleasing but powerful. Nikolai was struck by the peculiar moral beauty he remarked in her at this time. He had, however, been preparing to go away and it had not entered his head to regret that in leaving Voronezh he was depriving himself of the chance of seeing her. But that morning's encounter with her in church had, he felt, gone more deeply into his heart than was desirable for his general peace. That pale, delicate, sad face, those luminous eyes, the gentle, graceful gestures, and especially the profound and tender melancholy pervading all her features, troubled him and exacted his sympathy. In men Rostov could not endure to see the expression of a lofty spiritual life (that was why he did not like Prince Andrei) – he referred to it scornfully as philosophy and moonshine; but in Princess Maria that very sorrowfulness which revealed the depth of a whole spiritual world foreign to him was an irresistible attraction.

'She must be a marvellous girl! A real angel!' he said to himself. 'Why am I not free? Why was I in such a hurry with Sonya?' And involuntarily he compared the two: the poverty in the one and the abundance in the other of those spiritual gifts which he himself lacked and therefore prized so highly. He tried to picture what would have been were he free. How he would have wooed her and made her his wife. No, he could not imagine that. A chill came over him and nothing clear would present itself to his imagination. He had long ago pictured to himself the future with Sonya, and it was all simple and clear just because it had been thought out and he knew all about Sonya; but it was impossible to picture a future with Princess Maria, because he did not understand her but only loved her.

Reveries to do with Sonya had something gay and playful about them. But to dream of Princess Maria was always difficult and rather frightening.

'How she prayed!' he thought. 'One could see that her whole soul was in her prayer. Yes, that was the prayer that moves mountains, and I am convinced her prayers will be answered. Why don't I pray for what I want?' he bethought himself. 'What do I want? Freedom, release from Sonya. She was right,' he mused, remembering what the governor's wife had said, 'nothing but misery can come of my marrying Sonya. Entanglement, grief for Mamma ... our position ... business difficulties, fearful difficulties! Besides, I don't love her – not as I should. O God, get me out of this dreadful, hopeless situation!' he suddenly began to pray. 'Yes, prayer can move mountains but one must have faith and not just pray as Natasha and I used to as children, for the snow to turn to sugar, and then run out into the yard to see whether it had done so. No, but I am not praying for trifles now,' he said, putting his pipe down in a corner and standing with clasped hands before the icon. And, his heart melted by thoughts of Princess Maria, he started to pray as he had not prayed for a long time. He had tears in his eyes and a lump in his throat when Lavrushka came in at the door with some papers.

'Stupid fool! Bursting in when you're not wanted!' cried Nikolai, quickly changing his attitude.

'From the governor,' said Lavrushka in a sleepy voice. 'A courier has arrived and there's a letter for you.'

'Oh, very well, thanks, you can go!'

Nikolai took the two letters. One was from his mother, the other from Sonya. He recognized them by the handwriting and opened Sonya's first. He had only read a few lines when he turned pale and his eyes opened wide with dismay and joy.

'No, it's not possible!' he exclaimed aloud.

Unable to sit still, he strode up and down the room, holding the letter in both hands as he read. He skimmed through it, read it once, read it a second time, then with shoulders raised and arms stretched out, stood still in the middle of the room, mouth wide open and eyes staring. What he had just been praying for with confidence that God would hear him had come to pass; but Nikolai was as much astonished as if it were something extraordinary and unexpected, and as though the very fact of its happening so quickly proved that it had not come from God, to whom he had been praying, but was some ordinary coincidence.

The knot fastening his freedom, that had seemed so impossible to undo, had been cut by this unexpected (and to Nikolai quite chance) letter from Sonya. She wrote that recent unfortunate events – the loss of almost the whole of the Rostovs' property in Moscow – and the countess's frequently expressed wish that Nikolai should marry Princess Bolkonsky, together with his silence and coldness of late, had all combined to decide her to release him from his promise and set him completely free.

It would be too painful to me to think that I could be a cause of sorrow or discord in the family that has been so good to me [she wrote], and the one aim of my affections is the happiness of those I love; and so, Nicolas, I beg you to consider yourself free, and to know that, in spite of everything, no one can love you more truly than

Your Sonya

Both letters were written from Troitsa. The other, from the countess, described their last days in Moscow, their departure, the fire and the destruction of all their property. In her letter the countess also mentioned that Prince Andrei was among the wounded travelling with them. His condition was critical but the doctor said there was now more hope. Sonya and Natasha were nursing him.

With this letter Nikolai went next day to call on Princess Maria. Neither he nor she spoke a word as to the possible implications of Natasha attending Prince Andrei, but thanks to this letter Nikolai suddenly became almost as intimate with the princess as if they were relations.

The following morning he saw Princess Maria off on her journey to Yaroslavl, and a few days later left to rejoin his regiment.

<h1 style="text-align:center">8</h1>

SONYA'S letter to Nikolai, which had come as an answer to his prayer, had been written from Troitsa. This was how it had come about. The idea of getting Nikolai married to a wealthy bride obsessed the old countess's mind more and more. She knew that Sonya was the chief obstacle in the way of this. And Sonya's life had of late, and especially after the letter in which Nikolai described his meeting with Princess Maria at Bogucharovo, become more and more difficult in the countess's house. The countess never missed an opportunity of making humiliating or cruel allusions to Sonya.

But a few days before they left Moscow, distressed and over-wrought by all that was happening, the countess had sent for Sonya and, instead of upbraiding and demanding, had implored her with tears to sacrifice herself, and repay all that the family had done for her, by breaking off her engagement to Nikolai.

'I shall never know a moment's peace till you make me this promise,' she said.

Sonya sobbed hysterically, replied through her sobs that she would do anything, was ready for anything, but she did not promise in so many words and in her heart she could not bring herself to do what was demanded of her. She must deny herself for the happiness of the family which had brought her up and provided for her. To deny herself for the happiness of others was second nature to Sonya. Her position in the house was such that only thus could she show her quality, and she was used to sacrificing herself and liked to do so. But hitherto in all her acts of self-immolation she had been happily conscious that they raised her in her own esteem and in that of others, and so made her more worthy of Nikolai, whom she loved more than all the world; but now they wanted her to renounce what constituted for her the whole reward of renunciation and the entire meaning of life. And for the first time in her existence she felt bitterness against the people who had befriended her only to torture her the more agonizingly: she envied Natasha who had never experienced anything of this sort, had never been required to sacrifice herself but made others sacrifice themselves for her and yet was beloved by everybody. And for the first time Sonya felt that out of her pure, quiet love for Nikolai a passionate feeling was beginning to grow up which was stronger than principle, virtue or religion; and under the influence of this feeling Sonya, whose life of dependence had taught her instinctively to be secretive, having answered the countess in vague general terms, avoided further conversation with her and resolved to wait until she saw Nikolai, not with the idea of giving him his freedom but, on the contrary, of binding him to her for ever.

The bustle and horror of the Rostovs' last days in Moscow had stifled the gloomy thoughts that weighed on Sonya. She was glad to find escape from them in practical activity. But when she heard of Prince Andrei's presence in their house, in spite of all her very genuine compassion for him and for Natasha, a blithe and superstitious feeling that God did not mean her to be parted from Nikolai enveloped her. She knew Natasha loved no one but Prince Andrei, and had never ceased to love him. She knew that brought together now, in such terrible circumstances, they would fall in love with one another again, and that then Nikolai would not be able to marry Princess Maria as they would be within the prohibited degrees of affinity as stipulated by the Orthodox Church. Notwithstanding all the horror of what had happened during those last days and during the early part of their journey, this feeling, this consciousness that Providence was intervening in her personal affairs, cheered Sonya.

At the Troitsa monastery the Rostovs made the first break in their journey.

Three large rooms were assigned to them in the monastery hostel, one of which Prince Andrei occupied. The wounded man was much better that day. Natasha was sitting with him. In the next room the count and countess were respectfully conversing with the father superior, who was paying a visit to his old acquaintances and patrons.

Sonya was there, too, tormented by curiosity as to what Prince Andrei and Natasha were talking about. She could hear the sound of their voices through the door. The door of Prince Andrei's room opened. Natasha came out, looking agitated, and, not noticing the monk, who had risen to greet her and was drawing back the wide sleeve over his right hand, she went up to Sonya and took her hand.

'Natasha, what are you thinking of? Come here,' said the countess.

Natasha went up to receive the monk's blessing, and he counselled her to turn to God for help, and to the patron saint of the monastery, the blessed St Sergii.

As soon as the father superior withdrew, Natasha took her friend by the hand and went with her into the empty third room.

'Sonya, say yes! Say he will live?' she urged. 'Sonya, I am so happy and so wretched! Sonya, dearest, everything is as it was before. If only he lives! He cannot ... because ... because of ...' and Natasha burst into tears.

'Yes! I knew it! Thank God!' murmured Sonya. 'He will live.'

Sonya was no less overcome than her cousin by the latter's fears and distress, and by her own private thoughts, which she shared with no one. Sobbing, she kissed and comforted Natasha. 'If only he lives!' she said to herself. Having wept and talked together, and wiped away their tears, the two friends stole to Prince Andrei's door. Natasha opened it cautiously and glanced into the room. Sonya stood beside her at the half-open door.

Prince Andrei was lying raised high on three pillows. His pale face looked peaceful, his eyes were closed, and they could see his regular breathing.

'Oh, Natasha!' Sonya suddenly almost shrieked, grabbing her cousin's arm and stepping back from the door.

'What? What is it?' asked Natasha.

'It's the same, it's that ...' said Sonya, with a white face and trembling lips.

Natasha softly closed the door and walked away with Sonya to the window, not yet understanding what the latter was trying to tell her.

'Do you remember' – said Sonya, with a scared and solemn face – 'do you remember when I looked into the mirror for you ... at Otradnoe, at Christmas-time? ... You remember what I saw?'

'Yes, yes!' cried Natasha, opening her eyes wide, and vaguely recalling that Sonya had said something then about seeing Prince Andrei lying down.

'Do you remember?' Sonya went on. 'I saw him then and told everybody, you and Dunyasha too. I saw him lying on a bed,' said she, at each item making a gesture with her hand and a lifted finger, 'and that he had his eyes shut and was covered with a pink quilt, and had his hands folded,' she concluded, convincing herself that the details she had seen were exactly what she had seen in the mirror.

At the time she had seen nothing but had described the first thing that came into her head; but what she had invented then seemed to her now as real as any other recollection. She not only remembered what she had said at the time – that he looked round at her and smiled and was covered with something red – but was firmly convinced that she had seen and said then that he was covered with a pink quilt – yes, pink – and that his eyes were closed.

'Yes, yes, pink it was,' cried Natasha, who now fancied that she too remembered the word *pink*, and saw in this the most extraordinary and mysterious part of the vision.

'But what does it mean?' she added meditatively.

'Oh, I don't know, it's all so queer,' replied Sonya, clutching her head.

A few minutes later Prince Andrei rang and Natasha went to him; but Sonya, in a rare state of excitement and emotion, remained at the window, pondering over the strangeness of what had occurred.

*

That day there was an opportunity of sending letters to the army, and the countess was writing to her son.

'Sonya!' said the countess, raising her eyes from her letter as her niece passed. 'Sonya, won't you write to dear Nikolai?' She spoke in a soft, tremulous voice, and in the weary eyes that looked through her spectacles Sonya read all that the countess meant by those words. Those eyes expressed entreaty, dread of a refusal, shame at having to beg, and readiness for relentless hostility in case of such refusal.

Sonya went up to the countess and, kneeling down, kissed her hand.

'Yes, *maman*, I will write,' said she.

Sonya was softened, excited and moved by all that had happened that day, especially by the mysterious fulfilment she had just seen of her vision. Now that she knew that the renewal of Natasha's relations with Prince Andrei would prevent Nikolai from marrying Princess Maria she was joyfully conscious of a return of that self-sacrificing spirit in which she was accustomed and loved to live. So with a glad sense of performing a magnanimous action – held up several times by the tears that dimmed her velvety black eyes – she wrote the touching letter, the reception of which had so amazed Nikolai.

9

IN the guard-room to which Pierre had been taken the officer and soldiers who had arrested him treated him with hostility but at the same time with respect. Their attitude towards him betrayed both their uncertainty as to who he might be – perhaps someone of great importance – and animosity in consequence of the struggle they had just had with him.

But when the guard was relieved the following morning Pierre felt that for the new guard – officers and men alike – he was not as interesting as he had been to his captors. And indeed those on duty the second day saw nothing in this big, stout man in a peasant coat of the vigorous person who had fought so desperately with the pillaging soldier and the convoy, and had uttered those exalted words about saving a child: they saw in him only No. 17 of the Russian prisoners, arrested and detained for some reason by order of the higher authorities. If they noticed anything remarkable about Pierre, it was only his undaunted air of concentrated thought, and the way he spoke French, which struck them as surprisingly good. Nevertheless that very day Pierre was put in with the other suspicious characters, as the separate room he occupied was wanted for an officer.

All the Russians detained with Pierre were men of the lowest class. And all of them, recognizing Pierre as a gentleman, held aloof from him, the more so as he spoke French. Pierre listened sadly to their jeers at his expense.

That evening Pierre learned that all the prisoners (with himself, probably, in their number) were to be tried for incendiarism. The day after, he was taken with the rest to a house where a French general with a white moustache sat with two colonels and other Frenchmen with scarves sewn on their sleeves. With a sharp precision customary in the examination of prisoners, and which is supposed to preclude human frailty, Pierre, like the others, was interrogated as to who he was, where he had been, with what object, and so on.

These questions, like those generally put at trials, left the essence of the living fact aside, shut out the possibility of that essence being discovered, and were designed only at supplying a channel along which the examining officials desired the accused's answers to flow so as to lead to the goal of the inquiry, namely, a conviction. The moment Pierre began to say anything that did not contribute to this end the channel was removed and the water allowed to flow to waste. Pierre felt, moreover, what the accused always do feel at all trials – a puzzled wonder as to why these questions were put to him. He had a feeling that it was only out of condescension or a kind of courtesy that this device of a directing channel was employed. He knew he was in the power of these men, that only by force had they brought him here, that force alone gave them the right to exact answers to their questions, that the sole object of the proceedings was to prove him guilty. And so, since they had the power and the wish to incriminate him, there was no need for this expedient of an inquiry and trial. It was obvious that any answer was bound to lead to his conviction. When asked what he was doing when he was arrested, Pierre replied in a rather tragic manner that he was restoring to its parents a child he had saved from the flames. Why had he fought the marauder? Pierre answered that he was 'protecting a woman', and that 'to protect a woman who was being insulted was the duty of every man; that …' They pulled him up: this was not to the point. With what object had he been in the courtyard of a burning house, where he had been seen by witnesses? He replied that he had gone out to see what was happening in Moscow. They stopped him again: he had not been asked where he was going, but why he was found near the fire. Who was he? they inquired, repeating their first question, to which he had declined to answer. Again he replied that he could not answer that.

'Make a note of that, that's bad … very bad,' sternly remarked the general with the white whiskers and the florid red face.

On the fourth day fires broke out on the Zubovsky rampart.

Pierre and thirteen others were moved to a coach-house belonging to a merchant's mansion near the Crimean ford. As they marched through the streets Pierre could hardly breathe for the smoke which seemed to hang over the whole city. Fires were visible on all sides.

Pierre did not at that time grasp the significance of the burning of Moscow, and gazed with horror at the fires.

He passed another four days in the coach-house near the Crimean ford, and in the course of those four days he learned, from the conversation of the French soldiers, that all those in detention there were awaiting a decision which might come at any moment from the marshal. What marshal this was, Pierre could not find out from the soldiers. Evidently for them 'the marshal' represented the highest and somewhat mysterious symbol of power.

These first days, up to the 8th of September when the prisoners were brought up for a second examination, were the hardest of all for Pierre.

10

ON the 8th of September an officer – of very great consequence, judging by the respect the guards showed him – entered the coach-house where the prisoners were. This officer, probably someone from the Staff, held a memorandum in his hand, and called over all the Russians there, naming Pierre as 'the man who will not give his name'. Glancing indifferently and indolently at all the prisoners, he ordered the officer in charge to have them decently dressed and tidied up before bringing them before the marshal. An hour later a squad of soldiers arrived and Pierre with the thirteen others was taken to the Dyevichy meadow. It was a fine day, sunny after rain, and the air was exceptionally clear. The smoke did not hang low, as it had on the day Pierre had been removed from the guard-room on the Zubovsky rampart, but rose in columns into the pure atmosphere. Flames were nowhere to be seen but columns of smoke were rising on all sides, and all Moscow, so far as Pierre could make out, was one vast, charred ruin. On every side were devastated spaces with only stoves and chimney-pieces still standing, and here and there the blackened walls of a stone house. Pierre stared at the ruins and did not recognize districts he had known well. Here and there he found churches that had not been touched by the fire. The Kremlin, undamaged, gleamed white in the distance, with its towers and the belfry of Ivan the Great. Close at hand the dome of the Novo-Dyevichy convent glittered brightly and its bells pealed out particularly sonorously. These chimes reminded Pierre that it was Sunday, and the feast of the Nativity of the Virgin. But there seemed to be no one to celebrate the festival;

everywhere were blackened ruins, and the few Russians they met were ragged, panic-stricken folk who tried to hide themselves at sight of the French.

It was plain that the Russian nest was wrecked and destroyed; but Pierre felt dimly that behind the overthrow of the Russian order of life, in place of this ruined nest, an entirely different, stable French order had been established. He was conscious of this when he looked at the soldiers, briskly and gaily marching along in a steady file escorting him and the other delinquents; he was aware of it when his eyes fell on an important French official in a carriage and pair driven by a soldier, whom they met on the way. He felt it at the cheerful sounds of regimental music which floated across from the left of the open space, and especially he felt it and realized it from the list of prisoners the French officer had read off when he came that morning. Pierre had been taken by one set of soldiers and led first to one place and then to another, with dozens of other men; it seemed to him they might easily have forgotten him, have got him mixed up with the others. But no: the answers he had given at his interrogation had come back to him in his designation as 'the man who will not give his name'. And under that appellation, which was dreadful to Pierre, they were now conducting him somewhere with unhesitating assurance on their faces that he and all the other prisoners were the right ones and were being taken to the proper place. Pierre felt himself an insignificant chip fallen among the wheels of a machine whose mechanism he did not understand but which worked without a hitch.

He and his fellow-prisoners were brought to the right side of the Dyevichy meadow, to a big white house with an immense garden, not far from the convent. This was Prince Shcherbatov's house, where Pierre had often visited in other days and which, as he gathered from the talk of the soldiers, was at present occupied by the marshal, the Duke of Eckmühl (Davoust).

They were taken to the entrance, and led into the house one at a time. Pierre was the sixth to go in. Through a glass gallery, an ante-room and a hall, all familiar to him, he was escorted to a long low study at the door of which stood an adjutant.

Davoust, spectacles on nose, was sitting bent over a table at the far end of the room. Pierre went close up to him. Davoust, apparently engaged in consulting some document that lay before him, did not look up. Without raising his eyes he asked in a quiet voice:

'Who are you?'

Pierre was silent because he was incapable of uttering a word. To him Davoust was not merely a French general but a man notorious for his cruelty. Looking at the cold face – Davoust sat like a stern schoolmaster who was willing to be patient for a time and wait for an answer – Pierre felt that every instant's delay might cost him his life; but he did not know what to say. He could not make up his mind to repeat what he had said at his first examination, yet to disclose his rank and position would be both dangerous and humiliating. He stood silent. But before he had time to arrive at a decision Davoust raised his head, pushed his spectacles up on his forehead, screwed up his eyes and looked intently at him.

'I know this man,' he said in an icy, measured tone, obviously calculated to frighten Pierre.

The chill that had been running down Pierre's back seemed to clutch his head in a vice.

'You cannot know me, General, I have never seen you. ...'

'He is a Russian spy,' Davoust interrupted him, addressing another general in the room, whom Pierre had not noticed.

And Davoust turned away. With an unexpected vibration in his voice Pierre suddenly began rapidly:

'*Non, Monseigneur*,' he said, all at once remembering that Davoust was a duke. '*Non, Monseigneur*, you cannot possibly know me. I am a militia-officer and have not been out of Moscow.'

'Your name?' repeated Davoust.

'Bezuhov.'

'What proof have I that you are not lying?'

'*Monseigneur!*' exclaimed Pierre in a tone that betrayed not offence but entreaty.

Davoust lifted his eyes and gazed searchingly at him. For some seconds they looked at one another, and that look saved Pierre. It went beyond the circumstances of war and the court-room, and established human relations between the two men. Both of them in that one instant were dimly aware of an infinite number of things, and they realized that they were both children of humanity, that they were brothers.

When Davoust had first half raised his head from his memorandum, where men's lives and doings were indicated by numbers, Pierre had been only a case, and Davoust could have had him shot without burdening his conscience with an evil deed; but now he saw in him a human being. He reflected for a moment.

'How can you prove to me that you are telling the truth?' said Davoust coldly.

Pierre thought of Ramballe, and mentioned his name and regiment and the street and house where he could be found.

'You are not what you say you are,' returned Davoust.

In a trembling, faltering voice Pierre began adducing proofs of the truth of his statements.

But at this point an adjutant entered and reported something to Davoust.

Davoust immediately beamed at the news the adjutant brought, and began buttoning up his uniform. Apparently he quite forgot Pierre.

When the adjutant reminded him of the prisoner he jerked his head in Pierre's direction with a frown and ordered him to be taken away. But where they were to take him Pierre did not know: back to the coach-house or to the place of execution his companions had pointed out to him as they crossed the Dyevichy meadow.

He turned his head and saw that the adjutant was repeating some question.

'Yes, of course!' said Davoust, but what that 'Yes' referred to Pierre did not know.

Pierre had no idea afterwards how or where he went, or whether it was a long way. In a state of complete stupefaction and bewilderment, seeing nothing around him, he moved his legs in company with the others till they all stopped and he stopped too.

His brain was racked with a single thought. Who – who was it really that had sentenced him to death? Not the men on the commission who had first examined him – not one of them had wished to, or in all probability could have done so. It was not Davoust, who had looked at him in such a human fashion. Another moment and Davoust would have realized that he was making a bad mistake, but just then the adjutant had come in and interrupted. And the adjutant had obviously had no evil intent, though he might have refrained from coming in. Then who was it who was executing him, killing him, taking his life – his, Pierre's, with all his memories, yearnings, hopes and ideas? Who was doing it? And Pierre felt that it was no one's doing.

It was the system, the concatenation of circumstances.

A system of some sort was killing him – Pierre – robbing him of life, of everything, annihilating him.

11

FROM Prince Shcherbatov's house the prisoners were conducted straight down the Dyevichy meadow to the left of the nunnery as far as a kitchen-garden where a post had been set up. Beyond the post a big pit had been freshly dug in the ground, and a great crowd formed a semicircle about the post and the pit. The crowd consisted of a few Russians and a large proportion of soldiers from Napoleon's army not on duty – there were Germans, Italians and Frenchmen in a variety of uniforms. To right and left of the post stood rows of French soldiers in blue uniforms with red epaulets and high boots and shakos.

The prisoners were placed in a certain order, in accordance with a written list (Pierre was sixth), and led up to the post. A number of drums suddenly began beating on both sides of them, and Pierre felt that with the roll of the drums part of his soul had been torn away. He lost all capacity to think and understand. He could only look and listen. And he had only one desire – the desire that the dreadful thing which had to be done should be done as quickly as possible. Pierre looked round at his companions and studied their faces.

The first two were convicts with shaven heads. One was tall and thin; the other a dark, shaggy, muscular fellow with a flat nose. No. 3 was a house-serf, a man of five-and-forty, with grizzled hair and a plump, well-nourished body. The fourth was a peasant, a very handsome fellow with a full flaxen beard and black eyes. The fifth was a factory hand, a thin, sallow-faced lad of eighteen in a loose coat.

Pierre heard the French deliberating whether to shoot them singly or two at a time. 'In couples,' the officer in command replied in a voice of cold indifference. There was a stir in the ranks of the soldiers and it was observable that they were all in a hurry – not as men hurry to execute an order they understand but as people make haste to have done with an essential but unpleasant and incomprehensible task.

A French official wearing a scarf came up to the right of the file of prisoners, and read out the sentence in Russian and in French.

Then two pairs of French soldiers advanced to the criminals, and at the officer's command took the two convicts who stood first in the row. The convicts stopped when they reached the post and, while the sacks were being brought, looked dumbly about them, as a wounded animal watches the approaching huntsman. One of them kept crossing himself, the other scratched his back and worked his lips into the semblance of a smile. With hasty fingers the soldiers blindfolded them, drawing the sacks over their heads, and pinioned them to the post.

A dozen sharpshooters with muskets stepped out of the ranks with a firm, regular tread, and halted eight paces from the post. Pierre turned away so as not to see what was about to happen. There was a sudden rattle and crash which seemed to him louder than the most terrific thunderclap, and he looked round. There was some smoke, and the French soldiers, with pale faces and trembling hands, were doing something near the pit. Two more prisoners were led up. They, too, with the same silent appeal for protection in their eyes, gazed vainly round at the onlookers, evidently unable to comprehend or believe what was coming. They were incredulous because they alone knew what their life meant to them, and so they could not understand, could not believe that it could be taken from them.

Pierre wanted not to look, and again turned away; but again his ears were assailed by the sound as of a frightful explosion, and with the report he saw smoke, blood, and the white, scared faces of the Frenchmen who were again doing something by the post, their shaking hands knocking against each other. Breathing heavily, Pierre stared about him as though asking, 'What does it mean?' The same question was repeated in all the eyes that met his.

On the faces of all the Russians, on the faces of the French soldiers and officers, without exception, he read the same dismay, horror and conflict that he felt in his own heart. 'But who, after all, is doing this? They are all as much sickened as I am. Whose doing is it, then? Whose?' flashed for a second through his mind.

'Sharpshooters of the 86th, forward!' shouted someone. The fifth prisoner, the one next to Pierre, was led forward – alone. Pierre did not realize that he had been spared, that he and the rest had been brought there simply to witness the executions. With mounting horror, and no sense of joy or relief, he gazed at what was taking place. No. 5 was the factory hand in the loose coat. The moment they laid their hands on him he sprang back in terror and clung to Pierre. (Pierre shuddered and shook him off.) The lad was unable to walk. They dragged him along, holding him under the arms, while he shrieked something. When they got him to the post he was suddenly quiet, as if he had all at once understood something. Whether he understood that screaming was useless, or felt that it was impossible these men should kill him, at any rate he took his stand at the post, waiting to be blindfolded like the others, and like a wounded wild beast looked around him with glittering eyes.

Pierre could no longer bring himself to turn away and close his eyes. His curiosity and agitation, which was shared by the crowd, reached their highest pitch at this fifth murder. Like the other four this new victim seemed composed: he wrapped his loose coat closer round him and rubbed one bare foot against the other.

When they proceeded to bind his eyes he himself adjusted the knot which hurt the back of his head; then when they propped him against the blood-stained post he leaned back and, not being comfortable in that position, straightened himself, carefully placed his feet and settled at his ease. Pierre never took his eyes off him and did not miss the slightest movement he made.

The word of command must have been given, the reports of eight muskets must have followed; but try as he would to recollect it afterwards Pierre could never remember having heard the smallest whisper of a shot. He only saw the factory lad suddenly sag in the ropes that held him, blood oozing in two places, saw the ropes give under the weight of the hanging body and the factory lad, his head drooping unnaturally and one leg bent under him, sink down into a sitting position. Pierre ran up to the post. No one stopped him. Pale, frightened people were doing something round the factory hand. The lower jaw of one whiskered old Frenchman trembled as he untied the ropes. The body collapsed. The soldiers dragged it awkwardly from the post and hurriedly began shoving it into the pit.

They all plainly and beyond a doubt knew that they were criminals who must hide the traces of their crime as quickly as possible.

Pierre glanced into the pit and saw the factory lad lying with his knees close to his head and one shoulder higher than the other. And that shoulder was convulsively, rhythmically rising and falling. But earth in spadesful was already being shovelled over the whole body. One of the soldiers, in a tortured voice of angry impatience, shouted to Pierre to go back. But Pierre did not understand him, and remained near the post, and no one drove him away.

When the pit was quite filled up a command was given. Pierre was taken back to his place, and the French troops faced about on both sides of the post, made a half incline and marched past the stake with measured tread. The twenty-four sharpshooters, their muskets discharged, standing in the middle of the ring, ran back to their places as their companies passed by.

Pierre stared now with dazed eyes at these sharpshooters, who were running together in couples out of the circle. All but one had rejoined their companies. This one, a young soldier, face deadly pale, shako pushed to the back of his head, musket resting on the ground, still stood facing the pit on the spot from which he had fired. He swayed like a drunken man, taking a few steps forward and then back to save himself from falling. An old non-commissioned officer ran out of the ranks and, seizing the youngster by the elbow, hauled him back to his company. The crowd of Russians and Frenchmen began to disperse. They all walked off in silence, with lowered heads.

'That will teach them to start fires,' said one of the French.

Pierre glanced round at the speaker and saw that it was a soldier trying to reconcile himself somehow with what had been done, but without success. Without finishing what he had been going to say, he made a hopeless movement with his arm and went on his way.

12

AFTER the execution Pierre was separated from the other prisoners and put by himself in a small, ravaged and befouled church.

Towards evening a patrol-sergeant entered with two soldiers and informed him that he had been pardoned and would now proceed to the barracks for prisoners-of-war. Without understanding what was said to him, Pierre got up and went with the soldiers. They took him to the upper end of the open space, where some sheds had been rigged up out of charred planks, beams and battens, and led him into one of them. In the darkness some twenty various individuals surrounded Pierre. He stared at them, with no idea who they were, why they were there or what they wanted of him. He heard what they said but did not grasp the meaning of the words: his mind made no kind of deduction or interpretation of them. He replied to the questions put to him but had no notion who was listening, or how they would understand his answers. He looked at faces and figures, and they all seemed equally meaningless.

From the moment Pierre had witnessed that hideous massacre committed by men who had no desire to do it, it was as if the spring in his soul, by which everything was held together and given the semblance of life, had been suddenly wrenched out, and all had collapsed into a heap of senseless refuse. Though he did not realize it, his faith in the right ordering of the universe, in humanity, in his own self and in God had been destroyed. He had experienced this state of mind before but never with such intensity. When similar doubts had assailed him in the past they had had their origin in his own wrong-doing, and at the bottom of his heart he had felt that salvation from his despair and those doubts was to be found within himself. But this time he could not blame himself that the world had crumbled before his eyes, leaving only meaningless ruins. He felt that to get back to faith in life was not in his power.

Around him in the darkness stood a number of men: evidently something about him interested them greatly. They were telling him something, asking him about something, then leading him some-where, and at last he found himself in a corner of the shed among men who were talking on all sides, and laughing.

'And so, friends ... the prince himself *who* ...' a voice was saying in the opposite corner of the shed, with special stress on the word *who*.

Sitting mute and motionless on a heap of straw against the wall, Pierre now opened, now closed his eyes. But as soon as he shut them he saw again the dreadful face of that factory lad – dreadful from its very simplicity – and the faces of the unwilling executioners, still more dreadful in their uneasiness. And he would open his eyes again and stare vacantly about him in the darkness.

Beside him, in a stooping position, squatted a little man of whose presence Pierre was first made aware by a powerful odour of pers-piration which emanated from him every time he moved. This man was engaged in doing something to his legs in the darkness, and though Pierre could not see his face he was conscious that the man kept glancing at him. When his eyes were more accustomed to the dark Pierre made out that the man was taking off his leg-bands, and the way he did it aroused Pierre's attention.

Having unwound the string that tied the band round one leg, he carefully coiled it up and at once set to work on the other leg, glancing at Pierre. While with one hand he hung up the length of string, with the other he was already unwinding the band round the second leg.

In this fashion, with precise, rounded, rapid movements which lost no time in following one another, the man removed his leg-bands and hung them on pegs knocked in the wall just above his head, took out a knife, cut off something, shut the knife, put it under his bolster and, settling himself more comfortably, clasped both arms round his knees, which were drawn up, and stared straight at Pierre. Pierre was conscious of something pleasant, soothing and satisfying in those deft movements, in the man's well-ordered establishment of his belongings in his corner, even in the very smell of the man, and he returned his gaze, without dropping his eyes.

'Seen a lot o' trouble, sir, eh?' said the little man suddenly. And there was so much kindliness and simplicity in the sing-song voice that Pierre felt his jaw tremble and the tears rise to his eyes as he tried to reply. At the same second, giving Pierre no time to betray his confusion, the little fellow continued in the same pleasant tones:

'Eh, lad, don't fret now,' said he in the tender, sing-song, caressing voice in which old Russian peasant-women talk. 'Don't fret, my friend: suffering lasts an hour but life goes on for ever! That's the way it is, lad. And we get on here fine, thank God, there's no offence. They're men too, with good ones among 'em as well as bad,' he said, and, while still speaking, twisted agilely on to his knees, got up, cleared his throat and walked off to another part of the shed.

'Hi, you've come back again, have you?' Pierre heard the same soft voice from the far end of the hut. 'So you remember me, do you? There, there, that'll do!' And pushing away a little dog that was jumping up at him the soldier returned to his place and sat down. In his hands he held something wrapped in a bit of cloth.

'Here, you have a taste of this, sir,' said he, resuming the respectful tone he had used at first, and unwrapping and passing Pierre some baked potatoes. 'We had soup for dinner. But these potatoes are a treat!'

Pierre had not eaten all day and the smell of the potatoes struck him as extraordinarily good. He thanked the soldier and began to eat.

'What do you eat 'em like that for?' inquired the soldier with a smile. 'You should try 'em like this.'

He took a potato, got out his clasp-knife, cut the potato in the palm of his hand into two equal halves, sprinkled them with salt from the rag and offered them to Pierre.

'The potatoes are a treat,' he reiterated. 'You try 'em like that!'

Pierre thought he had never tasted anything more delicious.

'Oh, I'm right enough,' said he, 'but why did they shoot those poor fellows? ... The last was a lad of barely twenty.'

'Tst, tst ...' said the little man. 'What a sin, what a sin ...' he added quickly, and just as though the words were always waiting ready in his mouth and flew out by chance he went on: 'And how was it, sir, you stayed in Moscow?'

'I didn't think they would come so soon. I stayed by accident,' replied Pierre.

'And how came they to arrest you, friend? Was it in your own house?'

'No, I went out to look at the fire, and it was then they took me up and tried me for being an incendiary.'

'Where there's law there's injustice,' put in the little man.

'And have you been here long?' asked Pierre, chewing the last of the potato.

'Me? It was last Sunday they fetched me out of hospital in Moscow.'

'Why, are you a soldier then?'

'Yes, we were all from the Apsheron regiment. Dying of fever, I was. We were never told nothing. There were twenty or more of us lying sick. And we had no idea – we never guessed nothing.'

'And are you cut up at being here?' asked Pierre.

'To be sure, friend. My name's Platon – Platon Karatayev,' he added, evidently to make it easier for Pierre to address him. 'In the regiment they called me the little falcon. How can a man help feeling cut up? Moscow – she's the mother of cities. How can us look on at all this and not feel sick at 'eart? But the worm that gnaws the cabbage is the first to die: that's what the old folk used to tell us,' he added quickly.

'What? What did you say?' asked Pierre.

'Who? Me?' said Karatayev. 'Man proposes, God disposes, I say,' he replied, supposing that he was repeating what he had said at first, and immediately went on: 'And you, you must have a family estate? And a house of your own? Your cup must be full. And a wife maybe? And your old parents living?' he asked.

And though it was too dark for Pierre to see, he felt that the soldier's lips were twisted into a restrained smile of kindliness as he put these questions. He seemed grieved to learn that Pierre had no parents, especially no mother.

'A wife for good sense, a mother-in-law for kind welcome, but there's none so dear as a man's own mother!' said he. 'Well, and have you little ones?' he went on to ask.

Again Pierre's negative answer seemed to distress him, and he hastened to add:

'Never mind, you're young, and please God there'll be bairns yet. The great thing is to live on good terms. ...'

'But it makes no difference now,' Pierre could not help saying.

'Ah, my good man,' rejoined Platon, 'you can't be sure a beggar's sack or the prison-house will never fall to your lot!'

He settled himself more comfortably and cleared his throat, evidently preparatory to a long story. 'For instance, my dear friend, I was still living at home,' he began. 'We had a nice place with no end of land. Peasants we were, and we lived well, our house was one to thank God for. When father and we went out mowing there were seven of us. Lived well, we did, like proper Christians. But one day ...'

And Platon Karatayev told a long story of how he had gone into someone else's copse after wood, how he had been caught by the keeper, had been tried, flogged and sent to serve in the army.

'Well, lad,' and a smile changed the tone of his voice, 'we thought it was a misfortune but it turned out to be a blessing. If I 'adn't done wrong it would have been my brother for the army, and him – my younger brother, with five little ones, but me, you see, I only left a wife behind. We had a little girl once but the good Lord took her before I went for a soldier. I comes home on leave, and what do you think – I finds 'em all better off than they was before. Yard full of live-stock, the women-folk at home, two brothers out earning wages. Only Mihailo, the youngest, at home. My old dad says to me, "A bairn's a bairn to me," he says. "No matter which finger gets nipped, it hurts just the same. And if they hadn't shaved Platon for a soldier, then Mihailo would've had to go." He gathered us all together and – if you'll believe me, he stands us all up in front of the holy icons. "Mihailo," he says, "come you here and kneel down before him; and you, woman, kneel; and all you grandchillun, kneel at his feet. Understand?" he says. And that's the way it is, my good sir. There's no escaping fate. But we are always findin' fault and complainin': this ain't right, and the other don't suit us. Happiness, friend, is like water in a drag-net – pull it along and it bulges: take it out and it's empty! Yes, that's the way of it.'

And Platon shifted his seat on the straw.

After a short pause he got up.

'Well, I dare say you're sleepy?' said he, and began rapidly crossing himself and repeating:

'Lord Jesus Christ, holy St Nikola, Frola and Lavra! Lord Jesus Christ, holy St Nikola, Frola and Lavra! Lord Jesus Christ, have mercy on us and save us!' he concluded, then touched the ground with his forehead, got up, straightened himself, sighed and sat down again on the straw. 'That's the way of it. Lay me down like a stone, O God, and raise me up like new bread,' he muttered as he lay down, pulling his coat over him.

'What prayer was that you were saying?' asked Pierre.

'Eh?' murmured Platon, who was already half asleep. 'What was I saying? I was saying me prayers. Don't you say your prayers?'

'To be sure I do,' said Pierre. 'But what was that about Frola and Lavra?'

'Why,' replied Platon quickly, 'they're the horses' saints. We mustn't forget the poor dumb creatures. See the little rascal – she's curled up and warm all right,' he said, stroking the dog that lay at his feet; and turning over again he fell asleep at once.

Sounds of crying and screaming came from somewhere in the distance outside and the glare of fire was visible through the cracks in the walls, but inside the shed it was quiet and dark. It was a long time before Pierre got to sleep: he lay in the darkness with wide open eyes, listening to the rhythmical snoring of Platon at his side, and he felt that the world that had been shattered was once more stirring to life in his soul, in new beauty and on new and steadfast foundations.

13

In the shed, where Pierre spent four weeks, there were twenty-three soldiers, three officers and two civilian functionaries, all prisoners like himself.

Pierre remembered them afterwards as misty figures, except Platon Karatayev, who for ever remained in his mind as a most vivid and precious memory, and the very personification of all that was Russian, warm-hearted and – 'round'. When Pierre beheld his neighbour next morning at dawn the first impression of him as something rotund was fully confirmed: Platon's whole figure – in a French military coat belted round the waist with rope, a soldier's cap and bast shoes – was round. His head was as round as a ball; his back, his chest, his shoulders, even his arms, which he always held as though he were about to embrace something, were round; his pleasant smile and his large gentle brown eyes were round, too.

Platon Karatayev must have been on the far side of fifty to judge by his stories of the campaigns he had taken part in as an old soldier. He himself had no idea, and could never have determined with any accuracy, how old he was. But his shining white, strong teeth, which showed in two unbroken semicircles whenever he laughed – which was often – were all sound and good; there was not a grey hair in his beard or on his head, and his whole physique gave an impression of suppleness and of unusual hardiness and endurance.

His face, in spite of a multitude of curving wrinkles, held an expression of innocence and youth; his voice had an agreeable sing-song note. But the chief peculiarity of his speech was its spontaneity and shrewdness. It was evident that he never considered what he had said or was going to say, and this lent an especial and irresistible persuasiveness to the quick, true modulations of his voice.

His physical strength and agility during the first period of his imprisonment were such that he seemed not to know what fatigue or sickness meant. Every night before going to bed he repeated: 'O Lord, lay me down like a stone and raise me up like new bread;' and when he got up in the morning he would give his shoulders a certain shake and say: 'Lie down and curl up, get up and shake up.' And indeed he had only to lie down to fall asleep like a stone, or give himself a shake and be ready without a second's delay for any sort of work, just as children are ready for their toys directly they open their eyes. He knew how to do everything, not particularly well but not badly either. He could bake, cook, sew, carpenter and cobble boots. He was always busy, and only at night allowed himself to indulge in conversation, which he loved, and singing. He sang not as a trained singer does who knows he is being listened to, but like the birds, obviously because he was as much obliged to give vent to those sounds as one sometimes is to stretch oneself or move about; and his singing was always light, sweet, plaintive, almost feminine, and his face the while was very serious.

Being in prison, and having let his beard grow, he had apparently cast off everything alien and military that had been forced upon him, and unconsciously relapsed into his old peasant habits.

'A soldier away from the army is the shirt worn outside the breeches again,' he would say.

He did not like talking about his soldiering days, though he had no complaints to make and was proud of repeating that he had never once been flogged in all his years of service. When he had stories to tell they were generally of some old and evidently precious memory of the time when he lived the life of a *Kristianin* – a Christian – as he called it, instead of *krestianin*.* The proverbs of which he made so much use were not the mainly coarse and indecent expressions common among soldiers but the popular saws which taken without a context seem to have so little meaning, but which suddenly acquire a profoundly wise significance when applied appropriately.

He would often say the exact opposite of what he had said on a previous occasion, yet both would be right. He liked to talk and he talked well, adorning his speech with terms of endearment and proverbial sayings, which Pierre fancied he often invented himself; but the great charm of his stories lay in the fact that he clothed the simplest incidents – incidents which Pierre might easily have witnessed without taking any particular notice – in a grave seemliness to befit their nature. He liked listening to the folk-tales which one of the soldiers used to tell of an evening (they were always the same ones), but most of all he liked to hear stories of real life. He would listen with a happy smile, now and then putting in a word or asking a question for the purpose of elucidating for himself the moral excellence of what was related to him. Karatayev had no attachments, friendships or loves, as Pierre understood them; but he felt affection for and lived on sympathetic terms with every creature with whom life brought him in contact, and especially with man – not any particular man but those with whom he happened to be. He loved his dog, loved his comrades and the French, loved Pierre who was his neighbour; but Pierre felt that for all Karatayev's warm-heartedness towards him (thus involuntarily paying tribute to Pierre's spiritual life) he would not suffer a pang if they were parted. And Pierre began to feel the same way about Karatayev.

In the eyes of the other prisoners Platon Karatayev was just an

* The Russian word for *peasant*. – [Tr.]

ordinary soldier like the rest of his kind. They called him 'Little falcon' or 'Platosha', chaffed him good-naturedly and sent him on errands. But to Pierre he always remained what he had seemed that first night – an unfathomable, rounded-off, eternal personification of the spirit of simplicity and truth.

Platon Karatayev knew nothing by rote except his prayers. When he opened his mouth to speak he appeared to have no idea how, having once begun, he would finish up.

Sometimes Pierre, struck by the force of his remarks, would ask him to repeat them, but Platon could never recall what he had said a moment before, just as he could never tell Pierre the words of his favourite song. *Mother, little birch-tree* and *my heart is sick* came in but they made no coherent sense. He did not understand and could not grasp the meaning of words apart from their context. Every utterance and action of his was the manifestation of a force uncomprehended by him, which was his life. But his life, as he looked at it, held no meaning as a separate entity. It had meaning only as part of a whole of which he was at all times conscious. His words and actions flowed from him as smoothly, as inevitably and spontaneously as fragrance exhales from a flower. He could not understand the value or significance of any word or deed taken separately.

14

WHEN Princess Maria heard from Nikolai that her brother was with the Rostovs at Yaroslavl she immediately prepared, in spite of her aunt's efforts to dissuade her, to go to him – and to go not alone but to take her nephew with her. She did not ask, and was not interested to find out, whether this would be difficult or not difficult, possible or impossible: it was her duty not only to be with her brother, who might be dying, but to do everything in her power to bring his son to him, and so she set to and made her arrangements. If Prince Andrei had not communicated with her himself no doubt it was because he was too weak to write, or because he considered the long journey too hard and perilous for her and little Nikolai.

In a few days Princess Maria was ready to start. She used the huge family coach in which she had travelled to Voronezh, a semi-open trap and a baggage-wagon, and was accompanied by Mademoiselle

Bourienne, little Nikolai and his tutor, her old nurse, three maids, Tikhon, a young footman and a courier whom her aunt was sending with her.

It was out of the question even to think of going by the usual route, through Moscow, and the roundabout way which Princess Maria was obliged to follow, via Lipetsk, Ryazan, Vladimir and Shuya, was very long and, owing to the dearth of post-horses, extremely arduous; and in the neighbourhood of Ryazan, where the French were said to have shown themselves, positively dangerous.

During this trying journey Mademoiselle Bourienne, Dessalles and Princess Maria's servants were astonished at her tenacity of spirit and energy. She was the last to bed and the first up in the morning, and no obstacle could daunt her. Thanks to her assiduity and verve, which infected her fellow-travellers, by the end of the second week they found themselves approaching Yaroslavl.

The last few days of her stay in Voronezh had been the happiest period of her life. Her love for Rostov no longer tormented or agitated her. It filled her whole soul, had become an integral part of herself, and she no longer struggled against it. Latterly she had become convinced – though she never plainly, in so many words, admitted it to herself – that she loved and was loved. Her last meeting with Nikolai, when he had come to tell her that her brother was with the Rostovs, had persuaded her of this. Not by a single syllable had Nikolai alluded to the possibility of Prince Andrei's engagement to Natasha being renewed (should he recover), but Princess Maria saw by his face that he was aware of this and that it was constantly in his mind. And yet his manner to her – so considerate, gentle and affectionate – not only underwent no change but it sometimes seemed to Princess Maria that he was even glad of the family connexion between them because it allowed him greater liberty to express his loving friendship. She knew that she loved for the first and only time in her life, and felt that she was loved in her turn, and she was happy and at peace with this state of things.

But this happiness did not prevent her feeling the keenest concern for her brother – on the contrary, this spiritual tranquillity, in one sense, left her mind the freer to surrender to her anxiety about Prince Andrei. Her anguish was so intense at the moment of setting out from Voronezh that those who saw her off felt sure as they looked at her care-worn despairing face that she would fall ill on the journey. But its very difficulties and trials, which she tackled so forthrightly, saved her for the time being from her grief, and lent her strength.

As is always the case when one is travelling, Princess Maria was entirely preoccupied with its progress, ignoring the object of it. But as they approached Yaroslavl the thought presented itself of what might await her there – not now at some future date, at the end of many days, but that very evening – and her agitation increased to its utmost.

The courier, whom she had sent on ahead to find out where the Rostovs were staying in Yaroslavl, and the condition of Prince Andrei, was appalled, when he met the great travelling coach just entering the town gates, by the ghastly pallor of the princess's face that looked out at him from the window.

'I have ascertained everything, your Excellency: the Rostovs are staying in the square, at the merchant Bronnikov's house. It's not far from here, on the banks of the Volga,' said the courier.

Princess Maria gazed at him with frightened inquiry, not understanding why he did not answer what she chiefly wanted to know: How was her brother? Mademoiselle Bourienne put the question for her.

'How is the prince?' she asked.

'His Excellency is staying in the same house with them.'

'Then he is alive,' thought Princess Maria, and asked in a low voice: 'How is he?'

'The servants say there is no change in his condition.'

What 'no change' might mean Princess Maria did not inquire, and with a swift, scarcely noticeable glance at the little seven-year-old Nikolai, who was sitting in front of her, delighted at the town, she bowed her head and did not look up again till the heavy coach, rumbling, jolting and swaying, came to a stop. The steps were let down with a clatter.

The carriage-door was opened. On the left there was water – a broad river; on the right a porch. There were people at the entrance: servants, and a rosy-faced girl with a thick coil of black hair, smiling as it seemed to Princess Maria in an unpleasantly affected manner. (This was Sonya.) Princess Maria ran up the steps. 'Come in, come in!' said the girl, with the same artificial smile, and the princess found herself in the hall facing an elderly woman with Oriental features, who advanced rapidly to meet her, looking moved. This was the countess.

She put her arms round Princess Maria and proceeded to kiss her.

'My child!' she said in French. 'I love you dearly and have known you a long while.'

In spite of her agitation Princess Maria realized that this was the countess and that she must say something to her. Hardly knowing how she did it, she contrived to utter a few polite phrases in French in the tone in which she had been addressed, and asked: 'How is he?'

'The doctor says there is no danger,' said the countess, but as she spoke she raised her eyes to heaven with a sigh that contradicted her words.

'Where is he? Can I see him, can I?' asked the princess.

'Directly, princess, directly, my dear. Is this his son?' said the countess, turning to little Nikolai who came in with Dessalles. 'We shall find room for everybody, this is a big house. Oh, what a sweet little boy!'

The countess led Princess Maria into the drawing-room, where Sonya was talking to Mademoiselle Bourienne. The countess fondled the child and the old count appeared to welcome the princess. He was extraordinarily changed since Princess Maria had seen him last. Then he had been an alert, cheerful, self-confident little old man: now he seemed a pitiful, bewildered creature. All the time he talked to Princess Maria he kept looking about him, as though he were asking everyone whether he was doing the right thing. After the destruction of Moscow and the loss of his property, thrown out of his accustomed groove, he seemed to have lost his bearings and to feel that there was no longer a place for him in life.

In spite of her one desire to see her brother as speedily as possible, and her vexation that at the moment when all she wanted was to see him they should be trying to entertain her conventionally with praises of her nephew, the princess took note of all that was going on around her, and felt it incumbent upon her to conform for the time being to the new order of things into which she had stepped. She knew that all this was inevitable, and though it was hard for her she bore no grudge against them for it.

'This is my niece,' said the count, introducing Sonya. 'I do not think you have met her, have you, princess?'

Princess Maria turned to Sonya and, trying to smother the rising hostility she felt towards the girl, kissed her. But she was growing painfully aware of the wide gap between the mood of everyone around her and the emotions filling her own breast.

'Where is he?' she asked again, addressing them all.

'He is downstairs. Natasha is with him,' answered Sonya, colouring. 'We have sent to find out if it will be all right. You are tired, I expect, princess?'

Tears of vexation showed in Princess Maria's eyes. She turned away and was about to ask the countess again where to go to him when light, impetuous footsteps that sounded almost gay were heard at the door. The princess looked round and saw Natasha nearly running in – the Natasha whom she had so disliked at their meeting long ago in Moscow.

But Princess Maria had hardly looked at Natasha's face before she realized that here was a true comrade in her grief, and hence a friend. She flew to meet her, hugged her and burst into tears on her shoulder.

As soon as Natasha, sitting by Prince Andrei's bedside, learned of Princess Maria's arrival, she had softly left the room and hastened to her with those swift steps that had sounded so light-hearted to Princess Maria.

There was only one expression on her agitated face when she ran into the drawing-room – an expression of love, of boundless love for him, for her, for all that was near to the man she loved; an expression of pity, of suffering for others, of passionate desire to give herself completely to the task of helping them. It was plain that Natasha's heart at that moment held no thought of self, or of her own relations with Prince Andrei.

Princess Maria with her sensitive intuition saw all this at the first glance, and with sorrowful relief wept on her shoulder.

'Come, let us go to him, Marie,' said Natasha, drawing her away into the next room.

Princess Maria lifted her head, dried her eyes and turned to Natasha. She felt that from her she would be able to know and find out everything.

'How ...' she was beginning but stopped short. She felt that no question or answer could be put into words. Natasha's face and eyes would have to tell her all more clearly and with profounder meaning.

Natasha was gazing at her but she seemed to be in dread and in doubt: ought she, or ought she not, to say all she knew? She seemed to feel that before those luminous eyes, piercing to the very depths of her heart, it would be impossible not to tell the truth, the whole truth as she saw it. Natasha's lip suddenly twitched, ugly wrinkles creased her mouth and she broke into sobs, hiding her face in her hands.

Princess Maria understood.

But still she hoped, and asked, though she had no faith in words: 'But how is his wound? What is his general condition?'

'You – you ... will see,' was all Natasha could say.

They sat for a little while downstairs near his room till they had left off crying and were able to go in to him with calm faces.

'What has been the course of his illness? Did the change for the worse occur recently? When did *this* happen?' asked Princess Maria.

Natasha told her that at first his high temperature and the great pain he was in had made his condition dangerous, but when they were at Troitsa this had passed off and the doctor had been afraid of one thing only – gangrene. But the risk of that too was almost over. On their arrival at Yaroslavl the wound had begun to fester (Natasha knew all about such things as festering), and the doctor had said that the festering might take a normal course. Fever had set in. The doctor said this fever was not particularly serious.

'But two days ago *this* suddenly happened,' said Natasha, struggling with her sobs. 'I don't know what it means, but you will see how he is.'

'Has he grown weaker? Is he thinner? ...' queried the princess.

'No, it's not that, but worse. You will see. Oh, Marie, he is too good, he cannot, cannot live because ...'

15

WHEN Natasha with a practised movement opened Prince Andrei's door for Princess Maria to go in first, the princess felt the sobs rising in her throat. In spite of every effort she made to prepare and control herself she knew that she would be unable to see him without tears.

She understood what Natasha had meant when she said: 'Two days ago *this* suddenly happened.' She understood it to signify that he had suddenly become gentle and resigned, and that this sweet humility could only be the precursor of death. As she approached the door she already saw in her imagination Andrei's face as she remembered it in childhood – tender, diffident, full of feeling. In later life he had rarely looked like that, and so when he did it always affected her deeply.

She was sure he would speak soft, loving words to her such as her father had uttered before his death, and that she would not be able to bear it and would break into sobs in his presence. Yet sooner or later it had to be, and she went into the room. The sobs rose higher and higher in her throat the clearer her short-sighted eyes distinguished his form and tried to make out his features, and then she saw his face and met his gaze.

He was lying on a couch, propped up with pillows, in a squirrel-lined dressing-gown. He was thin and pale. One thin, transparently white hand held a handkerchief; with the other he stroked the delicate moustache that had grown long, moving his fingers slowly. His eyes were turned towards them as they came in.

When she saw his face, and their eyes met, Princess Maria's step suddenly slackened; she felt her tears dry up and her sobs cease. As she caught the expression of his face and eyes she all at once felt shy and guilty.

'But how am I in fault?' she asked herself. 'Because you are alive and your thoughts are on living, while I ...' his cold, stern look replied.

In the deep gaze that seemed to look not outwards from within but inwards upon himself there was something that was almost hostility as he slowly scanned his sister and Natasha.

He kissed his sister, holding her hand in his as was their wont.

'How are you, Marie? How did you manage to get here?' he said in a voice as steady and aloof as his look. Had he uttered a shriek of despair the cry would have struck less horror into Princess Maria's heart than the tone of his voice.

'And have you brought little Nikolai?' he asked in the same slow, quiet manner and with an obvious effort to remember.

'How are you now?' said Princess Maria, wondering herself at what she was saying.

'That, my dear, you must ask the doctor,' he replied, and, evidently making another effort to be affectionate, he said with his lips only (his mind was clearly not on what he was saying):

'Thank you for coming, my dear.'

Princess Maria pressed his hand. The pressure made him wince just perceptibly. He was silent, and she did not know what to say. She understood the change that had come over him two days ago. His speech, his voice, and especially that calm, almost antagonistic look betrayed the detachment from all earthly things which is so terrible for a living man to witness. He plainly found it difficult to understand the concerns of this world; yet at the same time one felt that he failed to understand, not because he had lost the power of understanding but because he understood something else – something the living did not and could not understand, and that entirely absorbed him.

'Yes, see how strangely fate has brought us together again,' he said, breaking the silence and pointing to Natasha. 'She looks after me all the time.'

Princess Maria listened and could not believe her ears. How could he, the sensitive, tender-hearted Prince Andrei, say such a thing before the girl he loved and who loved him? If he had any thought of living he could not have said that in that cold, hurtful tone. If he had not known he was dying how could he have failed to feel for her, how could he have spoken like that in her presence? There could only be one explanation – that he was indifferent to everything, and indifferent because of a revelation of something of far greater importance.

The conversation was unimpassioned, desultory and continually stopping short.

'Marie came by Ryazan,' remarked Natasha.

Prince Andrei did not notice that she called his sister *Marie*. And Natasha only noticed it then for the first time herself.

'Really?' he said.

'They told her Moscow has been burnt down, right to the ground, as if ...'

Natasha broke off; it was impossible to talk. He was plainly making an effort to listen but yet could not manage to.

'Yes, so they say,' he murmured. 'It is very sad,' and he stared straight before him, his fingers straying absently about his moustache.

'And so you have met Count Nikolai, Marie?' said Prince Andrei suddenly, apparently trying to say something to please them. 'He wrote home here that he had taken a great liking to you,' he went on, simply and calmly, obviously unable to realize all the complex significance his remark had for living people. 'If you liked him too, it would be a very good thing ... if you were to marry,' he added rather more quickly, as if pleased at having at last found words for which he had long been seeking. Princess Maria heard what he said but it had no significance for her, except inasmuch as it showed how terribly far he was now from all earthly interests.

'Why talk of me?' she said quietly, and glanced at Natasha. Natasha, conscious of this glance, did not look at her. Again the three of them were silent.

'André, would you like ...' Princess Maria said suddenly in a shaky voice. 'Would you like to see little Nikolai? He is always talking of you!'

For the first time Prince Andrei almost smiled, but Princess Maria, who knew his face so well, saw with horror that it was not a smile of pleasure, or of affection for his son, but of quiet, gentle irony at his sister's trying what she believed to be the last means of rousing him.

'Yes, I should like to see little Nikolai very much. Is he all right?'

*

When the little boy was brought into Prince Andrei's room he stared with dismay at his father but did not cry, because nobody else was crying. Prince Andrei kissed him and apparently did not know what to say to him.

After the child had been taken away Princess Maria went up to her brother again, kissed him and, unable to restrain her tears any longer, began to weep.

He looked at her attentively.

'Is it about little Nikolai?' he asked.

Princess Maria nodded her head, sobbing.

'Marie, you know the New Tes –' but he broke off.

'What did you say?'

'Nothing. You mustn't cry here,' he said, looking at her with the same cold expression.

*

When Princess Maria burst into tears he understood that she was crying at the thought of little Nikolai being left without a father. With a great effort he tried to return to life and see things from their point of view.

'Yes, it must seem sad to them,' he thought. 'But how simple it is!

'The fowls of the air sow not, neither do they reap, yet your Father feedeth them,' he said to himself and wanted to say to Princess Maria; 'but no, they would interpret it their own way and not understand! They can't understand that all these feelings of theirs which they set such store by – all the ideas which seem so important to us –

do not matter. We cannot understand one another,' and he remained silent.

*

Prince Andrei's little son was seven years old. He could scarcely read, he knew almost nothing. He was to go through much after that day, gaining knowledge, observation, experience; but had he enjoyed the mastery at that time of all he acquired later he could not have had a truer or more profound comprehension of the meaning of the scene he had witnessed between his father, Princess Maria and Natasha than he had then. He understood it from beginning to end and, without shedding a tear, left the room, crept up to Natasha who followed him out and looked shyly at her with his beautiful, dreamy eyes. His uplifted, rosy upper lip quivered, he leaned his head against her and wept.

From that day he avoided Dessalles and the countess, who would have petted him, and either stayed by himself or timidly joined Princess Maria or Natasha, of whom he seemed even fonder than of his aunt, and clung to them quietly and shyly.

Princess Maria left Prince Andrei's side, realizing to the full what Natasha's face had told her. She spoke no more to Natasha about any hope of saving his life. She took turns with her in sitting beside his couch, and shed no more tears but prayed without ceasing, addressing her spirit to the Eternal and Unfathomable Whose presence about the dying man was now so palpable.

16

PRINCE ANDREI not only knew he was going to die but felt that he was dying, that he was already half dead. He felt remote from everything earthly and was conscious of a strange and joyous lightness in his being. Neither impatient nor anxious, he awaited what lay before him. That sinister, eternal, unknown and distant something which he had sensed throughout his life was now close upon him and – as he knew by the strange lightness of being that he experienced – almost comprehensible and tangible. ...

In the past he had dreaded the end. Twice he had experienced the frightful agony which is the fear of death, of the end, but now that fear meant nothing to him.

The first time was when the shell was spinning like a top before him, and he had looked at the stubble-field, at the bushes, at the sky, and known that he was face to face with death. When he had recovered consciousness after his wound, and instantly, as though set free from the cramping bondage of life, the flower of eternal unfettered love had opened out in his soul, he had had no more fear and no more thought of death.

During the hours of solitude, suffering and half-delirium that he spent after he was wounded, the more deeply he penetrated this new principle of eternal love which had been revealed to him, the more he unconsciously detached himself from earthly life. To love everything and everybody, always to sacrifice self for love, meant to love no one in particular, meant not to live this mundane life. And the more imbued he became with this principle of love, the more he let go of life and the more completely he annihilated that fearful barrier which – in the absence of such love – stands between life and death. Whenever, during that first period, he remembered that he had to die, he said to himself: 'Well, what of it? So much the better!'

But after the night at Mytishchy when, half delirious, he had seen her for whom he longed appear before him, and pressing her hand to his lips had wept soft, happy tears, love for one particular woman had stolen unobserved into his heart and bound him again to life. And glad and agitating thoughts began to occupy his mind. Recalling the moment at the ambulance-station when he had seen Kuragin, he could not now regain the feeling he had then. He was tormented by the question: 'Is he alive?' And he dared not inquire.

His illness pursued its normal physical course, but what Natasha referred to when she said 'This suddenly happened' had occurred two days before Princess Maria's arrival. It was the last spiritual struggle between life and death, in which death gained the victory. It was the unexpected realization that life, in the shape of his love for Natasha, was still precious to him, and a last, though ultimately vanquished, onslaught of terror before the unknown.

It happened in the evening. As usual after dinner he was slightly feverish, and his thoughts were preternaturally clear. Sonya was sitting at the table. He fell into a doze. Suddenly he was conscious of a glow of happiness.

'Ah, she has come!' he thought.

And so it was: in Sonya's place sat Natasha who had just crept noiselessly in.

Ever since she had begun looking after him he had always had this instinctive awareness of her presence. She was sitting in a low chair placed sideways so as to screen the light of the candle from him, and was knitting a stocking. (She had learned to knit after Prince Andrei had casually remarked that no one made such a good sick-nurse as an old nanny who knitted stockings, and that there was something soothing about knitting.) The needles clicked in her swiftly moving fingers, and then he could see quite clearly the pensive profile of her bent head. She shifted a little, and the ball of wool rolled from her lap. She started, glanced round at him, and shading the candle with her hand stooped carefully with a supple, precise movement, picked up the ball and sat back as before.

He watched her without stirring and saw that she wanted to draw a deep breath after picking up the wool, but refrained from doing so and breathed cautiously.

At the Troitsa monastery they had spoken of the past, and he had told her that if he lived he would always thank God for his wound, which had brought them together again; but since then they had never mentioned the future.

'Could it be, or could it not?' he was wondering now as he looked at her and listened to the light click of the steel needles. 'Can fate have brought us together so strangely only for me to die? ... Can the truth of life have been revealed to me only to give my whole life the lie? I love her more than anything in the world! But what am I to do if I love her?' he said to himself, and he involuntarily groaned, from a habit he had fallen into in the course of his sufferings.

Hearing the sound, Natasha laid down her stocking, leaned nearer to him and suddenly, noticing his shining eyes, went up to him with a light step and bent over him.

'You are not asleep?'

'No, I have been looking at you a long time. I felt you come in. No one else gives me that sweet sense of tranquillity ... that radiance. I could weep for joy.'

Natasha moved closer to him. Her face shone blissful with happiness.

'Natasha, I love you too much. More than anything in the world.'

'And I?' She turned away for a second. 'But why too much?' she asked.

'Why too much? ... Well, what do you think, what do you feel in your heart – in your heart of hearts: am I going to live? What do you think about it?'

'I am sure of it, sure of it!' Natasha almost shouted, seizing both his hands in hers with a passionate gesture.

He was silent awhile.

'How good that would be!' – and taking her hand he kissed it.

Natasha felt happy and deeply stirred; but at once remembered that this would not do and that he must be kept quiet.

'But you have not slept,' she said, subduing her joy. 'Try and sleep ... please!'

He pressed her hand and let it go, and she moved back to the candle and sat down again in the same position as before. Twice she glanced round at him and met his shining eyes fixed on her. She set herself a stint on the stocking and resolved not to look round till she had finished it.

He did, in fact, soon shut his eyes and fall asleep. He did not sleep long, and woke with a start and in a cold perspiration.

As he fell asleep he was still thinking of the subject which now occupied his mind all the time – of life and death. And of death more than life. He felt nearer to death.

'Love? What is love?' he mused.

'Love hinders death. Love is life. Anything at all that I understand, I understand only because I love. Everything is – everything exists – only because I love. All is bound up in love alone. Love is God, and to die means that I, a tiny particle of love, shall return to the universal and eternal source.' These thoughts seemed comforting to him. But they were only thoughts. There was something lacking in them, they were confused and too one-sidedly personal, too intellectual. And he was a prey to the same restlessness and uncertainty. He fell asleep.

He dreamed that he was lying in the room in which he actually was lying, but that he had not been wounded and was quite well. Many various people, indifferent, insignificant people, appear before him. He is talking to them, arguing about some trifle. They are preparing to set off somewhere. Prince Andrei dimly realizes that all this is trivial and that he has other far more serious matters to attend to, but still he continues to speak, surprising them by empty witticisms. Gradually, imperceptibly, all these persons begin to disappear, to be replaced by a single question, that of the closed door. He gets up and goes towards the door in order to shoot the bolt and lock it. Everything depends on whether he can lock it quickly enough. He starts, tries to hurry but his legs refuse to move and he knows he will not be in time to lock the door, yet he still frenziedly strains every effort to get there. Agonizing fear seizes him. And this fear is the fear of death: *It* stands behind the door. But while he is helplessly and clumsily stumbling towards the door that dreadful something is already pushing against it on the other side and forcing its way in. Something not human – death – is breaking in through the door and he must hold the door to. He grapples with the door, straining every ounce of his strength – to lock it is no longer possible – but his efforts are feeble and awkward, and the door, under the pressure of that awful thing, opens and shuts again.

Once more *It* pushes on the door from without. His last superhuman struggles are vain and both leaves of the door are noiselessly opened. *It* comes in, and it is *death*. And Prince Andrei died.

But at the very instant when in his dream he died Prince Andrei remembered that he was asleep, and at the very instant when he died he exerted himself and was awake.

'Yes, that was death. I died – and woke up. Yes, death is an awakening!' His soul was suddenly flooded with light, and the veil which till then had concealed the unknown was lifted from his spiritual vision. He felt as if powers hitherto confined within him had been set free, and was aware of that strange lightness of being which had not left him since.

When, waking in a cold perspiration, he stirred on the couch, Natasha went up and asked him what was the matter. He did not answer and looked at her oddly, not understanding.

This was what had taken place two days before Princess Maria's arrival. From that hour the wasting fever assumed a malignant character, as the doctor expressed it, but Natasha was not interested in what the doctor said: she saw the terrible psychological symptoms which to her were far more convincing.

With his awakening from sleep that day there began for Prince Andrei an awakening from life. And in relation to the duration of life it did not seem to him more prolonged than the awakening from sleep compared to the duration of his dream.

There was nothing terrible or violent in this relatively slow awakening.

His last days and hours passed in an ordinary and simple way.

Both Princess Maria and Natasha, who never left his side, felt this. They did not weep or shudder, and towards the end felt that they were attending not on him (he was no longer there, he had gone from them) but on their most immediate remembrance of him – his body. Both were so deeply conscious of this that the external, horrible side of death did not affect them, and they did not find it necessary to foment their grief. Neither in his presence nor away from him did they weep, nor did they ever talk of him to one another. They felt that they could not express in words what was real to their understanding.

The two of them saw that he was slowly and quietly slipping farther and farther away from them, and both knew that this had to be so and that it was well.

He was confessed and given the sacrament; everyone came to bid him farewell. When they brought his son to him he pressed his lips to the boy's and turned away, not because his heart ached and was sorrowful (Princess Maria and Natasha saw that) but simply because he supposed he had done all that was required of him; but when they told him to give the child his blessing he did what was demanded, and looked round as though to ask whether there was anything else he must do.

When the last convulsions of the body occurred, which the spirit was leaving, Princess Maria and Natasha were in the room.

'Is it over?' said Princess Maria after the body had lain for some moments motionless and growing cold before them. Natasha went up, looked into the dead eyes and made haste to close them. She closed them and did not kiss them but clung to that which was the most actual reminder of him – his body.

'Where has he gone? Where is he now? ...'

When the body, washed and clothed, lay in the coffin on the table everyone went up to take leave of him, and everyone wept.

Little Nikolai cried because his heart was torn with perplexity. The countess and Sonya cried from pity for Natasha and because he was no more. The old count cried because he felt that before long he too must step over the same terrible threshold.

Natasha and Princess Maria wept too now, but they wept not because of their own personal grief: they wept from the emotion and awe which took possession of their souls before the simple and solemn mystery of death that had been accomplished before their eyes.

PART TWO

I

IT is beyond the power of the human intellect to encompass *all* the causes of any phenomenon. But the impulse to search into causes is inherent in man's very nature. And so the human intellect, without investigating the multiplicity and complexity of circumstances conditioning an event, any one of which taken separately may seem to be the reason for it, snatches at the first most comprehensible approximation to a cause and says: 'There is the cause!' In historical events (where the actions of men form the subject of observation) the primeval conception of a cause was the will of the gods, succeeded later on by the will of those who stand in the historical foreground – the heroes of history. But we have only to look below the surface of any historical event, to inquire, that is, into the activity of the whole mass of people who took part in the event, to become convinced that the will of our historical hero, so far from ruling the actions of the multitude, is itself continuously controlled. It might be thought that it is a matter of indifference whether historical events are interpreted this way or that. But between the man who says that the nations of the West marched into the East because Napoleon wished it and the man who believes that it happened because it had to happen, the difference is as wide as between those who maintained that the earth is stationary and the planets revolve round it, and those who admitted that they did not know what holds the earth in place but knew there were laws directing its movement and that of the other planets. There is, and can be, no cause of an historical event save the one cause of all causes. But there are laws governing events: some we are ignorant of, others we are groping our way to. The discovery of these laws becomes possible only when we finally give up looking for such causes in the will of any one man, just as the discovery of the laws of the motion of the planets was possible only when men renounced the conception of the earth as stationary.

After the battle of Borodino and the enemy occupation of Moscow and its destruction by fire, the most important episode of the war of 1812, in the opinion of historians, was the movement of the Russian army from the Ryazan to the Kaluga road and to the Tarutino camp – the so-called flank march across the Krasnaya Pakhra river. Historians ascribe the glory of this achievement of genius to various commanders, and dispute as to whom the honour is due. Even foreign – even French – historians admit the genius of the Russian generals when speaking of that flank march. But why military writers, and others following their lead, should assume this oblique movement to be the perspicacious design of some one individual who thereby saved Russia and destroyed Napoleon – it is extremely difficult to see. In the first place it is difficult to see where the acumen and genius of this march lies; for no great mental effort is needed to perceive that the best position for an army (when it is not being attacked) is where supplies are most plentiful. And anyone, even a not very bright boy of thirteen, might have supposed that the most advantageous position for the army after its retreat from Moscow in 1812 would be on the Kaluga road. And so it is impossible to understand, in the first place, what conclusions lead the historians to see some profound wisdom in this manoeuvre. Secondly, it is even more difficult to understand just why they should attribute the salvation of Russia and the downfall of the French to this manoeuvre; for this flank march, had it been preceded, accompanied or followed by other circumstances, might have meant the ruin of the Russians and the saving of the French. If the position of the Russian army did, in fact, begin to improve from the time of that march, it does not at all ensue that the improvement was consequent on the march.

That flank march might not only have brought no advantage to the Russian army: it might have been fatal but for the conjunction of other circumstances. What would have happened had Moscow not been burned? If Murat had not lost track of the Russians? If Napoleon had not remained inactive? If, as Bennigsen and Barclay advised, the Russian army had given battle at Krasnaya Pakhra? What would have happened had the French attacked the Russians when they were on the march the other side of the Pakhra? What would have happened if later on Napoleon, on reaching Tarutino, had attacked the Russians with one-tenth of the energy he had displayed at Smolensk? What would have happened had the French moved on Petersburg?

... On any one of these hypotheses the oblique march that brought salvation might have proved disastrous.

The third point, and the most difficult of all to understand, is that students of history deliberately shut their eyes to the fact that this flank march cannot be ascribed to any one man, that no one ever anticipated it, that, like the retreat to Fili, the manoeuvre was, in reality, never conceived of as a whole but came about step by step, incident by incident, moment by moment, as the result of an infinite number of most diverse conditions, and was only seen in its entirety when it was a *fait accompli* and belonged to the past.

At the council at Fili the prevailing thought in the minds of the Russian command was retreat by the most direct and obvious route — the Nizhni Novgorod road. Evidence of this is that the majority of votes at the council were for adopting this course, and, above all, the commander-in-chief's famous conversation after the council with Lansky, who was in charge of the commissariat. Lansky reported to the commander-in-chief that the army supplies were for the most part stored along the Oka, in the Tula and Kaluga provinces, and that if they retreated along the Nizhni Novgorod road the army would be separated from its supplies by the broad river Oka, across which transport in early winter was impossible. This was the first indication of the necessity for revising the plan of a direct retreat on Nizhni, which had previously seemed so natural. The army kept more to the south, along the Ryazan road, closer to its supplies. Subsequently the inactivity of the French, who actually lost sight of the Russian army, concern for the defence of the arsenal at Tula and, in the main, the advantages of getting nearer to its provisions, made the army incline still further south, to the Tula road. Having crossed over, by a forced march, to the Tula road beyond the Pakhra, the Russian commanders intended to halt at Podolsk and had no thought of taking up a position at Tarutino; but innumerable circumstances, as well as the reappearance on the scene of the French troops, who for a time had lost touch with the Russians, and plans for giving battle and, above all, the abundance of supplies in Kaluga constrained our army to turn still more south and switch from the Tula to the Kaluga road and on to Tarutino, through the country where those supplies lay. Just as it is impossible to say at what date the decision was taken to abandon Moscow, so it is impossible to say precisely when and by whom it was decided to move to Tarutino. It was only after the army had got there, as the result of an infinite number of diverse factors, that people began to assure themselves that they had long desired and foreseen this move.

2

THE famous flank movement consisted simply in this: the Russian army, which had been retreating directly back as the invaders pushed forward, as soon as the French attack ceased digressed from the straight course they had embarked on at first and, finding they were not pursued, naturally inclined towards the locality where supplies were abundant.

If we imagine, instead of generals of genius at the head of the Russian army, an army acting alone, without leadership of any kind, such an army could not have done anything else but retire towards Moscow, describing a semicircle through country where provisions were the most plentiful and which was richest.

So natural was this transfer from the Nizhni to the Ryazan, Tula and Kaluga roads that even the stragglers from the Russian army fled in that direction, and Petersburg ordered Kutuzov to take that route. At Tarutino Kutuzov received what was almost a reprimand from the Emperor for moving the army to the Ryazan road, and he was enjoined to occupy the very position facing Kaluga in which he was encamped at the time the Tsar's letter reached him.

Having rolled like a ball in the direction of the impetus given by the campaign as a whole and by the battle of Borodino, the Russian army, as the force of the blow spent itself and no new blows came, assumed the position natural to it.

Kutuzov's merit lay, not in any strategic manoeuvre of genius, as it is called, but in the fact that he alone appreciated the significance of what had happened. He was the only one at the time to understand the meaning of the French army's inactivity; he alone persisted in maintaining that the battle of Borodino was a victory; he alone – who as commander-in-chief might have been expected to favour aggressive measures – did everything in his power to hold the Russian army back from useless fighting.

The wild beast wounded at Borodino lay where the fleeing huntsman had left him; but whether he was still alive, whether he still had his strength and was only lying low, the huntsman did not know. Suddenly the animal was heard to moan. The moan of the wounded

1171

creature (the French army) which betrayed its hopeless plight was the dispatch of Lauriston to Kutuzov's camp with overtures for peace.

Napoleon, with his usual assurance, not that right was right but that whatever occurred to his mind was right, wrote to Kutuzov the first words to come into his head, words that were quite meaningless.

Monsieur le prince Koutouzov [he wrote],

I am sending you one of my adjutants-general to discuss with you various matters of interest. I beg your Highness to credit what he says to you, *especially when he expresses the sentiments of esteem and particular regard that I have long entertained for your person.* ... This letter having no other object, I pray God, *Monsieur le prince Koutouzov*, to have you in His holy and gracious keeping.

(Signed) NAPOLÉON

Moscow, 30th October, 1812.

Kutuzov replied:

I should be cursed by posterity were I regarded as the first to take any steps towards a settlement of any sort. *Such is the spirit of my nation.*

And he continued to put forth all his energies to restrain his troops from attacking.

During the month spent by the French in pillaging Moscow and by the Russian army quietly encamped at Tarutino a change had taken place in the relative strength of the two belligerent forces – a change both in spirit and in numbers – which was all to the advantage of the Russian side. Although the condition of the French army and its numerical strength were unknown to the Russians, as soon as that change occurred signs in plenty appeared urgently calling attention to the indispensability of attacking. These signs were: Lauriston's mission; the abundance of provisions at Tarutino; the reports coming in from all sides of the inactivity and disorder of the French; the flow of recruits to our regiments; the fine weather; the long spell of rest the Russian soldiers had enjoyed, and their impatience (usual in troops that have been resting) to do the work for which they had been brought together; curiosity as to what was going on in the French army, of which nothing had been seen for so long; the audacity with which our outposts now scouted around the French encamped at Tarutino; the news of easy successes gained by peasants and guerilla bands over the French, and the envy thus aroused; the desire for vengeance that lay in the heart of every Russian so long as the French were in Moscow; and – paramount factor – the vague consciousness in every soldier's mind that the relative strength of the armies was reversed, and now that we had the superiority. A substantial change had occurred in the relative strength of the opposing forces, and advance had become inevitable. And at once, as surely as a clock begins to strike and chime when the minute hand has completed a full circle, this change was reflected in an increased activity, whirring and chiming in the higher spheres.

3

THE Russian army was commanded by Kutuzov and his Staff, and by the Emperor from Petersburg. Even before the news of the abandonment of Moscow had reached Petersburg a detailed plan for the whole campaign had been drawn up and sent to Kutuzov for his guidance. Although this plan had been conceived on the supposition that Moscow was still in our hands, it was approved by the Staff and accepted as the basis for action. Kutuzov replied only that movements arranged from a distance were always difficult to execute. So fresh instructions were dispatched for the solution of problems that might be encountered, as well as fresh people whose duty it would be to watch Kutuzov's actions and report upon them.

Besides this, the entire high command of the Russian army was now reorganized. The posts left vacant by Bagration, who had been killed, and Barclay, who had gone away in dudgeon, had to be filled. Very serious consideration was given to the question whether it would be better to put A in B's place and B in D's, or on the contrary to put D in A's place, and so on – as though anything more than A's or B's satisfaction depended on this.

In consequence of the hostility between Kutuzov and his chief of staff, Bennigsen, of the presence of confidential representatives of the Emperor, and of these transfers, the play of party intrigue at headquarters was more than usually complicated: A was trying to undermine B, B was undermining C, and so on in all possible combinations and permutations. In all these plottings the subject of intrigue was for the most part the conduct of the war, which all these people believed they were controlling; but this affair of the war continued independently of them, following the course it had to – that is, a course that never corresponded to the schemes of these men but was the outcome of the intrinsic reaction of the masses. Only in the higher spheres did all these schemes, thwarting and conflicting with one another, appear as a true index of what must inevitably come to pass.

Prince Mihail Ilarionovich [wrote the Emperor on the 2nd of October in a letter that reached Kutuzov after the battle of Tarutino] Since the 2nd of September Moscow has been in the hands of the enemy. Your last reports were dated the 20th, and in all this time not only has no action been attempted against the enemy or for the relief of the ancient capital but according to your last reports you have even made a further retreat. Serpuhov is already occupied by an enemy detachment, and Tula with its famous arsenal, so indispensable to the army, is in danger. From General Wintzingerode's reports I see that an enemy corps ten thousand strong is moving on the Petersburg road. Another, numbering several thousand men, is marching upon Dmitrov. A third has advanced along the Vladimir road. A fourth, of considerable size, is concentrated between Ruza and Mozhaisk. Napoleon himself was in Moscow as late as the 25th. In view of all this information, with the enemy having split up his effectives in these large detachments, with Napoleon himself and his Guards in Moscow, is it possible that the enemy force confronting you is so considerable as not to allow of your taking the offensive? One may, with far more probability, assume that you are being pursued by detachments, or at most an army corps far inferior to the army under your command. It would seem that, availing yourself of these circumstances, you might with advantage have attacked an enemy weaker than yourself, and annihilated him, or at least have obliged him to retreat, and have kept in our hands a goodly part of the provinces now occupied by the enemy, and thereby have averted danger from Tula and the other towns of the interior. You will be responsible if the enemy is able to direct a considerable body of men against Petersburg, to menace that capital in which it has not been possible to retain any great number of troops; for with the army entrusted to you, and acting with energy and decision, you have ample means at your disposal for averting this fresh calamity. Remember that you have still to answer to your injured country for the loss of Moscow. You have had experience of my readiness to reward you. That readiness will not grow less, but I and Russia have a right to expect from you all the zeal, firmness and success which your intellect, your military talents and the valour of the troops under your command presage.

But while this letter – which showed that the change in the relative strength of the opposing forces was by now making itself felt in

Petersburg too – was on the road Kutuzov had found himself unable to hold his army back, and a battle had already been fought.

On the 2nd of October a Cossack, Shapovalov, out scouting, shot a hare and wounded a second. In pursuit of the wounded hare, he made his way deep into the forest and stumbled upon the left flank of Murat's army encamped there and quite off its guard. The Cossack laughingly told his comrades how he had all but fallen into the hands of the French. An ensign who heard the story informed his commander.

The Cossack was sent for and questioned. The officers of the Cossacks wanted to take advantage of this chance to capture some horses from the French, but one of the superior officers, who was intimate with the higher authorities, reported the incident to a general on the Staff. Latterly, relations on the Staff had been strained to the limit. A few days back Yermolov had gone to Bennigsen and besought him to use his influence with the commander-in-chief to induce him to take the offensive.

'If I did not know you I should think you did not want what you are asking for. I have only to advise one course for his Serene Highness without fail to do exactly the opposite,' replied Bennigsen.

The news brought by the Cossacks, confirmed by scouts riding out on horseback, proved conclusively that the time was ripe. The tight coil sprang, the clock-wheels whirred and the chimes began to play. Despite all his supposed power, his intellect, his experience and his knowledge of men, Kutuzov – in view of a note from Bennigsen (who sent personal reports to the Emperor), the desire expressed by all the generals alike, the wishes the Emperor was presumed to hold, and the information brought by the Cossacks – could no longer restrain the inescapable move forward, and gave the order for what he regarded as useless and mischievous – gave his assent, that is, to the accomplished fact.

4

BENNIGSEN'S note pressing for aggressive action and the report received from the Cossacks that the French left flank was uncovered were merely the final indications that the signal for an offensive could no longer be delayed, and the attack was fixed for the 5th of October.

On the morning of the 4th of October Kutuzov signed the dispositions. Toll read them to Yermolov, asking him to attend to the further arrangements.

'Very good, very good, but I can't possibly see about it now,' replied Yermolov, and left the hut.

The dispositions as drawn up by Toll were perfectly satisfactory. Just as for the battle of Austerlitz it was stated – though not in German thi₋ time – that 'the first column will proceed this way and that way, the second column will proceed to this place and that place', and so on. And on paper all these columns arrived in their places at the appointed moment and routed the enemy. Everything had been admirably thought out, as dispositions always are, and as is always the case not a single column reached its objective at the appointed time.

When the necessary number of copies of the dispositions were ready an officer was summoned and sent to deliver them to Yermolov to deal with. A young officer of the Horse Guards, Kutuzov's orderly, pleased with the importance of the mission entrusted to him, set off for Yermolov's quarters.

'The general has ridden out,' Yermolov's orderly told him.

The officer of the Horse Guards went to the lodgings of a general in whose company Yermolov was often to be found.

'Not here, nor the general either.'

The officer, mounting his horse again, rode off to someone else.

'No, he's gone out,'

'Hope I shan't be held accountable for this delay! Deuce take it!' thought the officer.

He rode all over the camp. One man declared he had seen Yermolov ride past with some other generals; others, that he must have returned home by now. Without stopping to eat, the officer searched till six o'clock in the evening. Yermolov was nowhere to be found, and no one knew where he was. The officer snatched a hasty meal at a comrade's and started off again to the vanguard to see Miloradovich. Miloradovich too was away, but here he was told that he had gone to a ball at General Kikin's and that Yermolov was probably there as well.

'But where is that?'

'Over yonder at Yechkino,' said a Cossack officer, pointing to a country house in the far distance.

'What, beyond our lines?'

'Two regiments of our fellows have been sent out to the outposts.

The devil of a spree they're having! A couple of bands, three sets of singers!'

The officer rode out beyond our lines to Yechkino. When he was still a long way from the house he heard the cheerful strains of a soldier's dance boisterously sung in chorus.

'In the mea-dows ... in the mea-dows!' he heard, accompanied by whistling and the sound of an instrument like a balalaika, drowned every now and then in a roar of voices. The officer's spirits rose as he listened, but at the same time he was afraid that he would be blamed for having been so long in delivering the weighty message entrusted to him. It was by now past eight o'clock. He dismounted and walked up to the porch of a large country house which had remained intact, half-way between the Russians and the French. In an ante-room and in the hall footmen were bustling about with wines and refreshments. Groups of singers stood under the windows. The officer was admitted and immediately saw all the chief generals of the army together, among them the big, imposing figure of Yermolov. They all had their coats unbuttoned and were standing in a semicircle with flushed and animated faces. In the middle of the room a short, handsome general with a red face was performing the steps of the *trepak* with much skill and spirit.

'Ha, ha, ha! Bravo, Nikolai Ivanovich! Ha, ha, ha! ...'

The officer felt doubly guilty at breaking in with important business at such a moment, and he would have waited; but one of the generals caught sight of him, and on hearing what he had come about, informed Yermolov. Yermolov came forward with a frown, listened to what the officer had to say and took the papers from him without a word.

'Do you suppose it was mere chance that he had gone off?' said a comrade of the Horse Guards officer, who was on the Staff, speaking of Yermolov that evening. 'Not a bit of it! It was done on purpose, to get Konovnitsyn into trouble. You see, there'll be a pretty kettle of fish tomorrow!'

5

NEXT day the decrepit old Kutuzov rose early, said his prayers, dressed and, with an unpleasant consciousness that he must now direct a battle he did not approve of, got into his carriage and drove to Letashovka (a village three and a half miles from Tarutino) to the place where the attacking columns were to meet. As he was driven along in the calèche he kept dozing and waking again, and listening for any sound of firing on the right which might indicate that the action had begun. But all was still quiet. A damp, overcast autumn morning was just dawning. As they approached Tarutino Kutuzov noticed cavalrymen leading their horses to water across the road along which he was driving. Kutuzov looked at them searchingly, stopped his carriage and inquired what regiment they belonged to. They were part of a column which should have been far to the front and in ambush long ago. 'It may be a mistake,' thought the old commander-in-chief. But a little farther on he saw infantry with their arms stacked, and the men in their drawers busy cooking rye-porridge and fetching wood. He sent for their officer. The officer reported that no order to advance had been received.

'No or – ' Kutuzov began, but checked himself immediately and summoned a senior officer. He climbed out of his calèche and paced silently up and down as he waited, with drooping head and breathing heavily. When Eykhen, the officer of the General Staff whom he had sent for, appeared Kutuzov turned purple with rage, not because that officer was to blame for the blunder but because he was an officer of sufficient status for him to vent his wrath on. Shaking and spluttering, the old man fell into one of those paroxysms of fury in which he would sometimes roll on the ground in frenzy, and flew at Eykhen, shaking his fists at him and shouting abuse in the language of the gutter. Another officer, Captain Brozin, who happened to appear and who was in no way to blame, came in for the same fate.

'And – what *canaille* are you? I'll have you shot! Scoundrels!' yelled Kutuzov in a hoarse voice, waving his arms and reeling.

He was in a state of actual physical suffering. He, the commander-in-chief, his Serene Highness who, everybody kept saying, had more power than any man had ever possessed in Russia, to be placed in such a position – made the laughing-stock of the whole army! 'Worrying and praying about today, staying awake the whole night going over and over everything – all sheer waste!' he thought to himself. 'Why, when I was a mere junior officer no one would have dared make a fool of me like this ... but now!' He felt real physical pain as though he had suffered corporal punishment, and could not help giving expression to it by cries of anger and distress. But soon his strength was exhausted, and looking about him, conscious of having said a great deal that was amiss, he got into his carriage and drove back in silence.

His fury once spent did not return, and, feebly blinking his eyes, Kutuzov listened to excuses and self-justifications (Yermolov kept out of sight till next day), and to the urgent representations of Bennigsen, Konovnitsyn and Toll that the movement that had miscarried should be executed on the morrow. And once more Kutuzov had to consent.

6

NEXT day the troops assembled at their appointed places in the evening and advanced during the night. It was an autumn night with dark purple clouds but no rain. The ground was damp but not muddy, and the troops proceeded noiselessly, except for an occasional faint clanking of the artillery. The men had been forbidden to talk above a whisper, to smoke their pipes or strike a light, and they tried to keep the horses from neighing. The secrecy of the enterprise heightened its attraction. The men tramped on blithely. Several columns halted, stacked their arms and lay down on the chilly ground, supposing they had reached their destination; others (the majority) marched all night and arrived at places that were obviously not intended.

Count Orlov-Denisov with his Cossacks (the least important detachment of all) was the only one to get to the right place at the right time. This detachment halted at the outskirts of a forest, on the path leading from the village of Stromilovo to Dmitrovsk.

Towards dawn Count Orlov-Denisov, who had dozed off, was awakened. A deserter from the French camp had been brought in. It was a Polish sergeant of Poniatowski's corps. He explained in Polish that he had come over because he had been slighted in the Service: he ought long ago to have been made an officer, he was braver than any of them, and so he had left and wanted to pay them out. He said that Murat was spending the night less than three-quarters of a mile away, and if they would let him have a convoy of a hundred men he would capture him alive. Count Orlov-Denisov consulted with his fellow-officers. The offer was too tempting to be refused. Everyone clamoured to go, everyone was in favour of the attempt. After much disputing and arguing Major-General Grekov, with two regiments of Cossacks, decided to go with the Polish sergeant.

'But mark my words,' said Count Orlov-Denisov to the Polish deserter, as he dismissed him, 'if you have been lying I'll have you hanged like a dog; but if your story's true there'll be a hundred gold pieces for you.'

The sergeant made no reply, and with a resolute air sprang into the saddle and rode away with Grekov, who had quickly mustered his men. The party disappeared into the forest. Count Orlov, having seen Grekov off, returned, shivering from the freshness of the early dawn and strung up by the step he had undertaken on his own responsibility, and began scanning the enemy camp, now just discernible in the deceptive light of approaching daybreak and the dying camp-fires. Our columns ought by now to be showing themselves on an open declivity to his right. He looked in that direction, but though they would have been visible a long way off there were no columns to be seen. In the French camp the count fancied – and his keen-sighted adjutant confirmed the impression – that things were beginning to stir.

'Oh, of course it's too late,' said Count Orlov, staring at the camp.

As often happens when someone we have trusted is no longer before our eyes, it suddenly seemed perfectly clear and obvious that the deserter was an impostor, that he had told them a pack of lies, and that the whole attack would now be ruined because of the absence of those two regiments, which the man would lead away heaven only knew where. How could they possibly seize and capture a commander-in-chief from among such a mass of troops?

'Of course the wretch was lying,' said the count.

'We could recall Grekov,' said one of his suite, who like Count Orlov felt doubtful of the adventure when he looked at the enemy's camp.

'Ha? You really think so? What would you do – let them go on, or not?'

'Are your orders to fetch them back?'

'Yes, fetch them back!' said Count Orlov with sudden determination, glancing at his watch. 'It would be too late. It's quite light.'

And the adjutant galloped into the woods after Grekov. When Grekov came back Count Orlov-Denisov, keyed up by the abandoned venture and the vain wait for the infantry column which still did not appear, as well as by the proximity of the enemy, decided to advance. (All his men were feeling the same way.)

'To horse!' he commanded in a whisper. Every man fell into his place and crossed himself. ...

'In God's name, forward!'

'Hurrah-ah-ah!' reverberated through the forest, and the Cossacks, trailing their lances, one company after another as though poured out of a sack, flew gaily across the brook towards the enemy camp.

One desperate frightened yell from the first French soldier to catch sight of the Cossacks, and all in the camp, half-dressed, half-asleep, fled blindly, abandoning artillery, muskets and horses.

Had the Cossacks chased the French, instead of turning their attention to what they left behind and around them, they could have taken both Murat and everything else that was there. This was what the officers tried to make them do. But it was impossible to budge the Cossacks once they got to capturing booty and prisoners. No one heeded the word of command. Fifteen hundred prisoners and thirty-eight guns were taken on the spot, besides standards and, what was of most consequence in the eyes of the Cossacks, horses, saddles, blankets and the like. All this they wanted to see after, to secure prisoners and guns, to divide the spoils – not without some shouting and even a certain amount of fighting – and it was on this that the Cossacks busied themselves.

The French, finding that they were no longer pursued, began to rally: they formed up into detachments and began firing. Orlov-Denisov was still waiting for the other columns to arrive, and did not advance farther.

Meanwhile, in accordance with the dispositions – *the first column will proceed*, and so on – the infantry of the belated columns, under the command of Bennigsen and the direction of Toll, had started off in due order and had, in the usual way, arrived somewhere but not at the place that was intended. As always happens, men who had started out cheerfully began to falter; murmurs were heard, it was felt that a muddle had occurred, and they were marched back to some point. Adjutants and generals galloped to and fro, shouted, lost their tempers, quarrelled, told each other that they had come quite wrong and were late, gave vent to a little abuse, etc., and finally all washed their hands of the whole business and went forward simply in order to get somewhere. 'We must arrive at some place or other!' And so they did, indeed, though not where they should have got – the few who did eventually reach their proper destination reached it too late to be of any use and only in time to be fired on. Toll, who in this battle played the part that Weierother had filled at Austerlitz, galloped assiduously from place to place, always finding everything at sixes and sevens. Thus he stumbled on Bagovut's corps in a wood when it was already broad daylight, though the corps ought long ago to have joined Orlov-Denisov. Exasperated at the miscarriage, and supposing that someone must be to blame, Toll galloped up to the commander of the corps and began upbraiding him severely, saying that he deserved to be shot. Bagovut, a sturdy old general of placid temperament, also being upset by all the delay, confusion and contradictory orders, to everybody's amazement fell into a rage, quite out of keeping with his usual character, and answered Toll somewhat offensively.

'I am not going to be lectured by anyone. I know as well as the next man how to face death with my soldiers,' and he moved forward with a single division.

Coming out on to a field under the enemy's fire, the valiant general, without stopping to consider in his agitation whether (now and with only one division) his advance into action was likely to be of use or not, marched his men straight ahead into the enemy's fire. Danger, shell and shot were just what he needed in his angry mood. One of the first bullets killed him, others killed many of his men. And his division remained under fire for some time and to no avail.

7

MEANWHILE another column was to have attacked the French from the front, but Kutuzov was with this column. He knew only too well that nothing but muddle would come of this battle, undertaken against his judgement, and so far as was in his power he held his forces back. He did not advance.

He rode mutely about on his small grey horse, giving languid replies to the suggestions that were made to him to attack.

'The word *attack* is for ever on your lips, but you don't see that we are unable to execute these complicated manoeuvres,' he said to Miloradovich, who asked permission to advance.

'You weren't smart enough to take Murat prisoner this morning, or to be in your place on time: now there's nothing to be done!' he answered another.

When Kutuzov was informed that there were now two battalions of Poles in the rear of the French, where according to the earlier reports from the Cossacks there had been none, he gave a sidelong glance at Yermolov who was behind him and to whom he had not spoken since the previous day.

'That is the way! They come begging to attack, proposing all sorts of plans, but as soon as it comes to action nothing is ready, and the enemy, forewarned, takes his measures accordingly.'

Yermolov screwed up his eyes and smiled faintly as he heard these words. He realized that so far as he was concerned the storm had blown over, and that Kutuzov would content himself with this innuendo.

'That's his little joke at my expense,' said Yermolov softly, nudging Raevsky with his knee, who was at his side.

Shortly after this Yermolov approached Kutuzov and respectfully submitted:

'It is not too late yet, your Highness – the enemy has not gone away. If you were to give the word to attack. Otherwise the Guards won't see so much as a puff of smoke.'

Kutuzov said nothing, but when it was reported to him that Murat's troops were in retreat he ordered an advance, although at every hundred yards he halted for three-quarters of an hour.

The whole battle amounted to no more than what had been done by Orlov-Denisov's Cossacks: the rest of the army simply lost several hundred men for nothing.

The consequence to Kutuzov was a diamond decoration; Bennigsen, too, was rewarded with diamonds and a hundred thousand roubles; and the other generals received agreeable recognition corresponding to their rank; and following the engagement more changes were made on the Staff.

'That's how things always are with us – the cart before the horse!' said the Russian officers and generals after the Tarutino affair, just as people do to this day, implying that some fool is handling matters all wrong, which we ourselves would have arranged quite otherwise. But people who talk like that either do not know what they are talking about, or purposely deceive themselves. No battle – be it Tarutino, Borodino, Austerlitz – ever comes off as those who planned it anticipated. That is the *sine qua non*.

An infinite number of freely acting forces (and nowhere is a man freer than during a life and death struggle) influence the course taken by a battle, and that course can never be known beforehand and never coincides with the direction it would take under the impulsion of any single force.

If many simultaneously and variously directed forces act on a given body, the direction which that body will take cannot be the course of any one of the forces individually – it will always follow an inter-mediate, as it were, shortest path, or what is represented in mechanics by the diagonal of a parallelogram of forces.

If in the accounts given us by historians, especially French histor-ians, we find their wars and battles conforming to previously pre-scribed plans, the only conclusion to be drawn is that their accounts are not true.

The battle of Tarutino obviously did not attain the aim which Toll had in view – to lead the troops into action in the order laid down by the dispositions; nor that which Count Orlov-Denisov may have had – to take Murat prisoner; nor the aim of destroying at one blow the whole corps, which Bennigsen and others may have entertained; nor the aim of the officer who wished to go into action to distinguish himself; nor that of the Cossack who wanted more booty than he got, and so on. But if the aim of the battle was what actually resulted and what was the universal desire of the country – the expulsion of the French from Russia and the destruction of their army – it is quite clear that the battle of Tarutino, just because of its incongruities, was exactly what was wanted at that stage of the campaign. It would be difficult and even impossible to imagine any issue of that battle more opportune than its actual outcome. With a minimum of effort and at the cost of trifling losses, despite almost unexampled muddle the most important results of the whole campaign were obtained: the transi-tion from retreat to advance, exposure of the weakness of the French, and the administration of the shock which was all that was needed to start Napoleon's army on its flight.

8

NAPOLEON enters Moscow after the brilliant victory *de la Moskowa*; there can be no doubt about the victory, since the French are left in possession of the field of battle. The Russians retire, abandoning their ancient capital. Moscow, crammed with provisions, arms, munitions and incalculable wealth, is in Napoleon's hands. The Russian army, only half the strength of the French, during the course of a whole month makes not a single attempt to assume the offensive. Napoleon's position could hardly be more brilliant. He can either, with doubly superior forces, fall upon the remains of the Russian army and exterminate it; negotiate an advantageous peace; or, in the case of his offer being rejected, make a threatening move on Petersburg, or – should that somehow not be successful – return to Smolensk or Vilna, or stay on in Moscow: in short, no extraordinary genius would seem to be required in order to retain the brilliant position the French held at that time. To do so it was only necessary to take the simplest and easiest measures: to keep the troops from looting; to prepare winter clothing – there was enough in Moscow for the whole army; and to organize systematic collection of provisions, of which (on the showing of the French historians) Moscow had sufficient to supply the entire army for six months. Napoleon, that greatest of all military geniuses, with absolute power, so the historians assert, took none of these steps.

He not only did nothing of all this but, on the contrary, used his power to select out of all the various courses open to him the one that was the most foolish and the most disastrous. Of all the different things Napoleon might have done – such as wintering in Moscow, going on to Petersburg, on to Nizhni Novgorod, or back a little more to the north or south (say, by the route Kutuzov afterwards took) – nothing more stupid or ruinous can be thought of than what he actually did. He remained in Moscow till October, letting his troops plunder the city, then – after hesitating whether to leave a garrison behind him – he quitted Moscow, marched within reach of Kutuzov without giving battle, turned to the right and went as far as Malo-Yaroslavets, again without attempting to break through, and finally retired not by the route Kutuzov had taken but along the devastated Smolensk road to Mozhaisk. Nothing could have been more stupid or more pernicious to the army than this, as the sequel proved. Assuming that Napoleon's object was to destroy his army, the most expert strategist could hardly conceive of any other series of actions which would so completely and infallibly have accomplished that purpose, independently of anything the Russian army might do.

Napoleon, the man of genius, did just this! But to say that Napoleon sacrificed his army because he wished to, or because he was very stupid, would be as inaccurate as to say that he brought his troops to

Moscow because he wanted to, and because he was very clever and a genius.

In both cases his personal activity, which was of no more consequence than the personal action of the meanest private, merely coincided with the laws that guided the event.

Quite falsely (and simply because consequent happenings did not vindicate his action) the historians represent Napoleon's faculties as having failed in Moscow. He employed all his ability and powers to do the best thing possible for himself and his army, just as he had always done before and as he did afterwards in 1813. His activity at this time was no less astounding than in Egypt, in Italy, in Austria and in Prussia. We cannot know with any certainty how much actual genius there was about Napoleon's operations in Egypt, where forty centuries looked down upon his glory, for the reason that all his great exploits there are described to us exclusively by Frenchmen. We cannot fairly assess his genius in Austria or Prussia, for we have to draw our information from French or German sources, and the incomprehensible surrender of whole corps without a blow struck, and of fortresses without a siege, must incline Germans to postulate his genius as the unique explanation of the war as it was waged in Germany. But we, thank God, have no need to plead his genius to cloak our shame. We have paid for the right to look facts simply and squarely in the face, and we shall not relinquish that right.

His genius operated as fully and amazingly in Moscow as elsewhere. Order after order and plan after plan were issued by him from the time he entered Moscow till the time he left it. The absence of the inhabitants and of a deputation, and even the burning of Moscow, did not daunt him. He did not lose sight of the welfare of his army or of the doings of the enemy, or of the well-being of the people of Russia, or of the conduct of affairs in Paris, or of diplomatic considerations concerning the terms of the anticipated peace.

9

ON the military side Napoleon, immediately on his entry into Moscow, gives General Sebastiani strict orders to keep a watch on the movements of the Russian army, sends army corps out along the different roads, and charges Murat to find Kutuzov. Then he gives careful instructions about the fortification of the Kremlin; then draws up a brilliant plan for a future campaign over the whole map of Russia. On the diplomatic side Napoleon summons Captain Yakovlev, who had been robbed and was in rags and did not know how to get out of Moscow, expounds to him at full length his whole policy and his magnanimity, and, after writing a letter to the Emperor Alexander in which he deems it his duty to inform his friend and brother that Rostopchin has managed affairs very badly in Moscow, he dispatches Yakovlev with it to Petersburg.

Having similarly expatiated on his view and his chivalry to Tutolmin, he dispatches that old man too to Petersburg to open negotiations.

On the judicial side orders were issued, immediately after the fires broke out, for the guilty persons to be found and executed. And the miscreant Rostopchin was punished by having his own houses burnt down.

On the administrative side Moscow was presented with a constitution. A municipal council was founded, and the following proclamation posted about the town:

CITIZENS OF MOSCOW!

Your miseries are cruel, but his Majesty the Emperor and King desires to arrest their course. Terrible examples have shown you how he punishes disobedience and crime. Stern measures have been taken to put an end to disorder and to restore public security. A paternal administration, composed of men chosen from among yourselves, will form your municipality or city government. It will care for your welfare, your needs and your interests. Its members will be distinguished by a red ribbon worn across the shoulder, and the mayor of the city will, in addition, wear a white belt. But except when discharging their duties they will only wear a red ribbon round the left arm.

The city police is established on its former footing, and thanks to its vigilance better order already prevails. The government has appointed two commissioners-general, or chiefs of police, and twenty commissioners, or inspectors, for the different wards of the city. You will recognize them by the white band they will wear around the left arm. A number of churches of various denominations are open, and divine service continues in them unhindered. Your fellow-citizens are daily returning to their homes, and instructions have been given that they should find in them the help and protection to which misfortune entitles. These are the measures the government has adopted for the restoration of order and easement of your position. But to attain this end it is necessary that you should second these efforts by your own and should, so far as is possible, forget your past sufferings; should cherish the hope of a less cruel destiny; should be fully persuaded that inevitable and ignominious death awaits those who make any attempt on your persons or on what remains of your property, and, finally, that you should not doubt that these will be safeguarded, since such is the will of the greatest and most just of monarchs. Soldiers and citizens, of whatever nation you may be – re-establish public confidence, the source of the prosperity of a state. Live like brothers. Render mutual aid and protection one to another. Combine to frustrate the designs of the evil-minded. Obey the military and civil authorities, and soon your tears will cease to flow.

On the commissariat side Napoleon decreed that all the troops should take turns in plundering Moscow for supplies, which would suffice to victual the army for a certain time.

In the matter of religious worship Napoleon ordered the priests to be brought back and services resumed in the churches.

Concerning trade and the provisioning of the army the following manifesto was placarded everywhere:

PROCLAMATION

Peaceable inhabitants of Moscow, artisans and working men whom misfortune has driven from the city, scattered tillers of the soil who are still kept in the fields by causeless terror – listen! Tranquillity is returning to this capital, and order is being restored in it. Finding that they are respected, your fellow-countrymen are boldly emerging from their hiding-places. Any violence to them or to their property brings prompt punishment. His Majesty the Emperor and King protects them, and considers none among you his enemy but such as disobey his commands. His desire is to put an end to your sufferings and restore you to your homes and families. Co-operate, therefore, with his beneficent purposes and come to us without fear. Citizens, return with confidence to your dwellings! You will soon find means of satisfying your needs. Craftsmen and industrious artisans, return to your work! Your houses, your shops, and guards to protect them, await you. For your labour you shall receive the wage which is your due. And lastly you too, peasants, come out from the woods where you are lurking in terror. Return without fear to your huts, and be assured that you will find protection. Markets have been organized in the city where peasants can bring their surplus produce and the fruits of the earth. The government has taken the following measures to ensure the free sale of this produce: (1) From this day peasants, husbandmen and those living in the environs of Moscow may, without any danger, bring their goods of whatever nature to two appointed markets – Moss street and the Poultry market. (2) Such goods will be bought from them at prices agreed upon between seller and buyer; but if a seller is unable to obtain a fair price he will be at liberty to take his goods back to his village, and no one may hinder his doing so on any pretext whatsoever. (3) Sunday and Wednesday of each week are appointed as chief market days; on this score a sufficient number of troops will be stationed along the high roads on Tuesdays and Saturdays at such distances from the town as to protect carts coming in. (4) Similar measures will be taken that peasants and their carts and horses may meet with no hindrance on their return journey. (5) Steps will immediately be taken to re-establish ordinary trading.

Inhabitants of town and country, and you, working men and artisans, whatever your nationality – you are called upon to carry into effect the paternal designs of his Majesty the Emperor and King, and to co-operate with him for the public welfare. Lay your respect and trust at his feet, and do not delay in uniting with us!

To raise the spirits of troops and civilians reviews were constantly held and decorations distributed. The Emperor rode through the streets on horseback to console the people, and despite his preoccupation with state affairs himself visited the theatres set up by his orders.

In the matter of philanthropy – the fairest jewel in a monarch's crown – Napoleon also did all that lay in his power. He caused the words *Maison de ma Mère* to be inscribed on the charitable institutions – thereby combining tender filial piety with beneficent majesty. He visited the Foundling Hospital and, allowing the orphans saved by him to kiss his white hands, conversed graciously with Tutolmin. Then, as Thiers eloquently recounts, gave instructions for his troops to be paid in forged Russian money which he had prepared.

To enhance the employment of these methods by an act worthy of himself and of the French army, he saw to it that relief was distributed to those who had suffered loss from the fire. But as food was too precious to be given away to foreigners, who were for the most part hostile to him, Napoleon preferred to bestow money with which to procure provisions from outside, and had this money paid in paper roubles.

With reference to army discipline orders were continually being issued providing for severe punishment for non-fulfilment of military duties and for the suppression of pillaging.

BUT, strange to say, all these arrangements, these efforts and plans, which were no whit inferior to others made in similar circumstances, never touched the root of the matter. Like the hands of a clock disconnected from the mechanism behind the dial, they swung about in an arbitrary, aimless fashion without engaging the cogwheels.

On the military side the plan of campaign – that prodigious work *à propos* of which Thiers remarks that 'his genius never devised anything more profound, more skilful, or more admirable', and enters into a polemical discussion with Monsieur Fain to prove that this composition of genius must be referred not to the 4th but to the 15th of October – that plan never was and never could have been put into execution, because it was quite out of touch with the actual facts of the position. The fortifying of the Kremlin, for which *la Mosquée* (as Napoleon called the church of Vasili Blazhenny) was to have been razed to the ground, turned out to be perfectly useless. The mining of the Kremlin only helped towards the fulfilment of Napoleon's wish to see the Kremlin blown up – in other words, that the floor on which the child has hurt himself might be beaten. The pursuit of the Russian army, on which Napoleon laid so much stress, produced an unheard-of phenomenon. The French generals lost track of the sixty thousand men of the Russian army, and, according to Thiers, it was only thanks to the skill, and also apparently the genius, of Murat that they eventually succeeded in discovering, like a needle in a haystack, the whereabouts of this Russian army sixty thousand strong.

On the diplomatic side all Napoleon's arguments to prove his magnanimity and justice, both to Tutolmin and to Yakovlev (who was principally interested to obtain a greatcoat and a conveyance for travelling) were thrown away; Alexander would not receive these envoys and returned no answer to the message they brought.

As to his judicial administration: after the execution of the supposed incendiaries the other half of Moscow was burnt down.

Administratively, the establishment of a municipality did not check pillage, and was of no benefit to anyone but the few persons who were members of it and so able – on the pretext of preserving order – to loot Moscow or to save their own property from being looted.

In matters of religion, though the Imperial visit to a mosque had been a great success in Egypt, a similar visit had no effect in Moscow. Two or three priests, picked up in the city, did attempt to carry out Napoleon's wishes but one of them got slapped in the face by a French soldier during the service, while of another a French official reported that 'the priest whom I found and invited to say mass cleaned and locked up the church. That night the doors were forced open again, the padlocks smashed, the books torn and other disorders perpetrated.'

As for commerce, the proclamation to 'industrious artisans and peasants' met with no response. There were no industrious artisans, and the peasants set upon the commissioners who ventured too far from the town with their proclamation and killed them.

The attempts to entertain the people and the troops with theatres were equally unsuccessful. The theatres set up in the Kremlin and in Poznyakov's house had to be closed again at once because the actors and actresses were robbed of their belongings.

Even philanthropy did not have the desired results. The genuine as well as the counterfeit paper money which flooded Moscow lost its value. The French, accumulating booty, cared for nothing but gold. Not only were the counterfeit notes worthless which Napoleon so graciously bestowed on the unfortunate – even silver fell below its standard value in relation to gold.

But the most striking example of the ineffectiveness of the orders issued by the authorities at that time was Napoleon's endeavour to check looting and restore discipline.

Here are some of the reports which the army authorities were sending in:

'Looting continues in the city, in spite of injunctions to the contrary. Order is not yet restored, and there is not a single merchant engaging in legitimate trade. Only the sutlers venture to sell anything, and the articles they have for sale are stolen goods.'

'My district continues to be pillaged by soldiers of the 3rd Corps, who, not content with stripping the poor creatures hiding in underground cellars of what little they have left, are brutal enough to wound them with sword-cuts, as I have repeatedly witnessed.'

'Nothing new to report, except that the soldiers are given up to theft and pillage – 9th October.'

'Robbery and pillaging continue. There is a band of thieves in our district who ought to be put down by forceful measures – 11th October.'

'The Emperor is exceedingly displeased that, despite strict orders to stop pillage, parties of marauding Guards are continually seen returning to the Kremlin. In the Old Guards the disorder and pillage have been more violent than ever last night and today. The Emperor finds with regret that the picked soldiers appointed to guard his person, who should be setting an example of good discipline, carry insubordination to such a point that they break into the cellars and stores containing army supplies. Others have fallen so low that they defy sentinels and officers of the watch, abusing and even striking them.'

'The Grand Marshal of the Palace [wrote the governor] complains bitterly that, notwithstanding repeated prohibitions, the soldiers continue to perform the offices of nature in all the courtyards, and even under the Emperor's very windows.'

The army, like a herd of cattle run wild and trampling underfoot the fodder which might have saved it from starvation, was disintegrating and perishing with every day it remained in Moscow.

But it did not stir.

It started in flight only when suddenly seized by panic at the capture of transport trains on the Smolensk road, and the battle of Tarutino. The news of that battle of Tarutino, which reached Napoleon unexpectedly in the middle of a review, fired him with a desire to punish the Russians (so Thiers tells us), and he issued the order for departure which the whole army was clamouring for.

In their flight from Moscow the soldiers carried away with them all the booty they had stolen. Napoleon, too, had his own personal *trésor* to take with him. Seeing the baggage-trains that encumbered the army, Napoleon (Thiers says) was horror-struck. And yet, for all his experience of war, he did not order the collection of superfluous vehicles to be burnt, as he had done with those of a certain marshal on the way to Moscow; he gazed at the calèches and carriages in which the soldiers were riding and remarked that it was a very good thing – all those conveyances would come in useful for carrying provisions, the sick and the wounded.

The plight of the whole army was like the plight of a wounded animal which feels its death is at hand and does not know what it is doing. To study the ingenious manoeuvres and objectives of Napoleon and his army from the time of entering Moscow up to the hour of the final catastrophe is like watching the convulsions and death throes of a mortally wounded animal. Very often the wounded creature, hearing a rustle, rushes straight at the sportsman's gun, runs forward and back again, and itself hastens its end. Napoleon, under the pressure of his entire army, did likewise. The rustle of the battle of Tarutino alarmed the beast and it made a rush towards the shot, reached the hunter and turned back again; and at last, like any wild creature, fled along the most inexpedient, the most perilous but the best known track – its former trail.

Napoleon, who is presented to us as the leader of all this movement backwards and forwards (just as the figure-head over the prow of a ship seems to the savage to be the power directing the vessel in its course) – Napoleon in whatever he did throughout this period was like a child holding on to the straps inside a carriage and imagining that he is driving it.

II

EARLY in the morning of the 6th of October Pierre stepped outside the prison-shed, and then, turning back, stood in the doorway to play with the little bluish-grey mongrel with the long body and short bandy legs, who was gambolling around him. This little dog had made her home in the shed, sleeping beside Karatayev at night, though occasionally she went off on excursions into the town from which she would always return again. Probably she had never had an owner, and still belonged to nobody and had no name. The French called her Azor; the story-teller christened her Jenny Daw, while Karatayev and the others called her Grey, or sometimes Floppy. The fact that she belonged to no one, and had no name or breed or definite colour, did not seem to trouble the blue-grey bitch in the least. Her fluffy tail stood up firm and round like a plume, her bandy legs served her so well that often, as though disdaining to use all four, she would gracefully raise one hind leg and run very easily and quickly on three. Everything was a source of satisfaction to her. At one moment she would be rolling on her back squealing with delight, or basking in the sun looking thoughtful and solemn. Now she would frolic about playing with a chip of wood or a straw.

Pierre's attire by now consisted of a dirty town shirt (the sole relic from the clothes he was originally wearing), a pair of soldier's drawers which by Karatayev's advice he tied with string round the ankles, for the sake of warmth, and a peasant coat and cap. Physically he had altered a great deal during this time. He no longer seemed stout, though he still retained the appearance of solidity and strength that was hereditary in his family. A beard and moustache covered the lower part of his face, and a tangle of hair, infested with lice, curled round his head like a cap. His eyes had a steady, quiet look of alert readiness they had never held before. The old laxity, which had shown even in his eyes, had given place to an energetic preparedness for action and resistance. His feet were bare.

Pierre gazed alternately below at the plain across which wagons and men on horseback were passing that morning, across the river into the distance, at the dog pretending she was going to bite him, and at his own bare feet which he shifted about with pleasure from one position to another, moving his dirty thick big toes. And every time he looked at his bare feet a smile of lively self-satisfaction flitted across his face. The sight of those bare feet reminded him of all he had experienced and learned during these weeks, and the recollection pleased him.

For some days the weather had been mild and clear, with light frosts in the mornings – what is called an 'old wives' summer'.

It was warm out of doors in the sun, and this warmth was particularly agreeable with the invigorating freshness of the morning frost still in the air.

Over everything, far and near, lay the magic crystal glitter only seen at this time in the autumn. The Sparrow hills were visible in the distance, with the village, the church and a large white house. And the leafless trees, the sand, the bricks and roofs of the houses, the green steeple of the church and the angles of the white house in the distance all stood out in the limpid air, in most delicate outline and with unnatural distinctness. Close by could be seen the familiar ruins of a half-burnt mansion, occupied by the French, with lilac bushes still showing dark green beside the fence. And even this charred and begrimed house – which in dull weather was repulsively ugly – now in the clear, still brilliance seemed soothingly beautiful.

A French corporal in a night-cap, with his coat carelessly unbuttoned, came round the corner of the shed, a short pipe between his teeth, and approached Pierre with a friendly wink.

'What sunshine, eh, Monsieur Kirill?' (This was the name the French had given Pierre.) 'Just like spring.'

And the corporal leaned against the door and offered Pierre his pipe, though he was always offering it and Pierre always declined. 'This is the weather to be on the march ...' he began.

Pierre asked what news there was of the departure of the French, and the corporal told him that nearly all the troops were starting to leave and that instructions about prisoners were expected that day. In Pierre's shed one of the Russian soldiers – Sokolov – was dangerously ill, and Pierre reminded the corporal that something ought to be done about this soldier. The corporal replied that Pierre need not worry – they had mobile as well as permanent hospitals, and arrangements would be made for the sick, and in fact every possible contingency was provided for by the authorities.

'Besides, Monsieur Kirill, you have only to say a word to the captain, you know. Oh, he's a ... he's a man who never forgets anything. Speak to the captain when he makes his round: he will do anything for you. ...'

(The captain in question often had long chats with Pierre and showed him all sorts of favours.)

'"You see, St Thomas," he says to me t'other day, "That Kirill's got education, he talks French; he is a Russian lord who has been unfortunate but he's a proper man. He knows what's what. ... If he wants anything, let him tell me – I won't refuse him. When a person's a scholar himself, he likes a bit of education, you see, and genuine, real refined people." It is for your sake I mention it, Monsieur Kirill. That job the other day now – if it hadn't been for you things would have ended bad.'

And after chatting a little while longer the corporal went away. (The affair he had alluded to was a fight a few days before between the prisoners and the French soldiers, in which Pierre had succeeded in restraining his comrades.) Some of the prisoners had seen Pierre talking to the corporal, and they immediately came up to ask what the Frenchman had said. While Pierre was repeating what he had been told about the army leaving Moscow a thin, sallow, ragged French soldier sidled up to the door of the shed. With a quick, timid gesture he raised his fingers to his forehead by way of a salute and addressed himself to Pierre, inquiring of him whether the soldier 'Platoche', who was making a shirt for him, was in that shed.

Seven or eight days before, the French had been issued with boot-leather and linen, which they had given out to the prisoners to make up into boots and shirts for them.

'Ready, ready, me duck!' cried Karatayev, coming out with a neatly folded shirt.

On account of the warm weather and for convenience at work, Karatayev was wearing nothing but a pair of drawers and a tattered shirt as black as soot. He had tied a wisp of bast round his hair, workman-fashion, and his round face looked rounder and more good-natured than ever.

'Make a bargain and stick to it!' said he. 'I promised it for Friday, and here it is all finished,' and Platon smilingly unfolded the shirt he had made.

The Frenchman glanced round uneasily and then, as if overcoming some hesitation, quickly stripped off his uniform and put on the shirt. Under his uniform he had no shirt but a long greasy flowered-silk waistcoat next to his thin yellow body. He was evidently afraid that the prisoners looking on would laugh at him, and lost no time in thrusting his head into the shirt. None of the prisoners said a word.

'There's a good fit now!' Platon kept saying, pulling the shirt down.

The Frenchman, having pushed his head and hands through without looking up, inspected the shirt and examined the seams.

'You see, me duck, this 'ere place ain't exactly a tailor's bench, and I 'adn't no proper sewing gear; and as the saying is, without the right 'strument you can't even kill a louse,' said Platon, with one of his round smiles and obviously pleased with his own work.

'C'est bien, c'est bien, merci,' said the Frenchman. 'But there must be some of the stuff left over.'

'It'll fit better still when it sets to your body,' Platon went on, still admiring his handiwork. 'Nice and comfortable you'll be. ...'

'Merci, merci, mon vieux. ... And the pieces?' insisted the Frenchman, smiling. And taking out a note, he gave it to Karatayev. 'But let me have the pieces.'

Pierre saw that Platon did not want to understand what the Frenchman was saying, and he looked on without interfering. Karatayev thanked the Frenchmen for the money and went on admiring his own work. The Frenchman persisted in his demands for the pieces that were left and asked Pierre to translate what he said.

'What does he want with them bits?' said Karatayev. 'Fine leg-bands they'd make us. Oh well, never mind.'

And, his face suddenly crestfallen and melancholy, Karatayev took a small bundle of scraps from inside his shirt and gave it to the Frenchman without looking at him. 'Alas! Alack!' muttered Karatayev, and turned on his heel. The Frenchman looked at the linen, deliberated for a moment, then glanced inquiringly at Pierre, and, as though Pierre's eyes had told him something, blushed all at once and called in a squeaky voice:

'Here, Platoche – Platoche! You can keep them!' And handing back the odd bits he swung round and hurried away.

'There, look at that,' said Karatayev, nodding his head. 'They say they're heathens, but that one has a soul. The old folk were right: "A sweaty hand's an open hand, a dry fist's a close fist." 'Adn't a rag to 'is back, and 'e goes an' gives me this.'

Karatayev smiled thoughtfully, gazing at the bits of stuff in silence for a moment.

'But they'll come in fine for leg-bands, me boy,' he said, and went back into the shed.

12

FOUR weeks had passed since Pierre had been taken prisoner. Although the French had offered to transfer him to the officer's shed, he had stayed on in the shed where he had been put from the first, with the ordinary soldiers.

In burnt and devastated Moscow Pierre experienced almost the extreme limits of privation a man can endure; but thanks to his physical strength and good health, of which he had hardly been aware till then, and still more to the fact that these privations came upon him so gradually that it was impossible to say when they began, he bore his position not only lightly but cheerfully. And it was just at this time that he attained to the peace and content with himself for which before he had always striven in vain. He had spent long years in the search for that tranquillity of mind, that inner harmony, which had so impressed him in the men at the battle of Borodino. He had sought it in philanthropy, in Freemasonry, in the dissipations of society life, in wine, in heroic feats of self-sacrifice, in romantic love for Natasha; he had sought it by the path of intellectual reasoning –

and all these efforts and experiments had failed him. And now, without any thought on his part, he had found that peace and that inner harmony simply through the horrors of death, through privation, and through what he had seen in Karatayev. Those dreadful moments of anguish he had gone through at the executions had, as it were, washed for ever from his imagination and his memory the restless ideas and feelings that had formerly seemed so important. It did not now occur to him to cogitate about Russia, or the war, or politics, or Napoleon. He realized that all that was no business of his, that he was not called upon to pronounce on such matters and therefore could not judge. 'Russia and summer don't mix together,' he would think, repeating words of Karatayev's which he found strangely comforting. His intention of assassinating Napoleon and his calculations round the cabalistic number of the beast of the Apocalypse struck him now as incomprehensible and positively ludicrous. His indignation against his wife, and his anxiety that his name should not be smirched, now seemed not merely trivial but even amusing. What concern was it of his that somewhere or other the woman was leading the life she preferred? What did it matter to anybody – least of all to him – whether or not they found out that their prisoner was Count Bezuhov?

He often recalled now his conversation with Prince Andrei, and fully agreed with his friend, except that he interpreted Prince Andrei's idea rather differently. Prince Andrei had been wont to reflect that happiness was purely negative – but he had said so with a shade of bitterness and irony, as though he were really saying that all our cravings for positive happiness were implanted in us merely for our torment, since they could never be satisfied. But Pierre acknowledged the truth of this without any qualification. The absence of suffering, the satisfaction of elementary needs and consequent freedom in the choice of one's occupation – that is, of one's mode of living – now seemed to Pierre the sure height of human happiness. Here and now for the first time in his life Pierre fully appreciated the enjoyment of eating because he was hungry, of drinking because he was thirsty, of sleep because he was sleepy, of warmth because he was cold, of talking to a fellow creature because he felt like talking and wanted to hear a human voice. The satisfaction of one's needs – good food, cleanliness, freedom – now that he was deprived of these seemed to Pierre to constitute perfect happiness; and the choice of occupation, that is, of his manner of life, now that that choice was so restricted, seemed to him such an easy matter that he forgot that a superfluity of the comforts of life destroys all joy in gratifying one's needs, while too much liberty in choosing our occupations – liberty which in his case arose from his education, his wealth and his social position – is just what makes the choice of occupation hopelessly difficult, and destroys the very desire and possibility of having an occupation.

All Pierre's dreams were now centred on the time when he would be free; though afterwards, and to the end of his days, he thought and spoke with enthusiasm of that month of captivity, of those irrecoverable, intense, joyful sensations, and above all, of the perfect spiritual peace, the complete inner freedom, which he experienced only during that period of his life.

On the first morning of his imprisonment, when he got up early and went out of the shed at dawn, and saw the cupolas and crosses of the Novo-Dyevichy convent, dim and dark at first, saw the hoar-frost on the dusty grass, saw the Sparrow hills and the wooded banks above the winding river disappearing into the purple distance, when he felt the contact of the fresh air and heard the cawing of the jack-daws flying from Moscow across the field, and when a little later flashes of light suddenly gleamed from the east and the sun's rim floated triumphantly up from behind a cloud, and cupolas and crosses and hoar-frost and distant horizon and river began to sparkle in the glad light, Pierre knew an unaccustomed feeling of vigour and *joie de vivre* such as he had never known before.

And this feeling not only stayed with him during the whole of his imprisonment but even grew in strength as the hardships of his position increased.

This feeling of being ready for anything, of moral alertness, was still further reinforced by the high opinion his fellow-prisoners formed of him soon after his arrival in the shed. His knowledge of languages, the respect shown him by the French, the frank simplicity with which he gave away anything he was asked for (he received the allowance of three roubles a week made to officers), his physical strength, which the soldiers saw when he pushed nails into the walls of the hut with his fingers, his gentleness to his companions and his capacity – which they could not understand – for sitting stock-still, doing nothing, and thinking, made him appear to the soldiers a somewhat mysterious and superior being. The very qualities that had been a source of embarrassment if not actually prejudicial to him in the world he had previously lived in – his strength, his disdain for the amenities of life, his absent-mindedness and simplicity – here among these people gave him almost the status of a hero. And Pierre felt that their opinion placed responsibilities upon him.

13

THE French evacuation began on the night of the 6th of October: kitchens and sheds were dismantled, carts loaded up, and troops and baggage-trains moved off.

At seven in the morning a French convoy in marching trim, wearing shakos and carrying muskets, knapsacks and enormous sacks, stood in front of the sheds, and a running fire of eager French talk, interlarded with oaths, was kept up all along the line.

Inside the shed everyone was ready dressed, belted and shod, only awaiting the order to start. The sick soldier Sokolov, pale and thin, with dark shadows round his eyes, alone lay in his corner, barefoot and not dressed. His eyes – the emaciation of his face made him seem all eyes – gazed inquiringly at his comrades, who were paying no heed to him, and at regular intervals he moaned quietly. It was evidently not so much his sufferings that caused him to moan (he was ill with dysentery) as his fear and grief at being abandoned.

Pierre, with a length of rope tied round his waist for a belt, and shod in shoes Karatayev had made for him out of some strips of raw leather which a French soldier had brought to have his boots mended with, went up to the sick man and squatted on his heels beside him.

'You know, Sokolov, they are not going away altogether! They have a hospital here. Very likely you'll be better off than the rest of us,' said Pierre.

'O Lord! Oh, it'll be the death of me! O Lord!' groaned the soldier more loudly.

'I'll go and ask them straight away,' said Pierre, and getting up, he went to the door of the shed.

Just as Pierre reached the door the corporal who had offered him a pipe the day before came up with two soldiers. Both the corporal and the soldiers were in marching kit with knapsacks and shakos with chin-straps buttoned, which altered their familiar faces.

The corporal approached the door for the purpose of locking it in accordance with his orders. The prisoners had to be counted before being let out.

'Corporal, what is to become of the sick man ? ...' Pierre was beginning; but even as he spoke doubts arose in his mind whether this was the corporal he knew, or some stranger, so unlike himself did the corporal look at that moment. Moreover, just as Pierre was speaking a sharp rattle of drums was suddenly heard from both sides. The corporal frowned at Pierre's words, and uttering a meaningless oath slammed the door to. It was half-dark now in the shed; the drums beat a crisp tattoo on two sides, drowning the sick man's moans.

'Here it is! ... Here's *that* again! ...' said Pierre to himself, and an involuntary shudder ran down his spine. In the changed face of the corporal, in the sound of his voice, in the agitating, deafening din of the drums, Pierre recognized that mysterious, callous force which drove men against their will to murder their kind – that force the workings of which he had witnessed during the executions. To be afraid or to try to escape that force, to address entreaties or exhortations to those who were serving as its tools, was useless. Pierre knew this now. One could but wait and endure. He did not go near the sick man again, nor look round at him. He stood scowling in silence at the door of the shed.

When the door was opened and the prisoners, crowding against one another like a flock of sheep, squeezed into the exit, Pierre elbowed his way in front of them and went up to the very captain who was, so the corporal had assured him, ready to do anything for him. The captain was also in marching dress, and on his cold face appeared that same *it* which Pierre had recognized in the corporal's words and the roll of the drums.

'Get on, get on!' the captain was saying, frowning sternly and looking at the prisoners as they pushed past.

Pierre knew that his venture would be in vain, but still he went up to him.

'Well, what is it ?' asked the officer, scanning him coldly as though he did not recognize him.

Pierre told him about the sick man.

'He can walk, damn him!' said the captain. 'Get on, get on!' he continued, without looking at Pierre.

'No, he is dying ...' Pierre was beginning.

'Be so good ...' shouted the captain, frowning angrily.

Drrram-da-da-dam, dam-dam rattled the drums. And Pierre realized that this mysterious force had already complete possession of these men and that to say anything more now was useless.

The officers among the prisoners were separated from the soldiers and ordered to march in front. There were about thirty officers, with Pierre in their number, and some three hundred men.

These officers, who had come from other sheds, were all strangers to Pierre and much better dressed than he. They looked at him and his queer foot-gear with aloof, mistrustful eyes. Not far from Pierre walked a stout major with a bloated, sallow, irascible countenance. He was wearing a Kazan dressing-gown, belted with a towel, and evidently enjoyed the general respect of his fellow-prisoners. He kept one hand, in which he clasped a tobacco-pouch, inside the bosom of his dressing-gown, and clutched the stem of his pipe firmly with the other. Panting and puffing, this major grumbled and growled at everybody because he thought he was being pushed and that they were all hurrying when they had nowhere to hurry to, and were all wondering when there was nothing to wonder at. Another, a thin little officer, addressed remarks to everyone, speculating as to where they were being taken now, and how far they would get that day. An official in felt high boots and a commissariat uniform ran from one side to another to spy out the ruins of Moscow, making loud observations as to what had been burnt down, and what this or that part of the city was that they could see. A third officer, of Polish extraction by his accent, disputed with the commissariat official, arguing that he was mistaken in his identification of the various quarters of Moscow.

'What are you quarrelling about?' said the major angrily. 'What does it matter whether it's St Nicolai or St Vlas, it's all one. You can see 'tis all burnt down, and there's an end of it. ... What are you shoving for? Isn't the road wide enough?' he demanded angrily of a man behind him who was not pushing him at all.

'Oh, I say! Look what they have done!' was heard on all sides as the prisoners gazed at the charred ruins. 'All beyond the river there, and Zubovo, and in the Kremlin ... see, half of it's gone! I told you the whole quarter beyond the river went, and so it has.'

'Well, you know it's burnt down, so what's the point of talking about it?' said the major.

As they passed near a church in the Khamovniky area (one of the few unscathed quarters of Moscow) the whole mass of prisoners suddenly swerved to one side, and exclamations of horror and aversion were heard.

'Oh, the swine!'

'What heathens!'

'Yes, it's a dead man, a dead man all right. ... And they've smeared his face with something!'

Pierre, too, drew near the church where the object that had called forth these exclamations was, and he vaguely discerned a figure leaning against the palings round the church. From the words of his comrades, who saw better than he did, he learned that this was the dead body of a man, propped on its feet against the fence, with its face dirtied with lamp-black.

'Move on there! What the devil. ... Get on! Thirty thousand devils! ...' they heard the escort swearing, and the French soldiers, with renewed vindictiveness, used the flat of their swords to drive on the prisoners who had crowded to stare at the dead man.

14

THROUGH the by-ways and alleys of the Khamovniky quarter the prisoners marched alone with their guards, followed by the carts and baggage-wagons belonging to the escort; but as they emerged near the provision stores they found themselves in the midst of a huge and closely packed train of artillery mixed up with a number of private vehicles.

At the bridge they all halted, waiting for those in front to cross. From the bridge the prisoners had a view of endless lines of moving baggage-trains before and behind. To the right, where the Kaluga road twisted round by the Neskuchny Gardens, troops and carts dragged never-ending into the distance. These were the troops of Beauharnais's corps which had set off before any of the others. Behind, along the quays and across Kamenny bridge, stretched the troops and transport commanded by Ney.

Davoust's troops, in whose charge were the prisoners, were crossing the Crimean ford and some were already debouching on to the Kaluga road. But the baggage-trains were so long that the vanguard of Ney's army was already emerging from Great Ordynka before the last of Beauharnais's wagons had got on to the Kaluga road out of Moscow.

After crossing the Crimean ford the prisoners moved a few steps at a time and halted, then moved forward again, and from all sides vehicles and men pressed up closer and closer. When they had advanced the few hundred paces that separated the bridge from the Kaluga road, taking over an hour to do so, and got as far as the square where the streets of the Transmoskva ward and the Kaluga road converge, the prisoners stopped, jammed together, and were kept standing for some hours at the cross-roads. From all sides, like the roar of the sea, came an unceasing sound of the rumble of wheels, the tramp of feet, and continuous angry shouting and abuse. Pierre stood flattened up against the wall of a charred house, listening to the din, which in his imagination was one with the roll of drums.

To have a better view several of the officer-prisoners climbed on to the wall of the burned house against which Pierre was leaning.

'What a jam! Just look at the crowds! ... They've even loaded goods on to the cannon! And see over there – those are furs! ...' they exclaimed. 'Oh look what the vermin have been looting! Look what that one has got behind there, in the cart. ... It's – yes, it's the mount from an icon, by heaven! ... Those must be Germans! ... And there's a peasant of ours, by Jove! ... Oh, the scum! See how that fellow's loaded himself up – he can hardly walk! Good Lord, they've even grabbed those chaises! ... See that man there perched on the trunks. Saints alive! they've started fighting! ...

'That's right, fetch him one on the nose – right on the nose! At this rate we shan't get by before nightfall. Look – I say, look! Those must be Napoleon's own! See what horses – and the monograms with a crown! It's like a portable house. ... That fellow's dropped his sack and hasn't noticed. Fighting again. ... A woman with a baby, and not bad-looking either. Yes, I dare say, that's the way they'll let you through, my lass! ... Look, there's no end to it. Russian wenches, I do declare, so they are! In carriages – see how comfortably they've settled themselves!'

Again, as at the church in Khamovniky, a wave of general curiosity bore all the prisoners forward on to the road, and Pierre, thanks to his height, saw over the heads of the others what it was that so attracted the prisoners' interest. In three carriages caught among the ammunition-caissons rode a party of women with rouged faces and decked out in glaring colours. They were squeezed closely together, shouting something in shrill voices.

From the moment when Pierre had recognized the manifestation of that mysterious force nothing had seemed to him strange or terrible; neither the corpse with its face smeared for a jest with lampblack, nor these women hurrying away, nor the burnt ruins of Moscow. All that he, Pierre, now saw hardly made any impression on him – as though his soul, preparing itself for a hard struggle, was refusing to receive any impressions that might weaken it.

The carriages with the women drove by. Behind them followed more carts, soldiers, baggage-wagons, soldiers, carriages, soldiers, caissons, more soldiers, and here and there women.

Pierre could not make out individuals separately: he saw only their general movement.

All these people and horses seemed as if they were impelled forward by some invisible power. During the hour Pierre spent watching them they all came pouring from the different streets with one and the same desire, to get along as quickly as possible; all alike, they jostled one another, became angry and started fighting. White teeth flashed, brows scowled, the same oaths were bandied to and fro, and every face bore the same look of reckless determination and cold inhumanity that had struck Pierre that morning in the corporal's expression when the drums were beating.

It was not until towards nightfall that the officer commanding the escort rallied his men and with shouting and angry argument forced his way in among the baggage-trains; and the prisoners, hemmed in on all sides, emerged on to the Kaluga road.

They proceeded very rapidly, not stopping to rest, and halted only when the sun began to set. The baggage-carts drew up close to one another, and the men began preparing for the night. Everyone seemed sulky and bad-tempered. Cursing, rancorous shouts and blows continued until late into the night. A private carriage following the prisoners' guard drove into one of the carts and ran a shaft through it. Several soldiers rushed across, some to flog the carriage-horses about the head as they pushed them aside, others to fight among themselves, and Pierre saw a German receive a severe scalp wound from a short sabre.

It seemed that all these men, now that they had halted amid fields in the chill dusk of the autumn evening, were experiencing one and the same disagreeable feeling of reaction from the hurry and eagerness to push on that had possessed them at the start. It was as if they realized, now that they had come to a stop, that they did not yet know where they were going, and that much misery and hardship lay in store for them on the journey.

During this halt the soldiers in charge of the prisoners treated them more brutally even than at the outset. It was here that the prisoners for the first time received horse-flesh for their meat ration.

From the officers down to the lowest ranks all displayed a sort of personal spite against every one of the prisoners, in surprising contrast to their former friendliness.

This spite increased still more when the roll was called and it was found that in the bustle of leaving Moscow one Russian soldier, pretending to be ill with colic, had managed to get away. Pierre saw a Frenchman beat a Russian soldier unmercifully for straying too far from the road, and heard his friend the captain reprimand and threaten to court-martial a non-commissioned officer for the escape of the Russian. To the non-commissioned officer's excuse that the prisoner was ill and could not walk the officer replied that their orders were to shoot those who lagged behind. Pierre felt that that blind force which had trampled over him during the executions, and which he had not been conscious of during his imprisonment, again had him in its clutches. He was filled with dread; but he felt too that the harder that fatal force strove to crush him the more did his own individual vitality assert itself in his soul.

Pierre ate his supper of rye-flour soup with horse-flesh, and chatted with his comrades.

Neither Pierre nor any of his companions spoke of what they had seen in Moscow, or of the roughness of their treatment at the hands of the French, or of the order to shoot stragglers which had been announced to them. As though to counteract the worsening of their position they were all particularly lively and gay. They reminisced, they talked of comical incidents they had seen during the march, and avoided any reference to their present plight.

The sun had set long since. Here and there a star flashed bright in the sky. The rising full moon spread a red glow along the horizon like the glare from a fire, and soon the vast red ball hung swaying strangely in the grey haze. The sky was growing lighter. The evening was over but night had not yet begun. Pierre got up and leaving his new companions walked between the camp-fires to the other side of the road, where he had been told the common prisoners were camping. He wanted to talk to them. On the way he was stopped by a French sentinel, who ordered him back.

Pierre returned, not to his companions by the camp-fire but to an unharnessed wagon where there was nobody. Tucking his legs under him and dropping his head, he sat down on the cold ground against a wheel of the wagon, and sat there a long while without moving, deep in thought. Over an hour went by. No one disturbed Pierre. Suddenly he burst into a burly peal of jovial laughter, so loud that men looked round on every side in astonishment at this odd and plainly solitary hilarity.

'Ha-ha-ha!' laughed Pierre. And he said aloud to himself: 'The soldier did not let me pass. They took me and shut me up They keep me prisoner. What "me"? Me? Me – my immortal soul! Ha-ha-ha! Ha-ha-ha! ...' he laughed with the tears starting to his eyes.

Someone got up and came to see what this queer big fellow was laughing at all by himself. Pierre stopped laughing, scrambled o his feet, walked away from the inquisitive intruder and looked about him.

The immense, endless bivouac which shortly before had hummed with the crackling of camp-fires and the voices of many men was now quiet; the red camp-fires paled and died down. High overhead in the luminous sky hung the full moon. Forests and fields beyond the confines of the camp, unseen before, now stretched visible in the distance. And still farther beyond those forests and fields the bright, quivering, limitless distance lured the eye into its depths. Pierre glanced up at the sky and the stars twinkling remote and far-away. 'And all that is mine, all that is in me, and all that is *me*,' thought Pierre. 'And they took all that and shut it up in a shed barricaded with planks!' He smiled and went to lie down and sleep beside his companions.

15

EARLY in October Napoleon sent another envoy to Kutuzov with overtures for peace and a letter falsely professing to come from Moscow, though in fact Napoleon was not far from Kutuzov on the old Kaluga road. Kutuzov replied to this letter as he had done to the previous one brought by Lauriston: he said that there could be no question of peace.

Soon after this a report was received from Dorohov's guerrilla squad operating to the left of Tarutino that French troops had been seen at Fominsk, that these troops belonged to Broussier's division, and that that division being separated from the rest of the French army might easily be destroyed. Soldiers and officers again clamoured for action. Generals on the Staff, elated by the easy victory at Tarutino, urged Kutuzov to act upon Dorohov's suggestion. Kutuzov did not consider any move necessary. The result, inevitably, was a compromise: a small detachment was sent to Fominsk to attack Broussier.

By a strange coincidence this operation – which turned out to be a most difficult and important one – was entrusted to Dokhturov, that same modest little Dokhturov whom no one has ever described to us as elaborating plans of campaign, rushing about at the head of regiments, showering crosses on batteries, and so on; who was thought to be and was spoken of as lacking decision and discernment – but nevertheless that same Dokhturov whom we always find in command, all through the Russo-French wars, from Austerlitz to the year 1813, wherever the position was most difficult. At Austerlitz he was the last to leave the Augest dam, rallying the regiments, saving what he could when all was rout and ruin and not a single general left in the rearguard. Ill with fever, he marches with twenty thousand men to Smolensk to defend the town against the whole of Napoleon's army. At Smolensk no sooner had he dozed off by the Malahov gate in a paroxysm of fever than he was roused by the roar of cannon bombarding the city – and Smolensk held out all day long. In the battle of Borodino when Bagration was killed and nine-tenths of the men of our left flank had fallen and the full force of the French artillery was directed against it, no other than the hesitating, undiscerning Dokhturov is dispatched there when Kutuzov hastens to repair his blunder in first sending someone else. And off goes the quiet little Dokhturov, and Borodino became the greatest glory of the Russian arms. Many are the heroes whose praises have been sung to us in verse and prose, but of Dokhturov hardly a word.

It is Dokhturov again who is sent to Fominsk, and from there to Malo-Yaroslavets, the scene of the last battle fought with the French and where the disintegration of the French army obviously began. And, again, accounts of this period of the campaign tell of many a genius and hero, but of Dokhturov nothing, or very little – and that half-heartedly – is said. This very silence about Dokhturov is the clearest testimony to his merit.

It is natural for a man who does not understand the workings of a machine to imagine that the most important part of the mechanism is the shaving which has fallen in by accident and is seen tossing about and interfering with its action. Anyone who does not understand the construction of the machine cannot conceive that it is not the shaving, which merely gets in the way and does damage, but the small connecting cogwheel, noiselessly revolving, that is one of the most essential parts of the mechanism.

On the 10th of October, the same day on which Dokhturov had gone half-way to Fominsk and stopped at the village of Aristovo, in readiness faithfully to carry out the orders given him, the entire French army, its convulsive jerking having brought it as far as Murat's position, apparently for the purpose of giving battle, abruptly, without any reason, swerved off to the left on to the new Kaluga highway and began marching into Fominsk, where until then only Broussier had been. Dokhturov at this time had under his command, besides Dorohov's guerillas, the two small detachments of Figner and Seslavin.

On the evening of October the 11th Seslavin came to the Aristovo headquarters with a captured French guardsman. The prisoner said that the troops which had that day entered Fominsk were the vanguard of the whole army, that Napoleon was with them and the whole army had marched out of Moscow four days previously. That same evening a house-serf, who had come from Borovsk, brought word that he had seen an immense mass of soldiery entering the town. Some Cossacks of Dokhturov's detachment reported having sighted the French Guards marching along the road to Borovsk. From all these reports it was evident that where they had expected to meet a single division there was now the entire French force marching from Moscow in an unexpected direction – along the old Kaluga highway. Dokhturov was unwilling to take any action as it was not clear to him now where his duty lay. His orders had been to attack Fominsk. But then only Broussier had been there, and now there was the whole French army. Yermolov wanted to act on his own judgement, but Dokhturov insisted that he must have instructions from his Serene Highness, Kutuzov. It was decided to send a dispatch to the Staff.

For this mission a capable officer, Bolhovitinov, was chosen, who, in addition to delivering a written report, was to explain the whole affair by word of mouth. Towards midnight Bolhovitinov, having received the dispatch and his verbal instructions, galloped off to Headquarters, accompanied by a Cossack with spare horses.

16

THE autumn night was warm and dark. Rain had been falling for the last four days. Changing horses twice and galloping twenty miles in an hour and a half over a sticky muddy road, Bolhovitinov reached Letashovka between one and two in the morning. Dismounting at a cottage, on the wattle fence of which hung a sign-board 'General Staff', and throwing down the reins, he entered the dark passage.

'The general on duty, instantly! It's very important!' he cried to someone who started up, wheezing in the darkness of the passage.

'His Honour has been very unwell since last evening, he hasn't slept for two nights,' pleaded the orderly in a whisper. 'Better wake the captain first.'

'This is most urgent, I tell you, from General Dokhturov,' said Bolhovitinov, groping his way through an open door behind the orderly who had gone in and was waking someone.

'Your Honour, your Honour! A courier.'

'What? What's that? From whom?' asked a sleepy voice.

'From Dokhturov and from Alexei Petrovich. Napoleon is at Fominsk,' said Bolhovitinov, unable to see the speaker in the dark but surmising by the sound of the voice that it was not Konovnitsyn.

The man who had been roused yawned and stretched.

'I don't like waking him,' he said, fumbling for something. 'He's a very sick man. And this may be only a rumour.'

'Here is the dispatch,' said Bolhovitinov. 'My orders are to deliver it at once to the general on duty.'

'Wait till I strike a light. You damned rascal, where is it you always hide things?' said the voice of the officer who was stretching himself, to the orderly. (The speaker was Shcherbinin, Konovnitsyn's adjutant.) 'I've found it, I've found it!' he added.

The orderly was striking a light. Shcherbinin was feeling round the candlestick.

'Oh, the swine!' said he with disgust.

By the light of the sparks Bolhovitinov caught a glimpse of Shcherbinin's youthful face as he held the candle, and, in the front corner of the room, of another man still asleep. This was Konovnitsyn.

When the flame of the sulphur splinters kindled by the tinder flared up, first blue and then red, Shcherbinin lighted a tallow candle – the cockroaches that had been gnawing it scurried from the candle-stick – and looked at the messenger. Bolhovitinov was bespattered all over with mud and in wiping his face with his sleeve had daubed it also.

'Where did the report come from?' inquired Shcherbinin, taking the envelope.

'The news is trustworthy enough,' said Bolhovitinov. 'Prisoners and Cossacks and spies all tell the same story.'

'Well, there's no help for it, we shall have to wake him,' said Shcherbinin, getting up and going to the sleeping man who wore a nightcap and was wrapped in a military greatcoat. 'Piotr Petrovich!' he said. Konovnitsyn did not stir. 'Wanted at Headquarters!' he said with a smile, knowing those words would be sure to rouse him.

And the head in the night-cap was, in fact, lifted immediately. On Konovnitsyn's handsome, resolute face, with cheeks flushed by fever, there still lingered for an instant a far-away, dreamy expression remote from reality, but he gave a sudden start and his face assumed its usual quiet firm look.

'Well, what is it? From whom?' he asked at once but with no haste, blinking at the light.

As he listened to what the officer had to tell him, Konovnitsyn broke the seal and read the dispatch. Hardly had he done so before he lowered his legs in their worsted stockings to the earth floor and began putting on his boots. Then he pulled off the night-cap and, running the comb through the locks on his temples, donned his forage-cap.

'Did you get here quickly? Let us go to his Serene Highness.'

Konovnitsyn had realized directly that the news brought was of great importance and there was no time to lose. As to whether it was good news or bad, he had no opinion and did not even put the question to himself. That did not interest him. He regarded the whole business of the war not with his intellect nor with his reason but with something else. In his heart he had a deep, unexpressed conviction that all would be well; but that one must not trust to this, and still less speak about it, but must simply do one's duty. And this he did, giving all his energies to it.

Piotr Petrovich Konovnitsyn, like Dokhturov, seems to have been included merely as a matter of form in the list of so-called heroes of 1812 – the Barclays, Raevskys, Yermolovs, Platovs and Milorado-viches. Like Dokhturov he had the reputation of being a man of very limited ability and knowledge; and again, like Dokhturov, Konov-nitsyn never drew up plans of campaign but was always to be found where the situation was most critical. Ever since he had been ap-pointed general on duty he had slept with his door open, insisting that he should be roused whenever any courier arrived. In battle he was always under fire, so that Kutuzov even chided him about it and was afraid to send him to the front; and like Dokhturov, Konovnitsyn was one of those inconspicuous cogwheels which, without chatter or noise, constitute the most essential part of the machine.

Emerging from the hut into the damp dark night, Konovnitsyn frowned – partly because the pain in his head was worse and partly from the disagreeable thought that occurred to him of the stir this news would make in the nest of all the bigwigs on the Staff, especially Bennigsen, who ever since Tarutino had been at daggers drawn with Kutuzov. The suggestions they would make, the quarrelling there would be, the orders and counter-orders! And the presentiment was not a pleasant one, though he knew there was no getting round the fact.

And, indeed, Toll, to whom he went to communicate the news, immediately began to expound his ideas to the general who shared his quarters, until Konovnitsyn, after listening in weary silence, re-minded him that they must go to his Serene Highness.

17

KUTUZOV, like all old people, did not sleep much at night. In the daytime he would often drop off unexpectedly into a doze; but at night he lay on his bed without undressing, and generally remained awake thinking.

He was lying on his bed like that now, leaning his large, heavy, disfigured head on his plump hand and meditating, his one eye wide open staring into the darkness.

Since Bennigsen, who was in correspondence with the Emperor and had more influence than all the rest of the Staff, had taken to avoiding him, Kutuzov was more at ease on the score of not finding himself obliged to lead his men into useless aggressive actions. The lesson of Tarutino and the day before the battle, a memory that rankled in Kutuzov's mind, must, he thought, have some effect on others too.

'They must see,' he thought, 'that we can only lose by taking the offensive. Patience and time are my two valiant allies!' He knew the apple was better not picked while it was still green. It would fall of itself when ripe, but if you pick it green you spoil the apple, and the tree, and set your teeth on edge. Like an experienced huntsman he knew the beast was wounded – wounded as only the whole might of Russia could wound it. But was the hurt mortal? That was a point not yet decided. The fact that Lauriston and Barthélemy had been sent to him, and the reports of the guerrillas, made Kutuzov almost sure that the wound was a deadly one. But further proofs were wanted: it was necessary to wait.

'They would like to run and look at the damage they have done. Wait a bit, and you'll see. This everlasting talk of manoeuvres, of attacks!' thought he. 'What for? Only to gain distinction for themselves! As if fighting were some sort of jolly exercise! They are like children from whom there's no getting a sensible account of what has happened because they all want to show how well they can fight. But that's not the point now.

'And what ingenious manoeuvres all these fellows propose to me! They think that when they have thought of one or two contingencies' (he had in mind the general plan sent him from Petersburg) 'they have exhausted the list. But there's no end to them.'

The unanswered question whether the wound inflicted at Borodino was mortal or not had been hanging about over Kutuzov's head for a whole month. On the one hand the French had occupied Moscow. On the other, Kutuzov felt convinced in every fibre of his being that the terrible blow into which he and the whole Russian people had put the last ounce of their strength must have been mortal. But in any case proofs were needed, and he had been waiting for them a month now, and the longer he waited the more impatient he became. Lying on his bed through those sleepless nights of his, he did the very thing the younger generals did – the very thing he found fault with them for doing. He imagined all sorts of possible contingencies, just like the younger men but with this difference, that he based nothing on them and saw them, not in twos or threes but in thousands. The more he conjectured, the more numerous the hypotheses that presented themselves. He worked out every kind of diversion the Napoleonic army might make, acting as a whole or in sections – against Petersburg, against himself, or to outflank him. He thought too of the possibility (which he feared most of all) that Napoleon might fight him with his own weapon – might settle down in Moscow and wait for him to move. Kutuzov even pictured Napoleon's army turning back via Medyn and Yukhnov; but the one thing he could not foresee was the very thing that happened – the insane, convulsive doubling to and fro of Napoleon's army during the first eleven days of its march from Moscow: the stampede which rendered possible what Kutuzov had not till then dared even to think of – namely, the complete annihilation of the French. Dorohov's report about Broussier's division, the guerrillas' accounts of the miseries of Napoleon's army, rumours of preparations for evacuating Moscow – all confirmed the presumption that the French army was worsted and about to take to its heels. But all this was only supposition, which appealed to the younger men but not to Kutuzov. With his sixty years' experience he knew how much dependence to put upon hearsay, knew how apt people are when they want anything to arrange all the evidence so that it appears to confirm what they desire, and how ready they are in such circumstances to overlook anything that makes for the contrary. And the more Kutuzov hoped, the less he allowed himself to believe that it might be so. This question engaged all the energies of his mind. All else was for him merely the ordinary routine of life. To such customary routine belonged his conversations with the Staff, the letters he wrote from Tarutino to Madame de Staël, the novels he read, the distribution of awards, his correspondence with Petersburg, and so on. But the destruction of the French, which he alone foresaw, was his heart's one desire.

On the night of the 11th of October he lay leaning on his arm and thinking of that.

There was a stir in the next room and he heard the steps of Toll, Konovnitsyn and Bolhovitinov.

'Eh, who's there? Come in, come in! Anything new?' the field-marshal called to them.

While a footman was lighting a candle Toll related the gist of the news.

'Who brought it?' asked Kutuzov with a face that impressed Toll when the candle was lighted by its cold severity.

'There can be no doubt about it, your Highness.'

'Call him in, call him here!'

Kutuzov sat up with one leg hanging down from the bed and his big paunch resting against the other leg which was bent under him. He screwed up his sound eye the better to scan the messenger, as though he hoped to read in his features the answer to what was occupying him.

'Speak up, tell me, my friend,' he said to Bolhovitinov in his low, aged voice, pulling the shirt together that gaped open over his chest. 'Come here, come closer. What is this news you have brought me? Eh? That Napoleon has left Moscow? Are you sure? Eh?'

Bolhovitinov gave him a detailed account from the beginning of all that had been committed to him.

'Out with it, make haste! Don't keep me in suspense,' Kutuzov interrupted him.

Bolhovitinov told the whole story and was then silent, awaiting instructions. Toll was about to speak but Kutuzov checked him. He tried to say something but all at once his face began to work and pucker up; waving his arm at Toll, he turned to the opposite corner of the hut which was dark with the icons hanging there.

'O Lord, my Creator, Thou hast heard our prayer ...' he said in a trembling voice, clasping his hands. 'Russia is saved! I thank Thee, O Lord!' And he wept.

18

FROM the time he received the news of the French leaving Moscow, to the end of the campaign, all Kutuzov's activity was directed exclusively towards restraining his troops, by the exercise of authority, by guile, by entreaty, from useless attacks, manoeuvres or encounters with the doomed enemy. Dokhturov goes to Malo-Yaroslavets, but Kutuzov lingers with the main army and gives orders for the evacuation of Kaluga – a retreat beyond that town seeming to him quite possible.

Kutuzov falls back on all sides, but the enemy, without waiting for him to retire, flees in the opposite direction.

Napoleon's historians describe to us his skilful manoeuvres at Tarutino and Malo-Yaroslavets, and make conjectures as to what would have happened had Napoleon managed to penetrate into the rich provinces of the south.

But not to speak of the fact that nothing hindered Napoleon from marching into these southern provinces (since the Russian army left the road open) the historians forget that nothing could have saved Napoleon's army, for it already carried within itself the germs of inevitable ruin. How could that army – which had found abundant supplies in Moscow and had trampled them underfoot instead of conserving them, and on arriving at Smolensk had looted instead of storing provisions – how could that army have recovered in the province of Kaluga, where the inhabitants were of the same stock as the Russians of Moscow, and where fire had the same property of consuming whatever they set fire to?

That army could not have retrieved itself anywhere. After Borodino and the sacking of Moscow it was to bear within itself, as it were, the chemical elements of dissolution.

The men of what had once been an army fled with their leaders, not knowing whither they went, Napoleon and every soldier with him concerned only to extricate themselves as quickly as might be from the hopeless position of which they were all, if but dimly, aware.

So it came about that at the council at Malo-Yaroslavets when the French generals, affecting to be conferring together, expressed their various views, the last opinion of all, uttered by General Mouton, a blunt soldier, who said what everyone was thinking – that the only course was to get away as quickly as possible – closed all mouths; and no one, not even Napoleon, could say anything against a truth which all recognized.

But though everybody knew it was necessary to get away, there still remained the shame of confessing that they must take to flight. Some external shock was needed to overcome that shame, and that shock came in due time. It was 'le Hourra de l'Empereur', as the French called it.

On the day after the council Napoleon rode out early in the morning amid the lines of his army, with a suite of marshals and an escort, on the pretext of inspecting the troops and the scene of battle, past and to come. A party of Cossacks on the prowl for booty fell in with the Emperor and very nearly captured him. What saved Napoleon from the Cossacks on this occasion was the very thing that was proving the downfall of the French: the booty, which here as at Tarutino, tempted the Cossacks to go after plunder and let the enemy slip. Disregarding Napoleon, they flung themselves on the spoils, and Napoleon succeeded in getting away.

With matters at such a pass that the 'children of the Don' might actually have snatched the Emperor himself in the midst of his army, it was clear that there was nothing else for it but to fly with all possible haste by the nearest familiar road. Napoleon, forty and paunchy, and not so nimble and daring as of old, accepted the intimation; and under the influence of the fright the Cossacks had given him he at once agreed with Mouton and issued the order – as the historians tell us – to retreat along the Smolensk road.

The fact that Napoleon agreed with Mouton and that the army retreated does not prove that Napoleon instigated the retreat but that the forces influencing the whole army to take to the Mozhaisk (the Smolensk) road were simultaneously exerting their influence on Napoleon too.

19

WHEN a man finds himself in motion he always devises some purpose for his bodily exertion. To be able to walk hundreds of miles a man must believe that something good awaits him at the end of those hundreds of miles. He needs the prospect of a promised land to give him the strength to keep on.

When the French invaded Russia their promised land was Moscow; when they were retreating it was their mother country. But their mother country was too far off, and a man who has six or seven hundred miles to walk before reaching his destination must be able to put his final goal out of his mind and say to himself that he will 'do thirty miles today and then spend the night somewhere'; and during this first stage of the journey that resting-place for the night eclipses the image of his ultimate goal and absorbs all his hopes and desires. And the instinctive impulses manifest in the individual are always magnified in a crowd.

For the French, marching back along the old Smolensk road the final goal – their native land – was too remote, and their immediate objective on which all their desires and hopes, enormously intensified in the mass, were concentrated, was Smolensk. It was not that they expected plentiful supplies and reinforcements awaiting them in Smolensk, nor that they were told any such thing (on the contrary, the higher ranks of the army and Napoleon himself knew that provisions were scant there), but because this alone could give them the strength to keep on and endure their present hardships. So both those who knew better, and those who did not, alike deceived themselves and struggled on to Smolensk as to a promised land.

Once out on the high road the French fled with surprising energy and unheard-of rapidity towards the goal they had fixed on. Besides the common impulse which united the French hosts into one whole and imparted a certain momentum there was something else which held them together – their great numbers. As with the law of gravity in physics, the enormous mass of the retreating army attracted the individual human atoms to itself. In their hundreds of thousands they moved like a solid empire.

Every man among them had but one longing – to give himself up and be taken prisoner, to escape from all this horror and misery. But on the one hand the driving force of the common impulse towards their goal, Smolensk, carried each one in the same direction; on the other hand, an army corps could not surrender to a company, and though the French availed themselves of every convenient opportunity to stray off and surrender on the smallest decent pretext such pretexts did not always occur. Their very numbers and the compact swiftness with which they moved ruled out that possibility and made it not only difficult but out of the question for the Russians to arrest the progress on which the entire energies of the French mass were bent. Beyond a certain limit no mechanical disruption of the body could accelerate the process of decomposition.

A lump of snow cannot be melted instantaneously. There is a certain measure of time in less than which no amount of heat can thaw the snow. On the contrary, the greater the heat the harder the remaining snow becomes.

Of the Russian generals Kutuzov was the only one to understand this. When the retreat of the French army took the definite shape of flight along the Smolensk road, what Konovnitsyn had foreseen on the night of the 11th of October began to come to pass. The entire high command of the Russian army were fired with a desire to distinguish themselves, to cut off, to seize, to capture, to overthrow the French, and all clamoured for action.

Kutuzov alone employed all his powers (and the powers of any commander-in-chief are very inconsiderable) to prevent an attack.

He could not tell them what we can say now: 'Why fight, why

block the road, losing our own men and inhumanly slaughtering poor unfortunate wretches? What is the point of that when from Moscow to Viazma, without battle, a third of their army melted away of itself?' Instead, drawing from his aged wisdom what they could understand, he reminded them of the golden bridge (of self-destruction), and they mocked him and slandered him, and swooped cock-a-hoop and hacked at the dying beast.

In the neighbourhood of Viazma, Yermolov, Miloradovich, Platov and others, finding themselves near the French, could not resist their desire to cut off and break up two French corps. In sending to inform Kutuzov of their intention, they enclosed a blank sheet of paper in the envelope instead of the dispatch.

And in spite of all Kutuzov's efforts to restrain the troops our men assailed the French and tried to bar the road. Infantry regiments, we are told, advanced to the attack with music and beating of drums, and slew and were slain in thousands.

But as for cutting off retreat – no one was cut off and no one was turned aside. And the French army, closing its ranks tighter at the danger, continued its fatal path to Smolensk, steadily melting away as it went.

PART THREE

I

THE battle of Borodino with the occupation of Moscow that followed and the flight of the French, without any more engagements, is one of the most instructive phenomena in history.

All historians are agreed that the external activity of states and peoples in their clashes with one another finds expression in wars; that the political power of states and peoples increases or diminishes in proportion to success or defeat in war.

Strange as we may find historical accounts of how some king or emperor, having quarrelled with some other emperor or king, levies an army, fights his enemy's army, gains a victory, killing three, five or ten thousand men, and consequently subjugates a whole dominion of several million souls; and unintelligible as it may be why the defeat of an army – a hundredth part of a nation's strength – should oblige that whole nation to submit, yet all the facts of history (so far as we know history) confirm the truth of the statement that the greater or lesser success of one army against another is the cause, or at least a material indication, of an increase or decrease in the power of that nation. An army gains a victory, and at once the rights of the conquering nation are increased to the detriment of the defeated. An army suffers defeat, and at once a people loses its rights in proportion to the severity of the reverse, and if its army is completely routed the nation is reduced to complete subjection.

So (according to history) it has been from the most ancient times, and up to our own day. All Napoleon's wars serve to confirm this rule. In proportion to the defeat of the Austrian army Austria is shorn of her rights, and the rights and might of France increase. The victories of the French at Jena and Auerstädt destroy the independent existence of Prussia.

But suddenly, in 1812, the French gain a victory near Moscow. Moscow is taken, and after that, with no more battles, it is not Russia that ceases to exist but the French army of six hundred thousand, and then Napoleonic France itself. To stretch the facts to fit the rules of history – to say that the Russians remained in possession of the field of Borodino, or that after Napoleon's army left Moscow it was cut up in a series of pitched battles – is impossible.

After the French victory at Borodino there was no general engagement, nor even a skirmish of any great importance, yet the French army ceased to exist. What does this signify? If such a thing had occurred in the history of China, we might say that it was not an historical reality (the favourite loophole of historians when facts do not fit theories); if it were a question of some brief conflict in which only a small number of troops took part, we might treat it as an exception to the general rule; but all this took place before the eyes of our fathers, for whom it was a matter of the life or death of their country, and the war was the most momentous of all known wars. ...

That period of the campaign of 1812, from Borodino to the final expulsion of the French, proved that the winning of a battle does not necessarily lead to conquest and may not even be a sure promise of conquest; it proved that the force which decides the fate of peoples lies not in the conquerors, nor even in armies and battles, but in something else.

French historians, describing the condition of the French forces before they marched out of Moscow, assert that everything was in good order in the *Grande Armée*, except the cavalry, the artillery and the transport – there being no forage for the horses and cattle. That was a misfortune no one could remedy, for the peasants of the surrounding country burnt their hay rather than let the French have it.

Victory did not bring forth its usual results because Tom, Dick and Harry, who were by no means burdened with heroic sentiment – after the French had evacuated Moscow they drove in in their carts to pillage the city – and the whole vast multitude of others like them refused to bring their hay to Moscow, in spite of the high prices offered them, but burnt it instead.

Let us imagine two men who have come out to fight a duel with swords in accordance with all the rules of the art of fencing. The parrying has continued for some time. Suddenly one of the combatants, aware that he has been wounded and realizing that the affair is no joke but that his life is at stake, throws down his sword and seizing the first cudgel that comes handy begins to brandish it. Then let us imagine that the combatant who thus so sensibly employed the best and simplest means for his purpose was at the same time influenced by traditions of chivalry and, wanting to conceal the facts of the case, insisted afterwards that he won his victory with the sword according to all the rules of the art of fencing. How confusing and unintelligible we should find the story of such a duel!

The fencer who demanded a contest in accordance with the rules of fencing is the French army; his opponent who threw away his sword and snatched up a club did like the Russian people; those who try to give an account of the issue consistent with the rules of fencing are the historians who have described the event.

After the burning of Smolensk a war began which did not fit any of the old traditions of warfare. The burning of towns and villages, the withdrawal after every battle, the blow dealt at Borodino, followed by another retreat, the burning of Moscow, the hunting down of marauders, the seizing of provision-trains, guerrilla fighting – all this was a departure from the rules.

Napoleon was conscious of it, and from the time he took up the correct attitude of the fencer in Moscow and instead of his opponent's rapier saw a cudgel raised against him he never ceased complaining to Kutuzov and to the Emperor Alexander that the war was being conducted contrary to all the rules – as if there were any rules for killing people. In spite of the complaints of the French that the rules were not being kept to, in spite of the fact that to some highly placed Russians it seemed rather disgraceful to fight with a club – they would have liked to take up the correct position *en quarte* or *en tierce* and make an adroit thrust *en prime*, and so on – the cudgel of the people's war was lifted with all its menacing and majestic might, and, caring nothing for good taste and procedure, with dull-witted simplicity but sound judgement it rose and fell, making no distinctions, and belaboured the French until the whole army of invaders had perished.

And it is well for the people who, unlike the French in 1813, will not salute their magnanimous conqueror according to all the rules of the art, gracefully and ceremoniously presenting him with the hilt of their swords. Happy the people who in the moment of trial, without stopping to ask what rules others have observed in similar cases, simply and nimbly pick up the first cudgel to hand and deal blow after blow until the resentment and revenge in their souls give way to contempt and compassion.

2

ONE of the most tangible and advantageous departures from the so-called rules of warfare is the action of scattered groups against a body of men obliged to operate in a dense mass. This sort of independent action is always seen in wars which assume a national character. In fighting of this kind, instead of combining into a crowd to attack a crowd, men divide, attack separately and at once run away when threatened by superior forces, only to resume the offensive at the first favourable opportunity. Such were the methods of the guerrillas in Spain, of the mountain tribes in the Caucasus and of the Russians in 1812.

People have called this kind of war 'guerrilla warfare' and assumed that by giving it this label they have explained its meaning. Incidentally, this sort of warfare not only fails to come under any rules but is in direct contradiction to a well-known law of tactics which is accepted as infallible. This law lays down that the attacking party shall concentrate his forces in order to be stronger than his adversary at the moment battle is joined.

Guerrilla warfare (always successful, as history testifies) operates in flat contradiction to this rule.

The paradox arises from the fact that military science assumes the strength of an army to be identical with its numerical proportions. Military science says, the greater the numbers the greater the strength. *Les gros bataillons ont toujours raison* – God is on the side of the big battalions.

For military science to make this assertion is like defining momentum in mechanics by reference to the mass only. It is like saying that the momenta of moving bodies will be equal or unequal according to the equality or inequality of their masses. But momentum (or 'quantity of motion') is the product of mass and velocity.

So too in warfare the strength of an army is the product of its mass and of something else, some unknown factor x.

Military science, finding in history innumerable instances of the size of an army not coinciding with its strength, and of small detachments defeating larger ones, vaguely admits the existence of this 'unknown' and tries to discover it – now in some geometrical disposition of the troops, now in superiority of weapons, or (more frequently) in the genius of the commanders. But none of these hypothetical identifications of the unknown factor yields results which accord with the historical facts.

Yet it is only necessary to renounce the false notion (flattering though it may be to the 'heroes') of the efficacy of dispositions issued in war-time by the higher authorities, and we shall arrive at our unknown x.

This x is the spirit of the army – in other words, the greater or lesser readiness to fight and face danger on the part of all the men composing an army, quite independently of whether they are, or are not, fighting under leaders of genius, of whether they fight in two- or three-line formation, with cudgels or with rifles that repeat thirty times a minute. Men who are eager to fight will always put themselves in the most advantageous conditions for fighting.

The spirit of an army is the factor which multiplied by the mass gives the resulting force. To define and formulate the significance of this unknown factor, the spirit of the army, constitutes the scientific problem.

The problem is only solvable if we stop arbitrarily substituting for the unknown x the conditions under which it is seen to operate – such as the dispositions of the general, the military equipment, and so on – mistaking these for the significant factor. We must accept the unknown and see it for what it is: the more or less active desire to fight and to face danger. Only then, expressing the known historical facts by means of equations, shall we be able to compare the relative values of the unknown factor; only then may we hope to arrive at the unknown itself.

If ten men, battalions or divisions, fighting fifteen men, battalions or divisions, beat the fifteen – that is, kill or capture them all while losing four themselves, the loss will have been four on one side and fifteen on the other. Therefore the four were equal to the fifteen, and we may write $4x = 15y$. In other words, x is to y as 15 is to 4. Though this equation does not yet give us the absolute value of the unknown factor, it does give us a ratio between two unknowns. And by putting a whole variety of historical data (battles, campaigns, periods of warfare and so on) into the form of such equations, a series of figures will be obtained which must involve the laws inherent in equations and will in time reveal them.

The principle of tactics, that armies should act in masses when on the offensive and should break up into smaller groups for retreat, unconsciously confirms the truth that the strength of an army depends on its spirit. To lead men forward under fire requires more discipline (obtainable only by movement in compact formation) than is needed for self-defence when attacked. But as the rule leaves out of account the spirit of the army, it continually proves fallacious. Above all it is in flagrant contrast to the facts when some strong rise or fall in the spirit of the troops occurs, as in all national wars.

The French during their retreat in 1812, instead of separating – according to tactics – into small detachments to defend themselves, clung together in a horde because the spirit of the troops had fallen so low that it was only their number that kept them going. The Russians on the contrary ought, according to tactics, to have attacked in a body, whereas in actual fact they split up into small units, because the spirit of the men ran so high that individual men struck at the French without waiting for orders and needed no compelling to expose themselves to hardships and dangers.

3

THE so-called partisan war began with the entry of the French into Smolensk.

Before guerrilla warfare had been officially recognized by the government many thousands of enemy soldiers – marauding stragglers, foraging parties – had been exterminated by Cossacks and peasants, who killed them off as instinctively as dogs set upon a mad stray. Denis Davydov was the first to appreciate with his Russian instinct the value of this terrible cudgel which, regardless of the rules of military science, was annihilating the French, and to him belongs the credit of taking the first step towards regularizing this method of warfare.

On August the 24th Davydov's first partisan detachment was formed, and others soon followed. As the campaign proceeded so more and more of these detachments were organized.

The partisans destroyed the *Grande Armée* piecemeal. They swept up the fallen leaves that were dropping of themselves from that withered tree – the French army – and sometimes shook the tree itself. By October, when the French were fleeing back to Smolensk, there were hundreds of these bands, of various sizes and characters.

There were some that kept up the appearance of regular troops, had infantry, artillery and army staffs, and the comforts and decencies of life. Others consisted solely of Cossack cavalry. There were small haphazard collections of mixed infantry and cavalry, and little knots of peasants and landed proprietors who remained anonymous. A sacristan commanded one such party which captured several hundred prisoners in the course of a month. There was the village elder's wife, Vasilisa, who killed hundreds of the French.

The latter days of October saw this guerrilla warfare at its height. The first period of this kind of war – with the partisans themselves amazed at their own audacity, in continual fear of being surrounded and captured by the French, and never unsaddling, hardly daring to dismount, hiding in the woods and expecting to be pursued at any moment – was past. By the end of October this kind of warfare had taken definite shape: it had become clear to everybody what could be ventured against the French and what could not. By now it was only the commanders of detachments marching with staff-officers who kept at a respectful distance from the French, according to the rules, and still regarded many things as impossible. The small bands that had started their activities long before and had already had the French under close observation considered feasible what the leaders of the big detachments would not even dare contemplate. The Cossacks and the peasants, who crept in and out among the French, reckoned everything possible now.

On the 22nd of October Denisov (who was one of the irregulars) was with his group at the height of the guerrilla enthusiasm. Since early morning he and his party had been on the move. All day long, keeping under cover of the forest that skirted the high road, he had been stalking a large French convoy of cavalry baggage and Russian prisoners, which, separated from the rest of the army and moving under a powerful escort – as was learned from scouts and prisoners – was making its way to Smolensk. Not only Denisov and Dolohov (who also was a leader of a small band operating in Denisov's vicinity) but the generals in charge of some big detachments with proper staffs were aware of the presence of this convoy and, as Denisov expressed it, 'were sharpening their teeth for it'. Two of these generals, one a Pole and the other a German, sent almost simultaneously to Denisov, inviting him to join forces with them to attack the convoy.

'No, thank you, bwother, I wasn't born yesterday!' said Denisov on reading these missives, and he wrote to the German that, despite his heartfelt desire to serve under so valiant and renowned a general, he must forgo that pleasure because he was already under the command of the Polish general. To the Pole he replied in the same strain, informing him that he was already under the command of the German.

Having arranged matters thus, Denisov, without referring to the higher authorities, intended with Dolohov to attack and seize the convoy with their own small forces. On October the 22nd the transport was proceeding from the village of Mikulino to that of Shamshevo. On the left of the road between the two villages were great forests, in some places extending to the very edge of the road, in others receding up to three-quarters of a mile or more. It was through these forests that Denisov and his party rode all day, sometimes keeping well back and sometimes emerging to the fringe but never losing sight of the moving French. That morning, not far from Mikulino, where the forest ran close to the road, Cossacks of Denisov's party had pounced on two wagons loaded with cavalry-saddles which had stuck in the mud, and made off with them into the forest. From that time right on to evening they had been watching the movements of the French without attacking. Denisov's idea was to let the French continue quietly on to Shamshevo, without alarming them, and then, joining Dolohov (who was to come that evening to a watchman's hut in the wood, three-quarters of a mile from Shamshevo, to concert measures with him), surprise the French at dawn, falling like an avalanche of snow on their heads, and rout and capture the whole lot at one blow. Six Cossacks had been left behind a mile and a half from Mikulino where the forest bordered the road, to bring word at once should any fresh columns of French show themselves.

Beyond Shamshevo Dolohov was to observe the road in the same way, to find out at what distance there were other French troops. They reckoned that the convoy had fifteen hundred men. Denisov had a couple of hundred, Dolohov about the same number. But numerical disparity did not deter Denisov. All that he now needed to know was what troops these were, and for this purpose he had to capture a 'tongue' – that is, a man from the enemy column. The morning's attack on the wagons had been accomplished in such haste that the French soldiers in charge of the two wagons had all been killed, and only a little drummer-boy had been taken alive, who had strayed away and could tell them nothing definite about the troops forming the column.

To make a second raid Denisov considered would be too dangerous – it might put the whole contingent on the alert – so he sent Tikhon Shcherbaty, a peasant who was with them, on ahead to Shamshevo to see if he could capture at least one of the French quartermasters from the vanguard.

4

It was a mild, rainy autumn day. Sky and horizon were both the colour of muddy water. At times a sort of mist descended, and then suddenly there would be a heavy downpour of slanting rain.

Denisov, in a felt cloak and an astrakhan cap from which the water streamed down, was riding a lean, pinched-looking thoroughbred. Like his horse, which had its head down and its ears laid back, he shrank from the driving rain and peered anxiously before him. His face was somewhat thinner than of old, and with its short growth of thick black beard had an irate look.

Beside Denisov, also in felt cloak and astrakhan cap, and mounted on a sleek, sturdy Don horse, rode the hetman of the Cossacks – Denisov's collaborator.

This hetman – Esaul Lovaisky the Third – was a tall creature, flat as a board, pale-faced, fair-haired, and with narrow, light eyes. His face and bearing were expressive of quiet self-confidence. Though it would have been very difficult to say what it was gave horse and rider their particular character, a glance at the hetman and at Denisov was enough to tell one that the latter was wet and uncomfortable and a man who merely rode his horse, while looking at the hetman it was plain that he was as comfortable and as much at ease as always – not a man who merely rode his horse but a man who was one with his steed, and thus possessed of twofold strength.

A little ahead of them walked a peasant guide, soaked to the skin through his grey kaftan and white woollen cap.

A little behind, on a thin, scraggy Kirghiz pony with a huge tail and mane and its mouth bloody and torn, rode a young officer in a blue French military coat.

Beside him rode a hussar, with a boy in a tattered French uniform and blue cap perched behind him on his horse's crupper. The lad clung to the hussar, his hands red with cold, and, wriggling his bare feet in an effort to warm them, gazed about him with bewildered eyes and uplifted brows. This was the French drummer-boy captured that morning.

Behind them along the narrow, sodden, churned-up forest track came hussars in threes and fours, and then Cossacks, some in felt cloaks, some in French greatcoats, and some with horse-cloths over their heads. The horses, whether chestnut or bay, all looked black from the drenching rain. Their necks seemed curiously narrow with their wet clinging manes. Steam rose from the horses in clouds. Everything – clothes, saddles, bridles – was wet, slippery and dank, like the ground and the fallen leaves that strewed the path. The men sat huddled up, their arms pressed close to their sides so as to keep the chill off the water that had already trickled through to their skins, and not to admit the fresh cold rain that leaked in under their seats, behind their knees and at the back of their necks. In the middle of the file of Cossacks two wagons drawn by French horses, and Cossack saddle-horses hitched on in front, rumbled over tree-stumps and branches, and splashed through ruts full of water.

Denisov's horse swerved to avoid a puddle in the track and bumped his rider's knee against a tree.

'Oh, the devil!' exclaimed Denisov angrily, and showing his teeth he struck the horse three times with his whip, splashing himself and his comrades with mud.

Denisov was in a bad temper, because of the rain and also from hunger (none of them had eaten anything since morning), but most of all because he still had no news from Dolohov, and the man sent to capture a 'tongue' had not returned.

'We aren't likely to get another chance to fall on a twansport twain like today. To attack them alone is too much of a wisk, and if we put it off till another day one of the big guewwilla detachments will snatch the pwey from under our vewy noses,' thought Denisov, continually peering ahead in the hope of discerning a messenger from Dolohov.

Emerging into a clearing in the forest from which he could see a long way to the right, Denisov reined in.

'There's someone coming,' said he.

The hetman looked in the direction Denisov was pointing.

'There are two of them – an officer and a Cossack. Only I wouldn't be *prepositive* that it is the lieutenant-colonel himself,' said the hetman, who was fond of using words the Cossacks did not know.

The two horsemen, riding down a hill, were lost to sight but they reappeared again a few minutes later. In front, at a weary gallop and using his leather whip, rode the officer, dishevelled and soaked through. His trousers had worked up to above his knees. Behind him, standing in the stirrups, trotted a Cossack. The officer, a very young lad with a broad, rosy face and keen, merry eyes, galloped up to Denisov and handed him a sopping envelope.

'From the general,' he said, 'I must apologize for its not being quite dry.'

Denisov, frowning, took the envelope and opened it.

'There now, they kept telling us it was so dangerous,' said the officer, addressing the hetman while Denisov was reading the letter. 'But Komarov here' – he indicated his Cossack – 'Komarov and I made our preparations. We each of us have two pisto ... But what's this?' he asked, noticing the French drummer-boy. 'A prisoner? You've already been in action? May I speak to him?'

'Wostov! Petya!' exclaimed Denisov, having skimmed through the dispatch. 'Why didn't you say who you were?' – and turning with a smile he held out his hand to the lad.

The officer was Petya Rostov.

All the way Petya had been rehearsing in his mind how he should behave with Denisov as befitted a grown man and an officer, making no reference to their previous acquaintance. But as soon as Denisov smiled at him Petya beamed at once, blushed with pleasure, forgot the official demeanour he had been intending to preserve, and began telling him how he had ridden past the French, and how glad he was to have been given this commission, and how he had already been in a battle near Vyazma, and how a certain hussar had distinguished himself there.

'Well, I'm wight glad to see you,' Denisov interrupted him, and his face again assumed its anxious expression.

'Mihail Feoklitych,' he said to the hetman, 'this is fwom the German again, you know. He' (he meant Petya) 'is serving under him.'

And Denisov told the hetman that the letter just delivered reiterated the German general's request that they should join forces with him for an attack on the transports.

'If we don't gwab it tomowwow he'll snatch it fwom under our noses,' he ended up.

While Denisov was talking to the hetman, Petya, mortified by

Denisov's cold tone and supposing that it might be due to the state of his trousers, did his best to work them down again under his cloak without attracting attention, at the same time maintaining as martial an air as possible.

'Has your Honour any orders for me?' he asked of Denisov, putting his hand to the peak of his cap in a salute and resuming the comedy of adjutant and general for which he had rehearsed himself, 'or am I to remain with your Honour?'

'Orders? ...' Denisov repeated thoughtfully. 'What about we-maining till tomowwow?'

'Oh yes, please ... May I stay with you?' cried Petya.

'But just what did your genewal tell you? To weturn at once?' asked Denisov.

Petya blushed.

'He didn't give me any instructions. I think I could, couldn't I?' he replied inquiringly.

'All wight, then,' said Denisov.

And turning to his men he directed a party of them to go on to the watchman's hut in the forest, the halting-place arranged on, and told the officer on the Kirghiz pony (this officer performed the duties of adjutant) to go and look for Dolohov, find out where he was and whether he would be coming that evening. Denisov himself intended riding with the hetman and Petya to the edge of the forest where it reached out to Shamshevo, to reconnoitre the position of the French and determine the best spot for the attack next day.

'Now, old gweybeard,' said he to the peasant who was acting as their guide, 'take us to Shamshevo.'

Denisov, Petya and the hetman, accompanied by a few Cossacks and the hussar who had charge of the prisoner, rode off to the left across a ravine to the edge of the forest.

5

THE rain had stopped; only a mist was falling, and drops from the trees. Denisov, the hetman and Petya rode in silence, following the peasant in the woollen cap who, stepping lightly, toes turned out, and moving noiselessly in his bast shoes over roots and wet leaves, led them to the fringe of the forest.

At the top of a slope he paused, looked about him and advanced to where the screen of foliage was less dense. He stood still under a big oak which had not yet shed its leaves, and mysteriously beckoned with his hand.

Denisov and Petya rode up to him. From the place where the peasant was standing they could see the French. Immediately beyond the forest a field of spring corn ran sharply downhill. To the right, the other side of a steep ravine, was a small village and a manor-house with a dilapidated roof. In this hamlet, in the house, over the whole little hump, in the garden, by the wells, by the pond and all along the road leading up from the bridge to the village, not more than five hundred yards distant, masses of men could be seen in the rolling mist. Their shouts in a foreign tongue at the horses straining uphill with the carts, and their calls to one another, rang out clearly.

'Bwing the pwisoner here,' said Denisov in a low voice, not taking his eyes off the French.

A Cossack dismounted, lifted the boy down and took him to Denisov. Pointing to the French, Denisov asked the lad what troops those were – and those? The drummer-boy, stuffing his benumbed hands into his pockets and lifting his eyebrows, looked at Denisov in dismay and, in spite of his obvious anxiety to tell all he knew, got confused in his answers and merely said Yes to everything Denisov asked him. Denisov turned away from him, frowning, and addressed the hetman, conveying his own conjectures to him.

Petya, moving his head round quickly, looked from the drummer-boy to Denisov, and from him to the hetman and then at the French in the village and along the road, trying not to miss anything of importance.

'Whether Dolohov comes or not, we must make the attempt ... eh?' said Denisov with a merry sparkle in his eye.

'It is a very convenient spot,' said the hetman.

'We'll send the infantwy down below, by the swamps,' Denisov went on. 'They can cweep up to the garden. You wide up from there with the Cossacks' – he pointed to the woods beyond the village – 'while I swoop from here with my hussars. And at the signal shot ...'

'It won't do to go by the hollow – it's all bog,' said the hetman. 'The horses would sink. You must skirt round more to the left.'

While they were talking in undertones there was the crack of a shot from the low ground by the pond, then another. Two puffs of white smoke appeared, and the voices of hundreds of Frenchmen half-way up the slope rose as it were in merry chorus. Denisov and the hetman involuntarily started back. They were so close that they thought they were the cause of the firing and shouting. But the shots and cries had nothing to do with them. Down below, a man wearing something red was running through the marsh. The French were evidently firing and shouting at him.

'Why, that's our Tikhon!' said the hetman.

'So it is! So it is!'

'Oh, the wascal!' exclaimed Denisov.

'He'll get away!' said the hetman, screwing up his eyes.

The man whom they called Tikhon, having run down to the stream, plunged in so that the water splashed in the air and, disappearing for an instant, scrambled out on all fours, looking black with the wet, and dashed on. The French in pursuit stopped.

'Smart fellow!' said the hetman.

'What a knave!' snarled Denisov with the same look of vexation. 'And what has he been up to all this time?'

'Who is he?' asked Petya.

'It's our scout. I sent him to capture a "tongue" for us.'

'Ah, to be sure,' said Petya, nodding immediately, as though he knew all about it, though he really did not understand a word.

*

Tikhon Shcherbaty was one of the most useful members of the party. He was a peasant from the village of Pokrovsk, near the river Gzhat. When Denisov had come to Pokrovsk at the beginning of his operations as a guerrilla leader and had as usual summoned the village elder to ask him what he knew about the French, the elder replied, as all village elders did, in self-defence as it were, that he knew nothing whatever about them and had never set eyes on them. But when Denisov explained that his object was to kill Frenchmen and inquired whether no French had strayed that way, the elder replied that there had been some 'miroderers' certainly but that Tikhon Shcherbaty was the only person in their village to busy himself with such matters. Denisov had Tikhon fetched, and after praising him for his activity continued with a few words, said in the elder's presence, on the subject of loyalty to Tsar and country, and the hatred of the French that all sons of the Fatherland should cherish in their hearts.

'We don't do the French no harm,' said Tikhon, evidently intimidated by Denisov's speech. 'We only just amused ourselves a bit, as you might say. Them *miroderers* now – we done in a score or so o' they fellows but we didn't do no other 'arm. ...'

Next day after Denisov, who had forgotten all about the peasant, had left Pokrovsk, it was reported to him that Tikhon had attached himself to their party and wanted to stay with them. Denisov instructed that he should be allowed to remain.

Tikhon who at first undertook the rough work of laying camp-fires, fetching water, skinning dead horses, and so on, soon showed a great liking and aptitude for partisan warfare. He would go out after booty at night and always returned with some French clothing and weapons, and when told to he would also bring back a French prisoner or two. Denisov then relieved him from the rough jobs and began taking him with him on expeditions and had him enrolled among the Cossacks.

Tikhon did not like riding and always went on foot, never lagging behind the cavalry. His weapons were a carbine (which he carried rather as a joke), a pike and an axe, which latter he wielded as skilfully as a wolf uses its teeth – to crunch either a bone or a flea. Tikhon with equal accuracy could swing his axe to split a log, or hold it by the head and cut thin skewers or carve spoons. Among Denisov's followers Tikhon was on a special footing of his own. When anything particularly difficult or obnoxious had to be done – such as heaving a cart out of the mud with one's shoulder, dragging a horse by its tail out of a swamp and flaying it, slinking into the very midst of the French, or walking thirty miles in a day – everybody pointed laughingly to Tikhon.

'It won't hurt that devil – he's as strong as an ox!' they would say of him.

Once a Frenchman Tikhon was trying to capture fired a pistol at him and shot him in the buttock. The wound (which Tikhon treated exclusively with applications of vodka – internal and external) was the subject of the liveliest jesting by the whole detachment – jesting to which Tikhon willingly lent himself.

'Hullo, me boy, had enough, eh? That put a kink in you, didn't it?' the Cossacks would banter him. And Tikhon, purposely making a long face, pretended to be angry and abuse the French with the most comical oaths. The only effect of the incident on Tikhon was to make him chary of bringing in prisoners, after his wound.

Tikhon was the bravest and most useful man in the guerrilla band. No one was so quick to find opportunities for attack, no one captured or killed so many Frenchmen, and consequently he was the butt of all the Cossacks and hussars, and willingly accommodated himself to the rôle. Now he had been sent by Denisov overnight to Shamshevo to capture a 'tongue'. But either because he was not satisfied to get only one French prisoner, or because he had slept through the night, he had crept by day among some bushes right in the very middle of the French, and, as Denisov had witnessed from the hill, had been discovered by them.

6

AFTER talking a little while longer with the hetman about the next day's attack, which now, seeing how near they were to the French, he seemed finally to have decided upon, Denisov turned his horse and rode back.

'Now, my lad, we'll go and get dwy,' he said to Petya.

As they approached the forester's hut Denisov stopped, peering into the trees. A man in a short jacket, bast shoes and a Kazan hat, with a gun over his shoulder and an axe stuck in his belt, was striding lightly through the forest on his long legs, his long arms swinging at his side. Catching sight of Denisov, he hastily threw something into the bushes, removed his sodden cap, the brim of which drooped limply, and walked up to his commander. It was Tikhon. His wrinkled, pock-marked face and narrow little eyes beamed with self-satisfied mirth. He lifted his head high and gazed at Denizov as though he could hardly refrain from laughing.

'Well, where have you been?' inquired Denisov.

'Where have I been? I went after the French,' answered Tikhon boldly and hurriedly, in a husky but melodious bass.

'What was the idea of crawling in among them in daylight? Ass! Well, why didn't you get one?'

'Oh, I got one all right.'

'Where is he, then?'

'Yes, I got one at daybreak, to go on with, as you might say,' pursued Tikhon, straddling his flat feet with their turned-out toes, in bast shoes. 'I takes 'im into forest. I sees 'e's no good, so I says to meself, I says, "Better go and fetch a likelier one".'

'You see? ... What a wogue – just as I thought,' said Denisov to the hetman. 'Why didn't you bwing that one?'

'Why, what use to bring him?' Tikhon, angry, interrupted quickly. 'That one wouldn't have done for you. Don't I know what sort you want?'

'What a wascal! ... Well?'

'Off I goes to get another,' Tikhon continued, 'and I creeps this-ways into forest and lays flat.' And abruptly he dropped down on his stomach to show them how he had crawled along. 'One shows up and I grabs 'im, like this.' Tikhon leaped lightly to his feet. '"Come along to the colonel," says I. He starts yelling and all on a sudden there were four of 'em. 'Urled themselves at me with they little swords. So I goes for 'em with me axe – this fashion. "What a to-do!" I says to 'em. "Taking on like that!"' cried Tikhon, waving his arms and squaring his chest with a menacing scowl.

'Oh yes, we saw from the hill how you took to your heels through the puddles and pools!' said the hetman, screwing up his glittering eyes.

Petya badly wanted to laugh but he noticed that all the others refrained from laughing. He turned his eyes rapidly from Tikhon's face to the hetman's and Denisov's, not knowing what to make of it all.

'Don't play the fool!' said Denisov, coughing angrily. 'Why didn't you bwing the first man?'

Tikhon began scratching his back with one hand and his head with the other, and suddenly his whole face expanded into a beaming, foolish grin, disclosing the gap where he had lost a tooth – the gap that had earned him his name Shcherbaty – the gap-toothed. Denisov smiled, and Petya went off into a peal of laughter in which Tikhon himself joined.

'Oh, but that was a reg'lar good-for-nothing,' said Tikhon. 'The clothes on 'im – poor stuff! How could I bring 'im? And such a coarse fellow, your Honour! "Why," says 'e, "me, I be a gineral's son. I'm not coming," he says.'

'Ugh, you wogue!' said Denisov. 'I wanted to question him. ...'

'Oh, I questioned him all right,' said Tikhon. ''E said 'e didn't rightly know much. "A powerful lot of us, there be," 'e said, "but not up to much. Not real soldiers at all at all. Shout at 'em loud enough," says 'e, "and you'll capture the whole lot of 'em",' Tikhon concluded, with a cheerful and determined look at Denisov.

'I'll have you thwashed a hot hundwed – that'll teach you to play the fool!' said Denisov severely.

'What's there to fly into a rage about?' protested Tikhon. 'Don't I know the sort of Frenchmen you want? Wait till it be dark and I'll fetch in any kind you like – three on 'em, so I will.'

'Well, let's go,' said Denisov, and all the way to the forester's hut he rode in silence, frowning angrily.

Tikhon fell in behind and Petya heard the Cossacks laughing and teasing him about a pair of boots he had thrown into the bushes.

When he had recovered from the fit of laughter that had overcome him at Tikhon's words and his grin, and understood in a flash that this Tikhon had killed the man, Petya had an uneasy feeling. He looked round at the captive drummer-boy and felt a pang in his heart. But this uneasiness lasted only a moment. He felt it necessary to hold his head higher, to brace himself and question the hetman with an air of importance about tomorrow's expedition, that he might not be unworthy of the company in which he found himself.

The officer who had been sent to find out about Dolohov met Denisov on the way with news that Dolohov would be there soon and that all was well with him.

Denisov at once recovered his spirits, and beckoning Petya to him, said: 'Well now, tell me about yourself.'

7

LEAVING his people after their departure from Moscow, Petya had joined his regiment and was soon taken on as orderly by the general of a large guerrilla detachment. From the time he received his commission, and especially after his transfer into the army in the field, and his introduction to active service at Vyazma, Petya had been in a constant state of blissful excitement at being grown-up, and chronically eager not to miss the slightest chance of covering himself with glory. He was highly delighted with what he saw and experienced in the army but at the same time it seemed to him that the really heroic exploits were always being performed just where he did not happen to be. And he was always in a hurry to get where he was not.

When on the 21st of October his general expressed a wish to send somebody to Denisov's detachment, Petya had begged so piteously to go that the general could not refuse. But as he was seeing him off he recalled Petya's foolhardy behaviour at the battle of Vyazma, where instead of keeping to the road Petya had galloped across the front line of sharpshooters under the fire of the French, and had there discharged a couple of pistol-shots. So in letting him go the general explicitly forbade Petya to take part in any enterprise whatever that Denisov might be planning. This was why Petya had blushed and been disconcerted when Denisov asked him if he could stay. Until he reached the outskirts of the forest Petya had fully intended to carry out his instructions to the letter and return at once. But when he saw the French and met Tikhon, and learned that there would certainly be an attack that night, he decided, with the swiftness with which young people change their opinions, that the general for whom up to that moment he had had the greatest respect was a rubbishy German, that Denisov was a hero, the hetman a hero, and Tikhon a hero too, and that it would be shameful of him to desert them at a critical moment.

It was growing dark when Denisov, Petya and the hetman rode up to the forester's hut. In the twilight they could see saddled horses, and Cossacks and hussars rigging up rough shelters in the clearing and kindling a glowing fire in a hollow where the smoke would not be seen by the French. In the entrance of the little watch-house a Cossack with sleeves rolled up was cutting up a sheep. In the hut itself three officers of Denisov's were converting a door into a table-top. Petya pulled off his wet clothes, gave them to be dried, and at once set to work helping the officers to fix up the dinner-table.

In ten minutes the table was ready, covered with a napkin, and spread with vodka, a flask of rum, white bread, roast mutton and salt.

Sitting at the table with the officers and tearing the fat, savoury mutton with greasy fingers, Petya was in an ecstatic childlike state of melting love for all men and a consequent belief that in the same way they loved him.

'So what do you think, Vasili Fiodorovich?' he said to Denisov. 'It won't matter my staying just one day with you, will it?' And not waiting for Denisov to reply he supplied an answer for himself: 'You see, I was told to find out – well, I am finding out.... Only do let me into the very ... into the real ... I don't care about rewards and decorations. ... I just want ...'

Petya clenched his teeth and looked about him, tossing his head and waving his arm.

'The real thing …' Denisov said with a smile.

'Only please give me a command, just the smallest command to command myself,' Petya went on. 'What difference could it make to you? Oh, is it a knife you want?' he said to an officer who was trying to sever himself a piece of mutton. And he handed him his clasp-knife.

The officer admired the blade.

'Please keep it! I have several others like it …' said Petya, blushing. 'Heavens! I was quite forgetting,' he cried suddenly. 'I have some wonderful raisins with me – you know, those seedless ones. Our new sutler has such first-rate things. I bought ten pounds. I always like sweet things. Will you have some? …' And Petya ran out to his Cossack in the passage and returned with baskets containing about five pounds of raisins. 'Help yourselves, gentlemen, help yourselves.'

'Don't you need a coffee-pot?' he said to the hetman. 'I got a marvellous one from our sutler. His things are first-rate. And he's very honest. That's the great thing. I'll be sure and send it to you. Or perhaps your flints are giving out, or you are out of them – that does happen sometimes. I've got some here' – he pointed to the baskets – 'a hundred flints. I bought them dirt cheap. Do take them – have as many as you want, all of them if you like. …'

Then suddenly, dismayed at the thought that he had let his tongue run away with him, Petya stopped short and blushed.

He tried to remember whether he had been guilty of any other folly. And passing the events of the day in review he remembered the French drummer-boy. 'We are very snug here, but what of him? Where have they put him? Have they given him anything to eat? I hope they aren't being nasty to him?' he wondered. But, having caught himself saying too much about the flints, he was afraid to speak now.

'I have a great mind to ask,' he thought. 'But won't they say: "He's a boy himself, so of course he feels for the other boy"? I'll show them tomorrow whether I'm a boy! Would I be embarrassed to ask?' Petya wondered. 'Oh well, I don't care,' and on the spur of the moment, colouring and looking anxiously at the officers to see if they would laugh at him, he said:

'May I call in that boy who was taken prisoner? Give him something to eat, perhaps? …'

'Yes, poor little chap,' said Denisov, who evidently saw nothing to be ashamed of in this thought. 'Fetch him in. His name is Vincent Bosse. Fetch him in.'

'I'll go,' said Petya.

'Yes, yes, do. Poor little chap,' said Denisov again.

Petya was standing at the door when Denisov said this. He slipped in between the officers and went up to Denisov.

'I must embrace you for that, my dear fellow!' he exclaimed. 'Oh, how good of you, how kind!'

And having embraced Denisov he ran out of the hut.

'Bosse! Vincent!' called Petya, stopping outside the door.

'Who is it you want, sir?' asked a voice from the darkness.

Petya explained that he wanted the French lad who had been taken prisoner that day.

'Oh, Vesenny?' said a Cossack.

The boy's name, Vincent, had already been transformed by the Cossacks into Vesenny, and by the peasants and the soldiers into Vesenya, and both these words which have to do in Russian with the spring-time seemed appropriate to the young lad who was little more than a child.

'He's warming himself by the fire there. Hey, Vesenya! Vesenya! – Vesenny!' laughing voices called, catching up the cry one after another.

'He's a sharp little fellow,' remarked an hussar standing near Petya. 'We gave him a meal not long ago. He was frightfully hungry!'

There was the sound of footsteps in the darkness, and the drummer-boy came towards the door, bare feet splashing through the mud.

'Ah, there you are!' said Petya in French. 'Would you like some food? Don't be afraid, no one will hurt you,' he added, shyly laying a friendly hand on his arm. 'Come along, come in.'

'Merci, monsieur,' said the drummer-boy in a trembling, almost childish voice, and he began wiping his muddy feet against the threshold. Petya had a great many things he longed to say to the drummer-boy but he did not dare. He stood irresolutely beside him in the passage. Then he took the boy's hand in the darkness and pressed it.

'Come along, come in!' he repeated in an encouraging whisper.

'Oh, I wonder what I could do for him?' he thought, and opening the door he ushered the boy in before him.

When the drummer-boy was in the hut Petya sat down at some distance from him, feeling that it would be lowering his dignity to take much notice of him. But he was fingering the money in his pocket and asking himself whether it would seem ridiculous if he gave some to the little prisoner.

8

THE arrival of Dolohov diverted Petya's attention from the drummer-boy, who on Denisov's orders had been given some mutton and a drink of vodka, and clad in Russian garments so that he might be kept with their band and not sent away with the other prisoners. Petya had heard a great many stories in the army about Dolohov's extraordinary courage and of his barbarity to the French, and so from the moment Dolohov entered the hut Petya could not take his eyes off him but put on more and more of a swagger, and held his head high, that he might not be unworthy even of such company as Dolohov.

Dolohov's appearance amazed Petya by its simplicity.

Denisov, dressed in a Cossack coat, wore a beard and had an icon of St Nikolai the Miracle-worker on his breast, and his way of speaking and his whole manner indicated his unusual position. But Dolohov, who in Moscow had affected Persian dress, now looked like the most meticulous of Guards officers. He was clean-shaven; he wore the padded coat of the Guards with a St George ribbon in his button-hole, and an ordinary forage-cap set straight on his head. He took his wet cloak off in the corner of the room, and without greeting anyone went straight up to Denisov and immediately began asking questions about the matter in hand. Denisov told him of the designs the large detachments had on the transport, of the message Petya had brought, and his own replies to both generals. Then he related all he knew about the position of the French convoy.

'That is all very well, but we must know what troops they are and their numbers,' said Dolohov. 'We must go and have a look. We can't rush into the business without knowing for certain how many there are of them. I like to do things properly. Here, I wonder, wouldn't one of you gentlemen like to ride over to the French camp with me? I have an extra uniform with me.'

'I, I ... I'll go with you!' cried Petya.

'You are pwecisely the one not to go,' said Denisov, addressing Dolohov, 'and as for him, I wouldn't let him go on any account.'

'I like that!' cried Petya. 'Why shouldn't I go?'

'Why, because there's no point.'

'Well, you must excuse me because ... because ... I'm going and that's all about it. You will take me, won't you?' he said, turning to Dolohov.

'Why not? ...' Dolohov answered absently, staring at the French drummer-boy. 'That youngster been with you long?' he asked Denisov.

'They took him today but he knows nothing. I'm keeping him with me.'

'Oh, and what do you do with the others?' inquired Dolohov.

'What do I do with them? Send 'em in and get a weceipt,' cried Denisov, suddenly flushing. 'And I may tell you fwankly, I haven't one single man's life on my conscience. What's the twouble of sending thirty, or for that matter thwee hundwed under escort to the city as against staining – I speak bluntly – one's honour as a soldier?'

'Such squeamishness would be all very well from this sixteen-year-old little countlet here,' said Dolohov with a cold sneer, 'but it's high time you dropped all that.'

'Well, I don't say anything! I only say I'm certainly coming with you,' put in Petya shyly.

'But you and I, my friend, are too old for such fads,' Dolohov went on, apparently deriving particular satisfaction from insisting on a subject which irritated Denisov. 'Now, why have you kept this lad?' he said, shaking his head. 'Because you are sorry for him, eh? Don't we know those "receipts" of yours! You send off a hundred prisoners and hardly more than a couple of dozen arrive. The rest either die of starvation or get killed. So isn't it just as well to make short work of them?'

The hetman, screwing up his light-coloured eyes, nodded approvingly.

'That's not the point. There's nothing to weason about here. I don't care to have their lives on my conscience. You say they die on the woad. All wight. Only it's not my doing.'

Dolohov laughed.

'Do you suppose they haven't been told to grab me twenty times over? And if they should catch me – or you either, for all your chivalry – they'd string us up from the nearest aspen-tree.' He paused. 'However, we must be getting to work. Have my Cossack bring in my pack. There are a couple of French uniforms in it. Well, are you coming with me?' he asked Petya.

'Me? Yes, yes, certainly!' cried Petya, blushing almost to tears and glancing at Denisov.

While Dolohov had been arguing with Denisov what should be done with prisoners, Petya had again had that uncomfortable, restless feeling; but once more he had no time to form a clear idea of what they were talking about. 'If famous grown-up men think like that, then that's the way to think and it must be all right, I suppose,' he reflected. 'And the great thing is, that Denisov shouldn't imagine I'll listen to him – that he can order me about. Most certainly I shall go with Dolohov to the French camp. If *he* can, so can I!'

And to all Denisov's efforts to dissuade him Petya replied that he too liked doing things properly and not just anyhow, and that he never thought about danger to himself.

'For – as you'll admit – if we don't know for sure how many of them there are, it might cost the lives of hundreds, as against the two of us. Besides, I badly want to go, and I certainly shall, so don't you try to stop me,' said he. 'It would only make it worse. ...'

9

HAVING put on French greatcoats and shakos, Petya and Dolohov rode to the clearing from which Denisov had reconnoitred the French camp, and emerging from the forest in pitch darkness descended into the hollow. When they reached the bottom of the hill Dolohov told the Cossacks accompanying them to wait there, and started off at a quick trot along the road towards the bridge. Petya, his heart in his mouth with excitement, rode by his side.

'If we're caught, I won't be taken alive. I have a pistol,' he whispered.

'Don't speak Russian,' said Dolohov in a hurried whisper, and at that moment they heard through the darkness the challenge 'Who goes there?' and the click of a musket.

The blood rushed into Petya's face and he clutched at his pistol.

'Lancers of the 6th Regiment,' replied Dolohov, neither hastening nor slackening his horse's pace.

The black figure of a sentinel stood on the bridge.

'Password ?'

Dolohov reined in his horse and advanced at a foot-pace.

'Tell me, is Colonel Gérard here ?' he asked.

'Password ?' repeated the sentinel, barring his way and not replying.

'When an officer is making his round sentinels don't ask him for the password .,.' cried Dolohov, suddenly losing his temper and riding straight at the sentinel. 'I ask you, is the colonel here ?'

And not waiting for an answer from the sentinel, who had stepped aside, Dolohov rode up the incline at a walk.

Noticing the black outline of a man crossing the road, Dolohov hailed him and inquired where the commander and officers were. The man, a soldier with a sack over his shoulder, stopped, came close up to Dolohov's horse, patted it and explained in a simple, friendly way that the colonel and the officers were higher up the hill, on the right, in the courtyard of the farm, as he called the little manor-house.

Having ridden farther along the road, on both sides of which French talk could be heard round the camp-fires, Dolohov turned into the courtyard of the manor-house. Riding in at the gateway, he dismounted and walked towards a big blazing camp-fire, around which sat a number of men engaged in loud conversation. Something was boiling in a small cauldron on one side of the fire and a soldier in a peaked cap and blue coat was kneeling in the bright glow, stirring the contents with a ramrod.

'Oh, he's a tough nut to crack,' said one of the officers, sitting in the shadow on the opposite side of the fire.

'He'll make those fellows get a move on !' said another, laughing.

Both fell silent, peering into the darkness at the sound of Dolohov's and Petya's steps as they advanced to the fire, leading their horses.

'Bonjour, messieurs!' called Dolohov loudly and distinctly.

There was a stir in the shadow beyond the fire, and one tall officer with a long neck skirted the fire and came up to Dolohov.

'That you, Clément ?' he asked. 'Where the devil ...' but perceiving his mistake he broke off and with a slight frown greeted Dolohov as a stranger, inquiring what he could do for him. Dolohov said that he and his companion were trying to overtake their regiment, and addressing the company in general asked whether they knew anything of the 6th Regiment. None of them could tell him anything and Petya fancied the officers were beginning to look at him and Dolohov with hostility and suspicion. For several seconds no one spoke.

'If you're reckoning on some supper, you have come too late,' said a voice from behind the fire, with a smothered laugh.

Dolohov replied that they were not hungry and must push on farther that night.

He handed the horses over to the soldier who was stirring the pot, and squatted down on his heels by the fire beside the officer with the long neck. The latter never took his eyes off Dolohov and asked him a second time what regiment he belonged to. Dolohov appeared not to hear the question. Making no answer, he lighted a short French pipe which he took from his pocket, and began asking the officers how far the road ahead of them was safe from Cossacks.

'The brigands are everywhere,' replied an officer from behind the fire.

Dolohov remarked that the Cossacks were only a danger to stragglers like himself and his companion but he supposed they would not venture to attack large detachments. 'Would they ?' he added inquiringly. No one replied.

'Now surely he'll come away,' Petya was thinking every moment as he stood by the fire, listening to the talk.

But Dolohov re-started the conversation which had dropped, and proceeded to ask point-blank how many men they had in their battalion, how many battalions there were, and how many prisoners. Asking about their Russian prisoners, Dolohov said:

'Nasty business dragging these carcasses about with one ! Far better shoot the vermin dead !' and burst into such a strange loud laugh that Petya thought the French must immediately see through their disguise, and he involuntarily took a step back from the fire.

Dolohov's remark and laughter elicited no response, and a French officer whom they had not seen (he lay wrapped in a greatcoat) sat up and whispered something to his neighbour. Dolohov got to his feet and called to the soldier who was holding their horses.

'Will they let us have the horses or not ?' wondered Petya, instinctively drawing nearer to Dolohov.

The horses were brought.

'Good evening, gentlemen,' said Dolohov.

Petya wanted to say '*Bonsoir*' too, but he could not utter a sound. The officers were whispering together. Dolohov was a long time getting into the saddle, for his horse was restive; then he rode out of the yard at a foot-pace. Petya rode beside him, longing to look round to see whether the Frenchmen were running after them, but not daring to.

When they came out on to the road Dolohov did not turn back towards the open country but continued along through the village. At one spot he reined in and listened. 'Hear that?' he asked. Petya recognized the sound of Russian voices and saw the dark outlines of Russian prisoners round their camp-fires. Reaching the bridge again, Petya and Dolohov rode past the sentinel, who, without saying a word, paced morosely up and down the bridge, and descended into the hollow where the Cossacks were waiting for them.

'Well, now, good-bye. Tell Denisov, at sunrise, at the first shot,' said Dolohov and was about to ride away but Petya seized him by the arm.

'Oh!' he cried, 'you are such a hero! Oh, how splendid! How glorious! How I like you!'

'That's all right,' said Dolohov, but Petya did not let go of him and in the dark Dolohov perceived that he was bending towards him and wanted to embrace him. Dolohov embraced him laughingly, turned his horse and vanished into the night.

10

REACHING the hut in the forest, Petya found Denisov in the passage. He was waiting for Petya's return in a great state of agitation, anxiety and vexation with himself for having let him go.

'Thank God!' he exclaimed. 'Thank God now!' he repeated, listening to Petya's ecstatic account. 'But, damn you, I haven't had a wink of sleep because of you! Well, thank God! Now go and lie down. We can still get a nap before morning.'

'Yes ... no,' said Petya. 'I don't feel sleepy yet. Besides I know what I am – if I once fall asleep there'll be no waking me. And then I'm used to not sleeping before a battle.'

Petya sat for a little while in the hut gleefully going over the details of his adventure and vividly picturing to himself what would happen next day. Then, observing that Denisov was asleep, he got up and went out of doors.

Outside it was still quite dark. The rain was over but the trees were still dripping. Close by could be seen the black shapes of the Cossacks' shanties and the horses tethered together. Behind the hut there was a dark blur where two wagons stood with their horses beside them, and in the hollow the dying camp-fire glowed red. Not all the Cossacks and hussars were asleep: here and there, mingling with the sounds of the falling rain-drops and the munching of the horses near by, low voices seemed to be whispering.

Petya came out, peered about him in the darkness, and went up to the wagons. Someone was snoring underneath one of the carts, and around them stood saddled horses munching their oats. In the dark Petya recognized his own horse, which he called Karabach (though it was a Ukrainian horse and not from Karabach in the Caucasus, famous for its breed of horses), and went up to it.

'Well, Karabach! We have work before us tomorrow,' he said, sniffing its nostrils and kissing it.

'What, sir, aren't you asleep?' said a Cossack who was sitting beneath a wagon.

'No, I ... your name's Lihachov, isn't it? You see, I've only just come back. We've been calling on the French.'

And Petya gave the Cossack a detailed account not only of his expedition but also of his reasons for going, and why he thought it better to risk his life than to do things in a haphazard way.

'Well, you should get some sleep now,' said the Cossack.

'No, I am used to this,' said Petya. 'I say, aren't the flints in your pistols worn out? I brought some with me. Could you do with any? You can have some.'

The Cossack popped out from under the wagon to take a closer look at Petya.

'Because I'm accustomed to seeing to things properly,' said Petya. 'Some men, you know, leave things to chance. They don't think of preparing beforehand, and then afterwards they regret it. I don't like that.'

'That's a fact,' said the Cossack.

'Oh yes, and another thing – please, my dear fellow, sharpen my sabre for me, will you? It got blunted ...' (but Petya could not bring out the lie). 'It has never been sharpened. Can you do it for me?'

'To be sure.'

Lihachov got up, rummaged in his pack, and soon Petya heard the warlike sound of steel on whetstone. He climbed on to the wagon and perched on the edge of it. The Cossack sharpened the sabre below.

'I say! Are the lads asleep?' asked Petya.

'Some are, and some aren't – like us.'

'And what about that boy?'

'Vesenny, you mean? Oh, he stowed himself away in the hay over there. Fast asleep after his fright. He was that pleased.'

For a long time after this Petya remained silent, listening to the noises. He heard footsteps in the darkness and a black figure loomed up.

'What are you sharpening?' asked a man, coming up to the wagon.

'A sabre for the gentleman here.'

'That's right,' said the man, whom Petya took to be an hussar. 'Was the cup left over here with you?'

'There it is by the wheel.'

The hussar took the cup.

'It must be getting on for daylight,' said he, yawning, as he walked off.

Petya ought to have needed no second thoughts to know that he was in a forest with Denisov's guerrilla band, three-quarters of a mile from the road, perched on a wagon captured from the French, with horses tethered round it, and the Cossack Lihachov sitting underneath sharpening his sabre for him; that the big dark blur to the right was the forester's hut and the bright red patch below on the left – the dying embers of a camp-fire; that the man who had come for the cup was an hussar who was thirsty. But he knew nothing of all this, and did not want to. He was in a fairy kingdom where nothing resembled reality. The big dark blur might be a hut certainly, but it might be a cavern leading down into the very depths of the earth. The red patch could be the camp-fire but perhaps it was the eye of a huge monster. Perhaps he, Petya, was in fact perched on a wagon but it might very well be that he was not sitting on a wagon but on a fearfully high tower, and if he fell off it would take him a whole day, a whole month, to reach the earth – he might fall for ever and never reach it! Perhaps it was merely the Cossack Lihachov sitting under the wagon, but it might be the kindest, bravest, most wonderful, marvellous man in the world, whom no one knew of. Perhaps it really was an hussar who came after water and went back into the hollow, or perhaps he had simply vanished – disappeared altogether and dissolved into nothingness.

Whatever Petya had seen now, it would not have surprised him. He was in a magic kingdom where everything was possible.

He looked up at the sky. And the sky was a fairy realm like the earth. It had begun to clear and the clouds were scudding over the tree-tops as though unveiling the stars. Sometimes it looked as if the clouds were passing, and a stretch of black sky appeared. At other times these black patches seemed to be storm-clouds. At still others it was as if the sky were lifting high, high above his head, and then it seemed to sink so low that he could have touched it with his hand.

Petya's eyes began to close and he swayed a little.

Rain-drops dripped from the trees. There was a low hum of talk. The horses neighed and jostled one another. Someone snored.

Ozhik-zhik, ozhik-zhik ... hissed the sabre on the whetstone. And all at once Petya heard a melodious orchestra playing some unknown, sweet, solemn hymn. Petya was as musical as Natasha, and more so than Nikolai, but he had never learnt music or thought about it and so the harmonies that suddenly filled his ears were to him absolutely new and intoxicating. The music swelled louder and louder. The air was developed and passed from one instrument to another. And what was played was a fugue – though Petya had not the slightest idea what a fugue was. Each instrument – now the violin, now the horn, but better and purer than violin and horn – played its own part, and before it had played to the end of the *motif* melted in with another, beginning almost the same air, and then with a third and a fourth; and then they all blended into one, and again became separate and again blended, now into solemn church music, now into some brilliant and triumphant song of victory.

'Oh yes, of course, I must be dreaming,' Petya said to himself as he lurched forward. 'It's only in my ears. Perhaps, though, it's music of my own. Well, go on, my music! Now! ...'

He closed his eyes. And from different directions, as though from a distance, the notes fluttered, swelled into harmonies, parted, came together and again merged into the same sweet and solemn hymn. 'Oh, this is lovely! As much as I like, and as I want it!' said Petya to himself. He tried to conduct this tremendous orchestra.

'Hush, now, softly die away!' and the sounds obeyed him. 'Now fuller, still livelier. More and more joyful now!' And from unknown depths rose the swelling triumphal chords. 'Now the voices!' commanded Petya. And, at first from afar, he heard men's voices, then women's, steadily mounting in a slow *crescendo*. Awed and rejoicing, Petya drank in their wondrous beauty.

The singing fused into a march of victory, and the rain dripped, and *ozhik-zhik, ozhik-zhik* ... hissed the sabre, and the horses jostled one another again, and neighed, not disturbing the chorus but forming part of it.

Petya did not know how long this lasted: he revelled in it, all the while wondering at his enjoyment and regretting that there was no one to share it. He was awakened by Lihachov's friendly voice.

'Here it is, your Honour – all ready to split a Frenchie in half.'

Petya opened his eyes.

'Why, it's getting light – really getting light!' he exclaimed.

The horses, invisible before, could now be seen to their very tails, and a watery light showed through the leafless boughs. Petya shook himself, jumped down, took a rouble from his pocket and gave it to Lihachov, brandished his sabre to try it and slipped it into the sheath. The Cossacks were busy untying their horses and tightening the saddle-girths.

'And here's the commander,' said Lihachov.

Denisov came out of the hut and, calling to Petya, bade him get ready.

II

In the half-light of dawn the men speedily picked out their horses, tightened up their saddle-girths and fell into line. Denisov stood by the hut, giving final instructions. The infantry of the detachment, hundreds of feet splashing through the mud, passed along the road and quickly vanished among the trees in the early morning mist. The hetman gave some orders to the Cossacks. Petya held his horse by the bridle, impatiently awaiting the signal to mount. His face, and especially his eyes, burned after the cold water he had splashed over them; cold shivers ran down his spine and his whole body shook with a rapid, rhythmic trembling.

'Well, is ev'wything weady?' asked Denisov. 'Bwing the horses.'

The horses were led up. Denisov flew at the Cossack because the saddle-girths were slack, and swore at him as he mounted. Petya put his foot in the stirrup. His horse made to nip his leg (its general practice) but Petya leaped into the saddle, unconscious of having any weight, and, turning to look round at the hussars moving up from behind in the darkness, rode up to Denisov.

'Vasili Fiodorovich, you will give me some assignment or other, won't you? Please ... for God's sake ...' said he.

Denisov seemed to have forgotten Petya's very existence. He glanced round at him.

'One thing I beg of you,' he said sternly, 'and that is to obey me and not shove yourself fo'ward anywhere.'

He did not say another word to Petya but rode in silence all the way. By the time they reached the edge of the forest it had grown quite light in the open country. Denisov held a whispered consultation with the hetman, and the Cossacks rode past Petya and Denisov. When they had all passed Denisov touched his horse and started off down the slope. Slipping and sinking back on their haunches, the horses slid down into the hollow with their riders. Petya kept beside Denisov. The trembling of his whole body kept increasing. It was getting lighter and lighter, only distant objects were still concealed in the mist. Having reached the valley, Denisov looked back and nodded to a Cossack standing near him.

'The signal!' he said.

The Cossack raised his arm and a shot rang out, followed immediately by the tramp of horses galloping in front, and shouts from different directions, and more shots.

At the first sound of trampling hooves and yelling Petya lashed his horse and, loosening his rein, galloped forward, heedless of Denisov who shouted at him. It seemed to Petya that it suddenly became broad daylight, as though it were midday, at the moment the shot was fired. He galloped to the bridge. The Cossacks were dashing along the road in front of him. On the bridge he collided with a Cossack who had fallen behind, but he tore on. In front Petya saw men of some sort – the French, he supposed – running from right to left across the road. One of them slipped in the mud under his horse's legs.

Cossacks were crowding round one peasant's cottage, doing something. A fearful shriek rose from the middle of the crowd. Petya galloped up, and the first thing he saw was the white face and trembling jaw of a Frenchman clutching the staff of a lance directed at his breast.

'Hurrah! ... Our lads! ...' shouted Petya, and giving rein to his excited horse he galloped on down the village street.

He could hear shooting ahead of him. Cossacks, hussars and tattered Russian prisoners, who had come running up from both sides of the road, were all shouting unintelligibly at the tops of their voices. A gallant-looking Frenchman in a blue coat, capless, and with a frowning red face, had been defending himself against the hussars. When Petya dashed up the Frenchman had already fallen. 'Too late again!' flashed through Petya's mind and he flew on to the spot where there was brisk firing. The shots came from the courtyard of the manor-house he had visited the night before with Dolohov. The French were making a stand behind a wattle fence in a garden thickly overgrown with bushes, and shooting at the Cossacks clustering at the gateway. Through the smoke as he rode up to the gates Petya caught a glimpse of Dolohov's pale, greenish face, as he shouted something to his men. 'Go round. Wait for the infantry!' he was yelling, just as Petya appeared.

'Wait? ... Hurra-a-h! ...' roared Petya, and without pausing a second threw himself into the fray where the firing and smoke were thickest. A volley rang out, bullets whistled past and landed with a thud. The Cossacks and Dolohov galloped in at the gates of the yard after Petya. In the dense billowing smoke some of the French flung down their arms and ran out of the bushes to meet the Cossacks, while others fled downhill towards the pond. Petya was tearing round the courtyard, but instead of holding the reins he was waving both arms about in a strange, wild manner, and slipping farther and farther to one side in the saddle. His horse stepped on the ashes of the camp-fire that was smouldering in the morning light, stopped short, and Petya fell heavily on to the wet ground. The Cossacks saw his arms and legs jerk rapidly, though his head was quite still. A bullet had pierced his skull.

After parleying with the senior French officer, who came out of the house with a handkerchief tied to his sword to announce that they surrendered, Dolohov got off his horse and went up to Petya, who lay motionless with outstretched arms.

'Done for!' he said with a frown, and walked to the gate to meet Denisov who was riding towards him.

'Dead?' cried Denisov, recognizing from a distance the unmistakably lifeless attitude – only too familiar to him – in which Petya's body was lying.

'Done for!' repeated Dolohov, as though the utterance of the words afforded him satisfaction, and he hastened over to the prisoners, who were surrounded by Cossacks who had hurried up. 'We're giving no quarter!' he called out to Denisov.

Denisov did not reply. He rode up to Petya, dismounted, and with trembling hands turned Petya's blood-stained, mud-bespattered face – which had already gone white – towards himself.

'I always like sweet things. Wonderful raisins, take them all,' he recalled Petya's words. And the Cossacks looked round in amazement at the sound, like the howl of a dog, which broke from Denisov as he quickly turned away, walked to the wattle fence and held on to it.

Among the Russian prisoners rescued by Denisov and Dolohov was Pierre Bezuhov.

12

DURING the whole of their march from Moscow no new orders had been issued by the French authorities concerning the party of prisoners with whom Pierre was. On the 22nd of October that party was no longer with the troops and transport in whose company they had left Moscow. Half the wagons laden with hard-biscuit ration that had travelled the first stages with them had been carried off by Cossacks, the other half had gone on ahead. Of the cavalrymen on foot who had marched in front of the prisoners, not one was left: all had disappeared. The artillery the prisoners had seen in front of them during the early days was now replaced by Marshal Junot's enormous baggage-train, convoyed by Westphalians. Behind the prisoners came a transport of cavalry accoutrements.

From Vyazma onwards the French army, which had till then moved in three columns, now pushed on in one mass. The signs of disorder which Pierre had observed at the first halt outside Moscow had by now reached their climax.

The road along which they moved was strewn on both sides with the carcasses of dead horses. Ragged soldiers, stragglers from various regiments, constantly shifted about, now tacked on to the marching column, now dropped behind again.

Several times during the progress there had been false alarms and the soldiers of the escort had raised their muskets, fired and run headlong, trampling one another underfoot, but had afterwards rallied again and abused each other for their needless panic.

These three bodies travelling together – the cavalry stores, the convoy of prisoners, and Junot's baggage-train – still made up a complete and separate whole, though each of its constituent parts was rapidly melting away.

Of the cavalry transport, which had at first consisted of a hundred and twenty wagons, not more than sixty were left, the others having been captured or abandoned. Several wagon-loads of Junot's baggage had likewise been discarded or seized. Three wagons had been attacked and rifled by stragglers from Davoust's corps. Pierre overheard the Germans saying that this baggage-train was more strongly guarded than the prisoners, and that one of their comrades, a German soldier, had been shot by the marshal's own order, because a silver spoon belonging to the marshal had been found in his possession.

The group of prisoners had dwindled even more than the other two convoys. Of the three hundred and thirty men who had set out from Moscow less than a hundred still survived. The prisoners were even more of a burden to the escort than the cavalry-stores or Junot's baggage. The cavalry-saddles and Junot's spoons they could understand might be of some use, but that cold and starving soldiers should have to stand and guard equally cold and starving Russians who froze and lagged behind on the road (in which case the order was to shoot them) was not merely incomprehensible but an offence. And the escort, as though afraid, in the miserable plight they themselves were in, of giving way to the pity they felt for the prisoners, and so making their own lot harder, treated them with marked sullenness and severity.

At Dorogobuzh while the soldiers of the convoy, leaving the prisoners locked up in a stable, went off to plunder their own stores several of the prisoners had tunnelled under the wall and run away, but they were caught by the French and shot.

The arrangement adopted on the departure from Moscow, by which the officers among the prisoners were kept apart from the common run, had been dropped long since: all who could walk went together, and after the third stage Pierre had rejoined Karatayev and the bluey-grey, bow-legged dog who had chosen Karatayev for her master.

On the third day out from Moscow Karatayev fell ill with another bout of the fever which had kept him in hospital in Moscow, and as he grew worse Pierre held more aloof from him. Pierre could not have said why it was but from the time Karatayev's strength began to fail it had needed an effort to go near him. And when he did so and heard the subdued moaning with which Karatayev generally lay down at the halting-places, and smelt the increasing odour emanating from the sick man, Pierre moved farther away and would not think about him.

While imprisoned in the shed Pierre had learned, not through his intellect but through his whole being, through life itself, that man is created for happiness, that happiness lies in himself, in the satisfaction of simple human needs; and that all unhappiness is due, not to privation but to superfluity. But now, during these last three weeks of the march, he had learned still another new and comforting truth – that there is nothing in the world to be dreaded. He had learned that just as there is no condition in which man can be happy and absolutely free, so there is no condition in which he need be completely unhappy and not free. He had learned that there is a limit to suffering and a limit to freedom, and that these limits are not far away; that the person in a bed of roses with one crumpled petal suffered as keenly as he suffered now, sleeping on the bare damp earth with one side of him freezing as the other got warm; that in the old days when he had put on his tight dancing-shoes he had been just as uncomfortable as he was now, walking on bare feet that were covered with sores – his footwear having long since fallen to pieces. He discovered that when he had married his wife – of his own free will as it had seemed to him – he had been no more free than now when they locked him up for the night in a stable. Of all that he himself subsequently termed his sufferings, but which at the time he scarcely felt, the worst was the state of his bare, rubbed, scabbed feet. (Horse-flesh was palatable and nourishing, the saltpetre flavour of the gunpowder they used instead of salt was positively pleasant, the weather was not very cold – it was always warm on the march in the daytime, and at night there were the camp-fires – and the lice that devoured him helped to keep his body warm.) The one thing that gave him a bad time of it at the beginning was – his feet.

Examining his sores by the camp-fire on the second day, Pierre thought he could not possibly go another step; but when everybody got up he hobbled along, and presently, when he had warmed to it, he walked without feeling the pain, though at night his feet were a still more shocking sight than before. But he did not look at them and thought of other things.

Now for the first time Pierre realized the full strength of the vitality in man, and the saving power innate in him of being able to transfer his attention, like the safety-valve in a boiler that lets off the surplus steam as soon as the pressure exceeds a certain point.

He did not see and did not hear the prisoners being shot who lagged behind, though more than a hundred had perished in that way. He did not think of Karatayev, who was growing weaker every day and would soon no doubt have to meet the same fate. Still less did Pierre think about himself. The harder his lot and the more appalling the future, the more independent of his present plight were the glad and consoling thoughts, memories and imaginings that came to him.

13

At midday on the 22nd Pierre was walking uphill along the muddy, slippery road, looking at his feet and at the unevenness of the road surface. Occasionally he glanced at the familiar crowd around him, and then again at his feet. The crowd was as familiar to and as much part of him as his own feet. The bluey-grey, bow-legged dog was scampering merrily along by the side of the road, every now and then, in token of her agility and contentment, picking up a hind leg and skipping along on three legs before again darting off on all four to bark at the crows that perched on the carrion. 'Floppy' was more frolicksome and sleeker than she had been in Moscow. All around lay the flesh of different animals – from men to horses – in various stages of decomposition, and as the wolves were kept off by the continual procession of marching men, 'Floppy' was able to eat her fill.

Rain had been falling since early morning, and although it continually seemed as if at any moment it would cease, and the skies would clear, after a short break the downpour would be heavier than ever. The road, saturated with rain, could not soak up any more, and the water ran along the ruts in streams.

Pierre plodded on, looking from side to side, counting his steps and reckoning them off in threes on his fingers. Mentally addressing the rain, he repeated over and over: 'Rain, rain, come again!'

It seemed to him that he was not thinking of anything at all; but somewhere deep down within him his soul was pondering grave and comfortable thoughts of a most subtle spiritual nature to do with a conversation the night before with Karatayev.

Half-frozen at a fire that had gone out, on the previous night's halt Pierre had got up and moved to the next fire, which was burning better. There Platon Karatayev was sitting, with his greatcoat over his head, like a priest's vestment, telling the soldiers in his flowing, pleasant voice, though feeble now and ailing, a story Pierre knew. It was past midnight, the time when Karatayev was usually free of his fever and particularly lively. As Pierre drew near the fire and heard Platon's weak, sickly voice, and saw his pathetic face in the bright firelight, he felt a painful prick at his heart. He was alarmed at his own pity for the man and would have gone away but there was no other fire, so, trying not to look at Platon, he sat down.

'Well, how are you?' he asked.

'How am I? Grumble at sickness, and God won't grant you death,' said Karatayev, and at once went back to the story he had begun.

'And so, brother,' he continued, with a smile on his thin, white face and a peculiar, happy light in his eyes. 'And so, brother ...'

Pierre had heard the story long before. Karatayev had told it to him quite half a dozen times, always taking particular pleasure in it. But, well as Pierre knew the story, he listened to it now as to something new, and the quiet rapture Karatayev evidently felt in telling it communicated itself to Pierre too. It was the tale of an old merchant who lived a good and God-fearing life with his family, and who set out one day to go to the annual fair at Makary with a friend of his, a rich merchant.

They put up for the night at an inn and both retired to bed, and next morning his friend was found robbed and with his throat cut. A blood-stained knife was discovered under the old merchant's pillow. The old man was tried, knouted, and after having the end of his nose slit off – all in due order, as Karatayev put it – he was sent to hard labour in Siberia.

'And so, brother' (it was at this point in the story that Pierre came up), 'ten years or more pass. The good old man is living as a convict, in proper submission and never doing no harm. Only he prays to God to let him die. Well, and one night the convicts was gathered together, just like it might be us here, and the old 'un with 'em. And they starts telling what each is being punished for, and what they was guilty of in the sight of God. This one had taken his brother's life, that one was sentenced for a couple of murders, a third had set a house on fire, while another had simply been a vagrant and 'adn't done nought. "What about you, grandad?" they asks the old man. "What are you here for?" they ask. "Me," says the old 'un. "Me, I'm here to suffer for my own sins, yes and for the sins of others. I have never taken life, nor another man's goods, and I used to give to any needy fellow-creature. A merchant I was, my friends, and great wealth was mine." And so on and so on, he tells the whole story, chapter and verse how it all came about. "For myself," says he, "I don't complain. 'Twas the Lord's doing to try me, no doubt. Only," says he, "'tis the old woman and the bairns I be sorry for." And the old man falls a-weeping. Now it so happened the very man who had murdered the other merchant, you know, was there in the company. "Where was it all, grandad?" he inquires. "What season of the year, and what was the month of it?" He asks this question and that, and his heart grows full, and 'e goes up to the old 'un and falls – plump! – at the feet of him. "Good old man," he says, "'tis me that has brought you here. Gospel truth it is, lads – the old 'un 'ere's innocent as a baby. I done it," says he, "I done the thing: I puts the knife under your pillow whilst you was asleep. Forgive me, grandad," he says, "forgive me, for Christ's sake!"'

Karatayev paused, smiling blissfully as he gazed into the fire and then drew the logs together.

'And the old man said, "God will forgive you," he says, "we are all sinners in His sight. I am suffering for my own sins," and he wept with bitter tears. Well, and what do you think, my friends?' exclaimed Karatayev, his face brightening more and more with a beatific smile, as though the great charm and whole point of his tale lay in what he was about to tell now, 'what do you think, my dear fellow – that murderer went and confessed to the authorities. "Six souls are on me conscience," he says (for he was a great evil-doer), "but it's the old 'un that worries me most. Don't let 'im suffer no more 'cause of what I done." So he explained the whole matter, and it was wrote down and the paper sent in the proper way. The place was a long way off, and the time goes by while they was judging and all the papers to be made out in right order, the authorities, I mean. The matter gets to the Tsar. Whiles, a decree comes from the Tsar: to set the merchant free and give him compensation like it had been awarded. The paper comes, and they begin looking for the old man. "Where is the old man who has been suffering innocently and in vain? A paper has come from the Tsar." And they fell to searching for him.'

Karatayev's lower jaw trembled. 'But God had pardoned him already – dead, he was! That was the way of it, my dears,' Karatayev concluded, and for a long time he sat staring before him with a smile on his lips.

It was not the story itself but its mysterious import and the solemn happiness which irradiated Karatayev's face as he told it, and the mystic significance of that happiness, which filled Pierre's soul with a vague sense of joy.

14

'FALL in!' a voice shouted suddenly.

There was a cheerful commotion among the prisoners and soldiers of the convoy – an air of expecting something festive and solemn. On every side commands were shouted and a party of smartly dressed cavalry on good horses came trotting up from the left, making a circuit round the prisoners. Every face wore the look of tension seen at the approach of important personages. The prisoners huddled together and were pushed off the road. The convoy formed up.

'*L'Empereur! L'Empereur! Le maréchal! Le duc!*' – and hardly had the sleek cavalry passed before a carriage drawn by six greys rattled by. Pierre caught a glimpse of a man in a three-cornered hat with a tranquil look on his handsome, fat white face. It was one of the marshals. His eye fell on Pierre's large and imposing figure, and in the expression with which he frowned and looked away Pierre fancied he detected sympathy and a desire to conceal it.

The general in charge of the transport galloped after the carriage with a red, panic-stricken face, whipping up his skinny horse. Several officers grouped together; the soldiers pressed round them. Everybody looked excited and uneasy.

'What did he say? What did he say? ...' Pierre heard them ask.

While the marshal was driving by, the prisoners had crowded in a bunch, and Pierre noticed Karatayev, whom he had not yet seen that morning. He was sitting in his little military coat leaning against a birch tree. His face still bore the look of joyful emotion with which he had told the story the night before of the merchant who had suffered innocently, but now it had an added quiet solemnity.

Karatayev turned on Pierre his kindly round eyes which at this moment were filled with tears, and there was unmistakable appeal in them – he wanted Pierre to come up so that he could say something to him. But Pierre was afraid for himself. He pretended not to see, and hastily moved away.

When the prisoners set off again Pierre looked back. Karatayev was sitting at the side of the road under the birch-tree, and two Frenchmen were bending over him talking. Pierre did not look round again. He limped on up the hill.

From behind, from the spot where Karatayev had been sitting, came the sound of a shot. Pierre heard the report distinctly but at the moment he heard it he remembered that he had not yet finished reckoning up how many stages were left to Smolensk – a calculation he had begun before the marshal drove by. And he began to count. Two French soldiers, one of them carrying his smoking musket in his hand, ran past Pierre. They both looked pale and in their expressions – one of them glanced timidly at Pierre – there was something resembling what he had seen on the face of the young soldier at the execution. Pierre looked at the soldier and remembered that this man, two days before, had scorched his shirt in drying it at the camp-fire, and how they had all laughed at him.

The dog began to howl behind at the spot where Karatayev had been sitting. 'Silly creature! What is she howling for?' thought Pierre.

The prisoners, his companions marching at his side, like him refrained from looking back to the place where the shot had been fired and the dog was howling; but there was a set look on all their faces.

15

THE cavalry-transport, and the prisoners and the marshal's baggage-train, halted at the village of Shamshevo. They all piled up together round the camp-fires. Pierre made his way to a fire, ate his roast horse-flesh, lay down with his back to the blaze and immediately fell asleep. He fell into the same sort of sleep that he had slept at Mozhaisk, after the battle of Borodino.

Once more real events mingled with his dreams, and once more someone, either himself or another person, was uttering thoughts in his ear, the same thoughts even as had been spoken to him at Mozhaisk.

'Life is everything. Life is God. Everything changes and moves to and fro, and that movement is God. And while there is life there is joy in consciousness of the Godhead. To love life is to love God. More difficult and more blessed than all else is to love this life in one's sufferings, in undeserved sufferings.

'Karatayev!' flashed into Pierre's mind.

And suddenly there rose before him, as vivid as though alive, the image of a long-forgotten, gentle old man who had given him geography lessons in Switzerland. 'Wait,' said the little old man, and he showed Pierre a globe. This globe was a living thing – a quivering ball of no fixed dimensions. Its whole surface consisted of drops closely squeezed together. And all these drops were shifting about, changing places, sometimes several coalescing into one, or one dividing into many. Each drop tried to expand and occupy as much space as possible, but others, striving to do the same, crushed it, sometimes absorbed it, at others melted into it.

'That is life,' said the old teacher.

'How simple and clear,' thought Pierre. 'How is it I never knew that before?'

'In the centre is God, and each drop does its best to expand so as to reflect Him to the greatest extent possible. And it grows, and is absorbed and crowded out, disappears from the surface, sinks back into the depths and emerges again. That was the case with Karatayev: he overflowed and vanished. Do you understand, my child?' said the teacher.

'Do you understand, damn you?' shouted a voice, and Pierre woke up.

He raised his head and sat up. A Frenchman who had just shoved a Russian soldier aside was squatting by the fire roasting a lump of meat on the end of a ramrod. His sleeves were rolled up and his sinewy, hairy red hands with their stubby fingers were deftly twirling the ramrod. The glow of the charcoal lighted up his tanned, melancholy face with its sullen brows.

'Much he cares,' he muttered, quickly addressing a soldier standing behind him. 'Brigand! Clear off!'

And twisting the ramrod he glanced gloomily at Pierre, who turned away and gazed into the darkness. A prisoner, the Russian soldier the Frenchman had pushed away, was crouched near the fire patting something with his hand. Looking more closely, Pierre recognized the bluey-grey dog, sitting beside the soldier wagging her tail.

'Followed us, has she?' said Pierre. 'But Plat –' he began, but did not finish. Suddenly several pictures sprang into his mind all at the same time and all sliding into each other – he saw the look Platon had fixed on him, as he sat under the tree; heard the shot from that same place, and the dog's howl; remembered the guilty faces of the two Frenchmen as they ran past him, and the lowered, smoking gun; was aware of Karatayev's absence at this halt – and he was on the point of letting the realization sink in that Platon had been killed but at that very instant a sudden recollection flashed into his memory, suggested by Heaven knew what, of a summer evening he had spent with a beautiful Polish lady on the veranda of his house in Kiev. And still without linking up the impressions of the day, or drawing any conclusion from them, Pierre closed his eyes and the vision of the country in summer-time mingled with memories of bathing and of that liquid, quivering globe, and he sank deep down into water, until the waters closed over his head.

*

Before sunrise he was awakened by loud and rapid firing and yells. French soldiers were flying past him.

'The Cossacks!' one of them shouted, and a moment later Pierre was surrounded by a throng of Russians.

For a long time he could not take in what was happening to him. All about him he heard his comrades sobbing with joy.

'Brothers! Our own folk! Friends!' Old soldiers were weeping as they embraced Cossacks and hussars.

The hussars and Cossacks crowded round the prisoners, one offering them clothing, another boots and a third bread. Pierre sat choked with tears in their midst, unable to utter a word; he hugged the first soldier who came up, and kissed him, weeping.

*

Dolohov was standing at the gate of the dilapidated manor-house letting the collection of disarmed Frenchmen file past him. The French, excited by all that had happened, were talking loudly among themselves; but as they passed before Dolohov, who stood lightly flicking his boots with his riding-whip and watching them with cold, glassy eyes that boded no good, they became silent. On the other side stood a Cossack of Dolohov's, counting the prisoners and marking off each hundred with a chalk stroke on the gate.

'How many?' Dolohov asked.

'Into the second hundred,' replied the Cossack.

'Get on, get on! – *filez, filez!*' Dolohov kept urging (having picked up the word from the French), and when his eyes met those of the passing prisoners they flashed with a cruel gleam.

Denisov, bare-headed and with a sombre face, walked behind some Cossacks who were carrying the body of Petya Rostov to a hole that had been dug in the garden.

16

AFTER the 28th of October, when the frosts began, the flight of the French assumed a still more tragic character, with men freezing, or roasting themselves to death by the camp-fires, while the Emperor, kings and dukes pursued their homeward way wrapped in furs and riding in carriages, with the treasures they had stolen; but in its essentials the process of the flight and disintegration of the French army continued unchanged.

From Moscow to Vyazma the French forces numbering seventy-three thousand – not counting the Guards (who did nothing all through the war except pillage) – was reduced to thirty-six thousand, though not more than five thousand had perished in battle. Such was the first term in the progression, from which the succeeding ones might be deduced with mathematical precision.

The French army went on melting away and being destroyed in the same proportions from Moscow to Vyazma, from Vyazma to Smolensk, from Smolensk to the Berezina, from the Berezina to Vilna, irrespective of the greater or lesser degree of cold, of pursuit by the Russians, of the barring of their way, or of any other particular conditions, operating separately. Beyond Vyazma the French army, instead of moving in three columns, huddled together into one mass, and went on thus to the end. Berthier wrote to his Emperor (and we know commanding officers feel it permissible to depart rather widely from the truth in describing the condition of their armies), and this is what he said:

I deem it my duty to acquaint your Majesty with the condition of the various corps which have come under my observation on the march the last two or three days. They are almost disbanded. Scarcely a quarter of the men remain with the standards of their regiments; the rest wander off on their own in different directions, with the idea of finding food and escaping discipline. In general they look to Smolensk as the place where they hope to pick up again. During the last few days many of the men have been seen to throw away their cartridges and muskets. In such a state of affairs, whatever your Majesty's ultimate plans may be, the interests of your Majesty's service demand that the army should be rallied at Smolensk and rid, first and foremost, of ineffectives, such as cavalrymen without horses, unnecessary baggage, and artillery-material that is no longer in proportion to our present numbers. As well as a few days' rest the soldiers, who are exhausted by hunger and fatigue, need supplies. Many in these last days have died by the roadside or at the bivouacs. This state of things continually worsens and makes one fear that unless swift measures are taken to avert the evil we shall be exposed to the risk of being unable to control the troops in the event of an engagement.

9th November: 20 miles from Smolensk.

After staggering into Smolensk, the promised land of their dreams, the French fell to fighting one another over the food there, sacking their own stores, until everything had been plundered, when they fled farther.

All hastened on, not knowing whither or why. Still less did that genius Napoleon know why they did so, for there was no one to issue any orders to him. But still he and those about him clung to their old habits: wrote commands, letters, reports, orders of the day; addressed one another as *sire, mon cousin, Prince d'Eckmühl, roi de Naples*, and so on. But the orders and reports were only on paper, no attempt was made to carry them out, because they could not be carried out, and though they called each other Majesty, Highness or Cousin, they all felt that they were miserable wretches who had done much evil, for which they now had to pay the penalty. And though they pretended to be concerned for the army each was thinking selfishly of how to get away quickly and save himself.

17

THE movements of the Russian and French armies during the retreat from Moscow back to the Niemen resemble a game of Russian blindman's-buff, in which two players are blindfolded and one of them rings a bell at intervals to let the other know of his whereabouts. At first he rings the bell with no fear of his opponent, but when he finds himself in a tight corner he tries to steal away noiselessly, and often, thinking to escape, runs straight into his adversary's arms.

At first Napoleon's army made its whereabouts known – that was in the early period of the retreat along the Kaluga highway – but afterwards, when they had taken to the Smolensk road, they ran holding the clapper of the bell, and often, supposing that they were getting away, blundered right into the Russians.

Owing to the rapidity of the French flight and the Russian pursuit, and the consequent exhaustion of the horses, the chief method of ascertaining the enemy's position – reconnaissance by cavalry – was not available. Moreover, in consequence of frequent and rapid changes of position by both armies, what news did come always came too late. If word was received one day that the enemy had been in a certain position on the day before, by the day after when the information could be acted upon the army in question was already a couple of days' march farther on and occupying an entirely different position.

One army fled, the other pursued. Beyond Smolensk the French had a choice of routes and one would have thought that during their four-day stay there they might have found out where the enemy was, have contrived some profitable plan, and tried something new. But after a four-day halt the mob took to the road again, without plan or purpose, running not to the right or to the left but along their old beaten tracks – the worst route they could have chosen – through Krasnoe and Orsha.

Believing that the enemy lay in their rear and not in front, the French hastened on, spreading out and scattering twenty-four hours' march from one another. In front of them all fled the Emperor, then the kings, then the dukes. The Russian army, expecting Napoleon to take the road to the right beyond the Dnieper – the only sensible course – themselves turned to the right and came out on the high road at Krasnoe. And here, just as in the game of blindman's-buff, the French ran into our vanguard. Seeing their enemy thus unexpectedly, the French were thrown into confusion and stopped short in sudden panic but then resumed their flight, abandoning their comrades in the rear. Then for three days separate portions of the French army – first Murat's (the viceroy's), then Davoust's, then Ney's – ran the gauntlet, as it were, of the Russian army. They all abandoned one another, shed their heavy baggage, their artillery, half their men, working their way past the Russians by moving in semicircles only by night.

Ney, who came last because he had lingered to blow up the unoffending walls of Smolensk (in spite of their wretched plight or, rather, in consequence of it, they wanted to beat the floor against which they had hurt themselves) – Ney, coming last, reached Napoleon at Orsha with only a thousand men left of his corps of ten thousand, having forsaken all the rest and all his cannon and got across the Dnieper by stealth at night, at a wooded spot.

From Orsha they fled along the road to Vilna, still playing at blindman's-buff with the pursuing army. At the Berezina there was confusion again, numbers were drowned and many surrendered, but those who managed to ford the river dashed on. Their chief commander donned a fur coat and, seating himself in a sledge, was off, deserting his companions. Those who could escaped the same way; those who could not surrendered or perished.

18

ONE might have supposed that the historians, who ascribe the actions of the masses to the will of one man, would have found it impossible to fit the flight of Napoleon's armies into their theory, considering that during this period of the campaign the French did all they could to bring about their own ruin, and that not one single movement of that rabble of men, from the time they turned on to the Kaluga road up to the day their leader fled from his army, betrayed a hint of rhyme or reason. But no! Mountains of volumes have been written by historians about this campaign and in all of them we find accounts of Napoleon's masterly arrangements and deeply considered plans; of the manoeuvres executed by the troops, of the strategy with which they were led and the military genius shown by the marshals.

The withdrawal from Malo-Yaroslavets, when nothing hindered Napoleon from taking to country amply stocked with supplies, and the parallel road was open to him along which Kutuzov afterwards pursued him – this wholly unnecessary return via a devastated road is explained to us as being the outcome of profound considerations. We are offered similar profound considerations to account for his retreat from Smolensk to Orsha. Then we have a description of his heroism at Krasnoe, where he is reported to have been prepared to put himself at the head of his troops and give battle, and to have marched about with a birch-stick, saying:

'I have played the Emperor long enough: it is now time to be the general.'

And yet in spite of this, and immediately after, he takes to flight again, leaving to their fate the scattered fragments of his army struggling after him.

Then we are told of the nobility of some of the marshals, especially Ney – nobility which consisted in his sneaking by a roundabout way through the forest by night, and across the Dnieper and escaping into Orsha without his standards and his artillery, and with nine-tenths of his men gone.

And lastly, the final departure of the great Emperor from his heroic army is presented to us by the historians as something sublime – a stroke of genius. Even that final act of running away, which in ordinary language would be characterized as the lowest depth of baseness, such as every child is taught to be ashamed of – even that act finds justification in the historian's language.

When it is impossible to stretch the very elastic thread of historical ratiocination any farther, when an action flagrantly contradicts all that humanity calls good and even right, the historians fetch out the saving idea of 'greatness'. 'Greatness' would appear to exclude all possibility of applying standards of right and wrong. For the 'great' man nothing is wrong; there is no atrocity for which a 'great' man can be blamed.

'*C'est grand!*' cry the historians, and that is enough. Goodness and evil have ceased to be: there is only '*grand*' and not '*grand*'. *Grand* is good, not-*grand* is bad. To be *grand* is according to them the necessary attribute of certain exceptional beings called by them 'heroes'. And Napoleon, taking himself off home wrapped in a warm fur cloak and abandoning to their fate not only his comrades but men who (in his belief) were there because he had brought them there, feels *que c'est grand*, and his soul is at ease.

'From the sublime' (he saw something sublime in himself) 'to the ridiculous there is only one step,' said he. And for fifty years the whole world has gone on repeating, '*Sublime! Grand! Napoléon le grand!*'

Du sublime au ridicule il n'y a qu'un pas!

And it never enters anyone's head that to admit a greatness not commensurable with the standard of right and wrong is merely to admit one's own nothingness and immeasurable littleness.

For us who have the standard of good and evil given us by Christ, nothing can claim to be outside the law. And there is no greatness where simplicity, goodness and truth are absent.

19

WHAT Russian, reading the accounts of the latter period of the campaign of 1812, has not known an irksome feeling of vexation, dissatisfaction and perplexity? Who has not asked himself: How was it the French were not all captured or wiped out when all three of our armies surrounded them in superior numbers, when the French were a disorderly, starving, freezing rabble, surrendering in droves, and when (as history relates) the aim of the Russians was precisely to stop, cut off and take them all prisoner?

How was it that the Russian army, which when numerically weaker than the French had given battle at Borodino, did not achieve its purpose when it had surrounded the French on three sides and its intention was to capture them? Can the French be so immensely superior to us that we are not equal to beating them after surrounding them with stronger and more numerous forces?

History (or what is called by that name) in reply to these questions declares that we must look for an explanation in the failure of Kutuzov and Tormasov and Tchichagov, and this general and that general, to execute such and such manoeuvres.

But why did they not execute these manoeuvres? And why if they were guilty of not carrying out a prearranged plan were they not tried and punished? But even if we admit that Kutuzov and Tchichagov and the rest were responsible for the Russian non-success it is still incomprehensible why, the position of the Russian army being what it was at Krasnoe and the Berezina (in both cases our forces were numerically superior), the French army with its marshals, kings and Emperor, was not captured if that was the Russian intention.

This strange phenomenon cannot be explained – as Russian military historians explain it – by saying that it was because Kutuzov prevented offensive operations, for we know that he was unable to restrain the troops from attacking at Vyazma and Tarutino.

Why was it that the Russian army, which with inferior forces had withstood the enemy in full strength at Borodino, was defeated at Krasnoe and the Berezina when fighting in superior numbers against the demoralized mob of the French?

If the aim of the Russians really was to cut off and take prisoner Napoleon and his marshals – and that aim was not only frustrated but every attempt in its direction failed most disgracefully – then this last period of the campaign is quite rightly considered by the French to be a series of victories, and quite wrongly represented by the Russians as redounding to our glory.

Russian military historians, in so far as they have any regard for logic, must come to this conclusion and, for all their lyrical rhapsodies about valour and devotion and so forth, are reluctantly obliged to admit that the French retreat from Moscow was a series of victories for Napoleon and of defeats for Kutuzov.

But, putting national vanity entirely aside, one cannot help feeling that such a conclusion involves a contradiction, seeing that the series of French victories brought them to complete annihilation, while the series of Russian defeats culminated in the absolute overthrow of their enemy and the liberation of their own country.

The source of this contradiction lies in the fact that historians, studying events in the light of the letters of kings and generals, of memoirs, reports, projects and so on, have attributed to this last period of the war of 1812 an aim that never existed – that of cutting off and capturing Napoleon with his marshals and his army.

Such a plan never was, and never could have been: there was no reason for it, and it would have been quite impossible to execute.

There was no object in such a plan, firstly because Napoleon's demoralized army was flying from Russia with all possible speed – that is to say, was doing just what every Russian desired. Where would have been the point in performing various military operations against the French who were running away as fast as they could go?

Secondly, it would have been senseless to try and block the passage of men whose whole energies were bent on flight.

Thirdly, it would have been absurd to sacrifice troops in order to destroy the French army which without external interference was destroying itself at such a rate that, although every road lay open and undisputed, they could carry across the frontier only the small number that remained to them in the month of December, namely, one-hundredth part of the original army.

Fourthly, it would have been senseless to wish to seize the Emperor, kings and dukes – whose capture would have been in the highest degree embarrassing for the Russians, as the ablest diplomatists of the time (Joseph de Maistre and others) recognized. Still more nonsensical would have been any desire to capture the French army, when our own forces had dwindled to half before reaching Krasnoe and a whole division would have been needed to convoy every corps of prisoners, and when our own soldiers were not always getting full rations and the prisoners already taken were dying of hunger.

All the deep-laid schemes to cut off and capture Napoleon and his army would have been like a market-gardener who, with the idea of driving out a herd of cattle trampling his beds, rushes to the gate to belabour them about the head as they come out. The only thing that could be said in the gardener's justification would be that he was very angry. But not even this excuse could be made for those who devised this project, for they were not the ones who had suffered from the trampled vegetable-beds.

But, besides being absurd, it would have been impossible to cut off Napoleon and his army.

Impossible, first, because, since experience shows that the movement of columns of soldiers about a battle area of two or three miles never quite coincides with the plans, the probability that Tchichagov, Kutuzov and Wittgenstein effecting a junction at a designated place on time was so remote as to be tantamount to impossibility, which, in fact, was what Kutuzov was thinking when he received the plan from Petersburg and remarked that diversions conceived over great distances never produce the desired results.

Secondly, it was impossible because to paralyse the force of inertia with which Napoleon's army was retiring back along its track would have required incomparably larger forces than the Russians possessed.

Thirdly, it was impossible because the military term 'to cut off' has no meaning. One can cut off a slice of bread, but not an army. To cut off an army – to bar its road – is quite impossible: there is always some way of making a *détour*, and there is the night, when nothing can be seen. The military strategist has only to look at Krasnoe and the Berezina to be convinced of this. Again, it is only possible to capture prisoners if they agree to be captured, just as it is only possible to catch a swallow if it perches on your hand. Men can be taken prisoner if they surrender, like the Germans, in due form by all the rules of strategy and tactics. But the French troops quite rightly did not see that there was anything to be gained by this, since death by hunger and cold awaited them alike in flight or captivity.

The fourth and chief reason why it was impossible is that never since the world began has a war been fought under such terrible conditions as those which obtained in 1812, and the Russian army strained every nerve to the utmost in its pursuit of the French, and could not have done more without perishing itself.

In its march from Tarutino to Krasnoe the Russian army lost fifty thousand sick or stragglers, that is, a number equal to the population of a large provincial town. Half of them fell out without a battle.

And it is in regard to this period of the campaign – when the troops lacked boots and sheepskin coats, were short of provisions and without vodka, and camping out at night for months in the snow with fifteen degrees of frost; when there were only seven or eight hours of daylight and the rest of the twenty-four was night during which discipline cannot exert the same influence; when men were put in peril of death (and death knows no discipline), not for a few hours only, as in a battle, but for months on end, every minute seeing a mortal struggle against hunger and cold; when half the army gave up the ghost in a single month – it is in regard to this period of the campaign that the historians tell us how Miloradovich ought to have executed a flank movement on one side, while Tormasov did the same on the other, and Tchichagov should have crossed over somewhere else (with the snow more than knee-deep), and how this one 'routed' and that one 'cut off' the French, and so forth, and so on.

The Russians, half of whom died, did all that could and should have been done to attain an end worthy of the nation, and they are not to blame because other Russians, comfortably ensconced in warm studies, proposed that they should do the impossible.

All the strange discrepancies, which we find incomprehensible to-day, between the events as they happened and the official records arise solely because the historians writing their histories have described the noble sentiments and fine speeches of various generals, instead of giving us a history of the facts.

They attach great consequence to what Miloradovich said, to the honours bestowed on this general or that, and their conjectures; but the question of those fifty thousand men who were left in hospitals or their graves holds not the slightest interest for them, for it does not come within the scope of their investigations.

And yet we have only to discard our researches among the reports and plans of the generals and consider the movements of those hundreds of thousands of men who took a direct part in the events, and all the questions that seemed insoluble before will at once be satisfactorily answered with extraordinary ease and simplicity.

The aim of cutting off Napoleon and his army never existed save in the imagination of some dozen individuals. It could not have existed because it was absurd and impracticable.

The people had but one object: to rid their land of invaders. That aim was effected primarily of itself, when the French ran away and all that was necessary was not to check their flight. In the second place it was promoted by the guerrilla warfare which exterminated the French piecemeal; and thirdly, by the fact of a large Russian army following in the rear of the French, ready to use its strength in case of any pause in their retreat.

The Russian army had to act like a whip urging on a springing animal. And the experienced driver knew that it was far more effective to threaten with whip upraised rather than lash the running animal about the head.

PART FOUR

I

WHEN a man sees an animal dying, horror seizes him: substance similar to his own is perishing before his eyes, is ceasing to be. But when the dying creature is a human being, and a beloved one, over and above horror at the extinction of life there is a severance, a spiritual wound, which like a physical wound is sometimes fatal, sometimes heals, but always aches and shrinks from any external chafing touch.

After Prince Andrei's death Natasha and Princess Maria both felt this alike. Crushed in spirit, they closed their eyes under the menacing cloud of death that hovered about them, and dared not look life in the face. Carefully they guarded their open wounds from every rough and painful contact. Everything – a carriage driving swiftly along the street, the announcement that dinner was ready, the maid asking which dress to put out; worse still, any word of insincere, perfunctory sympathy – set the wound throbbing, seemed an affront, and violated the urgent silence in which they were both striving to listen to the stern and terrible choir still echoing in their ears, and hindered their contemplation of the mysterious, limitless vistas which for an instant had opened out before them.

Only when they were alone together were they free from such outrage and hurt. They spoke little to one another. When they did speak it was of the most insignificant matters. And both of them alike avoided any allusion to the future.

To admit the possibility of a future seemed to them an insult to his memory. Still more sedulously did they shun in their talk everything that had reference to the departed. It seemed to them that what they had lived through and felt could not be expressed in words, and that any allusion to the details of his life profaned the majesty and sacredness of the mystery that had been accomplished before their eyes.

Continual restraint in what they said, their constant and studious avoidance of everything that might lead to mention of him – this halting on all sides at the barriers fencing off what might not be spoken about – brought before their minds with still greater purity and clearness what they were both feeling.

But pure, unmitigated grief is as impossible as pure, unmitigated joy. Princess Maria in her position as absolute and independent arbiter of her own fate and guardian and instructor of her nephew was the first to be called back by the exigencies of life from that world of sorrow in which she dwelt for the first fortnight. She received letters from her relatives which had to be answered; the room in which little Nikolai had been put was damp and he began to cough; Alpatych came to Yaroslavl with reports on the state of their affairs, and advice and suggestions that they should return to Moscow to the house in Vozdvizhenka street, which had not been damaged and only needed some trifling repairs. Life would not stand still, and it was necessary to live. Hard as it was for Princess Maria to emerge from the secluded realm of contemplation in which she had been living till then, and sorry and almost ashamed as she felt at leaving Natasha alone, the cares of everyday life demanded her participation, and against her will she had to give herself up to them. She went through the accounts with Alpatych, conferred with Dessalles about her nephew, and began her arrangements and preparations for the journey to Moscow.

Natasha was left to herself, and from the time Princess Maria started to be taken up with preparations for departure she held aloof from her too.

Princess Maria asked the countess to let Natasha come with her to Moscow, and both parents eagerly agreed to this suggestion, for they could see their daughter's physical strength declining more every day and hoped that a change of scene and the advice of Moscow doctors might do her good.

'I am not going anywhere,' Natasha replied, when the idea was put to her. 'All I ask is to be left in peace!' And she ran out of the room, scarcely able to restrain her tears – tears of vexation and irritation rather than of sorrow.

Since she had felt herself deserted by Princess Maria and alone in her grief, Natasha spent most of the time in her room by herself, sitting with her feet curled up in a corner of the sofa and, while her slender nervous fingers kept tearing or crumpling something or other, staring with fixed eyes at whatever fell under her gaze. This solitude exhausted her, tortured her, but it was exactly what she needed. As soon as anyone went in to her she would get up quickly, change her position and expression, and pick up a book or some needlework, obviously waiting impatiently for the intruder to leave.

She felt all the time as if she were on the verge of understanding, of penetrating the mystery on which her spiritual vision was fastened with a terrible questioning too terrible for her to bear.

One day towards the end of December Natasha, thin and pale, dressed in a black woollen gown, with her plait of hair coiled up into a careless knot, was sitting with her feet tucked under her at one end of the sofa, nervously crumpling and smoothing the ends of her sash while she looked at a corner of the door.

She was gazing as it were towards the place where he had vanished, to that farther shore on the other side of life. And that shore, of which she had never thought in the old days and which had seemed to her so far away and improbable, was now nearer and more familiar and comprehensible to her than this side of life where everything was emptiness and desolation, or suffering and indignity.

She was gazing into the world where she knew him to be; but she could not picture him otherwise than as he had looked here on earth. She saw him again as he had been at Mytishchy, at Troitsa, at Yaroslavl.

She saw his face, heard his voice, repeated his words and words which she had said to him, and sometimes imagined other words they might have spoken.

She remembered seeing him lying back in a low chair in his velvet, fur-lined cloak, leaning his head on his thin pale hand. His chest looked dreadfully hollow, his shoulders hunched. His lips were firmly set, his eyes glittered and a wrinkle was coming and going on his pale forehead. One of his legs was just perceptibly twitching with a rapid tremor. Natasha knew that he was struggling with terrible pain. 'What is that pain like? Why did he have it? What does he feel? What pain he is in!' thought Natasha. He had noticed her watching him, had raised his eyes and begun to speak gravely:

'One thing would be awful,' he said, 'to bind oneself for ever to a suffering invalid. It would be continual torture.' And he had looked searchingly at her. Natasha, as usual, had answered without giving herself time to think. She had said: 'It can't go on like this – it won't. You will get well – quite well.'

She was seeing him now as she had then, and living over in her memory all that she had felt at the time. She recalled the long, sad, stern look he had given her at those words, and she understood all the reproach and despair in that protracted gaze.

'I agreed,' Natasha said to herself now, 'that it would be dreadful if he always continued to suffer. I said so only meaning that it would be awful for him, but he meant that it would be awful *for me*. He still wanted to live then, and was afraid of dying. And I said it so crudely and stupidly. I wasn't meaning it that way. I was thinking of something quite different. If I had said what I meant, I should have said: even if he had to go on dying – dying all the time before my eyes – I should have been happy compared with what I am now. Now ... there is nothing, nobody. Did he know that? No. He didn't know and never will know. And now it can never, never be put right.' And again he was saying the same words but this time Natasha in her imagination made him a different answer. She stopped him and said: 'Horrible for you, but not for me. You know that for me life without you would be nothing, and to suffer with you is the greatest happiness for me,' and he took her hand and pressed it, just as he had pressed it on that terrible evening four days before his death. And in her imagination she said other words of tenderness and love which she might have uttered then but only spoke now: 'I love you ... you ... I love you, I love you ...' she said, wringing her hands convulsively and clenching her teeth in her extremity.

And the bitter sweetness of grief was taking possession of her, and her eyes were filling with tears, but all at once she asked herself to whom she was saying this. 'Where is he and *what* is he now?'

And again everything was shrouded in a dull aching perplexity, and again with a strained frown she tried to peer into the world where he was. And – yes – yes – surely she was just penetrating the mystery. ... But at the very instant when the incomprehensible seemed about to reveal itself a loud rattling of the door handle struck painfully on her ears. With a frightened look on her face, and not thinking of Natasha, Dunyasha the maid burst abruptly into the room.

'Come, miss, come quickly to your papa,' said Dunyasha with a strange, excited expression. 'A misfortune ... Count Petya ... a letter,' she gasped out, sobbing.

2

NATASHA at this time was feeling generally remote from everybody, and most of all from her own family. All of them – her father, mother and Sonya – were so near to her, so familiar, so *everyday*, that every word they uttered, every sentiment they expressed, seemed to her to desecrate the world in which she had been living of late, and she looked upon them with eyes not only indifferent but positively hostile. She heard Dunyasha's cry about Count Petya, and a misfortune, but did not take them in.

'What misfortune could they have? What misfortune could happen to them? They just continue on in their old, humdrum, quiet way,' she thought to herself.

As she went into the drawing-room her father was hastily coming out of her mother's room. His face was puckered up and wet with tears. He had evidently run out of the room to give vent to the sobs that were choking him. Seeing Natasha, he waved his arms despairingly and broke into convulsive, painful sobs that distorted his soft round face.

'Pe ... Petya. ... Go to her ... go ... she ... she ... is calling ...' and weeping like a child he tottered on feeble legs to a chair and almost fell into it, covering his face with his hands.

Suddenly as it were an electric shock ran through Natasha's whole being. Terrible anguish stabbed her heart. She felt a dreadful agony as if something were being rent within her and she were dying. But the pain were immediately followed by a feeling of release from the impression of being suspended from life. At the sight of her father and the sound of a fearful harsh cry from her mother through the door she instantly forgot herself and her own grief.

She ran to her father but with a feeble gesture he pointed towards her mother's door. Princess Maria, pale and with trembling lower jaw, came out from the countess's room and took Natasha by the hand, saying something to her. Natasha neither saw nor heard her. With swift steps she went to the door, paused for a moment as if struggling with herself, and then ran to her mother.

The countess was lying back in a low chair in a strange awkward position, stiffening herself and beating her head against the wall. Sonya and some of the maids were holding her by the arms.

'Natasha! Natasha! ...' the countess was screaming. 'It's not true ... it's not true. ... He's lying. ... Natasha!' she shrieked, pushing Sonya and the maids away. 'Go away, all of you, it's not true! Killed! ... ha, ha, ha! ... It's not true!'

Natasha leaned a knee on the low chair, stooped over her mother, put her arms round her and with unexpected strength lifted her up, turned her face towards herself and pressed her close.

'Mamma! ... darling! ... I'm here, dearest mamma!' she murmured again and again, without a second's intermission.

She did not let go of her mother but struggled gently with her, demanded a pillow and water, and unfastened and tore open her mother's dress.

'Dearest, my darling ... mamma ... my precious,' she kept whispering while she kissed her hair, her hands, her face, and feeling the streaming, irrepressible tears tickling her nose and cheeks.

The countess squeezed her daughter's hand, closed her eyes and was quieter for a moment. All at once she sat up, unnaturally quickly, looked vacantly about her and, seeing Natasha, began hugging her head to her with all her might. Then she turned her daughter's face, wincing with pain, towards her and gazed long and searchingly into it.

'Natasha, you love me?' she said in a soft, trusting whisper. 'Natasha, you would not deceive me? You will tell me the whole truth?'

Natasha looked at her with eyes brimming with tears, her whole face a single entreaty for forgiveness and love.

'Mamma ... dearest!' she repeated over and over, putting forth all the strength of her love to try and find some way of taking on herself a little of the load of grief crushing her mother.

And again in the impotent struggle against reality her mother, refusing to believe that she could still exist when her beloved boy was killed in the bloom of life, took refuge from fact in the world of delirium.

Natasha could never afterwards remember how that day passed, nor that night, nor the following day and night. She did not sleep and did not leave her mother's side. Natasha's love, patient and persistent, seemed to enfold the countess every second, not with consolation, not with explanation, but simply beckoning her back to life. On the third night the countess was very quiet for a few minutes, and

Natasha rested her head on the arm of her chair and closed her eyes. The bedstead creaked; Natasha opened her eyes. The countess was sitting up in bed and speaking softly.

'How glad I am my boy has come. You are tired. Would you like some tea?' Natasha went up to her. 'You have grown so handsome and manly,' continued the countess, taking her daughter's hand.

'Mamma, what are you saying! …'

'Natasha, he is dead, he is no more!'

And, embracing her daughter, the countess for the first time began to weep.

3

PRINCESS MARIA postponed her departure. Sonya and the count tried to take turns with Natasha but could not. They saw that she was the only one able to keep the mother from wild despair. For three weeks she stayed in her mother's room, sleeping on a lounge chair, feeding her and talking to her without pause because her tender caressing voice was the only thing that calmed the countess.

There was no healing the wound in the mother's heart. Petya's death had torn half her life away. When the news had come she had been a fresh and vigorous woman of fifty; a month later she emerged from her room a listless old woman with no interest in the world. But the same blow which almost killed the countess – this new blow brought Natasha back to life.

A spiritual wound caused by laceration of the spirit is like a physical wound and, strange as it may seem, slowly closes over. And after the deep wound – spiritual or physical – has cicatrized, and the torn edges have come together, it only heals completely as the result of a vital force thrusting up from within.

So healed Natasha's wound. She had believed that her life was over. But suddenly her love for her mother showed her that the essence of life – love – was still active within her. Love awoke, and life awoke.

Prince Andrei's last days had bound Princess Maria and Natasha together. This fresh trouble united them still more closely. Princess Maria put off her departure and for three weeks tended Natasha as though she were a sick child. Those weeks spent by Natasha in her mother's room had been a severe drain on her strength.

One afternoon, noticing Natasha shivering feverishly, Princess

Maria brought her to her own room and made her lie down on the bed. Natasha submitted, but when Princess Maria had drawn the blinds and was going away she called her back.

'I'm not sleepy, Marie, stay with me.'

'You are tired – try and have a sleep.'

'No, no. Why did you bring me away? She will be asking for me.'

'She is much better. She was talking so naturally today,' said Princess Maria.

Natasha lay on the bed and in the semi-darkness of the room studied Princess Maria's face.

'Is she like him?' Natasha wondered. 'Yes, and no. But there is something original, peculiar to herself about her – she's a quite new, unknown person. And she loves me. What is she like underneath? Entirely good. But what is it – what does she think? What is her opinion of me? Yes, she's a beautiful person.'

'Marie, dearest,' she said timidly, drawing Princess Maria's hand towards her. 'Marie, don't think that I'm wicked. You don't, do you? Marie, precious, I do so love you! Let us be real, bosom friends.'

And Natasha, throwing her arms round Princess Maria, began kissing her face and hands. Princess Maria felt both shy and happy at this demonstration of feeling.

From that day one of those tender and passionate friendships such as exist only between women was established between Princess Maria and Natasha. They were constantly kissing and saying tender things to one another, and spent most of their time together. If one went out the other became restless and hastened to join her. They felt more at peace together than when alone. A tie stronger than friendship sprang up between them: a singular feeling of life being possible only in each other's company.

Sometimes they were silent for hours on end; sometimes, in their beds at night they would begin talking and talk on till morning. They talked for the most part of the remote past. Princess Maria would speak of her childhood, of her mother, her father, her hopes and dreams; and Natasha, who with a carefree lack of understanding would have been repelled in the old days by this life of devotion and resignation, this poetry of Christian self-sacrifice, now with the sympathy born of the affection that bound her to Princess Maria, learnt to love her past too and to understand a side of life of which she had had no conception before. She had no thought of applying that humility and abnegation to her own life, because she was accustomed to look for other joys, but she understood and loved in another those previously incomprehensible virtues. Princess Maria, too, as she listened to Natasha's stories of her childhood and early girlhood, had a glimpse of horizons she knew nothing of – of a belief in life and the joys of life.

They still refrained from mentioning *him*, for fear of profaning (as it seemed to them) the exalted feeling in their hearts by words, but this reticence led them, though they would not have believed it, into gradually forgetting him.

Natasha had grown thin and pale, and physically so run down that everyone was always talking about her health, and she was glad it was so. But sometimes she was suddenly overcome by a dread not simply of death but of sickness, of ill-health, of losing her looks, and she would find herself examining her bare arm, surprised at its thinness, or gazing at her drawn, pitiful face in the looking-glass in the morning. It seemed to her that this was as it should be, and yet it was awfully sad.

One day after hurrying upstairs she noticed she was out of breath. Immediately, in spite of herself, she invented some excuse to go down, and then ran upstairs again, to try her strength and see what she could do.

Another time when she called Dunyasha her voice cracked, so she called again – though she could hear Dunyasha coming – called her in the deep chest tones in which she used to sing, and listened attentively.

She did not suspect it and would not have thought it possible, but underneath what seemed to her the impenetrable layer of mould which covered her soul tender, delicate young shoots of grass were already sprouting, destined to take root and with their living verdure so shroud the grief that weighed her down that soon it would no longer be seen or noticed. The wound had begun to heal from within.

At the end of January Princess Maria left for Moscow, and the count insisted on Natasha's going with her to consult the doctors.

4

AFTER the encounter at Vyazma, where Kutuzov had been unable to restrain the eagerness of his troops to overrun and cut off the enemy, and so on, the further flight of the French and pursuit by the Russians continued as far as Krasnoe without any pitched battle. The flight was so rapid that the Russian army racing after the French could not keep up with them: cavalry- and artillery-horses dropped on the road, and information as to the movements of the French was never reliable.

The Russian soldiers were so spent by this unbroken march at the rate of some twenty-seven miles a day that they could not move a step faster.

To appreciate the degree of exhaustion of the Russians it is only necessary to realize the significance of the fact that the army – a hundred thousand strong on leaving Tarutino, and losing no more than five thousand killed and wounded, and not a hundred prisoners – numbered only fifty thousand on reaching Krasnoe.

The rapidity of the Russian pursuit was as disintegrating to our army as the flight of the French was to theirs. The only difference was that the Russian army moved at will, free from the threat of annihilation that hung over the French, and that French sick and stragglers fell into enemy hands while Russian stragglers were among their own people. The principal cause of the reduction of Napoleon's army was the swiftness of its flight, and indubitable proof of this is furnished by the corresponding dwindling of the Russian army.

Just as at Tarutino and Vyazma, all Kutuzov's energies were directed not to arresting – so far as lay in his power – the fatal movement of the French (which was what Petersburg and the Russian army generals wanted) but to promoting it, and slackening the speed of his own troops.

But, in addition to the exhaustion of the men and the tremendous losses due to the swiftness of their advance, another reason for easing the pace and not being in a hurry presented itself to Kutuzov. The object of the Russian army was the pursuit of the French. The route the French would take was uncertain, and therefore the more closely our soldiers followed on their heels the greater the distance they had to traverse. Only by keeping some way in the rear could they take short cuts across the zigzags made by the enemy. All the artful manoeuvres proposed by our generals would have meant forced marches over longer distances, whereas the only reasonable course was to reduce these marches. And this was the aim to which Kutuzov devoted himself throughout the whole campaign from Moscow to

Vilna – not casually or intermittently, but so consistently that he never once deviated from it.

Kutuzov knew, not by reasoning or science but with every fibre of his Russian being – knew and felt, as did every Russian soldier, that the French were beaten, that the enemy was on the run and must be seen off the premises; but together with his soldiers he was aware of all the hardships of a campaign unprecedented for the speed of its marches and the time of year.

But to the generals (especially the foreign ones), burning to distinguish themselves, to dazzle the world, for some reason or other to take some duke or king prisoner, it seemed that now – just when any battle must be horrible and senseless – was the very time for fighting battles and conquering somebody. Kutuzov simply shrugged his shoulders when one after another they came to him with plans for manoeuvres to be executed by the ill-shod, insufficiently-clad and half-starved soldiers whose numbers in one month, and without a battle, had fallen to half, and who would even in the most favourable circumstances have a longer distance to traverse before they reached the frontier than they had come already.

This desire on the part of the generals to distinguish themselves, to perform manoeuvres, to overthrow and cut off, was particularly conspicuous whenever the Russian army came up against the French.

Such was the case at Krasnoe, where they had expected to find one of the three French columns and stumbled instead on Napoleon himself with a force of sixteen thousand. Despite all Kutuzov's efforts to avoid this disastrous engagement and to preserve his troops, the massacre of the shattered concourse of Frenchmen was kept up by the weary, worn-out Russians for three days at Krasnoe.

Toll wrote a disposition: 'First column to advance to this spot,' etc. And as usual everything took place otherwise than as laid down. Prince Eugène of Württemberg fired away from the hill-top at the mob of French as they raced by, and asked for reinforcements which did not arrive. By night the French dispersed to get round the Russians, hid themselves in the forest, and all who could struggled on again.

Miloradovich, who used to say that he cared nothing whatever about the commissariat arrangements of his detachment, and who could never be found when he was wanted – that self-styled *chevalier sans peur et sans reproche* – always eager for parleys with the French, sent envoys demanding their surrender, wasted time and did not carry out the orders he had received.

'I make you a present of that column, lads,' he said, riding up to his men and pointing out the French to his cavalry.

And the cavalry, with spur and sabre urging on horses that could scarcely move, trotted with great effort to the column he had bestowed on them – that is to say, a rabble of frozen, benumbed and famished Frenchmen – and the column that had been presented to them threw down their weapons and surrendered, which was what they had been longing to do for weeks past.

At Krasnoe they took twenty-six thousand prisoners, several hundred cannon, a stick of some sort which was promptly dubbed a 'marshal's baton', and disputed as to who had distinguished himself, and were well content with their achievement, though they much regretted not having captured Napoleon, or at least some hero, a marshal, say, and blamed one another, and especially Kutuzov, for having failed to do so.

These men, carried away by their passions, were but the blind instruments of the most melancholy law of necessity; but they believed themselves heroes and imagined that they were doing most noble and honourable work. They criticized Kutuzov, and declared that from the very beginning of the campaign he had prevented them from vanquishing Napoleon, that he thought of nothing but the comforts of the flesh and was unwilling to leave the neighbourhood of the Linen Mills because he was comfortable there, that at Krasnoe he had checked the advance, having completely lost his head when he heard of Napoleon's presence, and that it was quite probable that he had a secret understanding with Napoleon, that he had been bought over by him,* and so on and so forth.

Not only did his contemporaries, misled by the violence of their feeling, speak thus: posterity and history have acclaimed Napoleon as *grand*, while Kutuzov is qualified by foreigners as a sly, dissolute, feeble old intriguer, and by Russians as a nondescript creature – a sort of puppet, useful only because he had a Russian name. ...

* Wilson's *Diary*. L.T.

5

In 1812 and 1813 Kutuzov was openly accused of blundering. The Emperor was dissatisfied with him. And in a recent history inspired by promptings from the highest quarters Kutuzov is spoken of as a cunning Court liar, quaking at the name of Napoleon, and guilty through his mismanagement at Krasnoe and the Berezina of robbing the Russian army of the glory of complete victory over the French.*

Such is the lot, not of great men – *grands hommes* – whom the Russian mind does not acknowledge – but of those rare and always solitary individuals who, divining the will of Providence, subordinate their personal will to it. The hatred and contempt of the multitude is their punishment for discerning the higher laws.

For Russian historians (strange and terrible to say!) Napoleon, that most insignificant tool of history who never anywhere, even in exile, showed human dignity – Napoleon is the object of adulation and enthusiasm: he is *grand*. But Kutuzov, the man who from first to last in the year 1812, from Borodino to Vilna, was never once, by word or deed, false to himself, who presents an example, exceptional in history, of self-denial and present insight into the future significance of what was happening – Kutuzov appears to them as some colourless, pitiable being, and whenever they speak of him in connexion with the year 1812 they always seem a little ashamed of the whole episode.

And yet it is difficult to recall an historical character whose activity was so unswervingly and constantly directed to a single aim; and it would be difficult to imagine an aim more worthy or more consonant with the will of a whole people. Still more difficult would it be to find an instance in history where the aim of any historical personage has been so completely accomplished as that towards which all Kutuzov's efforts were devoted in 1812.

Kutuzov never talked of 'forty centuries looking down from the Pyramids,' of the sacrifices he was making for the Fatherland, of what he meant to do or had done. He did not as a rule talk about himself, adopted no pose, always appeared to be the plainest and most ordin-

* *History of the Year 1812: The character of Kutuzov and reflections on the unsatisfactory results of the battles at Krasnoe,* by Bogdanovich. L.T.

ary man, and said the plainest and most ordinary things. He wrote letters to his daughters and to Madame de Staël, read novels, liked the company of pretty women, joked with generals, officers and the soldiers, and never contradicted anybody who tried to argue with him. When Count Rostopchin galloped up to Kutuzov on the Yauza bridge and charged him personally with having lost Moscow, and said: 'Didn't you promise not to abandon Moscow without a battle?' Kutuzov replied: 'And I shall not abandon Moscow without a battle,' although Moscow was in fact already abandoned. When Arakcheyev arrived from the Emperor to say that Yermolov should be appointed to the command of the artillery Kutuzov answered: 'Yes, I was just saying so myself,' though a moment before he had said just the opposite. What did it matter to him – the one man amid a foolish crowd to grasp the whole mighty significance of what was happening – what did it matter to him whether Count Rostopchin attributed the disasters of the capital to him or to himself? Still less could it concern him who was appointed chief of artillery.

Not merely in these instances but on all occasions this old man, whose experience of life had taught him that ideas and the words which serve to express them are not what move men to action, frequently said things which were quite meaningless – uttering the first words which came into his head.

And yet this same man, so heedless of his words, never in the whole period of his command let fall a syllable which would have been inconsistent with the single aim towards the attainment of which he was working all through the war. With obvious reluctance, with bitter conviction that he would not be understood, he more than once, in very diverse circumstances, gave expression to his real thoughts. The battle of Borodino saw his first difference of opinion with those about him: he alone persisted in declaring that *the battle of Borodino was a victory*, and this view he continued to assert both verbally and in his dispatches and reports and right to his dying day. He alone said that *the loss of Moscow is not the loss of Russia*. His reply to Lauriston with his overtures for peace was: *There can be no peace, for such is the people's will*. He alone during the retreat of the French said that *all our manoeuvres are unnecessary, everything is being accomplished of itself better than we could desire*; that *what we have to do is to give the enemy a 'golden bridge'* (*and let them destroy themselves*); that *the battles of Tarutino, Vyazma and Krasnoe were none of them necessary*; that *as many men as possible must be saved to reach the frontier*; and that *he would not sacrifice one Russian for ten Frenchmen*.

And he alone, this intriguing courtier, as he is described to us, who lies to Arakcheyev to propitiate the Emperor – in Vilna he is the only one to say (thereby incurring the Emperor's displeasure) that *to carry the war beyond the frontier would be mischievous and useless*.

But words alone would be no proof that he grasped the significance of events at the time. His actions – without the smallest deviation – were all directed to one and the same threefold aim: (1) to brace all his forces to meet the French; (2) to defeat them; and (3) to drive them out of Russia, mitigating as far as possible the sufferings of the population and the army.

This procrastinator Kutuzov, whose motto was always 'Patience and Time', the sworn opponent of precipitate action, gives battle at Borodino, investing the preparations for it with unparalleled solemnity. This Kutuzov who at Austerlitz, before the battle began, declares that it will be lost, at Borodino, in the face of the conviction of the generals that the battle ended in defeat and the unprecedented instance of an army having to retire after winning a victory – he alone, in opposition to everyone else, persists to his dying day that Borodino was a victory. He was alone during the whole of the retreat in insisting that battles which now had no point should not be fought, that a new war should not be begun nor the frontiers of Russia crossed.

It is easy enough now that all the events with their consequences lie before us to understand their significance, provided we abstain from attributing to the masses the aims that existed in the brains of only a dozen individuals.

But how came that old man, alone, in opposition to universal opinion, so accurately to appreciate the import of events for the nation that never once throughout his career was he untrue to it?

This extraordinary power of insight into the significance of contemporary events sprang from the purity and fervour of his identification with the people.

It was their recognition of this feeling of his of oneness with them that led the people by such strange paths to choose him, an old man out of favour, to be their representative in the national war, against the wish of the Tsar. And it was this feeling alone which lifted him to the lofty pinnacle from which he, the commander-in-chief, exerted all his efforts, not to maim and exterminate men but to spare and have pity on them.

This simple, modest, and therefore truly great figure could not be cast in the lying mould invented by history for the European hero and so-called leader of men.

No great man is great to the flunkey, for the flunkey has menial ideas about what constitutes greatness.

6

THE 5th of November was the first day of what is called the battle of Krasnoe. Towards evening – after endless discussions and delays caused by generals not reaching their proper places; after much galloping to and fro of adjutants with counter-orders – when it was already self-evident that the enemy was everywhere in flight and that there could and would be no battle, Kutuzov left Krasnoe for Dobroe, to which place his Headquarters had that day been transferred.

It had been a clear, frosty day. Kutuzov, mounted on his plump little white horse, followed by an enormous suite of disgruntled generals whispering their discontent behind his back, rode towards Dobroe. All along the road knots of French prisoners taken that day (they numbered seven thousand) huddled round camp-fires warming themselves. Not far from Dobroe a huge buzzing crowd of tattered prisoners, bandaged and muffled up in anything they had been able to lay hands on, were standing beside a long row of unlimbered French cannon. At the approach of the commander-in-chief the hum died down and all eyes were fixed on Kutuzov, who moved slowly along the highway, wearing a white cap with a red band and a padded overcoat that bulged over his round shoulders. One of the generals started informing Kutuzov where the guns and prisoners had been captured.

Kutuzov seemed preoccupied and did not listen to what the general was saying. He screwed up his eyes with displeasure as he gazed attentively and fixedly at the prisoners who made a particularly wretched spectacle. Most of them were disfigured by frost-bitten noses and cheeks, and nearly all of them had red, swollen and festering eyes.

One group of Frenchmen was standing close by the road, and two soldiers – the face of one covered with sores – were tearing at a piece of raw meat with their hands. There was something horrible and bestial in the fleeting look they cast at the riders, and the malevolent scowl with which the soldier with the sores, after a glance at Kutuzov, turned away and went on with what he was doing.

Kutuzov stared long and intently at these two soldiers. Puckering his face still more, he half-closed his eyelids and shook his head thoughtfully. Farther on he noticed a Russian soldier laughingly clapping a Frenchman on the shoulder and making some friendly remark to him. Kutuzov shook his head again, with the same expression on his face.

'What were you saying?' he asked the general, who had continued with his report and was calling the commander-in-chief's attention to the captured French colours set up in front of the Preobrazhensky regiment.

'Ah, the standards!' said Kutuzov, rousing himself with an effort from the subject absorbing his thoughts.

He looked about him absently. Thousands of eyes were directed on him from all sides, waiting for him to speak.

He stopped in front of the Preobrazhensky regiment, sighed heavily and closed his eyes. One of his suite beckoned to the soldiers holding the standards to come forward and set up the flagstaffs round the commander-in-chief. Kutuzov was silent for a few seconds, and then with obvious reluctance, yielding to the obligations of his position, raised his head and began to speak. Crowds of officers gathered round him. He ran an attentive glance over the circle of officers, recognizing some of them.

'I thank you all!' he said, addressing the soldiers and then turning to the officers again. In the silence which reigned about him his slowly-spoken words were audible and distinct. 'I thank you all for your hard and faithful service. The victory is complete and Russia will not forget you. Honour and glory to you without end!'

He paused and looked round.

'Lower, lower with its head!' he said to a soldier holding the French eagle who had accidentally inclined it before the Preobrazhensky colours. 'Down with it, lower still, that's it! Hurrah, lads!' he cried, with a quick movement of his chin to the soldiers.

'Hur-rah-ah-ah!' roared thousands of voices.

While the soldiers were cheering, Kutuzov, leaning forward in his saddle, bowed his head, and his eye glinted with a mild and as it were ironic light.

'Yes, my men ...' he said when the shouts had ceased.

And all at once his voice and the expression of his face changed. It was not the commander-in-chief speaking now but an ordinary old man who wanted to tell his comrades something very important.

There was a stir among the throng of officers and in the ranks of soldiers, as they pressed forward to catch what he was going to say.

'Yes, men, I know you're having a bad time but it can't be helped. Have patience – it won't last much longer. We'll see our visitors off and then we'll rest. The Tsar won't forget your services. It is hard for you but at any rate you are at home, whereas they – you see what they are reduced to,' he said, pointing to the prisoners. 'Worse off than the poorest of beggars. While they were strong we did not spare them but now we may even have pity on them. They are human beings too. Isn't that so, lads?'

He looked about him and in the unflinching, respectfully wondering eyes staring at him read sympathy with what he had said. His face grew brighter and brighter with the gentle smile of old age which brought clusters of wrinkles to the corners of his mouth and eyes. He paused and bowed his head, as though uncertain.

'But with all said and done, who invited them here? It serves them right, the b — b — s!' he cried suddenly, lifting his head.

And flourishing his whip he rode off at a gallop for the first time during the whole campaign, leaving the soldiers guffawing gleefully and shouting 'Hurrah!' as they broke ranks.

Kutuzov's words were barely understood by the rank and file. No one could have repeated the field-marshal's address, solemn to begin with and ending up with the homely simplicity of an old man; but the sincerity behind his words was not only understood but the exalted feeling of triumph combined with pity for the enemy and consciousness of the justice of their cause – exactly expressed by the old man's good-natured expletives – found an echo in every man's breast and inspired their delighted long-sustained cheering. After this, when one of the generals went up and asked the commander-in-chief whether he wished his calèche to be sent for, Kutuzov, evidently deeply moved, could only answer with a sob.

7

When the troops reached their halting-place for the night on the 8th of November, the last day of the Krasnoe battles, it was already growing dusk. All day it had been still and frosty with a steady fall of light snow. Towards evening the snow-clouds began to clear, and a purplish starry sky appeared through the last of the falling flakes, and it got much colder.

A regiment of musketeers, which had left Tarutino three thousand strong but now numbered nine hundred, was one of the first to arrive at the halting-place – a village on the high road. The quartermasters who met the regiment announced that all the cottages were full of sick and dead Frenchmen, cavalrymen and staff-officers. There was only one hut left for the colonel.

The colonel rode up to his hut. The regiment went on through the village and stacked their arms near the last cottages on the road.

Like a huge, many-limbed monster the regiment set to work to prepare a lair and food. One party of men trudged off, knee-deep in the snow, to the right of the village, into a birch-forest which a few minutes later reverberated with the ring of axes and short sabres, the crash of falling branches and the sound of merry voices. Another party bustled round the regimental baggage-wagons and horses, which were drawn up together, getting out cauldrons and rye biscuit and feeding the horses. A third section dispersed about the village arranging quarters for the staff-officers, carrying out the dead bodies of the French that lay in the huts, and dragging away planks, dry wood and thatch from the roofs for the camp-fires, or wattle fencing to throw up some form of shelter.

Behind the cottages at the end of the village a dozen soldiers shouting boisterously were trying to shake down the high wattle wall of a barn from which they had already removed the roof.

'Now then, all together, heave!' cried the voices; and in the dark the fabric of the great snow-sprinkled wall began to give with a frosty creak. The lower stakes cracked more and more until at last the wattle wall collapsed, dragging down in its fall the men who had been pushing it. There was a loud exclamation, and then roars of coarse laughter.

'Come on, in pairs now! Give us a lever here! That's it. What the hell d'you think you're doing?'

'Now – heave. ... But wait a minute, boys. ... What about a song?'

They all stood silent, and a soft, pleasant, velvety voice began to sing. At the end of the third verse, as the last note died away, twenty voices roared out in chorus: 'Oo-oo-oo-oo! It's coming! All together! Heave, lads! ...' but in spite of their united efforts the wattle hardly moved, and in the silence that followed the men could be heard breathing heavily.

'Hi, you there of the 6th Company! You devils, you! Lend us a hand ... we'll do the same for you one day.'

Some twenty men of the 6th Company, who were on their way into the village, joined forces with them, and the wattle wall, about thirty-five feet long and seven wide, curving under its own weight, moved slowly along the village street, crushing and bruising the shoulders of the panting soldiers.

'Keep step there, can't you! ... Look out, you clumsy fathead. ... What are you stopping for? There now. ...'

The cheerful rough exchange of abuse never ceased.

'What are you up to?' cried a peremptory voice, as a sergeant came upon the party hauling their burden. 'There are staff here – the gen'ral 'imself's in that there 'ut and you foul-mouthed devils, you curs – I'll learn you!' shouted the sergeant, hitting the nearest soldier a swinging blow on the back.

The soldiers were quiet. The man who had been struck grunted and wiped his face, which was scratched and bleeding: he had been knocked forward against the wattle.

'The b — knows how to hit! My face's all bloody,' he muttered under his breath when the sergeant had walked away.

'And you don't like it? Fancy that!' mocked someone, and lowering their voices the soldiers continued on their way. Out of the village, they began again as loudly as before, punctuating their talk with the same aimless expletives.

In the hut which the men had passed were assembled officers of the higher command eagerly discussing over their tea the events of the day and the manoeuvres suggested for the morrow. It was proposed to execute a flank march to the left, to cut off and capture the viceroy (Murat).

By the time the soldiers had dragged the wattle fence to its place camp-fires ready for cooking were blazing on all sides. Wood crackled, the snow was melting and black shadowy figures flitted to and fro over the space where the snow had been trodden down.

Axes and choppers plied all around. Everything was done without any orders being given. Supplies of wood were piled high for the night, shanties rigged up for the officers, cauldrons put to boil and arms and accoutrements seen to.

The wattle wall brought in by the men of the 8th Company was curved in a semicircle and propped up by musket-rests to give shelter from the north, and a camp-fire built in front of it. The drums beat the tattoo, the roll was called, and the men had supper and settled themselves for the night round the fires – some repairing their foot-gear, some smoking pipes, others stripped naked and trying to steam the lice out of their clothes.

8

ONE might have supposed that under the almost inconceivably wretched conditions of the Russian soldiery at that time – lacking thick boots and sheepskin coats, without a roof over their heads in the snow with the temperature eight degrees below zero, and often without full rations (the commissariat did not always keep up with the troops) – they would have presented a most melancholy and depressing spectacle.

On the contrary, never, even in the happiest material circumstances, had the army worn a livelier and more cheerful aspect. This was because day by day it was able to shake off the weak or dejected. All the physically or morally frail had long since been left behind and only the flower of the army – physically and mentally – remained.

More men collected behind the wattle fence of the 8th Company than anywhere else. A couple of sergeant-majors were sitting by their camp-fire which blazed brighter than the others. A contribution of fuel was demanded in exchange for the right to shelter under the wattle screen.

'Hi, Makeyev – you lost? Or did the wolves get you? Fetch us some wood,' shouted a red-faced, red-haired man, screwing up his eyes and blinking from the smoke but not stirring from the fire. 'You, Jackdaw, you run and get us something to burn,' he cried to another soldier.

The red-headed man was neither a sergeant nor a corporal but being tough and strong he ordered the weaker ones about. The soldier they called 'Jackdaw', a thin little fellow with a sharp nose, got up submissively and was about to obey but at that moment there stepped into the light of the fire the slender, handsome figure of a young soldier carrying a load of wood.

'Give it here – that's fine!'

They broke up the wood and heaped it on the fire, blew at it with their mouths and fanned it with the skirts of their greatcoats, making the flames hiss and crackle. The men drew nearer and lit their pipes. The handsome young soldier who had brought the wood stuck his arms akimbo and began a brisk and nimble shuffle with his frozen feet on the spot where he stood.

'Ah me mother dear, the dew's cold an' clear, for a musketeer ...' he sang, with a sort of hiccough at each syllable.

'Look out, your soles will fly off!' shouted the red-haired man, noticing that one of the dancer's soles was loose. 'He's a rare devil for dancing!'

The dancer stopped, tore off the loose piece of leather and flung it on the fire.

'You're right there, old man,' said he, and sitting down he took out of his knapsack a strip of French blue cloth and proceeded to wrap it round his foot. 'It's the steam what spoils 'em,' he added, stretching his feet towards the fire.

'They'll soon be issuing us new ones. They say once we've finished *them* off we're all to get a double lot of stuff.'

'I say, that son of a bitch Petrov seems to have stayed behind after all,' remarked one of the sergeants.

'I've had an eye on him this long while,' said the other.

'Oh well, he's a rotten soldier. ...'

'The 3rd Company now – it appears they 'ad nine men missing at roll-call yesterday.'

'Yes, but when a man's feet are frozen off how's he to walk ?'

'Oh b — s!' said one of the sergeants.

'Why – you thinking of doing the same maybe ?' said an old soldier reproachfully to the man who had spoken of feet frozen off.

'Well, what do you take us for ?' the sharp-nosed soldier they called Jackdaw exclaimed in a squeaky, unsteady voice, suddenly getting up from the other side of the fire. 'The fat grows lean, and the lean dies. Look at me now – I got no strength left in me. Tell 'em to cart me off to 'ospital,' he said with sudden resolution, turning to the sergeant. 'I aches all over with t'rheumatiz. It's me'll be the next to drop on the road.'

'That'll do – that's enough of that,' replied the sergeant calmly.

The soldier said no more and the talk went on.

'A rare lot of Frenchies been taken today, and not a decent pair of boots among the lot – nothing you could properly call a boot,' observed one of the soldiers, starting a new topic.

'The Cossacks took care of that. We was clearing out a hut for the colonel when they carried 'em out. A pitiful sight an' all it was, lads,' put in the dancer. 'They rolled 'em over, and one was alive, would you believe it, jabbering something in that lingo of theirs.'

'And they're clean in themselves,' the first man went on. 'White – why, 'e was white as birch-bark, and there're some brave-looking fellows among 'em, I must say – gentry too.'

'Well, what do you expect? They takes 'em from all stations for their army.'

'But they don't understand nothing,' said the dancer with a puzzled smile. 'I says to 'im: "Which king do you belong to?" and 'e gives me a string of gibberish. A queer lot!'

'It's a funny thing, mates,' continued the man who had wondered at the white skins of the French. 'The peasants round Mozhaisk way were saying as how when they went to take away the dead – where the battle was, you understand – well, them dead 'ad been lyin' there nigh on a month, and, the peasant says – "they was lying there clean and white as paper, and not a whiff of smell of powder-smoke about 'em".'

'Was it the cold, perhaps?' asked someone.

'That's good, that is! Cold! Why, 'twas hot. If it'd 'ad bin cold, our chaps wouldn't 'ave rotted neither. "But no, go up to ours," 'e says, "and they'd be all maggoty rotten. We 'ad to tie 'ankerchiefs round our faces an' turn our 'eads away whiles we was shifting 'em. Almost more'n we could stomach. But them," 'e says, "they was white as paper, not a smell about 'em".'

All were silent.

'Most likely 'tis the food,' said the sergeant. 'They bin livin' like princes.'

No one contradicted him.

'That peasant at Mozhaisk, where the battle was, was tellin' us they was fetched out from a dozen villages round and was three weeks carting the dead away, and still there was more of 'em. And as for the wolves, he says. ...'

'That was something like a battle,' said an old trooper. 'The only one worth remembering. But since then ... it's been nothing but just goin' through with it.'

'Well, grandpa, we did 'ave a go at 'em day afore yesterday. But you can't get at 'em, they're that quick laying down their arms an' flopping on their knees. "*Pardong!*" they say. Take an example. I heard tell Platov twice took 'Poleon hisself. But 'e don't know t'right charm, see. Catches 'old on 'im and phttt! 'e turns into a bird in 'is 'ands and flies off. And no chance of killing 'im neither.'

'You be a prime liar, Kiselov, by the looks er you.'

'What d'ye mean – liar? 'Tis the honest-to-God truth.'

'Well, if you ask me, I'd bury 'im in the earth, if I caught 'un. With an aspen-stake to fix 'un down. The number of folk 'e's bin the death of!'

'Anyhows, we're soon going to make an end of 'im. 'E won't come 'ere again,' remarked the old soldier, yawning.

The conversation flagged and the soldiers began settling themselves for the night.

'Look at all them stars! Shining wonderful! Anyone'd say the women 'ad been spreading their washing out over the sky,' said one of the men, marvelling at the Milky Way.

'That's a sign of a good harvest for next year.'

'We shall want some more wood.'

'Warm your back and your belly freezes. That's funny!'

'O Lord!'

'What you shoving for? Think the fire's only for you, eh? Look at the way 'e's sprawled out!'

In the ensuing silence the snoring could be heard of those who had fallen asleep. The others kept turning over to warm themselves, now and again exchanging a few words. From a camp-fire a hundred paces off came a chorus of merry laughter.

'Hark at 5th Company guffawing over there,' said a soldier. 'And what a terrific lot of them there are!'

One of the men got up and walked across to the 5th Company.

"Aving a high old time, they are,' he said, coming back. 'A couple of Frenchies have turned up. One's pretty frozen but t'other's lively enough. Singing songs 'e is.'

'Oh? Let's go and have a squint. ...'

And several of the soldiers strolled over to the 5th Company.

9

THE 5th Company was bivouacking at the very edge of the forest. An immense camp-fire was blazing brightly in the midst of the snow, lighting up the branches of the trees heavy with hoar-frost.

About midnight the soldiers had heard footsteps in the snow of the forest and the cracking of dry boughs.

'A bear, lads,' said one of the men.

They all raised their heads to listen, and out of the forest into the bright firelight stepped two strangely garbed human figures clinging to one another.

They were two Frenchmen who had been hiding in the forest. They came up to the fire, hoarsely uttering something in a tongue our soldiers did not understand. One was taller than the other and wore an officer's hat; he seemed utterly spent. Approaching the fire, he tried to sit but fell to the ground. The other, a stumpy little soldier with his head tied round with a scarf, was stronger. He lifted his companion and said something, pointing to his mouth. The soldiers surrounded the Frenchmen, spread a greatcoat under the sick man, and brought both of them porridge and vodka.

The exhausted French officer was Ramballe and the man with a scarf tied round his head was his orderly, Morel.

When Morel had drunk some vodka and finished his bowl of porridge he suddenly became painfully hilarious and chattered incessantly to the soldiers, who could not understand him. Ramballe refused food and lay silently leaning on his elbow by the fire, staring at the Russians with red, vacant eyes. At intervals he emitted a long-drawn groan, and then relapsed into silence again. Morel, pointing to his shoulders, tried to make the soldiers understand that Ramballe was an officer and that what he needed was warmth. A Russian officer who had come up to the fire sent to ask his colonel whether he would take a French officer into his hut to warm him, and when the messenger returned and said that the colonel bade them bring the officer Ramballe was invited to go. He got up and tried to walk but staggered and would have fallen had not a soldier standing by caught hold of him.

'A drop too much, eh?' said a soldier with a humorous wink to Ramballe.

'Silly clown! Can't you talk sense? What an oaf the man is!' voices exclaimed on all sides, rebuking the jesting soldier.

They gathered round Ramballe, lifted him on to the crossed arms of two soldiers and carried him to the hut. Ramballe put his arms around their necks and as they carried him along he kept repeating plaintively:

'Oh you good fellows! Oh my kind, kind friends! Real decent fellows! Oh my brave, kind friends!' and he leaned his head against the shoulder of one of the men like a child.

Morel meanwhile was sitting in the best place by the fire, surrounded by soldiers.

Morel, a short, thickset Frenchman with inflamed, streaming eyes, was wearing a woman's shabby sheepskin jacket and had a kerchief tied over his forage-cap after the fashion of a peasant woman. He was unmistakably tipsy, and with one arm thrown round the soldier sitting next to him was singing a French song in a husky, broken voice. The soldiers held their sides as they looked at him.

'Now then, come on, teach us how it goes! I'll soon get the hang of it! How does it go? ...' said the soldier Morel was clasping – he was a singer and a wag.

> *Vive Henri quatre,*
> *Vive ce roi vaillant!**

sang Morel, winking.

> *Ce diable à quatre ... †*

'Vivarika! Vif-seruvaru! Sedyablyaka! ...' repeated the soldier, beating time with a flourish and really catching the tune.

'Bravo! Ha, ha, ha!' rose a rough cheerful guffaw from the audience. Morel, wrinkling up his face, laughed with them.

'Come on, what next, what next?'

* Long live Henry the Fourth,
Long live that valiant king! etc. (French song).
† That devil incarnate.

Qui eut le triple talent,
De boire, de battre,
Et d'être un vert galant ...★

'That sounds all right too! Now, Zaletayev! ...'

'Kiu ...' Zaletayev articulated with a struggle. 'Kiu-iu-iu ...' he drawled, laboriously pursing his lips, 'le-trip-ta-la-de-bu-de-bat-eh-de-tra-va-ga-la!' he sang.

'Fine! Just like the Frenchie! Ha-ha-ha! Like some more to eat, would you?'

'Give him some porridge. It takes a long time to fill up when you've been starving.'

They gave him some more porridge, and Morel with a laugh set to work on a third bowlful. Jovial smiles broadened the faces of all the young soldiers as they watched him. The older men, regarding such puerilities as beneath them, remained stretched out on the opposite side of the fire, raising themselves on an elbow now and then to glance at Morel with a smile.

'They are men like ourselves, after all,' said one, rolling himself up in his coat. 'Even wormwood has its roots and grows.'

'O Lord, just look at all those stars! No end to 'em! A sure sign of frost. ...'

And silence descended.

The stars, as though they knew no one would see them now, began to disport themselves in the dark sky: flashing bright, disappearing again, shimmering and signalling some glad mystery to one another.

10

THE French army melted away with the regularity of some mathematical progression. And the passage of the Berezina, about which so much has been written, was only one of the intermediate stages in its destruction, and not at all the decisive episode of the campaign. If so much has been and still is written about the Berezina it is, so far as the French are concerned, only because at the broken bridge across the river the calamities their army had met with one by one were suddenly concentrated at a single moment into a tragic catastrophe

★ *With the threefold talent,*
For drinking, for fighting,
For being a gallant.

no one ever forgot. On the Russian side the reason so much has been made of the Berezina was simply that in Petersburg – far from the theatre of war – a plan (again one of Pfuhl's) had been devised for drawing Napoleon into a strategic trap on the banks of the Berezina. Everyone was persuaded that the plan would work out exactly as arranged, and so they insisted that it was just the crossing of the Berezina that proved fatal to the French army. In reality the results of the Berezina crossing were far less disastrous to the French – in loss of guns and men – than Krasnoe had been, as the statistics show.

The sole significance of the passage of the Berezina lies in the fact that it proved beyond a doubt the fallacy of all plans for cutting off the enemy's retreat, and the soundness of the only possible line of action (the one Kutuzov demanded) – the idea of merely following on the enemy's heels. The mob of French fled at a continually increasing speed, with all their energies directed to reaching their goal. It fled like a wounded animal and it was impossible to stop its headlong flight. This was shown not so much by the arrangements made for the passage as by what occurred at the bridges. When the bridges broke, unarmed soldiers, people from Moscow and women and children who were with the French transport, all, carried forward by *vis inertiae*, instead of surrendering made a rush for the boats or threw themselves into the ice-covered water.

The impulse was a reasonable one. The state of fugitives and pursuers was equally wretched. So long as they remained with those of their own side each might hope for help from his fellows and from the fact of belonging with them. But those who surrendered to the Russians found themselves in the same miserable plight, and worse off when it came to getting a share of the necessities of life. The French had no need to be told that half the prisoners – whom the Russians did not know what to do with – perished of cold and hunger however much their captors might want to save them: they felt that it could not be otherwise. The most compassionate and pro-French Russian generals, Frenchmen in the Russian service, could do nothing for the prisoners. The French perished of the miseries which attended the Russian troops. It was not possible to take bread and clothing from our hungry soldiers, whom we needed, to give to Frenchmen – who might not be objectionable, were not hated, were not to blame but who were simply not needed. A few Russians even did this but they were exceptions.

Behind the French lay certain destruction: in front there was hope. They had burned their boats, massed flight was their only salvation, and to this the French devoted all their strength.

The farther they fled, the more pitiable the condition of the French remnant, especially after the Berezina, on which (in consequence of the Petersburg plan) great hopes had been placed by the Russians, the more violent waxed the passions of the Russian generals who railed at each other and most of all at Kutuzov. Taking for granted that the failure of the Petersburg Berezina plan would be laid at his door, they expressed their dissatisfaction with him, their contempt and ridicule, more and more openly. Their ridicule and contempt were, of course, couched in a respectful form – in such a form that Kutuzov could not even ask what he was accused of. They did not treat him seriously: they submitted their reports and asked for his sanction with the air of performing a melancholy ritual, while behind his back they winked and tried to mislead him at every turn.

Because they could not understand him it was accepted as the recognized thing by all these people that it was useless to talk to the old man, that he could never grasp the profundity of their plans and would only reply with one of his phrases (it seemed to them they were nothing but phrases) about a 'golden bridge' or that crossing the frontier with a troop of vagabonds was not to be thought of, and so forth. They had heard all that before. And everything he said – that it was necessary to wait for provisions, for instance, or that the men had no boots – was so simple, whereas what they proposed was so complicated and clever, that it was obvious to them that he was an old dotard, while they were commanders of genius, without authority to take the lead.

This mood and this gossip of the Staff rose to a climax with the arrival in the army of Wittgenstein, the brilliant admiral and favourite hero of Petersburg. Kutuzov saw it and simply sighed and shrugged his shoulders. Only once, after the affair of the Berezina, did he lose his temper and wrote the following note to Bennigsen (who made separate reports to the Emperor):

On account of your Excellency's bouts of ill-health your Excellency will retire to Kaluga, on receipt of this present, there to await further commands and appointments from his Imperial Majesty.

But this dismissal of Bennigsen was followed by the arrival on the scene of the Grand Duke Konstantin Pavlovich, who had taken part in the beginning of the campaign but had subsequently been removed by Kutuzov. Now the Grand Duke, on rejoining the army, informed Kutuzov of the Emperor's displeasure at the poor success of our forces and the slowness of their advance. The Emperor himself intended to be with his troops in a few days.

The old man, as experienced in Court methods as in warfare – this same Kutuzov who in the August of that year had been chosen commander-in-chief against the Sovereign's will, who had removed the Grand Duke and heir-apparent from the army, and acting on his own authority and contrary to the Emperor's wishes had decreed the abandonment of Moscow – realized at once that his day was over, that his part was played, and that the semblance of power he had been allowed to wield was no more. And it was not only the attitude of the Court which told him this. He saw on the one hand that the military business in which he had played his part was at an end, and felt that his work was accomplished. And at the same time he began to be conscious of the physical weariness of his aged body and of the necessity of physical rest.

On the 29th of November Kutuzov entered Vilna – his dear Vilna, as he called it. Twice during his career Kutuzov had been governor of Vilna. In that wealthy town, which had escaped damage, he found old friends and associations, as well as the amenities of life of which he had so long been deprived. And at once turning his back on military and political cares and, so far as the passions raging all around him would permit, he immersed himself in the quiet routine of ordinary life, as if all that was taking place and all that had still to be done in the realm of history did not concern him in the slightest.

Tchichagov, one of the most zealous of the 'cutters-off' and 'over-throwers', who had at first advocated effecting a diversion in Greece and then in Warsaw but was never willing to go where he was sent – Tchichagov, who was famous for the boldness of his remarks to the Emperor – Tchichagov, who considered Kutuzov to be under an obligation to him because when he had been sent in 1811 to make peace with Turkey over Kutuzov's head and found on arriving that peace had already been concluded, he had frankly admitted to the Emperor that the credit for having secured that peace really belonged to Kutuzov – this same Tchichagov was the first to meet Kutuzov at the castle at Vilna where the latter was to stay. In undress naval uniform, with a dirk, and holding his cap under his arm, he handed the commander-in-chief a garrison report and the keys of the town. The contemptuously respectful attitude of youth to old age in its dotage was expressed in the most marked manner by the behaviour of Tchichagov, who was aware of the charges being levelled against Kutuzov.

In conversation with Tchichagov Kutuzov happened to mention that the vehicles packed with china that had been captured from him at Borisov had been recovered and would be restored to him.

'You mean to imply that I have nothing to eat from. ... On the contrary, I can supply you with everything you are likely to require, even if you should wish to give dinner-parties,' replied Tchichagov hotly in French. The motive behind Tchichagov's every word was always to demonstrate his own correctness and therefore he imagined Kutuzov to be animated by the same desire.

Shrugging his shoulders, Kutuzov replied, also in French, with his subtle, shrewd smile:

'I mean only what I say.'

In opposition to the Emperor's wishes Kutuzov detained the greater part of the army in Vilna. Those about him said that he went downhill to an extraordinary extent and grew very feeble physically during his stay in that town. He attended to army matters with a bad grace, left everything to his generals and while waiting for the Emperor to arrive gave himself up to a life of dissipation.

The Emperor with his suite – Count Tolstoy, Prince Volkonsky, Arakcheyev and others – left Petersburg on the 7th of December and reached Vilna on the 11th, and drove straight to the castle in his travelling sledge. In spite of the severe frost some hundred generals and staff-officers in full parade uniform stood outside the castle, as well as a guard of honour of the Semeonovsk regiment.

A courier, dashing up to the castle ahead of the Tsar in a troika drawn by three foam-flecked horses, shouted: 'He's here!' and Konovnitsyn rushed into the vestibule to inform Kutuzov, who was waiting in the porter's little lodge.

A minute later the old man's big, heavy figure in full dress uniform, his breast covered with orders and a scarf pulled tight about his stomach, waddled out into the porch. He put on his *bicorne*, one peak over each ear, and, carrying his gloves, with an effort lowered himself sideways down the steps to the bottom, and took in his hand the report he had prepared for the Emperor.

There was much running to and fro and whispering, another troika flew furiously up, and all eyes were turned on an approaching sledge in which the figures of the Tsar and Volkonsky could already be descried.

From the habit of half a century all this had a physically agitating effect on the old general. He ran a nervous hand over his paunch, re-adjusted his hat and pulling himself together straightened his back and at the very moment the Emperor alighted from the sledge lifted his eyes to him, presented the report and began to speak in his measured, ingratiating voice.

The Emperor scanned Kutuzov from head to foot with a rapid glance, frowned for an instant but immediately mastering himself stepped forward and, stretching out his arms, embraced the old general. Once more, owing to old and long-standing habit of impression, this embrace, stirring some deep personal association, had its usual effect on Kutuzov and he gave a sob.

The Emperor greeted the officers and the Semeonovsk guard, and pressing the old man's hand again went with him into the castle.

When he was alone with the field-marshal the Emperor did not attempt to hide his dissatisfaction at the slowness of the pursuit and with the blunders made at Krasnoe and the Berezina, and informed him of his intentions for a future campaign abroad. Kutuzov offered no rejoinder or observation. The same submissive, vacant look with which he had listened to the Emperor's commands on the field of Austerlitz seven years before settled on his face now.

When Kutuzov came out of the study and with downcast head was crossing the ball-room with his heavy lurching gait he was arrested by a voice saying:

'Your Serene Highness!'

He raised his head and looked long into the eyes of Count Tolstoy, who stood before him holding a silver salver on which lay a small object. Kutuzov seemed not to grasp what was expected of him.

Suddenly he rallied as it were: a faint smile flashed across his puffy face, and with a low, respectful bow he picked up the object lying on the salver. It was the order of St George of the first class.

THE next day the field-marshal gave a dinner and ball which the Emperor honoured with his presence. Kutuzov had received the order of St George of the first class; the Emperor had conferred on him the highest marks of respect; but everyone was aware that the Tsar was displeased with the commander-in-chief. The proprieties were observed, and the Emperor was the first to set the example in doing so; but everybody knew that the old man was at fault and had shown his incapacity. When Kutuzov, conforming to a custom of Catherine's day, ordered the captured standards to be lowered at the Emperor's feet as he entered the ball-room the Emperor frowned and muttered something in which those nearest caught the words, 'the old comedian'.

The Emperor's displeasure was increased at Vilna in particular by the fact that Kutuzov evidently could not or would not see the importance of the coming campaign.

On the following morning when the Emperor said to the officers gathered about him: 'You have not only saved Russia, you have saved Europe!' they all understood that the war was not ended.

Kutuzov alone refused to see this and openly expressed his opinion that no fresh war could improve the position or add to the glory of Russia but could only spoil matters and detract from the lofty pinnacle of glory on which, to his mind, Russia was now standing. He tried to point out to the Emperor the impossibility of levying fresh troops, spoke of the hardships the people were suffering, of the possibility of failure, and so on.

This being the field-marshal's attitude, he was naturally regarded merely as a hindrance and an obstacle in the path of the impending war.

To avoid friction with the old man the obvious resource was to do as had been done at Austerlitz and with Barclay at the beginning of the Russian campaign – shift the ground from under the commander-in-chief's feet without upsetting the old man by informing him of the change, and transfer authority to the Emperor himself.

With this object his staff was gradually reconstructed and its real strength removed and passed to the Emperor. Toll, Konovnitsyn and Yermolov received new appointments. Everyone spoke loudly of how infirm the field-marshal had grown, and of his failing health.

It was necessary for him to be in poor health in order that his place could be given to his successor. And his health was, in fact, failing.

So just as naturally and simply and gradually as Kutuzov had come from Turkey to the Treasury in Petersburg to recruit the militia, and then to the army when he was needed there, now, his part being played, the new actor that was required took Kutuzov's place.

The war of 1812, besides its national significance dear to every Russian heart, was to assume another – a European – character.

The movement of peoples from west to east was to be followed by a movement from east to west, and for this fresh war another leader was needed, having other qualities and views and prompted by other impulses than Kutuzov's.

Alexander I was as necessary for the movement from east to west and for the re-establishment of national frontiers as Kutuzov had been for the salvation and glory of Russia.

Kutuzov had no notion of what was meant by the balance of power, or Napoleon. He could not understand all that. For the representative of the Russian people, after the enemy had been annihilated and Russia liberated and raised to the summit of her glory, there was nothing left for a Russian as a Russian to do. Nothing remained for the representative of the national war but to die. And Kutuzov died.

12

As is generally the case, Pierre only felt the full effects of the physical privations and strain he had suffered as a prisoner when they were over. After his rescue he arrived at Orel and on the third day there, as he was preparing to start for Kiev, he fell ill and was laid up for three months. He had what the doctors termed 'bilious fever'. But in spite of the fact that they treated him, bled him and made him swallow drugs – he recovered.

All that had happened to him from the time of his rescue till his illness had left hardly any impression on his mind. He only remembered dull grey weather, now rainy, now snowy, internal physical aches, pains in his feet and side. He had a hazy memory of unhappy, suffering people, of the plaguing curiosity of officers and generals who persisted with their questions, of his difficulty in obtaining a conveyance and horses; and above all he remembered his incapacity all that time to think and feel. On the day that he was rescued he had seen the body of Petya Rostov. That same day he had learned that Prince Andrei, after surviving for upwards of a month after the battle of Borodino, had only a short time before died in the Rostovs' house at Yaroslavl. On that day, too, Denisov, who told him this piece of news, in the course of conversation happened to mention Hélène's death, supposing that Pierre had heard of it long before. All this had at the time seemed merely strange to Pierre. He felt that he could not take in these tidings in all their bearings. Just then his one idea was to get away as fast as possible from the places where men were slaughtering each other to some quiet refuge where he could recover, rest and think over all the strange new things he had learned during this period. But as soon as he reached Orel he fell ill. When he came to himself after his illness he found in attendance on him two of his servants, Terenty and Vasska, who had come from Moscow, and the eldest of his cousins, who had been living on his estate at Elets, and hearing of his rescue and illness had come to nurse him.

It was only gradually during his convalescence that Pierre got rid of the impressions of the last few months and accustomed himself to the idea that no one would drive him forth tomorrow, that no one would dispossess him of his warm bed, and that he was quite sure of having dinner and tea and supper. But for a long time in his dreams he continued to see himself in the conditions of captivity. In the same way, little by little, he came to realize the significance of the news he had been told after his rescue: the news of the death of Prince Andrei, the death of his wife and the annihilation of the French.

A joyous feeling of freedom – that complete, inalienable freedom inherent in man of which he had first had a consciousness at the first halt outside Moscow – filled Pierre's soul during his convalescence. He was surprised to find that this inner freedom, independent as it was of external circumstances, now had as it were an additional setting of external liberty. He was alone in a strange town, without acquaintances. No one made any demands on him; no one forced him to go anywhere against his will. He had everything that he wanted; the thought of his wife which had been a continual torment to him in the old days was no longer there, since she herself was no more.

'Oh, how good! How nice!' he said to himself when a cleanly laid table was moved up to him with savoury beef-tea, or when he settled down for the night in his soft clean bed, or when he remembered that his wife and the French no longer existed. 'Oh, how good, how nice!' And from old habit he would ask himself the question: 'Well, what next? What am I going to do now?' And immediately he would answer himself: 'Nothing. I am going to live. Oh, how splendid!'

The very thing that had haunted him in the old days and that he had constantly sought in vain – an object in life – did not exist for him now. That search for an object in life was over not merely temporarily, for the time being – he felt that it no longer existed for him and could not present itself again. And it was precisely this absence of an aim which gave him the complete and joyful sense of freedom that constituted his present happiness.

He could have no object, because now he had faith – not faith in any rules or creed or dogma, but faith in a living, ever-manifest God. In the old days he had sought Him in the aims he set himself. That search for an aim had simply been a search for God, and suddenly during his captivity he had learnt, not through words or arguments but by direct feeling, what his old nurse had told him long ago: that God is here and everywhere. In his captivity he had come to see that God in Karatayev was grander, more infinite and unfathomable than in the Architect of the Universe recognized by the masons. He felt like a man who finds what he has been looking for at his very feet, when he has been straining his eyes to seek it in the far distance. All his life he had been seeking over the heads of those around him, while he had only to look straight in front without straining his eyes.

In the past he had been unable to see the great, the inscrutable, the infinite in anything. He had only felt that it must exist somewhere and had looked for it. In all that was near and comprehensible he had seen only what was limited, narrow, commonplace, meaningless. He had armed himself with a mental telescope and gazed into space, where what was petty and everyday, hidden in the misty distance, had seemed to him great and infinite merely because it was not clearly seen. This was the way European life, politics, freemasonry, philosophy and philanthropy had appeared to him. But even then, at moments of weakness as he had accounted them, his mind had penetrated that distance too and he had remarked the same triviality, worldliness and emptiness. But now he had learnt to see the great, the eternal, the infinite in everything; and therefore – to see it and revel in its contemplation – he naturally threw away the telescope through which he had hitherto been gazing over men's heads, and joyfully feasted his eyes on the ever-changing, eternally great, unfathomable and infinite life around him. And the closer he looked, the more tranquil and happier he was. The awful question that had shattered all his mental edifices in the past – the question *Why?* – no longer existed for him. To that question *Why?* he now had always ready in his soul the simple answer: *Because God is* – the God without whose will not one hair falls from a man's head.

13

IN external ways Pierre had hardly changed at all. In appearance he was just the same as before. As he always had been, he was absent-minded and seemingly absorbed not in what was before his eyes but in something special of his own. The difference between his former and his present self was that in the old days when he was oblivious of what was before him, or of what was being said to him, he had wrinkled his brows painfully as though striving, without success, to distinguish something far away. Now he still forgot what was said to him and still did not see what confronted him, but now he looked with a faint, apparently ironical smile at what was before him and listened to what was said, though it was evident that his eyes and his mind were concerned with something quite different. Hitherto he had seemed to be a kind-hearted person but unhappy, and so people had been inclined to hold a little aloof from him. Now a smile of *joie de vivre* constantly played round his lips and his eyes radiated sympathetic interest in others – in the question 'Were they as happy as he was?' – and people liked to be with him.

In the past he had talked a great deal, had got excited when he talked and had listened very little; now he was seldom carried away in conversation and knew how to listen, so that people were eager to tell him their most intimate secrets.

The princess, who had never had any affection for Pierre and had cherished a particular feeling of animosity towards him since she had felt herself under obligation to him following the old count's death, after a short stay at Orel, whither she had come with the intention of showing Pierre that in spite of his 'thanklessness' she considered it her duty to nurse him – the princess, to her surprise and annoyance, quickly felt that she was fond of him. Pierre did nothing to ingratiate himself with his cousin: he merely studied her with interest. In the old days she had always suspected him of mockery and indifference, and so had shrunk into herself as she did with others, and had shown him only the combative side of her nature; now, on the contrary, she felt that he seemed to be trying to read and understand the most sacred recesses of her heart, and, mistrustfully at first and then with gratitude, she let him see the hidden, kindly sides of her character.

The craftiest of men could not have stolen into the princess's confidence more dexterously, tempting forth her memories of the best times of her youth, and entering into them. Yet the extent of Pierre's artfulness consisted in seeking his own pleasure in drawing out the human qualities in the embittered, hard and, after her own fashion, proud princess.

'Yes, he's a most excellent creature when he is not under bad influence but under the influence of people like myself,' thought the princess.

The change that had taken place in Pierre was noticed, in their own way, by his servants Terenty and Vasska too. They found that he had grown vastly more natural and human. Often after he had helped his master to undress and wished him good-night, Terenty would linger with boots and clothes in his hand in the hope that he would start a talk. And Pierre, seeing that Terenty was longing for a chat, generally kept him.

'Well, tell me ... now how did you manage to get food?' he would ask.

And Terenty would begin about the destruction of Moscow or speak of the late count, and would stand for a long time with the clothes over his arm, telling stories or sometimes listening to Pierre's yarns, and then with a pleasant sense of intimacy with his master and affection for him finally withdrew.

The doctor who was attending Pierre and visited him every day, though he felt it incumbent on him, after the manner of doctors, to pose as a man whose every moment was precious for suffering humanity, sat for hours with Pierre, repeating his favourite anecdotes and observations on the *mœurs* of his patients in general, and of the ladies in particular.

'Yes, it's a pleasure to talk to a man like that – very different from what we are used to in the provinces,' he would say of Pierre.

There were several prisoners from the French army in Orel, and the doctor brought one of them, a young Italian, to see Pierre.

This officer became a frequent visitor, and the princess used to make fun of the sentimental affection which the Italian expressed for her cousin.

The Italian was apparently only happy when he could come to see Pierre and talk with him and tell about his past, his life at home, and his love, and pour out his indignation against the French and especially against Napoleon.

'If all Russians are in the least like you,' he would say to Pierre, 'it is sacrilege to wage war on such a people. You, who have suffered so much at the hands of the French, do not even bear a grudge against them.'

And this passionate devotion Pierre earned merely by bringing out what was best in the soul of the Italian and delighting in it.

During the latter part of Pierre's stay in Orel he received a visit from his old masonic acquaintance, Count Willarski, who had introduced him to the Lodge in 1807. Willarski was married to a Russian heiress who had large estates in the province of Orel, and he was filling a temporary post in the commissariat department in the town.

Hearing that Bezuhov was in Orel, Willarski, though they had never been in very close touch, called upon him with the professions of friendship and intimacy that men commonly display on meeting one another in the desert. Willarski was bored in Orel and rejoiced to meet a man of his own circle with, as he supposed, similar interests.

But to his surprise Willarski soon noticed that Pierre had quite dropped behind the times and was sunk, as he expressed it to himself, in apathy and egoism.

'You are turning into a fossil, my dear fellow,' he said.

But for all that Willarski felt much more at home with Pierre now than he had done in the past, and came to see him every day. To Pierre, as he looked at and listened to Willarski, it seemed strange and incredible to think that he had been the same sort of person himself until quite lately.

Willarski was a married man with a family, whose time was taken up in managing his wife's property, in performing his official duties and in looking after family affairs. He regarded all these occupations as hindrances to life, and considered them all despicable because their purpose was the welfare of himself and his family. Military, administrative, political and masonic questions constantly engrossed his attention. And Pierre, without criticizing or trying to change the other's views, watched this strange yet only too familiar phenomenon with the smile of quiet, amused irony now habitual with him.

There was a new feature in Pierre's relations with Willarski, with the princess, the doctor and all the people he met now, which gained for him universal goodwill. This was his acknowledgement of the freedom of everybody to think, feel and see things in his own way – his recognition of the impossibility of altering a man's convictions by words. This legitimate individuality of every man's views, which in the old days used to trouble and irritate Pierre, now formed the basis of the sympathy he felt for and the interest he took in other people. The diversity, sometimes the complete contradiction between men's opinions and their lives, and between one man and another, pleased Pierre and drew from him a gentle, satirical smile.

In practical affairs Pierre now suddenly felt within himself a centre of gravity he had previously lacked. Hitherto, every question concerning money, especially requests for money to which, as a wealthy man, he was very frequently exposed, had reduced him to a helpless state of worry and perplexity. 'To give or not to give ?' he was always asking himself. 'I have the money and he needs it. But there's another who needs it more. Who needs it most ? And perhaps both of them are impostors ?' And in the days gone by he had been unable to discover any solution to all these conjectures, and had given to all and sundry so long as he had anything to give. He used to find himself in precisely the same quandary with regard to his property, when one person would advise him to adopt one course and another would recommend something else.

Now he found to his amazement that he was no longer troubled with misgivings and hesitation. Now there was a judge within him, settling, by some laws of which he himself was unaware, what should or should not be done.

He was just as unconcerned about money matters as before, but now he knew infallibly what he ought and what he ought not to do. The first time he had recourse to this new judgement was when a prisoner, a French colonel, came to him and after boasting for some time of his exploits ended by making what almost amounted to a demand that Pierre should give him four thousand francs to send to his wife and children. Without the least difficulty or effort Pierre refused, amazed afterwards to find how simple and easy it was to do what before had always seemed so insurmountably difficult. At the same time as he refused the French colonel he made up his mind that he must certainly resort to some stratagem when he left Orel to induce the Italian officer to accept assistance of which he was evidently in need. A further proof to Pierre of his own more stable outlook on practical matters was furnished by decisions he took in regard to his wife's debts and the rebuilding of his houses in and near Moscow.

His head steward came to Orel and with him Pierre went into the question of his diminished income. He had lost, according to the steward's calculations, about two million roubles by the burning of Moscow.

With the idea of compensating this loss the head steward pointed out that Pierre's income, far from being reduced, would be positively increased if he refused to honour his wife's debts, which he was under no obligation to meet, and did not rebuild his Moscow house or the country villa on his Moscow estate, which cost him eighty thousand a year to keep up and brought in nothing.

'Yes, yes, of course,' said Pierre with a beaming smile. 'I don't need any of all that. By being ruined I have become much richer!'

But in January Savelich arrived from Moscow and gave him an account of the state of things there, and the estimate the architect had made for restoring the house and the villa in the suburbs, speaking of this as though it were a matter already confirmed. At the same time he received from Prince Vasili and other acquaintances in Petersburg letters in which his wife's debts were mentioned. And Pierre decided that the steward's proposals which had so pleased him at first were wrong, and that he must go to Petersburg to wind up his wife's affairs and must rebuild in Moscow. Why he ought to do so he did not know, but he was convinced that he ought. His income would be reduced by three-quarters. But it had to be so; he felt that.

Willarski was going to Moscow and they agreed to travel together.

During the whole period of his convalescence in Orel Pierre had experienced a feeling of delight, of freedom, of life; but when he came out into the wide world and saw hundreds of new faces that feeling intensified. Throughout the journey he felt like a schoolboy on holiday. Everyone – the stage-coach driver, the overseers at the posting-stations, the peasants on the road and in the villages – all had a new significance for him. The presence and the observations of

Willarski, who was continually deploring the poverty and ignorance of Russia and her backwardness compared with Europe, only heightened Pierre's appreciation. Where Willarski saw lethargy Pierre saw an extraordinary strength of vitality, the strength which in the snow over a vast latitude sustained the life of that homogeneous, peculiar and unique people. He did not contradict Willarski, and even seemed to agree with him – apparent agreement being the simplest way of avoiding arguments which could lead to nothing – and smiled cheerfully as he listened.

14

Just as it is difficult to explain why and whither ants speed about a scattered ant-hill, some dragging bits of rubbish, eggs and corpses away from it, others hurrying back to the wreck; or their object in jostling, overtaking and fighting one another – so it would be hard to give the reasons that induced the Russians, after the departure of the French, to flock to the place which had been known as Moscow. But just as when one watches the scurrying ants round their ruined ant-heap it is evident from the tenacity, the energy and the immense number of the delving insects that, though the ant-hill is totally destroyed, something indestructible, intangible – something that is the real strength of the colony – remains; so Moscow in the month of October, without a government, without church services or sacred icons, without its wealth and its houses – was still the Moscow it had been in August. Everything was shattered except something intangible yet mighty and indestructible.

The motives of those who rushed from all sides to Moscow after it had been cleared of the enemy were most diverse and personal, and at first mainly savage and animal. One impulse only they all had in common: attraction to the place which had been called Moscow, in order to set their energies to work there.

Within a week Moscow had fifteen thousand inhabitants; in a fortnight twenty-five thousand, and so it went on, the figures increasing until by the autumn of 1813 the population exceeded what it had been in 1812.

The first Russians to enter Moscow were the Cossacks of Wintzingerode's detachment, peasants from the adjacent villages and residents who had fled the capital to hide in the outskirts. The returning

Russians, finding Moscow plundered, plundered in their turn. They continued what the French had begun. Trains of peasant carts drove into Moscow to carry away to the villages all that had been abandoned in the ruined houses and streets. The Cossacks carried off what they could to their camps, and house-owners snatched everything possible from other houses, on the pretence that they were recovering their own property.

But the first pillaging parties were followed by a second and a third contingent, and as the numbers swelled plundering became more and more difficult and assumed more definite forms.

The French had found Moscow deserted but with all the machinery of an organically normal town life still existent – with diverse branches of commerce and craftsmanship, of luxury, of local government and religion. The machinery was inert but it still existed. There were markets, stalls, shops, corn-exchanges, bazaars – for the most part still stocked with goods; there were factories and workshops; there were palaces and stately houses filled with luxuries; there were hospitals, prisons, government offices, churches and cathedrals. The longer the French stayed the more these forms of town life fell away, until towards the end everything disintegrated into one confused, lifeless scene of pillage.

The longer the rapine by the French continued the more the wealth of Moscow and the strength of the pillagers was demolished. But the plundering which marked the return of the Russians to their capital – the longer that lasted, and the greater the number of people taking part in it, the more rapidly was the wealth of Moscow and the regular life of the city restored.

Besides the plunderers, people of all sorts, drawn some by curiosity, some by the duties of office, some by self-interest – householders, clergy, officials of high and low degree, tradesmen, artisans and peasants – streamed into Moscow from all directions, as blood flows to the heart.

Within a week the peasants who came with empty carts to carry off plunder were stopped by the authorities and made to cart away dead bodies from the town. Other peasants, hearing of their comrades' discomfiture, drove into the capital with corn, oats and hay, by competition with one another knocking prices down to lower than they had been in former days. Gangs of carpenters, hoping for fat jobs, arrived in Moscow daily, and on all sides new houses began to go up and burnt-out skeletons were repaired. Tradesmen carried on their business from booths. Cook-shops and taverns were set up in houses that had been through the flames. The clergy resumed services of divine worship in many of the churches that had escaped the fire. The faithful contributed ecclesiastical furnishings which had been stolen. Government clerks planted their baize-covered tables and pigeon-holes of documents in small rooms. The higher authorities and the police organized the distribution of goods left by the French. The owners of houses in which much property was found that had come from other houses complained of the injustice of the order to bring everything to the Granovitaya palace in the Kremlin; others insisted that as the French had collected things from different places into this or that house it would be unfair to allow the master of the house to keep the contents. The police were abused and they were bribed. Estimates were made out at ten times its value for Crown property destroyed in the conflagration. Demands for relief poured in. Count Rostopchin wrote his proclamations.

15

AT the end of January Pierre arrived in Moscow and put up in the wing of his house which had not been damaged. He called on Count Rostopchin and various acquaintances who were back in Moscow, and made plans to leave for Petersburg after a couple of days. Everybody was celebrating the victory; there was a ferment of life in the shattered but reviving city. Everyone was glad to see Pierre; everyone was eager to meet him and they all plied him with questions about what he had seen. Pierre felt particularly friendlily disposed to everyone he encountered; but now he was instinctively on his guard not to entangle himself in any way. To all the inquiries put to him, important or trivial – such as, Where did he mean to live ? Was he going to rebuild ? When was he leaving for Petersburg and would he mind taking a small parcel for someone ? – he would answer 'Yes, very possibly,' 'I dare say I may,' and so on.

He heard that the Rostovs were in Kostroma but he seldom thought of Natasha. If she did come into his mind it was only as a pleasant memory of time long past. He felt himself set free, not only from social obligations but also from that feeling which, it seemed to him, he had wittingly let loose on himself.

On the third day after his arrival he learned from the Drubetskoys that Princess Maria was in Moscow. The death, the sufferings and the last days of Prince Andrei had often engaged his thoughts and now recurred to him with fresh vividness. Having heard at dinner that Princess Maria was in Moscow and living in her own house – which had escaped the fire – in Vozdvizhenka street, he drove that same evening to call upon her.

On his way to Princess Maria's Pierre's mind was full of Prince Andrei, of their friendship, of the different occasions when they had met, and especially of the last time at Borodino.

'Can he have died in the bitter mood he was in then? Is it possible that the meaning of life was not revealed to him before he died?' mused Pierre. He thought of Karatayev and his death and involuntarily began to compare the two men, so different and yet so alike in the love he had felt for them both and in that both had lived and both were dead.

In the most serious of humours Pierre drove up to the house of the old prince. The house had been spared: traces of damage were to be seen but its general aspect was unchanged. The old footman met Pierre with a stern face, as if wishing to impress on the visitor that the absence of the prince made no difference to the order of the establishment, and said that the princess had retired to her own apartments, and received on Sundays.

'Tell her I am here. Perhaps she will see me,' said Pierre.

'Yes, sir,' answered the man. 'Please step into the portrait-gallery.'

A few minutes later the footman returned accompanied by Dessalles with a message from the princess that she would be very glad to see Pierre if he would excuse her want of ceremony and come upstairs to her apartment.

In a low room lighted by a single candle he found the princess and someone with her dressed in black. Pierre recalled that the princess always had lady companions but who they were and what they were like he never knew or remembered. 'This must be one of her companions,' he thought, glancing at the lady in the black dress.

The princess rose quickly to meet him and held out her hand.

'Yes,' she said, studying his altered face after he had kissed her hand, 'so this is how we meet again. He often talked of you even towards the end,' she went on, turning her eyes from Pierre to her companion with a hesitancy that surprised him for an instant.

'I was so glad to hear of your safety. It was the only piece of good news we had for a long time.'

Again the princess glanced round still more uneasily at her companion and was about to add something but Pierre interrupted her.

'Just imagine – I knew nothing about him!' he said. 'I thought he had been killed. All my news I have had second-hand from others. I only know that he fell in with the Rostovs. ... What a strange coincidence!'

Pierre spoke rapidly, with animation. He glanced once at the companion's face, saw her friendly, interested eyes fixed attentively on him, and, as often happens in the course of conversation, he gathered a general impression that this companion in the black dress was a good, kind, nice creature, who need be no hindrance to his conversing freely with Princess Maria.

But when he mentioned the Rostovs the embarrassment in Princess Maria's face became even more marked. She shot another quick look from Pierre to the lady in black, and said:

'Don't you recognize her?'

Pierre looked again at the companion's pale, delicate face with its black eyes and strange mouth. Something near and dear, something long forgotten and more than sweet, gazed at him from those intent eyes.

'But no, it can't be!' he thought. 'This austere, thin, pale face that looks so much older? It cannot be she. It merely reminds me of her.' But at that moment Princess Maria said 'Natasha!' And the face with the attentive eyes painfully, with effort, like a rusty door opening, smiled, and through that opened door there floated to Pierre a breath of fragrance suffusing him with a happiness he had long forgotten and which, certainly of late, had had no place in his thoughts. It breathed about him, penetrated his being and enveloped him entirely. When she smiled doubt was no longer possible: it was Natasha, and he loved her.

In that first moment Pierre involuntarily betrayed to her and to Princess Maria, and most of all to himself, a secret of which he himself had been unaware. He flushed joyfully and with agonizing distress. He tried to mask his emotion. But the more he tried to hide it the more clearly – more clearly than any words could have done – did he disclose to himself and to her, and to Princess Maria, that he loved her.

'No, it's only the unexpectedness of it,' thought Pierre. But as soon as he tried to go on with the conversation he had begun with Princess Maria he glanced again at Natasha, and a still deeper flush spread over his face and a still more violent agitation of rapture and terror flooded his soul. He tripped over his words and stopped short in the middle of a sentence.

Pierre had not noticed Natasha because he had never expected to see her there; but he had not recognized her because of the immense change in her since they had last met. She had grown thin and pale. But it was not that which made her unrecognizable: she was unrecognizable when he first entered the room and glanced at her because there was no trace of a smile in the eyes that in the old days had always shone with suppressed *joie de vivre*; he saw only intent, kindly eyes full of mournful inquiry.

Pierre's confusion roused no answering confusion on Natasha's part, but only a look of pleasure that faintly lighted up her whole face.

16

'She has come to stay with me,' said Princess Maria. 'The count and countess will be here in a few days. The countess is in a dreadful state. But it was necessary for Natasha herself to see a doctor. They insisted on her coming away with me.'

'Yes, is there a family free of sorrow these days?' said Pierre, turning to Natasha. 'You know it happened the very day we were rescued. I saw him. What a charming boy he was!'

Natasha looked at him, and in response to his words her eyes only widened and grew brighter.

'What can one say or think of by way of comfort?' exclaimed Pierre. 'Nothing! Why should such a glorious young fellow, so full of life, have to die?'

'Yes, in our times it would be hard to live if one had not faith ...' remarked Princess Maria.

'Yes, yes, that is true, indeed!' Pierre put in hastily.

'Why is it true?' Natasha asked, looking closely into Pierre's eyes.

'How can you ask that?' said Princess Maria. 'Why, only the thought of what awaits ...'

Natasha, without waiting for Princess Maria to finish, looked again inquiringly at Pierre.

'And because,' Pierre continued, 'only one who believes that there is a God guiding us can bear such a loss as hers and ... yours.'

Natasha had already opened her mouth to speak but suddenly she stopped.

Pierre hurriedly turned away from her and again addressed Princess Maria, to ask about his friend's last days.

Pierre's agitation had now almost subsided but at the same time he felt that his freedom had vanished too. He felt that there was now a judge criticizing his every word and action, a judge whose verdict was of greater consequence to him than that of all the rest of the world. As he talked now he was considering what impression his words were making on Natasha. He did not purposely say things to please her but whatever he said he looked at from her point of view.

Princess Maria – reluctantly, as is usual – began telling Pierre of the condition in which she had found Prince Andrei. But Pierre's questions, the eager, restless look in his eyes, his face quivering with emotion, gradually induced her to go into details which she shrank for her own sake to recall.

'Yes, yes, and so ... ?' Pierre kept saying as he lent towards her with his whole body, listening earnestly. 'Yes; so he found peace? He grew gentler? With his whole soul he was always striving for one thing only – to be completely good – so he could not have been afraid of death. The faults he had – if he had any – were not of his making. So he did soften? ... What a happy thing that he saw you again,' he added, suddenly turning to Natasha and looking at her with eyes full of tears.

Natasha's face twitched. She frowned and for an instant looked down. For a moment she hesitated: should she speak or not?

'Yes, that was a great happiness,' she said in her quiet voice with its deep chest notes. 'For me it was happiness indeed.' She paused 'And he ... he ... he said he was wishing for just that at the very moment I entered the room. ...'

Natasha's voice broke. She flushed, pressed her clasped hands on her knees, and then, controlling herself with an evident effort, lifted her head and began to speak rapidly.

'We knew nothing about it when we started from Moscow. I had not dared to ask about him. Then suddenly Sonya told me he was travelling with us. I had no idea – I could not imagine what state he was in, all I wanted was to see him, to be with him,' she said, trembling and choking.

And, not letting them interrupt her, she went on to tell of what she had never yet mentioned to anyone – all she had gone through during those three weeks of their journey and their stay in Yaroslavl.

Pierre listened with parted lips and eyes full of tears fastened upon her. As he listened he was not thinking of Prince Andrei, nor of death, nor of what she was saying. He listened to her, conscious only of pity for the pain she was suffering as she told her story.

The princess, frowning in her effort to hold back her tears, sat by Natasha's side and heard for the first time the history of those last days of her brother's and Natasha's love.

It was evidently a pressing necessity for Natasha to speak of that agonizing yet joyful time.

She talked on, mingling the most trivial details with her most sacred feelings, and it seemed as though she would never come to an end. Several times she repeated the same thing twice.

Dessalles' voice was heard at the door asking whether little Nikolai might come in to say good-night.

'Well, that's all – everything ...' said Natasha.

She got up quickly just as little Nikolai was coming in and almost running to the door, which was hidden by a curtain, knocked her head against it and with a moan of mingled pain and grief rushed from the room.

Pierre gazed at the door through which she had disappeared, and wondered why he suddenly felt alone in the wide world.

Princess Maria roused him from his abstraction, calling his attention to her nephew who had come in.

Little Nikolai's face, so like his father, affected Pierre so deeply at this moment of emotional tension that after kissing the child he got up quickly, took out his handkerchief and walked over to the window. He would have taken leave of Princess Maria but she would not let him go.

'No, Natasha and I often sit up until past two, so please don't go. We will have some supper. Go downstairs, we will follow directly.'

Before Pierre went down the princess said to him:

'This is the first time she has talked of him like that.'

17

PIERRE was shown into the large brightly-lit dining-room. In a few minutes he heard footsteps and the princess entered with Natasha. Natasha was calm, though the severe, unsmiling expression had settled on her face again. Princess Maria, Natasha and Pierre were all three suffering under that sense of awkwardness which usually follows after a serious and intimate conversation. To continue on the same subject is impossible; to discuss trifles does not seem right; and silence is disagreeable because the desire to talk is there and silence feels like affectation. They sat down to table without a word. The footmen drew the chairs back and pushed them up again. Pierre unfolded his cold table-napkin, and making up his mind to break the silence glanced at Natasha and Princess Maria. They had evidently both reached the same decision at the same moment: in the eyes of both shone a satisfaction with life and an admission that there was gladness in it as well as sorrow.

'Do you drink vodka, count?' asked Princess Maria, and these words suddenly banished the shadows of the past. 'Now tell us about yourself,' said she. 'One hears such incredible stories about you.'

'Yes,' replied Pierre with the gentle smile of irony now habitual to him. 'I am even told of wonders I myself never dreamed of! Maria Abramovna invited me to her house and kept telling me what had happened to me, or was supposed to have happened. Stepan Stepanych also gave me a lesson in the way I should relate my experiences. Altogether I have noticed that it is a very comfortable matter to be an interesting person (I am now an interesting person); people invite me out and tell me all about myself.'

Natasha smiled and started to say something.

'We heard,' said Princess Maria, forestalling her, 'that you lost two millions in Moscow. Is that true?'

'Oh, I am three times as rich as before,' said Pierre.

Though his circumstances were altered by his decision to pay his wife's debts and the necessity of rebuilding, Pierre still said that he was three times as rich as before.

'What I have undoubtedly gained is freedom ...' he began seriously, but on second thoughts did not continue, feeling that this was too egotistic a theme.

'And are you building?'

'Yes, Savelich says I must!'

'So you did not know of the countess's death when you stayed on in Moscow?' asked Princess Maria, and at once flushed crimson, having seen that in putting this question to him immediately after his reference to 'freedom' she was ascribing a significance to his words which was perhaps not intended.

'No,' answered Pierre, obviously not finding anything awkward in the interpretation Princess Maria had given to his remark about his freedom. 'I heard of it in Orel and you cannot imagine how it affected me. We were not a model couple,' he added quickly, glancing at Natasha and observing in her face curiosity as to how he would speak of his wife, 'but her death was a terrible shock. When two people cannot agree, the fault always lies on both sides. And one's own guilt suddenly becomes horribly serious when the other is no longer alive. And then to die like that ... alone, away from friends, without consolation! I felt very, very sorry for her,' he concluded, and was pleased to see a glad look of approval on Natasha's face.

'And so you are single and an eligible *parti* again,' remarked Princess Maria.

Pierre blushed crimson and for a long time tried not to look at Natasha. When he ventured a glance her way her face was cold and severe – even, he fancied, disdainful.

'But did you really see and speak to Napoleon, as we have been told?' asked Princess Maria.

Pierre laughed.

'No, not once, ever! To hear people, one might imagine that to be a prisoner is synonymous with being on a visit to Napoleon. Not only did I never see him – I never even heard him mentioned. I was in much lower company!'

Supper was over and Pierre, who had at first declined to talk about his captivity, was gradually led on to do so.

'But it's true, isn't it, that you stayed behind in Moscow to kill Napoleon?' Natasha asked him with a slight smile. 'I guessed as much when we met you at the Suharev tower – remember?'

Pierre acknowledged that this was true and, thus started, allowed himself to be drawn by Princess Maria's questions, and still more by Natasha's, into giving them a detailed account of his adventures.

At first he spoke with the light irony with which he now always used towards others and especially towards himself; but when he came to describe the horrors and sufferings he had witnessed he was unconsciously carried away and began speaking with the suppressed emotion of a man re-living in imagination experiences which made an acute impression on him.

Princess Maria looked from Pierre to Natasha with a gentle smile. In the whole narrative from beginning to end she saw only Pierre and his goodness. Natasha, leaning on her elbow, the expression on her face continually changing with the story, watched Pierre without taking her eyes off him, evidently living with him through all that he was telling them. Not only her look but her exclamations and the brief questions she put showed Pierre that she understood just what he wanted to convey. It was plain that she understood not only what he said but also what he would have liked to say and could not express in words. The episode with the child and the woman whom he had tried to defend and so got himself arrested Pierre related in the following manner:

'It was an awful sight – children abandoned, some of them in the flames. ... I saw one child dragged out. ... There were women who had their things pulled off, their ear-rings snatched. ...'

Pierre coloured and hesitated.

'Then a patrol arrived on the scene and all those who were not looting – all the men, I mean – were arrested. And me with them.'

'I am sure you're not telling us everything – I am sure there was something you did ...' said Natasha, and after a pause added: 'something fine.'

Pierre continued. When he came to the execution he would have passed over the horrible details but Natasha insisted on his leaving nothing out.

Pierre was going on to Karatayev but stopped. (By this time he had risen from the table and was walking up and down the room, Natasha following him with her eyes.)

'No, you just can't understand what I learned from that illiterate man – that simple creature.'

'Go on, go on,' urged Natasha. 'What became of him?'

'They killed him, almost before my eyes.'

And Pierre went on to tell them about the last part of the retreat, and about Karatayev falling ill (his voice shook continually) and then his death.

Pierre told of his adventures as he had never thought of them before. He now saw as it were a new significance in all he had been through. Now that he was telling it all to Natasha he experienced the rare happiness men know when women listen to them – not *clever* women who when they listen are either trying to assimilate what they hear for the sake of enriching their minds and, when opportunity offers, repeating it, or to apply what is told them to their own ideas and promptly bring out the clever comments elaborated in their own little mental workshop; but the happiness true women give who are endowed with the capacity to select and absorb all that is best in what a man shows of himself. Natasha, without knowing it, was all attention: she did not miss one word, one inflection of his voice, no twitch of a muscle in his face nor a single gesture. She caught the still unspoken word on the wing and took it straight into her open heart, divining the secret import of all Pierre's spiritual travail.

Princess Maria understood his story and sympathized with him but she was seeing something else that absorbed her entire interest. She saw the possibility of love and happiness between Natasha and Pierre. And this idea, which struck her now for the first time, filled her heart with gladness.

It was three o'clock in the morning. The footmen appeared with sad, forbidding faces, bringing fresh candles, but no one noticed them.

Pierre finished his story. Natasha still gazed intently and persistently at him with shining, eager eyes, as if wishing to read the portions of his story that he had perhaps not told. In shamefaced and happy confusion Pierre occasionally glanced at her and cudgelled his brains what to say next to change the subject. Princess Maria was silent. It did not occur to any of them that it was three o'clock in the morning and time to go to bed.

'People talk about adversity bringing suffering,' remarked Pierre, 'but if I were asked at this moment whether I would rather be what I was before I was taken prisoner, or go through all that again, my answer would be: "For heaven's sake give me captivity and horse-flesh!" We imagine that as soon as we are thrown out of our customary ruts all is over, but it is only then that the new and the good begins. While there is life there is happiness. There is a great deal, a great deal before us. I say that for you,' he added, turning to Natasha.

'Yes, yes,' she murmured, answering something quite different.

'I too would ask for nothing better than to go through it all again from the beginning.'

Pierre looked at her keenly.

'No, I could ask for nothing more,' Natasha repeated.

'No, no!' cried Pierre. 'I am not to blame for being alive and wanting to live – nor you either.'

Suddenly Natasha let her head drop into her hands, and burst into tears.

'What is it, Natasha?' said Princess Maria.

'Nothing, nothing.' She smiled at Pierre through her tears. 'Good-night, it's bedtime.'

Pierre got up and took his leave.

*

Natasha, as she always did, went with Princess Maria into her bed-room. They talked of what Pierre had told them. Princess Maria did not express her opinion of Pierre. Nor did Natasha speak of him.

'Well, good-night, Marie,' said Natasha. 'Do you know, I am often afraid that by not speaking of him' (she meant Prince Andrei) 'for fear of desecrating our feelings, we forget him.'

Princess Maria sighed deeply and by this sigh acknowledged the justice of Natasha's remark, but she did not agree with her in words.

'Is it possible to forget?' said she.

'It did me so much good to tell all about it today. It was hard and painful, yet I was glad to ... very glad,' said Natasha. 'I am sure he really loved him. That was why I told him ... it didn't matter my telling him?' she asked suddenly, blushing.

'Telling Pierre? Oh, no! What a fine man he is!' said Princess Maria.

'Do you know, Marie,' said Natasha all of a sudden, with a mischievous smile such as Princess Maria had not seen on her face for a long time, 'he has somehow grown so fair and smooth and fresh-looking – as though he had just come out of a bath: do you understand? Out of a moral bath, I mean. Don't you agree?'

'Yes,' replied Princess Maria. 'He has improved very much.'

'And his short jacket and his cropped hair; exactly as though ... well, exactly as though he had come straight out of the bath. ... Papa used sometimes ...'

'I can understand how it was *he*' [Prince Andrei] 'cared for him more than anyone else,' said Princess Maria.

'Yes, and they were quite different. They say men are better friends when they are not alike. That must be true. He is not a bit like him in anything, is he?'

'No, and he's a marvellous person.'

'Well, good-night,' said Natasha.

And the same mischievous smile lingered for a long time on her face as though it had been forgotten there.

18

IT was a long while before Pierre could go to sleep that night. He strode up and down his room, at one moment frowning, deep in some difficult train of thought, or shrugging his shoulders and giving a start, at the next smiling blissfully.

He was thinking of Prince Andrei, of Natasha, and of their love, now jealous of her past, now reproaching now forgiving himself for the feeling. It was six o'clock in the morning and still he paced the room.

'Well, what's to be done if it cannot be otherwise? What's to be done? It must be so then,' he said to himself; and hurriedly undressing he got into bed, happy and agitated but free from doubt and hesitation.

'Yes, strange and impossible as such happiness may seem, I must do everything to make her my wife,' he told himself.

Several days previously Pierre had appointed to go to Petersburg on the Friday. When he woke next morning – Thursday – Savelich came to ask about packing for the journey.

'Petersburg? What about Petersburg? Who is there in Petersburg?' he asked involuntarily, though only to himself. 'Oh yes, a long while ago, before this happened, I had some such thought – I was going to Petersburg for some reason or other,' he remembered. 'Why was it? And perhaps I shall go. How good and attentive he is, and how he remembers everything!' he thought, looking at Savelich's old face. 'And what a nice smile he has!'

'Well, Savelich, do you still not want your freedom?' Pierre asked him.

'What would be the good of freedom to me, your Excellency? We lived well while the old count was alive – God rest his soul! – and now with you we're comfortable-like and have nothing to complain of.'

'Yes, but what about your children?'

'The children too will do very well, your Excellency. With a master like you there is nothing to fear.'

'Well, but my heirs?' suggested Pierre. 'Supposing I suddenly marry ... that might happen, you know,' he added with an involuntary smile.

'If I may take the liberty – it would be a very good thing, your Excellency.'

'How lightly he thinks of it,' thought Pierre. 'He doesn't know how terrible it is, how perilous. Whether too soon or too late ... it is terrible!'

'What orders, your Excellency? Will you be going tomorrow?' asked Savelich.

'No, I am deferring it for a bit. I'll let you know later. I am sorry for the trouble I have put you to,' said Pierre, and watching Savelich smile he thought how odd it was, though, he should not know that now there is no Petersburg for me, that *that* must be settled before anything else. 'But of course he must know and is only pretending. Shall I have a talk with him and see what he thinks?' Pierre wondered. 'No, some other time.'

At breakfast Pierre told his cousin that he had been to call on Princess Maria the previous evening and had there met – 'Whom do you think? Natasha Rostov!'

The princess looked as though she saw nothing more extraordinary in that fact than if Pierre had seen Anna Semeonovna.

'Do you know her?' asked Pierre.

'I met the princess once,' she replied. 'I did hear they were arranging a match for her with young Rostov. It would be a fine thing for the Rostovs – they are said to be utterly ruined.'

'No, I meant, do you know Natasha Rostov?'

'I heard about that affair of hers at the time. A great pity.'

'No, either she doesn't understand or is pretending,' thought Pierre. 'Better not say anything to her either.'

The princess, too, had prepared provisions for Pierre's journey.

'How kind they all are,' thought Pierre, 'to take so much trouble about all this now, when it certainly can be of no interest to them. And all for my sake – that is what's so marvellous.'

That same morning the chief of police came to Pierre with the suggestion that he send someone to the Granovitaya palace to recover the things that were to be restored to their owners that day.

'And this man too,' thought Pierre, looking into the face of the chief of police. 'What a fine, good-looking officer, and how kind! Fancy bothering about such trifles *now*! And they actually say he is not honest and takes bribes. What nonsense! Besides, why shouldn't he take bribes? That's the way he has been brought up. And they all do it. But such a pleasant, good-tempered face, and he smiles when he looks at me.'

Pierre went to Princess Maria's to dinner.

As he drove through the streets past the charred remains of houses he was surprised at the beauty of the ruins. The picturesqueness of the chimney-stacks and fallen walls in the burned-out quarters of the town, stretching in long rows and hiding one another, reminded him of the Rhine and the Colosseum. The hack-drivers he met and their passengers, the carpenters at work squaring timber for new houses, the women hawkers and shopkeepers all looked at Pierre with cheerful, beaming eyes that seemed to say: 'Ah, there he is! We shall see what comes of it.'

When he reached Princess Maria's house Pierre was beset by a sudden doubt whether he really had been there the night before and really had seen Natasha and talked to her. 'Perhaps I imagined it: perhaps I shall go in and find no one.' But he had hardly entered the room before an instantaneous feeling of loss of freedom made him aware with his whole being of her presence. She was wearing the same black dress that hung in soft folds, and her hair was done in the same way as the night before, yet she was quite different. Had she looked like this when he came in the day before he could not for a second have failed to recognize her.

She was just as he had known her almost as a child, and later on as Prince Andrei's betrothed. A bright, questioning light shone in her eyes; there was a friendly and strangely roguish expression on her face.

Pierre dined and would have spent the whole evening there; but Princess Maria was going to vespers and Pierre went with them.

Next day he arrived early, had dinner with them and stayed on. Although Princess Maria and Natasha were obviously glad to see their visitor, and although all the interest of Pierre's life was now centred in that house, by the evening they had said all they had to say and the conversation passed from one trivial topic to another and often broke off altogether. Pierre stayed so late that Princess Maria and Natasha exchanged glances, evidently wondering when he would go. Pierre noticed, and yet could not tear himself away. He began to feel uncomfortable and awkward but sat on because he simply *could not* get up and take his departure.

Princess Maria, foreseeing no end to the situation, was the first to rise, and complaining of a sick headache began to say good-night.

'So tomorrow you are off to Petersburg?' she asked.

'No, I am not going,' Pierre replied hastily, in a surprised and what sounded an offended tone. 'To Petersburg, you say? Tomorrow – only I won't say good-bye now. I'll call round in case you have any commissions for me,' he added, standing in front of Princess Maria and turning red but not leaving.

Natasha gave him her hand and retired. Princess Maria, on the contrary, instead of going away sank into an arm-chair and looked sternly and intently at him with her deep, luminous eyes. The weariness she had unmistakably betrayed just before had now quite passed off. She drew a deep, prolonged sigh, as though she were preparing for a lengthy talk.

The moment Natasha left the room all Pierre's confusion and awkwardness vanished, to be replaced by eager excitement. He quickly moved up an arm-chair close to Princess Maria.

'Yes, I wanted to tell you,' said he, replying to her look as though she had spoken. 'Princess, help me! What am I to do? Can I hope? Princess, my dear friend, listen! I know it all. I know I am not worthy of her; I know this is not the time to speak. But I want to be a brother to her. No, not that. ... I don't want, I can't ...'

He paused and passed his hands over his face and eyes.

'It's like this,' he went on, with an evident effort to control himself and speak coherently, 'I don't know when I first began to love her. But my whole life long I have loved her, and her alone, and I love her so that I cannot imagine life without her. I cannot ask for her hand at present, but the thought that she might be mine and that I may be letting the opportunity slip ... the opportunity ... is awful. Tell me, can I hope? Tell me, what shall I do? Dear princess!' he added, after a little silence, touching her hand when she did not answer.

'I am thinking of what you have told me,' returned Princess Maria. 'This is what I think. You are right – to speak to her of love just at present ...' Princess Maria stopped. She had been going to say that to speak of love now was impossible; but she stopped because she had seen by the sudden change in Natasha that her friend would not only not be upset if Pierre were to confess his love but that this was the very thing she was longing for.

'To speak to her now ... wouldn't do,' said the princess all the same.

'But what am I to do?'

'Leave it to me,' said Princess Maria. 'I know ...'

Pierre was looking into Princess Maria's eyes.

'Well? ... Well? ...' he said.

'I know that she loves ... will love you,' Princess Maria corrected herself.

Before her words were out Pierre had sprung up and, with a startled face, clutched at Princess Maria's hand.

'What makes you think so? You think I may hope? You really ...?'

'Yes, I believe so,' said Princess Maria with a smile. 'Write to her parents. And leave it to me. I will tell her when the moment comes. I hope for it. And I feel in my heart that it will be.'

'No, it can't! How happy I am! But it can't be. ... How happy I am – no, it's not possible!' Pierre kept saying, kissing Princess Maria's hands.

'You go to Petersburg, that will be best. And I will write to you,' she said.

'To Petersburg? Go away? Very well, I'll go. But may I come and see you again tomorrow?'

Next day Pierre came to say good-bye. Natasha was less animated than on the preceding occasions; but that day when he now and again looked into her eyes Pierre felt that he was vanishing away, that neither he nor she existed any more, that nothing existed but happiness. 'Is it possible? No, it can't be,' he told himself at every glance she gave, every gesture, every word of hers, that filled his heart with bliss.

When he took her thin slender hand and was saying good-bye he could not help holding it somewhat longer in his own.

'Is it possible that this hand, this face, these eyes, all this treasure of womanly charm, so far from me now – is it possible that one day it may all be mine for ever, as familiar to me as I am to myself? ... No, surely not! ...'

'Good-bye, count,' she said to him, and then added in a whisper: 'I shall look forward very much to your return.'

And those simple words, with the look in her eyes and the expression on her face that accompanied them, for two whole months formed the subject of inexhaustible memories, interpretations and exquisite day-dreams for Pierre. '*I shall look forward very much to your return. ... Yes*, yes, how did she say it? I remember – *I shall look forward very much to your return.* Oh, how happy I am! What is happening – how can I be so happy?' said Pierre to himself.

19

PIERRE'S soul knew nothing this time of what had troubled it in similar circumstances during his courtship of Hélène.

He did not go over, as he had then, with a sickening sense of shame the words he had uttered, or ask himself: 'Oh, why did I not say that?' and 'Whatever made me say "*Je vous aime*"?' Now, on the contrary, every word Natasha had said, every word of his own, he went over in his imagination and pictured every detail of her look and smile, and had no wish to add or take away anything but only to have it repeated again and again. As for doubts – whether what he contemplated doing was right or wrong – there was never a trace of them now. Only one terrible anxiety sometimes assailed his mind: 'Wasn't it all a dream? Isn't Princess Maria mistaken? Am I not too conceited and self-confident? I believe in it – but isn't this what is bound to happen: Princess Maria will tell her, and she will smile and say: "How strange! He is certainly deluding himself. Doesn't he know that he is just an ordinary mortal, a man like any other man, while I – I am something altogether different, and far superior"?'

This was Pierre's only doubt, and it frequently recurred to him. And he made no plans of any sort now. The happiness before him appeared so incredible that if only he could attain it anything more would be a matter of supererogation. Everything ended with it.

A joyous, unexpected frenzy, which Pierre had not believed himself capable of feeling, possessed him. The whole meaning of life – not for him alone but for all the world – seemed to him centred in his love and the possibility of her loving him. At times he thought that everybody was occupied by one thing only – his future happiness. At times it seemed to him that other people were all rejoicing as he himself was, and only tried to conceal their gladness by pretending to be busy with other interests. In every word and gesture he saw intimations of his own happiness. He often surprised those he met by his momentous, blissful looks and smiles, which they fancied expressed some secret understanding between him and them. But when he realized that people could not be aware of his happiness he pitied them from the bottom of his heart and longed somehow to explain to them that they were wasting their time on fiddlesticks and nonsense not worthy of attention.

When it was suggested to him that he should take some official post, or when the war or public affairs in general were discussed with the assumption that the welfare of the human race depended on this or that issue of events, he would listen with a gentle smile of commiseration and astound those who were conversing with him by his odd observations. But at this period he saw everybody – both those who seemed to him to grasp the true significance of life (that is, what he was feeling) and those unfortunates who obviously had no notion of his state – in the brilliant light of the emotion that radiated within him, so that without the slightest effort he immediately saw in whoever came his way everything that was good and deserving of love.

As he went through the papers and belongings of his dead wife her memory aroused no feeling in him but pity that she had not known the bliss which was now his. Prince Vasili, particularly puffed up at that time, having obtained some new office and a decoration, struck him as a pathetic, kindly, pitiful old man.

Often in after life Pierre recalled this period of blissful insanity. All the opinions he had then formed for himself of men and circumstances remained true for him always. He not only did not renounce them subsequently, but when he was in doubt or inwardly at variance he flew back to the view he had held at this time of his madness, and that view always turned out to be a true one.

'I may have appeared strange and queer then,' he thought, 'but I was not so mad as I seemed. On the contrary, I was wiser and had more insight than at any other time; and I understood all that is worth understanding in life, because ... I was so happy.'

Pierre's insanity consisted in not waiting, as he used to do, to discover personal grounds, which he called 'good qualities', in people before loving them: love filled his heart to overflowing and in loving his fellow-men without cause he never failed to discover incontestable reasons that made them worth loving.

20

From that first evening after Pierre had left them, when Natasha had said to Princess Maria with a gay, mischievous smile that he looked exactly – yes, exactly – as if he had just come out of a bath, with his short jacket and cropped hair – from that moment something hidden and unrecognized by herself, yet irresistible, awoke in Natasha's soul.

Everything: her face, the way she walked, her expression and her voice, underwent a sudden change. To her own surprise the sap of life and hopes of happiness rose to the surface and clamoured to be satisfied. From that first evening Natasha seemed to have forgotten all that had happened to her. From that time she never once bewailed her state or said a single word about the past, and no longer feared to make light-hearted plans for the future. She spoke little of Pierre, but when Princess Maria mentioned him a light that had long been dimmed kindled in her eyes and her lips curved into an odd smile.

The change that took place in Natasha at first surprised Princess Maria; but when she understood its meaning she felt grieved. 'Can she have loved my brother so little that she can so soon forget him?' she thought when she brooded over the transformation. But when she was with Natasha she was not vexed with her and did not blame her. Natasha's reawakening to life was obviously so overwhelming, so unexpected for the girl herself, that in her presence Princess Maria felt that she had no right to reproach her even in her heart.

Natasha gave herself up so fully and frankly to this new feeling that she made no attempt to mask the fact that sorrow had given way to gladness.

When Princess Maria returned to her room that night after her talk with Pierre, Natasha met her on the threshold.

'Has he spoken? Yes? He has?' she repeated. And a joyful and at the same time piteous expression, which seemed to plead forgiveness for her joy, settled on Natasha's face.

'I wanted to listen at the door but I knew you would tell me.'

Understandable and touching as was the look Natasha fastened on Princess Maria, and sorry as Princess Maria was for her friend's agitation, the words wounded her for a moment. She remembered her brother and his love.

'But what's to be done? She can't help it,' thought Princess Maria.

And with a sad and rather stern face she told Natasha all that Pierre had said. When she heard that he was going to Petersburg Natasha was shattered.

'To Petersburg!' she repeated, as though unable to take it in.

But noticing the mournful expression of Princess Maria's face she surmised the reason for her melancholy and suddenly burst into tears.

'Marie,' she said, 'tell me what to do: I am so afraid of behaving badly. I'll do whatever you say. Tell me. ...'

'You love him?'

'Yes,' whispered Natasha.

'What are you crying for, then? I am glad for you,' said Princess Maria, moved by those tears to complete forgiveness of Natasha's joy.

'It won't be just yet ... some day. Only think how happy we'll be when I am his wife and you marry Nicolas.'

'Natasha, I asked you not to speak of that. Let us talk about you.'

They were silent.

'But why must he go to Petersburg?' cried Natasha suddenly, and hastened to answer herself. 'Well, well, it is best so. ... Eh, Marie? It is best so. ...'

WAR AND PEACE

*

EPILOGUE

PART ONE

I

SEVEN years had passed. The storm-tossed sea of European history had sunk to rest upon its shores. The sea appeared to be calm; but the mysterious forces that move humanity (mysterious because the laws that govern their action are unknown to us) were still at work.

Though the surface of the ocean of history seemed motionless, the movement of humanity continued as uninterrupted as the flow of time. Coalitions of men came together and separated again; the causes that would bring about the formation and the dissolution of empires and the displacement of peoples were in course of preparation.

The ocean of history was no longer, as before, swept from shore to shore by squalls: it seethed in its depths. The personages of history were not borne by the waves from coast to coast as before; now they seemed to revolve in stationary eddies. Historical personages who had lately been leading armies and reflecting the movement of the masses by decreeing wars, campaigns and battles now reflected the turbulent flux by political and diplomatic combinations, statutes, treaties, and so on.

This activity of the figures of history the historians call *reaction*.

In dealing with the part played by these historical personages the historians are severe in their criticism, supposing them to be the cause of what they describe as *reaction*. All the famous people of that period, from Alexander and Napoleon to Madame de Staël, Photius, Schelling, Fichte, Chateaubriand, and the rest, are arraigned before their stern tribunal and acquitted or condemned according to whether they conduced to *progress* or *reaction*.

Russia too is described by the historians as the scene at this time of reaction, and for this they throw the chief responsibility on Alexander I – the same Alexander I to whom they also give the credit for the liberal enterprises at the beginning of his reign, and for the saving of Russia.

There is no one in Russian literature today, from schoolboy essay-writer to learned historian, who does not throw his little stone at Alexander for one or another ill-considered measure at this later period of his sovereignty.

'He ought to have acted in such and such a way. In this case he did well, on that occasion badly. He conducted himself admirably at the beginning of his reign and during 1812; but he erred in granting a constitution to Poland, in establishing the Holy Alliance, in entrusting power to Arakcheyev, in encouraging first Golitsyn and his mysticism and afterwards Shishkov and Photius. He did wrong in interfering with the army on active service, did wrong in disbanding the Semeonovsk regiment, and so on.'

It would take a dozen pages to enumerate all the faults the historians find in him on the strength of the knowledge they possess of what is for the good of humanity.

What do these strictures signify?

Do not the very actions for which the historians applaud Alexander I – the attempts at liberalism at the beginning of his reign, his struggle with Napoleon, the firmness he displayed in 1812 and the campaign of 1813 – proceed from those very sources – the circumstances of birth, breeding and life that made his personality what it was – from which also flowed the actions for which they censure him, like the Holy Alliance, the restoration of Poland and the reaction of the 1820s?

What is the substance of these strictures?

In this – that an historical character like Alexander I, standing on the highest possible pinnacle of human power with the blinding light of history focused upon him; a character exposed to those most potent of influences – the intrigues, flatteries and self-delusion inseparable from power; a character who at every moment of his life felt a responsibility for all that was being done in Europe; and a character, not from fiction but as much alive as any other man, with his own personal bent, passions, and impulses towards goodness, beauty and truth – that this character, though not lacking in virtue (the historians do not accuse him on that score), living fifty years ago,* had not the same conception concerning the welfare of humanity as a present-day professor who from his youth up has been engaged in study, *i.e.* in reading, listening to lectures and making notes on those books and lectures in a note-book.

* *War and Peace* was written between 1864 and 1869. — [Tr.]

But if we are going to assume that Alexander I, fifty years ago, was mistaken in his view of what was good for the peoples we can hardly help considering that the historian who criticizes Alexander may, after a certain lapse of time, prove to be equally incorrect in his idea of what is for the good of humanity. This assumption is all the more natural and inevitable because, watching the development of history, we see that every year, with each new writer, opinion as to what constitutes the welfare of humanity changes; so that what once seemed good, ten years later seems bad, and vice versa. That is not all: we even find in history, at one and the same time, quite contradictory views as to what was good and what was bad. Some people place the giving of a constitution to Poland, and the Holy Alliance, to Alexander's credit, while others censure him for them.

The activity of Alexander or of Napoleon cannot be termed beneficial or harmful, since we cannot say for what it was beneficial or harmful. If that activity fails to please someone, this is only because it does not coincide with his restricted conception of what constitutes good. I may regard the preservation of my father's house in Moscow in 1812, or the glory of Russian arms, or the prosperity of Petersburg (or any other) university, or the independence of Poland, or the might of Russia, or the balance of power in Europe, or a certain kind of European enlightenment called 'progress' – I may regard all these as good but I am still bound to admit that, besides these ends and aims, the action of every historic character has other more general purposes beyond my grasp.

But let us suppose that what we call science has the power of reconciling all contradictions and possesses an invariable standard of right and wrong by which to try historical persons and events.

Let us say that Alexander could have done everything differently. Let us assume that he might – in accordance with the prescriptions of those who accuse him and who profess to know the ultimate goal of the movement of humanity – have arranged matters in harmony with the programme of nationalism, freedom, equality and progress (for there would seem to be nothing newer) with which his present-day critics would have provided him. Let us assume that this programme could have been possible and had actually been formulated at the time, and that Alexander could have acted in accordance with it. What then would become of the activity of all those who opposed the tendency of the government of the day – of the activity which in the opinion of the historians was good and beneficial? Their activity would not have existed: there would have been no life, nothing.

Once say that human life can be controlled by reason, and all possibility of life is annihilated.

2

If we assume, as the historians do, that great men lead humanity towards the attainment of certain ends – such as the majesty of Russia or of France, the balance of power in Europe, the propagation of the ideas of the Revolution, progress in general, or anything else you like – it becomes impossible to explain the phenomena of history without intruding the concepts of *chance* and *genius*.

If the object of the European wars of the beginning of this century had been the aggrandizement of Russia, that object might have been attained without any of the preceding wars and without the invasion. If the object was the aggrandizement of France, that might have been attained without either the Revolution or the Empire. If the object was the propagation of ideas, the printing-press could have accomplished that much more effectually than soldiers. If the object was the progress of civilization, one may very readily suppose that there are other more expedient means of diffusing civilization than by slaughtering people and destroying their wealth.

Why then did things happen thus and not otherwise?

Because they did so happen. '*Chance* created the situation; *genius* made use of it,' says history.

But what is *chance*? What is *genius*?

The words *chance* and *genius* do not denote anything that actually exists, and therefore they cannot be defined. These two words merely indicate a certain degree of comprehension of phenomena. I do not know why a certain event occurs; I suppose that I cannot know: therefore I do not try to know, and I talk about *chance*. I see a force producing effects beyond the scope of ordinary human agencies; I do not understand why this occurs, and I cry *genius*.

To a flock of sheep, the one the shepherd drives into a separate enclosure every night to feed, and that becomes twice as fat as the others, must seem to be a genius. And the circumstance that every evening this particular sheep, instead of coming into the common fold, chances into a special pen with extra oats, and that this sheep, this particular one, fattens up and is killed for mutton, doubtless impresses the rest of the flock as a remarkable conjunction of genius with a whole series of fortuitous chances.

But the sheep need only rid themselves of the idea that all that is done to them is done solely for the furtherance of their sheepish ends; they have only to concede that what happens to them may also have purposes beyond their ken, and they will immediately perceive a unity and coherence in what happens with their brother that is being fattened. Although it may not be given to them to know to what end he was being fattened, they will at least know that all that happened to him did not occur accidentally, and will no longer need to resort to conceptions of *chance* or *genius*.

It is only by renouncing our claim to discern a purpose immediately intelligible to us, and admitting the ultimate purpose to be beyond our ken, that we shall see a logical connexion in the lives of historical personages, and perceive the why and wherefore of what they do which so transcends the ordinary powers of humanity. We shall then find that the words *chance* and *genius* have become superfluous.

We have only to admit that we do not know the purpose of the convulsions among the European nations, and that we know only the hard facts – the butchery, first in France, then in Italy, in Africa, in Prussia, in Austria, in Spain and in Russia – and that the movements from west to east and from east to west constitute the essence and end of those events, and we shall not only find it no longer necessary to see some exceptional ability – *genius* – in Napoleon and Alexander: we shall be unable to regard them as being anything but men like other men. And far from having to turn to *chance* to explain the little incidents which made those men what they were, it will be clear to us that all those little incidents were inevitable.

If we give up all claim to a knowledge of the ultimate purpose we shall realize that, just as it is impossible to imagine for any given plant other more appropriate blossom or seed than those it produces, so it is impossible to imagine any two persons, with all their antecedents, more completely adapted, down to the smallest detail, to the mission which Napoleon and Alexander were called upon to fulfil.

3

THE fundamental and essential feature of European events at the beginning of the present century is the militant mass movement of the

European peoples from west to east and then from east to west. The first impulse to this flux was given by the movement from west to east. For the peoples of the west to be able to achieve their militant advance as far as Moscow they had to (1) form themselves into a military group of sufficient magnitude to sustain a collision with the military group of the east; (2) renounce all established traditions and customs; and (3) have at their head, during their military movement, a man able to justify to himself and to them the guile, robbery and murder which must be the concomitants of their progress.

So, beginning with the French Revolution, the old group which is not large enough is destroyed; old habits and traditions are abolished; and step by step a group of new dimensions is elaborated, new customs and traditions are developed, and a man is prepared who is to stand at the head of the coming movement and bear the whole responsibility for what has to be done.

A man of no convictions, no habits, no traditions, no name, not even a Frenchman, emerges – by what seems the strangest freak of chance – from among all the seething parties of France, and, without attaching himself to any one of them, is borne forward to a prominent position.

The incompetence of his colleagues, the weakness and inanity of his rivals, the frankness of his falsehoods and his brilliant and self-confident mediocrity raise him to the head of the army. The brilliant quality of the soldiers of the army sent to Italy, his opponents' reluctance to fight and his own childish insolence and conceit secure him military glory. Innumerable so-called *chance* circumstances attend him everywhere. The disfavour into which he falls with the French Directorate turns to his advantage. His attempts to avoid his pre-destined path are unsuccessful: Russia refused to receive him into her service and the appointment he seeks in Turkey comes to nothing. During the wars in Italy he more than once finds himself on the brink of disaster and each time is saved in some unexpected manner. Owing to various diplomatic considerations the Russian armies – the very armies which have the power to extinguish his glory – do not appear upon the European scene while he is there.

On his return from Italy he finds the government in Paris in the process of dissolution in which all those who are in that government are doomed to erasure and extinction. And by chance an escape from this dangerous situation offers itself to him in the nonsensical, gratuitous expedition to Africa. Again so-called *chance* accompanies him. Malta the impregnable surrenders without a shot; his most reckless schemes are crowned with success. The enemy's fleet, which later on does not let a single row-boat through, now suffers a whole army to elude it. In Africa a whole series of outrages is perpetrated against the practically defenceless inhabitants. And the men committing these atrocities, and their leader most of all, persuade themselves that this is admirable, this is glory, this is like Caesar and Alexander the Great.

This ideal of *glory* and *greatness* – which consists not merely in the assurance that nothing one does is to be considered wrong but in glorying in one's every crime and ascribing to it an incomprehensible, supernatural significance – this ideal, destined to guide this man and his associates, is provided with fertile ground for its development in Africa. Whatever he does succeeds. The plague does not touch him. Responsibility for the cruel massacring of prisoners is not laid at his door. His childishly incautious, unreasoning and ignoble departure from Africa, leaving his comrades in distress, is accounted to his credit, and again the enemy's fleet twice lets him slip past. Completely intoxicated by the success of his crimes and ready for his new rôle, though without any plan, he arrives in Paris just when the disintegration of the Republican government, which a year before might have made an end of him, has reached its utmost limit and his presence there now, as a newcomer free from party entanglements, can only lift him to the heights.

He has no plan of any kind; he is afraid of everything; but the parties hold out their hands to him and insist on his participation.

He alone – with the ideal of glory and grandeur built up in Italy and Egypt, his insane self-adulation, his insolence in crime and frankness in lying – he alone can justify what has to be done.

He is needed for the place that awaits him and so, almost apart from his own volition and in spite of his indecision, his lack of a plan and all the blunders he makes, he is drawn into a conspiracy that aims at seizing power, and the conspiracy is crowned with success.

He is dragged into a meeting of the legislature. In alarm he tries to flee, believing himself in danger; pretends to be falling into a faint; says the most senseless things which should have meant his ruin. But the once proud and discerning rulers of France, feeling their part is over, are even more panic-stricken than he, and fail to pronounce the word they should have spoken to preserve their power and crush him.

Chance, millions of *chances*, invest him with authority, and all men everywhere, as if by agreement together, co-operate to confirm that power. *Chance* forms the characters of the rulers of France who cringe before him; *chance* forms the character of Paul I of Russia who recognizes his power; *chance* contrives a plot against him which not only fails to injure him but strengthens his position. *Chance* throws the duc d'Enghien into his hands and unexpectedly impels him to assassinate him – thereby convincing the mob by the most potent of all arguments that he has right on his side since he has might. *Chance* sees to it that though he strains every nerve to prepare an expedition against England (which would undoubtedly have been his downfall) he never carries this enterprise into execution but abruptly falls upon Mack and the Austrians, who surrender without a battle. *Chance* and *genius* give him the victory at Austerlitz; and by *chance* it comes to pass that all men, not only the French but all Europe – except England, who takes no part in the events about to happen – forget their former horror and detestation of his crimes and now recognize his consequent authority, the title he has bestowed upon himself and his ideal of grandeur and glory, which seems to one and all something excellent and reasonable.

As though measuring and making ready for the movement to come, the forces of the West several times – in 1805, 1806, 1807, 1809 – sally eastwards, gaining strength and growing. In 1811 the body of men that had formed in France unites into one enormous body with the peoples of Central Europe. Every increase in the size of this group adds further justification for Napoleon's power. During the ten-year preparatory period before the great push this man forms relations with all the crowned heads of Europe. The discredited rulers of the world have no rational ideal to oppose to the meaningless Napoleonic *mystique* of *glory* and *grandeur*. One after another they rush to display to him their insignificance. The King of Prussia sends his wife to curry favour with the great man; the Emperor of Austria is gratified that this man should take the daughter of the Kaisers to his bed; the Pope, guardian of all that the nations hold sacred, utilizes religion to raise the great man higher. It is less that Napoleon prepares himself for the performance of his rôle than that all about him lead him on to acceptance of entire responsibility for what is happening and has to happen. There is no act, no crime, no petty deceit he might commit, which would not immediately be proclaimed by those about him as a great deed. The most suitable fête the Teutons can think of to observe in his honour is a celebration of Jena and Auerstädt. Not only is he great but so are his forefathers, his brothers, his stepsons and his brothers-in-law. Everything is done to deprive him of the last vestige of his reason and to prepare him for his terrible part. And when he is ready so too are the forces.

The invasion streams eastwards and reaches its final goal – Moscow. The capital is taken: the Russian army suffers heavier losses than the enemy ever suffered in previous wars from Austerlitz to Wagram. But all at once, instead of the *chance* happenings and the *genius* which hitherto had so consistently led him by an uninterrupted series of successes to the predestined goal, an innumerable sequence of reverse *chances* occur – from the cold in his head at Borodino to the frosts and the spark which set Moscow on fire – and, instead of *genius*, folly and baseness without parallel appear.

The invaders run, turn back, run again, and all the *chances* are now not for Napoleon but always against him.

A counter-movement follows, from east to west, bearing a remarkable resemblance to the preceding movement from west to east. There are similar tentative drives westward as had in 1805, 1807 and 1809 preceded the great eastward movement; there is the same coalescence into a group of colossal proportions; the same adhesion of the peoples of Central Europe to the movement; the same hesitation midway and the same increased velocity as the goal is approached.

Paris, the ultimate goal, is reached. The Napoleonic government and army are overthrown. Napoleon himself is no longer of any account; all his actions are manifestly pitiful and mean; but again inexplicable chance steps in: the allies detest Napoleon whom they regard as the cause of their troubles. Stripped of his power and authority, his crimes and his treacheries exposed he should have appeared to them what he had appeared ten years previously and was to appear a year later – a bandit and an outlaw. But by some strange freak of chance no one perceives this. His rôle is not yet played to a finish. The man who ten years before and a year later was looked on as a miscreant outside the law is sent to an island a couple of days' journey from France, which is given to him as his domain, with guards and millions of money, as though to pay him for some service rendered.

4

THE flood of nations begins to subside into its normal channels. The waves of the great movement abate, leaving a calm surface ruffled by eddies where the diplomatists busy themselves (in the belief that the calm is the result of their work).

But suddenly the smooth sea is convulsed again. The diplomats imagine that their dissensions are the cause of this new upheaval of the elements; they anticipate war between their sovereigns; the position seems to them insoluble. But the wave they feel to be gathering does not come from the quarter expected. It is the same wave as before, and its source the same point as before – Paris. The last backwash of the movement from the west occurs – a backwash which serves to solve the apparently insuperable diplomatic difficulties and put an end to the militant flux of the period.

The man who has devastated France returns to France alone, without any conspiracy and without soldiers. Any gendarme might apprehend him; but by a strange chance not only does no one touch him – they all rapturously acclaim the man they had cursed the day before and will be cursing again within a month.

This man is still needed to justify the final collective act.

The act is performed. The last part is played. The actor is bidden to disrobe and wash off his powder and paint: he will not be wanted any more.

And several years pass during which, in solitude on his island, this man plays his pitiful farce to himself, intriguing and lying to justify his conduct when justification is no longer needed, and revealing to the world at large what it was that people had mistaken for strength so long as an unseen hand directed his actions.

The stage manager, having brought the drama to a close and stripped the puppet of his motley, shows him to us.

'Look – this is what you believed in! Here he stands! Do you see now that it was not he but *I* who moved you?'

But, dazed by the violence of the movement, it was long before people understood this.

A still more striking example of logical sequence and inevitability is to be seen in the life of Alexander I, the figure who stood at the head of the counter-movement from east to west.

What qualities should the man possess if he were to overshadow everyone else and head the counter-movement westwards?

He must have a sense of justice and a sympathy with European affairs, but a detached sympathy not obscured by petty interests; a moral superiority over his peers – the other sovereigns of the day; a gentle and attractive personality; and a personal grievance against Napoleon. And all this is found in Alexander I; all this has been prepared by countless so-called *chance* circumstances in his life: his upbringing and early liberalism, the advisers who surrounded him; by Austerlitz and Tilsit and Erfurt.

So long as the war is a national one he remains inactive because he is not needed. But as soon as the necessity for a general European war becomes apparent, at the given moment he is in his place and, uniting the nations of Europe, leads them to the goal.

The goal is reached. After the final war of 1815 Alexander finds himself at the summit of human power. How does he use it?

Alexander I, the peacemaker of Europe, the man who from his youth up had striven only for the welfare of his peoples, the first champion of liberal reforms in his country, now when it seems that he possesses the utmost power and therefore the possibility of achieving the welfare of his peoples (while Napoleon in exile is drawing up childish and mendacious plans of how he would have made mankind happy had he retained power) – Alexander I, having fulfilled his mission and feeling the hand of God upon him, suddenly recognizes the nothingness of the supposed power that is his, turns away from it and hands it over to contemptible men whom he despises, saying only:

'"Not unto us, not unto us, but unto Thy Name!" I too am a man like the rest of you. Let me live like a man, and think of my soul and of God.'

*

Just as the sun and every particle of the ether is a sphere complete in itself and at the same time only a part of a whole too immense for the comprehension of man, so every individual bears within himself his own aims and yet bears them so as to serve a general purpose unfathomable by man.

A bee poised on a flower has stung a child. And so the child is afraid of bees and declares that bees are there to sting people. A poet delights in the bee sipping honey from the calyx of a flower and says the bee exists to suck the nectar of flowers. A bee-keeper, seeing the bee collect pollen and carry it to the hive, says that the object of bees is to gather honey. Another bee-keeper, who has studied the life of the swarm more closely, declares that the bee gathers pollen-dust to feed the young bees and rear a queen, and that it exists for the propagation of its species. The botanist, observing that a bee flying with pollen from one dioecious plant to the pistil of another fertilizes the latter, sees in this the purpose of the bee's existence. Another, remarking the hybridization of plants and seeing that the bee assists in this work, may say that herein lies the purpose of the bee. But the ultimate purpose of the bee is not exhausted by the first or the second or the third of the processes the human mind can discern. The higher the human intellect soars in the discovery of possible purposes, the more obvious it becomes that the ultimate purpose is beyond our comprehension.

Man cannot achieve more than a certain insight into the correlation between the life of the bee and other manifestations of life. And the same is true with regard to the final purpose of historical characters and nations.

5

NATASHA'S marriage to Bezuhov, which took place in 1813, was the last happy event for the older generation of the Rostov family. Count Ilya Rostov died that same year and, as is always the case, with the father's death the family was broken up.

The events of the previous year – the burning of Moscow and the flight from the capital, the death of Prince Andrei and Natasha's despair, Petya's death and the old countess's grief – rained, blow upon blow, on the old count's head. He seemed not to understand, and to feel that he lacked the strength to understand, the meaning of all these events and, figuratively speaking, bowed his old head as though expecting and inviting further blows to make an end of him. He would appear alternately frightened and distraught or alert and active.

The arrangements for Natasha's wedding occupied him for a while. He ordered dinners and suppers and obviously tried to give the impression of being cheerful; but his cheerfulness was not infectious as it used to be: on the contrary, it evoked the compassion of those who knew and were fond of him.

After Pierre and his bride had taken their departure he grew very quiet and began to complain of depression. A few days later he fell ill and took to his bed. Despite the doctors' assurances, he realized from the first that he would never get up again. For two weeks the countess did not take her clothes off, sitting in a low chair by his bedside. Every time she gave him his medicine he sobbed and mutely kissed her hand. On the closing day of his life, sobbing, he begged forgiveness of his wife and his absent son for having squandered their property – the chief sin that lay on his conscience. Having received communion and the last anointing, he quietly died; and next day a throng of acquaintances, come to pay their final respects to the deceased, filled the house rented by the Rostovs. All these acquaintances, who had so often dined and danced at his house, and had so often made fun of him, now said, with a unanimous feeling of self-reproach and emotion, as though seeking to justify themselves: 'Well, anyhow, he was a most worthy man. One doesn't meet his like nowadays. ... And we all have our failings, have we not? ...'

It was precisely when the count's fortunes had become so entangled that it was impossible to conceive what would happen if he lived another year that he unexpectedly died.

Nikolai was with the Russian army in Paris when the news of his father's death reached him. He at once resigned his commission and without waiting for his discharge took leave of absence and went to Moscow. The position of the count's finances became quite obvious within a month of his death, astounding everyone by the immense total of various petty debts, the existence of which no one had suspected. The debts amounted to double the value of the estate.

Friends and relations advised Nikolai to decline the inheritance. But Nikolai saw in such a course a slur on his father's memory, which he held sacred, and therefore would not hear of refusing, and so accepted the inheritance together with the obligation to pay the debts.

The creditors, who had so long been silent, kept in check while the old count was alive by the vague but powerful influence which his easy-going good-nature exerted upon them, all beset Nikolai at once. As always happens, rivalry sprang up as to which of them should get paid first, and the very people who, like Mitenka, held promissory notes given them as presents, now showed themselves the most exacting of creditors. Nikolai was allowed no respite and no peace, and those who had apparently had pity on the old man – the cause of their losses (if they really had lost money by him) – now remorselessly pursued the innocent young heir who had voluntarily assumed responsibility for payment.

Not one of the plans that Nikolai resorted to was successful: the estate was sold by auction for half its value, leaving half the debts still unpaid. Nikolai took thirty thousand roubles offered him by his brother-in-law, Bezuhov, to settle what he regarded as genuine monetary obligations. And to avoid being thrown into prison for the remaining debts, as creditors threatened, he re-entered government service.

To return to the army, where he would have been made colonel at the next vacancy, was out of the question, for his mother now clung to him as her last hold on life; and so, despite his reluctance to remain in Moscow among people who had known him in former days, and in spite of his distaste for the civil service, he accepted an official post in Moscow, doffed his beloved uniform and moved with his mother and Sonya to a small house in one of the poorer quarters.

Natasha and Pierre were living in Petersburg at the time and had no very distinct idea of Nikolai's circumstances. Having borrowed money from his brother-in-law, Nikolai did his utmost to conceal his poverty-stricken state from him. His situation was rendered the more difficult because on his salary of twelve hundred roubles he had not only to keep himself, his mother and Sonya but had to support his mother in such a way that she would not be sensible of their poverty. The countess could not conceive of life without the conditions of luxury to which she had been accustomed from her childhood and, without realizing how hard it was for her son, was continually requiring, now a carriage (which they did not have) to send for a friend, now some expensive delicacy for herself, or wine for her son, or money to buy a surprise-present for Natasha, for Sonya or for Nikolai himself.

Sonya kept house, waited on her aunt, read to her, bore with her caprices and secret ill-will, and helped Nikolai to conceal their poverty from the old countess. Nikolai felt himself irredeemably indebted to Sonya for all she was doing for his mother; he admired her patience and devotion but tried to keep aloof from her.

In his heart of hearts he seemed to harbour a sort of grudge against her for being too perfect, and because there was nothing to reproach her with. She had all the qualities for which people are prized, but little that could have made him love her. And he felt that the more he appreciated her the less he loved her. He had taken her at her word when she wrote giving him his freedom, and now behaved as though all that had passed between them had been forgotten ages ago and could never in any circumstances be renewed.

Nikolai's position was growing worse and worse. His hope of putting something aside out of his salary proved an idle dream. Far from saving anything, he was even running up small debts to satisfy his mother's exigencies. He could see no way out of his difficulties. The idea of marrying some rich woman, which his female relatives suggested, was repugnant to him. The only other solution – his mother's death – never entered his head. He wished for nothing and hoped for nothing, and deep in his heart experienced a grim, melancholy enjoyment in enduring his position with resignation. He tried to avoid his old acquaintances with their commiseration and mortifying offers of assistance, shunned every sort of entertainment and recreation, and even at home did nothing but play patience with his mother or pace silently up and down the room, smoking one pipe after another. He seemed bent on preserving in himself the gloomy frame of mind which alone enabled him to bear his position.

6

At the beginning of the winter Princess Maria came to Moscow. From the gossip of the town she heard of the Rostovs' situation, of how 'the son was sacrificing himself for his mother', as people were saying. 'It is just what I should have expected him to do,' said Princess Maria to herself, finding in it a delightful confirmation of her love for him. Remembering her friendly relations with the whole household – which made her almost one of the family – she decided that it was her duty to go and see them. But when she thought of her contact with Nikolai in Voronezh she felt timid about doing so. A few weeks after her arrival in Moscow she did however nerve herself to the effort and went to call on the Rostovs.

Nikolai was the first to meet her, since it was impossible to reach the countess's room without passing through his. But instead of the delight Princess Maria had expected to see on his face, after a first glance at her his features assumed a cold, stiff, haughty expression she had never seen in him before. He inquired after her health, conducted her to his mother's room, where he sat with them for five or six minutes and then departed.

When the princess left the countess Nikolai met her again and with marked formality and reserve accompanied her to the hall. To her remarks about his mother's health he made no reply. 'What's that to you? Leave me in peace,' his look seemed to say.

'Why should she come prowling about here? What does she want? I can't stand these *mesdames* and all this sweet amiableness!' he said aloud in Sonya's presence, evidently unable to repress his vexation, after the princess's carriage had rolled away from the house.

'Oh, Nicolas, how can you talk like that!' exclaimed Sonya, scarcely concealing her delight. 'She is so kind, and *maman* likes her so much!'

Nikolai made no reply and would have preferred not to mention the princess again. But after her visit the old countess spoke of her several times a day.

She sang her praises, insisted that her son must call on her, expressed a wish to see more of her, and yet was always out of temper when she had been talking of her.

Nikolai tried to hold his tongue when his mother spoke of the princess, but his silence irritated her.

'She is a very admirable and excellent young woman,' she would say, 'and you must go and call on her. You would at least be seeing somebody; I am sure it is dull for you here with only us.'

'But I don't in the least want to see people, mamma.'

'You used to be keen enough but now it's all "I don't want to". Really, my dear, I don't understand you. One minute you are bored and the next you suddenly don't care to see anyone.'

'Why, I never said I was bored.'

'Well, at all events you've just said you didn't wish even to see her. She is a very praiseworthy girl, and you always liked her; but now all of a sudden you have got some notion or other into your head. I am always kept in the dark.'

'Not at all, mamma.'

'If I were asking you to do something disagreeable now – but all I ask of you is to return a call. Why, one would think mere politeness required that. ... Well, I have asked you, and now I shall not interfere any more, since you choose to have secrets from your mother.'

'All right, I'll go if you wish it.'

'It doesn't matter to me. I only wish it for your own sake.'

Nikolai sighed, bit his moustache and laid out the cards for patience, trying to divert his mother's attention to something else.

Next day and the day after and the day after that the same conversation was repeated.

After her visit to the Rostovs and the unexpectedly chilly reception she had met with from Nikolai, Princess Maria confessed to herself that she had been right in not wanting to be the first to call.

'I wasn't expecting anything else,' she told herself, summoning pride to her aid. 'I have no concern with him and I only wanted to see the old lady, who has always been kind to me and to whom I am under many obligations.'

But she could not soothe herself with these reflections: a feeling akin to remorse fretted her whenever she thought of her visit. Although she was firmly resolved not to call on the Rostovs again and to forget the matter altogether, she felt uncomfortable all the time. And when she asked herself what it was that was worrying her she was obliged to admit that it was her encounter with Rostov. His frigid, formal manner did not proceed from his feeling for her (she knew that) but it was a cover for something. What that something was she must find out; and until she did so she felt she would never have any peace.

One day in midwinter she was sitting in the schoolroom superintending her nephew's lessons when she was informed that Rostov was below. With the firm resolve not to betray herself or evince any sign of her agitation she sent for Mademoiselle Bourienne and went with her to the drawing-room.

Her first glance at Nikolai's face told her that he had only come to fulfil the obligations of civility, and she resolutely determined to keep to the tone he adopted towards her.

They talked of the countess's health, of mutual acquaintances, of the latest news of the war, and when the ten minutes demanded by etiquette had elapsed, after which the visitor may rise, Nikolai got up to say good-bye.

With Mademoiselle Bourienne's help the princess had maintained the conversation very well; but at the very last moment, just when he had risen to his feet, she was so weary of talking of what did not interest her, and she was so absorbed in wondering why she alone was granted so little happiness in life, that in a fit of absent-mindedness she sat still, her luminous eyes staring straight before her, oblivious of the fact that he had risen.

Nikolai glanced at her, and anxious to appear not to notice her abstraction made some remark to Mademoiselle Bourienne and then glanced at the princess again. She still sat motionless with a look of suffering on her gentle face. He suddenly felt sorry for her and a dim idea came to him that perhaps he might be the cause of the sadness in her face. He longed to help her, say something nice to her, but he could not think what to say.

'Good-bye, princess,' he said.

She started, flushed and sighed heavily.

'Oh, I beg your pardon!' she murmured, as though waking from a dream. 'You are going already, count: well, good-bye! Oh, but the cushion for the countess!'

'Wait, I'll fetch it,' said Mademoiselle Bourienne, and she left the room.

Both sat in silence, with an occasional glance at one another.

'Yes, princess,' said Nikolai at last, with a mournful smile, 'it doesn't seem so long ago since we first met at Bogucharovo, but how much water has flowed under the bridges since then! We all seemed to be in trouble enough then, but I would give a great deal to have that time back ... but there's no bringing it back.'

Princess Maria gazed intently at him with her luminous eyes as he said this. She seemed to be trying to fathom the secret import of his words which would make clear his feelings towards her.

'Yes, yes,' she replied, 'but you have no reason to regret the past, count. As I conceive of your life now, I think you will always recall it with satisfaction, because the self-sacrifice that fills it today ...'

'I cannot accept your praise,' he interrupted her hurriedly; 'on the contrary, I am always reproaching myself. ... But this is not at all an interesting or cheerful subject.'

And again the stiff and cold expression came back into his face. But the princess had caught a glimpse of the man she had known and loved and it was to him that she spoke now.

'I thought you would allow me to say that,' she told him. 'You and I ... your family and I have been brought so near together that I thought you would not feel my sympathy out of season; but I was mistaken.' Her voice suddenly shook. 'I don't know why,' she went on, recovering herself, 'but you used to be different, and ...'

'There are a thousand reasons *why*' – he laid special emphasis on the word *why*. 'Thank you, princess,' he added softly. 'Sometimes it is hard.'

'So that's why! That's why!' cried a voice in Princess Maria's heart. 'No, it was not only that gay, kind, frank look, not only that handsome exterior, that I loved in him: I divined his noble, indomitable, self-sacrificing spirit too,' she said to herself. 'Yes, he is poor now, and I am rich. ... Yes, that is the only reason. ... Yes, if it were not for that ...' And remembering his former tenderness, and looking now at his kind, sorrowful face, she suddenly understood the cause of his coldness.

'But why, count, why?' she almost cried, unconsciously moving closer to him. 'Why? Tell me. You must tell me!'

He was silent.

'I don't understand your *why*,' she continued. 'But I am heavy-hearted, I ... I do not mind confessing to you. For some reason you wish to deprive me of our old friendship. And that hurts.' There were tears in her eyes and in her voice. 'I have had so little happiness in my life that every loss is hard for me. ... Excuse me, good-bye!' and suddenly she burst into tears and was hurrying from the room.

'Princess, wait, for God's sake!' he called, trying to detain her. 'Princess!'

She looked round. For a few seconds they gazed dumbly into one another's eyes, and all at once what had seemed impossible and remote became possible, near at hand and inevitable. ...

7

IN the autumn of 1814 Nikolai married Princess Maria and moved to Bald Hills with his wife, his mother and Sonya.

Within four years he had settled his remaining debts, without selling any of his wife's property, and having come into a small legacy on the death of a cousin he repaid what he had borrowed from Pierre too.

In another three years, by 1820, Nikolai had managed his pecuniary affairs so successfully that he was able to purchase a modest estate adjoining Bald Hills and was negotiating to buy back his ancestral home of Otradnoe – that being his pet dream.

At first his own steward of necessity, he soon grew so passionately interested in farming that it came to be his favourite and almost his sole occupation.

Nikolai was a plain farmer: he did not like innovations, especially the English ones then coming into fashion. He laughed at theoretical treatises on estate management, did not care for home refineries and expensive processes, or for sowing costly grain, and as a general thing did not confine himself to one department of agriculture alone: he always kept before his eye the welfare of the *estate* as a whole, and not one particular part of it. The chief thing to his mind was not the nitrogen in the soil or the oxygen in the air, nor manures or special ploughs, but the principal agent by which nitrogen, oxygen, manure and plough were made effective – the peasant labourer. When Nikolai first took up farming and began to go into its different branches it was the peasant who especially attracted his attention: the peasant seemed to him not merely a tool but also an end in himself and his critic. At first he studied the peasants attentively, trying to understand what they were after, what they considered good and bad, and only made a pretence of supervising and giving orders while in reality he was learning from them their methods, their manner of speech and their judgement of what was good and bad. And it was only when he had gained an insight into the peasants' tastes and aspirations, had learnt to talk their language, to grasp the inner meaning of their sayings and felt akin to them, that he began boldly giving them orders – in other words, fulfilling towards them the duties expected of him. And Nikolai's management produced the most brilliant results.

On taking over the control of the property Nikolai had at once by some unerring instinct appointed as bailiff, village elder and peasant representative the very men the peasants would have elected themselves had the choice been theirs, and these posts never changed hands. Before analysing the properties of manure, before entering into 'debits and credits' (his ironic term for book-keeping), he found out how many cattle the peasants possessed and did his utmost to increase the number. He kept the peasant families together in the largest possible groups and would not allow them to split up into separate households. The lazy, the dissolute and the feeble he pursued and tried to banish from the community.

He was as careful of the sowing and reaping of the peasants' hay and corn as of his own, and few landowners had their crops sown and harvested so early and so well as Nikolai.

He disliked having anything to do with the domestic serfs – the *parasites*, as he called them – and everybody said that he demoralized and spoilt them. When a decision had to be taken regarding a house-serf, especially if one had to be punished, he could never make up his mind and consulted the opinion of all in the house: only whenever it was possible to have a domestic serf conscripted in place of a peasant he did so without the smallest hesitation. In all his dealings with the peasants he never experienced the slightest diffidence. Every order he gave would, he knew, be approved by the great majority with very few exceptions.

He never allowed himself either to be hard on or punish a man just because he felt like it, or to make things easy for or reward anyone because that happened to be his own wish. He could not have advanced any definition of this standard of his, of what he should or should not do, but the standard lived firm and inflexible inside him.

Often in vexation at some failure or irregularity he would complain hopelessly of 'these Russian peasants of ours', and imagine that he could not bear them.

But heart and soul he loved 'these Russian peasants of ours' and their way of life, and so he understood and was able to adopt the one method of managing the land which could produce good results.

Countess Maria was jealous of this passion of her husband's and regretted that she could not share it; but the joys and heart-aches he met with in that world, to her so remote and alien, were beyond her comprehension. She could not understand why it should make him so brisk and cheerful to rise at dawn, to spend a whole morning in the fields or on the threshing-floor before he returned from the sowing or mowing or reaping to have tea with her. She did not understand why he was so delighted and enthusiastic about the thrifty and well-to-do peasant Matvey Yermishin, who had been up all night with his family, carting his sheaves, and had got his corn stacked before anyone else had so much as reaped their fields. She did not understand why he chuckled under his moustaches and winked when he stepped out of the window on to the balcony and saw a warm, fine rain falling on the dry and thirsty shoots of the young oats, or why, when the wind carried away a threatening cloud during the hay harvest, he would come in from the barn, flushed, sunburnt and perspiring, with a smell of wormwood and gentian in his hair, and, gleefully rubbing his hands together, exclaim: 'Well, another day of this and my stuff and the peasants' will all be under cover.'

Still less could she understand how it was that with his kind heart and never-failing readiness to anticipate her wishes he should be driven almost frantic when she brought him a petition from a peasant or his woman who had appealed to her for relief from some drudgery or other – why it was that he, her good-natured Nikolai, should obstinately refuse her and angrily request her not to interfere in what was not her business. She felt he had a world apart, which he loved passionately, governed by laws she had not fathomed.

Sometimes, in her endeavours to understand him, she would talk to him of the good work he was doing for his serfs, but he would only grow vexed and reply: 'Not in the least! Such an idea never even enters my head; and I wouldn't lift my little finger for their good! That's all romantic nonsense and old wives' cackle – all that doing-good-to-one's-neighbour business. What I want is that our children should not have to go begging: I want to build up our fortunes in my lifetime, that's all. And to do that, order and discipline are necessary.... That's all about it!' he would declare, clenching a confident fist. 'And fairness too, of course,' he would add. 'Because if the peasant is naked and starving, and has only one wretched horse, he can do no good for himself or me.'

And doubtless because Nikolai did not allow himself to entertain the idea that he was doing anything for others, for the sake of virtue, everything he touched was fruitful. His fortune rapidly increased; serfs from neighbouring estates came to beg him to buy them, and long after he was dead and gone the peasantry cherished a pious memory of his rule. 'He was a proper master ... the peasants' welfare first and then his own. And of course he allowed no liberties. Yes, a real good master he was!'

8

THE one thing which occasionally troubled Nikolai in connexion with the administration of his affairs was his hasty temper and his old habit, acquired in the hussars, of making free use of his fists. At first he saw nothing reprehensible in this, but in the second year of his marriage his views on that form of correction underwent a sudden change.

One summer day he had sent for the village elder from Bogucharovo, a man who had succeeded to the post when Dron died and who now stood accused of various instances of fraud and negligence. Nikolai went out to him on the porch and the man had scarcely opened his mouth to reply before the sound of shouts and blows was heard. Going indoors later on for lunch, Nikolai joined his wife, who was sitting with her head bent low over her embroidery frame. As usual, he began to tell her what he had been doing that morning and among other things mentioned the Bogucharovo elder. Countess Maria, turning first red and then white, continued to sit with bowed head and compressed lips, offering no rejoinder to her husband.

'The insolent scoundrel!' he cried, growing hot again at the mere recollection. 'Well, he should have told me he was drunk and did not see. ... Why, what is it, Marie?' he asked suddenly.

Countess Maria raised her head and tried to say something but hastily looked down again and her lips gathered.

'Why, whatever is the matter, my dearest?'

Tears always improved the plain looks of Countess Maria. She never cried from pain or vexation: it was always from sorrow or pity. And when she wept her luminous eyes acquired an irresistible charm.

The moment Nikolai took her hand she could restrain herself no longer and burst into tears.

'Nicolas, I saw you ... he was in the wrong but you, why did you ...? Oh, Nicolas! ...' and she hid her face in her hands.

Nikolai said nothing. He flushed crimson, left her side and began pacing up and down the room in silence. He understood why she was weeping but he could not all at once agree with her in his heart that what he had been used to from childhood, what he took as a matter of course, was wrong. 'Is it just sentimentality, a feminine foible, or is she right?' he asked himself. Before he had decided the point he glanced again at her suffering, loving face and suddenly realized that she was right and that he had been sinning against himself.

'Marie,' he said softly, going up to her, 'it shall never happen again: I give you my word. Never,' he repeated in a trembling voice, like a boy begging for forgiveness.

The tears flowed faster still from the countess's eyes. She took her husband's hand and kissed it.

'Nikolai, when did you break your cameo?' she asked to change the subject, examining the finger on which he wore a ring with a cameo representing the head of Laocoön.

'This morning – at the same time. Oh, Marie, don't remind me of it!' and he flushed again. 'I give you my word of honour it shan't occur any more. And let this always be a reminder to me.' And he pointed to the broken ring.

After that, whenever he was having it out with village elders and foremen and the blood rushed to his face and his fists began to clench, Nikolai would twist the broken ring on his finger and look away from the man who was making him angry. But he did forget himself once or twice within a twelvemonth and then he would go and confess to his wife and promise her again that this should really be the very last time.

'Marie, you must despise me, don't you?' he would say. 'I deserve it.'

'You should walk away, walk away as fast as you can if you don't feel strong enough to control yourself,' she would tell him sadly, trying to comfort him.

Among the gentry of the province Nikolai was respected but not liked. The local politics of the Nobility did not interest him and so some thought him stuck up and others a fool. In summer, from spring-sowing to harvest, he spent his every minute on the land. In the autumn he gave himself up with the same business-like earnestness to sport, going out for a month or two at a time with his hunt. During the winter he rode off to visit his other villages, or occupied himself with reading. The books he read were mainly historical works on which he spent a certain sum every year. He was building up for himself, as he said, a 'serious library', and he made it a principle to read through every book he bought. He would sit in his study with a grave air for this reading which at first he imposed on himself as a duty but which afterwards became a habit affording him a special kind of gratification to think that he was engaging in a 'serious' pursuit. Except for business excursions he passed most of the winter at home, entering into the domestic life of his family and interesting himself in all the details of his children's relations with their mother. He grew steadily closer to his wife, every day discovering fresh spiritual treasures in her.

Sonya had lived with them since their marriage. Before that, however, Nikolai had told his wife all that had happened between him and Sonya, blaming himself and extolling her. He had begged Princess Maria to be kind and affectionate to his cousin. The princess was fully sensible of the wrong he had done Sonya and felt guilty herself, fancying that her wealth had influenced Nikolai's choice. She had no fault to find with Sonya and tried to be fond of her but simply could not: indeed, she often found herself cherishing uncharitable feelings towards her which she could not overcome.

Once she had a talk with her friend Natasha about Sonya and her own unfairness towards her.

'You know,' said Natasha, 'you are always reading the Gospels. There's a passage in them that just fits Sonya.'

'Is there?' Countess Maria asked in surprise.

'"To him that hath shall be given, but from him that hath not shall be taken away" – remember? She is one that hath not: why, I don't know. Perhaps she lacks egoism – I don't know, but from her is taken away, and everything has been taken away. Sometimes I am dreadfully sorry for her. I used to be awfully anxious for Nicolas to marry her but I always had a sort of presentiment that it would not happen. She is a *barren flower* – you know, like one of those unfertilized flowers one finds on a strawberry plant. Sometimes I am sorry for her and sometimes I think she doesn't feel it as you or I would.'

And although Countess Maria explained to Natasha that those words in the Gospel were meant in a different sense, still, looking at Sonya, she could not help agreeing with her friend's interpretation. It did really seem that Sonya was not fretted by her position and was quite reconciled to her lot as a *barren flower*. She appeared to be fond not so much of individuals as of the family as a whole. Like a cat, she had attached herself not to people but to the house. She waited on the old countess, petted and spoiled the children, was always ready to perform the small services for which she had a gift – but all this was unconsciously accepted from her with a less than adequate measure of gratitude.

The manor-house at Bald Hills had been restored, though not on the same scale as under the old prince.

The structure, begun in the days of straitened circumstances, was more than simple. The huge house on the old stone foundations was of wood, plastered only on the inside. The great rambling mansion had bare deal floors, was furnished with the plainest hard sofas, armchairs, tables and chairs made from their own birch-trees by their own serf-carpenters. The house was very roomy, with quarters for the domestic-serfs and apartments for visitors. Sometimes whole families of Rostov and Bolkonsky relations would come to Bald Hills with almost a score of horses and dozens of servants, and stay for months. And four times a year, on the name-days and birthdays of the master and mistress, as many as a hundred visitors would gather there for a day or two. The rest of the year life pursued its unbroken routine with its ordinary occupations, with breakfasts, lunches, dinners and suppers provided out of the produce of the estate.

9

IT was the eve of St Nikolai, the fifth of December, 1820. That year Natasha had been staying at her brother's with her husband and children since early autumn. Pierre had gone to Petersburg on business of his own for three weeks, as he said, but had remained nearly seven and was expected back every minute.

On this 5th of December, besides the Bezuhov family, Nikolai's old friend, the retired General Vasili Fiodorovich Denisov, was staying with the Rostovs.

On the 6th, which was his name-day, when the house would be full of visitors, Nikolai knew he would have to exchange his Tartar tunic for a frock-coat, and put on narrow boots with pointed toes and drive to the new church he had built; after which he would be expected to receive congratulations, offer refreshments to his guests and talk about the elections of the Nobility and the year's crops. But the eve of that day he considered he had a right to spend as usual. By dinner-time Nikolai had gone over the bailiff's accounts from the Ryazan estate, the property of his wife's nephew, written two business letters and walked through the granaries, the cattle-yards and the stables. Having taken precautions against the general drunkenness to be expected on the morrow because it was a great saint's day, he returned to dinner and without having time for a private talk with his wife sat down to the long table laid with twenty covers, at which all the household were assembled. At the table were his mother, his mother's old companion Mademoiselle Byelov, his wife, their three children with their governess and tutor, his wife's nephew with his tutor, Sonya, Denisov, Natasha, her three children, their governess, and old Mihail Ivanych, the late prince's architect, who was living in retirement at Bald Hills.

Countess Maria was sitting at the opposite end of the table. As soon as her husband took his place she knew by the gesture with which he picked up his table-napkin and quickly pushed back the tumbler and wine-glass set before him that he was out of humour, as he sometimes was – especially before the soup, and when he came in to dinner straight from the farm. Countess Maria was thoroughly familiar with this mood of his, and when she herself was in a good temper she would wait quietly till he had swallowed his soup and only then begin to talk to him and make him admit that there was no cause for his ill-humour. But today she quite forgot, and was hurt and felt miserable that he should be angry with her for no reason. She asked him where he had been. He told her. Then she inquired whether everything was going well on the estate. He scowled disagreeably at her unnatural tone and made a curt reply.

'So I was not mistaken,' thought Countess Maria. 'Now, why is he vexed with me?' In the tone in which he answered her she detected ill-will towards herself and a desire to cut short the conversation. She was aware that her remarks sounded artificial but could not refrain from asking several other questions.

Thanks to Denisov, talk round the table soon became general and lively and she did not say any more to her husband. When they rose and came round to thank the old countess, Countess Maria held out her hand and kissed her husband and asked him why he was angry with her.

'You always have such strange fancies. I had no thought of being angry with you,' he replied.

But the word *always* seemed to her to imply: 'Yes, I am angry and I don't choose to say why.'

Nikolai and his wife lived on such excellent terms that even Sonya and the old countess, who felt jealous and would have been pleased to see them disagree, could find nothing to reproach them with; but even they had their moments of mutual antagonism. At times, and particularly after a more than usually happy period, a feeling of estrangement and hostility assailed them both. This feeling occurred most frequently when Countess Maria was with child. Such was her condition now.

'Well, *messieurs et mesdames*,' said Nikolai loudly and with a show of cheerfulness (it seemed to his wife that this was on purpose to wound her), 'I have been on my feet since six o'clock this morning.

Tomorrow I shall have to be a victim and suffer, but today I'm off to have a rest.'

And without a word to his wife he disappeared into the little sitting-room and lay down on the sofa.

'That's always the way,' thought Countess Maria. 'He talks to everyone except me. I see … I see that I am repulsive to him, especially when I am in this condition.' She looked down at her swollen figure and then into the glass at her pale, sallow, sunken face in which the eyes appeared bigger than ever.

And everything jarred on her: Denisov's clamour and boisterous laughter, Natasha's chatter and, above all, the hasty glance Sonya stole at her.

Sonya was always the first excuse Countess Maria found for feeling irritated.

After sitting a little while with her guests and not taking in a word of what they were saying, she slipped out and went to the nursery.

The children were perched on chairs playing at driving to Moscow, and invited her to join them. She sat down and played with them a little but the thought of her husband and his unreasonable crossness worried her all the time. She got up and with difficulty walking on tiptoe went to the small sitting-room.

'Perhaps he is not asleep and I can have it out with him,' she said to herself. Andrusha, her eldest boy, tiptoed behind her, imitating her, but she did not notice him.

'*Chère Marie*, I think he is asleep – he was so tired,' said Sonya, meeting her in the larger divan-room (it seemed to Countess Maria that Sonya was everywhere). 'Mind Andrusha doesn't wake him.'

Countess Maria looked round, saw Andrusha behind her, felt that Sonya was right, and for that very reason flushed angrily and with obvious difficulty refrained from a harsh retort. She said nothing but, to avoid heeding Sonya, beckoned to Andrusha to follow her without making a noise, and went to the door. Sonya moved towards the other door. From the room where Nikolai was asleep came the sound of even breathing, every tone of which was familiar to his wife. As she listened to it she could see before her mind's eye his smooth handsome forehead, his moustaches, the whole face she had so often gazed at in the stillness of the night when he slept. Suddenly Nikolai stirred and cleared his throat. And at the same instant Andrusha called from the other side of the door: 'Mamma's here, papa!'

Countess Maria turned pale with dismay and made signs to the boy. He was quiet at once and for a moment or two there ensued what seemed to Countess Maria a dreadful silence. She knew how Nikolai hated being waked. Then through the door she heard him clear his throat again and move, and his voice said crossly:

'I'm never given a moment's peace. Marie, is that you? Why did you bring him here?'

'I only came to see if – I did not notice ... forgive me. ...'

Nikolai coughed and said no more. His wife stepped away from the door and took the boy back to the nursery. Five minutes later little black-eyed, three-year-old Natasha, her father's favourite, hearing from her brother that papa was asleep and mamma in the sitting-room, ran in to her father without her mother seeing. The dark-eyed little girl rattled boldly at the door, scampered energetically up to the sofa on her sturdy little legs and, having taken stock of the attitude her father was lying in – he was asleep with his back to her – rose on tiptoe and kissed the hand which lay under his head. Nikolai turned round with a smile of tenderness on his face.

'Natasha, Natasha!' came Countess Maria's frightened whisper from the door. 'Papa is trying to have a nap.'

'No, he isn't, mamma,' answered little Natasha with conviction. 'He's laughing.'

Nikolai lowered his legs, sat up and took his daughter in his arms.

'Come in, Marie,' he called to his wife.

She went in and sat down beside her husband.

'I did not notice him following me,' she said timidly. 'I just glanced in.'

Holding his little girl on one arm, Nikolai looked at his wife and, perceiving the apologetic expression on her face, put his other arm round her and kissed her hair.

'May I kiss mamma?' he asked Natasha.

Natasha smiled demurely.

'Again!' she commanded, pointing with an imperious gesture to the spot where Nikolai had kissed her mother.

'I don't know why you should think I am in a bad temper,' said Nikolai, replying to the question he knew was in his wife's mind.

'You have no idea how unhappy, how lonely I feel when you are like that. It always seems to me ...'

'Marie, stop! What nonsense! Aren't you ashamed of yourself?' he asked gaily.

'I always think you can't care for me, that I am so plain ... always ... and now ... in this condi ...'

'Oh, how absurd you are! "Handsome is, as handsome does," you know – not the other way about. It's only the Malvinas who are loved because they are beautiful; but do I love my wife? I don't love her but ... I don't know how to put it. Without you, or when something comes between us like this, I feel quite lost and can't do anything. Do I love my own finger? No, but just try cutting it off. ...'

'No, I am not like that myself, but I understand. So you're not vexed with me?'

'Horribly vexed!' he said, smiling and getting up. And smoothing his hair he began walking about the room.

'Do you know, Marie, what I've been thinking?' he began, immediately starting to think aloud to his wife now that they had made it up. He did not inquire whether she were disposed to listen: he took it for granted. An idea occurred to him and so it must to her, too. Accordingly he told her of his intention to persuade Pierre to stay with them till spring.

Countess Maria listened till he had finished, made some comment and then in her turn began thinking aloud. Her thoughts ran on about the children.

'One can see the woman in her already,' she said in French, pointing to little Natasha. 'You reproach us women with being illogical. There's an example of our logic. I say: "Papa is trying to have a nap!" but she answers, "No, he's laughing." And she was right,' said Countess Maria with a contented smile.

'Yes, yes!' And Nikolai picked his little daughter up with a powerful grip, set her on his shoulder, held her by the legs and paced the room with her. The faces of father and daughter shone with light-hearted happiness.

'But, you know, you may be unfair. You are too fond of this one,' his wife whispered in French.

'Yes, but what can I do? ... I try not to show it. ...'

At that moment they heard the sound of the door-pulley and footsteps in the hall and ante-room, as if someone had arrived.

'Somebody has come.'

'I am sure it's Pierre. I'll go and find out,' said Countess Maria.

While she was gone Nikolai allowed himself to give his little daughter a gallop round the room. Panting for breath, he took the laughing child quickly from his shoulder and pressed her to his heart. His capers reminded him of dancing, and looking at the little mite's round happy face he wondered what she would be like when he was an old man, taking her into society and dancing the mazurka with her as his old father had danced the *Daniel Cooper* with his daughter.

'Yes, it *is* he, Nicolas,' said Countess Maria, returning a few minutes later. 'Now our Natasha has come to life again. You should have seen her delight, and what a scolding he got for having stayed away longer than he said he would! Well, come along now, quick, make haste! It's time you two were parted,' she added, looking smilingly at the little girl nestling close to her father.

Nikolai went out, holding his daughter by the hand.

Countess Maria lingered behind in the sitting-room.

'Never, never would I have believed that one could be so happy,' she whispered to herself. Her face broke into a smile; but at the same time she sighed and a gentle melancholy showed itself in the depths of her eyes, as though over and above the happiness she was feeling there existed another sort of happiness, unattainable in this life, which she had involuntarily thought of at that instant.

10

NATASHA had married early in the spring of 1813, and by 1820 had three daughters and the son she had longed for and was now nursing herself. She had filled out and grown broader, so that it was difficult to recognize in the buxom young mother the slim, vivacious Natasha of old. Her features were more defined and wore a sedate expression of quiet serenity. Her face had lost the ever flashing, eager light which had once constituted its charm. Now one often saw only her face and physical presence, without anything of the animating soul. The impression one had was of fine, vigorous maternity. Very seldom now was the old fire kindled. That happened only when, as today, her husband returned after absence, or a sick child recovered, or when she and Countess Maria spoke of Prince Andrei (she never mentioned him to her husband, fancying he might be jealous of Prince Andrei's memory), or when some unusual occasion induced her to sing – a practice which she had quite abandoned since her marriage. And at such times as these the revival of the old fire in her ample, comely form made her more attractive than she had ever been in the past.

Since their marriage Natasha and her husband had lived in Moscow, in Petersburg, on their estate near Moscow, or with her mother – that is to say, at Nikolai's. Society saw little of the young Countess Bezuhov, and those who did see her found her unsatisfactory, since she was neither sociable nor ingratiating. It was not that Natasha liked solitude – she hardly knew whether she liked it or not: indeed, she rather supposed that she did not – but with her pregnancies, her confinements, the nursing of her children, and sharing every moment of her husband's life, she had demands enough, which could only be fulfilled by renouncing society. Everyone who had known Natasha before her marriage marvelled at the change in her, as though it were something extraordinary. Only the old countess, whose maternal instinct had always told her that Natasha's waywardness proceeded solely from the need of children and a husband – as Natasha herself had cried more in earnest than in jest at Otradnoe – was surprised at the wonder of people who had never understood her daughter, and kept saying that she had always known Natasha would make an exemplary wife and mother.

'Only,' the old countess would add, 'she carries her love for her husband and children to extremes; so much so that it becomes positively absurd.'

Natasha did not follow the golden rule preached by so many clever folk, especially the French, which lays down that a girl should not let herself go when she marries, should not neglect her accomplishments, should be even more careful of her appearance than when she was single, and should try to captivate her man as much as she had before he became her husband. Natasha, on the contrary, had instantly dropped all her witchery, in the armoury of which she had one extraordinarily powerful weapon – her singing. She gave up even her singing just because it was such a great attraction. Natasha bothered no more about charm of manner or graceful speech, or her clothes; nor did she think of striking attractive attitudes before her husband, or to avoid wearying him with her demands. In fact, she contravened every one of these rules. She felt that the allurements instinct had taught her to use before would now seem merely ridiculous in the eyes of her husband, to whom she had from the first moment surrendered herself entirely – that is, with her whole soul, leaving no corner of it hidden from his sight. She felt that the bond between them rested not on the romantic feelings which had attracted him to her but on something else, as indefinable but as firm as the bond between her own body and soul.

To fluff out her curls, put on a fashionable gown and sing sentimental songs in order to fascinate her husband would have seemed as strange as to adorn herself so as to attract herself. To adorn herself for others might perhaps have given her pleasure – she did not know – but she simply had not the time. The chief reason she neglected her singing, her wardrobe and pretty turns of speech was that there was absolutely not a moment to spare for such things.

It is a well-known fact that man has the faculty of becoming completely absorbed in one subject, however trivial that subject may appear to be. And it is well known that no subject is so trivial as to be incapable of boundless development if one's entire attention is devoted to it.

The subject in which Natasha was completely absorbed was her family, that is, her husband, whom she had to keep so that he should belong entirely to her and to the home, and the children whom she had to carry, to bear, to nurse and bring up.

And the more she put, not her mind only but her whole soul, her whole being, into the subject that absorbed her the more that subject seemed to enlarge under her eyes and the feebler and more inadequate did her own powers appear, so that she concentrated them all on that one thing and still had not the time to do all that she considered necessary.

In those days, just as now, there were arguments and discussions on the rights of women, the relations of husband and wife, their freedoms and rights – only people did not then call them *questions*, as we do today. But it was not that Natasha was not interested in them: she had absolutely no comprehension of them.

Those questions, then as now, existed only for those who see nothing in marriage but the pleasure married people may derive from one another – who see only the first beginnings of a marriage and not its whole significance, the family.

Such discussions and arguments, which are like the question of how to get the utmost possible gratification out of one's dinner, did not then, and do not now, exist for those for whom the object of dinner is the nourishment it affords and the object of wedlock is – the family.

If the purpose of dinner is to nourish the body the man who eats two dinners at a sitting may perhaps attain greater enjoyment but not his object, since the stomach will not digest two dinners.

If the purpose of marriage is the family the person who seeks to have a number of wives or husbands may possibly obtain much pleasure therefrom, but will not in any case have a family.

If the purpose of food is nourishment and the purpose of marriage is the family the whole question resolves itself into not eating more than the stomach can digest and not having more wives or husbands than are needed for the family – that is, one wife or one husband. Natasha needed a husband. A husband was given her. And her husband gave her a family. And she not only saw no need of any other or better husband but as all her spiritual energies were devoted to serving that husband and family she could not imagine, and found no interest in imagining, how it would be if things were different.

Natasha did not care for society in general but this made her all the fonder of being with her relatives – with Countess Maria, her brother, her mother and Sonya. She took delight in the society of those to whom she could come striding dishevelled from the nursery in her dressing-gown and with joyful face show a diaper stained yellow instead of green, and from whom she could hear reassuring words to the effect that baby was much better.

Natasha was so neglectful of herself that her dresses, the way she did her hair, her untimely remarks, her jealousy – she was jealous of Sonya, of the governess, of every woman, pretty or plain – were stock jests among her friends. The general opinion was that Pierre was tied to his wife's apron strings, which really was the case. From the very earliest days of their married life Natasha had intimated her claims. Pierre had been greatly surprised at his wife's view, to him a totally novel idea, that every moment of his life belonged to her and the home. His wife's demands astonished him but they also flattered him and he submitted.

Pierre's subjection entailed not daring not only to flirt but even to speak smilingly to another woman; not daring to dine at the club without good reason, *merely* as a pastime, not daring to spend money on a whim or to absent himself for any length of time, except on business – in which category his wife included his scientific pursuits, to which, although not in the least understanding them, she attributed great importance. To make up for this, Pierre had full licence to regulate life at home as he chose, for himself and his family. Natasha in her own home placed herself on the footing of a slave to her husband, and the whole household went on tiptoe when he was occupied – that is, was reading or writing in his study. Pierre had only to manifest a leaning, to find his desire instantly being fulfilled. He had only to express a wish and Natasha would jump up and perform it.

The entire household was governed according to the imaginary injunctions of the master, in other words in accordance with Pierre's wishes which Natasha tried to anticipate. Their manner of life and place of residence, their acquaintance and ties, Natasha's occupations, the children's upbringing – all followed not only Pierre's expressed wishes but what Natasha supposed his wishes to be from the ideas he gave voice to in conversation. And she deduced the essentials of his wishes quite correctly and, having once arrived at them, clung to them tenaciously. When Pierre himself showed signs of wanting to change his mind she would meet him with his own arguments.

Thus in the anxious time, which Pierre would never forget, after the birth of their first child, when they tried three different wet-nurses for the delicate baby and Natasha fell ill with worry, Pierre one day told her of Rousseau's views (with which he was in complete agreement) of how unnatural and deleterious it was to have wet-nurses at all. When the next baby was born, in spite of vigorous opposition from her mother, the doctors and even from her husband himself – who were all against her nursing the baby, which to them was something unheard of and pernicious – she insisted on having her own way, and after that nursed all her children herself.

It very often happened that in a moment of irritation husband and wife would quarrel, but long after the dispute Pierre, to his delight and surprise, would find his wife reflecting, not only in theory but in practice, the very idea of his against which she had rebelled – and not the idea alone but the idea purged of any personal element which he had imported into it in the heat of argument.

After seven years of married life Pierre was able to feel a comforting and assured conviction that he was not a bad fellow after all. This he could do because he saw himself mirrored in his wife. In himself he felt the good and bad inextricably mixed and overlapping. But in his wife he saw reflected only what was really good in him, since everything else she rejected. And this reflection was not the result of a logical process of thought but came from some other mysterious, direct source.

II

Two months previously, when Pierre was already staying with the Rostovs, he had received a letter from a certain Prince Fiodr asking him to come to Petersburg to discuss various important questions that were agitating the members of a society of which Pierre had been one of the principal founders.

As soon as she had read the letter (she read all her husband's letters) Natasha had urged him to go to Petersburg, acutely though she would feel his absence. She attributed immense weight to all her husband's intellectual and abstract interests, though she did not understand them, and was always in dread of being a hindrance to him in such matters. To Pierre's timid look of inquiry after reading the letter she replied by begging him to go, but to fix a definite date for his return. And leave of absence was given him for four weeks.

This term had expired a fortnight ago, and Natasha had since been in a constant state of alarm, depression and irritability.

Denisov, now a general on the retired list and much dissatisfied with the present progress of public affairs, had arrived during that fortnight, and gazed at Natasha with pained amazement, as at a bad likeness of a once dear one. Dejected, melancholy looks, random replies and talk about the nursery were all he saw and heard from his former enchantress.

Natasha was mournful and bad-tempered the whole of this time, but never more so than when her mother, her brother, Sonya or Countess Maria sought to comfort her, and tried to excuse Pierre and suggest reasons for his delay in returning.

'It's all nonsense, all rubbish – those discussions which never lead to anything, and all those stupid societies!' Natasha would declare of the very affairs in the immense importance of which she firmly believed. And she would march off to the nursery to feed Petya, her only boy.

No one could give her such soothing and sensible consolation as this little three-months-old creature when he lay at her breast and she felt the movement of his lips and the snuffling of his tiny nose. The diminutive being said to her: 'You are angry, you are jealous, you would like to pay him out, you are afraid – but he is here in me, he is here in me! ...' And to that there was no answer. It was more than true.

During those two weeks of restlessness Natasha resorted to the infant for comfort so often, and fussed over him so much, that she overfed him and he fell ill. She was terrified by his illness, and at the same time it was just what she needed. In caring for him she found it easier to bear her uneasiness about her husband.

She was nursing the baby when the sound of Pierre's sledge was heard at the front door, and the old nurse, knowing how to please her mistress, hurried noiselessly into the room with a beaming face.

'Has he come?' asked Natasha quickly in a whisper, afraid to stir for fear of waking the baby who was dropping off to sleep.

'The master's here, ma'am,' whispered the nurse.

The blood rushed to Natasha's face and her feet involuntarily moved; but to jump up and run was out of the question. The baby opened his eyes and glanced at her as much as to say, 'You are here?', and again lazily smacked his lips.

Cautiously withdrawing her breast, Natasha rocked her son a little, handed him to the nurse and went with swift steps towards the door. But at the door she stopped as though her conscience pricked her for letting her joy take her away from the child so soon, and she looked back. The nurse, with her elbows raised, was lifting the infant over the rail of the cot.

'Yes, you go, ma'am, you go. Don't worry, run along,' she whispered, smiling, with the sort of familiarity that grows up between nurse and mistress.

And Natasha fled on light feet to the ante-room.

Denisov, issuing pipe in hand from the library into the hall, now recognized the old Natasha again for the first time. A flood of radiant, joyous light streamed from her transfigured face.

'He's come!' she exclaimed as she flew past, and Denisov felt that he was delighted that Pierre, whom he did not much care for, had returned.

Running into the vestibule, Natasha saw a tall figure in a fur coat unwinding his scarf. 'It's he! It's really he! He's here!' she said to herself, and darting up to him she hugged him, pressing his head to her breast and then pushing him away and gazing into his red, happy face which was all over hoar-frost. 'Yes, it's he, happy and contented....'

And all at once she remembered the tortures of suspense she had gone through during the last two weeks: the joy that had lit up her face vanished; she frowned and a torrent of reproaches and bitter words broke over Pierre.

'Yes, it's all very well for you to look pleased – you have been having a good time. ... But what about me? You might at least have shown some consideration for your children. I am nursing, my milk went wrong. ... Petya was at death's door. But you were enjoying yourself. Yes, you were enjoying ...'

Pierre knew he was not in the wrong, for he could not have come sooner; he knew this outburst was unseemly and would blow over in a minute or two; above all, he knew that he himself was glad and happy. He wanted to smile but dared not even think of doing so. He put on a piteous, frightened face and bowed before the storm.

'I swear I could not get away sooner. But how is Petya?'

'All right now. Come along! I wonder you aren't ashamed! If only you could see what a state I am in without you, how wretched I was. ...'

'You are well?'

'Come along, come along!' she said, not letting go of his arm. And they went off to the suite of rooms they were occupying.

When Nikolai and his wife came to look for Pierre they found him in the nursery dandling his baby son, who was awake again, on the great palm of his right hand. There was a fixed and gleeful smile on the baby's broad face with its open toothless mouth. The storm had spent itself long since and Natasha's face was all sunshine as she gazed tenderly at her husband and son.

'And did you manage to say all you wanted to to Prince Fiodr?' Natasha was saying.

'Yes, indeed.'

'You see, he can hold his head up.' (Natasha meant the baby.) 'But what a fright I've had with him! ... And you saw the princess? Is it true she's in love with that —'

'Yes, just fancy ...'

At that moment Nikolai and Countess Maria came in. Pierre, still with the baby in his arms, stooped down, kissed them and replied to their inquiries. But it was obvious that in spite of the many interesting things they had to discuss the baby with its little wobbling night-capped head was absorbing all Pierre's attention.

'What a pet!' said Countess Maria, looking at the baby and beginning to play with it. 'That's a thing I can't understand, Nicolas,' she went on, turning to her husband. 'I can't understand how it is you don't appreciate the charm of these exquisite little marvels.'

'I don't, I can't,' replied Nikolai, looking at the baby with indifferent eyes. 'Just a lump of flesh, that's all. Come along, Pierre.'

'And yet really he's such an affectionate father,' said Countess Maria in defence of her husband, 'but only after they are a year or fifteen months old. ...'

'Now Pierre makes a capital nurse,' said Natasha. 'He says his hand is just made for a baby's seat. Look there!'

'Well, only not for this ...' Pierre suddenly exclaimed with a laugh, and shifting the baby he handed him back to the nurse.

12

As is the way with every large household, several quite separate microcosms lived together at Bald Hills and, while each preserved its own individuality but made concessions to the rest, merged into one harmonious whole. Every event that happened in the house was important, joyful or sad for all these microcosms, though each circle had its own private grounds for independent rejoicing or mourning over a given event.

Thus Pierre's return was a happy and important occurrence affecting them all.

The servants (always the most reliable judges of their masters since they assess not on words or expressions of sentiment but on actions and manner of life) were glad when Pierre came back because they knew that when he was there their count would cease his daily round of the estate and would be in better spirits and temper, and also because they knew there would be handsome presents for them all for the fête day.

The children and their governesses rejoiced to see him back because there was no one like Pierre for drawing them into the social life of the household. He alone could play on the harpsichord that *écossaise* – his one piece! – which, as he said, would do for every sort of dance, and he was sure to have brought presents for everyone.

Young Nikolai Bolkonsky, now a slim, delicate, intelligent lad of fifteen with curly light-brown hair and beautiful eyes, was delighted:

'Uncle Pierre,' as he called him, was the object of his passionate adoration and affection. No one had tried to instil into Nikolai any special love for Pierre, whom he only saw occasionally. His aunt and guardian, Countess Maria, had done her utmost to induce the boy to love her husband as she loved him, and Nikolai did like his uncle, but with just a shade of contempt in his liking. Pierre, however, he worshipped. He had no ambitions to be a hussar or a Knight of St George like his uncle Nikolai: he wanted to be learned, wise and good like Pierre. In Pierre's presence his face was always beaming, and he blushed and choked whenever Pierre addressed him. He never missed anything Pierre said, and afterwards, with Dessalles or on his own, he would recall and ponder the meaning of his every word. Pierre's past life and his unhappiness before 1812 (of which young Nikolai had formed a vague, romantic picture from fragmentary phrases he had overheard), his adventures in Moscow, his captivity, Platon Karatayev (whom he knew about from Pierre), his love for Natasha (to whom the boy himself was particularly devoted) and, above all, Pierre's friendship with the father Nikolai did not remember, all made Pierre in his eyes a hero and a being apart.

From stray references to his father and Natasha, from the emotion with which Pierre spoke of the dead man, and the thoughtful reverent tenderness with which Natasha spoke of him too, the boy, who was only just beginning to guess at love, conceived for himself the idea that his father had been in love with Natasha and had bequeathed her to his friend when he was dying. This father of his, whom the boy did not remember, seemed to him a divinity who could not even be imagined, and of whom he never thought without an aching heart and tears of grief and rapture.

And so the boy too was happy at Pierre's return.

The guests in the house were glad to see Pierre because he always helped to enliven and unite any company he was in.

The grown-up members of the family, to say nothing of his wife, were pleased to have back a friend whose presence made life run more smoothly and tranquilly.

The old ladies were pleased both at the presents he brought them and, above all, because Natasha would now be herself again.

Pierre sensed these attitudes towards him of the different sections of the household and hastened to satisfy the expectations of each.

Though he was the most absent-minded and forgetful of men, with the aid of a list his wife drew up he had bought everything, not forgetting his mother- and brother-in-law's commissions, nor the presents of a dress for Mademoiselle Byelov and toys for his nephews. In the early days of marriage it had seemed strange to him that his wife should expect him to remember all the items he had undertaken to buy, and he had been taken aback by her serious annoyance when he returned after his first absence, having forgotten everything. But in time he had grown used to this. Knowing that Natasha never asked him to get anything for herself, and only gave him commissions for others when he himself volunteered, he now found an unforeseen and childlike pleasure in this purchase of presents for the whole household, and never forgot anything. If he incurred Natasha's censure now, it was only for buying and spending too much. To her other defects (as most people thought them but which to Pierre were virtues) of untidiness and neglect of herself Natasha certainly added that of thriftiness.

From the time that Pierre set up as a family man on a scale entailing heavy expenditure he had noticed to his astonishment that he spent only half as much as in the past, and that his circumstances, somewhat straitened latterly (mainly owing to his first wife's debts) were beginning to improve.

Living was cheaper because it was circumscribed: that most expensive of luxuries, the sort of life which allows of going somewhere else or doing something different at a moment's notice, was his no longer, nor did he have any desire for it. He felt that his manner of life was determined now, once and for all, till death, and that to alter it was not in his power, and so that order of life proved economical.

With a jovial, smiling face Pierre was unpacking his purchases.

'What do you think of this?' he cried, unrolling a length of material like a shopman.

Natasha, who was sitting opposite him with her eldest daughter on her knee, turned her sparkling eyes from her husband to the things he was showing her.

'Is that for Mademoiselle Byelov? Splendid!' She felt the quality of the material. 'A rouble a yard, I suppose?'

Pierre told her the price.

'Very dear,' remarked Natasha. 'However, how pleased the children and *maman* will be! Only you shouldn't have bought me this,' she added, unable to suppress a smile as she admired the gold comb set with pearls, in a style just then coming into fashion.

'Adèle tempted me – she kept on at me to buy it,' said Pierre.

'When am I to wear it?' and Natasha stuck it in her coil of hair. 'It will do when I have to bring little Masha out; perhaps they will be fashionable again by then. Well, let's go now.'

And collecting the presents they went first to the nursery and then to see the old countess.

The countess was sitting with her companion, Mademoiselle Byelov, playing grand-patience as usual, when Pierre and Natasha came into the drawing-room with parcels under their arms.

The countess was now turned sixty. Her hair was quite grey and she wore a cap with a frill which framed her whole face. Her face was shrivelled, her upper lip had sunk in and her eyes were misted.

After the deaths in such rapid succession of her son and husband she felt herself a being accidentally forgotten in this world, with no object and no interest in life. She ate and drank, slept and lay awake, but did not live. Life made no impression on her. She wanted nothing from life but peace, and that peace only death could give her. But until death came she had to go on living, that is, employ her vital forces. She evinced to a remarkable degree a trait noticeable in the very young and the very old. Her existence had no manifest aim but was merely, so far as could be seen, occupied by the need to exercise her various functions and proclivities. She had to eat, have a little sleep, ruminate and reminisce, shed a few tears, do some handwork, lose her temper occasionally, and so forth, simply because she had a stomach, brains, muscles, nerves and a liver. She did all these things not at the promptings of any external impulse, like people in the full vigour of life when the aim towards which they strive screens from our view that other aim of exercising their functions. She spoke only because it was a physical necessity to her to use her tongue and lungs. She cried as a child cries, because its nose is stuffed up, and so on. What to people possessed of full health and strength appears as a final aim for her was merely a pretext.

Thus in the morning – especially if she had eaten anything too rich the day before – she was apt to feel a need to be cross, and would select the handiest excuse – Mademoiselle Byelov's deafness.

From the other end of the room she would begin to say something in a low voice.

'I fancy it is a little warmer today, my dear,' she would murmur. And when Mademoiselle Byelov replied: 'Yes, they've come to be sure,' she would mutter angrily: 'Mercy on us, how deaf and stupid she is!'

Another excuse would be her snuff, which was either too dry or too damp or not rubbed fine enough. After these outbursts of irritability her face would grow yellow, and her maids knew by infallible tokens when Mademoiselle Byelov would be deaf again, and the snuff damp, and the countess look bilious. Just as she needed to work off her spleen, so she had sometimes to exercise another of her remaining faculties – namely, the one of thinking, and for this the pretext was her game of patience. When she needed to cry, the late count would be the pretext. When she needed anxiety, there was Nikolai and his health. When she felt a need to say something spiteful, Countess Maria provided the excuse. When her vocal organs required exercise, which usually happened towards seven o'clock, after her after-dinner rest in a darkened room, the pretext would be the re-telling of the same stories over and over again to the same audience.

The old lady's condition was understood by the whole household, though no one ever spoke of it, and they all made every possible effort to satisfy her needs. Only a rare glance exchanged with a sad half-smile between Nikolai, Pierre, Natasha and Countess Maria expressed their common realization of her condition.

But those glances said something more: they said that she had played her part in life, that what they now saw was not her whole self, that we must all come to the same extremity one day, and that they were glad to give way to her, to forbear for the sake of this poor creature, once so dear, once as full of life as themselves, but now so pitiful. '*Memento mori,*' said those glances.

Only the really heartless and stupid members of the household, and the little ones, failed to understand this, and kept away from her.

13

WHEN Pierre and his wife entered the drawing-room the countess was in her recurring condition of needing the mental exercise of a game of patience, and so – though by force of habit she repeated the formula she always employed when Pierre or her son returned after an absence: 'High time, my dear boy, high time! We got tired of waiting for you. Well, thanks be to God you are home again!' and received her presents with another stock phrase: 'It's not the gift that counts, my dear. ... Thank you for thinking of an old woman like me. ...' – it was clear that Pierre's arrival at that moment was unwelcome, since it distracted her in dealing out the cards. She finished her game and only then turned her attention to the presents. They consisted of a beautifully worked card-case, a bright blue Sèvres cup with a lid and shepherdesses painted on it, and a gold snuff-box with the count's portrait in the lid which Pierre had had executed by a miniature-painter in Petersburg. The countess had long wished for such a box; but just now she had no inclination to weep and so she glanced indifferently at the portrait and took more notice of the card-case.

'Thank you, my dear, you have cheered me up,' said she, as she always did. 'But best of all you have brought yourself back. Why, I never saw anything like it – you really must give your wife a good scolding! Would you believe it: she is like a crazed creature when you are not there. No eyes for anything, forgets everything,' she said, going on in her usual strain. 'Look, Anna Timofeyevna,' she added to her companion, 'see what a beautiful case for cards my son has brought us!'

Mademoiselle Byelov duly admired the presents and was in raptures over her dress material.

Though Pierre, Natasha, Nikolai, Countess Maria and Denisov had much to talk about that they could not discuss before the old countess – not because anything was concealed from her but simply because she had dropped so far out of things that had they started on any topic in her presence they would have had to answer so many random questions and repeat for her benefit what had already been repeated over and over again: that this person was dead and that one married, which she would not be able to remember this time any more than the last – yet they sat at tea round the samovar in the drawing-room as usual, and Pierre answered the countess's questions as to whether Prince Vasili had aged, and whether Countess Maria Alexeyevna sent greetings and still thought of them, and other matters that interested none of them and to which she herself was indifferent.

Conversation of this kind, which entertained no one but could not be avoided, lasted all through tea-time. All the adult members of the family were gathered about the round table at which Sonya presided beside the samovar. The children with their tutors and governesses had had tea and their voices could be heard in the next room. In the drawing-room everyone sat in his accustomed place: Nikolai by the stove at a small table where his tea was handed to him, while Milka, the old borzoi bitch (daughter of the first Milka), with her large black eyes looking more prominent than ever in her now completely grey muzzle, lay on an arm-chair beside him. Denisov, whose curly hair, moustaches and whiskers were liberally streaked with grey, sat next to Countess Maria with his general's tunic unbuttoned. Pierre sat between his wife and the old countess, talking of things he knew might interest the old lady and be intelligible to her. He was telling her of the superficial events of society and of the people who had once made up the circle of her contemporaries and in the days gone by had been an active, lively, distinct coterie but who were now for the most part scattered here and there, like herself living out their remnant of life, garnering the last ears of the crop they had sown in earlier years. But to the old countess those contemporaries of hers seemed to make up the only real world that was worth considering. Natasha saw by Pierre's animation that his visit had been full of interest and that he had much to talk about which he could not say before the countess. Denisov, who was not a member of the family, did not understand Pierre's reserve and, being a malcontent, was concerned to hear what was going on in Petersburg. He kept urging Pierre to tell them about the recent scandal in the Semeonovsk regiment, or about Arakcheyev, or about the Bible Society. Once or twice Pierre let himself be drawn into discussing these subjects but Nikolai and Natasha always brought him back to the health of Prince Ivan and Countess Maria Antonovna.

'Now what about all this idiocy – Gossner and Madame Tatawinov?' asked Denisov. 'Is that weally still going on?'

'Going on!' Pierre exclaimed. 'It's worse than ever! The Bible Society has absorbed the whole government!'

'What is that, *mon cher ami*?' inquired the countess, who had finished her tea and was evidently casting about for some excuse for a little peevishness after her meal. 'What were you saying about the government? I don't understand.'

'Why, you see, *maman*,' put in Nikolai, who knew how to translate things into his mother's language, 'Prince Alexander Golitsyn has founded a society, so he has great influence, they say.'

'Arakcheyev and Golitsyn,' remarked Pierre incautiously, 'are practically the government now. And what a goverment! They see conspiracy everywhere and are afraid of everything.'

'Oh, but what fault could anyone find with Prince Golitsyn, I should like to know?' demanded the old countess in an offended tone. 'He is a most estimable man. I used to meet him in the old days at Maria Antonovna's.' And still more aggrieved by the general silence she went on: 'Nowadays people find fault with everyone. A Gospel Society – what harm is there in that?' and she got up (everybody else rose too) and with a forbidding air sailed back to her table in the sitting-room.

The rather glum silence that followed was broken by the sound of children's voices and laughter from the next room. Evidently some joyful excitement was afoot there.

'Finished, finished!' little Natasha's gleeful shriek rose above all the rest.

Pierre exchanged glances with Countess Maria and Nikolai (Natasha he never lost sight of) and smiled happily.

'That's delightful music!' he said.

'Anna Makarovna must have finished her stocking,' said Countess Maria.

'Oh, I'm going to have a look,' said Pierre, jumping up. 'You know,' he added, stopping at the door, 'why it is I'm so particularly fond of that music? It is always the first thing to tell me that everything is all right. When I was driving back today the nearer I got to the house the more nervous I grew. Then as I entered the ante-room I heard Andrusha in peals of laughter, and I knew all was well. ...'

'I know. I know that feeling,' Nikolai chimed in. 'But I mustn't come – those stockings are to be a surprise for me.'

Pierre went in to the children, and the shrieks and laughter were louder than ever.

'Now then, Anna Makarovna,' Pierre's voice was heard saying, 'step into the middle of the room and at the word of command – one, two, and when I say three. ... (That's right, you stand there. And you I'll have in my arms.) Now – one, two ...' said Pierre; there was dead silence. 'Three!' – and children's voices filled the room with a rapturous shout.

'There *are* two, there *are* two!' they roared.

There were two stockings which by a secret method known only to herself Anna Makarovna used to knit at the same time on the same needles and produce one out of the other in the children's presence, when the pair was done.

14

SOON after this the children came in to say good-night. The children kissed everyone; the tutors and governesses made their bows and went away. Only Dessalles and his charge remained. Dessalles whispered to the boy to come downstairs.

'No, Monsieur Dessalles, I shall ask my aunt to let me stay,' young Nikolai Bolkonsky replied, also in a whisper.

'*Ma tante*, please let me stay,' he pleaded, going up to his aunt. His face was full of entreaty, agitation and excitement. Countess Maria glanced at him and turned to Pierre.

'When you are here he can't tear himself away ...' she said.

'I will bring him to you directly, Monsieur Dessalles. Good-night,' said Pierre, giving his hand to the Swiss tutor, and he turned to young Nikolai with a smile. 'You and I haven't seen anything of one another yet. ... Marie, how like he is growing!' he added, addressing Countess Maria.

'Like my father?' asked the boy, flushing crimson and looking up at Pierre with rapturous, shining eyes.

Pierre nodded, and went on with what he had been saying when the children interrupted. Countess Maria had some canvas embroidery in her hands; Natasha sat with her eyes fixed on her husband. Nikolai and Denisov got up, asked for pipes, smoked and went to fetch more tea from Sonya, still sitting with weary pertinacity at the samovar, as they plied Pierre with questions. The curly-haired, delicate boy sat with shining eyes unnoticed in a corner, starting every now and then and murmuring something to himself, evidently thrilling to a new and violent emotion as he turned his curly head with the slender neck showing above the folded-down collar in Pierre's direction.

The conversation ran on the scandals of the day in the higher administrative circles, a subject in which most people see the chief interest of home politics. Denisov, who bore a grudge against the government because of his own disappointments in the Service, rejoiced to hear of the follies (so he deemed them) being committed in Petersburg, and commented in harsh, cutting terms.

'In the old days one had to be a German to be anybody – now you must dance with Mesdames Tatawinov and Kwüdner, and wead Ecka'tshausen and the bwethwen. Ugh, I would let good old Bonaparte loose again! He'd knock all the nonsense out of 'em. Fancy giving the command of the Semeonovsk wegiment to a fellow like that Schwa'tz!' he cried.

Nikolai, though he had not Denisov's disposition to find everything amiss, also thought it dignified and becoming to criticize the government, and believed that the fact that *A* had been appointed minister of this department and *B* governor-general of that province, and that the Emperor had said this and this minister had said that, were all matters of the greatest importance. And so he thought it incumbent upon him to take an interest in these things and interrogate Pierre. Hence the questions put by Nikolai and Denisov kept the discussion from ranging beyond the ordinary lines of gossip about the upper spheres of the administration.

But Natasha, who knew her husband's every manner and thought, saw that Pierre had long been trying, though in vain, to divert the conversation into another channel and open his heart on another idea – the idea concerning which he had gone to Petersburg to consult his new friend, Prince Fiodr, and she came to the rescue with the query: How had he settled things with Prince Fiodr?

'What was that?' asked Nikolai.

'Oh, the same old thing over again,' said Pierre, looking about him. 'Everybody perceives that matters are going so badly that they cannot be allowed to continue so, and that it's the duty of all honest men to counteract it as far as they can.'

'Why, what can honest men do?' Nikolai inquired, frowning slightly. 'What can be done?'

'Well, this ...'

'Let us go into the study,' said Nikolai.

Natasha, who had for some time been expecting to be fetched to her baby, now heard the nurse calling and went off to the nursery. Countess Maria accompanied her. The men adjourned to the study and young Nikolai Bolkonsky stole in, unnoticed by his uncle, and sat down at the writing-table in a dark corner by the window.

'Well, what would you suggest doing?' asked Denisov.

'Still another hare-brained scheme!' said Nikolai.

'Why this,' Pierre began, not sitting down but pacing the room, occasionally stopping short, and lisping and gesticulating rapidly as he talked. 'The position in Petersburg is this: the Emperor lets everything go. He is entirely wrapped up in this mysticism.' (Pierre could not tolerate mysticism in anyone now.) 'All he asks for is peace, and he can only get peace through these men of no faith and no conscience, who recklessly hack at and strangle everything – I mean men like Magnitsky, Arakcheyev and *tutti quanti*. ... You will agree that if you did not look after your estates yourself, and only asked for peace and quiet, the more savage your bailiff was the more readily your object might be attained,' he said, turning to Nikolai.

'Well, but what is the drift of all this?' inquired Nikolai.

'Why, everything's going to pieces. Larceny in the law-courts, in the army nothing but flogging, drill and forced labour in military settlements. Civilization is being crushed. Anything that is youthful and honourable is persecuted! Everybody sees that it can't go on like this. The strain is too great, something's bound to snap,' said Pierre (as men examining the performance of any government have always said since governments began). 'One thing I told them in Petersburg.'

'Told whom?' asked Denisov.

'Oh, you know whom,' said Pierre, with a meaning glance from under his brows. 'Prince Fiodr and all of them. Zeal in the encouragement of culture and philanthropy is all very well of course. The aim is excellent, but in present circumstances something else is needed.'

At that moment Nikolai noticed the presence of his nephew. His face darkened and he went up to the boy.

'Why are you here?'

'Why not? Let him be,' said Pierre, taking hold of Nikolai's arm and continuing. 'That is not enough, I told them: something else is needed now. While you stand expecting the overstrained cord to snap at any moment; while everyone waits for the inevitable upheaval, as many people as possible should join hands as closely as they can to withstand the general calamity. All that is young and strong in the nation is being enticed away and corrupted. One is lured by women, another by honours, a third by ambition or money, and over they go to the other camp. As for independent, free men such as you or me – there are none left. What I say is, widen the scope of our Society, let the *mot d'ordre* be not virtue alone but independence and action!'

Nikolai, moving away from his nephew, irritably pushed up an arm-chair, sat down in it and listened to Pierre, uttering the while an occasional grunt of dissatisfaction and frowning more and more.

'Yes, but what action to what end?' he cried. 'And what attitude will you adopt towards the government?'

'Why, the attitude of supporters. The Society need not be a secret one if the government will sanction it. So far from being hostile to the government, we are the true conservatives – a Society of *gentlemen* in the full meaning of the word. Our object: to prevent another Pugachov from coming to cut the throats of your children and mine, to prevent Arakcheyev from dispatching me to a military settlement. We band together exclusively for the common weal and general security.'

'Yes, but a secret society must necessarily be an inimical and mischievous one, which can only breed evil.'

'Why? Was the *Tugendbund* which saved Europe' (people did not then venture to suggest that Russia had saved Europe) 'productive of anything harmful? The *League of Virtue* is an alliance of virtue: it means love, mutual help ... it is what Christ preached on the Cross ...'

Natasha, who had come into the room in the middle of the conversation, looked joyfully at her husband. It was not what he was saying that pleased her – that did not even interest her because it all seemed so perfectly simple, and something she had known long ago. It appeared so to her because she knew so well the source from which it all sprang – Pierre's heart and soul. She was glad, looking at his eager, enthusiastic face.

Pierre was watched with even more passionate joy by the boy with the thin neck sticking out from the turn-down collar, whom everyone had forgotten. Every word of Pierre's burned into his heart, and with nervous movements of his fingers he unconsciously picked up and snapped the sealing-wax and quill pens on his uncle's table.

'It's not at all what you imagine; but that is what the German *Tugenbund* was and that is what I am proposing.'

'No, my fwiend! A *Tugendbund* is all vewy well for the sausage-eaters but I don't understand it and can't even pwonounce it,' interposed Denisov in a loud, positive voice. 'Evewything is wotten and cowwupt, I agwee, but I still do not fathom that *Tugendbund* of yours, nor do I care about it. A pwoper wevolt now, and I'm your man!'

Pierre smiled, Natasha laughed, but Nikolai only scowled the more and began arguing with Pierre that no revolution was to be expected, and that the danger he talked of existed only in his imagination. Pierre maintained the contrary, and as his intellectual faculties were keener and more resourceful Nikolai soon found himself nonplussed.

This made him still angrier, for in his heart he knew – not by reasoning but by something stronger than reason – that his opinion was the right one.

'Let me tell you this,' he said, rising and trying with nervously twitching fingers to prop up his pipe in a corner, and finally letting it fall. 'I can't prove it to you. You say everything is all rotten in Russia and a revolution is coming. I don't see it. But you also say that our oath of allegiance is a conditional matter, and to that I reply: "You are my best friend, as you know, but if you formed a secret society and began working against the government – whatever government – I know it would be my duty to obey the government. And if Arakcheyev bid me lead a squadron against you and mow you down, I shouldn't hesitate for a second, I should do it! Now make what you like of that.'

An awkward silence followed. Natasha was the first to speak, taking her husband's side and attacking her brother. Her defence was weak and clumsy but she attained her object. The discussion began again, and no longer in the unpleasantly hostile tone in which Nikolai's last words had been spoken.

When they all got up to go in to supper young Nikolai Bolkonsky went up to Pierre, pale and with shining luminous eyes.

'Uncle Pierre ... you ... no ... If Papa were alive ... he would agree with you, wouldn't he?' he asked.

In a flash Pierre realized what an extraordinary, independent, complex and strenuous travail of thought and feeling must have been going on in this boy during the conversation, and remembering all he had been saying he regretted that the lad should have heard him. He had to give him an answer, however.

'Yes, I believe he would,' he said reluctantly, and left the study.

The boy looked down and then for the first time seemed to become aware of the havoc he had wrought with the things on the writing-table. He flushed and went up to Nikolai.

'Uncle, forgive me, I did that ... but not on purpose,' he said, pointing to the broken sealing-wax and pens.

Nikolai started angrily.

'Very well, very well,' he said, throwing the pieces under the table. And, evidently suppressing his fury with difficulty, he turned away from the boy.

'You ought not to have been here at all,' he said.

15

At supper no more was said about politics or societies, and conversation turned on the subject Nikolai liked best – reminiscences of 1812, which Denisov started and over which Pierre was particularly genial and amusing. And the family separated on the friendliest terms.

After supper Nikolai, having undressed in his study and given instructions to the steward who had been waiting for him, went in his dressing-gown to the bedroom, where he found his wife still at her writing-table.

'What are you writing, Marie?' Nikolai asked.

Countess Maria reddened. She was afraid that what she was writing would not be understood or approved of by her husband.

She would have liked to conceal what she was writing from him, but at the same time was glad that he had caught her and that she would now have to tell him.

'It's my diary, Nicolas.' she replied, handing him a blue exercise-book filled with her firm, bold script.

'Diary? ...' echoed Nikolai with a shade of irony, and he took up the book. It was in French.

December 4th

Today when Andrusha [the eldest boy] woke up he did not want to dress, and Mademoiselle Louise sent for me. He was naughty and obstinate. I tried threatening him but it only made him more wilful. Then I took things in hand: I left him alone and helped nurse to get the other children up, declaring that I did not love him. For a long while he was quiet, as though wondering, then he jumped up out of bed and rushed to me in his night-shirt, sobbing so that I could not soothe him for a long time. It was plain that what troubled him most was having grieved me. Then when I gave him his report in the evening he cried again most pitifully as he kissed me. One can do anything with him by tenderness.

'What does his "report" mean?' asked Nikolai.

'I have begun giving the elder ones little marks every evening, showing how they have behaved.'

Nikolai looked into the brilliant eyes that were watching him, and continued to turn over the pages and read. The diary recorded everything in the children's lives which seemed to the mother of interest as indicative of their characters, or suggesting general reflections on educational methods. The entries consisted mainly of the most trifling details but they did not seem so to the mother or the father now reading this journal about his children for the first time.

On the 5th of December there was the note:

Mitya was naughty at table. Papa said he was to have no pudding. He had none, but looked so miserably and greedily at the others while they were eating. To my mind punishing a child by not letting him have any sweet only encourages his greediness. Must tell Nicolas.

Nikolai put down the book and looked at his wife. The radiant eyes gazed at him questioningly: would he approve or disapprove of her diary? There could be no doubt not only of Nikolai's approval but also of his admiration of his wife.

Perhaps it need not be done so pedantically, Nikolai thought, perhaps it need not be done at all; but this constant, tireless spiritual application, the sole aim of which was the children's moral welfare, enchanted him. If Nikolai could have analysed his feelings he would have found that his proud, tender, assured love for his wife rested on this very feeling of awe at her spirituality, at the lofty moral world, almost beyond his reach, in which she had her being.

He was proud that she was so wise, and he fully recognized his own insignificance beside her in the spiritual world, and rejoiced all the more that a soul like that not only belonged to him but was part of his very self.

'I quite, quite approve, my dearest!' he said, with an expressive look. And after a short pause he added: 'And I behaved badly today. You weren't in the study. Pierre and I began arguing, and I lost my temper. But he is impossible – such a child! I don't know what would become of him if Natasha didn't keep him in hand. Can you imagine what he went to Petersburg about? ... They have formed ...'

'Yes, I heard,' said Countess Maria. 'Natasha told me.'

'Well, then, you know,' pursued Nikolai, growing hot at the mere recollection of the discussion, 'he wants to convince me that it's the duty of every honest man to go against the government, and that the oath of allegiance and duty ... I am sorry you weren't there. As it was, they all fell on me – Denisov and Natasha too. ... Natasha is too absurd. We know she can twist him round her little finger, but when it comes to an argument she hasn't an idea to call her own – she simply repeats what he says,' added Nikolai, succumbing to the irresistible inclination which tempts one into criticism of one's nearest and dearest. He forgot that what he was saying of Natasha could apply word for word to himself in relation to his wife.

'Yes, I have noticed that,' said Countess Maria.

'When I told him that duty and sworn allegiance come before everything, he began trying to prove the Lord knows what. A pity you were not there – what would you have said?'

'To my way of thinking, you were absolutely right. I told Natasha so. Pierre says everybody is wretched, and being persecuted and corrupted, and that it is our duty to help our neighbour. Of course he is right there,' said Countess Maria, 'but he forgets that we have other duties nearer home, which God Himself has marked out for us, and that we may run risks for ourselves but not for our children.'

'Yes, yes, that's just what I told him!' cried Nikolai, who fancied he actually had said just that. 'But they kept on about love for one's neighbour and Christianity and all the rest of it in front of young Nikolai, who slipped into the study and sat breaking all my things.'

'Ah, do you know, Nicolas, I often worry about young Nikolai. He is such a curious boy. And I am afraid I neglect him for my own. We all have children and parents, but he has no one. He is always alone with his thoughts.'

'Well, I don't think you have anything to reproach yourself with on his account. All that the fondest mother could do for her son you have done, and are doing, for him. And of course I am glad you do. He is a fine lad, a fine lad! This evening he listened to Pierre in a sort of trance. And only fancy – we got up to go in to supper and I looked, and he had broken everything on my table to bits, and he told me of it at once. I have never known him tell an untruth. A fine lad, a fine lad!' repeated Nikolai, who at heart was not fond of Nikolai Bolkonsky but always felt moved to acknowledge he was a fine lad.

'Still, I am not the same as a mother,' said Countess Maria. 'I feel I am not the same and it distresses me. He's a wonderful boy, but I am dreadfully afraid for him. It would be a good thing for him to have companionship.'

'Oh well, it won't be long now. Next summer I'll take him to Petersburg,' said Nikolai. 'Yes, Pierre always was a dreamer, and always will be,' he went on, returning to the discussion in the study, which had evidently stirred him deeply. 'Why, what can I care what goes on there – whether Arakcheyev is a villain, and so forth? How could I have cared at the time of our marriage when I had so many debts that they were going to put me in prison, and a mother who couldn't see or understand the situation? And then there are you and the children and our affairs. Is it for my own pleasure that I work on the estate or in the office from morning till night? No, I know I must work to be a comfort to my mother, to repay you, and not to leave the children such paupers as I was left myself.'

Countess Maria wanted to tell him that man does not live by bread alone; that he attached too much importance to this *work*; but she knew that it would be better not, and useless. She only took his hand and kissed it. He accepted this as a sign of approval and a confirmation of his ideas, and after a few minutes' silent reflection he continued to think aloud.

'Do you know, Marie,' he said, 'Ilya Mitrofanych' (this was one of their overseers) 'was here today from the Tambov estate, and he tells me they are already offering eighty thousand for the forest.' And with an eager face Nikolai began talking of the possibility of buying back Otradnoe before long. 'Given another ten years of life,' he said, 'and I shall leave the children ... well provided for.'

Countess Maria listened to her husband and took in all that he said. She knew that when he was thinking aloud he would sometimes ask her what he had been saying, and be vexed if he noticed that she had been thinking of something else. But she had to force herself to attend, for what he was saying in no way interested her. She looked at him and though she was not exactly thinking of other things her feelings were elsewhere. She felt a submissive, tender love for this man who would never understand all that she understood – and this seemed to make her love him the more, and added a touch of passionate tenderness. Besides this feeling which absorbed her entirely and prevented her from following the details of her husband's plans, thoughts that had no connexion with what he was saying kept flitting through her brain. She thought of her nephew (her husband's account of the boy's excitement over Pierre's discourse struck her forcibly) and various traits of his gentle, sensitive nature recurred to her. Thinking of her nephew led her to her own children. She did not compare him with them, but compared her feeling for him with her feeling for them, and was sadly conscious of something lacking in her feeling for young Nikolai.

Sometimes the idea had occurred to her that this difference arose from the difference in their ages, but she felt guilty towards him and vowed deep down in her heart to do better and to accomplish the impossible – in this life to love her husband, and her children, and young Nikolai, and all her fellow-creatures, as Christ loved mankind. Countess Maria's spirit was always striving towards the infinite, the eternal and the absolute, and could therefore never be at peace. An austere expression born of hidden, lofty suffering of spirit burdened by the flesh appeared on her face. Nikolai gazed at her. 'My God, what would become of us if she were to die, which is what I dread when she looks like that!' he thought, and placing himself before the icon he began to say his evening prayers.

16

As soon as Natasha and Pierre were alone they too began to talk as only husband and wife can talk – that is, exchanging ideas with extraordinary swiftness and perspicuity, by a method contrary to all the rules of logic, without the aid of premises, deductions or conclusions, and in a quite peculiar way. Natasha was so used to talking to her husband in this fashion that a logical sequence of thought on Pierre's part was to her an infallible sign of something being wrong between them. When he began proving anything or calmly arguing, and she, led on by his example, began to do the same, she knew that they were on the verge of a quarrel.

From the moment they were alone together and Natasha, with wide-open happy eyes, crept up to him and all at once, quickly seizing his head, pressed it to her bosom, saying, 'Now you are all mine, mine! You shan't escape!' – from that moment the conversation began that contravened every law of logic in that it turned at one and the same time upon entirely different topics. This simultaneous discussion of all sorts of subjects, far from being an obstacle to understanding, was the surest token that they understood one another fully.

Just as in a dream everything may be unreal, incoherent and contradictory except the feeling behind the dream, so in this communion of ideas, so contrary to all the laws of logic, the words that passed between husband and wife were not logical and clear, but the feeling that prompted them was.

Natasha was telling Pierre of the daily round of existence at her brother's; of how miserable and half-alive she had been without him; and of how she was fonder than ever of Marie, and how Marie was in every respect a better person than herself. In saying this Natasha was quite sincere in acknowledging Marie's superiority but at the same time she implied that she meant Pierre to prefer herself to Marie or any other woman, and that now, when he had just been seeing so many other women in Petersburg, was the moment for him to tell her so anew.

Accordingly Pierre told her how intolerable he had found the evening parties and dinners in the company of ladies in Petersburg.

'I have quite lost the art of small talk with ladies,' said he. 'It was horribly tedious. Especially as I was so busy.'

Natasha looked intently at him and went on:

'Marie, now she is wonderful!' she said. 'The way she understands children! She seems to see into their very souls. Yesterday, for instance, Mitya was naughty ...'

'How like his father he is,' Pierre interpolated.

Natasha knew why he made this remark about Mitya's likeness to Nikolai: he felt uncomfortable at the memory of his dispute with his brother-in-law and was longing to hear what she thought about it.

'It's a weakness of Nikolai's that unless a thing is generally accepted he will never agree with it. But I know you set great store on what opens up a fresh field,' said she, repeating words Pierre had once uttered.

'No, the truth of the matter is,' said Pierre, 'that to Nikolai ideas and discussions are only an amusement – almost a waste of time. There he is, collecting a library, and has made it a rule for himself not to buy a new book until he has read the last one – Sismondi and Rousseau and Montesquieu,' he added with a smile. 'You know how I ...' he began, to soften his criticism; but Natasha interrupted to show that this was unnecessary.

'So you say that ideas are just a pastime to him. ...'

'Yes, and for me everything else is pastime. All the while in Petersburg I saw everyone as in a dream. When an idea takes hold of me everything else seems waste of time.'

'Oh, what a pity I missed your meeting with the children!' remarked Natasha. 'Which was the most delighted? Liza, I'm sure.'

'Yes,' Pierre replied, and went on with what was in his mind.

'Nikolai says we have no business to reason. But I can't help it. Not to mention the fact that when I was in Petersburg I felt (I can say this to you) that without me the whole affair would go to pieces – every one was pulling his own way. But I succeeded in uniting them all; and then my idea is so clear and simple. You see, I don't say that we ought to oppose this and that. We may be mistaken. What I say is: Let those who love what is right join hands, and let us have but one banner – the banner of action and virtue. Prince Sergei is a capital fellow, and intelligent.'

Natasha would have had no doubt about Pierre's idea being a grand idea but that one thing disconcerted her. It was his being her husband. 'Could anyone so important and necessary to society also be my husband? How can it have happened?' She wanted to express this misgiving to him. 'Now who could decide whether he is really cleverer than all the others?' she wondered, and she passed in review all the people Pierre most respected. There was nobody whom, to judge by his account, he had held in higher regard than Platon Karatayev.

'Do you know what I'm thinking about?' she asked. 'About Platon Karatayev. What would he have said? Would he have approved of you now?'

Pierre was not at all surprised at this question. He understood the drift of his wife's thoughts.

'Platon Karatayev?' he said, and pondered, evidently sincerely trying to imagine what Karatayev's judgement would have been on the point. 'He would not have understood ... and yet, perhaps, he would.'

'I love you awfully!' said Natasha suddenly. 'Awfully, awfully!'

'No, he wouldn't have approved,' said Pierre, after reflection. 'What he would have approved of is our family life. He was always so anxious to find seemliness, happiness, peace in everything, and I could have pointed with pride to ourselves. You know, you talk about when we are parted, but you wouldn't believe what a special feeling I have for you after a time of separation. ...'

'Yes, I was going to say ...' Natasha began.

'No, it's not that. I never leave off loving you. And no one could love more; but this is something special. ... Oh well, you know ...' he did not finish because their eyes meeting said the rest.

'What nonsense it is,' Natasha exclaimed suddenly, 'about honeymoons, and that the greatest happiness is at the beginning. On the contrary, now is much the best. If only you wouldn't go away. Do you remember how we used to quarrel? And it was always my fault. Always. And what it was we quarrelled about – I don't remember even.'

'It was always the same thing,' said Pierre with a smile. 'Jealo ...'

'Don't say it! I can't bear it!' cried Natasha, and a cold, vindictive light glittered in her eyes. 'Did you see her?' she added, after a pause.

'No, and if I had I shouldn't have recognized her.'

They were silent.

'Oh, do you know? While you were talking in the study I was looking at you,' Natasha began, obviously anxious to disperse the cloud that had overtaken them. 'You are as like as two peas – you and the boy.' (She meant her baby son.) 'Ah, it's time I went to him ... my milk. ... But I'm sorry to go away.'

They were silent for a few seconds. Then suddenly turning to each other they both started to speak, Pierre with self-satisfaction and enthusiasm, Natasha with a quiet, happy smile. Immediately, they both stopped to let the other continue.

'No, what were you saying? Go on, go on.'

'No, you go on, mine was only nonsense,' said Natasha.

Pierre finished what he had been about to say. It was the sequel to his complacent reflections on his success in Petersburg. At that moment it seemed to him that he was chosen to give a new direction to the whole Russian community and the world at large.

'I only wanted to say,' he explained, 'that all ideas which have great results are always simple. My idea is just that if vicious people unite together into a power, then honest folk must do the same. That's simple enough, isn't it?'

'Yes.'

'Now what were you going to say?'

'Oh, nothing – only nonsense.'

'Say it, though.'

'Oh, nothing, only silly nonsense,' said Natasha, beaming with a still more radiant smile. 'I was only going to tell you about Petya: today nurse was coming to take him from me, and he laughed and shut his eyes and snuggled up to me – I'm sure he thought he was hiding. He's terribly sweet! There he is crying. Well, good-bye!' and she went out of the room.

Meanwhile, downstairs in young Nikolai Bolkonsky's bedroom a lamp was burning as usual. (The boy was afraid of the dark and could not be cured of his fear.) Dessalles was asleep propped up on four pillows, his Roman nose emitting rhythmic snores. Young Nikolai, who had just woken in a cold perspiration, sat up in bed and stared before him with wide-open eyes. He had awoken from a fearful dream. He had been dreaming that he and Uncle Pierre, wearing helmets like the helmets in his illustrated edition of Plutarch, were marching at the head of a huge army. The army was composed of slanting white threads, filling the air like the cobwebs which float about in autumn and which Dessalles called *le fil de la Vierge*. In front of them lay glory, also exactly like those threads, only somewhat stouter. They – he and Pierre – were being borne along lightly and joyously, nearer and nearer to their goal. Suddenly the threads that moved them began to slacken and become entangled, and everything was dark and confused. And Uncle Nikolai stood before them in a stern and menacing attitude.

'Is this your work?' he said, pointing to some broken pens and sticks of sealing-wax. 'I loved you once but Arakcheyev has given me orders and I shall kill the first of you to advance a step further.' The boy Nikolai looked round for Pierre but Pierre was no longer there. In his place stood his father – Prince Andrei – and his father had neither shape nor form but there he was, and seeing him young Nikolai grew faint with love: he felt himself without strength, without bones or marrow. His father caressed and was sorry for him. But Uncle Nikolai was moving down upon them, coming closer and closer. Horror seized Nikolai and he awoke.

'My father!' he thought. (Though there were two very good portraits of Prince Andrei in the house, Nikolai never imagined him in human form.) 'My father has been with me and made much of me. He was pleased with me; he approved of Uncle Pierre. Whatever Uncle Pierre says I will do. Mucius Scaevola burnt his hand. And why shouldn't the same sort of thing happen in my life? I know they want me to study. And I will. But one day I shall have finished learning, and then I will do something. I only ask one thing of God: that it may be with me as it was with Plutarch's men, and I will do as they did. I will do better. Everyone shall know of me, shall love and applaud me.' And all at once Nikolai felt his breast heaving with sobs, and he burst into tears.

'*Êtes-vous indisposé?*' he heard Dessalles' voice asking.

'*Non*,' answered Nikolai, and lay back on his pillow. 'He is good and kind and I am fond of him,' he said to himself, thinking of Dessalles. 'But Uncle Pierre! Oh, what a wonderful person he is! And my father? Oh, Father, Father! Yes, I will do something that even *he* would be content with....'

PART TWO

I

HISTORY has for its subject the life of nations and of humanity. To catch hold of and encompass in words – to describe exactly – the life of a single people, much less of humanity, would appear impossible.

The ancient historians all employed the same simple method for seizing the seemingly elusive and depicting the life of a people. They wrote of the parts played by the individuals who stood in authority over that people, and regarded their activity as an expression of the activity of the nation as a whole.

To the twofold question of how individuals could oblige nations to act as they wished, and by what the will of those individuals themselves was guided, the historians of old replied by recognizing a Divinity which, in the first case, made the nation subject to the will of one chosen person, and, in the second, guided the will of that chosen person to the accomplishment of predestined ends.

The question was thus resolved by belief in the direct participation of the Deity in human affairs.

Neither proposition finds a place in the theory of the new school of history.

It would seem that, having rejected the belief of the ancients in man's subjection to the Deity and in a predetermined aim towards which nations are led, the new school ought to be studying not the manifestations of power but the causes which create power. But modern history has not done this. Though it has repudiated the theory of the older historians it still follows their practice.

In place of men endowed with divine authority and governed directly by the will of God modern history has set up either heroes possessed of extraordinary, superhuman ability, or simply men of any and every degree, from monarchs to journalists, who dominate the masses. Instead of the former divinely appointed purposes of nations –

of the Jews, the Greeks, the Romans – which the old historians saw at the back of movements of humanity, the new school postulates aims of its own – such as the welfare of the French, German or English people, or, in its highest flights, the welfare and civilization of humanity in general, by which is usually meant the peoples inhabiting a small, north-western corner of a large continent.

Modern history has rejected the beliefs of the ancients without establishing any new conviction in place of them, and the logic of the situation has obliged the historians, who were under the impression that they had dismissed the hypothesis of the divine authority of kings and the *Fatum* of the ancients, to arrive at the same conclusion by another route – that is, to recognize that (1) nations are guided by individuals, and (2) there exists a certain goal towards which the nations and humanity are moving.

In the works of all the modern historians, from Gibbon to Buckle, in spite of their seeming differences of outlook and the apparent novelty of their opinions, these two time-honoured, unavoidable premisses lie at the basis of the argument.

In the first place the historian describes the activity of separate persons who in his opinion have dictated to humanity (one historian accepts only monarchs, military generals and ministers of state in this category, while another will also include orators, scholars, reformers, philosophers and poets). Secondly, the historians assume that they know the goal towards which humanity is being led: to one this goal is the majesty of the Roman or the Spanish or the French empire; for another it is liberty, equality and the kind of civilization that obtains in the little corner of the globe called Europe.

In 1789 fermentation starts in Paris: it develops and spreads, and finds expression in a movement of peoples from west to east. Several times this movement is directed towards the east and comes into collision with a counter-movement from the east westwards. In the year 1812 it reaches its extreme limit – Moscow – and then, with remarkable symmetry, the counter-movement follows from east to west, attracting to it, as the original movement had done, the peoples of middle Europe. The counter-movement reaches the departure-point in the west of the first movement – Paris – and subsides.

During this period of twenty years an immense number of fields are left untilled; houses are burned; trade changes its orientation; millions of people grow poor, grow rich, move from place to place;

and millions of Christian men professing the law of love for their neighbour murder one another.

What does all this mean? Why did it happen? What induced these people to burn houses and kill their fellow-creatures? What were the causes of these events? What force compelled men to act in this fashion? These are the instinctive, guileless and supremely legitimate questions humanity propounds to itself when it encounters the monuments and traditions of that bygone period of turmoil.

For an answer to these questions we turn to the science of history, whose purpose is to teach nations and humanity to know themselves.

Had history adhered to the old ideas it would have said that the Deity, to reward or punish His people, gave Napoleon power and guided his will for the attainment of His own divine ends. And this reply would have been complete and lucid. One might or might not believe in the divine significance of Napoleon; but for anyone who believed in it all the history of that period would be intelligible and free from contradictions.

But modern history cannot answer in that way. Science does not admit the conception of the ancients as to the direct participation of the Deity in human affairs, and must therefore give other answers.

Replying to these questions the new school of history says: 'You want to know what this movement means, what caused it, and what force produced these events? Listen:

'Louis XIV was a very proud and self-confident man; he had such and such mistresses and such and such ministers, and he ruled France vilely. Louis' successors, too, were weak men and they, too, ruled France vilely. And they had such and such favourites and such and such mistresses. Furthermore, certain people were at this time writing books. At the end of the eighteenth century there had gathered in Paris a couple of dozen persons who began talking about all men being equal and free. Because of this, over the length and breadth of France men fell to slaughtering and destroying one another. They killed the king and a good many others. At this time there was in France a man of genius – Napoleon. He got the upper hand of everybody everywhere – that is to say, he killed numbers of his fellows because he was a great genius. And for some reason he went to kill Africans, and killed them so well and was so cunning and clever that when he returned to France he ordered everyone to obey him. And they all did. Having made himself an Emperor he again went off to kill people in Italy, Austria and Prussia. There, too, he killed a great many. Now in Russia there was an Emperor, Alexander, who decided to restore order in Europe, and so he fought wars against Napoleon. But in '07 he suddenly made friends with him, until in 1811 they quarrelled again, and again began killing a lot of people. And Napoleon brought six hundred thousand men to Russia and captured Moscow; but afterwards he suddenly ran away from Moscow, and then the Emperor Alexander, aided by the counsels of Stein and others, united Europe into a coalition to march against the disturber of her peace. All Napoleon's allies suddenly turned into enemies; and their forces advanced against the fresh forces which he raised. The allies defeated Napoleon, entered Paris, forced Napoleon to abdicate, and sent him to the island of Elba, not depriving him of the dignity of Emperor or failing to show him every respect, though five years before and one year later they all regarded him as a bandit and an outlaw. Thereupon Louis XVIII, who till then had been a laughing-stock both to the French and the allies, began to reign. As for Napoleon, after shedding tears before the Old Guard he renounced his throne and went into exile. Next, astute statesmen and diplomats (in particular Talleyrand, who had managed to sit down before anyone else in the famous arm-chair and thereby to extend the frontiers of France) proceeded to hold conversations in Vienna, and by this means make the nations happy or unhappy. All at once the diplomats and monarchs almost came to blows; they were on the point of ordering their armies to massacre one another again; but at this point Napoleon arrived in France with a battalion, and the French, who had been abhorring him, immediately all submitted to him. But the allied monarchs got very annoyed at this and again went to war with the French. And they defeated the genius Napoleon and, suddenly confirming that he was a bandit, removed him to St Helena. And there the exile, parted from his dear ones and his beloved France, died a lingering death on the rocky island, and bequeathed his great deeds to posterity. As for Europe, reaction set in, and the sovereigns all took to outraging their subjects again.'

It would be a mistake to think this mere irony – a caricature of historical descriptions. On the contrary, it is a very mild expression of the incongruous answers which fail to answer given by *all* historians, from the compilers of memoirs and of histories of individual countries to the 'universal histories' and the new sort of histories of the *culture* of that period.

The grotesqueness of these answers arises from the fact that modern history is like a deaf man answering questions no one has put to him.

If the purpose of history is the description of the flux of humanity and of peoples, the first question to be answered, unless all the rest is to remain unintelligible, will be: What is the power that moves nations? To this the new school laboriously replies either that Napoleon was a great genius or that Louis XIV was very arrogant, or else that certain writers wrote certain books.

All that may well be so, and mankind is quite ready to say Amen; but it is not what was asked. All that might be very interesting if we recognized a divine power, self-subsisting and consistent, governing the nations by means of Napoleons, Louises and philosophical writers; but we acknowledge no such power, and therefore, before any talk of Napoleons, Louises and philosophical writers, we ought to be shown the relation obtaining between these persons and the movement of nations.

If divine power is to be replaced by some other force, then it should be explained what this new force consists of, in which the whole interest of history is contained.

History seems to take it for granted that this force is self-evident and known to everyone. But in spite of every desire to regard it as known the frequent reader of historical works will find himself doubting whether this new force, so variously understood by the historians themselves, is really quite so familiar to all and sundry.

2

WHAT is the force that moves nations?

Biographical historians and historians of individual peoples understand this force as a power inherent in heroes and rulers. According to their chronicles events occur solely at the will of a Napoleon, an Alexander or in general the personages of whom they treat. The answers which historians of this *genre* return to the question of what force causes events to happen are satisfactory only so long as there is but one historian to each event. But as soon as historians of different nationalities and views begin describing one and the same event, the replies they give immediately lose all meaning, since this force is understood by them not only differently but often in absolutely opposite ways. One historian will maintain that a given event owed its origin to Napoleon's power; another that it was Alexander's power; while a third ascribes the event to the influence of some other person. Moreover, historians of this type contradict one another even in their interpretation of the force on which the authority of one and the same figure was based. Thiers, a Bonapartist, says that Napoleon's power was based on his virtue and his genius; Lanfrey, a Republican, declares that it rested on his rascality and skill in deceiving the people. So that the historians of this class, by mutually destroying one another's position, destroy the conception of the force which produces events, and furnish no reply to history's essential question.

Universal historians, who deal with all the nations, appear to recognize the erroneousness of the specialist historians' view of the force that produces events. They do not recognize it as a power pertaining to heroes and rulers but regard it as the resultant of a multiplicity of variously directed forces. In describing a war, or the subjugation of a people, the general historian looks for the cause of the event not in the power of any one individual but in the interaction of many persons connected with the event.

According to this view, the power of historical personages conceived as the product of several different forces can hardly, it would seem, be regarded as the force which in itself produces events. Yet general historians do almost invariably make use of the concept of power as a force which itself produces events and stands to events in the relation of cause to effect. We find them (the historians) saying at one minute that an historical personage is the product of his time and his power only the outcome of various forces; and at the next that his power is itself a force producing events. Gervinus, Schlosser and others, for instance, in one place argue that Napoleon was the product of the Revolution, of the ideas of 1789 and so forth, and in another plainly state that the campaign of 1812 and other incidents not to their liking were simply the outcome of Napoleon's misdirected will, and that the very ideas of 1789 were arrested in their development by Napoleon's caprice. The ideas of the Revolution and the general temper of the age produced Napoleon's power. But Napoleon's power stifled the ideas of the Revolution and the general temper of the age.

This curious contradiction is no chance occurrence. It not only confronts us at every turn but volume upon volume of universal history is made up of a chain of such contradictions – which spring from the fact that after taking a few steps along the road of analysis the universal historians stop short half-way.

For component forces to give rise to a certain composite or resultant force the sum of the components must equal the resultant. This condition is never observed by the universal historians. Hence, to explain the resultant force they are obliged to admit, in addition to their inadequate components, a further, unexplained, force affecting the resultant.

The specialist historian describing the campaign of 1813, or the restoration of the Bourbons, asserts in so many words that these events were brought about by the will of Alexander. But the general historian, Gervinus, refuting this opinion of the specialist historian, seeks to prove that the campaign of 1813 and the restoration of the Bourbons were due not only to Alexander but to the activity of Stein, Metternich, Madame de Staël, Talleyrand, Fichte, Chateaubriand and others. He evidently decomposes Alexander's power into its component factors – Talleyrand, Chateaubriand and the rest – but the sum of these components, that is, the interaction of Chateaubriand, Talleyrand, Madame de Staël and the others, obviously does not equal the resultant, namely, the phenomenon of millions of Frenchmen submitting to the Bourbons. And therefore to explain how the submission of millions resulted from these components – that is, how component forces equal to a given quantity A gave a resultant equal to a thousand times A – he is obliged to fall back on the same force – power – which he has been denying inasmuch as he was regarding it as the resultant of the given forces; that is, he has to concede an unexplained force acting on the resultant. And this is just what the universal historians do. And consequently contradict not only the sectional historian but themselves too.

Country people having no clear idea of the cause of rain say, 'The wind has blown away the rain,' or 'The wind is blowing up for rain,' according to whether they want rain or fine weather. In the same way the universal historians at times when they want it to be so, when it fits in with their theory, say that power is the result of events; and at others, when it is necessary to prove the opposite, say that power produces the events.

A third class of historians – the so-called historians of *culture*, following on the lines laid down by the writers of universal history who sometimes accept *littérateurs* and *grandes dames* as forces producing events – interpret this force still differently. They see it in what is termed *culture*, in intellectual activity.

The historians of culture from first to last take after their progenitors, the writers of universal histories, for if historical events may be explained by the fact that certain persons treated one another in certain ways, why not explain them by the fact that certain people wrote certain books ? Out of all the immense number of tokens that accompany every vital phenomenon these historians select the manifestation of intellectual activity, and declare that this manifestation is the cause. But, despite their endeavours to prove that the cause of events lies in intellectual activity, only by a great stretch can one agree that there is any connexion between intellectual activity and the movement of peoples, and it is altogether impossible to agree that intellectual activity has controlled the actions of mankind, for such phenomena as the brutal murders of the French Revolution, which were the outcome of the doctrine of the equality of man, and the most wicked wars and executions resulting from the Gospel of Love belie this hypothesis.

But even admitting that all the cunningly devised arguments with which these histories abound are correct: admitting that nations are governed by some undefined force called an *idea*, the essential question of history either still remains unanswered or else to the power of monarchs and the influence of counsellors and other persons introduced by the universal historians we must add another, new force – the *idea*, the relation of which to the masses requires explanation. One can understand that Napoleon had power and so an event came to pass; with some effort one may even grant that Napoleon together with other influences was the cause of an event; but how a book, *Le Contrat social*, had the effect of making Frenchmen destroy one another is unintelligible without some explanation of the causal nexus of this new force with the event.

There undoubtedly exists a connexion between all the people alive at one time, and so it is possible to discover some sort of connexion between the intellectual activity of men and their historical movements, just as such a connexion may be discovered between the movements of humanity and commerce, handicrafts, horticulture, or anything else you please. But why intellectual activity should appear to the historians of culture to be the cause or expression of the whole historical movement is hard to understand. Only the following considerations can have led the historians to such a conclusion: (1) that history is written by learned men and so it is natural and agreeable for them to believe that the pursuit of their calling supplies the ruling element in the movement of all humanity, just as a similar belief is natural and agreeable to merchants, agriculturists or soldiers (only it does not find expression because merchants and soldiers do not write history); and (2) that spiritual activity, enlightenment, civilization, culture, ideas are all vague, indefinite conceptions under whose banner they can very conveniently employ words having a still less definite meaning and which can therefore be readily adapted to any theory.

But leaving aside the question of the intrinsic worth of histories of this kind (which may possibly even be of use to someone for something), the histories of culture, to which all general histories tend more and more to approximate, are remarkable for the fact that after examining seriously and in detail various religious, philosophic and political doctrines as causes of events, so soon as they have to describe an actual historical event, such as the campaign of 1812 for instance, they involuntarily describe it as resulting from an exercise of power – roundly declaring that that campaign was the result of Napoleon's will. In saying this, the historians of culture unconsciously contradict themselves; they show that the new force they have invented does not account for what happens in history, and that history can only be explained by introducing the power which they apparently do not recognize.

3

A LOCOMOTIVE is moving. Someone asks: 'What makes it move?' The peasant answers, ''Tis the devil moves it.' Another man says the locomotive moves because its wheels are going round. A third maintains that the cause of the motion lies in the smoke being carried away by the wind.

The peasant's contention is irrefutable: he has devised a complete explanation. To refute him someone would have to prove to him that there is no devil, or another peasant would have to tell him that it is not a devil but a German who makes the locomotive go. Only then, because of the contradiction, will they see that they are both wrong. But the man who argues that the movement of the wheels is the cause confounds himself, for having once started on analysis he ought to proceed further and explain why the wheels go round. And until he has reached the ultimate cause of the movement of the locomotive in the pressure of steam in the boiler he has no right to stop in his search for the cause. Finally, the man who explained the movement of the locomotive by the smoke that is borne back has noticed that the theory about the wheels does not furnish a satisfactory explanation, and has seized upon the first feature to attract his attention, and in his turn produces that as an explanation.

The only conception capable of explaining the movement of the locomotive is that of a force commensurate with the movement observed.

The only conception capable of explaining the movement of peoples is that of some force commensurate with the whole movement of the peoples.

Yet to supply this conception various historians assume forces of entirely different kinds, all of which are incommensurate with the movement observed. Some see it as a force directly inherent in heroes, as the peasant sees the devil in the steam-engine; others, as a force resulting from several other forces, like the movement of the wheels; others again, as an intellectual influence, like the smoke that is blown away.

So long as histories are written of separate individuals, whether Caesars, Alexanders, Luthers or Voltaires, and not the histories of *all* – absolutely *all* – those who take part in an event, it is impossible not to ascribe to individual men a force which can compel other men to direct their activity towards a certain end. And the only conception of such a kind known to historians is the idea of power.

This conception is the sole handle by means of which the material of history, as at present expounded, can be dealt with; and anyone who breaks that handle off, as Buckle did, without finding some other method of treating historical material, merely deprives himself of the last possible way of dealing with it. The necessity for the conception of power as an explanation of the phenomena of history is most strikingly illustrated by the universal historians and historians of culture themselves, who, after professedly rejecting the conception of power, inevitably have recourse to it at every step.

Up to now historical science in its relation to humanity's inquiry is like money in circulation – bank-notes and coin. The biographies and national histories are the paper money. They may pass and circulate and fulfil their function without mischief to anyone, and even to advantage, so long as no question arises as to the security behind them. One has only to forget to ask how the will of heroes produces events, and the histories of Thiers and his fellows will be interesting, instructive and not without their touch of poetry. But in exactly the same way as doubts of the real value of bank-notes arise either because, being easy to manufacture, too many of them get made, or because people try to exchange them for gold, so doubts concerning the real value of histories of this kind arise either because too many of them are written or because someone in the simplicity of his heart inquires: What force enabled Napoleon to do that? – that is, wants to exchange the current paper money for the pure gold of true understanding.

The writers of universal histories and the history of culture are like people who, recognizing the defects of paper money, decide to substitute for it coin of some metal inferior to gold. Their money will be 'hard coin', no doubt; but while paper money may deceive, the ignorant coin of inferior metal will deceive no one. Just as gold is gold only where it is employable not merely for barter but also for the real use of gold, so too the universal historians will only rank as gold when they are able to answer the cardinal question of history: What constitutes power? The universal historians give contradictory replies to this question, while the historians of culture thrust it aside altogether and answer something quite different. And as imitation gold counters can only be used among a community of persons who agree to accept them for gold or who are ignorant of the nature of gold, so the universal historians and historians of culture who fail to answer the essential questions of humanity only serve as currency for sundry purposes of their own – in the universities and among the legions who go in for 'serious' reading, as they are pleased to call it.

4

HAVING dismissed the conviction of the ancients as to the divinely ordained subjection of the will of a nation to the one chosen vessel and the subjection of the will of that chosen vessel to the Deity, history cannot take a single step without being involved in contradictions. It must choose one of two alternatives: either to return to its old belief in the direct intervention of the Deity in human affairs, or to find a definite explanation of the meaning of the force producing historical events which is termed 'power'.

A return to the first is impossible: the old belief has been shattered, and so an explanation must be found of what is meant by power.

'Napoleon commanded an army to be raised and to march forth to war.' Such a statement is so familiar, we are so entirely at home with such a point of view, that the question why six hundred thousand men go out to fight when Napoleon utters certain words seems to us foolish. He had the power and so what he ordered was done.

This solution is perfectly satisfactory if we believe that the power was given him by God. But, as soon as we discountenance that, it becomes essential to determine what this power is that one man has over others.

It cannot be the direct physical ascendancy of a strong creature over a weak one – an ascendancy based on the application or threat of physical force, like the power of Hercules; nor can it be founded on the possession of moral force, as in the innocence of their hearts some historians suppose, who say that the leading figures in history are cast in heroic mould, that is, are endowed with an extra-ordinary strength of soul and mind called genius. This power cannot be based on any preponderance of moral strength seeing that, not to mention heroes such as Napoleon concerning whose moral qualities opinions differ widely, history shows us that neither a Louis XI nor a Metternich, who ruled over millions of their fellows, had any particular moral qualities but on the contrary in most respects were morally weaker than any of the millions they ruled over.

If the source of power lies neither in the physical nor the moral qualities of the individual who possesses it, it is obvious that it must be looked for elsewhere – in the relation to the masses of the man who wields the power.

And that is how power is understood by the science of jurisprudence, that *bureau d'échange* of history, which undertakes to exchange history's concept of power for true gold.

Power is the collective will of the masses, transferred by their expressed or tacit consent to their chosen rulers.

In the domain of jurisprudence, deliberating as it does on how the State and its power ought to be constructed were it possible to do so *a priori*, all this is very clear; but when applied to actual history this definition of power calls for elucidation.

The science of jurisprudence regards the State and its power much as the ancients regarded fire – namely, as something existing absolutely. For history the State and its power are merely phenomena, in the same way as for modern physics fire is not an element but a phenomenon.

From this fundamental difference in the points of view of history and jurisprudence it follows that jurisprudence can discuss in detail how, in its opinion, power should be constituted and what power is in its immutable essence, outside the conditions of time; but to history's questions about the meaning of the mutations of power in time it can return no answer.

If power is the collective will of the masses transferred to their ruler, was Pugachov a representative of the will of the people? If not, then why was Napoleon I? Why was Napoleon III a criminal when he was apprehended at Boulogne, and why were those whom he afterwards apprehended criminals?

Do palace revolutions – in which sometimes only two or three people take part – transfer the will of the people to a new ruler? In international relations is the will of the people also transferred to their conqueror? Was the will of the Confederation of the Rhine transferred to Napoleon in 1808? Was the will of the Russian people transferred to Napoleon in 1809 when our army in alliance with the French made war upon Austria?

These questions may be answered in three different ways:

(1) by maintaining that the will of the people is always unconditionally transferred to the ruler or rulers whom they have chosen, and that therefore every emergence of a new power, every struggle against the power once delegated, must be regarded as a contravention of the real power; or

(2) by maintaining that the will of the masses is delegated to the rulers on certain definite and known conditions, and by showing that all restrictions on, conflicts with and even abolitions of power proceed from non-observance by the rulers of the conditions upon which their power was entrusted to them; or

(3) by maintaining that the will of the masses is delegated to the rulers conditionally but that the conditions are uncertain and undefined, and that the appearance of several authorities, their struggles

and their falls result solely from the greater or lesser fulfilment by the rulers of the uncertain conditions upon which the will of the people is transferred from one set of persons to another.

These are the three ways in which the historians explain the relation of the masses to their rulers.

Some historians, failing in their simplicity to understand the question of the meaning of power – those sectional and biographical historians already referred to – seem to believe that the collective will of the people is delegated to historical leaders unconditionally, and therefore in writing about some particular State they assume that Power to be the one absolute and real power, and that any other force opposing it is not a power but a violation of power – mere violence.

This theory of theirs, though convenient for covering primitive and peaceful periods of history, has the disadvantage when applied to complex and stormy periods in the life of nations, during which various powers arise simultaneously and come into collision, that the legitimist historian will try to prove that the Convention, the Directory and Bonaparte were only infringers of the true power, while the Republican and Bonapartist will argue, the one that the Convention and the other that the Empire was the true authority and all the rest a violation of authority. It is evident that the interpretations furnished by these historians, being mutually contradictory, can satisfy none but children of the tenderest age.

Recognizing the falsity of this view of history, another class of historians assert that power rests on a conditional delegation of the collective will of the people to their rulers, and that historical leaders possess power only conditionally on their carrying out the programme which the will of the people has by tacit agreement prescribed to them. But what this programme consists of, these historians do not tell us, or if they do they continually contradict one another.

Each historian, according to his view of what constitutes the goal of a nation's progress, conceives of this programme as, for instance, the greatness, the wealth, the freedom or the enlightenment of the citizens of France or some other country. But ignoring the mutual contradictions of the historians as to the nature of this programme – even granted the existence of some one general programme – we find that the facts of history almost always gainsay this theory. If the conditions on which power is vested in rulers consist in the wealth, freedom and enlightenment of the people, how is it that Louis XIV and Ivan the Terrible live out their reigns in peace, while Louis XVI and Charles I are put to death by their peoples? To this question such historians reply that the actions of Louis XIV, which ran counter to the programme, were visited on Louis XVI. But why did they not react on Louis XIV or Louis XV? – why expressly on Louis XVI? And what is the term for such reactions? To these questions there is and can be no reply. Equally little does this view explain why for several centuries the collective will remains vested in certain rulers and their heirs, and then suddenly in the course of fifty years is transferred to a Convention, to a Directory, to a Napoleon, to an Alexander, to a Louis XVIII, to a Napoleon again, to a Charles X, to a Louis Philippe, to a Republican government and to a Napoleon III. To explain these swift transferences of the people's will from one individual to another, especially when complicated by international relations, conquests and alliances, the historians are reluctantly obliged to allow that a proportion of these phenomena are not normal delegations of the popular will but accidents proceeding from the cunning or the craft, the blundering or the weakness, of a diplomatist, a monarch or a party leader. So that most of the phenomena of history – civil wars, revolutions, conquests – are presented by these historians not as the results of free transferences of the people's will but as the products of the ill-directed will of one or more individuals, that is, once again, as usurpations of power. And so these historians too see historical events as exceptions to their theory.

These historians are like a botanist who, having observed that some plants germinate with two cotyledons, should insist that every growing thing grows by dividing into a pair of leaflets; and that the palm-tree, therefore, and the mushroom, nay, even the oak – which in its full-grown ramification loses all resemblance to the twin-leaflet, dicotyledonous form – are departures from theory.

Historians of the third class assume that the will of the people is vested in historical personages conditionally, but that the conditions are not known to us. They say that historical leaders have powers only because they are carrying out the will of the people which has been delegated to them.

But in that case, if the force that moves nations lies not in their historical leaders but in the peoples themselves, where is the significance of those leaders?

Historical personages, so these historians tell us, are the expression of the will of the masses: the activity of the historical leader represents the activity of the people.

But in that case the question arises, Does all the activity of the leaders serve as an expression of the people's will, or only a certain side of it? If the whole activity of the leaders serves as the expression of the people's will, as some historians suppose, then all the *minutiae* of court scandal contained in the biographies of the Napoleons and the Catherines serve to express the life of the nation, which is obvious nonsense; but if it is only one side of the activity of an historical leader which serves to express the life of a people, as other so-called 'philosophical' historians believe, then in order to determine what side of the activity of the historical personage expresses the nation's life we have first of all to know in what the nation's life consists.

Confronted by this difficulty, historians of the kind I am speaking of will invent some most obscure and impalpable, generalized abstraction to cover the greatest possible number of occurrences, and then declare this abstraction to be the aim of mankind's movement. The most usual generalizations adopted by almost all historians are: freedom, equality, enlightenment, progress, civilization and culture. Having postulated some such generalization as the goal of the movements of humanity, the historians go on to study those personages in history who have left the greatest number of memorials behind them: kings, ministers, generals, authors, reformers, popes and journalists – according as these personages, in their judgement, have contributed to or hindered the abstraction in question. But as it is nowhere proven that the aim of humanity does consist in freedom, equality, enlightenment or civilization, and as the connexion of the masses with the rulers and enlighteners of humanity only rests on the arbitrary assumption that the collective will of the masses is always vested in these figures which attract our attention, it happens that the activity of the millions who migrate, burn their houses, abandon tilling the soil, and butcher one another, never does find expression in descriptions of the activity of some dozen persons who do not burn houses, have nothing to do with agriculture or killing their fellow-creatures.

History proves this at every turn. Is the ferment of the peoples of the west at the end of the last century and their drive eastwards explained by the activity of Louis XIV, XV and XVI, their mistresses and ministers, or by the lives of Napoleon, Rousseau, Diderot, Beaumarchais and others?

Is the movement of the Russian people eastwards to Kazan and Siberia expressed in the details of the morbid character of Ivan the Terrible and his correspondence with Kurbsky?

Is the movement of the peoples at the time of the Crusades explained by the life and activity of the Godfreys and the Louises and their ladies? For us that movement of the peoples from west to east, without any object, without leadership – a crowd of vagrants following Peter the Hermit – remains incomprehensible. And still more incomprehensible is the cessation of that movement when a rational and sacred aim for the Crusades – the deliverance of Jerusalem – had been clearly proclaimed by historical leaders. Popes, kings and knights urged the people to free the Holy Land; but the people did not move, for the unknown cause which had previously impelled them existed no longer. The history of the Godfreys and the Minnesingers evidently cannot be taken as an epitome of the life of the people. And the history of the Godfreys and Minnesingers has remained the history of Godfreys and Minnesingers, while the history of the life of the people and their incentives has remained unknown.

Even less explanatory of the life of the people is the history of writers and reformers.

The history of culture will explain to us the impelling motives and circumstances of the life and thoughts of a writer or a reformer. We may learn that Luther had a hasty temper and delivered such and such orations; we may learn that Rousseau was of a suspicious nature and wrote such and such books; but we shall not learn why the nations flew at one another's throats after the Reformation, or why men guillotined one another during the French Revolution.

If we unite both these kinds of history, as is done by the most modern historians, we shall get histories of monarchs and writers but not history of the lives of nations.

5

THE life of nations cannot be summarized in the lives of a few men, for the connexion between those men and the nations has not been discovered. The theory that this connexion is based on the transference of the collective will of a people to certain historical personages is a hypothesis not supported by the experience of history.

The theory of the transference of the collective will of the people to historical personages may perhaps explain much in the domain of jurisprudence and be essential for its purposes, but in its application to history, as soon as revolutions, conquests or civil wars make their appearance – as soon as history begins, in fact – this theory explains nothing.

The theory seems to be irrefutable just because the act of transference of the people's will cannot be verified.

No matter what event takes place, nor who directs it, the theory can always claim that such and such a person took the lead because the collective will was vested in him.

The replies this theory gives to historical questions are like the replies of a man who, watching the movements of a herd of cattle, and paying no attention to the varying quality of the pasturage in different parts of the field, or to the drover's stick, should attribute the direction the herd takes to what animal happens to be at its head.

'The herd goes in that direction because the animal in front leads it there and the collective will of all the other cattle is vested in that leader.' That is what historians in our first category say – those who assume an unconditional transference of power.

'If the animals leading the herd change, this happens because the collective will of all the cattle is transferred from one leader to another, according to whether the leader leads them in the direction selected by the whole herd.' Such is the reply of the historians who assume that the collective will of the masses is delegated to rulers on terms which they regard as known. (With this method of observation it very often happens that the observer, influenced by the direction he himself prefers, reckons as leaders those who, owing to the people's change of direction, are no longer in front but on one side or even in the rear.)

'If the beasts in front are continually changing and the direction of the whole herd constantly alters, this is because, in order to follow a given direction, the cattle transfer their will to those beasts which attract our attention, and to study the movements of the herd we must watch the movements of all the prominent animals moving on all sides of the herd.' So say the third class of historians who accept all historical characters, from monarchs to journalists, as the expression of their age.

The theory of the transference of the will of the masses to historical persons is merely a paraphrase – a re-statement of the question in other words.

What causes historical events? Power.

What is power? Power is the collective will of the masses vested in one person.

On what condition is the will of the people delegated to one person? On condition that that person expresses the will of the whole people.

That is, power is power. That is, power is a word the meaning of which we do not understand.

*

If the domain of human knowledge were confined to abstract thinking, then humanity, having subjected to criticism the explanation of power that *juridical science* gives us, would conclude that power is merely a word and has no existence in reality. But for the knowledge of phenomena man has, besides abstract reasoning, another instrument – experience – by which he verifies the results of his reasoning. And experience tells him that power is not merely a word but an actually existing phenomenon.

Not to speak of the fact that no description of the collective activity of men can dispense with the concept of power, the existence of power is proved both by history and by observation of contemporary events.

Whenever an event occurs one man or several men make their appearance, by whose will the event seems to take place. Napoleon III issues a decree and the French go to Mexico. The King of Prussia and Bismarck issue decrees and an army enters Bohemia. Napoleon I gives a command and soldiers march into Russia. Alexander I gives a command and the French submit to the Bourbons. Experience shows us that whatever event occurs it is always related to the will of one or of several men who decreed it should be so.

The historians, from the old habit of recognizing divine intervention in human affairs, are inclined to look for the cause of events in the exercise of the will of the person endowed with power, but this supposition is not confirmed either by reason or by experience.

On the one hand reflection shows that the expression of man's will – his words – are only part of the general activity expressed in an event, as for instance, in a war or a revolution; and so without assuming an incomprehensible, supernatural force – a miracle – it is impossible to admit that words can be the immediate cause of the movements of millions of men. On the other hand, even if we admitted that words could be the cause of events, history shows that the expression of the will of historical personages in the majority of cases does not produce any effect – that is, their commands are often not executed and sometimes the very opposite of what they order is done.

Without admitting divine intervention in the affairs of humanity we cannot accept 'power' as the cause of events.

Power, from the standpoint of experience, is merely the relation that exists between the expression of the will of a person and the execution of that will by others.

To explain the conditions of that relationship we must first of all establish a concept of the expression of will, referring it to man and not to the Deity.

If it were the Deity giving commands and expressing His will (as history written by the older school assures us), the expression of that will could never be dependent upon time nor evoked by temporal things, seeing that the Deity is in no way bound to the event. But when we speak of commands that are the expression of the will of men, functioning in time and having a relation to one another, we must, if we are to understand the connexion of commands with events, restore two conditions: (1) the uninterrupted connexion in the time process both of the events themselves and of the person issuing commands – a condition to which all that occurs is subject; and (2) the indispensable connexion between the person issuing commands and those who execute them.

6

ONLY the expression of the will of the Deity, not affected by time, can relate to a whole series of events that have to take place over a period of years or centuries; and only the Deity, who is stirred to action by no temporal agency, can by His sole will determine the direction of humanity's movement. Man is subject to time and himself takes part in the event.

Reinstating the first condition neglected – that of time – we perceive that no single command can be executed without some preceding command making the execution of the last command possible.

No command ever appears spontaneously (i.e. without any external stimulus), or itself covers a whole series of occurrences; but each command follows from another, and never refers to a whole series of events but always to one moment only of an event.

When we say, for instance, that Napoleon ordered armies to go to war we combine in one single expression a series of consecutive commands dependent one on another. Napoleon could not have commanded an invasion of Russia and never did so. One day he ordered certain documents to be dispatched to Vienna, to Berlin and to Petersburg; the following day saw such and such decrees and orders issued to the army, the fleet, the commissariat, and so on and so on – millions of separate commands making up a series of commands corresponding to a series of events which brought the French armies into Russia.

If throughout his reign Napoleon continues to issue commands concerning an invasion of England and expends on no other undertaking so much time and effort, and yet during his whole reign never once attempts to execute his design but undertakes an expedition into Russia, with which country, according to his repeatedly expressed conviction, he considers it to his advantage to be in alliance – then this results from the fact that his commands did not correspond to the course of events in the first case but did so in the latter.

For a command to be carried out to the letter it must be a command actually capable of fulfilment. But to know what can and what cannot be carried out is impossible, not only in the case of Napoleon's invasion of Russia, in which millions participated, but even in the case of the simplest event, seeing that both the one and the other are liable at any moment to find themselves confronted by millions of obstacles. Every command executed is always one of an immense number unexecuted. All the impossible commands are inconsistent with the course of events and do not get carried out. Only the possible ones link up into a consecutive series of commands corresponding to a series of events, and are carried out.

Our erroneous idea that the command which precedes the event causes the event is due to the fact that when the event has taken place and out of thousands of commands those few which were consistent with that event have been executed we forget about the others that were not executed because they could not be. Apart from that, the chief source of our error in this regard arises from the fact that in the historical account a whole series of innumerable, diverse and petty events, such, for example, as all those which led the French soldiers into Russia, is generalized into a single event in accord with the result produced by that series of events; and by a corresponding generalization a whole series of commands is also summed up into a single expression of will.

We say: Napoleon chose to invade Russia and he did so. In reality we never find in all Napoleon's career anything resembling an expression of that design. What we do find is a series of commands or expressions of his will of the most varied and indefinite tenor possible. Out of a countless series of unexecuted commands of Napoleon's one series, for the campaign of 1812, was carried out – not because they differed in any way from other commands that were *not* executed but because they coincided with the course of events which brought the French army into Russia; just as in stencil-work a certain figure comes out, not because the colour was laid on from this side or in a particular way but because colour was smeared all over the figure cut out in the stencil.

So that examining the relation in time of commands to events we find that a command can never in any case be the cause of the event but that a definite interdependence none the less exists between the two.

To understand what this interdependence is, it is necessary to reinstate the second of our two conditions governing every command which emanates from man and not from the Deity – the condition that the man who issues the command must also be a participator in the event.

It is this relation of commander to commanded which is called 'power'. This relation may be analysed as follows:

For the purpose of common action men always unite in certain combinations in which, regardless of the difference of the aims set for their common action, the relation between those taking part in it always remains the same.

Men uniting in these combinations always assume among themselves such a relationship that the larger number take a more direct part, and the smaller number a less direct part, in the collective action for which they have combined.

Of all such combinations in which men unite for joint action one of the most striking and precise is an army.

1421

Every army is composed of men of the lowest service grades – the rank and file – who always form the majority; then of those of a slightly higher military standing – corporals and non-commissioned officers, fewer in number than the privates; and of still higher officers, of whom there are still fewer, and so on up to the highest military command, which is concentrated in one person.

A military organization may very truly be likened to a cone, the base of which, with the largest diameter, consists of the rank and file; the next higher and smaller section of the cone consists of the next higher grades of the army, and so on to the apex, the point of which will represent the commander-in-chief.

The soldiers forming the majority constitute the lower section of the cone and its base. The soldier himself does the stabbing and hacking, the burning and pillaging, and always receives orders for these actions from the men above him: he himself never gives an order. The non-commissioned officer (there are not so many of him) does less of the immediate work of war than the private, but he gives commands. An officer takes an active part more rarely still but issues commands the more frequently. A general does nothing but command the army, indicates the objective and hardly ever uses a weapon himself. Finally the commander-in-chief: he never takes a direct part in the actual work of war but only makes general dispositions for the movement of the masses under him. A similar mutual relationship of individuals obtains in every combination of men for joint activity – in agriculture, commerce and every administrative department.

Thus, without exaggeratedly separating all the contiguous sections of the cone – all the ranks of an army, or the ranks and positions in any administrative or public body, from lowest to highest – we discern a law by which men concerned to take common action combine in such relations that the more directly they participate in performing the action the less they can command and the more numerous they are, while the less they take any direct part in the work itself the more they command and the fewer they are in number; rising in this way from the lowest strata to a single man at the top, who takes the least direct share in the action and devotes his energy to a greater extent than all the others to the giving of commands.

It is this relationship between commander and commanded which constitutes the essence of the concept called power.

Having restored the conditions of time under which all events take place, we find that a command is executed only when it is related to a corresponding course of events. Likewise restoring the essential condition of connexion between those who command and those who execute, we have seen that by the very nature of the case those who command take the smallest part in the action itself, and that their activity is exclusively directed to commanding.

7

WHEN some event takes place people express their various opinions and hopes in regard to it, and inasmuch as the event proceeds from the collective activity of many some one of the opinions or hopes expressed is sure to be fulfilled, if only approximately. When one of the opinions expressed is fulfilled that opinion gets connected with the event as the command preceding it.

Men are hauling a log. Each of them may be expressing opinion as to how and where it should be hauled. They haul the log to its destination, and it turns out that it has been done in accordance with what one of them said. He gave the command. This is commanding and power in their primary form. The man who laboured hardest with his arms was the least able to think what he was doing, or reflect on what would be the result of the common activity, or give a command; while the man who was doing the most commanding was obviously the least able of the party, by reason of his greater verbal activity, to perform direct manual labour. In a larger aggregate of men directing their efforts to a common end the category of those who, because their activity is devoted to giving commands, take less part in the joint enterprise stands out still more prominently.

When a man is acting alone he always keeps before him a certain set of considerations which, so he believes, have regulated his action in the past, justify his action in the present and guide him in planning future activity.

In exactly the same way amalgamations of people leave those who do not take a direct part in the activity to devise considerations, justifications and projects concerning their collective activity.

For reasons known or unknown to us the French began to shipwreck and butcher each other. And corresponding to and accompanying this phenomenon we have the justification of the people's expressed determination that this was necessary for the welfare of France, for liberty and for equality. The French cease to murder one another, and justify that on the ground of the necessity of a centralization of power, of resistance to Europe, and so on. Men march from west to east, slaying their fellow-men, and this proceeding is accompanied by figures of speech about the glory of France, the baseness of England, and so on. History shows us that these justifications of events have no general sense and are self-contradictory – like, for instance, killing a man pursuant to recognition of his rights, or the slaughter of millions in Russia for the humiliation of England. But these justifications have a very necessary significance in their own day.

These justifications relieve those who produce the events from moral responsibility. At the time they do the work of the brooms that are fixed in front of a locomotive to clear the snow from the rails ahead: they clear men's moral responsibilities from their path. Without such justifications there would be no reply to the exceedingly simple question which presents itself when we examine any historical event: How do millions of men come to combine to commit crimes, wars, massacres and so forth?

Under the present complex forms of political and social life in Europe can any event be imagined that is not prescribed, decreed or ordered by monarchs, ministers, parliaments or newspapers? Is there any collective action which cannot find its justification in political unity, in patriotism, in the balance of power or in civilization? So that every event that occurs inevitably coincides with some expressed desire and, having found justification for itself, appears as the product of the will of one or more persons.

In whatever direction a ship is moving the surge where the prow cuts the waves will always be noticeable ahead. To those on board the ship the movement of this wave-form will be the only movement they see.

Only by watching closely, moment by moment, the movement of this wave-form and comparing it with that of the ship shall we convince ourselves that it is entirely conditioned by the forward movement of the ship and that we were deluded by the fact that we ourselves are imperceptibly moving.

We see the same thing if we observe, moment by moment, the movement of historical personages (that is, restoring the inevitable condition of all that occurs – continuity in the flow of time) and do not lose sight of the essential connexion of historical figures with the masses.

When the ship keeps on in one direction the surge ahead of her stays constant; if she tacks about, it too will change. But wherever the ship may turn there will always be the surge ahead, anticipating her movement.

Whatever happens it will always appear that precisely this had been foreseen and decreed. Whichever way the ship turns, the surge which neither directs nor accelerates her movement will always foam ahead of her and at a distance seem to us not merely to be moving on its own account but to be governing the ship's movement also.

*

Examining only those expressions of the will of historical personages which may be considered to have borne to events the relation of commands, historians have assumed that events depend on commands. But examining the events themselves and the connexion in which the historical characters stand to the masses, we have found that historical characters and their commands are dependent on events. An incontestable proof of this deduction lies in the fact that, however many commands may be given, the event does not take place unless there are other causes for it; but as soon as an event does take place – whatever it may be – then out of all the incessantly expressed wishes of different people some will always be found which in meaning and time of utterance will bear to the event the relation of commands.

Arriving at this conclusion, we are able to give a direct and positive reply to those two essential questions of history:

(1) What is power?

(2) What force produces the movement of nations?

(1) Power is the relation of a given person to other persons, in which the more this person expresses opinions, theories and justifications of the collective action the less is his participation in that action.

(2) The movement of nations is caused not by power, nor by intellectual activity, nor even by a combination of the two, as historians have supposed, but by the activity of *all* the people who participate in the event, and who always combine in such a way that those who take the largest direct share in the event assume the least responsibility, and *vice versa*.

Morally, power appears to cause the event; physically, it is those who are subordinate to that power. But, inasmuch as moral activity is inconceivable without physical activity, the cause of the event is found neither in the one nor the other but in the conjunction of the two.

Or, in other words, the concept of a cause is not applicable to the phenomenon we are examining.

In the last analysis we reach an endless circle – that uttermost limit to which in every domain of thought the human intellect must come if it is not playing with its subject. Electricity produces heat; heat produces electricity. Atoms attract and atoms repel one another.

Speaking of the interaction of heat and electricity and of atoms we cannot say why this occurs, and we say that such is the nature of these phenomena, such is their law. The same applies to historical phenomena. Why do wars or revolutions happen? We do not know. We only know that to produce the one or the other men form themselves into a certain combination in which all take part; and we say that this is the nature of men, that this is a law.

8

IF history had to do with external phenomena the establishment of this simple and obvious law would suffice and we might end our discussion. But the law of history relates to man. A particle of matter cannot tell us that it is unconscious of the law of attraction and repulsion and that that law is not true; but man, who is the subject of history, says bluntly: I am free, and am therefore not subject to laws.

The presence of the problem of man's freewill, though unexpressed, is felt at every step in history.

All seriously thinking historians are involuntarily led to this question. All the contradictions and obscurities of history, and the false path historical science has followed, are due solely to the lack of a solution of this question.

If the will of every man were free, that is, if every man could act as he pleased, all history would be a series of disconnected accidents.

If one man only out of millions once in a thousand years had the power of acting freely, i.e. as he chose, it is obvious that one single free act of that man in violation of the laws would be enough to prove that laws governing all human action cannot possibly exist.

Again, if there is a single law controlling the actions of men, free-will cannot exist, for man's will will then be subject to that law.

In this contradiction lies the problem of freewill, which from earliest times has occupied the best intellects of mankind and has from earliest times appeared in all its colossal significance.

The problem lies in the fact that if we regard man as a subject for observation from whatever point of view – theological, historical, ethical or philosophic – we find the universal law of necessity to which he (like everything else that exists) is subject. But looking upon man from within ourselves – man as the object of our own inner consciousness of self – we feel ourselves to be free.

This inner consciousness is a source of self-cognition distinct from and independent of reason. With his reason man observes himself, but only through self-consciousness does he know himself.

Now without consciousness of self no observation or application of reason is conceivable.

In order to understand, to observe, to draw conclusions, man must first of all be conscious of himself as living. A man is only conscious of himself as a living being by the fact that he wills: he is conscious of his volition. And his own will – which is the very essence of his life – he is and cannot but be conscious of as being free.

If on submitting himself to observation man perceives that his will is directed by a constant law (say he observes the imperative need of taking food, or the way the brain works, or whatsoever it may be) he cannot regard this consistent direction of his will otherwise than as a limitation of it. But a thing can only be limited if it is free to begin with. Man sees his will to be limited just because he is conscious of it in no other way than as being free.

You tell me I am not free. But I have just lifted my arm and let it fall. Everyone understands that this reply, however illogical, is an irrefutable demonstration of freedom.

The reply is the expression of a consciousness that is not subject to reason.

If the consciousness of freedom were not a separate and independent source of self-knowledge it would be subject to reasoning and experience; but in fact it is not, and it is unthinkable that it could be so.

Man learns from a succession of experiments and reflections that he, as the object under observation, is subject to certain laws, to which he submits, and never, once he has become acquainted with them, will he resist the laws of gravitation or impermeability. But the same series of experiments and reflections proves to him that the complete freedom of which he is conscious in himself is impossible; that every action of his depends on his particular organism, on his character and the motives inspiring him; yet he never submits to the deductions of these experiments and arguments.

Having learned from experience and by reasoning that a stone falls downwards, man is convinced beyond doubt and in all cases expects to find this law operating which he has discovered.

But having learned just as surely that his will is subject to laws, he does not and cannot believe it.

However often experience and deliberation may show a man that in the same circumstances and with the same character he will do the same thing as before, he will feel none the less assured of being able to act as he pleases when in the same circumstances and with the same character, and for, perhaps, the thousandth time, he approaches the action which always ends in the same way. Every man, savage and sage alike, however incontestably reason and experience may prove to him that it is impossible to imagine two different courses of action in precisely identical circumstances, feels that without this nonsensical conception (which constitutes the essence of freedom) he cannot conceive of life. He feels that, however impossible it may be, it is so, for without this conception of freedom not only would he be unable to understand life but he would be unable to live for a single moment.

Life would be intolerable because all man's aspirations, all the interest that life holds for him, are so many aspirations and strivings after greater freedom. Wealth and poverty, fame and obscurity, power and subjection, strength and weakness, health and disease, culture and ignorance, work and leisure, repletion and hunger, virtue and vice are only greater or lesser degrees of freedom.

To imagine a man wholly destitute of freedom is the same thing as to imagine a man destitute of life.

If the concept of freedom appears to the reason as a senseless contradiction, like the possibility of performing two actions at one and the same instant of time, or the possibility of an effect without a cause, that only proves that consciousness is not subject to reason.

It is this unwavering, certain consciousness of freedom – a consciousness indifferent to experience or reason, recognized by all thinkers and felt by everybody without exception – it is this consciousness without which there is no imagining man at all, which forms the other side of the question.

Man is the creation of an almighty, infinitely good and omniscient God. What is sin, the conception of which springs from man's consciousness of freedom? That is the question for theology.

The actions of man are subject to general and immutable laws which can be expressed in statistics. What is man's responsibility to society, the conception of which follows from his consciousness of freedom? That is the question for jurisprudence.

Man's actions proceed from his natural character and the motives influencing him. What is conscience and the sense of right and wrong behaviour that follow from the consciousness of freedom? That is the question for ethics.

Man in connexion with the common life of humanity conceives himself as subject to the laws which determine that life. But the same man apart from this connexion conceives of himself as free. How is the past life of nations and of humanity to be regarded – as the product of the free or the unfree activity of man? That is the question for history.

Only in our conceited age of the popularization of knowledge – thanks to that most powerful engine of ignorance, the diffusion of printed matter – has the question of freedom of will been put on a level on which the question itself cannot exist. In our day the majority of so-called 'advanced' people – that is, a mob of ignoramuses – have accepted the result of the researches of natural science, which is occupied with one side only of the question, for a solution of the whole problem.

They say and they write and they print that the soul and freedom do not exist, since the life of man is expressed by muscular movements and muscular movements are conditioned by the working of the nervous system: soul and freewill do not exist because at some unknown period of time we sprang from the apes. They say this with no inkling that thousands of years ago that same law of necessity which they are now so strenuously trying to prove by physiology and comparative zoology was not merely acknowledged by all religions and all thinkers but has never been denied. They do not see that the rôle of the natural sciences in this matter is merely to illumine one side of it. For even if, from the point of view of observation, reason and the will are but secretions of the brain, and if man following the general law of evolution developed from lower animals at some unknown period of time, all this will only elucidate from a fresh angle the truth admitted thousands of years ago by all religious and philosophic theories – that from the standpoint of reason man is subject to the laws of necessity; but it does not advance by a hair's breadth the solution of the question, which has another, opposite, side, founded on the consciousness of freedom.

If men descended from apes at an unknown period of time, that is as intelligible as that they were made from a handful of dust at a known period of time (in the first case the unknown quantity is the date, in the second it is the origin); and the question of how man's consciousness of freedom is to be reconciled with the law of necessity to which he is subject cannot be solved by comparative physiology and zoology, seeing that in the frog, the rabbit and the ape we can observe only muscular and nervous activity, whereas in man we find muscular and nervous activity plus consciousness.

The naturalists and their disciples who suppose they are solving this question are like plasterers set to stucco one side of a church wall. In an access of zeal, in the absence of their foreman, they plaster over windows, icons, woodwork and still unbuttressed walls, and rejoice that from their plasterers' point of view everything is now so smooth and even.

9

IN this matter of freewill versus necessity history has the advantage over other branches of knowledge which have attempted a solution in that, so far as history is concerned, the question relates not to the essential nature of man's freewill but to our presentation of how this freewill actually manifested in the past and under certain conditions.

In this respect history stands to the other sciences in the same relation as empirical to speculative science.

The subject of history is not the will of man as such but our presentation of it.

And so for history the insoluble mystery presented by the union of freewill and necessity does not exist as it does for theology, ethics and philosophy. History deals with a presentation of the life of man in which the union of those two antinomies has already taken place.

In actual life every historical event, every human action, can be quite clearly and specifically comprehended without any sense of the contradictory, even though each event will be seen to be in part free and in part necessitated.

To solve the question of how freedom and necessity amalgamate and what constitutes the essence of these two concepts the philosophy of history can and must pursue a route contrary to that followed by other sciences. Instead of first defining the concepts of freedom and necessity *per se*, and then ranging the phenomena of life under those definitions, history must form her definitions of the concepts of free-will and necessity from the immense quantity of phenomena of which she is cognizant, and that are always dependent on those two elements.

Whatever presentation of the activity either of many men or of one man we may consider we always regard it as the product partly of freewill and partly of the law of necessity.

Whether we speak of the migration of peoples and the incursions of the barbarians, or the decrees of Napoleon III, or someone's action an hour ago in choosing one direction out of several for his walk, we are unconscious of the presence of any contradiction. The measure of freedom and necessity governing the actions of these men is clearly defined for us.

Very often indeed our conception of the degree of freedom varies with the point of view from which we examine the phenomenon; but every human action always appears to us alike as a certain combination of freedom and necessity. In every action we investigate we see a certain measure of freedom and a certain measure of necessity. And always, the more freedom we see in any action the less necessity do we perceive, and the more necessity the less freedom.

The ratio of freedom to necessity decreases and increases according to the point of view from which the action is regarded; but their relation is always one of inverse proportion.

A drowning man who clutches at another and drags him under; or a hungry mother exhausted by feeding her baby who steals food; or a well-disciplined soldier who slays a defenceless fellow-creature because he is ordered to do so – seem less guilty, that is less free and more subject to the law of necessity, to one who knows the circumstances in which they were placed, and more free to an observer unaware that the man was drowning, the mother starving, and the soldier under orders, and so on. Similarly a man who committed a murder twenty years ago and has since lived peaceably and harmlessly in society seems less guilty, and his deed more subject to the law of necessity, to someone who considers what he did after a lapse of twenty years than to one looking at the same act the day after it was committed. And in the same way every act of a madman, a drunkard or a man labouring under violent excitement appears less free and more inevitable to one who knows the mental condition of the person who performed the action, and more free and less inevitable to the one who does not know it. In all such cases the conception of freedom is increased or diminished, and that of compulsion is correspondingly diminished or increased, according to the point of view from which the action is regarded. So that the greater the estimate of necessity the smaller the estimate of freedom, and *vice versa*.

Religion, ordinary common sense, the science of jurisprudence and history itself appreciate alike this relation between necessity and freedom.

In every case, without exception, where our impression concerning the ratio of freewill to necessity may vary there are three points only to be taken into consideration.

(1) The relation to the external world of the man who commits the deed;

(2) his relation to time; and

(3) his relation to the causes leading to the deed.

In consideration (1) our judgement will be affected by the degree to which we realize the man's relation to the external world – by the more or less clear idea we form of the definite position occupied by the man generally in relation to everything co-existing with him. It is this sort of consideration which makes it evident that a drowning man is less free and more subject to necessity than a man standing on dry ground; and that makes the actions of a man living in close connexion with others in a thickly populated district, bound by family, official or business duties, seem undoubtedly less free and more subject to necessity than those of a man living in solitude and seclusion.

If we study one man by himself, if we isolate him from his environment, every action of his seems free to us. But if we see any relation of his whatever to what surrounds him, if we see any connexion with anything whatever – with another man talking to him, a book read by him, the work in which he is engaged, even with the air he breathes or the light that falls on the objects about him – we see that each of these circumstances has its influence on him and orders at least one side of his activity. And the more we perceive of these influences the less free does he seem to us and the greater the impression we have of the necessity to which he is subject.

(2) Here our conclusion will be affected by how far the man's relation in time to the world is apparent – by the degree to which we perceive the specific place of his action in the course of time. It is this consideration which causes the fall of the first man, resulting in the emergence of the human race, to appear obviously less free than a man's entry into wedlock today. It is this consideration which accounts for the fact that the life and activity of people who lived centuries ago and are connected with me in time cannot seem to me as free as the life of a contemporary, the consequences of which are as yet unknown to me.

Our scale of judgement as to the greater or lesser degrees of freedom and necessity will here depend on the greater or lesser interval of time between the performance of the action and our appraisal of it.

If I examine an act I performed a moment ago in circumstances approximately identical with those I am in now my action appears to me to have been wholly free. But if I examine an act performed a month ago, being now in different circumstances I cannot help recognizing that if that act had not been committed much that resulted from it – useful, agreeable and even indispensable – could never have taken place. If I reflect on a more remote action of ten or more years ago the consequences of my action are still plainer to me and I shall find it hard to imagine what would have been had that action not been performed. The farther I go back in memory or – which is the same thing – the longer I postpone my appraisal the more uncertain becomes my belief in the freedom of my action.

Precisely the same process operates in history, too, so that we find our convictions varying as to the part played by freewill in the general affairs of humanity. A contemporary event seems to us indubitably the doing of all the men we know of concerned in it; but in the case of a more remote event we have had time to observe its inevitable consequences, which prevent our conceiving of anything else as possible. And the farther back we go in our investigation of events the less arbitrary do they appear.

The Austro-Prussian war looks to us to be the undoubted consequence of the crafty conduct of Bismarck, and so on.

The Napoleonic wars, though less positively this time, seem to us the outcome of their heroes' will. But when we get to the Crusades we see an event occupying its definite place in history as an occurrence without which the modern history of Europe is unimaginable, although to the chroniclers of the Crusades that event appeared simply due to the will of certain individuals. In the migration of peoples it never enters anyone's head today to suppose that the renovation of the European world depended on a caprice of Attila's. The more remote in history the object of our observation the more doubtful we feel of the freewill of those concerned in the event and the more manifest becomes the law of necessity.

(3) The third element influencing our judgement is the degree to which we can apprehend that endless chain of causation demanded by reason, in which every phenomenon capable of being understood (and therefore every human action) must have its definite place as a result of what has gone before and as a cause of what will follow.

It is in virtue of this principle that the better we are acquainted with the physiological, psychological and historical laws deduced from observation and by which man is controlled, and the more correctly we discern the physiological, psychological and historical causes of the action, and the simpler the action we are investigating and the less complex the character and mind of the individual whose action it is, the more subject to necessity and the less free do our actions and those of others appear.

When we have absolutely no understanding of the cause of an action – whether it be a crime, a virtuous act or even one that is neither – we ascribe a greater element of freewill to it. In the case of a crime we are more urgent in demanding punishment for the deed; in the case of a virtuous act we are warmer in our appreciation of its merits. In cases of no moral bearing we recognize the maximum of individuality, originality and independence. Yet let but *one* of the countless causes of the act become known to us and we at once recognize a certain element of necessity and are less insistent on punishment for the crime, less ready to acknowledge merit in the virtuous act or freedom in the apparently original performance. The fact that the criminal was reared in vicious surroundings mitigates his fault in our eyes. The self-sacrifice of a father or a mother, or self-sacrifice in the hope of gain, is more intelligible than gratuitous self-sacrifice and therefore appears less deserving of sympathy and less the work of freewill. The founder of a sect or a party, or an inventor, impresses us less when we know how and by what the way was paved for him beforehand. If we have a large range of examples, if our observation is continually directed to seeking the correlation between cause and effect in people's actions, their actions appear to us more subject to compulsion and less free the more accurately we connect effects with causes. If the actions investigated are simple, and we have a vast number of such actions under observation, our conception of their inevitability will be still more complete. The dishonest conduct of the son of a dishonest father, the misbehaviour of a woman who has fallen into bad company, a reformed drunkard's relapse into drunkenness, and so on, are cases that seem to us less free the better we understand their cause. If, again, the human being whose conduct we are considering stands on a very low plane of mental development, like a child or a lunatic or an imbecile, we who know the causes of the act and the simplicity of the character and intelligence in question see forthwith so great a measure of necessity and so little freewill that as soon as we know the cause compelling the action we can foretell what will happen.

The concepts of legal disability, admitted by all legislative codes, and that of extenuating circumstances rest entirely on these three considerations. Responsibility appears greater or less according to our greater or lesser knowledge of the conditions in which the individual was placed whose action is under judgement, and according to the longer or shorter interval of time between the perpetration of the action and its investigation, and according to our greater or lesser understanding of the causes that led to the action.

10

THUS our impression of freewill and necessity is gradually diminished or increased according to the degree of connexion with the external world, the greater or lesser degree of remoteness in time and the degree of dependence on causes which we see in the phenomenon of a man's life that we examine.

So that if we select for observation a point in the life of a man at which his connexion with the external world is best known, where the interval of time between the action and our appraisal of it is as long as possible, and the causes of the action are as easy as possible to arrive at, we form the idea of a maximum of necessity and a minimum of freewill. On the other hand, if we select for observation a man in the least possible dependence on external conditions, and observe a given act of his which was accomplished at the nearest possible moment to the present time, and of which the causes are beyond our ken, we form the idea of a minimum of necessity and a maximum of freewill.

But in neither case – and however we shift our point of view – however clear we may make to ourselves the connexion between our man and the external world or however hopelessly we fail to trace any such connexion, however much we lengthen or shorten the period of time involved, however intelligible or incomprehensible the causes of the action may be to us, we can never conceive of either complete freedom or complete necessity of action.

(1) However hard we try to imagine a man exempt from the influence of the external world we never arrive at a conception of freedom in space. Every human action is inevitably conditioned by what surrounds him and by his own body. I raise my arm and let it fall. My action seems to me free; but on asking myself whether I could raise my arm in any direction I see that I raised it in the direction in which there was least resistance to the action either from things around me or from the construction of my own body. I chose one out of all the possible directions because in that direction I met with the least hindrance. For my action to be wholly free it would have to meet with no obstacles at all. To conceive of a man being absolutely free we must imagine him outside space, which is obviously impossible.

(2) However much we approximate the time of appraisal to the time of the deed we can never arrive at a conception of freedom in time. For if I examine an action committed a second ago I must still recognize it as not being free, since it is irrevocably linked to the moment at which it was committed. Can I lift my arm? I lift it; but I ask myself: Could I have refrained from lifting my arm at that moment which is already in the past? To satisfy myself on this score I do not lift it the next moment. But I am not now refraining from doing so at the first moment when I asked myself the question. Time has gone by which it was not in my power to detain, and the arm which I then raised and the air in which I raised it are no longer the same air which now surrounds me or the same arm which I now refrain from

lifting. The moment at which the first movement was made is irrevocable and at that moment I could perform one movement and no other and whatever movement I made it could have been the only one. The fact that I did not lift my arm a moment later does not prove that I could not have raised it. And since I could only make one movement at one moment of time it could not have been any other. To imagine it as free one would have to imagine it in the present, on the boundary between the past and the future – i.e. outside time, which is impossible.

(3) However much the difficulty of apprehending the causes of an act may be enlarged we never reach a conception of complete freewill – i.e. of absolute absence of cause. However much we may fail to see the cause of a given expression of will (as manifested in any act of our own or another) the first demand of the intellect is to assume and seek out a cause, without which no phenomenon is conceivable. I raise my arm in order to perform an action independent of any cause, but my wish to perform an action without a cause is the cause of my action.

But even if, imagining a man entirely exempt from all influences and examining a momentaneous act of his in the present which we assume to have had no cause, we were to reduce the element of necessity to an infinitesimal minimum equivalent to zero we should still not have arrived at a conception of complete freedom in man, for a being uninfluenced by the external world, standing outside of time and independent of causes would not be a human being at all.

In the same way we can never conceive of a human action quite devoid of freedom and entirely subject to the law of necessity.

(1) However we may increase our knowledge of the spatial conditions in which a man is situated this knowledge can never be complete, since the number of those conditions is as infinite as the infinity of space. And therefore so long as not *all* the conditions that may influence man are defined the circle of necessity is not complete and a certain measure of freedom enters in.

(2) However we may prolong the period of time between the action we are examining and our appraisal of it that period will be finite, while time is infinite, and so in this respect too there can never be absolute inevitability.

(3) However accessible may be the chain of causation of any action we shall never know the whole chain, since it is endless, and so again we never get a conception of absolute necessity.

Moreover, even if, having reduced the residuum of freedom to a minimum equalling zero, we were to assume in some given case – as, for instance, that of a dying man, an unborn babe or an idiot – a complete absence of freedom, by so doing we should destroy the very conception of man in the case we are examining, for as soon as there is no freedom there is no man either. And so the conception of the action of a man subject solely to the law of necessity, devoid of any particle of freedom, is just as impossible as the conception of a completely free human action.

Thus to imagine a human action subject only to the law of necessity, without any freedom, we must assume a knowledge of an *infinite* number of spatial conditions, an *infinitely* long period of time and an *infinite* chain of causation.

To imagine a man perfectly free and not subject to the law of necessity we must imagine him alone, *outside space, outside time* and *outside dependence on cause.*

In the first case, supposing necessity were possible without freewill, we should be brought to a definition of necessity by the law of necessity itself, i.e. mere form without content.

In the second case, if freewill were possible without necessity, we should come to unconditioned freewill outside space, time and cause, which by the fact of its being unconditioned and unlimited would be nothing, or mere content without form.

In general, then, we should have arrived at the two fundamentals on which man's whole cosmic philosophy is constructed – the incomprehensible essence of life and the laws defining that essence.

Reason says: (1) Space with all the forms of matter that give it visibility is infinite, and cannot be imagined otherwise. (2) Time is infinite progression without a moment's pause, and cannot be imagined otherwise. (3) The connexion between cause and effect has no beginning and can have no end.

Consciousness says: (1) I alone am, and all that exists is only I; consequently I include space. (2) I measure flowing time by the fixed moment of the present, in which moment alone I am conscious of myself as living; consequently I stand outside of time. (3) I am independent of cause, since I feel myself to be the cause of every manifestation of my life.

Reason gives expression to the laws of necessity. Consciousness gives expression to the reality of freewill.

Freedom not limited by anything is the essence of life in man's consciousness. Necessity without content is man's reason with its three forms of approach.

Freedom is the thing examined. Necessity is the examiner. Freedom is the content. Necessity is the form.

Only by separating the two sources of cognition, related to one another as form is to content, do we get the mutually exclusive and separately inapprehensible concepts of freedom and necessity.

Only by uniting them do we get a clear conception of the life of man.

Apart from these two concepts which in their synthesis mutually define one another as form and content no conception of life is possible.

All that we know of the life of man is merely a certain relation of freewill to necessity, that is, of consciousness to the laws of reason.

All that we know of the external world of nature is only a certain relation of the forces of nature to necessity, or of the essence of life to the laws of reason.

The great natural forces lie outside us and are not objects of our consciousness; we call these forces gravitation, inertia, electricity, vital force, and so on; but the force of life in man is an object of our consciousness and we call it freewill.

But just as the force of gravitation, inconceptible in itself but realized by every man, can only be understood by us to the extent to which we know the laws of necessity to which it is subject (from the initial fact that all bodies have weight and down to Newton's law), so too the force of freewill, inconceptible in itself but recognized by the consciousness of every human being, is only intelligible to us in so far as we know the laws of necessity to which it is subject (beginning with the fact that every man dies and continuing to the knowledge of the most complex laws of political economy and history).

All knowledge is but the bringing of the essence of life under the laws of reason.

Man's freewill differs from every other force in that man is directly conscious of it: but in the eyes of reason it in no way differs from any other force. The forces of gravitation, electricity or chemical affinity are only distinguished from one another in that they are differently defined by reason. Similarly the force of man's freewill is distinguished by reason from the other forces of nature only by the definition reason gives it. Freewill apart from necessity, that is, apart from the laws of reason that define it, differs in no way from gravitation or heat or the force that makes things grow – for reason it is only a momentary, undefinable sensation of life.

And as the undefinable essence of the force moving the heavenly bodies, the undefinable essence of the forces of heat and electricity, or of chemical affinity, or of the vital force, forms the subject-matter of astronomy, physics, chemistry, botany, zoology and so on, so the essence of the force of freewill constitutes the subject-matter of history. But just as the subject of every science is the manifestation of this unknown essence of life, while the essence itself can only be the subject of metaphysics, so too the manifestation of the force of freewill in space, in time and in dependence on cause forms the subject of history, while freewill itself is the subject of metaphysics.

In the biological sciences what we know we call the laws of necessity; what is unknown to us we call vital force. Vital force is only an expression for what remains unexplained by what we know of the essence of life.

So too in history: what is known to us we call the laws of necessity; what is unknown we call freewill. Freewill is for history only an expression connoting what we do not know about the laws of human life.

II

HISTORY examines the manifestations of man's freewill in connexion with the external world in time and in dependence on cause; that is, it defines this freedom by the laws of reason. And so history is a science only in so far as this freewill is defined by those laws.

The recognition of man's freewill as a force capable of influencing historical events, that is, as not subject to laws, is the same for history as the recognition of a free force moving the heavenly bodies would be for astronomy.

Such an assumption would destroy the possibility of the existence of laws, that is, of any science whatever. If there is even one heavenly body moving freely then the laws of Kepler and Newton are negated and no conception of the movement of the heavenly bodies any longer exists. If there is a single human action due to freewill then not a single historical law can exist, nor any conception of historical events.

History is concerned with the lines of movement of human wills, one extremity of which is hidden in the unknown while at the other end men's consciousness of freewill in the present moment moves on through space and time and causation.

The more this field of movement opens out before our eyes the more evident do the laws of the movement become. To discover and define those laws is the problem of history.

From the standpoint from which the science of history now regards its subject, by the method it now follows – seeking the causes of phenomena in the freewill of man – a scientific statement of those laws is impossible, for, whatever limits we may set to man's freewill, as soon as we recognize it as a force not subject to law the existence of law becomes impossible.

Only by reducing this element of freewill to the infinitesimal, that is, by regarding it as an infinitely small quantity, can we convince ourselves of the absolute inaccessibility of causes, and then instead of seeking causes history will adopt for its task the investigation of historical laws.

Research into those laws was begun long ago and the new methods of thought which history must adopt are being worked out simultaneously with the self-destroying process towards which the old kind of history with its perpetual dividing and dissecting of the causes of events is tending.

All human sciences have gone along this path. Reaching the infinitesimal or infinitely small, mathematics – the most exact of the sciences – leaves off dividing and sets out upon the new process of integrating the infinitesimal unknown. Abandoning the concept of causation, mathematics looks for laws, i.e. the properties common to all the infinitely small unknown elements.

The other sciences, too, have proceeded along the same path in their thinking, though it has taken another form. When Newton formulated the law of gravitation he did not say that the sun or the earth had a property of attraction. What he said was that all bodies, from the largest to the smallest, have the property of attracting one another; that is, leaving on one side the question of the cause of the movement of bodies, he expressed the property common to all bodies, from the infinitely large to the infinitely small. The natural sciences do the same thing: putting aside the question of cause, they seek for laws. History, too, is entered on the same course. And if the subject of history is to be the study of the movements of the nations and humanity, and not descriptions of episodes in the lives of individuals, it too is bound to lay aside the notion of cause and seek the laws common to all the equal and indissolubly interconnected infinitesimal elements of freewill.

12

IMMEDIATELY the law of Copernicus was discovered and demonstrated the mere recognition of the fact that it was not the sun but the earth that moves destroyed the whole cosmography of the ancients. It might have been possible by refuting that law to retain the old conception of the movements of the heavenly bodies; but without refuting it it would seem impossible to continue studying the Ptolemaic worlds. Yet long after the discovery of the law of Copernicus the Ptolemaic worlds continued to be a subject of study.

From the time the first person said and proved that the number of births or of crimes is subject to mathematical laws, and that this or that form of government is determined by certain geographical and politico-economic conditions, and that certain relations of population to soil lead to migrations of peoples – from that moment the foundations on which history had been built were destroyed in their essence.

By refuting the newer laws history's former approach might have been retained, but unless they were rejected it would appear impossible to continue studying historical events as though they were the arbitrary product of man's freewill. For if such and such a form of government was established or such and such a migration of peoples took place in consequence of certain geographical, ethnographical or economic conditions, then the freewill of those persons who are represented to us as having established that form of government or evoked the migrations can no longer be regarded as the cause of those phenomena.

And yet the old style of history continues to be studied *pari passu* with the laws of statistics, geography, political economy, comparative philology and geology, which flatly contradict its tenets.

The struggle between the old views and the new was long and stubborn in physical philosophy. Theology stood on guard over the old views and accused the new of violating revelation. But when truth emerged victorious theology rebuilt its house as firmly as before on the new ground.

Equally prolonged and obstinate is the conflict today between the old and the new conception of history, and in the same way theology mounts guard before the old view and accuses the new of subverting revelation.

In both cases and on both sides the struggle rouses passion and stifles truth. On the one side there is fear and regret at the loss of the whole edifice constructed through the centuries; on the other, the passion for destruction.

To the men who fought against the dawning truths of physical philosophy it seemed that if they were to admit those truths their belief in God, in the creation of the universe and in the miracle of Joshua the son of Nun would be shattered. To the defenders of the laws of Copernicus and Newton – to Voltaire, for example – it seemed that the laws of astronomy put an end to religion, and he made use of the law of gravitation as a weapon against religion.

In exactly the same way now it seems that we have only to admit the law of necessity in order to destroy the conception of the soul, of good and evil, and of all the institutions of State and Church that have been built up on those conceptions.

So too, like Voltaire in his day, uninvited defenders of the law of necessity use the law as a weapon against religion, though the law of necessity in history, like the law of Copernicus in astronomy, far from destroying, even strengthens the foundations on which the institutions of State and Church are erected.

As in the question of astronomy then, so in the question of history now, the whole difference of opinion rests on the recognition or non-recognition of some absolute unit serving as the measure of visible phenomena. In astronomy the standard measure was the immovability of the earth; in history it is the independence of the individual – freewill.

As with astronomy the difficulty in the way of recognizing that the earth moves consisted in having to rid oneself of the immediate sensation that the earth was stationary accompanied by a similar sense of the planets' motion, so in history the obstacle in the way of recognizing the subjection of the individual to the laws of space and time and causality lies in the difficulty of renouncing one's personal impression of being independent of those laws. But as in astronomy the new view said: 'True, we are not conscious of the movement of the earth but if we were to allow that it is stationary we should arrive at an absurdity, whereas if we admit the motion (which we do not feel) we arrive at laws,' likewise in history the new theory says: 'True, we are not conscious of our dependence but if we were to allow that we are free we arrive at an absurdity, whereas by admitting our dependence on the external world, on time and on causality we arrive at laws.'

In the first case it was necessary to surmount the sensation of an unreal immobility in space and to recognize a motion we did not feel. In the present case it is similarly necessary to renounce a freedom that does not exist and to recognize a dependence of which we are not personally conscious.